Lecture Notes in Artificial Intelligence   11700

Subseries of Lecture Notes in Computer Science

Series Editors

Randy Goebel
  University of Alberta, Edmonton, Canada
Yuzuru Tanaka
  Hokkaido University, Sapporo, Japan
Wolfgang Wahlster
  DFKI and Saarland University, Saarbrücken, Germany

Founding Editor

Jörg Siekmann
  DFKI and Saarland University, Saarbrücken, Germany

More information about this series at http://www.springer.com/series/1244

Wojciech Samek · Grégoire Montavon ·
Andrea Vedaldi · Lars Kai Hansen ·
Klaus-Robert Müller (Eds.)

Explainable AI: Interpreting, Explaining and Visualizing Deep Learning

 Springer

Editors
Wojciech Samek ⓘ
Fraunhofer Heinrich Hertz Institute
Berlin, Germany

Grégoire Montavon
Technische Universität Berlin
Berlin, Germany

Andrea Vedaldi ⓘ
University of Oxford
Oxford, UK

Lars Kai Hansen ⓘ
Technical University of Denmark
Kgs. Lyngby, Denmark

Klaus-Robert Müller ⓘ
Technische Universität Berlin
Berlin, Germany

ISSN 0302-9743   ISSN 1611-3349 (electronic)
Lecture Notes in Artificial Intelligence
ISBN 978-3-030-28953-9   ISBN 978-3-030-28954-6 (eBook)
https://doi.org/10.1007/978-3-030-28954-6

LNCS Sublibrary: SL7 – Artificial Intelligence

This Springer imprint is published by the registered company Springer Nature Switzerland AG
The registered company address is: Gewerbestrasse 11, 6330 Cham, Switzerland

Explainable AI – Preface

Shortly after the emergence of the first computers, researchers have been interested in developing 'intelligent' systems that can make decisions and perform autonomously [6]. Until then, some of these tasks were carried out by humans. Transferring the decision process to an AI system might in principle lead to faster and more consistent decisions, additionally freeing human resources for more creative tasks. AI techniques, such as machine learning, have made tremendous progress over the past decades and many prototypes have been considered for use in areas as diverse as personal assistants, logistics, surveillance systems, high-frequency trading, health care, and scientific research. While some AI systems have already been deployed, what remains a truly limiting factor for a broader adoption of AI technology is the inherent and undoubtable risks that come with giving up human control and oversight to 'intelligent' machines [1]. Clearly, for sensitive tasks involving critical infrastructures and affecting human well-being or health, it is crucial to limit the possibility of improper, non-robust, and unsafe decisions and actions [4]. Before deploying an AI system, we see a strong need to validate its behavior, and thus establish guarantees that it will continue to perform as expected when deployed in a real-world environment.

In pursuit of that objective, ways for humans to verify the agreement between the AI decision structure and their own ground-truth knowledge [7] have been explored. Simple models such as shallow decision trees or response curves are readily interpretable, but their predicting capability is limited. More recent deep learning based neural networks provide far superior predictive power, but at the price of behaving as a 'black-box' where the underlying reasoning is much more difficult to extract. Explainable AI (XAI) has developed as a subfield of AI, focused on exposing complex AI models to humans in a systematic and interpretable manner.

A number of XAI techniques [2, 3, 5, 8] have been proposed. Some of them have already proven useful by revealing to the user unsuspected flaws or strategies in commonly used ML models. However, many questions remain on whether these explanations are robust, reliable, and sufficiently comprehensive to fully assess the quality of the AI system. A series of workshops have taken place at major machine learning conferences on the topic of interpretable and explainable AI. The present book has emerged from our NIPS 2017 workshop "Interpreting, Explaining and Visualizing Deep Learning ... now what?". The goal of the workshop was to assess the current state of the research on XAI, and to discuss ways to mature this young field.

Therefore, in essence, this book does not provide final answers to the problem of interpretable AI. It is a snapshot of interpretable AI techniques that have been proposed recently, reflecting the current discourse in this field and providing directions of future development.

Our goal was to organize these contributions into a coherent structure, and to explain how each of them may contribute in the 'big picture' of interpretable and explainable AI. A number of chapters in this book are extensions of the workshop contributions. Other papers are contributions from non-participants that have been added to obtain a more comprehensive coverage of the current research flavors. Each chapter has received at least two peer-reviews and the revised contributions have greatly profited from this process.

The book is organized in six parts:

Part 1: Towards AI Transparency
Part 2: Methods for Interpreting AI Systems
Part 3: Explaining the Decisions of AI Systems
Part 4: Evaluating Interpretability and Explanations
Part 5: Applications of Explainable AI
Part 6: Software for Explainable AI

Although not being able to cover the full breadth of topics, the 22 chapters in this book provide a timely snapshot of algorithms, theory, and applications of interpretable and explainable AI. Many challenges still exist both on the methods and theory side, as well as regarding the way explanations are used in practice. We consider the book an excellent starting point that will hopefully enable future work resolving open challenges of this active field of research.

July 2019

Wojciech Samek
Grégoire Montavon
Andrea Vedaldi
Lars Kai Hansen
Klaus-Robert Müller

References

1. Amodei, D., Olah, C., Steinhardt, J., Christiano, P., Schulman, J., Mané, D.: Concrete Problems in AI Safety. arXiv preprint arXiv:1606.06565 (2016)
2. Bach, S., Binder, A., Montavon, G., Klauschen, F., Müller, K.-R., Samek, W.: On pixel-wise explanations for non-linear classifier decisions by layer-wise relevance propagation. PLoS ONE 10(7), e0130140 (2015)
3. Fong, R.C., Vedaldi, A.: Interpretable explanations of black boxes by meaningful perturbation. In: IEEE International Conference on Computer Vision (CVPR). pp. 3429–3437 (2017)
4. Lapuschkin, S., Wäldchen, S., Binder, A., Montavon, G., Samek, W., Müller, K.-R.: Unmasking clever hans predictors and assessing what machines really learn. Nature Communications 10, 1096 (2019)
5. Montavon, G., Samek, W., Müller, K.-R.: Methods for interpreting and understanding deep neural networks. Digital Signal Processing 73, 1–15 (2018)
6. Rosenblatt, F.: The perceptron, a perceiving and recognizing automaton (Project Para). Report No. 85-460-1. Cornell Aeronautical Laboratory (1957)

7. Samek, W., Müller, K.-R.: Towards explainable artificial intelligence. In: Samek, W., Montavon, G., Vedaldi, A., Hansen, L.K., Müller, K.-R. (eds.) Explainable AI: Interpreting, Explaining and Visualizing Deep Learning. LNCS, vol. 11700, pp. 5–22. Springer, Cham (2019)

8. Zeiler, M.D., Fergus, R.: Visualizing and understanding convolutional networks. In: European Conference Computer Vision (ECCV). pp. 818–833 (2014)

Contents

Part VI Software for Explainable AI

Part I
Towards AI Transparency

Towards AI Transparency – Preface

Since the beginning of artificial intelligence, researchers, engineers and practitioners felt the urge to understand their complex and non-linear models. While in the early days of AI, researchers aimed to find connections between models such as perceptrons and human neurodynamics [6], later work focused more on understanding the learned representations and the system's behavior, e.g. by extracting rules from neural networks [2] or visualizing them using saliency maps [5]. With the emergence of kernel machines and deep learning, the wish for AI transparency grew even stronger [1, 4, 8]. The broader usage of AI systems also for sensitive applications (e.g. medical domain) or as a tool enabling the sciences further increased the demand for explainable AI methods (XAI).

The following chapters discuss the different aspects of the explanation problem and give an overview over recent developments, open challenges and future research directions in XAI.

In Chapter 1, Samek and Müller [7] motivate the need for transparency and explainability in AI, from multiple angles, e.g. safety and dependability, social/legal, or the ability to extract new insights from a learned model. The chapter also discusses different facets of an explanation and summarizes the recent developments and open challenges.

In Chapter 2, Weller [9] focuses on the challenges of transparency. This chapter lists several types and goals of transparency, each requiring a different sort of explanation. Furthermore, it points to the possible dangers of transparency and discusses the relation of transparency to concepts such as fairness and trust.

In Chapter 3, Hansen and Rieger [3] comment on the history of explainable AI, in particular, the prevalence of the question of explanation in the earlier research on expert systems, attempts in this context to characterize explanations in terms of desiderata, and the need to quantify uncertainty associated to these explanations.

Altogether, these three introductory chapters pave the way for more detailed discussions on the theory, methods and applications of XAI presented in later parts of this book.

July 2019

Wojciech Samek
Grégoire Montavon
Andrea Vedaldi
Lars Kai Hansen
Klaus-Robert Müller

References

1. Baehrens, D., Schroeter, T., Harmeling, S., Kawanabe, M., Hansen, K., Müller, K.-R.: How to explain individual classification decisions. J. Mach. Learn. Res. **11**, 1803–1831 (2010)
2. Denker, J., Schwartz, D., Wittner, B., Solla, S., Howard, R., Jackel, L., Hopfield, J.: Large automatic learning, rule extraction, and generalization. Complex syst. **1**(5), 877–922 (1987)
3. Hansen, L.K., Rieger, L.: Interpretability in intelligent systems - a new concept?. In: Samek, W., Montavon, G., Vedaldi, A., Hansen, L.K., Müller, K.-R. (eds.) Explainable AI: Interpreting, Explaining and Visualizing Deep Learning. LNCS, vol. 11700, pp. 41–49. Springer, Cham (2019)
4. Lapuschkin, S., Wäldchen, S., Binder, A., Montavon, G., Samek, W., Müller, K.-R.: Unmasking clever hans predictors and assessing what machines really learn. Nat. Commun. **10**, 1096 (2019)
5. Morch, N., Kjems, U., Hansen, L.K., Svarer, C., Law, I., Lautrup, B., Strother, S., Rehm, K.: Visualization of neural networks using saliency maps. In: International Conference on Neural Networks (ICNN). vol. 4, pp. 2085–2090 (1995)
6. Rosenblatt, F.: Principles of neurodynamics. perceptrons and the theory of brain mechanisms. Report No. VG-II96-G-8. Cornell Aeronautical Laboratory (1961)
7. Samek, W., Müller, K.-R.: Towards explainable artificial intelligence. In: Samek, W., Montavon, G., Vedaldi, A., Hansen, L.K., Müller, K.-R. (eds.) Explainable AI: Interpreting, Explaining and Visualizing Deep Learning. LNCS, vol. 11700, pp. 5–22. Springer, Cham (2019)
8. Simonyan, K., Vedaldi, A., Zisserman, A.: Deep inside convolutional networks: Visualising image classification models and saliency maps. In: ICLR Workshop (2014)
9. Weller, A.: Transparency: motivations and challenges. In: Samek, W., Montavon, G., Vedaldi, A., Hansen, L.K., Müller, K.-R. (eds.) Explainable AI: Interpreting, Explaining and Visualizing Deep Learning. LNCS, vol. 11700, pp. 23–40. Springer, Cham (2019)

1
Towards Explainable Artificial Intelligence

Wojciech Samek[1]([✉]) [iD] and Klaus-Robert Müller[2,3,4] [iD]

[1] Fraunhofer Heinrich Hertz Institute, 10587 Berlin, Germany
wojciech.samek@hhi.fraunhofer.de
[2] Technische Universität Berlin, 10587 Berlin, Germany
klaus-robert.mueller@tu-berlin.de
[3] Korea University, Anam-dong, Seongbuk-gu, Seoul 02841, Korea
[4] Max Planck Institute for Informatics, 66123 Saarbrücken, Germany

Abstract. In recent years, machine learning (ML) has become a key enabling technology for the sciences and industry. Especially through improvements in methodology, the availability of large databases and increased computational power, today's ML algorithms are able to achieve excellent performance (at times even exceeding the human level) on an increasing number of complex tasks. Deep learning models are at the forefront of this development. However, due to their nested non-linear structure, these powerful models have been generally considered "black boxes", not providing any information about what exactly makes them arrive at their predictions. Since in many applications, e.g., in the medical domain, such lack of transparency may be not acceptable, the development of methods for visualizing, explaining and interpreting deep learning models has recently attracted increasing attention. This introductory paper presents recent developments and applications in this field and makes a plea for a wider use of *explainable* learning algorithms in practice.

Keywords: Explainable artificial intelligence · Model transparency · Deep learning · Neural networks · Interpretability

1.1 Introduction

Today's artificial intelligence (AI) systems based on machine learning excel in many fields. They not only outperform humans in complex visual tasks [16,53] or strategic games [56,61,83], but also became an indispensable part of our every day lives, e.g., as intelligent cell phone cameras which can recognize and track faces [71], as online services which can analyze and translate written texts [11] or as consumer devices which can understand speech and generate human-like answers [90]. Moreover, machine learning and artificial intelligence have become indispensable tools in the sciences for tasks such as prediction, simulation or

© Springer Nature Switzerland AG 2019
W. Samek et al. (Eds.): Explainable AI, LNAI 11700, pp. 5–22, 2019.
https://doi.org/10.1007/978-3-030-28954-6_1

exploration [15,78,89,92]. These immense successes of AI systems mainly became possible through improvements in deep learning methodology [47,48], the availability of large databases [17,34] and computational gains obtained with powerful GPU cards [52].

Despite the revolutionary character of this technology, challenges still exist which slow down or even hinder the prevailance of AI in some applications. Examplar challenges are (1) the large complexity and high energy demands of current deep learning models [29], which hinder their deployment in resource restricted environments and devices, (2) the lack of robustness to adversarial attacks [55], which pose a severe security risk in application such as autonomous driving[1], and (3) the lack of transparency and explainability [18,32,76], which reduces the trust in and the verifiability of the decisions made by an AI system.

This paper focuses on the last challenge. It presents recent developments in the field of *explainable artificial intelligence* and aims to foster awareness for the advantages–and at times–also for the necessity of transparent decision making in practice. The historic second Go match between Lee Sedol and AlphaGo [82] nicely demonstrates the power of today's AI technology, and hints at its enormous potential for generating new knowledge from data when being accessible for human interpretation. In this match AlphaGo played a move, which was classified as "not a human move" by a renowned Go expert, but which was the deciding move for AlphaGo to win the game. AlphaGo did not explain the move, but the later play unveiled the intention behind its decision. With explainable AI it may be possible to also identify such novel patterns and strategies in domains like health, drug development or material sciences, moreover, the explanations will ideally let us comprehend the reasoning of the system and understand why the system has decided e.g. to classify a patient in a specific manner or associate certain properties with a new drug or material. This opens up innumerable possibilities for future research and may lead to new scientific insights.

The remainder of the paper is organized as follows. Section 1.2 discusses the need for transparency and trust in AI. Section 1.3 comments on the different types of explanations and their respective information content and use in practice. Recent techniques of explainable AI are briefly summarized in Sect. 1.4, including methods which rely on simple surrogate functions, frame explanation as an optimization problem, access the model's gradient or make use of the model's internal structure. The question of how to objectively evaluate the quality of explanations is addressed in Sect. 1.5. The paper concludes in Sect. 1.6 with a discussion on general challenges in the field of explainable AI.

1.2   Need for Transparency and Trust in AI

Black box AI systems have spread to many of today's applications. For machine learning models used, e.g., in consumer electronics or online translation services,

---

[1] The authors of [24] showed that deep models can be easily fooled by physical-world attacks. For instance, by putting specific stickers on a stop sign one can achieve that the stop sign is not recognized by the system anymore.

transparency and explainability are not a key requirement as long as the overall performance of these systems is good enough. But even if these systems fail, e.g., the cell phone camera does not recognize a person or the translation service produces grammatically wrong sentences, the consequences are rather unspectacular. Thus, the requirements for transparency and trust are rather low for these types of AI systems. In safety critical applications the situation is very different. Here, the intransparency of ML techniques may be a limiting or even disqualifying factor. Especially if single wrong decisions can result in danger to life and health of humans (e.g., autonomous driving, medical domain) or significant monetary losses (e.g., algorithmic trading), relying on a data-driven system whose reasoning is incomprehensible may not be an option. This intransparency is one reason why the adoption of machine learning to domains such as health is more cautious than the usage of these models in the consumer, e-commerce or entertainment industry.

In the following we discuss why the ability to explain the decision making of an AI system helps to establish trust and is of utmost importance, not only in medical or safety critical applications. We refer the reader to [91] for a discussion of the challenges of transparency.

1.2.1   Explanations Help to Find "Clever Hans" Predictors

Clever Hans was a horse that could supposedly count and that was considered a scientific sensation in the years around 1900. As it turned out later, Hans did not master the math but in about 90% of the cases, he was able to derive the correct answer from the questioner's reaction. Analogous behaviours have been recently observed in state-of-the-art AI systems [46]. Also here the algorithms have learned to use some spurious correlates in the training and test data and similarly to Hans predict right for the 'wrong' reason.

For instance, the authors of [44, 46] showed that the winning method of the PASCAL VOC competition [23] was often not detecting the object of interest, but was utilizing correlations or context in the data to correctly classify an image. It recognized boats by the presence of water and trains by the presence of rails in the image, moreover, it recognized horses by the presence of a copyright watermark[2]. The occurrence of the copyright tags in horse images is a clear artifact in the dataset, which had gone unnoticed to the organizers and participants of the challenge for many years. It can be assumed that nobody has systematically checked the thousands images in the dataset for this kind of artifacts (but even if someone did, such artifacts may be easily overlooked). Many other examples of "Clever Hans" predictors have been described in the literature. For instance, [73] show that current deep neural networks are distinguishing the classes "Wolf" and "Husky" mainly by the presence of snow in the image. The authors of [46] demonstrate that deep models overfit to padding artifacts when classifying airplanes, whereas [63] show that a model which was

---

[2] The PASCAL VOC images have been automatically crawled from flickr and especially the horse images were very often copyrighted with a watermark.

trained to distinguish between 1000 categories, has not learned dumbbells as an independent concept, but associates a dumbbell with the arm which lifts it. Such "Clever Hans" predictors perform well on their respective test sets, but will certainly fail if deployed to the real-world, where sailing boats may lie on a boat trailer, both wolves and huskies can be found in non-snow regions and horses do not have a copyright sign on them. However, if the AI system is a black box, it is very difficult to unmask such predictors. Explainability helps to detect these types of biases in the model or the data, moreover, it helps to understand the weaknesses of the AI system (even if it is not a "Clever Hans" predictor). In the extreme case, explanations allow to detect the classifier's misbehaviour (e.g., the focus on the copyright tag) from a single test image[3]. Since understanding the weaknesses of a system is the first step towards improving it, explanations are likely to become integral part of the training and validation process of future AI models.

1.2.2   Explanations Foster Trust and Verifiability

The ability to verify decisions of an AI system is very important to foster trust, both in situations where the AI system has a supportive role (e.g., medical diagnosis) and in situations where it practically takes the decisions (e.g., autonomous driving). In the former case, explanations provide extra information, which, e.g., help the medical expert to gain a comprehensive picture of the patient in order to take the best therapy decision. Similarly to a radiologist, who writes a detailed report explaining his findings, a supportive AI system should in detail explain its decisions rather than only providing the diagnosis to the medical expert. In cases where the AI system itself is deciding, it is even more critical to be able to comprehend the reasoning of the system in order to verify that it is not behaving like Clever Hans, but solves the problem in a robust and safe manner. Such verifications are required to build the necessary trust in every new technology.

There is also a social dimension of explanations. Explaining the rationale behind one's decisions is an important part of human interactions [30]. Explanations help to build trust in a relationship between humans, and should therefore be also part of human-machine interactions [3]. Explanations are not only an inevitable part of human learning and education (e.g., teacher explains solution to student), but also foster the acceptance of difficult decisions and are important for informed consent (e.g., doctor explaining therapy to patient). Thus, even if not providing additional information for verifying the decision, e.g., because the patient may have no medical knowledge, receiving explanations usually make us feel better as it integrates us into the decision-making process. An AI system which interacts with humans should therefore be explainable.

1.2.3   Explanations Are a Prerequisite for New Insights

AI systems have the potential to discover patterns in data, which are not accessible to the human expert. In the case of the Go game, these patterns can be

---

[3] Traditional methods to evaluate classifier performance require large test datasets.

new playing strategies [82]. In the case of scientific data, they can be unknown associations between genes and diseases [51], chemical compounds and material properties [68] or brain activations and cognitive states [49]. In the sciences, identifying these patterns, i.e., explaining and interpreting what features the AI system uses for predicting, is often more important than the prediction itself, because it unveils information about the biological, chemical or neural mechanisms and may lead to new scientific insights.

This necessity to explain and interpret the results has led to a strong dominance of linear models in scientific communities in the past (e.g. [42, 67]). Linear models are intrinsically interpretable and thus easily allow to extract the learned patterns. Only recently, it became possible to apply more powerful models such as deep neural networks without sacrificing interpretability. These explainable non-linear models have already attracted attention in domains such as neuroscience [20, 87, 89], health [14, 33, 40], autonomous driving [31], drug design [70] and physics [72, 78] and it can be expected that they will play a pivotal role in future scientific research.

1.2.4 Explanations Are Part of the Legislation

The infiltration of AI systems into our daily lives poses a new challenge for the legislation. Legal and ethical questions regarding the responsibility of AI systems and their level of autonomy have recently received increased attention [21, 27]. But also anti-discrimination and fairness aspects have been widely discussed in the context of AI [19, 28]. The EU's General Data Protection Regulation (GDPR) has even added the *right to explanation* to the policy in Articles 13, 14 and 22, highlighting the importance of human-understandable interpretations derived from machine decisions. For instance, if a person is being rejected for a loan by the AI system of a bank, in principle, he or she has the right to know why the system has decided in this way, e.g., in order to make sure that the decision is compatible with the anti-discrimination law or other regulations. Although it is not yet clear how these legal requirements will be implemented in practice, one can be sure that transparency aspects will gain in importance as AI decisions will more and more affect our daily lives.

1.3 Different Facets of an Explanation

Recently proposed explanation techniques provide valuable information about the learned representations and the decision-making of an AI system. These explanations may differ in their information content, their recipient and their purpose. In the following we describe the different types of explanations and comment on their usefulness in practice.

1.3.1 Recipient

Different recipients may require explanations with different level of detail and with different information content. For instance, for users of AI technology it may be sufficient to obtain coarse explanations, which are easy to interpret, whereas AI researchers and developers would certainly prefer explanations, which give them deeper insights into the functioning of the model.

In the case of image classification such simple explanations could coarsely highlight image regions, which are regarded most relevant for the model. Several preprocessing steps, e.g., smoothing, filtering or contrast normalization, could be applied to further improve the visualization quality. Although discarding some information, such coarse explanations could help the ordinary user to foster trust in AI technology. On the other hand AI researchers and developers, who aim to improve the model, may require all the available information, including negative evidence, about the AI's decision in the highest resolution (e.g., pixel-wise explanations), because only this complete information gives detailed insights into the (mal)functioning of the model.

One can easily identify further groups of recipients, which are interested in different types of explanations. For instance, when applying AI to the medical domain these groups could be patients, doctors and institutions. An AI system which analyzes patient data could provide simple explanations to the patients, e.g., indicating too high blood sugar, while providing more elaborate explanations to the medical personal, e.g., unusual relation between different blood parameters. Furthermore, institutions such as hospitals or the FDA might be less interested in understanding the AI's decisions for individual patients, but would rather prefer to obtain global or aggregated explanations, i.e., patterns which the AI system has learned after analyzing many patients.

1.3.2   Information Content

Different types of explanation provide insights into different aspects of the model, ranging from information about the learned representations to the identification of distinct prediction strategies and the assessment of overall model behaviour. Depending on the recipient of the explanations and his or her intent, it may be advantageous to focus on one particular type of explanation. In the following we briefly describe four different types of explanations.

1. **Explaining learned representations**: This type of explanation aims to foster the understanding of the learned representations, e.g., neurons of a deep neural network. Recent work [12,38] investigates the role of single neurons or group of neurons in encoding certain concepts. Other methods [64,65, 84,93] aim to interpret what the model has learned by building prototypes that are representative of the abstract learned concept. These methods, e.g., explain what the model has learned about the category "car" by generating a prototypical image of a car. Building such a prototype can be formulated within the activation maximization framework and has been shown to be an effective tool for studying the internal representation of a deep neural network.

2. **Explaining individual predictions**: Other types of explanations provide information about individual predictions, e.g., heatmaps visualizing which

pixels have been most relevant for the model to arrive at its decision [60] or heatmaps highlighting the most sensitive parts of an input [84]. Such explanations help to verify the predictions and establish trust in the correct functioning on the system. Layer-wise Relevance Propagation (LRP) [9,58] provides a general framework for explaining individual predictions, i.e., it is applicable to various ML models, including neural networks [9], LSTMs [7], Fisher Vector classifiers [44] and Support Vector Machines [35]. Section 1.4 gives an overview over recently proposed methods for computing individual explanations.

3. **Explaining model behaviour**: This type of explanations go beyond the analysis of individual predictions towards a more general understanding of model behaviour, e.g., identification of distinct prediction strategies. The spectral relevance analysis (SpRAy) approach of [46] computes such meta explanations by clustering individual heatmaps. Each cluster then represents a particular prediction strategy learned by the model. For instance, the authors of [46] identify four clusters when classifying "horse" images with the Fisher Vector classifier [77] trained on the PASCAL VOC 2007 dataset [22], namely (1) detect the horse and rider, (2) detect a copyright tag in portrait oriented images, (3) detect wooden hurdles and other contextual elements of horseback riding, and (4) detect a copyright tag in landscape oriented images. Such explanations are useful for obtaining a global overview over the learned strategies and detecting "Clever Hans" predictors [46].

4. **Explaining with representative examples**: Another class of methods interpret classifiers by identifying representative training examples [37,41]. This type of explanations can be useful for obtaining a better understanding of the training dataset and how it influences the model. Furthermore, these representative examples can potentially help to identify biases in the data and make the model more robust to variations of the training dataset.

1.3.3   Role

Besides the recipient and information content it is also important to consider the purpose of an explanation. Here we can distinguish two aspects, namely (1) the intent of the explanation method (what specific question does the explanation answer) and (2) our intent (what do we want to use the explanation for).

Explanations are relative and it makes a huge difference whether their intent is to explain the prediction as is (even if it is incorrect), whether they aim to visualize what the model "thinks" about a specific class (e.g., the true class) or whether they explain the prediction relative to another alternative ("why is this image classified as car and not as truck"). Methods such as LRP allow to answer all these different questions, moreover, they also allow to adjust the amount of positive and negative evidence in the explanations, i.e., visualize what speaks for (positive evidence) and against (negative evidence) the prediction. Such fine-grained explanations foster the understanding of the classifier and the problem at hand.

Furthermore, there may be different goals for using the explanations beyond visualization and verification of the prediction. For instance, explanations can be potentially used to improve the model, e.g., by regularization [74]. Also since explanations provide information about the (relevant parts of the) model, they can be potentially used for model compression and pruning. Many other uses (certification of the model, legal use) of explanations can be thought of, but the details remain future work.

1.4 Methods of Explainable AI

This section gives an overview over different approaches to explainable AI, starting with techniques which are model-agnostic and rely on a simple surrogate function to explain the predictions. Then, we discuss methods which compute explanations by testing the model's response to local perturbations (e.g., by utilizing gradient information or by optimization). Subsequently, we present very efficient propagation-based explanation techniques which leverage the model's internal structure. Finally, we consider methods which go beyond individual explanations towards a meta-explanation of model behaviour.

This section is not meant to be a complete survey of explanation methods, but it rather summarizes the most important developments in this field. Some approaches to explainable AI, e.g., methods which find influential examples [37], are not discussed in this section.

1.4.1 Explaining with Surrogates

Simple classifiers such as linear models or shallow decision trees are intrinsically interpretable, so that explaining its predictions becomes a trivial task. Complex classifiers such as deep neural networks or recurrent models on the other hand contain several layers of non-linear transformations, which largely complicates the task of finding what exactly makes them arrive at their predictions.

One approach to explain the predictions of complex models is to locally approximate them with a simple surrogate function, which is interpretable. A popular technique falling into this category is Local Interpretable Model-agnostic Explanations (LIME) [73]. This method samples in the neighborhood of the input of interest, evaluates the neural network at these points, and tries to fit the surrogate function such that it approximates the function of interest. If the input domain of the surrogate function is human-interpretable, then LIME can even explain decisions of a model which uses non-interpretable features. Since LIME is model agnostic, it can be applied to any classifier, even without knowing its internals, e.g., architecture or weights of a neural network classifier. One major drawback of LIME is its high computational complexity, e.g., for state-of-the-art models such as GoogleNet it requires several minutes for computing the explanation of a single prediction [45].

Similar to LIME which builds a model for locally approximating the function of interest, the SmoothGrad method [85] samples the neighborhood of the input to approximate the gradient. Also SmoothGrad does not leverage the internals of the model, however, it needs access to the gradients. Thus, it can also be regarded as a gradient-based explanation method.

1.4.2   Explaining with Local Perturbations

Another class of methods construct explanations by analyzing the model's response to local changes. This includes methods which utilize the gradient information as well as perturbation- and optimization-based approaches.

Explanation methods relying on the gradient of the function of interest [2] have a long history in machine learning. One example is the so-called Sensitivity Analysis (SA) [10,62,84]. Although being widely used as explanation methods, SA technically explains the change in prediction instead of the prediction itself. Furthermore, SA has been shown to suffer from fundamental problems such as gradient shattering and explanation discontinuities, and is therefore considered suboptimal for explanation of today's AI models [60]. Variants of Sensitivity Analysis exist which tackle some of these problems by locally averaging the gradients [85] or integrating them along a specific path [88].

Perturbation-based explanation methods [25,94,97] explicitly test the model's response to more general local perturbations. While the occlusion method of [94] measures the importance of input dimensions by masking parts of the input, the Prediction Difference Analysis (PDA) approach of [97] uses conditional sampling within the pixel neighborhood of an analyzed feature to effectively remove information. Both methods are model-agnostic, i.e., can be applied to any classifier, but are computationally not very efficient, because the function of interest (e.g., neural network) needs to be evaluated for all perturbations.

The meaningful perturbation method of [25,26] is another model-agnostic technique to explaining with local perturbations. It regards explanation as a meta prediction task and applies optimization to synthesize the maximally informative explanations. The idea to formulate explanation as an optimization problem is also used by other methods. For instance, the methods [64,84,93] aim to interpret what the model has learned by building prototypes that are representative of the learned concept. These prototypes are computed within the activation maximization framework by searching for an input pattern that produces a maximum desired model response. Conceptually, activation maximization [64] is similar to the meaningful perturbation approach of [25]. While the latter finds a minimum perturbation of the data that makes $f(x)$ low, activation maximization finds a minimum perturbation of the gray image that makes $f(x)$ high. The costs of optimization can make these methods computationally very demanding.

1.4.3   Propagation-Based Approaches (Leveraging Structure)

Propagation-based approaches to explanation are not oblivious to the model which they explain, but rather integrate the internal structure of the model into the explanation process.

Layer-wise Relevance Propagation (LRP) [9,58] is a propagation-based explanation framework, which is applicable to general neural network structures, including deep neural networks [13], LSTMs [5,7], and Fisher Vector classifiers [44]. LRP explains individual decisions of a model by propagating the prediction from the output to the input using local redistribution rules. The propagation process can be theoretically embedded in the deep Taylor decomposition framework [59]. More recently, LRP was extended to a wider set of machine learning models, e.g., in clustering [36] or anomaly detection [35], by first transforming the model into a neural network ('neuralization') and then applying LRP to explain its predictions. The leveraging of the model structure together with the use of appropriate (theoretically-motivated) propagation rules, enables LRP to deliver good explanations at very low computational cost (one forward and one backward pass). Furthermore, the generality of the LRP framework allows also to express other recently proposed explanation techniques, e.g., [81,95]. Since LRP does not rely on gradients, it does not suffer from problems such as gradient shattering and explanation discontinuities [60].

Other popular explanation methods leveraging the model's internal structure are Deconvolution [94] and Guided Backprogagation [86]. In contrast to LRP, these methods do not explain the prediction in the sense "how much did the input feature contribute to the prediction", but rather identify patterns in input space, that relate to the analyzed network output.

Many other explanation methods have been proposed in the literature which fall into the "leveraging structure" category. Some of these methods use heuristics to guide the redistribution process [79], others incorporate an optimization step into the propagation process [39]. The iNNvestigate toolbox [1] provides an efficient implementation for many of these propagation-based explanation methods.

1.4.4   Meta-explanations

Finally, individual explanations can be aggregated and analyzed to identify general patterns of classifier behavior. A recently proposed method, spectral relevance analysis (SpRAy) [46], computes such meta explanations by clustering individual heatmaps. This approach allows to investigate the predictions strategies of the classifier on the whole dataset in a (semi-)automated manner and to systematically find weak points in models or training datasets.

Another type of meta-explanation aims to better understand the learned representations and to provide interpretations in terms of human-friendly concepts. For instance, the network dissection approach of [12,96] evaluates the semantics of hidden units, i.e., quantify what concepts these neurons encode. Other recent work [38] provides explanations in terms of user-defined concepts and tests to which degree these concepts are important for the prediction.

1.5   Evaluating Quality of Explanations

The objective assessment of the quality of explanations is an active field of research. Many efforts have been made to define quality measures for heatmaps which explain individual predictions of an AI model. This section gives an overview over the proposed approaches.

A popular measure for heatmap quality is based on perturbation analysis [6,9,75]. The assumption of this evaluation metric is that the perturbation of relevant (according to the heatmap) input variables should lead to a steeper decline of the prediction score than the perturbation of input dimensions which are of lesser importance. Thus, the average decline of the prediction score after several rounds of perturbation (starting from the most relevant input variables) defines an objective measure of heatmap quality. If the explanation identifies the truly relevant input variables, then the decline should be large. The authors of [75] recommend to use untargeted perturbations (e.g., uniform noise) to allow fair comparison of different explanation methods. Although being very popular, it is clear that perturbation analysis can not be the only criterion to evaluate explanation quality, because one could easily design explanations techniques which would directly optimize this criterion. Examples are occlusion methods which were used in [50,94], however, they have been shown to be inferior (according to other quality criteria) to explanation techniques such as LRP [8].

Other studies use the "pointing game" [95] to evaluate the quality of a heatmap. The goal of this game is to evaluate the discriminativeness of the explanations for localizing target objects, i.e., it is compared if the most relevant point of the heatmap lies on the object of designated category. Thus, these measures assume that the AI model will focus most attention on the object of interest when classifying it, therefore this should be reflected in the explanation. However, this assumption may not always be true, e.g., "Clever Hans" predictors [46] may rather focus on context than of the object itself, irrespectively of the explanation method used. Thus, their explanations would be evaluated as poor quality according to this measure although they truly visualize the model's prediction strategy.

Task specific evaluation schemes have also been proposed in the literature. For example, [69] use the subject-verb agreement task to evaluate explanations of a NLP model. Here the model predicts a verb's number and the explanations verify if the most relevant word is indeed the correct subject or a noun with the predicted number. Other approaches to evaluation rely on human judgment [66,73]. Such evaluation schemes relatively quickly become impractical if evaluating a larger number of explanations.

A recent study [8] proposes to objectively evaluate explanation for sequential data using ground truth information in a toy task. The idea of this evaluation metric is to add or subtract two numbers within an input sequence and measure the correlation between the relevances assigned to the elements of the sequence and the two input numbers. If the model is able to accurately perform the addition and subtraction task, then it must focus on these two numbers (other numbers in the sequence are random) and this must be reflected in the explanation.

An alternative and indirect way to evaluate the quality of explanations is to use them for solving other tasks. The authors of [6] build document-level representations from word-level explanations. The performance of these document-level representations (e.g., in a classification task) reflect the quality of the word-level explanations. Another work [4] uses explanation for reinforcement learning. Many other functionally-grounded evaluations [18] could be conceived such as using explanations for compressing or pruning the neural network or training student models in a teacher-student scenario.

Lastly, another promising approach to evaluate explanations is based on the fulfillment of a certain axioms [54,57,60,80,88]. Axioms are properties of an explanation that are considered to be necessary and should therefore be fulfilled. Proposed axioms include relevance conservation [60], explanation continuity [60], sensitivity [88] and implementation invariance [88]. In contrast to the other quality measures discussed in this section, the fulfillment or non-fulfillment of certain axioms can be often shown analytically, i.e., does not require empirical evaluations.

1.6   Challenges and Open Questions

Although significant progress has been made in the field of explainable AI in the last years, challenges still exist both on the methods and theory side as well as regarding the way explanations are used in practice. Researchers have already started working on some of these challenges, e.g., the objective evaluation of explanation quality or the use of explanations beyond visualization. Other open questions, especially those concerning the theory, are more fundamental and more time will be required to give satisfactory answers to them.

Explanation methods allow us to gain insights into the functioning of the AI model. Yet, these methods are still limited in several ways. First, heatmaps computed with today's explanation methods visualize "first-order" information, i.e., they show which input features have been identified as being relevant for the prediction. However, the relation between these features, e.g., whether they are important on their own or only whether they occur together, remains unclear. Understanding these relations is important in many applications, e.g., in the neurosciences such higher-order explanations could help us to identify groups of brain regions which act together when solving a specific task (brain networks) rather than just identifying important single voxels.

Another limitation is the low abstraction level of explanations. Heatmaps show that particular pixels are important without relating these relevance values to more abstract concepts such as the objects or the scene displayed in the image. Humans need to interpret the explanations to make sense them and to understand the model's behaviour. This interpretation step can be difficult and erroneous. Meta-explanations which aggregate evidence from these low-level heatmaps and explain the model's behaviour on a more abstract, more human understandable level, are desirable. Recently, first approaches to aggregate low-level explanations

[46] and quantify the semantics of neural representations [12] have been proposed. The construction of more advanced meta-explanations is a rewarding topic for future research.

Since the recipient of explanations is ultimately the human user, the use of explanations in human-machine interaction is an important future research topic. Some works (e.g., [43]) have already started to investigate human factors in explainable AI. Constructing explanations with the right user focus, i.e., asking the right questions in the right way, is a prerequisite to successful human-machine interaction. However, the optimization of explanations for optimal human usage is still a challenge which needs further study.

A theory of explainable AI, with a formal and universally agreed definition of what explanations are, is lacking. Some works made a first step towards this goal by developing mathematically well-founded explanation methods. For instance, the authors of [59] approach the explanation problem by integrating it into the theoretical framework of Taylor decomposition. The axiomatic approaches [54,60,88] constitute another promising direction towards the goal of developing a general theory of explainable AI.

Finally, the use of explanations beyond visualization is a wide open challenge. Future work will show how to integrate explanations into a larger optimization process in order to, e.g., improve the model's performance or reduce its complexity.

Acknowledgements. This work was supported by the German Ministry for Education and Research as Berlin Big Data Centre (01IS14013A), Berlin Center for Machine Learning (01IS18037I) and TraMeExCo (01IS18056A). Partial funding by DFG is acknowledged (EXC 2046/1, project-ID: 390685689). This work was also supported by the Institute for Information & Communications Technology Planning & Evaluation (IITP) grant funded by the Korea government (No. 2017-0-00451, No. 2017-0-01779).

References

1. Alber, M., et al.: iNNvestigate neural networks!. J. Mach. Learn. Res. **20**(93), 1–8 (2019)
2. Ancona, M., Ceolini, E., Öztireli, C., Gross, M.: Gradient-based attribution methods. In: Samek, W., Montavon, G., Vedaldi, A., Hansen, L.K., Müller, K.-R. (eds.) Explainable AI. LNCS, vol. 11700, pp. 169–191. Springer, Cham (2019)
3. Antunes, P., Herskovic, V., Ochoa, S.F., Pino, J.A.: Structuring dimensions for collaborative systems evaluation. ACM Comput. Surv. (CSUR) **44**(2), 8 (2012)
4. Arjona-Medina, J.A., Gillhofer, M., Widrich, M., Unterthiner, T., Hochreiter, S.: RUDDER: return decomposition for delayed rewards. arXiv preprint arXiv:1806.07857 (2018)
5. Arras, L., et al.: Explaining and interpreting LSTMs. In: Samek, W., Montavon, G., Vedaldi, A., Hansen, L.K., Müller, K.-R. (eds.) Explainable AI. LNCS, vol. 11700, pp. 211–238. Springer, Cham (2019)
6. Arras, L., Horn, F., Montavon, G., Müller, K.R., Samek, W.: What is relevant in a text document?: An interpretable machine learning approach. PLoS ONE **12**(8), e0181142 (2017)

7. Arras, L., Montavon, G., Müller, K.R., Samek, W.: Explaining recurrent neural network predictions in sentiment analysis. In: EMNLP 2017 Workshop on Computational Approaches to Subjectivity, Sentiment & Social Media Analysis (WASSA), pp. 159–168 (2017)
8. Arras, L., Osman, A., Müller, K.R., Samek, W.: Evaluating recurrent neural network explanations. In: ACL 2019 Workshop on BlackboxNLP: Analyzing and Interpreting Neural Networks for NLP (2019)
9. Bach, S., Binder, A., Montavon, G., Klauschen, F., Müller, K.R., Samek, W.: On pixel-wise explanations for non-linear classifier decisions by layer-wise relevance propagation. PLoS ONE 10(7), e0130140 (2015)
10. Baehrens, D., Schroeter, T., Harmeling, S., Kawanabe, M., Hansen, K., Müller, K.R.: How to explain individual classification decisions. J. Mach. Learn. Res. 11, 1803–1831 (2010)
11. Bahdanau, D., Cho, K., Bengio, Y.: Neural machine translation by jointly learning to align and translate. In: International Conference on Learning Representations (ICLR) (2015)
12. Bau, D., Zhou, B., Khosla, A., Oliva, A., Torralba, A.: Network dissection: quantifying interpretability of deep visual representations. In: IEEE Conference on Computer Vision and Pattern Recognition (CVPR), pp. 6541–6549 (2017)
13. Binder, A., Bach, S., Montavon, G., Müller, K.-R., Samek, W.: Layer-wise relevance propagation for deep neural network architectures. Information Science and Applications (ICISA) 2016. LNEE, vol. 376, pp. 913–922. Springer, Singapore (2016). https://doi.org/10.1007/978-981-10-0557-2_87
14. Binder, A., et al.: Towards computational fluorescence microscopy: machine learning-based integrated prediction of morphological and molecular tumor profiles. arXiv preprint arXiv:1805.11178 (2018)
15. Chmiela, S., Sauceda, H.E., Müller, K.R., Tkatchenko, A.: Towards exact molecular dynamics simulations with machine-learned force fields. Nat. Commun. 9(1), 3887 (2018)
16. Cireşan, D., Meier, U., Masci, J., Schmidhuber, J.: A committee of neural networks for traffic sign classification. In: International Joint Conference on Neural Networks (IJCNN), pp. 1918–1921 (2011)
17. Deng, J., Dong, W., Socher, R., Li, L.J., Li, K., Fei-Fei, L.: Imagenet: a large-scale hierarchical image database. In: IEEE Conference on Computer Vision and Pattern Recognition (CVPR), pp. 248–255 (2009)
18. Doshi-Velez, F., Kim, B.: Towards a rigorous science of interpretable machine learning. arXiv preprint arXiv:1702.08608 (2017)
19. Doshi-Velez, F., et al.: Accountability of AI under the law: the role of explanation. arXiv preprint arXiv:1711.01134 (2017)
20. Eitel, F., et al.: Uncovering convolutional neural network decisions for diagnosing multiple sclerosis on conventional MRI using layer-wise relevance propagation. arXiv preprint arXiv:1904.08771 (2019)
21. European Commission's High-Level Expert Group: Draft ethics guidelines for trustworthy AI. European Commission (2019)
22. Everingham, M., Eslami, S.A., Van Gool, L., Williams, C.K., Winn, J., Zisserman, A.: The PASCAL visual object classes challenge: a retrospective. Int. J. Comput. Vision 111(1), 98–136 (2015)
23. Everingham, M., Van Gool, L., Williams, C.K., Winn, J., Zisserman, A.: The pascal visual object classes (VOC) challenge. Int. J. Comput. Vision 88(2), 303–338 (2010)
24. Eykholt, K., et al.: Robust physical-world attacks on deep learning models. arXiv preprint arXiv:1707.08945 (2017)

25. Fong, R.C., Vedaldi, A.: Interpretable explanations of black boxes by meaningful perturbation. In: IEEE International Conference on Computer Vision (CVPR), pp. 3429–3437 (2017)
26. Fong, R., Vedaldi, A.: Explanations for attributing deep neural network predictions. In: Samek, W., Montavon, G., Vedaldi, A., Hansen, L.K., Müller, K.-R. (eds.) Explainable AI. LNCS, vol. 11700, pp. 149–167. Springer, Cham (2019)
27. Goodman, B., Flaxman, S.: European union regulations on algorithmic decision-making and a "right to explanation". AI Mag. **38**(3), 50–57 (2017)
28. Hajian, S., Bonchi, F., Castillo, C.: Algorithmic bias: from discrimination discovery to fairness-aware data mining. In: 22nd ACM SIGKDD International Conference on Knowledge Discovery and Data Mining, pp. 2125–2126 (2016)
29. Han, S., Pool, J., Tran, J., Dally, W.: Learning both weights and connections for efficient neural network. In: Advances in Neural Information Processing Systems (NIPS), pp. 1135–1143 (2015)
30. Heath, R.L., Bryant, J.: Human Communication Theory and Research: Concepts, Contexts, and Challenges. Routledge, New York (2013)
31. Hofmarcher, M., Unterthiner, T., Arjona-Medina, J., Klambauer, G., Hochreiter, S., Nessler, B.: Visual scene understanding for autonomous driving using semantic segmentation. In: Samek, W., Montavon, G., Vedaldi, A., Hansen, L.K., Müller, K.-R. (eds.) Explainable AI. LNCS, vol. 11700, pp. 285–296. Springer, Cham (2019)
32. Holzinger, A., Langs, G., Denk, H., Zatloukal, K., Müller, H.: Causability and explainabilty of artificial intelligence in medicine. Wiley Interdiscip. Rev. Data Min. Knowl. Discov. **9**, e1312 (2019)
33. Horst, F., Lapuschkin, S., Samek, W., Müller, K.R., Schöllhorn, W.I.: Explaining the unique nature of individual gait patterns with deep learning. Sci. Rep. **9**, 2391 (2019)
34. Karpathy, A., Toderici, G., Shetty, S., Leung, T., Sukthankar, R., Fei-Fei, L.: Large-scale video classification with convolutional neural networks. In: IEEE Conference on Computer Vision and Pattern Recognition (CVPR), pp. 1725–1732 (2014)
35. Kauffmann, J., Müller, K.R., Montavon, G.: Towards explaining anomalies: a deep Taylor decomposition of one-class models. arXiv preprint arXiv:1805.06230 (2018)
36. Kauffmann, J., Esders, M., Montavon, G., Samek, W., Müller, K.R.: From clustering to cluster explanations via neural networks. arXiv preprint arXiv:1906.07633 (2019)
37. Khanna, R., Kim, B., Ghosh, J., Koyejo, O.: Interpreting black box predictions using fisher kernels. arXiv preprint arXiv:1810.10118 (2018)
38. Kim, B., et al.: Interpretability beyond feature attribution: quantitative testing with concept activation vectors (TCAV). In: International Conference on Machine Learning (ICML), pp. 2673–2682 (2018)
39. Kindermans, P.J., et al.: Learning how to explain neural networks: patternnet and patternattribution. In: International Conference on Learning Representations (ICLR) (2018)
40. Klauschen, F., et al.: Scoring of tumor-infiltrating lymphocytes: from visual estimation to machine learning. Semin. Cancer Biol. **52**(2), 151–157 (2018)
41. Koh, P.W., Liang, P.: Understanding black-box predictions via influence functions. In: International Conference on Machine Learning (ICML), pp. 1885–1894 (2017)
42. Kriegeskorte, N., Goebel, R., Bandettini, P.: Information-based functional brain mapping. Proc. Nat. Acad. Sci. **103**(10), 3863–3868 (2006)
43. Lage, I., et al.: An evaluation of the human-interpretability of explanation. arXiv preprint arXiv:1902.00006 (2019)

44. Lapuschkin, S., Binder, A., Montavon, G., Müller, K.R., Samek, W.: Analyzing classifiers: fisher vectors and deep neural networks. In: IEEE Conference on Computer Vision and Pattern Recognition (CVPR), pp. 2912–2920 (2016)
45. Lapuschkin, S.: Opening the machine learning black box with layer-wise relevance propagation. Ph.D. thesis, Technische Universität Berlin (2019)
46. Lapuschkin, S., Wäldchen, S., Binder, A., Montavon, G., Samek, W., Müller, K.R.: Unmasking clever hans predictors and assessing what machines really learn. Nat. Commun. **10**, 1096 (2019)
47. LeCun, Y., Bengio, Y., Hinton, G.: Deep learning. Nature **521**(7553), 436–444 (2015)
48. LeCun, Y.A., Bottou, L., Orr, G.B., Müller, K.-R.: Efficient backprop. In: Montavon, G., Orr, G.B., Müller, K.-R. (eds.) Neural Networks: Tricks of the Trade. LNCS, vol. 7700, pp. 9–48. Springer, Heidelberg (2012). https://doi.org/10.1007/978-3-642-35289-8_3
49. Lemm, S., Blankertz, B., Dickhaus, T., Müller, K.R.: Introduction to machine learning for brain imaging. Neuroimage **56**(2), 387–399 (2011)
50. Li, J., Monroe, W., Jurafsky, D.: Understanding neural networks through representation erasure. arXiv preprint arXiv:1612.08220 (2016)
51. Libbrecht, M.W., Noble, W.S.: Machine learning applications in genetics and genomics. Nat. Rev. Genet. **16**(6), 321 (2015)
52. Lindholm, E., Nickolls, J., Oberman, S., Montrym, J.: NVIDIA tesla: a unified graphics and computing architecture. IEEE Micro **28**(2), 39–55 (2008)
53. Lu, C., Tang, X.: Surpassing human-level face verification performance on LFW with GaussianFace. In: 29th AAAI Conference on Artificial Intelligence, pp. 3811–3819 (2015)
54. Lundberg, S.M., Lee, S.I.: A unified approach to interpreting model predictions. In: Advances in Neural Information Processing Systems (NIPS), pp. 4765–4774 (2017)
55. Madry, A., Makelov, A., Schmidt, L., Tsipras, D., Vladu, A.: Towards deep learning models resistant to adversarial attacks. In: International Conference on Learning Representations (ICLR) (2018)
56. Mnih, V., et al.: Human-level control through deep reinforcement learning. Nature **518**(7540), 529–533 (2015)
57. Montavon, G.: Gradient-based vs. propagation-based explanations: an axiomatic comparison. In: Samek, W., Montavon, G., Vedaldi, A., Hansen, L.K., Müller, K.-R. (eds.) Explainable AI. LNCS, vol. 11700, pp. 253–265. Springer, Cham (2019)
58. Montavon, G., Binder, A., Lapuschkin, S., Samek, W., Müller, K.-R.: Layer-wise relevance propagation: an overview. In: Samek, W., Montavon, G., Vedaldi, A., Hansen, L.K., Müller, K.-R. (eds.) Explainable AI. LNCS, vol. 11700, pp. 193–209. Springer, Cham (2019)
59. Montavon, G., Lapuschkin, S., Binder, A., Samek, W., Müller, K.R.: Explaining nonlinear classification decisions with deep Taylor decomposition. Pattern Recogn. **65**, 211–222 (2017)
60. Montavon, G., Samek, W., Müller, K.R.: Methods for interpreting and understanding deep neural networks. Digit. Signal Process. **73**, 1–15 (2018)
61. Moravčík, M., et al.: Deepstack: expert-level artificial intelligence in heads-up no-limit poker. Science **356**(6337), 508–513 (2017)
62. Morch, N., et al.: Visualization of neural networks using saliency maps. In: International Conference on Neural Networks (ICNN), vol. 4, pp. 2085–2090 (1995)

63. Mordvintsev, A., Olah, C., Tyka, M.: Inceptionism: going deeper into neural networks (2015)
64. Nguyen, A., Dosovitskiy, A., Yosinski, J., Brox, T., Clune, J.: Synthesizing the preferred inputs for neurons in neural networks via deep generator networks. In: Advances in Neural Information Processing Systems (NIPS), pp. 3387–3395 (2016)
65. Nguyen, A., Yosinski, J., Clune, J.: Understanding neural networks via feature visualization: a survey. In: Samek, W., Montavon, G., Vedaldi, A., Hansen, L.K., Müller, K.-R. (eds.) Explainable AI. LNCS, vol. 11700, pp. 55–76. Springer, Cham (2019)
66. Nguyen, D.: Comparing automatic and human evaluation of local explanations for text classification. In: Conference of the North American Chapter of the Association for Computational Linguistics: Human Language Technologies (NAACL-HLT), pp. 1069–1078 (2018)
67. Phinyomark, A., Petri, G., Ibáñez-Marcelo, E., Osis, S.T., Ferber, R.: Analysis of big data in gait biomechanics: current trends and future directions. J. Med. Biol. Eng. **38**(2), 244–260 (2018)
68. Pilania, G., Wang, C., Jiang, X., Rajasekaran, S., Ramprasad, R.: Accelerating materials property predictions using machine learning. Sci. Rep. **3**, 2810 (2013)
69. Poerner, N., Roth, B., Schütze, H.: Evaluating neural network explanation methods using hybrid documents and morphosyntactic agreement. In: 56th Annual Meeting of the Association for Computational Linguistics (ACL), pp. 340–350 (2018)
70. Preuer, K., Klambauer, G., Rippmann, F., Hochreiter, S., Unterthiner, T.: Interpretable deep learning in drug discovery. In: Samek, W., Montavon, G., Vedaldi, A., Hansen, L.K., Müller, K.-R. (eds.) Explainable AI. LNCS, vol. 11700, pp. 331–345. Springer, Cham (2019)
71. Redmon, J., Divvala, S., Girshick, R., Farhadi, A.: You only look once: unified, real-time object detection. In: IEEE Conference on Computer Vision and Pattern Recognition (CVPR), pp. 779–788 (2016)
72. Reyes, E., et al.: Enhanced rotational invariant convolutional neural network for supernovae detection. In: International Joint Conference on Neural Networks (IJCNN), pp. 1–8 (2018)
73. Ribeiro, M.T., Singh, S., Guestrin, C.: Why should I trust you?: explaining the predictions of any classifier. In: ACM SIGKDD International Conference on Knowledge Discovery and Data Mining, pp. 1135–1144 (2016)
74. Ross, A.S., Hughes, M.C., Doshi-Velez, F.: Right for the right reasons: training differentiable models by constraining their explanations. In: 26th International Joint Conferences on Artificial Intelligence (IJCAI), pp. 2662–2670 (2017)
75. Samek, W., Binder, A., Montavon, G., Lapuschkin, S., Müller, K.R.: Evaluating the visualization of what a deep neural network has learned. IEEE Trans. Neural Netw. Learn. Syst. **28**(11), 2660–2673 (2017)
76. Samek, W., Wiegand, T., Müller, K.R.: Explainable artificial intelligence: understanding, visualizing and interpreting deep learning models. ITU J. ICT Discov. **1**(1), 39–48 (2018). Special Issue 1 - The Impact of Artificial Intelligence (AI) on Communication Networks and Services
77. Sánchez, J., Perronnin, F., Mensink, T., Verbeek, J.J.: Image classification with the fisher vector: theory and practice. Int. J. Comput. Vision **105**(3), 222–245 (2013)
78. Schütt, K.T., Arbabzadah, F., Chmiela, S., Müller, K.R., Tkatchenko, A.: Quantum-chemical insights from deep tensor neural networks. Nat. Commun. **8**, 13890 (2017)

79. Selvaraju, R.R., Cogswell, M., Das, A., Vedantam, R., Parikh, D., Batra, D.: Grad-CAM: visual explanations from deep networks via gradient-based localization. In: IEEE International Conference on Computer Vision (CVPR), pp. 618–626 (2017)
80. Shapley, L.S.: A value for n-person games. Contrib. Theory Games **2**(28), 307–317 (1953)
81. Shrikumar, A., Greenside, P., Kundaje, A.: Learning important features through propagating activation differences. arXiv preprint arXiv:1704.02685 (2017)
82. Silver, D., et al.: Mastering the game of Go with deep neural networks and tree search. Nature **529**(7587), 484–489 (2016)
83. Silver, D., et al.: Mastering the game of Go without human knowledge. Nature **550**(7676), 354–359 (2017)
84. Simonyan, K., Vedaldi, A., Zisserman, A.: Deep inside convolutional networks: visualising image classification models and saliency maps. In: ICLR Workshop (2014)
85. Smilkov, D., Thorat, N., Kim, B., Viégas, F., Wattenberg, M.: SmoothGrad: removing noise by adding noise. arXiv preprint arXiv:1706.03825 (2017)
86. Springenberg, J.T., Dosovitskiy, A., Brox, T., Riedmiller, M.: Striving for simplicity: the all convolutional net. In: ICLR Workshop (2015)
87. Sturm, I., Lapuschkin, S., Samek, W., Müller, K.R.: Interpretable deep neural networks for single-trial EEG classification. J. Neurosci. Methods **274**, 141–145 (2016)
88. Sundararajan, M., Taly, A., Yan, Q.: Axiomatic attribution for deep networks. In: International Conference on Machine Learning (ICML), pp. 3319–3328 (2017)
89. Thomas, A.W., Heekeren, H.R., Müller, K.R., Samek, W.: Analyzing neuroimaging data through recurrent deep learning models. arXiv preprint arXiv:1810.09945 (2018)
90. Van Den Oord, A., et al.: Wavenet: a generative model for raw audio. arXiv preprint arXiv:1609.03499 (2016)
91. Weller, A.: Transparency: motivations and challenges. In: Samek, W., Montavon, G., Vedaldi, A., Hansen, L.K., Müller, K.-R. (eds.) Explainable AI. LNCS, vol. 11700, pp. 23–40. Springer, Cham (2019)
92. Wu, D., Wang, L., Zhang, P.: Solving statistical mechanics using variational autoregressive networks. Phys. Rev. Lett. **122**(8), 080602 (2019)
93. Yosinski, J., Clune, J., Nguyen, A., Fuchs, T., Lipson, H.: Understanding neural networks through deep visualization. arXiv preprint arXiv:1506.06579 (2015)
94. Zeiler, M.D., Fergus, R.: Visualizing and understanding convolutional networks. In: Fleet, D., Pajdla, T., Schiele, B., Tuytelaars, T. (eds.) ECCV 2014. LNCS, vol. 8689, pp. 818–833. Springer, Cham (2014). https://doi.org/10.1007/978-3-319-10590-1_53
95. Zhang, J., Lin, Z., Brandt, J., Shen, X., Sclaroff, S.: Top-down neural attention by excitation backprop. In: Leibe, B., Matas, J., Sebe, N., Welling, M. (eds.) ECCV 2016. LNCS, vol. 9908, pp. 543–559. Springer, Cham (2016). https://doi.org/10.1007/978-3-319-46493-0_33
96. Zhou, B., Bau, D., Oliva, A., Torralba, A.: Comparing the interpretability of deep networks via network dissection. In: Samek, W., Montavon, G., Vedaldi, A., Hansen, L.K., Müller, K.-R. (eds.) Explainable AI. LNCS, vol. 11700, pp. 243–252. Springer, Cham (2019)
97. Zintgraf, L.M., Cohen, T.S., Adel, T., Welling, M.: Visualizing deep neural network decisions: prediction difference analysis. In: International Conference on Learning Representations (ICLR) (2017)

2
Transparency: Motivations and Challenges

Adrian Weller[1,2,3](✉) ⓘ

[1] University of Cambridge, Cambridge, UK
[2] The Alan Turing Institute, London, UK
[3] Leverhulme Centre for the Future of Intelligence, Cambridge, UK
adrian.weller@eng.cam.ac.uk

Abstract. Transparency is often deemed critical to enable effective real-world deployment of intelligent systems. Yet the motivations for and benefits of different types of transparency can vary significantly depending on context, and objective measurement criteria are difficult to identify. We provide a brief survey, suggesting challenges and related concerns, particularly when agents have misaligned interests. We highlight and review settings where transparency may cause harm, discussing connections across privacy, multi-agent game theory, economics, fairness and trust.

Keywords: Transparency · Interpretability · Explainable · Social good

2.1 Introduction

The case for transparency has been made in many settings, including for government policy [69], business [44], charity [63], and algorithms [48]. Within machine learning, there is a general feeling that "transparency" – like "fairness" – is important and good. Yet both concepts are somewhat ambiguous, and can mean different things to different people in different contexts. We discuss various types of transparency in the context of human interpretation of algorithms, noting their benefits, motivations, difficulties for measurement, and potential concerns.

We then consider settings where, perhaps surprisingly, transparency may lead to a worse outcome. Transparency is often beneficial but it is not a universal good. We draw attention to work in other disciplines and hope to contribute to an exploration of which types of transparency are helpful to whom in which contexts, while recognizing when conditions may arise such that transparency could be unhelpful.

We summarize our main themes:

(A) There are many types of transparency with different motivations – we need better ways to articulate them precisely, and to measure them (Sect. 2.2).

Supported by The Alan Turing Institute, Darwin College and the Leverhulme Trust.

(B) We should recognize that sometimes transparency is a means to an end, not a goal in itself (Sects. 2.2 and 2.3.3).
(C) Actors with misaligned interests can abuse transparency as a manipulation channel, or inappropriately use information gained (Sect. 2.3).
(D) In some settings, more transparency can lead to less efficiency (Sect. 2.4 reviews related work in economics, multi-agent game theory and network routing), fairness (Sect. 2.5) or trust (Sects. 2.3.2 and 2.6).

In Sect. 2.7, we note 'machine interpretability' as an important research direction, which may also provide insight into how to measure human understanding in some settings.

Related Work. There is a considerable literature on transparency and social good. Much of this focuses on the benefits of transparency but some earlier work, notably in economics and social science, also considers drawbacks of transparency and accountability [9, 19, 40, 51, 53]. We discuss related work throughout the text.

2.2   Types of Transparency: Benefits, Measurement and Motivations

Considering transparency of algorithmic systems broadly, there are important areas to consider beyond just the algorithm. For machine learning systems trained on data, knowing where and how the data was gathered can be critical, along with understanding who made those choices and what their motivations were. Further, we should look at the socio-technical context of a system to understand how it will be used in practice.

We briefly describe various types of transparency in the context of human interpretability of algorithmic systems, highlighting different possible motivations. We typically seek an explanation in understandable terms, which can often be framed as answering questions of "what", "how", or "why" (either *toward what purpose* in the future, or *due to what cause* in the past). Some of our observations have been made previously [16, 42, 46]. To our knowledge, in the setting of artificial intelligence, we make new points on motivations and on measuring understanding.

An automated explanation might arise immediately from the original system – typically if it has been constrained to lie in some set of classifiers deemed to be interpretable (e.g. a short decision list). Alternatively, a second explainer algorithm may have produced an explanation for the original system. We consider various classes of people: a *developer* is building the system; a *deployer* owns it and releases it to the public or some user group; a *user* is a typical user of the system. For example, developers might be hired to build a personalized recommendation system to buy products, which Amazon then deploys, to be used by a typical member of the public. People might be experts or not.

We list several types and goals of transparency. Each may require a different sort of explanation, requiring different measures of efficacy:

Type 1 For a developer, to understand how their system is working, aiming to debug or improve it: to see what is working well or badly, and get a sense for why.

Type 2 For a user, to provide a sense for what the system is doing and why, to enable prediction of what it might do in unforeseen circumstances and build a sense of trust in the technology.

Type 3 For society broadly to understand and become comfortable with the strengths and limitations of the system, overcoming a reasonable fear of the unknown.

Type 4 For a user to understand why one particular prediction or decision was reached, to allow a check that the system worked appropriately and to enable meaningful challenge (e.g. credit approval or criminal sentencing).

Type 5 To provide an expert (perhaps a regulator) the ability to audit a prediction or decision trail in detail, particularly if something goes wrong (e.g. a crash by an autonomous car). This may require storing key data streams and tracing through each logical step, and will facilitate assignment of accountability and legal liability.

Type 6 To facilitate monitoring and testing for safety standards.

Type 7 To make a user (the audience) feel comfortable with a prediction or decision so that they keep using the system. Beneficiary: deployer.

Type 8 To lead a user (the audience) into some action or behavior – e.g. Amazon might recommend a product, providing an explanation in order that you will then click through to make a purchase. Beneficiary: deployer.

We can differentiate between the intended *audience* of an explanation and the likely *beneficiary* (or beneficiaries). We suggest that types 1–6 are broadly beneficial for society provided that explanations given are *faithful*, in the sense that they accurately convey a true understanding without hiding important details. This notion of faithful can be hard to characterize precisely. It is similar in spirit to the instructions sometimes given in courts to tell "the truth, the whole truth, and nothing but the truth."

Defining criteria and tests for practical faithfulness are important open problems. We suggest that helpful progress may be made in future by focusing on one particular context at a time. We make a similar suggestion for the challenges of characterizing if an explanation is good at conveying faithful information in understandable form, and if a human has actually understood it well.[1] [16] suggest several methods, such as establishing a quantitative approximate measure (e.g. if we are restricting models to be decision trees then we can feel reasonably confident that a model becomes harder to understand as the number of nodes increases), or asking a human if they can correctly estimate what the system would output for given inputs. We suggest further approaches below and highlight a key challenge.

---

[1] Greater faithfulness of an explanation may challenge the ability of its audience to understand it well, perhaps requiring a greater investment of time and effort [54].

We use (as in [16]) the terms *global* interpretability or explanation for a general understanding of how an overall system works, as in our transparency types 2–3; and *local* interpretability for an explanation of a particular prediction or decision, as in types 4, 5, 7 and 8 (though both forms may be useful for a given type).

Fig. 2.1. An image (left) is given to a classification system. A separate explaining algorithm extracts the sub-image (right) which it estimates led the original system to output "beagle" (from [14]). Would it be better or not if the sub-image contained the legs of the dog? That depends on the classification system, and what exactly is desired, and is not simple to answer, demonstrating one challenge in defining a quantitative measure of the quality of the explanation.

For global interpretability, we mention two interesting possible approaches due to quotes attributed to the physicist Richard Feynman: (i) "What I cannot create, I do not understand" suggests that in some settings, a good test of understanding might be to see if the person could recreate the whole system (given expert help and allowing some reasonable tolerance); (ii) "If you can't explain it to a six year old, you don't really understand it" suggests a possible meta-approach to test clarity of an explanation – for any given test T of human understanding, ask the person to explain the system to someone new, then give that new person the test T. [35] introduced measures of human interpretability based on being able to describe a decision boundary, which would facilitate model reconstruction. Rudin [57] argues that in many settings, a global model which is constrained to be 'interpretable by construction', for example by being described by a simple, short, intuitive scoring system, will provide sufficiently high performance [58]. We discuss further notions of understanding in Sect. 2.7.

Highlighting a key challenge even for local interpretability, consider explaining the output of an image classification system, as illustrated in Fig. 2.1. Several recent approaches attempt to identify the parts of a given image which are most salient, i.e. those parts which in a sense were most responsible for leading to the system's prediction [54, 75]. Such approaches can be very helpful – e.g. for type 1 transparency, we might learn that a system which reliably tells apart wolves from huskies on a test set might in fact be relying on the presence or absence of snow in the background, rather than features of the animal itself, and hence may be unlikely to generalize well on test data [54]. Suppose we are given two such methods of generating a salient sub-image for a classification system. How should we measure which method provides a better explanation of what the system is doing? This is an important question, where the answer will depend on sharpening our understanding of exactly what we are seeking. Note that it is not helpful to compare against what a human thinks is relevant in the image. Rather, we want a sub-image which is high in predictive information *for the system* yet is not too large, focusing only on the relevant region. A promising possible direction for a quantitative solution was suggested by [14], who propose a measure of concentration of information.

[59] proposed a different quantitative metric for evaluating methods which return ordered collections of input pixels, based on region perturbation. On this metric, an approach called Layer-wise Relevance Propagation (LRP [7]) performed well for explaining classifications made by deep neural networks. Alternative 'axiomatic' approaches have been developed for identifying and quantifying the contributions of each input feature toward a particular classification, based on specifying reasonable desirable properties which an explanation should have [15,64,65]. Interestingly, these approaches link to earlier work by Shapley [60] on determining the value of contributions made in n-person games. Typically, it is computationally intractable to compute the appropriate contributions exactly, but various methods may be regarded as approximations to this approach [45].

We briefly note two other approaches to *ex post* explanations of a specific automated classification. Rather than provide an attribution over features of the input, [34] instead identifies which training data points were particularly influential for making the classification. [70] propose *counterfactual explanations*: suppose an individual applies to a bank for a loan but is classified as not being sufficiently creditworthy; a counterfactual explanation reveals the minimum change required in some feature(s), for example income, such that the loan would instead be classified as approved, thus potentially providing an action which could feasibly be taken by the individual to change the decision.

Other approaches seek to identify interpretable representations in order to help understand how an algorithm works [1,11,29]. We have not provided an exhaustive survey of interpretability methods, but hope that it is clear that different approaches yield different notions of transparency, each of which may be useful in different settings. There is no universally appropriate approach.

Transparency as a Proxy. Transparency can provide insight into other characteristics which may be hard to measure (as noted by [16]). We noted above how local explanations for an image classification system – revealing how wolves were differentiated from huskies – demonstrated the lack of robustness of the system. Other features where transparency can provide helpful insight include safety, fairness, verification and causality. There is a rapidly growing literature on methods to try to address these areas directly [3,17,21,27,31,46,52,67].

2.3   Possible Dangers of Transparency

In this section, we begin to examine ways that transparency may be unhelpful.

2.3.1   Divergence Between Audience and Beneficiary

There are some forms of transparency, such as types 7 and 8 in Sect. 2.2, where the intended audience for an explanation diverges from the beneficiary, hence the motivation may be suspect. This can lead to worrying types of manipulation and requires careful consideration.

Considering type 7 transparency, we draw attention to the remarkable 'Copy Machine' study. [37] arranged for researchers to try to jump in line to make a few photocopies at a busy library copy machine. The researcher either (i) gave no explanation, asking simply "May I use the xerox machine?"; (ii) provided an 'empty' explanation: "May I use the xerox machine, because I have to make copies?"; or (iii) provided a 'real' explanation: "May I use the xerox machine, because I'm in a rush?" The respective success rates were: (i) 60%; (ii) 93%; and (iii) 94%. The startling conclusion was that saying "*because* something" seemed to work effectively to attain compliance, even if the 'something' had zero information content. Hence, a possible worry is that a deployer might provide an empty explanation as a psychological tool to soothe users.

In fact there is a line of research which considers all communication often to be more a form of manipulation than a way to transfer information. This view is prominent when taking an evolutionary view of multiple agents [73], a perspective which we revisit throughout the remainder of this paper. Earlier work by [2] explored whether disclosures provided in financial reports are more aptly described as communication or manipulation.

For type 8 transparency, where the deployer has a clear motive which may not be in the best interests of the audience of the explanation, particular care and future study is warranted. Even if a faithful explanation is given, it may have been carefully selected from a large set of possible faithful explanations in order to serve the deployer's goals.

2.3.2   Government Use of Algorithms

In many states in the US, a private company provides the COMPAS system to judges to help predict the recidivism risk of a prisoner, i.e. the chance that the prisoner will commit a crime again if released. This information is an important factor in parole hearings to determine whether to release prisoners early or to keep them locked behind bars. Significant attention has focused on whether or not the prediction system is fair [4]. We discuss connections between fairness and transparency in Sects. 2.4.1 and 2.5. Here we consider the appropriate degree of transparency of such a system: a prisoner should at least have transparency type 4 from Sect. 2.2 in order to check if proper process has been followed and enable potential challenge, but can there be too much transparency?

Perhaps motivated by concerns in the US over the COMPAS system, Bulgaria passed legislation requiring that (many forms of) government software be open source, "after all, it's paid by tax-payers' money and they should... be able to see it" [12]. More recently, New York announced the creation of a task force to examine how city agencies use algorithms to make decisions, looking to find ways to make automated systems more transparent, fair and accountable [72]. Note that a machine learning system typically consists of both algorithms and data, and having access to just one of these may not provide much meaningful information. We consider the case of all algorithms and data being transparently available and note several concerns.

Gaming and IP Incentives. If all details are readily available, this can facilitate gaming of the rules [22].[2] In addition, if all code and data is open source, then this reduces incentives to develop relevant private intellectual property, which may delay progress significantly.

Transparency and Privacy. Indeed, in many cases, transparency may be viewed as the opposite of privacy. Many in society feel that some sort of right to privacy – and hence, a limit to transparency – is appropriate. Legal frameworks vary by country. A recent landmark decision by the Supreme Court of India is explicit, stating "The right to privacy is protected as an intrinsic part of the right to life and personal liberty under Article 21 and as a part of the freedoms guaranteed by Part III of the Constitution" [50]. Tensions between privacy and transparency can exist even for one user whose data is used in a system – the user may want their personal data to be kept private but might also like a right to an explanation of how that same system (algorithms + data) works.

Further, there are many settings where privacy (i.e. a lack of transparency to all) is critical to foster a trusting relationship of confidence. Examples include the relationship between a doctor and a patient, a lawyer and their client, or discussions of international diplomacy. Inside these relationships, it is interesting to question whether greater transparency leads to trust. We return to this topic in Sect. 2.6. Here we rather suggest that a prudent approach is to release private information only to a partner that is already trusted, hence trust can lead to transparency. Providing information to an agent empowers them [61], hence you should first be confident that their interests align with yours.

As one example, there has been discussion about the extent to which government agencies such as the NSA should be allowed to collect data on individuals. Some argue that "if you've got nothing to hide, you've got nothing to fear" [62] or suggest that collecting only 'metadata' is harmless. Yet [13] quotes General Michael Hayden, former director of the NSA and CIA, as saying "We kill people based on metadata."

---

[2] One view is that if rules are set up correctly, then transparency will not lead to 'gaming' since agents optimizing their own objectives subject to the rules will necessarily lead to a good outcome for all. However, it is often very challenging in practice to get the rules exactly right in this way – thus there may be a distinction between the 'letter' and the 'spirit' of the law. See Sect. 2.4 for a related example.

2.3.3   Means and Ends

In Sect. 2.2, we noted that transparency can serve as an imperfect proxy to gain insight into other desirable properties of a system, such as reliability or fairness. For example, transparency is often cited as critical for deployment of autonomous vehicles. We suggest that these transparency concerns are primarily for types 1, 2, 3, 5 and 6. Each of these involves somewhat different types of explanation or understanding, with some easier to implement than others. A key concern is reliable safety: how can we be certain that the vehicle will perform well in all circumstances if we do not understand exactly how it is working?

In such cases, we should take care not to stifle innovation by confusing transparency as an end in itself rather than a means to other goals. It is conceivable that much time and resources could be spent trying to gain an extremely transparent understanding, when those efforts might be better spent directly on the goal of improving safety. Being pragmatic, it is plausible that society will resort to implementing various safety tests, such as are used for aircraft autopilot systems. If such tests are passed by an autonomous vehicle system, and accidents are extremely rare in practice, then it may make sense to proceed even without full transparency. After all, which is preferable: full transparency and many deaths per year from accidents, or less transparency and fewer deaths per year? As [18] eloquently put it, we must beware the "perfection of means and confusion of goals."

2.4   Economics and Multi-agent Game Theory

In an economy, each individual can act as an autonomous agent. If each agent optimizes her own selfish utility, there is no guarantee in general that this will lead to the best outcome for society. Under restrictive assumptions, [5] famously proved the existence of a general equilibrium for a competitive economy. If *externalities* are present, i.e. if costs of one agent's actions fall on others, then we should expect that the result of each agent optimizing her own outcome may lead to a suboptimal result for the whole. This phenomenon is sometimes described as the *price of anarchy* [56].

We relate this to transparency by considering what happens if all agents are given additional faithful information about a system. This is a form of type 3 transparency from Sect. 2.2, which may seem the most innocuous of all. An engineering perspective might naturally lead one to suspect that more information should lead to a better outcome. However, the background of an economist or multi-agent game theorist helps to realize that more information empowers the agents to optimize their own agendas more efficiently, and thus may lead to a worse global outcome. We illustrate these ideas with a striking example of Braess' paradox [10] as given by [32].

Figure 2.2 (top) shows a traffic network where 6 cars enter s at the left, flow through the network via either u or v and exit from t at the right. The costs (delays) of each edge are shown in red, and importantly rise as the amount of flow through them increases. This is realistic in that greater traffic flow on a

Initial configuration. Everyone has cost (delay) of 83.

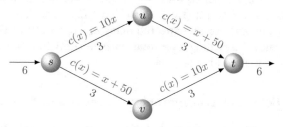

Edge $u \to v$ is revealed. Everyone has cost (delay) of 92.

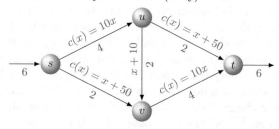

Fig. 2.2. An example of Braess' paradox for network flow from [32]. 6 cars of flow must pass from s to t. For each edge: red (above) shows the cost (i.e. delay incurred) as a function of the flow x through it; blue (below) shows the Wardrop equilibrium flow given the costs, based on each car selfishly optimizing. When the edge $u \to v$ is revealed, surprisingly everyone does worse.

road often leads to longer delays for everyone on it. Thus we have externalities. If each agent optimizes her own utility, the *Wardrop equilibrium* shown in blue is reached, where each car incurs a delay of $10 \cdot 3 + 3 + 50 = 83$ time units (details in [32]; at a Wardrop equilibrium, no individual can reduce her path cost by switching routes, hence all routes have the same cost).

Now consider what happens if all cars learn about an extra road from u to v as shown in Fig. 2.2 (bottom). We may assume that the $u \to v$ road was always there but that it was hidden until the faithful information about its existence was made transparent. Some cars on the $s \to u$ path save time by taking the new $u \to v$ road then $v \to t$, rather than going directly along $u \to t$. Cars on $s \to v$ see an opportunity to reduce their delay by switching to this new $s \to u \to v$ route. Although intuitively the additional road increases capacity for all and hence seemingly should only lead to a better outcome, in fact the new Wardrop equilibrium obtained by selfish optimization results in a greater delay for everyone of $10 \cdot 4 + 2 + 50 = 92$ units!

[32] provides an additional twist on this example. Suppose now that all users know that road works might be under way on the $u \to v$ road, which has delay $x + 10 + R$, where R is a random variable taking the values 0 or 30 with equal probability. If R is unknown, then the expected delay along $u \to v$ is $x + 25$, leading to the outcome in Fig. 2.2 (top) with delay of 83. On the other hand,

if instead R is known to everyone, then: we either have $R = 30$ which leads to the outcome in Fig. 2.2 (top); or we have $R = 0$ which leads to the outcome in Fig. 2.2 (bottom); for an expected delay of $\frac{1}{2}(83+92) = 87.5 > 83$. Hence, again transparency (providing everyone with faithful information) leads to a worse expected outcome for everyone.

2.4.1 Selective Transparency, Fairness and Policy

The examples above show that providing full transparency of information to everyone can sometimes result in a worse outcome for all. But what if transparency is provided selectively only to *some* participants?

Consider the original example of Braess' paradox in Fig. 2.2. Suppose the population is divided into a small privileged subgroup P of size ϵ, and everyone else Q. It is not hard to see that if the information about the $u \rightarrow v$ road is made available only to P, then P will do (significantly) better while Q will do (slightly) worse. But now consider if the flow cost functions for $s \rightarrow u$ and $v \rightarrow t$ are slightly changed to be locally flat for flows just above 3, before resuming their increase.[3] Now *everyone does better* if the $u \rightarrow v$ road is revealed *only to* P (though P does much better than Q), while everyone does worse if $u \rightarrow v$ is revealed to everyone!

This presents an intriguing dilemma for policy makers: should we prefer (i) a 'fair' outcome where everyone suffers equally, or (ii) an outcome which is better for everyone but where some are much better off than others? One imagines this scenario might often arise in practice if a large fraction of the population were being guided by a map application provided by one company – the company might defend a decision to provide faster routing to a select few in order to benefit all.

Now consider if the privileged few were chosen uniformly at random – perhaps that might be fair? Notions of fairness beyond equality, and the role of randomness in fairness, were recently explored [24, 74].

2.4.2 Algorithmic Trading

Algorithmic trading is one area where self-interested agents compete fiercely for high stakes. In many cases, increasing transparency may be beneficial – but when considering regulation such as the Markets in Financial Instruments Directive (MiFID II), which came into effect in the EU in 2018 and includes various requirements for transparency, one should take care to keep in mind the observation above that in some cases, providing more transparent information to self-interested agents can potentially have negative consequences.

---

[3] Consider $c(x) = \begin{cases} 10x & x \leq 3 \\ 30 & 3 \leq x \leq 3+\epsilon . \\ 10(x-\epsilon) & 3+\epsilon \leq x. \end{cases}$

2.4.3   Principals and Agents: Actions and Consequences

In economics, the *principal-agent* problem [55] occurs when one entity (the *agent*) takes actions on behalf of another entity (the *principal*). In general, an agent might act so as to benefit herself even though this could hurt the principal. An example is a fund manager (agent) making investment decisions for an investor (principal). The problem is typically worse when the agent has more information than the principal since this makes it hard for the principal to check if the agent is acting in the principal's interest. Hence, it is common to call for greater transparency about the agent.

[53] considers when in fact it might surprisingly be bad for a principal to observe more information about the agent. Prat distinguishes between information directly about the agent's *actions*, and information about the *consequences* thereof. While the latter is helpful, when more information about the actions is available, the agent has an incentive to disregard useful signals which are private to her, and instead to do what an able agent is expected to do a priori. Prat uses this insight to explain a phenomenon previously observed by [36]: US pension funds' performance in equity markets was worse than that of mutual funds. Typically mutual fund investors only see realized investment returns, whereas pension fund investors have much greater access to their fund managers who explain their investment strategy. Thus there may be an incentive for conformism in pension fund managers, leading to lower expected returns.

In a similar spirit, [53] discusses *executive privilege*, particularly the right of the US President and certain government officers to resist calls for transparent information about how they arrived at decisions in some settings. Prat provides a telling quote from a US Supreme Court ruling relating to the famous Watergate case (US vs. Nixon): "Human experience teaches us that those who expect public dissemination of their remarks may well temper candor with a concern for appearances and for their own interest to the detriment of the decision-making process."

2.5   Fairness and Discrimination

Much work on fairness in machine learning has focused on attempting to avoid discrimination against sub-groups as identified by sensitive features, such as race or gender. Typical metrics for discrimination are based on various types of *disparate impact* or *disparate treatment* [8]. Here we consider a theme which relates to transparency and a common fairness approach used to avoid disparate treatment: simply remove the sensitive feature(s) from the data. A valid objection to this method is that it may be possible to predict (and hence reconstruct) the sensitive feature(s) from other features with high confidence. Nevertheless, the approach is in widespread use and the example below may help to explain its intuitive appeal to some.

[6] describes fascinating work exploring the conditions under which cooperation naturally emerges in multi-agent populations. In many settings, repeated contact leading to iterated prisoner's dilemma interactions are supportive of the

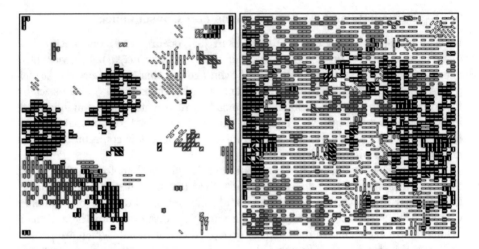

Fig. 2.3. Illustrations by [26] of the evolution of ethnocentrism. Four different tribes are shown as shades of gray. Agents which are {Ethnocentric (cooperate with their own tribe, defect against other tribes)/Pure cooperators (always cooperate)/Egoists (always defect)/Those who cooperate only with other tribes} have {Horizontal/Vertical/Diagonal up-right/Diagonal up-left} lines respectively. The left image shows one run after 100 periods; the right image is after 2000 periods. Over time, almost all agents are ethnocentric. See the reference for a video.eps

emergence of cooperation (for details of the prisoner's dilemma, see wikipedia or https://plato.stanford.edu/entries/prisoner-dilemma/).

In subsequent work, [26] expanded the framework to consider agents which have an extra feature of 'ethnicity' which might be regarded as their color or tribe. Now each agent could either cooperate or defect when interacting with other agents of the same tribe; and similarly could either cooperate or defect with agents of other tribes. Using a simple model of multi-agent evolution, it was strikingly demonstrated that a robust conclusion across a wide range of model parameters, is that 'ethnocentrism' emerges. That is, after many iterations, each agent is very likely to cooperate with others of the same tribe, but to defect against agents from other tribes. See Fig. 2.3.

Hence, in this setting, greater transparency (i.e. making faithful information on ethnicity available) leads to the emergence of discriminatory behavior. In general settings, there is no clear answer as to whether better outcomes will be achieved by hiding or revealing sensitive attributes. Some have attempted to use technical privacy methods to try simultaneously to get the benefits of both [33].

Recent work explores multi-agent reinforcement learning in repeated social interactions to begin to identify conditions on the environment and the agents' cognitive capacities which lead to the emergence of cooperation (see [39,43] and related blog entries). [68] show that bounded rationality with quantized priors may lead to discrimination.

2.6   Trust: Transparency and Honesty

Many support the view that transparency builds trust. For example, the Dalai Lama is reported to have warned "A lack of transparency results in distrust and a deep sense of insecurity." However, we suggest that the story is more nuanced. If we distinguish between transparency – i.e. the provision of information – and honesty – i.e. the accuracy of the information – then which is more important?

A common view is that trust relies on honesty. In order to judge trustworthiness, [49] claims we must examine three qualities: honesty, competence and reliability. Stressing honesty, Simon Sinek is reported to have said "Trust is built on telling the truth, not telling people what they want to hear." However, as we can sense from the following phrases themselves, it can be difficult to hear the 'harsh truth' from someone speaking with 'brutal honesty'.

In recent work, [41] demonstrated settings where *prosocial lies* increased trust. Prosocial lies are a form of deception – the transmission of information that intentionally misleads others – which benefits the target. Their work aims to separate the roles of benevolence and integrity in building interpersonal trust. They conclude that altruistic lies increase trust when deception is directly experienced, or even when it is merely observed.

These effects may make sense when we consider that humans evolved in a tribal multi-agent society. Trusting someone may reflect a belief that they are 'in our tribe' and will reliably look out for our interests. From a historic survival perspective, this benevolence may have been more important than truthful communication – perhaps a 'pre-truth' society?

Interestingly, work in psychology indicates that we are not good at estimating how transparent we are ourselves when communicating with others. [23] showed evidence for the *illusion of transparency* – a tendency for people to overestimate the extent to which others can discern their internal states. This is attributed to a tendency for people to adjust insufficiently from the 'anchor' of their own experience when attempting to adopt another's perspective. Consistent with this, [25] made the following observation: if someone is asked to tap a well-known melody on a tabletop and then to estimate the chance that a listener will be able to identify the song they have tapped, tappers grossly overestimate the listener's abilities.

2.7   Machine Interpretability and Understanding

Human interpretability – that is helping humans to understand machines – is of great importance. But we describe below two classes of 'machine interpretability' – that is helping machines to 'understand' – which are also valuable lines of research.

First, it will be increasingly helpful for machines to be able to follow humans and our motivations. As examples, consider automated care for the elderly, or how an autonomous vehicle waiting at a crossroad should perceive and respond reliably if a human in a car opposite is beckoning to advance.

Second, we believe that a fruitful line of work will be to help machines understand each other. Exciting work has begun to explore this direction, looking for ways to enable multiple agents to cooperate effectively [20, 28, 47]. Different paradigms of multi-agent organization should be explored [30]. One motivation is the goal of AI agents which can autonomously generate and communicate flexible, hierarchical *concepts* which can apply broadly, going beyond traditional transfer learning. Ideally, these concepts will capture high level structure in a way which can be transmitted efficiently and deployed flexibly. Although it is highly desirable for humans to understand this structure, we suggest that it will still be extremely useful, and perhaps easier, to begin by working on ways for machines to communicate with each other. Further, complex structures may be developed which are beyond easy human understanding.

It is possible that a relatively low capacity information bottleneck (as examined by [66]) will be a useful constraint between agents to develop such structures. Indeed, [38] has suggested that the low inter-human bandwidth of speech compared to the higher processing power of our brains may have helped lead to the development of our own intelligence and consciousness.

With this goal in mind, a useful metric of successful 'transfer of understanding' (here a metric for a good explanation) could be to measure how agent B's performance on some task, or range of tasks, improves after receiving some limited information from agent A – though important details will need to be determined, including suitable bandwidth constraints, and recognition that what is useful will depend on the knowledge that A has already.

A similar notion might be useful for measuring human interpretability. An example of a helpful conceptual explanation to improve a beginner's ability to play chess might be "try to control the center." One advantage is that only performance improvement need be measured, bypassing the difficult task of quantifying internal understanding directly.

2.8 Conclusion

There are many settings where transparency is helpful. We have described some of these settings and have begun to clarify just what sort of transparency may be desirable for each, with accompanying research challenges. This topic is timely given keen interest in laws such as the GDPR (introduced in the EU in 2018) which seek to provide users with some sort of meaningful information about algorithmic decisions.

One focus of this work is to highlight scenarios where transparency may cause harm. We have provided examples where greater transparency can lead to worse outcomes and less fairness. We hope to continue to develop frameworks to understand what sorts of transparency are helpful or harmful to whom in particular contexts, and to develop mechanisms which ensure that appropriate benefits are realized. This is a rich area which can draw on connections across economics and the social sciences, philosophy, multi-agent game theory, law, policy and cognitive science.

Acknowledgements. This article is an extended version of [71]. The author thanks Frank Kelly for pointing out the Braess' paradox example and related intuition; and thanks Vasco Carvalho, Stephen Cave, Jon Crowcroft, David Fohrman, Yarin Gal, Adria Gascon, Zoubin Ghahramani, Sanjeev Goyal, Krishna P. Gummadi, Dylan Hadfield-Menell, Bill Janeway, Frank Kelly, Aryeh Kontorovich, Neil Lawrence, Barney Pell and Mark Rowland for helpful discussions; and thanks the anonymous reviewers for helpful comments. The author acknowledges support from the David MacKay Newton research fellowship at Darwin College, The Alan Turing Institute under EPSRC grant EP/N510129/1 & TU/B/000074, and the Leverhulme Trust via the CFI.

References

1. Adel, T., Ghahramani, Z., Weller, A.: Discovering interpretable representations for both deep generative and discriminative models. In: ICML (2018)
2. Adelberg, A.: Narrative disclosures contained in financial reports: means of communication or manipulation? Acc. Bus. Res. **9**(35), 179–190 (1979)
3. Amodei, D., Olah, C., Steinhardt, J., Christiano, P., Schulman, J., Mané, D.: Concrete problems in AI safety. arXiv preprint. arXiv:1606.06565 (2016)
4. Angwin, J., Larson, J., Mattu, S., Kirchner, L.: Machine bias: There's software used across the country to predict future criminals. and it's biased against blacks. ProPublica, May 2016
5. Arrow, K., Debreu, G.: Existence of an equilibrium for a competitive economy. Econometrica J. Econometric Soc. **22**, 265–290 (1954)
6. Axelrod, R.: The Evolution of Cooperation. Basic Books, New York (2006)
7. Bach, S., Binder, A., Montavon, G., Klauschen, F., Müller, K.R., Samek, W.: On pixel-wise explanations for non-linear classifier decisions by layer-wise relevance propagation. PLoS ONE **10**(7), e0130140 (2015)
8. Barocas, S., Selbst, A.: Big data's disparate impact. Calif. Law Rev. **104**(3), 671–732 (2016)
9. Bernstein, E.: The transparency trap. Harv. Bus. Rev. **92**(10), 58–66 (2014)
10. Braess, D.: Über ein paradoxon aus der verkehrsplanung. Math. Methods Oper. Res. **12**(1), 258–268 (1968)
11. Chen, X., Duan, Y., Houthooft, R., Schulman, J., Sutskever, I., Abbeel, P.: InfoGAN: interpretable representation learning by information maximizing generative adversarial nets. In: NeurIPS (2016)
12. Coldewey, D.: Bulgaria now requires (some) government software be open source. TechCrunch, July 2016
13. Cole, D.: We kill people based on metadata. The New York Review of Books, May 2014
14. Dabkowski, P., Gal, Y.: Real time image saliency for black box classifiers. In: NeurIPS (2017)
15. Datta, A., Sen, S., Zick, Y.: Algorithmic transparency via quantitative input influence: theory and experiments with learning systems. In: 2016 IEEE Symposium on Security and Privacy (SP), pp. 598–617. IEEE (2016)
16. Doshi-Velez, F., Kim, B.: Towards a rigorous science of interpretable machine learning. CoRR abs/1702.08608 (2017)
17. Dwork, C., Hardt, M., Pitassi, T., Reingold, O.: Fairness through awareness. In: ITCSC (2012)

18. Einstein, A.: The common language of science. Adv. Sci. **2**(5) (1942). A 1941 recording by Einstein to the British Association for the Advancement of Science is available https://www.youtube.com/watch?v=e3B5BC4rhAU

19. Etzioni, A.: Is transparency the best disinfectant? J. Polit. Philos. **18**(4), 389–404 (2010)

20. Evtimova, K., Drozdov, A., Kiela, D., Cho, K.: Emergent communication in a multi-modal, multi-step referential game. In: ICLR (2018)

21. Feldman, M., Friedler, S.A., Moeller, J., Scheidegger, C., Venkatasubramanian, S.: Certifying and removing disparate impact. In: KDD (2015)

22. Ghani, R.: You say you want transparency and interpretability? (2016). http://www.rayidghani.com/you-say-you-want-transparency-and-interpretability

23. Gilovich, T., Savitsky, K., Medvec, V.: The illusion of transparency: biased assessments of others' ability to read one's emotional states. J. Pers. Soc. Psychol. **75**(2), 332 (1998)

24. Grgić-Hlača, N., Zafar, M.B., Gummadi, K.P., Weller, A.: On fairness, diversity and randomness in algorithmic decision making. In: FAT/ML Workshop at KDD (2017)

25. Griffin, D., Ross, L.: Subjective construal, social inference, and human misunderstanding. Adv. Exp. Soc. Psychol. **24**, 319–359 (1991)

26. Hammond, R., Axelrod, R.: The evolution of ethnocentrism. J. Conflict Resolut. **50**(6), 926–936 (2006). http://www-personal.umich.edu/~axe/vtmovie.htm

27. Hardt, M., Price, E., Srebro, N.: Equality of opportunity in supervised learning. In: NeurIPS (2016)

28. Havrylov, S., Titov, I.: Emergence of language with multi-agent games: learning to communicate with sequences of symbols. arXiv preprint. arXiv:1705.11192 (2017)

29. Higgins, I., et al.: beta-VAE: learning basic visual concepts with a constrained variational framework. In: ICLR (2017)

30. Horling, B., Lesser, V.: A survey of multi-agent organizational paradigms. Knowl. Eng. Rev. **19**(4), 281–316 (2004)

31. Joseph, M., Kearns, M., Morgenstern, J., Roth, A.: Fairness in learning: classic and contextual bandits. In: NeurIPS (2016)

32. Kelly, F.: Network routing. Philos. Trans. Royal Soc. Lond. A Math. Phys. Eng. Sci. **337**(1647), 343–367 (1991)

33. Kilbertus, N., Gascón, A., Kusner, M.J., Veale, M., Gummadi, K.P., Weller, A.: Blind justice: fairness with encrypted sensitive attributes. In: ICML (2018)

34. Koh, P.W., Liang, P.: Understanding black-box predictions via influence functions. In: ICML (2017)

35. Lakkaraju, H., Bach, S., Leskovec, J.: Interpretable decision sets: a joint framework for description and prediction. In: KDD, pp. 1675–1684. ACM (2016)

36. Lakonishok, J., Shleifer, A., Vishny, R.W., Hart, O., Perry, G.L.: The structure and performance of the money management industry. Brook. Pap. Econ. Act. Microecon. **1992**, 339–391 (1992)

37. Langer, E., Blank, A., Chanowitz, B.: The mindlessness of ostensibly thoughtful action: the role of "placebic" information in interpersonal interaction. J. Pers. Soc. Psychol. **36**(6), 635–642 (1978)

38. Lawrence, N.: Living together: mind and machine intelligence. CoRR abs/1705.07996 (2017)

39. Leibo, J., Zambaldi, V., Lanctot, M., Marecki, J., Graepel, T.: Multi-agent reinforcement learning in sequential social dilemmas. In: AAMAS (2017). https://deepmind.com/blog/understanding-agent-cooperation/

40. Lerner, J., Tetlock, P.: Accounting for the effects of accountability. Psychol. Bull. **125**(2), 255 (1999)
41. Levine, E., Schweitzer, M.: Prosocial lies: when deception breeds trust. Organ. Behav. Hum. Decis. Process. **126**, 88–106 (2015)
42. Lipton, Z.: The mythos of model interpretability. In: ICML Workshop on Human Interpretability in Machine Learning, New York, NY, pp. 96–100 (2016)
43. Lowe, R., Wu, Y., Tamar, A., Harb, J., Abbeel, P., Mordatch, I.: Multi-agent actor-critic for mixed cooperative-competitive environments. In: NeurIPS (2017). https://blog.openai.com/learning-to-cooperate-compete-and-communicate/
44. Lowenstein, L.: Financial transparency and corporate governance: you manage what you measure. Columbia Law Rev. **96**(5), 1335–1362 (1996)
45. Lundberg, S.M., Lee, S.I.: A unified approach to interpreting model predictions. In: NeurIPS (2017)
46. McAllister, R., et al.: Concrete problems for autonomous vehicle safety: advantages of Bayesian deep learning. In: IJCAI (2017)
47. Mordatch, I., Abbeel, P.: Emergence of grounded compositional language in multi-agent populations. In: AAAI (2018)
48. Mortier, R., Haddadi, H., Henderson, T., McAuley, D., Crowcroft, J.: Human-data interaction: the human face of the data-driven society. Social Science Research Network (2014)
49. O'Neill, O.: What we don't understand about trust. TED talk, June 2013
50. Pandey, G.: Indian Supreme Court in landmark ruling on privacy. BBC News, 24 August 2017. http://www.bbc.co.uk/news/world-asia-india-41033954
51. Peled, A.: When transparency and collaboration collide: the USA open data program. J. Am. Soc. Inf. Sci. Technol. **62**(11), 2085–2094 (2011)
52. Peters, J., Janzing, D., Schölkopf, B.: Elements of Causal Inference - Foundations and Learning Algorithms. Adaptive Computation and Machine Learning Series. MIT Press, Cambridge (2017)
53. Prat, A.: The wrong kind of transparency. Am. Econ. Rev. **95**(3), 862–877 (2005)
54. Ribeiro, M., Singh, S., Guestrin, C.: Why should I trust you?: Explaining the predictions of any classifier. In: KDD (2016)
55. Ross, S.A.: The economic theory of agency: the principal's problem. Am. Econ. Rev. **63**(2), 134–139 (1973)
56. Roughgarden, T.: Selfish routing and the price of anarchy. Technical report, Stanford University Dept of Computer Science (2006). http://www.dtic.mil/get-tr-doc/pdf?AD=ADA637949
57. Rudin, C.: Please stop explaining black box models for high stakes decisions. In: NeurIPS Workshop on Critiquing and Correcting Trends in Machine Learning (2018)
58. Rudin, C., Ustun, B.: Optimized scoring systems: toward trust in machine learning for healthcare and criminal justice. Interfaces **48**(5), 449–466 (2018)
59. Samek, W., Binder, A., Montavon, G., Lapuschkin, S., Müller, K.R.: Evaluating the visualization of what a deep neural network has learned. IEEE Trans. Neural Networks Learn. Syst. **28**(11), 2660–2673 (2017)
60. Shapley, L.S.: A value for n-person games. Contrib. Theory Games **2**(28), 307–317 (1953)
61. Solove, D.: Privacy and power: computer databases and metaphors for information privacy. Stanford Law Rev. **53**(6), 1393–1462 (2001)
62. Solove, D.: Why privacy matters even if you have 'nothing to hide'. Chronicle of Higher Education, 15 May 2011

63. Sridhar, D., Batniji, R.: Misfinancing global health: a case for transparency in disbursements and decision making. Lancet **372**(9644), 1185–1191 (2008)
64. Štrumbelj, E., Kononenko, I.: Explaining prediction models and individual predictions with feature contributions. Knowl. Inf. Syst. **41**(3), 647–665 (2014)
65. Sundararajan, M., Taly, A., Yan, Q.: Axiomatic attribution for deep networks. In: ICML (2017)
66. Tishby, N., Pereira, F., Bialek, W.: The information bottleneck method. In: Allerton Conference on Communication, Control, and Computing (1999)
67. Varshney, K.R., Alemzadeh, H.: On the safety of machine learning: cyber-physical systems, decision sciences, and data products. Big Data **5**(3), 246–255 (2017)
68. Varshney, L., Varshney, K.: Decision making with quantized priors leads to discrimination. Proc. IEEE **105**(2), 241–255 (2017)
69. Vishwanath, T., Kaufmann, D.: Toward transparency: new approaches and their application to financial markets. World Bank Res. Obs. **16**(1), 41–57 (2001)
70. Wachter, S., Mittelstadt, B., Russell, C.: Counterfactual explanations withoutopening the black box: automated decisions and the GDPR. Harv. J. Law Technol. **31**(2), 841 (2018)
71. Weller, A.: Challenges for transparency. In: ICML Workshop on Human Interpretability (2017)
72. Wiggers, K.: New York City announces task force to find biases in algorithms. VentureBeat, May 2018
73. Wiley, R.: The evolution of communication: information and manipulation. Anim. Behav. **2**, 156–189 (1983)
74. Zafar, M.B., Valera, I., Rodriguez, M.G., Gummadi, K.P., Weller, A.: From parity to preference-based notions of fairness in classification. In: NeurIPS (2017)
75. Zintgraf, L., Cohen, T., Adel, T., Welling, M.: Visualizing deep neural network decisions: prediction difference analysis. In: ICLR (2017)

3

Interpretability in Intelligent Systems – A New Concept?

Lars Kai Hansen[(✉)] and Laura Rieger

DTU Compute, Technical University of Denmark, Kgs. Lyngby, Denmark
lkai@dtu.dk

Abstract. The very active community for interpretable machine learning can learn from the rich 50+ year history of explainable AI. We here
give two specific examples from this legacy that could enrich current
interpretability work: First, *Explanation desiderata* were we point to the
rich set of ideas developed in the 'explainable expert systems' field and,
second, tools for *quantification of uncertainty* of high-dimensional feature importance maps which have been developed in the field of computational neuroimaging.

Keywords: Interpretable AI · Machine learning ·
Uncertainty quantification

3.1 Neural Network Interpretability

High activity research fields often develop to be somewhat myopic in their early
phases - simply because the large body of published work leaves little time to follow progress in other areas or even to look back at previous research in the field.
Independent component analysis is a prominent early example, for which a history
of lost insights was recalled in Comon's paper [6]. Deep learning interpretability
is a contemporary example: One could easily get the impression that the interpretability issue surfaced with the new wave of deep learning, however, this is not
the case. While end-to-end learning has hugely accentuated the need for explanations, interpretability is an active research topic with an over 50-year history. In
fact, since the early days of intelligent systems the importance and focus on interpretability has only increased [30]. From scientific contexts, where interpretability
methods can assist formulation of causal hypotheses, see e.g., work in bio-medicine
[43] and computational chemistry [40], to recent societal importance in the European Union's General Data Protection Regulatory, establishing the so-called *Right
to explanation* as coined by Goodman and Flaxman [15].

Here we make two dives into the rich history of explainability in intelligent
systems and we ask 'what can modern work learn'?

First a semantic note. The terms interpretability and explainability are often
used interchangeably in the literature. However, in a recent review [13] a useful distinction is made. The more general concept is explainability which covers

© Springer Nature Switzerland AG 2019
W. Samek et al. (Eds.): Explainable AI, LNAI 11700, pp. 41–49, 2019.
https://doi.org/10.1007/978-3-030-28954-6_3

interpretability, i.e., to communicate machine learning function to user, and completeness, i.e., that the explanation is a close enough approximation that it can be audited. The distinction is described: '...interpretability alone is insufficient. In order for humans to trust black-box methods, we need explainability – models that are able to summarize the reasons for neural network behavior, gain the trust of users, or produce insights about the causes of their decisions. While interpretability is a substantial first step, these mechanisms need to also be complete, with the capacity to defend their actions, provide relevant responses to questions, and be audited' [13]. In Montavon et al.'s comprehensive tutorial a related distinction is made: '... interpreting the concepts learned by a model by building prototypes, and explaining the model's decisions by identifying the relevant input variables' [30].

Explainability, in this broader sense, has been a key component in several intelligent systems communities and the central tenet of this paper is that future work can learn from looking back at this history. We will focus on two specific lines of research, the first concerns the broader foundation of explainability: What are the desiderata, i.e., the salient dimensions and issues that should be addressed? Our second focus area concerns the important specific challenge of understanding the dimensions of uncertainty in machine learning models and their explanations.

Going back in time prior to the new wave of deep learning, many have stressed the importance of interpretability. Breiman's classic paper *Statistical Modeling: The Two Cultures* has a strong focus on interpretability [3]. Breiman notes: 'Occam's Razor, long admired, is usually interpreted to mean that simpler is better. Unfortunately, in prediction, accuracy and simplicity (interpretability) are in conflict. For instance, linear regression gives a fairly interpretable picture of the y, x relation. But its accuracy is usually less than that of the less interpretable neural nets'. As we will see below, this dilemma has been acknowledged by the explainable expert systems community many years earlier. Breiman clearly expressed his preferences: 'On interpretability, trees rate an A+', however, it was already known that trees and rule based systems have severe limitations when it comes to both implementing and comprehending function, see e.g. [29].

The interest in intelligent systems' interpretability has earlier roots. In a 1988 position paper Mitchie discussed how AI would pass different criteria from weak to ultra-strong [28]: 'The ultra-strong criterion demands that the system be capable not only of explaining how it has structured its acquired skills: it should also be able to teach them'. This ambition is still very relevant.

Going further back in early expert system history, explanation and human interaction were key issues. Expert systems in the late 60's - like 'SCHOLAR' developed for instructional support - were designed for interaction [5], such as explaining why a student's answer was wrong in a mixed initiative dialogue. Stanford's widely discussed 'MYCIN' expert system for antimicrobial selection was designed with three components: A rule based decision support component that combined MYCIN and physicians judgment, an explanation module and a learning module [4,41,42]. This rule based system had about 200 rules in 1975.

MYCIN developers held it self-evident that AI could get medical acceptance only with convincing explanations [42]. Thus, MYCIN was equipped to map its internal rules to natural language and answer both 'why' and 'how' questions. By 1983 the MYCIN system had expanded to 500 rules and the state of the art was summarized in a review in Science [10]. In a 1984 book summarizing experiences with MYCIN no less than four chapters are devoted to MYCIN's explanation mechanisms [4].

Prior to Breiman's comments, earlier work on explainability in statistics includes Good's discussion of evidence in context of belief networks [14]. Good considered three dimensions of explanations: 'What', concerning semantic explanations as in a dictionary, 'How' as in natural or manufacturing process descriptions, and finally the 'Why' type explanations - hypothesizing causal mechanisms behind an event.

3.2   Desiderata of Explainable AI

Expert systems moved on and important principles can be learned from Swartout and Moore's 1993 review of 'second generation explainable expert systems' [47] listing five general desiderata for useful explanations of AI, adding significant perspective to recent work in the field:

$\mathcal{D}_1$ Fidelity: the explanation must be a reasonable representation of what the system actually does.

$\mathcal{D}_2$ Understandability: Involves multiple usability factors including terminology, user competencies, levels of abstraction and interactivity.

$\mathcal{D}_3$ Sufficiency: Should be able to explain function and terminology and be detailed enough to justify decision.

$\mathcal{D}_4$ Low Construction Overhead: The explanation should not dominate the cost of designing AI.

$\mathcal{D}_5$ Efficiency: The explanation system should not slow down the AI significantly.

Expert systems have developed through several generations. The notion of second versus first generation AI was based on the modes of explanation. First generation systems were characterized by explanations based directly on rules applied by the AI to reach decisions. This leads to high fidelity ($\mathcal{D}_1$), but often conflicts with understandability ($\mathcal{D}_2$) because the rules used for inference may be incomprehensive for the user [47]. So-called *Explainable Expert Systems* (EES) addressed this dilemma. The XPLAIN system [46] is an example. XPLAIN was based on two key principles to enhance understandability: 'explicitly distinguishing different forms of domain knowledge present in the knowledge base and formal recording of the system development process' [34]. The evaluation of XPLAIN is anecdotal, yet quite convincing. Cases are presented in which the system is able to answer 'why' questions - and even at times resorting to 'white lies' to create a smoother learning experience [46]. Computational complexity both in construction and execution (desiderata $\mathcal{D}_4 - \mathcal{D}_5$) are not so prominent in current literature, although the most widely used methods differ significant in complexity. The so-called Local Interpretable Model-agnostic Explanation (LIME) scheme, for example, is based on image segmentation, random sampling and multiple linear model fittings, hence rather complex at explanation time [37], hence a challenge to $\mathcal{D}_5$. An approach such a 'Testing with Concept Activation Vectors' (TCAV) comes at a significant initial cost [19], hence may pose a challenge to $\mathcal{D}_4$.

Much of the EES progress was produced in the context of rule based expert systems, while AI based on machine learning - so-called connectionists' methods - more often was considered 'black box'. Interest in connectionists' methods was primarily based on performance and not interpretability, c.f., the quote from [2] '...symbolic learning techniques produce more understandable outputs but they are not as good as connectionist learning techniques in generalization'. We already noted that this view was propagated by Breiman, hence, the sparking interest in converting existing neural networks to decision tree form [1,48,49] or even learn neural networks that more readily are converted to trees see for example work by Gallant [12] and by Craven and Shavlik [7]. But trees may not deliver on $\mathcal{D}_2$, in particular, as discussed above and noted by [46] - the intuitive appeal of trees fails in practice when trees get to be complex in structure or operate in high dimensional feature spaces. These challenges were also recently noted in [33]. For domains where modern neural networks excel such as image, audio and text data, tree based explanations are challenged.

Returning to the list of desiderata, several recent papers have aimed at framing the discourse of interpretability. Presumably unaware of [47], Lipton notes that interpretability is not a well-defined concept and goes on to discuss multiple dimensions of interpretability and formulates a set of desiderata [25,26] closely related to $\mathcal{D}_1 - \mathcal{D}_3$. Lipton's desiderata read (i) 'Trust', (ii) 'Causality', (iii) 'Transferability', (iv) 'Informativeness', and (v) 'Fair and Ethical Decision-Making'. Here Lipton discusses several dimensions of (i) 'Trust' mostly covered in desiderata $\mathcal{D}_1 - \mathcal{D}_2$, (ii) 'Causality' is roughly equivalent to [47]'s $\mathcal{D}_3$, while the notion of 'Transferability' and 'Informativeness' both refer to the user's ability to gain abstract 'knowledge' from explanations. This idea also appeared in the original paper's discussion of usability $\mathcal{D}_2$, viz. the need to explain a system at different levels of abstraction. 'Fair and Ethical Decision-Making' is noted by Lipton as an area that specifically requires interpretability. In [47] such considerations are framed in a general discussion of usability ($\mathcal{D}_2$). It is also noted that an explanation systems must be able to explain from different perspectives '.. e.g., form versus function in the biological domain or safety vs. profitability in the financial domain'.

The usability dimension ($\mathcal{D}_2$) remains an important issue in contemporary interpretability papers. The question 'Interpretable to Whom?' has been raised in several papers [8,33,50] focusing on the user and addressed by human factors evaluation. In fact, Doshi-Velez and Been open their paper with the more general statement 'Unfortunately, there is little consensus on what interpretability in machine learning is and how to evaluate it for benchmarking' [8]. Their key contribution is to point out that current machine learning workflows are incomplete in the sense that they have unspecified objectives from the application domain.

This can be important issues that were not included in the machine learning objective function: '...incompleteness that produces some kind of unquantified bias, e.g. the effect of including domain knowledge in a model selection process' [8]. Seemingly unaware of the results of the EES community they focus on usability, and in case there are human users involved, a fully specified application somehow will entail human factors evaluation, immediately making [47]'s discussion of desideratum $\mathcal{D}_2$ relevant. When evaluating AI explanation systems with human subjects, we should be aware of the users' potential cognitive biases [39]. In the context of explainability, it is interesting to note that users may suffer from biases, for example the interesting phenomenon 'choice blindness' discovered by Johansson et al. [18]. Choice blindness shows up in failure to make and explain consistent decisions. In the work of [18] magicians 'fool' users to explain decisions users did or did not make with similar strengths. Yet, we note that the importance of actual usability evaluation of explanation methods also appeared early. A 1990 AAAI workshop featured work on user scenarios [9] and later work was reported in [45].

Breiman equated simplicity and interpretability. However, it is well-known that seemingly simple models can be hard to interpret. Even simple linear classification models need careful tuning to optimize stability of feature importance maps [36]. The 'filters vs. pattern' discussion that first emerged in the context of neuroimaging is another example of unexpected complexity. In this context, there is an important difference between visualizing the classification model and the corresponding (causal) generative model. The difference is induced by correlated input noise and can lead to wrong conclusions if not handled appropriately as pointed out by Haufe et al. [17]. Similar challenges appear in deep networks [20]. Further examples of the dissociation of simplicity and interpretability are discussed by Lipton [25,26], citing the work on 'Interpretable Boosted Naïve Bayes Classification' by [38]. This paper opens with a statement aligned with the Breiman's dilemma: 'Efforts to develop classifiers with strong discrimination power using voting methods have marginalized the importance of comprehensibility'. The objective of the paper is to demonstrate that the interpretation problem for voting systems can be mitigated. Specifically, Madigan et al.'s tools for interpretation in Naive Bayes classifiers [27]' is shown to be useful for complex boosting ensembles.

3.3 Quantify Similarity and Uncertainty of Feature Importance Maps Using Resampling

In certain application domains of neural networks, including scientific computing and bio-medicine, interpretation have played an important role for long and tools have been developed for explanation of neural networks' function.

In early work on mind reading based on brain scanning interpretability was naturally in focus [24,31]. The dominating analysis paradigm at the time was Friston et al.'s SPM 'statistical parametric mapping' [11]. This approach produced intuitively appealing three dimensional brain maps of voxel-wise significant activation. These maps have had significant impact in the field and it was a strong aim of neural networks visualizations to produce matching SPMs. The tools developed included 3D mapping of voxel-wise saliency [32] and sensitivity [21]. The usability ($\mathcal{D}_2$) for neuroscientists was enhanced by embedding the maps in 3D 'anatomically informed' navigation tools, see e.g., [32] for examples. The brain map visualizations were further enriched with knowledge graph information to facilitate decision making and teaching [35].

Concerning the first desideratum ($\mathcal{D}_1$) - fidelity of explanations - we need to consider the two logical fundamental properties: 'Existence' and 'uniqueness'. Considering the many constraints imposed by the desiderata, the very existence of a satisfactory interpretability scheme is a non-trivial issue. Finding such schemes is the concern of current interpretability engineering literature. Given existence, we face an equally important issue of uniqueness. Note that at least two mechanisms of uncertainty can contribute to non-uniqueness: Firstly, epistemic uncertainty, i.e., uncertainty in the explainability model, typically induced by a combination of limited data and knowledge. Epistemic uncertainty gives rise to multiple competing paradigm of explainability. The second source of non-uniqueness is the inherent randomness of a given problem domain for which noise and finite samples can conspire to create large fluctuations in solutions ('aleatory uncertainty').

Epistemic uncertainty was discussed in detail in the work of Lange et al. [23]. Nine different interpretation schemes were evaluated to explore the diversity in model space and learn similarities. The idiosyncratic scales employed by different mapping procedures is a significant challenge for quantitative comparisons of visualizations. This problem was addressed in [16] proposing a simple nonparametric approach to standardization of maps, hence, allowing maps to be meaningfully combined, e.g., by simple averaging. Such consensus based methods allow reduction of model uncertainty and quantification of inter-map differences (epistemic uncertainty).

Aleatory uncertainty in brain maps was addressed by the so-called NPAIRS framework [44]. Statistical re-sampling techniques such as split-half, can provide unbiased estimates of variance of interpretability heat maps. This allows for mapping of the local visualization 'effect size', by scaling heat maps by their standard deviation. Application of these tools include imaging pipeline optimization [22]. Outside the original domain of these methods, they have been applied for skin cancer diagnosis support [43]. We foresee that future applications of deep learning within scientific computing will call for careful and unbiased quantification of aleatory uncertainty and methods to aggregate multiple explanation hypotheses.

3.4   Concluding Remarks

Explainability is at the core of modern machine learning. The transparency made possible by effective tools for explainability can improve design and debugging for the machine learning engineer and even more importantly, our users' trust and usability in the tools we develop. It would be productive if the very active community of scientist working in this field made an even bigger effort to embrace the rich 50+ year history of explainable AI. Here we focused on two specific topics from this legacy that could enrich current interpretability work: (1) Careful definition of the task via *Explanation desiderata*. Here we pointed to a rich set of ideas developed in the 'explainable expert systems' field and (2) Careful handling of *uncertainty*. Here we pointed to the comprehensive workflows for quantification of uncertainty of high-dimensional feature importance maps, originally developed in the field of computational neuroimaging.

References

1. Andrews, R., Diederich, J., Tickle, A.B.: Survey and critique of techniques for extracting rules from trained artificial neural networks. Knowl. Based Syst. **8**(6), 373–389 (1995)
2. Boz, O.: Converting a trained neural network to a decision tree dectext-decision tree extractor (2000)
3. Breiman, L.: Statistical modeling: the two cultures (with comments and a rejoinder by the author). Stat. Sci. **16**(3), 199–231 (2001)
4. Bruce, G., Buchanan, B., Shortliffe, E.: Rule-Based Expert Systems: The MYCIN Experiments of the Stanford Heuristic Programming Project. Addison-Wesley, Reading (1984)
5. Carbonell, J.R.: AI in CAI: an artificial-intelligence approach to computer-assisted instruction. IEEE Trans. Man Mach. Syst. **11**(4), 190–202 (1970)
6. Comon, P.: Independent component analysis, a new concept? Sign. Proc. **36**(3), 287–314 (1994)
7. Craven, M.W., Shavlik, J.W.: Using sampling and queries to extract rules from trained neural networks. In: Machine Learning Proceedings 1994, pp. 37–45. Elsevier (1994)
8. Doshi-Velez, F., Kim, B.: Towards a rigorous science of interpretable machine learning. arXiv preprint. arXiv:1702.08608 (2017)
9. Druzdzel, M.J., Henrion, M.: Using scenarios to explain probabilistic inference. In: Working notes of the AAAI-1990 Workshop on Explanation, pp. 133–141 (1990)
10. Duda, R.O., Shortliffe, E.H.: Expert systems research. Science **220**(4594), 261–268 (1983)
11. Friston, K.J., Holmes, A.P., Worsley, K.J., Poline, J.P., Frith, C.D., Frackowiak, R.S.: Statistical parametric maps in functional imaging: a general linear approach. Hum. Brain Mapp. **2**(4), 189–210 (1994)
12. Gallant, S.I.: Connectionist expert systems. Commun. ACM **31**(2), 152–169 (1988)
13. Gilpin, L.H., Bau, D., Yuan, B.Z., Bajwa, A., Specter, M., Kagal, L.: Explaining explanations: an approach to evaluating interpretability of machine learning. arXiv preprint. arXiv:1806.00069 (2018)
14. Good, I.: Explicativity: a mathematical theory of explanation with statistical applications. Proc. R. Soc. Lond. A **354**(1678), 303–330 (1977)
15. Goodman, B., Flaxman, S.: European union regulations on algorithmic decision-making and a "right to explanation". arXiv preprint. arXiv:1606.08813 (2016)
16. Hansen, L.K., Nielsen, F.Å., Strother, S.C., Lange, N.: Consensus inference in neuroimaging. NeuroImage **13**(6), 1212–1218 (2001)
17. Haufe, S., et al.: On the interpretation of weight vectors of linear models in multivariate neuroimaging. NeuroImage **87**, 96–110 (2014)

18. Johansson, P., Hall, L., Sikström, S., Olsson, A.: Failure to detect mismatches between intention and outcome in a simple decision task. Science **310**(5745), 116–119 (2005)

19. Kim, B., et al.: Interpretability beyond feature attribution: quantitative testing with concept activation vectors (TCAV). In: International Conference on Machine Learning, pp. 2673–2682 (2018)

20. Kindermans, P.J., et al.: Learning how to explain neural networks: PatternNet and PatternAttribution. arXiv preprint. arXiv:1705.05598 (2017)

21. Kjems, U., et al.: The quantitative evaluation of functional neuroimaging experiments: mutual information learning curves. NeuroImage **15**(4), 772–786 (2002)

22. LaConte, S., et al.: The evaluation of preprocessing choices in single-subject bold fMRI using NPAIRS performance metrics. NeuroImage **18**(1), 10–27 (2003)

23. Lange, N., et al.: Plurality and resemblance in fMRI data analysis. NeuroImage **10**(3), 282–303 (1999)

24. Lautrup, B., Hansen, L.K., Law, I., Mørch, N., Svarer, C., Strother, S.C.: Massive weight sharing: a cure for extremely ill-posed problems. In: Workshop on Supercomputing in Brain Research: From Tomography to Neural Networks, pp. 137–144 (1994)

25. Lipton, Z.C.: The mythos of model interpretability. arXiv preprint. arXiv:1606.03490 (2016)

26. Lipton, Z.C.: The mythos of model interpretability. Queue **16**(3), 30 (2018)

27. Madigan, D., Mosurski, K., Almond, R.G.: Graphical explanation in belief networks. J. Comput. Graph. Stat. **6**(2), 160–181 (1997)

28. Michie, D.: Machine learning in the next five years. In: Proceedings of the 3rd European Conference on European Working Session on Learning, pp. 107–122. Pitman Publishing (1988)

29. Minsky, M.L.: Logical versus analogical or symbolic versus connectionist or neat versus scruffy. AI Mag. **12**(2), 34 (1991)

30. Montavon, G., Samek, W., Müller, K.R.: Methods for interpreting and understanding deep neural networks. Digital Sign. Proces. **73**, 1–15 (2018)

31. Mørch, N., et al.: Nonlinear versus linear models in functional neuroimaging: learning curves and generalization crossover. In: Duncan, J., Gindi, G. (eds.) IPMI 1997. LNCS, vol. 1230, pp. 259–270. Springer, Heidelberg (1997). https://doi.org/10.1007/3-540-63046-5_20

32. Mørch, N.J., et al.: Visualization of neural networks using saliency maps. In: 1995 IEEE International Conference on Neural Networks. IEEE (1995)

33. Narayanan, M., Chen, E., He, J., Kim, B., Gershman, S., Doshi-Velez, F.: How do humans understand explanations from machine learning systems? An evaluation of the human-interpretability of explanation. arXiv preprint. arXiv:1802.00682 (2018)

34. Neches, R., Swartout, W.R., Moore, J.D.: Enhanced maintenance and explanation of expert systems through explicit models of their development. IEEE Trans. Softw. Eng. **11**, 1337–1351 (1985)

35. Nielsen, F.A., Hansen, L.K.: Automatic anatomical labeling of Talairach coordinates and generation of volumes of interest via the brainmap database. NeuroImage **16**(2), 2–6 (2002)

36. Rasmussen, P.M., Hansen, L.K., Madsen, K.H., Churchill, N.W., Strother, S.C.: Model sparsity and brain pattern interpretation of classification models in neuroimaging. Pattern Recogn. **45**(6), 2085–2100 (2012)

37. Ribeiro, M.T., Singh, S., Guestrin, C.: Why should I trust you?: Explaining the predictions of any classifier. In: Proceedings of the 22nd ACM SIGKDD International Conference on Knowledge Discovery and Data Mining, pp. 1135–1144. ACM (2016)
38. Ridgeway, G., Madigan, D., Richardson, T., O'Kane, J.: Interpretable boosted Naïve Bayes classification. In: KDD, pp. 101–104 (1998)
39. Saposnik, G., Redelmeier, D., Ruff, C.C., Tobler, P.N.: Cognitive biases associated with medical decisions: a systematic review. BMC Med. Inform. Decis. Mak. **16**(1), 138 (2016)
40. Schütt, K.T., Arbabzadah, F., Chmiela, S., Müller, K.R., Tkatchenko, A.: Quantum-chemical insights from deep tensor neural networks. Nat. Commun. **8**, 13890 (2017)
41. Shortliffe, E.H., Axline, S.G., Buchanan, B.G., Merigan, T.C., Cohen, S.N.: An artificial intelligence program to advise physicians regarding antimicrobial therapy. Comput. Biomed. Res. **6**(6), 544–560 (1973)
42. Shortliffe, E., Davis, R., Axline, S., Buchanan, B., Green, C., Cohen, S.: Computer-based consultations in clinical therapeutics: explanation and rule acquisition capabilities of the MYCIN system. Comput. Biomed. Res. **8**(4), 303–320 (1975)
43. Sigurdsson, S., Philipsen, P.A., Hansen, L.K., Larsen, J., Gniadecka, M., Wulf, H.C.: Detection of skin cancer by classification of Raman spectra. IEEE Trans. Biomed. Eng. **51**(10), 1784–1793 (2004)
44. Strother, S.C., Anderson, J., Hansen, L.K., Kjems, U., Kustra, R., Sidtis, J., Frutiger, S., Muley, S., LaConte, S., Rottenberg, D.: The quantitative evaluation of functional neuroimaging experiments: the NPAIRS data analysis framework. NeuroImage **15**(4), 747–771 (2002)
45. Suermondt, H.J., Cooper, G.F.: An evaluation of explanations of probabilistic inference. In: Proceedings of the Annual Symposium on Computer Application in Medical Care, p. 579. American Medical Informatics Association (1992)
46. Swartout, W.R.: XPLAIN: a system for creating and explaining expert consulting programs. University of Southern California Marina del Rey Information Sciences Institute, Technical report (1983)
47. Swartout, W.R., Moore, J.D.: Explanation in second generation expert systems. In: David, J.M., Krivine, J.P., Simmons, R. (eds.) Second Generation Expert Systems, pp. 543–585. Springer, Heidelberg (1993). https://doi.org/10.1007/978-3-642-77927-5_24
48. Thrun, S.: Extracting provably correct rules from artificial neural networks. Technical report IAI-TR-93-5, Institut for Informatik III Universitat Bonn, Germany (1994)
49. Thrun, S.: Extracting rules from artificial neural networks with distributed representations. In: Advances in Neural Information Processing Systems, pp. 505–512 (1995)
50. Tomsett, R., Braines, D., Harborne, D., Preece, A., Chakraborty, S.: Interpretable to whom? A role-based model for analyzing interpretable machine learning systems. arXiv preprint. arXiv:1806.07552 (2018)

Part II
Methods for Interpreting AI Systems

Methods for Interpreting AI Systems – Preface

Shallow decision trees and sparse linear models are simple and easy to interpret. A human can look at the decision structure, e.g. the nodes and the weights, and make sense of it. When the task is more complex, these simple ML models need to be substituted by more complex ones to represent the higher nonlinearity of the task. These models are a priori also more difficult for a user to interpret. For example, deep neural networks are often composed of millions of neurons that interact in a highly complex and seemingly opaque manner.

A direct downside of using these complex and blackbox-type models is the lack of trust humans can place in their predictions. Instead, we would like to verify whether the concepts that the model has learned are based on the correct input variables and whether the model combines them in a meaningful manner. Standard inspection techniques are usually able to get a first partial insight into the model, e.g. visual inspection of the first layer of a network. However, in order to gain deeper insights into these models, new techniques are needed. Developing such techniques has become an important research focus in the past few years.

The next four chapters give a snapshot of current research on bringing more interpretability into complex ML models.

In Chapter 4, Nguyen et al. [3], consider the setting where we are given a trained neural network, and we would like to understand what is modeled in its output neurons. The proposed solution builds a 'prototype' in input domain that maximally activates a certain output neuron of the model subject to the constraint that the prototype looks realistic. These prototypes can be visualized by a human so that the concept that has been learned can be interpreted. Here, it is implicitly assumed that the input domain is interpretable for a human.

In Chapter 5, Hong et al. [1] present an approach for converting text in another modality, here, images. The proposed approach trains a generative neural network of images that is conditioned on the text sequence received as input. It works similarly to a translation system but produces images as output. In contrast to Chapter 4, the input text rather than the model is here the quantity to interpret. Yet, both works share a common objective of synthesizing images that are as realistic as possible so that they are maximally interpretable for a human.

In Chapter 6, Hu et al. [2] present a learning algorithm for summarizing data into clusters or hashes. The cluster structure is driven to be human-interpretable via a self-augmented training strategy that brings useful invariances into the model. Invariances are key to enhance the interpretability of a model. For example, if the model has built abstractions to small local distortions, the user of that model can take this invariance for granted and focus his effort on the interpretation of higher-level concepts such as image classes.

In Chapter 7, Oh et al. [4] take a different viewpoint on the question of interpretability. In an adversarial setting, a fully transparent model may actually be exploited by a malicious user. For example, the latter may seek to extract unauthorized information from the model or to craft adversarial inputs that make the model behave in a improper way. The authors find that, without specific countermeasures, the model's decision behavior can leak a surprisingly large amount of information on its inner-workings and consequently reveal potential weaknesses.

Overall, these four chapters have highlighted the breadth of tasks that are covered by XAI. While some techniques have been developed to shed light on the inner working of the model, an important goal is often also to better understand the input data itself. Furthermore, while interpretability may generally appear as desirable, it ultimately depends on the intent of the user receiving or providing the interpretable feedback. In some sensitive applications, opacity may in fact become a desirable property [5].

July 2019

Wojciech Samek
Grégoire Montavon
Andrea Vedaldi
Lars Kai Hansen
Klaus-Robert Müller

References

1. Hong, S., Yang, D., Choi, J., Lee, H.: Interpretable text-to-image synthesis with hierarchical semantic layout generation. In: Samek, W., Montavon, G., Vedaldi, A., Hansen, L.K., Müller, K.-R. (eds.) Explainable AI: Interpreting, Explaining and Visualizing Deep Learning. LNCS, vol. 11700, pp. 77–95, Springer, Cham (2019)
2. Hu, W., Miyato, T., Tokui, S., Matsumoto, E., Sugiyama, M.: Unsupervised discrete representation learning. In: Samek, W., Montavon, G., Vedaldi, A., Hansen, L.K., Müller, K.-R. (eds.) Explainable AI: Interpreting, Explaining and Visualizing Deep Learning. LNCS, vol. 11700, pp. 97–119, Springer, Cham (2019)
3. Nguyen, A., Yosinski, J., Clune, J.: Understanding neural networks via feature visualization: A survey. In: Samek, W., Montavon, G., Vedaldi, A., Hansen, L.K., Müller, K.-R. (eds.) Explainable AI: Interpreting, Explaining and Visualizing Deep Learning. LNCS, vol. 11700, pp. 55–76, Springer, Cham (2019)
4. Oh, S.J., Schiele, B., Fritz, M.: Towards reverse-engineering black-box neural networks. In: Samek, W., Montavon, G., Vedaldi, A., Hansen, L.K., Müller, K.-R. (eds.) Explainable AI: Interpreting, Explaining and Visualizing Deep Learning. LNCS, vol. 11700, pp. 121–144, Springer, Cham (2019)
5. Weller, A.: Transparency: motivations and challenges. In: Samek, W., Montavon, G., Vedaldi, A., Hansen, L.K., Müller, K.-R. (eds.) Explainable AI: Interpreting, Explaining and Visualizing Deep Learning. LNCS, vol. 11700, pp. 23–40, Springer, Cham (2019)

4
Understanding Neural Networks via Feature Visualization: A Survey

Anh Nguyen[1]([⊠]), Jason Yosinski[2], and Jeff Clune[2,3]

[1] Auburn University, Auburn, AL, USA
anhnguyen@auburn.edu
[2] Uber AI Labs, San Francisco, CA, USA
yosinski@uber.com
[3] University of Wyoming, Laramie, WY, USA
jeffclune@uwyo.edu

Abstract. A neuroscience method to understanding the brain is to find and study the *preferred stimuli* that highly activate an individual cell or groups of cells. Recent advances in machine learning enable a family of methods to synthesize preferred stimuli that cause a neuron in an artificial or biological brain to fire strongly. Those methods are known as Activation Maximization (AM) [10] or Feature Visualization via Optimization. In this chapter, we (1) review existing AM techniques in the literature; (2) discuss a probabilistic interpretation for AM; and (3) review the applications of AM in debugging and explaining networks.

Keywords: Neural networks · Feature visualization · Activation Maximization · Generator network · Generative models · Optimization

4.1 Introduction

Understanding the human brain has been a long-standing quest in human history. One path to understanding the brain is to study what each neuron[1] codes for [17], or what information its firing represents. In the classic 1950's experiment, Hubel and Wiesel studied a cat's brain by showing the subject different images on a screen while recording the neural firings in the cat's primary visual cortex (Fig. 4.1). Among a variety of test images, the researchers found *oriented edges* to cause high responses in one specific cell [14]. That cell is referred to as an *edge detector* and such images are called its *preferred stimuli*. The same technique later enabled scientists to discover fundamental findings of how neurons along the visual pathway detect increasingly complex patterns: from circles, edges to faces and high-level concepts such as one's grandmother [3] or specific celebrities like the actress Halle Berry [37].

---

[1] In this chapter, "neuron", "cell", "unit", and "feature" are used interchangeably.

© Springer Nature Switzerland AG 2019
W. Samek et al. (Eds.): Explainable AI, LNAI 11700, pp. 55–76, 2019.
https://doi.org/10.1007/978-3-030-28954-6_4

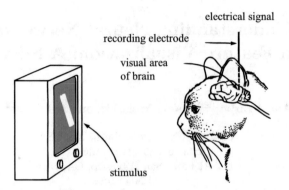

Fig. 4.1. In the classic neuroscience experiment, Hubel and Wiesel discovered a cat's visual cortex neuron (right) that fires strongly and selectively for a light bar (left) when it is in certain positions and orientations [14].

Similarly, in machine learning (ML), visually inspecting the preferred stimuli of a unit can shed more light into what the neuron is doing [48,49]. An intuitive approach is to find such preferred inputs from an existing, large image collection e.g. the training or test set [49]. However, that method may have undesired properties. First, it requires testing each neuron on a large image set. Second, in such a dataset, many informative images that would activate the unit may not exist because the image space is vast and neural behaviors can be complex [28]. Third, it is often ambiguous which visual features in an image are causing the neuron to fire e.g. if a unit is activated by a picture of a bird on a tree branch, it is unclear if the unit "cares about" the bird or the branch (Fig. 4.13b). Fourth, it is not trivial how to extract a holistic description of what a neuron is for from the typically large set of stimuli preferred by a neuron.

A common practice is to study the top 9 highest activating images for a unit [48,49]; however, the top-9 set may reflect only one among many types of features that are preferred by a unit [29].

Instead of finding real images from an existing dataset, one can synthesize the visual stimuli from scratch [10,25,27,29,32,42,46]. The synthesis approach offers multiple advantages: (1) given a strong image prior, one may synthesize (i.e. reconstruct) stimuli without the need to access the target model's training set, which may not be available in practice (see Sect. 4.5); (2) more control over the types and contents of images to synthesize, which helps shed light on more controlled research experiments.

Activation Maximization. Let θ be the parameters of a classifier that maps an image $\mathbf{x} \in \mathbb{R}^{H \times W \times C}$ (that has C color channels, each of which is W pixels wide and H pixels high) onto a probability distribution over the output classes. Finding an image $\mathbf{x}$ that maximizes the activation $a_i^l(\theta, \mathbf{x})$ of a neuron indexed i in a given layer l of the classifier network can be formulated as an optimization problem:

$$\mathbf{x}^* = \arg\max_{\mathbf{x}}(a_i^l(\theta, \mathbf{x})) \tag{4.1}$$

This problem was introduced as *activation maximization*[2] (AM) by Erhan, Bengio and others [10]. Here, $a_i^l(.)$ returns the activation value of a *single* unit as in many previous works [27–29]; however, it can be extended to return any neural response $a(.)$ that we wish to study e.g. activating a group of neurons [24,26,33]. The remarkable DeepDream visualizations [24] were created by running AM to activate all the units across a given layer simultaneously. In this chapter, we will write $a(.)$ instead of $a_i^l(.)$ when the exact indices l, i can be omitted for generality.

AM is a non-convex optimization problem for which one can attempt to find a local minimum via gradient-based [44] or non-gradient methods [30]. In *post-hoc* interpretability [23], we often assume access to the parameters and architecture of the network being studied. In this case, a simple approach is to perform gradient ascent [10,27,31,48] with an update rule such as:

$$\mathbf{x}_{t+1} = \mathbf{x}_t + \epsilon_1 \frac{\partial a(\theta, \mathbf{x}_t)}{\partial \mathbf{x}_t} \tag{4.2}$$

That is, starting from a random initialization $\mathbf{x}_0$ (here, a random image), we iteratively take steps in the input space following the gradient of $a(\theta, \mathbf{x})$ to find an input $\mathbf{x}$ that highly activates a given unit. ϵ_1 is the step size and is chosen empirically.

Note that this gradient ascent process is similar to the gradient descent process used to train neural networks via backpropagation [39], except that here we are optimizing the network input instead of the network parameters θ, which are frozen.[3] We may stop the optimization when the neural activation has reached a desired threshold or a certain number of steps has passed.

In practice, synthesizing an image from scratch to maximize the activation alone (i.e. an unconstrained optimization problem) often yields uninterpretable images [28]. In a high-dimensional image space, we often find *rubbish* examples (also known as *fooling* examples [28]) e.g. patterns of high-frequency noise that look like nothing but that highly activate a given unit (Fig. 4.2).

In a related way, if starting AM optimization from a real image (instead of a random one), we may easily encounter *adversarial* examples [44] e.g. an image that is slightly different from the starting image (e.g. of a school bus), but that a network would give an entirely different label e.g. "ostrich" [44]. Those early AM visualizations [28,44] revealed huge security and reliability concerns with machine learning applications and informed a plethora of follow-up adversarial attack and defense research [1,16].

Networks that We Visualize. Unless otherwise noted, throughout the chapter, we demonstrate AM on CaffeNet, a specific pre-trained model of the well-known AlexNet convnets [18] to perform single-label image classification on the ILSVRC 2012 ImageNet dataset [7,40].

---

[2] Also sometimes referred to as *feature visualization* [29,32,48]. In this chapter, the phrase "visualize a unit" means "synthesize preferred images for a single neuron".

[3] Therefore, hereafter, we will write $a(x)$ instead of $a(\theta, x)$, omitting θ, for simplicity.

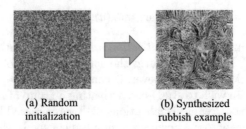

(a) Random
initialization

(b) Synthesized
rubbish example

Fig. 4.2. Example of activation maximization without image priors. Starting from a random image (a), we iteratively take steps following the gradient to maximize the activation of a given unit, here the "bell pepper" output in CaffeNet [18]. Despite highly activating the unit and being classified as "bell pepper", the image (b) has high frequencies and is not human-recognizable.

4.2   Activation Maximization via Hand-Designed Priors

Examples like those in Fig. 4.2b are not human-recognizable. While the fact that the network responds strongly to such images is intriguing and has strong implications for security, if we cannot interpret the images, it limits our ability to understand what the unit's purpose is. Therefore, we want to constrain the search to be within a distribution of images that we can interpret e.g. photo-realistic images or images that look like those in the training set. That can be accomplished by incorporating *natural image priors* into the objective function, which was found to substantially improve the recognizability of AM images [21, 27, 29, 32, 48]. For example, an image prior may encourage smoothness [21] or penalize pixels of extreme intensity [42]. Such constraints are often incorporated into the AM formulation as a *regularization* term $R(\mathbf{x})$:

$$\mathbf{x}^* = \arg\max_{\mathbf{x}}(a(\mathbf{x}) - R(\mathbf{x})) \tag{4.3}$$

For example, to encourage the smoothness in AM images, $R : \mathbb{R}^{H \times W \times C} \to \mathbb{R}$ may compute the total variation (TV) across an image [21]. That is, in each update, we follow the gradients to (1) maximize the neural activation; and (2) minimize the total variation loss:

$$\mathbf{x}_{t+1} = \mathbf{x}_t + \epsilon_1 \frac{\partial a(\mathbf{x}_t)}{\partial \mathbf{x}_t} - \epsilon_2 \frac{\partial R(\mathbf{x}_t)}{\partial \mathbf{x}_t} \tag{4.4}$$

However, in practice, we do not always compute the analytical gradient $\partial R(\mathbf{x}_t)/\partial \mathbf{x}_t$. Instead, we may define a regularization operator $r : \mathbb{R}^{H \times W \times C} \to \mathbb{R}^{H \times W \times C}$ (e.g. a Gaussian blur kernel), and map $\mathbf{x}$ to a more regularized (e.g. slightly blurrier as in [48]) version of itself in every step. In this case, the update step becomes:

$$\mathbf{x}_{t+1} = r(\mathbf{x}_t) + \epsilon_1 \frac{\partial a(\mathbf{x}_t)}{\partial \mathbf{x}_t} \tag{4.5}$$

Note that this update form in Eq. 4.5 is strictly more expressive [48], and allows the use of non-differentiable regularizers $r(.)$.

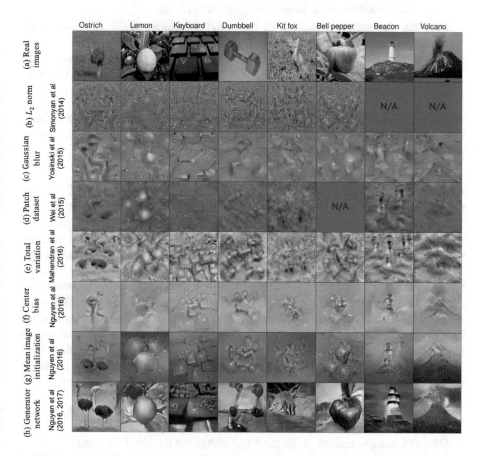

Fig. 4.3. Activation maximization results of seven methods in the literature (b–h), each employing a different image prior (e.g. L_2 norm, Gaussian blur, etc.). Images are synthesized to maximize the output neurons (each corresponding to a class) of the CaffeNet image classifier [18] trained on ImageNet. The categories were not cherry-picked, but instead were selected based on the images available in previous papers [21, 29, 42, 46, 48]. Overall, while it is a subjective judgement, Activation Maximization via Deep Generator Networks method (h) [27] produces images with more natural colors and realistic global structures. Image modified from [27].

Local Statistics. AM images without priors often appear to have high-frequency patterns and unnatural colors (Fig. 4.2b). Many regularizers have been designed in the literature to ameliorate these problems including:

- Penalize extreme-intensity pixels via α-norm [42, 46, 48] (Fig. 4.3b).
- Penalize high-frequency noise (i.e. smoothing) via total variation [21, 29] (Fig. 4.3e), Gaussian blurring [48, 54] (Fig. 4.3c) or a bilateral filter [45].

- Randomly jitter, rotate, or scale the image before each update step to synthesize stimuli that are robust to transformations, which has been shown to make images clearer and more interpretable [24,32].
- Penalize the high frequencies in the *gradient* image $\frac{\partial a(\mathbf{x}_t)}{\partial \mathbf{x}_t}$ (instead of the visualization $\mathbf{x}_t$) via Gaussian blurring [32,54].
- Encourage patch-level color statistics to be more realistic by (1) matching those of real images from a dataset [46] (Fig. 4.3d) or (2) learning a Gaussian mixture model of real patches [24].

While substantially improving the interpretability of images (compared to high-frequency rubbish examples), these methods only effectively attempt to match the *local* statistics of natural images.

Global Structures. Many AM images still lack *global* coherence; for example, an image synthesized to highly activate the "bell pepper" output neuron (Fig. 4.3b–e) may exhibit multiple bell-pepper segments scattered around the same image rather than a single bell pepper. Such stimuli suggest that the network has learned some *local* discriminative features e.g. the shiny, green skin of bell peppers, which are useful for the classification task. However, it raises an interesting question: Did the network ever learn the global structures (e.g. the whole pepper) or only the local discriminative parts? The high-frequency patterns as in Fig. 4.3b–e might also be a consequence of optimization in the image space. That is, when making pixel-wise changes, it is non-trivial to ensure global coherence across the entire image. Instead, it is easy to increase neural activations by simply creating more local discriminative features in the stimulus.

Previous attempts to improve the global coherence include:

- Gradually paint the image by scaling it and alternatively following the gradients from multiple output layers of the network [54].
- Bias the image changes to be near the image center [29] (Fig. 4.3g).
- Initialize optimization from an average image (computed from real training set images) instead of a random one [29] (Fig. 4.3h).

While these methods somewhat improved the global coherence of images (Fig. 4.3g–h), they rely on a variety of heuristics and introduce extra hyperparameters [29,54]. In addition, there is still a large realism gap between the real images and these visualizations (Fig. 4.3a vs. h).

Diversity. A neuron can be multifaceted in that it responds strongly to multiple distinct types of stimuli, i.e. *facets* [29]. That is, higher-level features are more invariant to changes in the input [19,49]. For example, a face-detecting unit in CaffeNet [18] was found to respond to both human and lion faces [48]. Therefore, we wish to uncover different facets via AM in order to have a fuller understanding of a unit.

However, AM optimization starting from different random images often converge to similar results [10, 29]—a phenomenon also observed when training neural networks with different initializations [20]. Researchers have proposed different techniques to improve image diversity such as:

- Drop out certain neural paths in the network when performing backpropagation to produce different facets [46].
- Cluster the training set images into groups, and initialize from an average image computed from each group's images [29].
- Maximize the distance (e.g. cosine similarity in the pixel space) between a reference image and the one being synthesized [32].
- Activate two neurons at the same time e.g. activating (bird + apron) and (bird + candles) units would produce two distinct images of *birds* that activate the same *bird* unit [27] (Fig. 4.10).
- Add noise to the image in every update to increase image diversity [26].

While obtaining limited success, these methods also introduce extra hyperparameters and require further investigation. For example, if we enforce two stimuli to be different, exactly how far should they be and in which similarity metric should the difference be measured?

4.3   Activation Maximization via Deep Generator Networks

Much previous AM research were optimizing the preferred stimuli directly in the high-dimensional image space where pixel-wise changes are often slow and uncorrelated, yielding high-frequency visualizations (Fig. 4.3b–e). Instead, Nguyen et al. [27] propose to optimize in the low-dimensional latent space of a deep generator network, which they call Deep Generator Network Activation Maximization (DGN-AM). They train an image *generator* network to take in a highly compressed code and output a synthetic image that looks as close to real images from the ImageNet dataset [40] as possible. To produce an AM image for a given neuron, the authors optimize in the input latent space of the generator so that it outputs an image that activates the unit of interest (Fig. 4.4). Intuitively, DGN-AM restricts the search to only the set of images that can be drawn by the prior and encourages the image updates to be more coherent and correlated compared to pixel-wise changes (where each pixel is modified independently).

Generator Networks. We denote the sub-network of CaffeNet [18] that maps images onto 4096-D fc6 features as an encoder $E : \mathbb{R}^{H \times W \times C} \to \mathbb{R}^{4096}$. We train a generator network $G : \mathbb{R}^{4096} \to \mathbb{R}^{H \times W \times C}$ to invert E i.e. $G(E(\mathbf{x})) \approx \mathbf{x}$. In addition to the reconstruction losses, the generator was trained using the Generative Adversarial Network (GAN) loss [13] to improve the image realism. More training details are in [9, 27]. Intuitively, G can be viewed as an artificial *general* "painter" that is capable of painting a variety of different types of images, given an arbitrary input description (i.e. a latent code or a condition vector). The idea is that G would be able to faithfully portray what a target network has learned, which may be recognizable or unrecognizable patterns to humans.

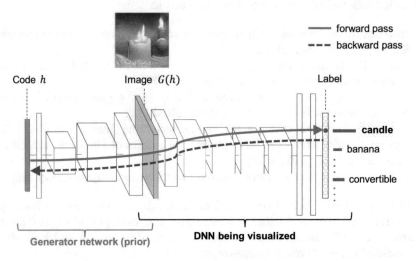

Fig. 4.4. We search for an input code (red bar) of a deep generator network (left) that produces an image (middle) that strongly activates a target neuron (e.g. the "candle" output unit) in a given pre-trained network (right). The iterative optimization procedure involves multiple forward and backward passes through both the generator and the target network being visualized.

Optimizing in the Latent Space. Intuitively, we search in the input code space of the generator G to find a code $\mathbf{h} \in \mathbb{R}^{4096}$ such that the image $G(\mathbf{h})$ maximizes the neural activation $a(G(\mathbf{h}))$ (see Fig. 4.4). The AM problem in Eq. 4.3 now becomes:

$$\mathbf{h}^* = \arg\max_{\mathbf{h}}(a(G(\mathbf{h})) - R(\mathbf{h})) \qquad (4.6)$$

That is, we take steps in the latent space following the below update rule:

$$\mathbf{h}_{t+1} = \mathbf{h}_t + \epsilon_1 \frac{\partial a(G(\mathbf{h}_t))}{\partial \mathbf{h}_t} - \epsilon_2 \frac{\partial R(\mathbf{h}_t)}{\partial \mathbf{h}_t} \qquad (4.7)$$

Note that, here, the regularization term $R(.)$ is on the latent code $\mathbf{h}$ instead of the image $\mathbf{x}$. Nguyen et al. [27] implemented a small amount of L_2 regularization and also clipped the code. These hand-designed regularizers can be replaced by a strong, learned prior for the code [26].

Optimizing in the latent space of a deep generator network showed a great improvement in image quality compared to previous methods that optimize in the pixel space (Fig. 4.5; and Fig. 4.3b–h vs. Fig. 4.3i). However, images synthesized by DGN-AM have limited diversity—they are qualitatively similar to the real top-9 validation images that highest activate a given unit (Fig. 4.6).

Fig. 4.5. Images synthesized from scratch via DGN-AM method [27] to highly activate output neurons in the CaffeNet deep neural network [15], which has learned to classify 1000 categories of ImageNet images. Image from [27].

To improve the image diversity, Nguyen et al. [26] harnessed a learned realism prior for **h** via a denoising autoencoder (DAE), and added a small amount of Gaussian noise in every update step to improve image diversity [26]. In addition to an improvement in image diversity, this AM procedure also has a theoretical probabilistic justification, which is discussed in Sect. 4.4.

4.4 Probabilistic Interpretation for Activation Maximization

In this section, we first make a note about the AM objective, and discuss a probabilistically interpretable formulation for AM, which is first proposed in Plug and Play Generative Networks (PPGNs) [26], and then interpret other AM methods under this framework. Intuitively, the AM process can be viewed as sampling from a generative model, which is composed of (1) an image prior and (2) a recognition network that we want to visualize.

4.4.1 Synthesizing Selective Stimuli

We start with a discussion on AM objectives. In the original AM formulation (Eq. 4.1), we only explicitly maximize the activation a_i^l of a unit indexed i in layer l; however, in practice, this objective may surprisingly also increase the activations $a_{j \neq i}^l$ of some other units j in the same layer and even higher than a_i^l [27]. For example, maximizing the output activation for the "hartebeest" class is likely to yield an image that also strongly activates the "impala" unit because these two animals are visually similar [27]. As the result, there is no guarantee that the target unit will be the highest activated across a layer. In that case, the resultant visualization may not portray what is unique about the target unit (l, i).

Instead, we are interested in *selective* stimuli that highly activate only a_i^l, but not $a_{j \neq i}^l$. That is, we wish to maximize a_i^l such that it is the highest single activation across the same layer l. To enforce that selectivity, we can either maximize the softmax or log of softmax of the raw activations across a layer [26,42] where the softmax transformation for unit i across layer l is given as $s_i^l = \exp(a_i^l)/\sum_j \exp(a_j^l)$. Such selective stimuli (1) are more interpretable and preferred in neuroscience [3] because they contain only visual features exclusively for one unit of interest but not others; (2) naturally fit in our probabilistic interpretation discussed below.

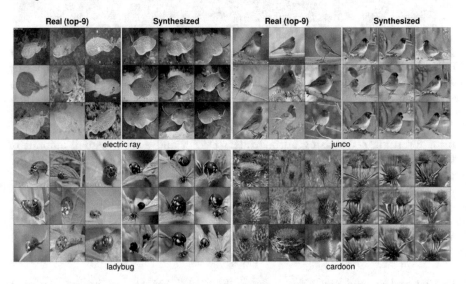

Fig. 4.6. Side-by-side comparison between real and synthetic stimuli synthesized via DGN-AM [27]. For each unit, we show the top 9 validation set images that highest activate a given neuron (left) and 9 synthetic images (right). Note that these synthetic images are of size 227×227 i.e. the input size of CaffeNet [18]. Image from [27].

4.4.2   Probabilistic Framework

Let us assume a joint probability distribution $p(\mathbf{x}, y)$ where $\mathbf{x}$ denotes images, and y is a categorical variable for a given neuron indexed i in layer l. This model can be decomposed into an image density model and an image classifier model:

$$p(\mathbf{x}, y) = p(\mathbf{x})p(y|\mathbf{x}) \tag{4.8}$$

Note that, when l is the output layer of an ImageNet 1000-way classifier [18], y also represents the image category (e.g. "volcano"), and $p(y|\mathbf{x})$ is the classification probability distribution (often modeled via softmax).

We can construct a Metropolis-adjusted Langevin [38] (MALA) sampler for our $p(\mathbf{x}, y)$ model [26]. This variant of MALA [26] does not have the accept/reject step, and uses the following transition operator:[4]

$$\mathbf{x}_{t+1} = \mathbf{x}_t + \epsilon_{12} \nabla \log p(\mathbf{x}_t, y) + N(0, \epsilon_3^2) \qquad (4.9)$$

Since y is a categorical variable, and chosen to be a fixed neuron y_c outside the sampler, the above update rule can be re-written as:

$$\mathbf{x}_{t+1} = \mathbf{x}_t + \epsilon_{12} \nabla \log p(y = y_c | \mathbf{x}_t) + \epsilon_{12} \nabla \log p(\mathbf{x}_t) + N(0, \epsilon_3^2) \qquad (4.10)$$

Decoupling ϵ_{12} into explicit ϵ_1 and ϵ_2 multipliers, and expanding the ∇ into explicit partial derivatives, we arrive at the following update rule:

$$\mathbf{x}_{t+1} = \mathbf{x}_t + \epsilon_1 \frac{\partial \log p(y = y_c | \mathbf{x}_t)}{\partial \mathbf{x}_t} + \epsilon_2 \frac{\partial \log p(\mathbf{x}_t)}{\partial \mathbf{x}_t} + N(0, \epsilon_3^2) \qquad (4.11)$$

An intuitive interpretation of the roles of these three terms is illustrated in Fig. 4.7 and described as follows:

- ϵ_1 term: take a step toward an image that causes the neuron y_c to be the *highest activated* across a layer (Fig. 4.7; red arrow)
- ϵ_2 term: take a step toward a generic, realistic-looking image (Fig. 4.7; blue arrow).
- ϵ_3 term: add a small amount of noise to jump around the search space to encourage image diversity (Fig. 4.7; green arrow).

Maximizing Raw Activations vs. Softmax. Note that the ϵ_1 term in Eq. 4.11 is not the same as the *gradient of raw activation* term in Eq. 4.2. We summarize in Table 4.1 three variants of computing this ϵ_1 gradient term: (1) derivative of logits; (2) derivative of softmax; and (3) derivative of log of softmax. Several previous works empirically reported that maximizing raw, pre-softmax activations a_i^l produces better visualizations than directly maximizing the softmax values s_i^l (Table 4.1a vs. b); however, this observation had not been fully justified [42]. Nguyen et al. [26] found the log of softmax gradient term (1) working well empirically; and (2) theoretically justifiable under the probabilistic framework in Sect. 4.4.2.

We refer readers to [26] for a more complete derivation and discussion of the above MALA sampler. Using the update rule in Eq. 4.11, we will next interpret other AM algorithms in the literature.

---

[4] We abuse notation slightly in the interest of space and denote as $N(0, \epsilon_3^2)$ a sample from that distribution. The first step size is given as ϵ_{12} in anticipation of later splitting into separate ϵ_1 and ϵ_2 terms.

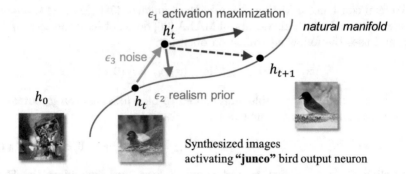

Fig. 4.7. AM can be considered as a sampler, traversing in the natural image manifold. We start from a random initialization h_0. In every step t, we first add a small amount of noise (green arrow), which pushes the sample off the natural-image manifold (h'_t). The gradients toward maximizing activation (red arrow) and more realistic images (blue arrow) pull the noisy h'_t back to the manifold at a new sample h_{t+1}.

Table 4.1. A comparison of derivatives for use in activation maximization methods. (a) has most commonly been used, (b) has worked in the past but with some difficulty, but (c) is correct under the sampler framework in Sect. 4.4.2 and [26].

a. Derivative of raw activations. Worked well in practice [10, 27] but may produce *non-selective* stimuli and is not quite the right term under the probabilistic framework in Sect. 4.4.2	$\dfrac{\partial a_i^l}{\partial x}$
b. Derivative of softmax. Previously avoided due to poor performance [42, 48], but poor performance may have been due to ill-conditioned optimization rather than the inclusion of logits from other classes	$\dfrac{\partial s_i^l}{\partial x} = s_i^l \left(\dfrac{\partial a_i^l}{\partial x} - \sum_j s_j^l \dfrac{\partial a_j^l}{\partial x} \right)$
c. Derivative of log of softmax. Correct term under the sampler framework in Sect. 4.4.2. Well-behaved under optimization, perhaps due to the $\frac{\partial a_i^l}{\partial x}$ term untouched by the s_i^l multiplier	$\begin{aligned} \dfrac{\partial \log s_i^l}{\partial x} &= \dfrac{\partial \log p(y = y_i \mid x_t)}{\partial x} \\ &= \dfrac{\partial a_i^l}{\partial x} - \dfrac{\partial}{\partial x} \log \sum_j \exp(a_j^l) \end{aligned}$

4.4.3   Interpretation of Previous Algorithms

Here, we consider four representative approaches in light of the probabilistic framework:

1. AM with no priors [10, 28, 44] (discussed in Sect. 4.1)
2. AM with a Gaussian prior [42, 46, 48] (discussed in Sect. 4.2)
3. AM with hand-designed priors [21, 29, 31, 42, 46, 48] (discussed in Sect. 4.2)
4. AM in the latent space of generator networks [26, 27] (discussed in Sect. 4.3)

Activation Maximization with No Priors. From Eq. 4.11, if we set $(\epsilon_1, \epsilon_2, \epsilon_3) = (1, 0, 0)$, we obtain a sampler that follows the neuron gradient directly without contributions from a $p(\mathbf{x})$ term or the addition of noise. In a high-dimensional space, this results in adversarial or rubbish images [28,44] (as discussed in Sect. 4.2). We can also interpret the optimization procedure in [28,44] as a sampler with a non-zero ϵ_1 but with a $p(\mathbf{x})$ such that $\frac{\partial \log p(\mathbf{x})}{\partial \mathbf{x}} = 0$ i.e. a uniform $p(\mathbf{x})$ where all images are equally likely.

Activation Maximization with a Gaussian Prior. To avoid producing high-frequency images [28] that are uninterpretable, several works have used L_2 decay, which can be thought of as a simple zero-mean Gaussian prior over images [42,46,48]. From Eq. 4.11, if we define a Gaussian $p(\mathbf{x})$ centered at the origin (assume the mean image has been subtracted) and set $(\epsilon_1, \epsilon_2, \epsilon_3) = (1, \lambda, 0)$, pulling Gaussian constants into λ, we obtain the following noiseless update rule:

$$\mathbf{x}_{t+1} = (1 - \lambda)\mathbf{x}_t + \frac{\partial \log p(y = y_c|\mathbf{x}_t)}{\partial \mathbf{x}_t} \tag{4.12}$$

The first term decays the current image slightly toward the origin, as appropriate under a Gaussian image prior, and the second term pulls the image toward higher probability regions for the chosen neuron. Here, the second term is computed as the derivative of the log of a softmax transformation of all activations across a layer (see Table 4.1).

Activation Maximization with Hand-Designed Priors. In an effort to outdo the simple Gaussian prior, many works have proposed more creative, hand-designed image priors such as Gaussian blur [48], total variation [21], jitter, rotate, scale [24], and data-driven patch priors [46]. These priors effectively serve as a simple $p(\mathbf{x})$ component in Eq. 4.11. Note that all previous methods considered under this category are noiseless ($\epsilon_3 = 0$).

Activation Maximization in the Latent Space of Generator Networks. To ameliorate the problem of poor mixing in the high-dimensional pixel space [5], several works instead performed optimization in a semantically meaningful, low-dimensional feature space of a generator network [6,26,27,47,53].

That approach can be viewed as re-parameterizing $p(\mathbf{x})$ as $\int_{\mathbf{h}} p(\mathbf{x}|\mathbf{h})p(\mathbf{h})$, and sampling from the joint probability distribution $p(\mathbf{h}, y)$ instead of $p(\mathbf{x}, y)$, treating $\mathbf{x}$ as a deterministic variable. That is, the update rule in Eq. 4.11 is now changed into the below:

$$\mathbf{h}_{t+1} = \mathbf{h}_t + \epsilon_1 \frac{\partial \log p(y = y_c|\mathbf{h}_t)}{\partial \mathbf{h}_t} + \epsilon_2 \frac{\partial \log p(\mathbf{h}_t)}{\partial \mathbf{h}_t} + N(0, \epsilon_3^2) \tag{4.13}$$

In this category, DGN-AM [27] follows the above rule with $(\epsilon_1, \epsilon_2, \epsilon_3) = (1,1,0)$.[5] Specifically, we hand-designed a $p(\mathbf{h})$ via clipping and L_2 regularization

---

[5] $\epsilon_3 = 0$ because noise was not used in DGN-AM [27].

(i.e. a Gaussian prior) to keep the code **h** within a "realistic" range. PPGNs follows exactly the update rule in Eq. 4.13 with a better $p(\mathbf{h})$ prior learned via a denoising autoencoder [26]. PPGNs produce images with better diversity than DGN-AM [26].

4.5   Applications of Activation Maximization

In this section, we review how one may use activation maximization to understand and explain a pre-trained neural network. The results below are specifically generated by DGN-AM [27] and PPGNs [26] where the authors harnessed a general image generator network to synthesize AM images.

Visualize Output Units for New Tasks. We can harness a general learned ImageNet prior to synthesize images for networks trained on a different dataset e.g. MIT Places dataset [50] or UCF-101 activity videos [27] (Figs. 4.5 and 4.8).

Fig. 4.8. Preferred stimuli generated via DGN-AM [27] for output units of a network trained to classify images on the MIT Places dataset [51] (left) and a network trained to classify videos from the UCF-101 dataset (right). The results suggested that the learned ImageNet prior generalizes well to synthesizing images for other datasets.

Visualize Hidden Units. Instead of synthesizing preferred inputs for output neurons (Fig. 4.5), one may apply AM to the hidden units. In a comparison with visualizing *real* image regions that highly activate a unit [50], we found AM images may provide similar but sometimes also complementary evidence suggesting what a unit is for [27] (Fig. 4.9). For example, via DGN-AM, we found that a unit that detects "TV screens" also detects people on TV (Fig. 4.9, unit 106).

Synthesize Preferred Images Activating Multiple Neurons. First, one may synthesize images activating a group of units at the same time to study the interaction between them [27,32]. For example, it might be useful to study how a network distinguishes two related and visually similar concepts such as "impala"

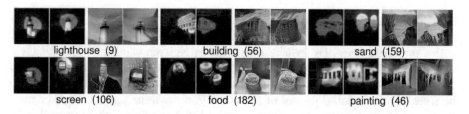

lighthouse (9)   building (56)   sand (159)

screen (106)   food (182)   painting (46)

Fig. 4.9. AM images for example hidden units at layer 5 of an CaffeNet [18] trained
to classify images of scenes [50]. For each unit: the left two images are masked-out real
images, each highlighting a region that highly activates the unit via methods in [50],
and humans provide text labels (e.g. "lighthouse") describing the common theme in
the highlighted regions. The right two images are AM images, which enable the same
conclusion regarding what feature a hidden unit has learned. Figure from [27].

and "hartebeest" animals in ImageNet [7]. One way to do this is to synthesize
images that maximize the "impala" neuron's activation but also *minimize* the
"hartebeest" neuron's activation. Second, one may reveal different facets of a
neuron [29] by activating different pairs of units. That is, activating two units at
the same time e.g. (castle + candle); and (piano + candle) would produce two
distinct images of candles that activate the same "candle" unit [27] (Fig. 4.10). In
addition, this method sometimes also produces interesting, creative art [12,27].

castle   candles

piano   candles

Fig. 4.10. Synthesizing images via DGN-AM [27] to activate both the "castle" and
"candles" units of CaffeNet [18] produces an image that resembles a castle on fire (top
right). Similarly, "piano" + "candles" produces a candle on a piano (bottom right).
Both rightmost images highly activate the "candles" output neuron.

Watch Feature Evolution During Training. We can watch how the features
evolved during the training of a target classifier network [27]. Example videos
of AM visualizations for sample output and hidden neurons during the training
of CaffeNet [15] are at: https://www.youtube.com/watch?v=q4yIwiYH6FQ and
https://www.youtube.com/watch?v=G8AtatM1Sts. One may find that features
at lower layers tend to converge faster vs. those at higher layers.

Synthesizing Videos. To gain insights into the inner functions of an activity recognition network [43], one can synthesize a single frame (Fig. 4.8; right) or an entire *preferred video*. By synthesizing videos, Nguyen et al. [27] found that a video recognition network (LRCN [8]) classifies videos without paying attention to temporal correlation across video frames. That is, the AM videos[6] appear to be a set of uncorrelated frames of activity e.g. a basketball game. Further tests confirmed that the network produces similar top-1 predicted labels regardless of whether the frames of the *original* UCF-101 videos [43] are randomly shuffled.

Activation Maximization as a Debugging Tool. We discuss here a case study where AM can be used as a debugging tool. Suppose there is a bug in your neural network image classifier implementation that internally and unexpectedly converts all input RGB images (Fig. 4.11a) into BRG images (Fig. 4.11b) before feeding them to the neural network. This bug might be hard to notice by only examining accuracy scores or attribution heatmaps [23]. Instead, AM visualizations could reflect the color space of the images that were fed to the neural network and reveal this bug (Fig. 4.11c).

Synthesize Preferred Images Conditioned on a Sentence. Instead of synthesizing images preferred by output units in an image classifier, we can also synthesize images that cause an image *captioning* network to output a desired sentence (examples in Fig. 4.12).

This reverse-engineering process may uncover interesting insights into the system's behaviors. For example, we discovered an interesting failure of a state-of-the-art image captioner [8] when it declares birds even when there is no bird in an image (Fig. 4.13).

Synthesize Preferred Images Conditioned on a Semantic Segmentation Map. We can extend AM methods to synthesize images with more fine-grained controls of where objects are placed by matching a semantic map output of a segmentation network (Fig. 4.14) or a target spatial feature map of a convolutional layer.

Synthesize Preferred Stimuli for Real, Biological Brains. While this survey aims at visualizing artificial networks, it is also possible to harness our AM techniques to study biological brains. Two teams of Neuroscientists [22,36] have recently been able to reconstruct stimuli for neurons in alive macaques' brains using either the ImageNet PPGN (as discussed in Sect. 4.4) [22] or the DGN-AM (as discussed in Sect. 4.3) [36]. The synthesized images surprisingly resemble monkeys and human nurses that the subject macaque meets frequently [36] or show eyes in neurons previously shown to be tuned for detecting faces [22]. Similar AM frameworks have also been interestingly applied to reconstruct stimuli from EEG or MRI signals of human brains [34,41].

---

[6] https://www.youtube.com/watch?v=IOYnIK6N5Bg.

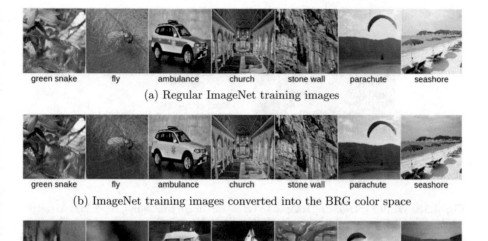

(a) Regular ImageNet training images

(b) ImageNet training images converted into the BRG color space

(c) Visualizations of the units that are trained on BRG ImageNet images above (b)

Fig. 4.11. The original ImageNet training set images are in RGB color space (a). We train CaffeNet [18] on their BRG versions (b). The activation maximization images synthesized by DGN-AM [27], faithfully portray the color space of the images, here BRG, where the network was trained on.

A **red** car parked on the side of a road

A **blue** car parked on the side of a road

Fig. 4.12. We synthesize input images (right) such that a pre-trained image captioning network (LRCN [8]) outputs the target caption description (left sentences). Each image on the right was produced by starting optimization from a different random initialization.

Fig. 4.13. While synthesizing images to cause an image captioning model [8] to output *"A bird is sitting on a branch"* via DGN-AM method [27], we only obtained images of branches or trees that surprisingly has no birds at all (a). Further tests on real MS COCO images revealed that the model [8] outputs correct captions for a test image that has a bird (b), but still insists on the existence of the bird, even when it is manually removed via Adobe Photoshop (c). This suggests the image captioner learned a strong correlation between birds and tree branches—a bias that might exist in the language or image model.

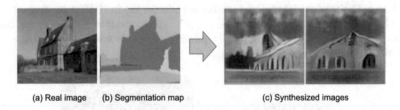

Fig. 4.14. A segmentation network from [52] is capable of producing a semantic segmentation map (b) given an input real image (a). The authors extend the DGN-AM method [27] to synthesize images (c) to match the target segmentation map (b), which specifies a scene with a building on green grass and under a blue sky background. Figure modified from [52].

4.6   Discussion and Conclusion

While activation maximization has proven a useful tool for understanding neural networks, there are still open challenges and opportunities such as:

– One might wish to harness AM to compare and contrast the features learned by different models. That would require a robust, principled AM approach that produces faithful and interpretable visualizations of the learned features for networks trained on different datasets or of different architectures. This is challenging due to two problems: (1) the image prior may not be general enough and may have a bias toward a target network or one dataset over the others; (2) AM optimization on different network architectures, especially of different depths, often requires different hyper-parameter settings to obtain the best performance.

– It is important for the community to propose rigorous approaches for evaluating AM methods. A powerful image prior may incur a higher risk of producing misleading visualizations—it is unclear whether a synthesized visual feature comes from the image prior or the target network being studied or both. Note that we have investigated that and surprisingly found the DGN-AM prior to be able to generate a wide diversity of images including the non-realistic ones (e.g. blurry, cut-up, and BRG images [27]).

– Concepts in modern deep networks can be highly distributed [4,11,44]; therefore, it might be promising to apply AM to study networks at a different, larger scale than individual neurons, e.g. looking at groups of neurons [33].

– It might be a fruitful direction to combine AM with other tools such as attribution heatmapping [33] or integrate AM into the testbeds for AI applications [35] as we move towards safe, transparent, and fair AI.

– One may also perform AM in the parameter space of a 3D renderer (e.g. modifying the lighting, object geometry or appearances in a 3D scene) that renders a 2D image that strongly activates a unit [2]. AM in a 3D space allows us to synthesize stimuli by varying a controlled factor (e.g. lighting) and thus might offer deeper insights into a model's inner-workings.

Activation maximization techniques enable us to shine light into the blackbox neural networks. As this survey shows, improving activation maximization techniques improves our ability to understand deep neural networks. We are excited for what the future holds regarding improved techniques that make neural networks more interpretable and less opaque so we can better understand how deep neural networks do the amazing things that they do.

Acknowledgements. Anh Nguyen is supported by the National Science Foundation under Grant No. 1850117, Amazon Research Credits, Auburn University, and donations from Adobe Systems Inc. and Nvidia.

References

1. Akhtar, N., Mian, A.: Threat of adversarial attacks on deep learning in computer vision: a survey. IEEE Access **6**, 14410–14430 (2018)
2. Alcorn, M.A., et al.: Strike (with) a pose: neural networks are easily fooled by strange poses of familiar objects. In: Proceedings of the IEEE Conference on Computer Vision and Pattern Recognition, pp. 4845–4854. IEEE (2019)
3. Baer, M., Connors, B.W., Paradiso, M.A.: Neuroscience: Exploring the brain (2007)
4. Bau, D., Zhou, B., Khosla, A., Oliva, A., Torralba, A.: Network dissection: quantifying interpretability of deep visual representations. In: Proceedings of the IEEE Computer Vision and Pattern Recognition (CVPR), pp. 3319–3327. IEEE (2017)
5. Bengio, Y., Mesnil, G., Dauphin, Y., Rifai, S.: Better mixing via deep representations. In: International Conference on Machine Learning, pp. 552–560 (2013)
6. Brock, A., Lim, T., Ritchie, J.M., Weston, N.: Neural photo editing with introspective adversarial networks. arXiv preprint arXiv:1609.07093 (2016)

7. Deng, J., et al.: Imagenet: a large-scale hierarchical image database. In: Proceedings of the IEEE Computer Vision and Pattern Recognition (CVPR), pp. 248–255 (2009)
8. Donahue, J., Hendricks, L.A., Guadarrama, S., Rohrbach, M., et al.: Long-term recurrent convolutional networks for visual recognition and description. In: Proceedings of the IEEE Computer Vision and Pattern Recognition (CVPR), pp. 2625–2634 (2015)
9. Dosovitskiy, A., Brox, T.: Generating images with perceptual similarity metrics based on deep networks. In: Advances in Neural Information Processing Systems (NIPS), pp. 658–666 (2016)
10. Erhan, D., Bengio, Y., Courville, A., Vincent, P.: Visualizing higher-layer features of a deep network. Dept. IRO, Université de Montréal, Technical report 4323 (2009)
11. Fong, R., Vedaldi, A.: Net2vec: quantifying and explaining how concepts are encoded by filters in deep neural networks. arXiv preprint arXiv:1801.03454 (2018)
12. Goh, G.: Image synthesis from Yahoo Open NSFW (2016). https://opennsfw.gitlab.io
13. Goodfellow, I., et al.: Generative adversarial nets. In: Advances in Neural Information Processing Systems (NIPS), pp. 2672–2680 (2014)
14. Hubel, D.H., Wiesel, T.N.: Receptive fields of single neurones in the cat's striate cortex. J. Physiol. **148**(3), 574–591 (1959)
15. Jia, Y., et al.: Caffe: convolutional architecture for fast feature embedding. arXiv preprint arXiv:1408.5093 (2014)
16. Kabilan, V.M., Morris, B., Nguyen, A.: Vectordefense: vectorization as a defense to adversarial examples. arXiv preprint arXiv:1804.08529 (2018)
17. Kandel, E.R., Schwartz, J.H., Jessell, T.M., Siegelbaum, S.A., Hudspeth, A.J., et al.: Principles of Neural Science, vol. 4. McGraw-Hill, New York (2000)
18. Krizhevsky, A., Sutskever, I., Hinton, G.E.: Imagenet classification with deep convolutional neural networks. In: Advances in Neural Information Processing Systems (NIPS), pp. 1097–1105 (2012)
19. Le, Q.V.: Building high-level features using large scale unsupervised learning. In: IEEE International Conference on Acoustics, Speech and Signal Processing (ICASSP), pp. 8595–8598. IEEE (2013)
20. Li, Y., Yosinski, J., Clune, J., Lipson, H., Hopcroft, J.: Convergent learning: do different neural networks learn the same representations? In: Feature Extraction: Modern Questions and Challenges, pp. 196–212 (2015)
21. Mahendran, A., Vedaldi, A.: Visualizing deep convolutional neural networks using natural pre-images. In: Proceedings of the IEEE Computer Vision and Pattern Recognition (CVPR), pp. 233–255 (2016)
22. Malakhova, K.: Visualization of information encoded by neurons in the higher-level areas of the visual system. J. Opt. Technol. **85**(8), 494–498 (2018)
23. Montavon, G., Samek, W., Müller, K.R.: Methods for interpreting and understanding deep neural networks. Digit. Signal Proc. **73**, 1–15 (2017)
24. Mordvintsev, A., Olah, C., Tyka, M.: Inceptionism: going deeper into neural networks. Google Research Blog (2015). Accessed 20 June
25. Nguyen, A., University of Wyoming. Computer Science Department, U.: AI Neuroscience: Visualizing and Understanding Deep Neural Networks. University of Wyoming (2017). https://books.google.com/books?id=QCexswEACAAJ
26. Nguyen, A., Clune, J., Bengio, Y., Dosovitskiy, A., Yosinski, J.: Plug & play generative networks: conditional iterative generation of images in latent space. In: Proceedings of the IEEE Computer Vision and Pattern Recognition (CVPR), pp. 3510–3520. IEEE (2017)

27. Nguyen, A., Dosovitskiy, A., Yosinski, J., Brox, T., Clune, J.: Synthesizing the preferred inputs for neurons in neural networks via deep generator networks. In: Advances in Neural Information Processing Systems, pp. 3387–3395 (2016)
28. Nguyen, A., Yosinski, J., Clune, J.: Deep neural networks are easily fooled: high confidence predictions for unrecognizable images. In: Proceedings of the IEEE Computer Vision and Pattern Recognition (CVPR), pp. 427–436 (2015)
29. Nguyen, A., Yosinski, J., Clune, J.: Multifaceted feature visualization: uncovering the different types of features learned by each neuron in deep neural networks. In: Visualization for Deep Learning Workshop, ICML Conference (2016)
30. Nguyen, A., Yosinski, J., Clune, J.: Understanding innovation engines: automated creativity and improved stochastic optimization via deep learning. Evol. Comput. 24(3), 545–572 (2016)
31. Nguyen, A.M., Yosinski, J., Clune, J.: Innovation engines: automated creativity and improved stochastic optimization via deep learning. In: Proceedings of the 2015 Annual Conference on Genetic and Evolutionary Computation, pp. 959–966. ACM (2015)
32. Olah, C., Mordvintsev, A., Schubert, L.: Feature visualization. Distill 2(11), e7 (2017)
33. Olah, C., et al.: The building blocks of interpretability. Distill 3(3), e10 (2018)
34. Palazzo, S., Spampinato, C., Kavasidis, I., Giordano, D., Shah, M.: Decoding brain representations by multimodal learning of neural activity and visual features. arXiv preprint arXiv:1810.10974 (2018)
35. Pei, K., Cao, Y., Yang, J., Jana, S.: DeepXplore: automated whitebox testing of deep learning systems. In: Proceedings of the 26th Symposium on Operating Systems Principles, pp. 1–18. ACM (2017)
36. Ponce, C.R., Xiao, W., Schade, P., Hartmann, T.S., Kreiman, G., Livingstone, M.S.: Evolving super stimuli for real neurons using deep generative networks. bioRxiv, p. 516484 (2019)
37. Quiroga, R.Q., Reddy, L., Kreiman, G., Koch, C., Fried, I.: Invariant visual representation by single neurons in the human brain. Nature 435(7045), 1102–1107 (2005)
38. Roberts, G.O., Rosenthal, J.S.: Optimal scaling of discrete approximations to langevin diffusions. J. Roy. Stat. Soc. Ser. B (Stat. Methodol.) 60(1), 255–268 (1998)
39. Rumelhart, D.E., Hinton, G.E., Williams, R.J.: Learning representations by back-propagating errors. Nature 323(6088), 533 (1986)
40. Russakovsky, O., et al.: Imagenet large scale visual recognition challenge. IJCV 115(3), 211–252 (2015)
41. Shen, G., Horikawa, T., Majima, K., Kamitani, Y.: Deep image reconstruction from human brain activity. PLoS Comput. Biol. 15(1), e1006633 (2019)
42. Simonyan, K., Vedaldi, A., Zisserman, A.: Deep inside convolutional networks: visualising image classification models and saliency maps. In: ICLR Workshop (2014)
43. Soomro, K., Zamir, A.R., Shah, M.: Ucf101: a dataset of 101 human actions classes from videos in the wild. arXiv preprint arXiv:1212.0402 (2012)
44. Szegedy, C., et al.: Intriguing properties of neural networks. CoRR abs/1312.6199 (2013)
45. Tyka, M.: Class visualization with bilateral filters. https://mtyka.github.io/deepdream/2016/02/05/bilateral-class-vis.html. Accessed 26 June 2018
46. Wei, D., Zhou, B., Torrabla, A., Freeman, W.: Understanding intra-class knowledge inside CNN. arXiv preprint arXiv:1507.02379 (2015)

47. Yeh, R., Chen, C., Lim, T.Y., Hasegawa-Johnson, M., Do, M.N.: Semantic image inpainting with perceptual and contextual losses. arxiv preprint. arXiv preprint arXiv:1607.07539 (2016)
48. Yosinski, J., Clune, J., Nguyen, A., Fuchs, T., Lipson, H.: Understanding neural networks through deep visualization. In: Deep Learning Workshop, ICML Conference (2015)
49. Zeiler, M.D., Fergus, R.: Visualizing and understanding convolutional networks. In: Fleet, D., Pajdla, T., Schiele, B., Tuytelaars, T. (eds.) ECCV 2014. LNCS, vol. 8689, pp. 818–833. Springer, Cham (2014). https://doi.org/10.1007/978-3-319-10590-1_53
50. Zhou, B., Khosla, A., Lapedriza, A., Oliva, A., Torralba, A.: Object detectors emerge in deep scene CNNs. In: International Conference on Learning Representations (ICLR) (2015)
51. Zhou, B., Lapedriza, A., Xiao, J., Torralba, A., Oliva, A.: Learning deep features for scene recognition using places database. In: Advances in Neural Information Processing Systems, pp. 487–495 (2014)
52. Zhou, B., Zhao, H., Puig, X., Fidler, S., Barriuso, A., Torralba, A.: Scene parsing through ade20k dataset. In: Proceedings of the IEEE Conference on Computer Vision and Pattern Recognition (CVPR), pp. 633–641. IEEE (2017)
53. Zhu, J.-Y., Krähenbühl, P., Shechtman, E., Efros, A.A.: Generative visual manipulation on the natural image manifold. In: Leibe, B., Matas, J., Sebe, N., Welling, M. (eds.) ECCV 2016. LNCS, vol. 9909, pp. 597–613. Springer, Cham (2016). https://doi.org/10.1007/978-3-319-46454-1_36
54. Øygard, A.M.: Visualizing GoogLeNet classes — audun m øygard. https://www.auduno.com/2015/07/29/visualizing-googlenet-classes/. Accessed 26 June 2018

5

Interpretable Text-to-Image Synthesis with Hierarchical Semantic Layout Generation

Seunghoon Hong[1], Dingdong Yang[1], Jongwook Choi[1], and Honglak Lee[1,2(✉)]

[1] University of Michigan, Ann Arbor, MI, USA
honglak@eecs.umich.edu
[2] Google Brain, Mountain View, CA, USA

Abstract. Generating images from natural language description has drawn a lot of attention in the research community for its practical usefulness and for understanding the method in which the model relates text with visual concepts by synthesizing them. Deep generative models have been successfully employed to address this task, which formulates the problem as a translation task from text to image. However, learning a direct mapping from text to image is challenging due to the complexity of the mapping and makes it difficult to understand the underlying generation process. To address these issues, we propose a novel hierarchical approach for text-to-image synthesis by inferring a semantic layout. Our algorithm decomposes the generation process into multiple steps. First, it constructs a semantic layout from the text using the layout generator and then converts the layout to an image with the image generator. The proposed layout generator progressively constructs a semantic layout in a coarse-to-fine manner by generating object bounding boxes and refining each box by estimating the object shapes inside the box. The image generator synthesizes an image conditioned on the inferred semantic layout, which provides a useful semantic structure of an image matching the text description. Conditioning the generation with the inferred semantic layout allows our model to generate semantically more meaningful images and provides interpretable representations to allow users to interactively control the generation process by modifying the layout. We demonstrate the capability of the proposed model on the challenging MS-COCO dataset and show that the model can substantially improve the image quality and interpretability of the output and semantic alignment to input text over existing approaches.

5.1 Introduction

Generating images from text description has been an active research topic in computer vision. Allowing users to describe visual concepts in natural language provides a natural and flexible interface for conditioning image generation. Also, the task describes the model's understanding of the visual concepts by

© Springer Nature Switzerland AG 2019
W. Samek et al. (Eds.): Explainable AI, LNAI 11700, pp. 77–95, 2019.
https://doi.org/10.1007/978-3-030-28954-6_5

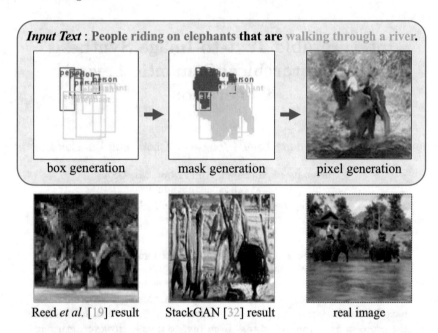

Fig. 5.1. Overall framework of the proposed algorithm. Given a text description, our algorithm sequentially constructs a semantic structure of a scene and generates an image conditioned on the inferred layout and text. Best viewed in color.

synthesizing images matching the text description. Recently, approaches based on conditional Generative Adversarial Network (GAN) have shown promising results on text-to-image synthesis task [6,23,25,28,38–40]. Conditioning both the generator and discriminator on text allows these approaches to generate realistic images that are both diverse and relevant to the input text. Based on the conditional GAN framework, recent approaches further improve the prediction quality by generating high-resolution images [38–40] or improving the text conditioning [4,7,28].

However, the success of existing approaches has been limited to simple datasets, such as birds [37] and flowers [19], while the generation of complicated real-world images, such as MS-COCO [15] remains an open challenge. As illustrated in Fig. 5.1, generating images from a general sentence, *"people riding on elephants that are walking through a river"*, requires multiple reasonings on various visual concepts, such as object category (*people* and *elephants*), spatial configurations of objects (*riding*), scene context (*walking through a river*), *etc.*, which is more complex than generating a single, large object as in simpler datasets [19,37]. Existing approaches have not been successful in generating reasonable images for such complex text description due to the complexity of learning a direct text-to-pixel mapping from general images. In addition, deep generative models often lack the mechanisms required to introspect its generation process, which limits the interpretability of the model since the learned mapping of the model is not explicitly interpretable only from the output images, especially when the generation quality is limited (Fig. 5.1).

Instead of learning a direct mapping from text to image, we propose an alternative approach that constructs a *semantic layout* as an intermediate representation between text and image. The semantic layout defines the structure of the scene based on object instances and provides fine-grained information of the scene, such as the number of objects, object category, location, size, shape, *etc.* (Fig. 5.1). Introducing a mechanism that explicitly aligns the semantic structure of an image to text allows the proposed method to generate complicated images of complex text descriptions. In addition, conditioning the image generation on a semantic structure allows our model to generate semantically more meaningful images that are recognizable and interpretable.

Our model for hierarchical text-to-image synthesis consists of two parts: the *layout generator* that constructs a semantic label map from a text description, and the *image generator* that converts the estimated layout to an image with using the text. Since learning a direct mapping from text to fine-grained semantic layout is challenging, we further decompose the task into two manageable subtasks: estimating the bounding box layout of an image using the *box generator*, and then refining the shape of each object inside the box using the *shape generator*. The generated layout is then used to guide the image generator for pixel-level synthesis. The box generator, shape generator, and image generator are implemented by independent neural networks and trained in parallel with corresponding supervisions.

Generating a semantic layout improves the quality of text-to-image synthesis and provides several potential benefits. First, the predicted semantic layout provides an interpretable representation of intermediate outputs in text-to-image mapping, which helps humans to understand the underlying mechanism of the model converting texts to images. Second, it offers an interactive interface for controlling the image generation process; users can modify the semantic layout to generate a desired image by removing/adding objects, changing size and location of objects, *etc.*. Third, the semantic layout provides instance-wise annotations on generated images, which can be directly exploited for automated scene parsing and object retrieval. The contributions of this paper are as follows:

- We propose a novel approach for synthesizing images from complicated text descriptions. Our model explicitly constructs a semantic layout from the text description and guides image generation using the inferred semantic layout.
- Conditioning image generation on explicit layout prediction allows our method to generate images that are semantically meaningful and well-aligned with input descriptions.
- We conduct extensive quantitative and qualitative evaluations on the challenging MS-COCO dataset and demonstrate substantial improvement on generation quality over existing works.

The remainder of the paper is organized as follows: we briefly review related work in Sect. 5.2 and provide an overview of the proposed approach in Sect. 5.3.

Our model for layout and image generation is introduced in Sect. 5.4 and 5.5, respectively. We discuss the experimental results on the MS-COCO dataset in Sect. 5.6.

5.2   Related Work

Generating images from text descriptions has recently drawn a lot of attention from the research community. Various approaches have been proposed to formulate the task as a conditional image generation problem based on Variational Auto-Encoders (VAE) [16], auto-regressive models [24], optimization techniques [18], *etc.* Recently, approaches based on conditional GANs [8] have shown promising results in text-to-image synthesis [4,6,7,23,25,28,38–40]. Reed *et al.* [23] proposed the first approach that formulates the task in the conditional GAN framework, which conditions both the generator and the discriminator on text embedding. They demonstrated the successful generation results on 64 × 64 images. Built upon this framework, recent approaches have improved the generation quality by synthesizing the higher-resolution images [39,40] or improving conditioning on text information [4,7,28,38]. To increase the resolution of output images, Zhang *et al.* [39] proposed a two-stage GAN that first generates low-resolution images from text and increases its resolution by another network conditioned on the low-resolution image. Zhang *et al.* [40] extended the approach by using an end-to-end trainable network that regularizes the generator outputs in multiple resolutions with a set of discriminators. On the other hand, to improve the conditioning on the text, Hao *et al.* [7] proposed to augment the text annotations by synthesizing captions using a pre-trained caption generator, and Dash *et al.* [4] proposed to augment the discriminator to predict additional class labels. To reduce the ambiguities in text, Sharma *et al.* [28] conditioned image generation on a dialogue instead of single caption. Xu *et al.* [38] employed a multi-stage generation method with an attention mechanism to condition the image generation on each word in a caption one at a time. Although these approaches have demonstrated impressive generation results on datasets of specific categories (*e.g.*, birds [37] and flowers [19]), the perceptual quality of generation tends to substantially degrade on datasets with complicated images (*e.g.*, MS-COCO [15]). We investigate a method to improve text-to-image synthesis on general images by conditioning generation on the inferred semantic layout.

The problem of generating images from pixel-wise semantic labels has been explored recently [3,11,14,24]. In these approaches, the task of image generation is formulated as translating semantic labels to pixels. Isola *et al.* [11] proposed a pixel-to-pixel translation network that converts dense pixel-wise labels to an image using conditional GAN. Chen *et al.* [3] proposed a cascaded refinement network that generates a high-resolution output from dense semantic labels using a cascade of upsampling layers conditioned on the layout. Karacan *et al.* [14] employed both dense layouts and attribute vectors for image generation using conditional GAN. Reed *et al.* [24] utilized sparse label maps defined on a few foreground objects, similar to our method. Unlike previous approaches that require ground-truth layouts for generation, our method *infers* the semantic layout, and thus is more applicable to various generation tasks. Note that our main contribution is complementary to these approaches and we can integrate existing segmentation-to-pixel generation methods to generate an image conditioned on a layout.

The idea of inferring scene structure for image generation has been explored by recent works in several domains. For example, Wang *et al.* [36] proposed to infer a surface normal map as an intermediate structure to generate indoor scene images, and Villegas *et al.* [33] predicted human joints for future frame prediction. Reed *et al.* [25] predicted local key-points of bird or human for text-to-image synthesis. Contrary to the previous approaches that predict specific types of structures for image generation, our proposed method aims to predict semantic label maps, which is a general representation of natural images. Concurrent to this work, Johnson *et al.* [13] developed a hierarchical text-to-image synthesis method based on a scene graph. In this approach, they first extract a scene-graph from an input text and construct an image in a coarse-to-fine manner with incorporating the relationship between objects encoded in the graph. Contrary to this work, we aim to infer a semantic layout directly from the text without information on scene structure, where the information required to organize and associate objects is implicitly learned from text.

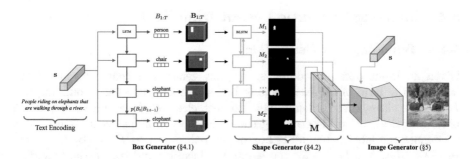

Fig. 5.2. Overall pipeline of the proposed algorithm. Given a text embedding, our algorithm first generates a coarse layout of the image by placing a set of object bounding boxes using the box generator (Sect. 5.4.1), and further refines the object shape inside each box using the shape generator (Sect. 5.4.2). Combining outputs from the box and the shape generator creates a semantic label map defining the semantic structure of the scene. Conditioned on the inferred semantic layout and the text, a pixel-wise image is finally generated by the image generator (Sect. 5.5).

5.3   Overview

The overall pipeline of the proposed framework is illustrated in Fig. 5.2. Given a text description, our model progressively constructs a scene by refining the semantic structure of an image using the following sequence of generators:

- **The box generator** takes a text embedding **s** as input and generates a coarse layout by composing object instances in an image. The output of the box generator is a set of bounding boxes $B_{1:T} = \{B_1, ..., B_T\}$, where each bounding box B_t defines the location, size, and category label of the t-th object (Sect. 5.4.1).
- **The shape generator** takes a set of bounding boxes generated from the box generator and predicts the shapes of the objects inside the boxes. The output of the shape generator is a set of binary masks $M_{1:T} = \{M_1, ..., M_T\}$, where each mask M_t defines the foreground shape of the t-th object (Sect. 5.4.2).
- **The image generator** takes the semantic label map **M** obtained by aggregating instance-wise masks and the text embedding as inputs and generates an image by translating a semantic layout to pixels matching the text description (Sect. 5.5).

By conditioning the image generation process on the semantic layouts that are explicitly inferred, our method is able to generate images that preserve detailed object shapes and therefore semantic contents are more recognizable. In our experiments, we show that the images generated by our method are semantically more meaningful and well-aligned with the input text, compared to images generated by previous approaches [23,39] (Sect. 5.6).

5.4   Inferring Semantic Layout from Text

5.4.1   Bounding Box Generation

Given an input text embedding **s**, we first generate a coarse layout of the image in the form of object bounding boxes. We associate each bounding box B_t with a class label to define which object class to place and where, which plays a critical role in determining the global layout of the scene. Specifically, we denote the labeled bounding box of the t-th object as $B_t = (\mathbf{b}_t, l_t)$, where $\mathbf{b}_t = [b_{t,x}, b_{t,y}, b_{t,w}, b_{t,h}] \in \mathbb{R}^4$ represents the location and size of the bounding box, and $l_t \in \{0,1\}^{L+1}$ is a one-hot class label over L categories. We reserve the $(L+1)$-th class as a special indicator for the end-of-sequence.

The *box generator* G_{box} defines a stochastic mapping from the input text **s** to a set of T object bounding boxes $B_{1:T} = \{B_1, ..., B_T\}$:

$$\widehat{B}_{1:T} \sim G_{\text{box}}(\mathbf{s}). \tag{5.1}$$

Model. We employ an auto-regressive decoder for the box generator by decomposing the conditional joint bounding box probability as $p(B_{1:T} \mid \mathbf{s}) = \prod_{t=1}^{T} p(B_t \mid B_{1:t-1}, \mathbf{s})$, where the conditionals are approximated by LSTM [10]. In the generative process, we first sample a class label l_t for the t-th object and then generate the box coordinates $\mathbf{b}_t$ conditioned on l_t, *i.e.*, $p(B_t \mid \cdot) = p(\mathbf{b}_t, l_t \mid \cdot) = p(l_t \mid \cdot) p(\mathbf{b}_t \mid l_t, \cdot)$. The two conditionals are modeled by a Gaussian Mixture Model (GMM) and a categorical distribution [9], respectively:

$$p(\boldsymbol{l}_t \mid B_{1:t-1}, \mathbf{s}) = \text{Softmax}(\mathbf{e}_t), \tag{5.2}$$

$$p(\mathbf{b}_t \mid \boldsymbol{l}_t, B_{1:t-1}, \mathbf{s}) = \sum_{k=1}^{K} \pi_{t,k} \mathcal{N}\left(\mathbf{b}_t; \boldsymbol{\mu}_{t,k}, \boldsymbol{\Sigma}_{t,k}\right), \tag{5.3}$$

where K is the number of mixture components. The softmax logit $\mathbf{e}_t$ in Eq. (5.2) and the parameters for the Gaussian mixtures $\pi_{t,k} \in \mathbb{R}, \boldsymbol{\mu}_{t,k} \in \mathbb{R}^4$ and $\boldsymbol{\Sigma}_{t,k} \in \mathbb{R}^{4\times4}$ in Eq. (5.3) are computed by the outputs from each LSTM step.

Training. We train the box generator by minimizing the negative log-likelihood of ground-truth bounding boxes:

$$\mathcal{L}_{\text{box}} = -\lambda_l \frac{1}{T} \sum_{t=1}^{T} \boldsymbol{l}_t^* \log p(\boldsymbol{l}_t) - \lambda_b \frac{1}{T} \sum_{t=1}^{T} \log p(\mathbf{b}_t^*), \tag{5.4}$$

where T is the number of objects in an image, and λ_l, λ_b are balancing hyper-parameters. $\mathbf{b}_t^*$ and $\boldsymbol{l}_t^*$ are ground-truth bounding box coordinates and a label of the t-th object, respectively, which are ordered based on their bounding box locations from left to right. Note that we drop the conditioning in Eq. (5.4) for notational brevity. The hyper-parameters are set to $\lambda_l = 4, \lambda_b = 1$, and $K = 20$ in our experiments.

At test time, we generate bounding boxes via ancestral sampling of box coordinates and class labels using Eqs. (5.2) and (5.3), respectively. We terminate the sampling when the sampled class label corresponds to the termination indicator $(L+1)$, thus the number of objects are determined adaptively based on the text.

5.4.2   Shape Generation

Given a set of bounding boxes obtained by the box generator, the shape generator predicts a more detailed image structure in the form of object masks. Specifically, for each object bounding box B_t obtained by Eq. (5.1), we generate a binary mask $M_t \in \mathbb{R}^{H \times W}$ that defines the shape of the object inside the box. To this end, we first convert the discrete bounding box outputs $\{B_t\}$ to a binary tensor $\mathbf{B}_t \in \{0,1\}^{H \times W \times L}$, whose element is 1 if and only if it is contained in the corresponding class-labeled box. Using the notation $M_{1:T} = \{M_1, ..., M_T\}$, we define the *shape generator* G_{mask} as

$$\widehat{M}_{1:T} = G_{\text{mask}}(\mathbf{B}_{1:T}, \mathbf{z}_{1:T}), \tag{5.5}$$

where $\mathbf{z}_t \sim \mathcal{N}(0, I)$ is a random noise vector.

Generating an accurate object shape requires two criteria: (i) First, each instance-wise mask M_t should match the location and class information of $\mathbf{B}_t$ and be recognizable as an individual instance (instance-wise constraints). (ii) Second, each object shape must be aligned with its surrounding context (global constraints). To satisfy both criteria, we design the shape generator as a recurrent neural network, which is trained with two conditional adversarial losses, as described below.

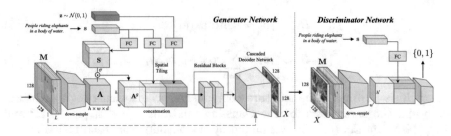

Fig. 5.3. Architecture of the image generator. Conditioned on the text description and the semantic layout generated by the layout generator, it generates an image that matches both inputs.

Model. We build the shape generator G_{mask} using a convolutional recurrent neural network [29], as illustrated in Fig. 5.2. At each step t, the model takes $\mathbf{B}_t$ through the encoder CNN and encodes the information of all object instances using bi-directional convolutional LSTM (Bi-convLSTM). In addition to the convLSTM output at the t-th step, we add noise $\mathbf{z}_t$ by spatial tiling and concatenation and generate a mask M_t by forwarding it through a decoder CNN.

Training. Training the shape generator is based on the GAN framework [8], in which the generator and the discriminator are alternately trained. To enforce both the global and the instance-wise constraints discussed earlier, we employ two conditional adversarial losses [17] with the instance -wise discriminator D_{inst} and the global discriminator D_{global}.

First, we encourage each object mask to be compatible with class and location information encoded by the object bounding box. We train an instance-wise discriminator D_{inst} by optimizing the following *instance-wise adversarial loss*:

$$\mathcal{L}_{\text{inst}}^{(t)} = \mathbb{E}_{(\mathbf{B}_t, M_t)}\Big[\log D_{\text{inst}}\big(\mathbf{B}_t, M_t\big)\Big] \tag{5.6}$$
$$+ \mathbb{E}_{\mathbf{B}_t, \mathbf{z}_t}\Big[\log\Big(1 - D_{\text{inst}}\big(\mathbf{B}_t, G_{\text{mask}}^{(t)}(\mathbf{B}_{1:T}, \mathbf{z}_{1:T})\big)\Big)\Big],$$

where $G_{\text{mask}}^{(t)}(\mathbf{B}_{1:T}, \mathbf{z}_{1:T})$ indicates the t-th output from mask generator. The instance-wise loss is applied for each of T instance-wise masks and aggregated over all instances as $\mathcal{L}_{\text{inst}} = (1/T)\sum_t \mathcal{L}_{\text{inst}}^{(t)}$.

On the other hand, the global loss encourages all the instance-wise masks to form a globally coherent context. To consider the relation between different objects, we aggregate them into a global mask[1] $G_{\text{global}}(\mathbf{B}_{1:T}, \mathbf{z}_{1:T}) = \sum_t G_{\text{mask}}^{(t)}(\mathbf{B}_{1:t}, \mathbf{z}_{1:t})$, and compute a global adversarial loss analogous to Eq. (5.6) as

$$\mathcal{L}_{\text{global}} = \mathbb{E}_{(\mathbf{B}_{1:T}, M_{1:T})}\Big[\log D_{\text{global}}\big(\mathbf{B}_{\text{global}}, M_{\text{global}}\big)\Big] \tag{5.7}$$
$$+ \mathbb{E}_{\mathbf{B}_{1:T}, \mathbf{z}_{1:T}}\Big[\log\Big(1 - D_{\text{global}}\big(\mathbf{B}_{\text{global}}, G_{\text{global}}(\mathbf{B}_{1:T}, \mathbf{z}_{1:T})\big)\Big)\Big],$$

---

[1] G_{global} is computed by summation to model overlaps between objects.

where $M_{\text{global}} \in \mathbb{R}^{H \times W}$ is an aggregated mask obtained by taking element-wise addition over $M_{1:T}$. $\mathbf{B}_{\text{global}} \in \mathbb{R}^{H \times W \times L}$ is an aggregated bounding box tensor obtained by taking element-wise maximum over $\mathbf{B}_{1:T}$.

Finally, we impose a reconstruction loss $\mathcal{L}_{\text{rec}}$ that encourages the predicted instance masks to be similar to the ground-truths. We implement this idea using perceptual loss [2,3,12,35], which measures the distance of real and fake images in the feature space of a pre-trained CNN by

$$\mathcal{L}_{\text{rec}} = \sum_l \left\| \Phi_l(G_{\text{global}}) - \Phi_l(M_{\text{global}}) \right\|, \tag{5.8}$$

where Φ_l is the feature extracted from the l-th layer of a CNN. We use the VGG-19 network [30] pre-trained on ImageNet [5] in our experiments. Since our input to the pre-trained network is a binary mask, we replicate masks to channel dimension and use the converted mask to compute Eq. (5.8). We found that using the perceptual loss improves the stability of GAN training and the quality of object shapes, as discussed in [2,3,35].

Combining Eqs. (5.6), (5.7) and (5.8) allows the overall training objective for the shape generator to become:

$$\mathcal{L}_{\text{shape}} = \lambda_i \mathcal{L}_{\text{inst}} + \lambda_g \mathcal{L}_{\text{global}} + \lambda_r \mathcal{L}_{\text{rec}}, \tag{5.9}$$

where λ_i, λ_g, and λ_r are hyper-parameters that balance different losses, which are set to 1, 1, and 10 in the experiment, respectively.

5.5   Synthesizing Images from Text and Layout

The outputs from the layout generator define the location, size, shape, and class information of objects, which provides semantic structure of a scene relevant to the text. Given the semantic structure and text, the objective of the image generator is to generate an image that conforms to both conditions. To this end, we first aggregate binary object masks $M_{1:T}$ to a semantic label map $\mathbf{M} \in \{0,1\}^{H \times W \times L}$, such that $\mathbf{M}_{ijk} = 1$ if and only if there exists an object of class k whose mask M_t covers the pixel (i,j). Then, given the semantic layout $\mathbf{M}$ and the text $\mathbf{s}$, the image generator is defined by:

$$\widehat{X} = G_{\text{img}}(\mathbf{M}, \mathbf{s}, \mathbf{z}), \tag{5.10}$$

where $\mathbf{z} \sim \mathcal{N}(0, I)$ is a random noise. We describe the network architecture and training procedures of the image generator below.

Model. Figure 5.3 illustrates the overall architecture of the image generator. Our generator network is based on a convolutional encoder-decoder network [11] with several modifications. It first encodes the semantic layout $\mathbf{M}$ through several down-sampling layers to construct a layout feature $\mathbf{A} \in \mathbb{R}^{h \times w \times d}$. We consider that the layout feature encodes various context information of the input layout

Table 5.1. Quantitative evaluation results. Two evaluation metrics based on caption generation and the Inception score are presented. The second and third columns indicate types of bounding box or mask layouts used in image generation, where "GT" indicates ground-truth and "Pred." indicates the predicted layouts by our model. The last row presents the caption generation performance on real images, which corresponds to the upper-bound of the caption generation metric. Higher values are more accurate in all columns.

Method	Box	Mask	Caption generation						Inception [26]
			BLEU-1	BLEU-2	BLEU-3	BLEU-4	METEOR	CIDEr	
Reed *et al.* [23]	-	-	0.470	0.253	0.136	0.077	0.122	0.160	7.88 ± 0.07
StackGAN [39]	-	-	0.492	0.272	0.152	0.089	0.128	0.195	8.45 ± 0.03
Ours	Pred.	Pred.	**0.541**	**0.332**	**0.199**	**0.122**	**0.154**	**0.367**	**11.46 ± 0.09**
Ours (control experiment)	GT	Pred.	0.556	0.353	0.219	0.139	0.162	0.400	11.94 ± 0.09
	GT	GT	0.573	0.373	0.239	0.156	0.169	0.440	12.40 ± 0.08
Real images (upper bound)	-	-	0.678	0.496	0.349	0.243	0.228	0.802	-

along the channel dimension. We use the layout feature to adaptively select context relevant to the text. Specifically, we compute a d-dimensional vector from the text embedding and spatially replicate it to construct $\mathbf{S} \in \mathbb{R}^{h \times w \times d}$. Then we apply gating on the layout feature by $\mathbf{A}^g = \mathbf{A} \odot \sigma(\mathbf{S})$, where σ is the sigmoid nonlinearity and $\odot$ denotes element-wise multiplication. To further encode text information on the background, we compute another text embedding with separate fully-connected layers and spatially replicate it to size $h \times w$. The gated layout feature $\mathbf{A}^g$, the text embedding, and the noises are then combined by concatenation along channel dimension and subsequently fed into several residual blocks and the decoder to be mapped to an image. We employ a cascaded network [3] for the decoder, which takes the semantic layout $\mathbf{M}$ as an additional input to every upsampling layer. We found that the cascaded network enhances conditioning on a layout structure and produces a more accurate object boundary.

For the discriminator network D_{img}, we first concatenate the generated image X and the semantic layout $\mathbf{M}$. It is fed through a series of down-sampling blocks, resulting in a feature map of size $h' \times w'$. We concatenate it with a spatially tiled text embedding, from which we compute a decision score of the discriminator.

Training. Conditioned on both the semantic layout $\mathbf{M}$ and the text embedding $\mathbf{s}$ extracted by [22], the image generator G_{img} is jointly trained with the discriminator D_{img}. We define the objective function by $\mathcal{L}_{\text{img}} = \lambda_a \mathcal{L}_{\text{adv}} + \lambda_r \mathcal{L}_{\text{rec}}$, where

$$\mathcal{L}_{\text{adv}} = \mathbb{E}_{(\mathbf{M}, \mathbf{s}, X)} \left[\log D_{\text{img}}(\mathbf{M}, \mathbf{s}, X) \right]$$
$$+ \mathbb{E}_{(\mathbf{M}, \mathbf{s}), \mathbf{z}} \left[\log \left(1 - D_{\text{img}}(\mathbf{M}, \mathbf{s}, G_{\text{img}}(\mathbf{M}, \mathbf{s}, \mathbf{z})) \right) \right], \tag{5.11}$$

$$\mathcal{L}_{\text{rec}} = \sum_l \| \Phi_l(G_{\text{img}}(\mathbf{M}, \mathbf{s}, \mathbf{z})) - \Phi_l(X) \|, \tag{5.12}$$

where X is a ground-truth image associated with semantic layout $\mathbf{M}$. As in the mask generator, we apply the same perceptual loss $\mathcal{L}_{\text{rec}}$, which is found to be effective. We set the hyper-parameters $\lambda_a = 1$, $\lambda_r = 10$ in our experiment.

Table 5.2. Human evaluation results.

Method	Ratio of ranking 1st	vs. Ours
StackGAN [39]	18.4%	29.5%
Reed et al. [23]	23.3%	32.3%
Ours	**58.3%**	-

5.6 Experiments

5.6.1 Experimental Setup

Dataset. We use the MS-COCO dataset [15] to evaluate our model. It contains 164,000 training images over 80 semantic classes, where each image is associated with instance-wise annotations (*i.e.*, object bounding boxes and segmentation masks) and five text descriptions. The dataset has complex scenes with many objects in a diverse context, which makes generation challenging. We use the official train and validation splits from MS-COCO 2014 for training and evaluating our model, respectively.

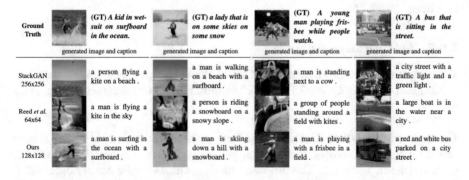

Fig. 5.4. Qualitative examples of generated images conditioned on text descriptions on the MS-COCO validation set with using our method and the baselines, method (StackGAN [39] and Reed et al. [23]). The input text and ground-truth image are shown in the first row. For each method, we provide a reconstructed caption conditioned on the generated image.

Evaluation Metrics. We evaluate text-conditional image generation performance using various metrics: Inception score, caption generation, and human evaluation.

Inception Score—We compute the Inception score [26] by applying a pre-trained classifier on synthesized images and investigating statistics of their score distributions. It measures the recognizability and the diversity of generated images and is correlated with human perceptions on visual quality [20]. We use the Inception-v3 [31] network pre-trained on ImageNet [5] for evaluation, and measure the score for all validation images.

Caption Generation—In addition to the Inception score, assessing the performance of text-conditional image generation necessitates measuring the relevance of the generated images to the input texts. To this end, we generate sentences from the synthesized image and measure the similarity between the input text and the predicted sentence. The underlying intuition is that if the generated image is relevant to input text and its contents are recognizable, one should be able to determine the original text from the synthesized image. We employ an image caption generator [34] trained on MS-COCO to generate sentences, where one sentence is generated per image by greedy decoding. We report three standard language similarity metrics: BLEU [21], METEOR [1], and CIDEr [32].

Human Evaluation—Evaluation based on caption generation is beneficial for large-scale evaluation, but may introduce unintended bias by the caption generator. To verify the effectiveness of caption-based evaluation, we conduct human evaluation using Amazon Mechanical Turk. For each text randomly selected from the MS-COCO validation set, we presented five images generated by various methods and asked users to rank the methods based on the relevance of generated images to text. We collected results for 1,000 sentences, each of which is annotated by five users. We report results based on the ratio of each method ranked as the most accurate one-to-one comparison between ours and the baselines.

5.6.2   Quantitative Analysis

We compare our method with two state-of-the-art approaches [23,39] based on conditional GANs. Tables 5.1 and 5.2 summarize the quantitative evaluation results.

Comparisons to Other Methods. We first present systemic evaluation results based on Inception scores and caption generation performance. The results are summarized in Table 5.1. The proposed method substantially outperforms existing approaches based on both evaluation metrics. In terms of Inception score, our method outperforms the existing approaches with a substantial margin, presumably because our method generates more recognizable objects. Caption generation performance shows that captions generated from our synthesized images are more strongly correlated with the input text than the baselines. This shows that images generated by our method are more accurately aligned with descriptions and the semantic contents are more recognizable.

Table 5.2 summarizes comparison results based on human evaluation. When users are asked to rank images based on their relevance to input text, they choose images generated by our method as the most accurate in approximately 60% of all presented sentences, which is substantially higher than the baselines (about 20%). This is consistent with the caption generation results in Table 5.1, in which our method substantially outperforms the baselines, while their performances are comparable.

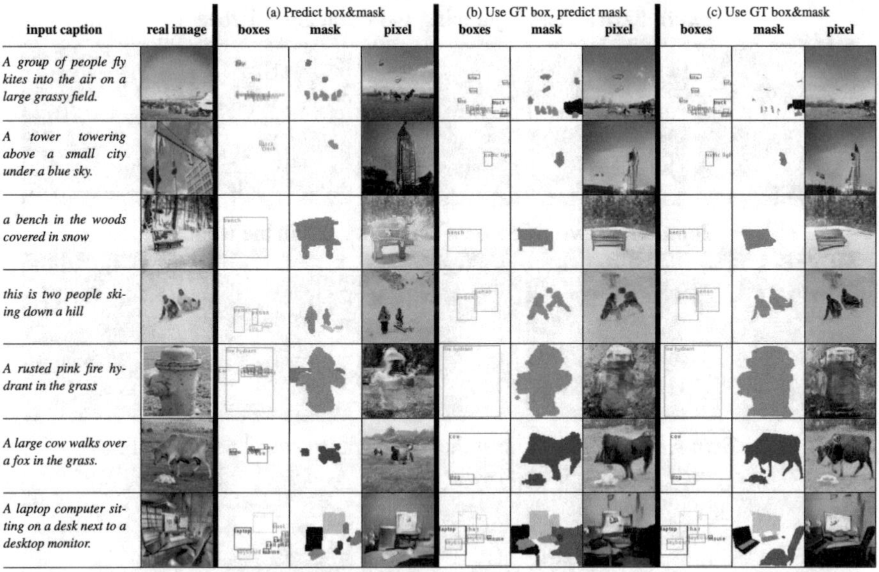

Fig. 5.5. Image generation results of our method. Each column corresponds to generation results conditioned on (a) predicted box and mask layouts, (b) ground-truth box and predicted mask layouts, and (c) ground-truth box and mask layouts. Classes are color-coded for illustration purpose. Best viewed in color.

Figure 5.4 illustrates qualitative comparisons. Due to adversarial training, images generated by the other methods, especially StackGAN [39], tend to be clear and exhibit high-frequency details. However, it is difficult to recognize contents from the images, since they often fail to predict important semantic structures of objects and scenes. As a result, the reconstructed captions from the generated images are usually not relevant to the input text. Compared to them, our method generates much more recognizable and semantically meaningful images by conditioning the generation with the inferred semantic layout, and is able to reconstruct descriptions that are more aligned with the input sentences.

Ablative Analysis. To understand the quality and the impact of the predicted semantic layout, we conduct an ablation study by gradually replacing the bounding box and mask layouts predicted by the layout generator with the ground-truths. Table 5.1 summarizes quantitative evaluation results. As it shows, replacing the predicted layouts with the ground-truths results in gradual performance improvements, which shows prediction errors in both the bounding box and mask layouts.

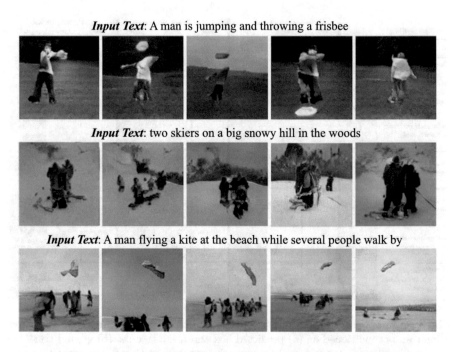

Fig. 5.6. Multiple samples generated from a text description.

5.6.3   Qualitative Analysis

Figure 5.5 shows qualitative results of our method. For each text, we present the generated images alongside the predicted semantic layouts. As in the previous section, we also present our results conditioned on ground-truth layouts. As it shows, our method generates reasonable semantic layouts and images matching the input text. It generates bounding boxes corresponding to fine-grained scene structures implied in texts (*i.e.* object categories and the number of objects) and object masks capturing class-specific visual attributes as well as the relation to other objects. Given the inferred layouts, our image generator produces correct object appearances and backgrounds compatible with the text. Replacing the predicted layouts with ground-truths makes the generated images have a similar context to the original images.

Diversity of Samples. To assess the diversity in the generation, we sample multiple images while fixing the input text. Figure 5.6 illustrates the example images generated by our method, which generates diverse semantic structures given the same text description, while preserving semantic details, such as the number of objects and object categories.

Fig. 5.7. Generation results by manipulating captions. The manipulated portions of texts are highlighted in **bold** characters, where the types of manipulation is indicated by different colors. **Blue**: scene context, Magenta: spatial location, Red: the number of objects, ahd Green: object category.

Text-Conditional Generation. To see how our model incorporates text description in the generation process, we generate images while modifying portions of the descriptions. Figure 5.7 illustrates the example results. When we change the context of descriptions, such as object class, number of objects, spatial composition of objects, and background patterns, our method correctly adapts the semantic structure and images based on the modified part of the text.

Controllable Image Generation. We demonstrate controllable image generation by modifying the bounding box layout. Figure 5.8 illustrates the example results. Our method updates object shapes and context based on the modified semantic layout (*e.g.* adding new objects and changing spatial configuration of objects) and generates accurate images.

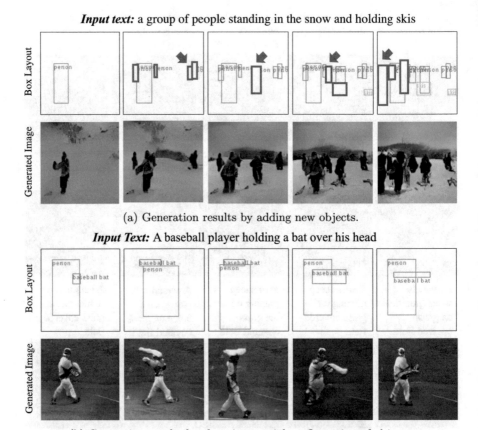

(a) Generation results by adding new objects.

(b) Generation results by changing spatial configuration of objects.

Fig. 5.8. Examples of controllable image generation.

5.7   Conclusion

We proposed an approach for text-to-image synthesis which explicitly infers and exploits a semantic layout as an intermediate representation from text to image. Our model hierarchically constructs a semantic layout in a coarse-to-fine manner by a series of generators. By conditioning image generation on explicit layout prediction, our method generates complicated images that preserve semantic details and are highly relevant to the text description. We also showed that the predicted layout can be used to interpret and control the generation process of the model.

Despite these advantages, training the proposed method requires heavier annotations than the previous methods, such as instance-level bounding box and mask annotations, which makes our method less scalable to large-scale generation problems. To resolve this limitation, we believe that there are several interesting future research directions to explore further. One option is an unsupervised discovery of intermediate semantic structures through end-to-end training. With properly designed regularization on the intermediate output structures, we believe that we can inject useful inductive bias that guides the model to discover meaningful structures from data. Another interesting direction is semi-supervised learning of the model using a large set of partially annotated data. For instance, we can exploit a small number of fully annotated images and a large number of partially annotated images (*e.g.* images with only text descriptions), which allows our model to exploit large-scale datasets, such as the Google Conceptual Caption dataset [27].

References

1. Banerjee, S., Lavie, A.: METEOR: an automatic metric for MT evaluation with improved correlation with human judgments. In: ACL, pp. 228–231 (2005)
2. Cha, M., Gwon, Y., Kung, H.T.: Adversarial nets with perceptual losses for text-to-image synthesis. In: 2017 IEEE 27th International Workshop on Machine Learning for Signal Processing (MLSP), pp. 1–6 (2017)
3. Chen, Q., Koltun, V.: Photographic image synthesis with cascaded refinement networks. In: ICCV (2017)
4. Dash, A., Gamboa, J.C.B., Ahmed, S., Afzal, M.Z., Liwicki, M.: TAC-GAN-Text Conditioned Auxiliary Classifier Generative Adversarial Network. arXiv preprint arXiv:1703.06412 (2017)
5. Deng, J., Dong, W., Socher, R., Li, L.J., Li, K., Fei-Fei, L.: Imagenet: a large-scale hierarchical image database. In: CVPR, pp. 248–255 (2009)
6. Dong, H., Yu, S., Wu, C., Guo, Y.: Semantic image synthesis via adversarial learning. In: ICCV, pp. 5707–5715 (2017)
7. Dong, H., Zhang, J., McIlwraith, D., Guo, Y.: I2T2I: learning text to image synthesis with textual data augmentation. In: ICIP, pp. 2015–2019 (2017)
8. Goodfellow, I.J., et al.: Generative adversarial networks. In: NIPS, pp. 2672–2680 (2014)
9. Ha, D., Eck, D.: A neural representation of sketch drawings. In: ICLR (2018)
10. Hochreiter, S., Schmidhuber, J.: Long short-term memory. Neural Comput. **9**(8), 1735–1780 (1997)
11. Isola, P., Zhu, J.Y., Zhou, T., Efros, A.A.: Image-to-image translation with conditional adversarial networks. In: CVPR, pp. 5967–5976 (2017)
12. Johnson, J., Alahi, A., Fei-Fei, L.: Perceptual losses for real-time style transfer and super-resolution. In: ECCV, pp. 694–711 (2016)
13. Johnson, J., Gupta, A., Fei-Fei, L.: Image generation from scene graphs. In: CVPR, pp. 1219–1228 (2018)

14. Karacan, L., Akata, Z., Erdem, A., Erdem, E.: Learning to generate images of outdoor scenes from attributes and semantic layouts. CoRR (2016)
15. Lin, T.Y., et al.: Microsoft COCO: common objects in context. In: ECCV, pp. 740–755 (2014)
16. Mansimov, E., Parisotto, E., Ba, J.: Generating images from captions with attention. In: ICLR (2016)
17. Mirza, M., Osindero, S.: Conditional generative adversarial nets. arXiv preprint arXiv:1411.1784 (2014)
18. Nguyen, A., Yosinski, J., Bengio, Y., Dosovitskiy, A., Clune, J.: Plug & play generative networks: conditional iterative generation of images in latent space. In: CVPR, pp. 3510–3520 (2017)
19. Nilsback, M.E., Zisserman, A.: Automated flower classification over a large number of classes. In: Proceedings of the Indian Conference on Computer Vision, Graphics and Image Processing, pp. 722–729 (2008)
20. Odena, A., Olah, C., Shlens, J.: Conditional image synthesis with auxiliary classifier GANs. In: ICML, pp. 2642–2651 (2017)
21. Papineni, K., Roukos, S., Ward, T., Zhu, W.J.: BLEU: a method for automatic evaluation of machine translation. In: ACL, pp. 311–318 (2002)
22. Reed, S., Akata, Z., Lee, H., Schiele, B.: Learning deep representations of fine-grained visual descriptions. In: CVPR, pp. 49–58 (2016)
23. Reed, S., Akata, Z., Yan, X., Logeswaran, L., Schiele, B., Lee, H.: Generative adversarial text to image synthesis. In: ICML, pp. 1060–1069 (2016)
24. Reed, S., et al.: Parallel multiscale autoregressive density estimation. In: ICML, pp. 2912–2921 (2017)
25. Reed, S.E., Akata, Z., Mohan, S., Tenka, S., Schiele, B., Lee, H.: Learning what and where to draw. In: NIPS, pp. 217–225 (2016)
26. Salimans, T., Goodfellow, I., Zaremba, W., Cheung, V., Radford, A., Chen, X.: Improved techniques for training GANs. In: NIPS, pp. 2234–2242 (2016)
27. Sharma, P., Ding, N., Goodman, S., Soricut, R.: Conceptual captions: a cleaned, hypernymed, image alt-text dataset for automatic image captioning. In: ACL, pp. 2556–2565 (2018)
28. Sharma, S., Suhubdy, D., Michalski, V., Ebrahimi Kahou, S., Bengio, Y.: Chatpainter: improving text to image generation using dialogue. In: ICLR (2018)
29. Shi, X., Chen, Z., Wang, H., Yeung, D.Y., Wong, W.K., Woo, W.C.: Convolutional LSTM network: a machine learning approach for precipitation nowcasting. In: NIPS, pp. 802–810 (2015)
30. Simonyan, K., Zisserman, A.: Very deep convolutional networks for large-scale image recognition. In: ICLR (2015)
31. Szegedy, C., Vanhoucke, V., Ioffe, S., Shlens, J., Wojna, Z.: Rethinking the inception architecture for computer vision. In: CVPR, pp. 2818–2826 (2016)
32. Vedantam, R., Zitnick, C.L., Parikh, D.: CIDEr: consensus-based image description evaluation. In: CVPR, pp. 4566–4575 (2015)
33. Villegas, R., Yang, J., Zou, Y., Sohn, S., Lin, X., Lee, H.: Learning to generate long-term future via hierarchical prediction. In: ICML, pp. 3560–3569 (2017)
34. Vinyals, O., Toshev, A., Bengio, S., Erhan, D.: Show and tell: a neural image caption generator. In: CVPR, pp. 3156–3164 (2015)
35. Wang, C., Xu, C., Wang, C., Too, D.: Perceptual adversarial networks for image-to-image transformation. IEEE Trans. Image Process. **27**(8), 4066–4079 (2017)
36. Wang, X., Gupta, A.: Generative image modeling using style and structure adversarial networks. In: ECCV, pp. 318–335 (2016)

37. Welinder, P., et al.: Caltech-UCSD Birds 200. Technical Report. CNS-TR-2010-001, California Institute of Technology (2010)
38. Xu, T., et al.: AttnGAN: fine-grained text to image generation with attentional generative adversarial networks. In: CVPR, pp. 1316–1324 (2018)
39. Zhang, H., et al.: StackGAN: text to photo-realistic image synthesis with stacked generative adversarial networks. In: ICCV, pp. 5908–5916 (2017)
40. Zhang, Z., Xie, Y., Yang, L.: Photographic text-to-image synthesis with a hierarchically-nested adversarial network. In: CVPR, pp. 1520–1529 (2018)

6
Unsupervised Discrete Representation Learning

Weihua Hu[1], Takeru Miyato[2], Seiya Tokui[2], Eiichi Matsumoto[2],
and Masashi Sugiyama[3,4(✉)]

[1] Stanford University, Stanford, CA, USA
weihuahu@stanford.edu
[2] Preferred Networks, Tokyo, Japan
{miyato,tokui,matsumoto}@preferred.jp
[3] RIKEN AIP, Tokyo, Japan
[4] The University of Tokyo, Tokyo, Japan
sugi@k.u-tokyo.ac.jp

Abstract. Learning discrete representations of data is a central machine learning task because of the compactness of the representations and ease of interpretation. The task includes clustering and hash learning as special cases. Deep neural networks are promising to be used because they can model the non-linearity of data and scale to large datasets. However, their model complexity is huge, and therefore, we need to carefully regularize the networks in order to learn useful and interpretable representations that exhibit intended invariance for applications of interest. To this end, we propose a method called Information Maximizing Self-Augmented Training (IMSAT). In IMSAT, we use data augmentation to impose the invariance on discrete representations. More specifically, we encourage the predicted representations of augmented data points to be close to those of the original data points in an end-to-end fashion. At the same time, we maximize the information-theoretic dependency between data and their predicted discrete representations. Our IMSAT is able to discover interpretable representations that exhibit intended invariance. Extensive experiments on benchmark datasets show that IMSAT produces state-of-the-art results for both clustering and unsupervised hash learning.

Keywords: Discrete representation learning · Clustering · Hash learning

6.1 Introduction

Many data in our world have natural underlying discrete structures. For instance, they can be categorized into distinct classes such as object categories [25], or they can be represented as composition of existence/inexistence of certain features [42]. Our goal is to discover such discrete structures from a huge number of

© Springer Nature Switzerland AG 2019
W. Samek et al. (Eds.): Explainable AI, LNAI 11700, pp. 97–119, 2019.
https://doi.org/10.1007/978-3-030-28954-6_6

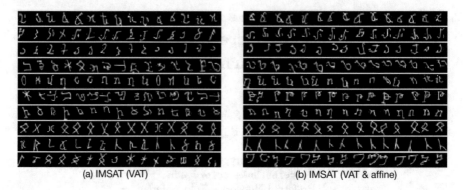

(a) IMSAT (VAT)   (b) IMSAT (VAT & affine)

Fig. 6.1. Randomly sampled clusters of Omniglot discovered using (a) IMSAT (VAT) and (b) IMSAT (VAT & affine). Each row contains randomly sampled data points in same cluster.

unlabeled data. This will not only allow us to represent data in a compact way but also enables us to easily interpret data and find their regularities, which are crucial in exploratory data analyses.

The task of unsupervised discrete representation learning is to obtain a function that maps *similar* (resp. *dissimilar*) data into similar (resp. dissimilar) discrete representations, where the *similarity* of data is defined according to applications of interest. It is a central machine learning topic and includes two important tasks as special cases: clustering and unsupervised hash learning. Clustering is widely applied to data-driven application domains [2], while hash learning is popular for an approximate nearest neighbor search for large scale information retrieval [51].

Deep neural networks are promising to be used thanks to their scalability and flexibility of representing complicated, non-linear decision boundaries. However, their model complexity is huge, and therefore, regularization of the networks is crucial to learn meaningful and interpretable representations of data. Particularly, in *unsupervised* representation learning, no explicit label supervision is provided to guide the representation learning. Therefore, we need to carefully regularize the networks in order to learn desirable representations that exhibit intended invariance for applications of interest, e.g., in many computer vision applications, we may want our obtained representations to be invariant to small perturbations or small affine transformation. Figure 6.1 shows clusters discovered by two variants of our method applied to a hand-written character recognition dataset (see Sect. 6.4 for the detailed experimental setting). We see that the cluster assignments in Fig. 6.1(b) are visually coherent and interpretable, being invariant to rotation and translation, while the clusters in Fig. 6.1(a) are less so, assigning characters with different shapes to the same clusters. How can we regularize the neural networks so that the obtained discrete representations are more interpretable and meaningful for humans?

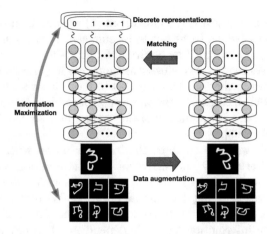

Fig. 6.2. Basic idea of our proposed method for unsupervised discrete representation learning. We encourage the prediction of a neural network to remain unchanged under data augmentation (the pair of one-way arrows), while maximizing the information-theoretic dependency between data and their representations (the two-way arrow).

Naïve regularization to use is a weight decay [11]. Such regularization, however, only encourages global smoothness of the function prediction; thus, does not necessarily give us interpretable and meaningful representations. Instead, our key idea is to directly encourage our model to learn meaningful representations by using data augmentation, i.e., the data transformation that we want our model output to be invariant to. More specifically, we map data points into their discrete representations by a deep neural network and regularize it by encouraging its prediction to be invariant to data augmentation that we have specified beforehand. The predicted discrete representations then exhibit the invariance specified by the augmentation; thus, they will be more interpretable for humans.

Our proposed regularization method is illustrated as the pair of one-way arrows in Fig. 6.2. As depicted, we encourage the predicted representations of augmented data points to be close to those of the original data points in an *end-to-end fashion*. We term such regularization *Self-Augmented Training (SAT)*. SAT is inspired by the recent success in regularization of neural networks in semi-supervised learning [1,36,45]. SAT is flexible to impose various types of invariances on the representations predicted by neural networks. For example, it is generally preferred for data representations to be locally invariant, i.e., remain unchanged under local perturbations on data points. Using SAT, we can impose the local invariance on the representations by pushing the predictions of perturbed data points to be close to those of the original data points. For image data, it may also be preferred for data representations to be invariant under affine distortion, e.g., rotation, scaling and parallel movement. We can similarly impose the invariance via SAT by using the affine distortion for the data augmentation.

Returning back to Fig. 6.1, the clusters in (a) are obtained by only imposing the local invariance (which turns out to be sufficient in many simpler datasets), while those in (b) are obtained by additionally imposing the invariance to affine transformation. We see that the cluster assignments in (b) indeed exhibit invariance to affine transformation. In general, the more invariance information we provide to our SAT framework, the more interpretable representations we can expect to obtain. Such invariance information can be also considered as a form of weak supervision [60].

Following [13], we then combine SAT regularization with the information maximization criterion [5], and arrive at our Information Maximizing Self-Augmented Training (IMSAT), an information-theoretic method for learning discrete representations using deep neural networks. We illustrate the basic idea of IMSAT in Fig. 6.2. Similarly, Regularized Information Maximization (RIM) [13], we maximize information theoretic dependency between inputs and their mapped outputs, while regularizing the mapping function. IMSAT differs from the original RIM in two ways. First, IMSAT deals with a more general setting of learning discrete representations; thus, is also applicable to hash learning. Second, it uses a deep neural network for the mapping function and regularizes it in an end-to-end fashion via SAT. Learning with our method can be performed by stochastic gradient descent (SGD); thus, scales well to large datasets.

In summary, our contributions are: (1) an information-theoretic method for unsupervised discrete representation learning using deep neural networks with the end-to-end regularization, and (2) adaptations of the method to clustering and hash learning to achieve the state-of-the-art performance on several benchmark datasets.

6.2 Related Work

Various methods have been proposed for clustering and hash learning. The representative ones include K-means clustering and hashing [17], Gaussian mixture model clustering, iterative quantization [14], and minimal-loss hashing [40]. However, these methods can only model linear boundaries between different representations; thus, cannot fit to non-linear structures of data. Kernel-based [27,56] and spectral [39,52] methods can model the non-linearity of data, but they are difficult to scale to large datasets.

Recently, clustering and hash learning using deep neural networks have attracted much attention. In clustering, [54] proposed to use deep neural networks to simultaneously learn feature representations and cluster assignments, while [9] and [59] proposed to model the data generation process by using deep generative models with Gaussian mixture models as prior distributions.

Regarding hash learning, a number of studies have used deep neural networks for supervised hash learning and achieved state-of-the-art results on image and text retrieval [28,34,53,55,58]. Relatively few studies have focused on unsupervised hash learning using deep neural networks. The pioneering work is semantic hashing, which uses stacked RBM models to learn compact binary representations [46]. [11] recently proposed to use deep neural networks for the mapping function and achieved state-of-the-art results. These unsupervised methods, however, did not explicitly impose the invariance on the learned representations. Consequently, the predicted representations may not be useful for applications of interest.

In supervised and semi-supervised learning scenarios, data augmentation has been widely used to regularize neural networks. [32] showed that applying data augmentation to a supervised learning problem is equivalent to adding a regularization to the original cost function. [1,36,45] showed that such regularization can be adapted to semi-supervised learning settings to achieve state-of-the-art performance.

In unsupervised representation learning scenarios, [10] proposed to use data augmentation to model the invariance of learned representations. Our IMSAT is different from [10] in two important aspects: (1) IMSAT *directly* imposes the invariance on the learned representations, while [10] imposes invariance on surrogate classes, *not directly* on the learned representations. (2) IMSAT focuses on learning *discrete* representations that are directly usable for clustering and hash learning, while [10] focused on learning *continuous* representations that are then used for other tasks such as classification and clustering.

Our method is related to denoising auto-encoders [50]. Auto-encoders maximize a lower bound of mutual information [8] between inputs and their hidden representations [50], while the denoising mechanism regularizes the prediction of the auto-encoder to be locally invariant. However, such a regularization does not necessarily impose the invariance on the *hidden representations* because the decoder network also has the flexibility to model the invariance to data perturbations. SAT is more direct in imposing the intended invariance on hidden representations predicted by the encoder network.

Contractive auto-encoders [44] impose the local invariance on the *encoder network* by minimizing the Frobenius norm of its Jacobian. One shortcoming of the approach might be that the Jacobian of the encoder is approximated only in the *layer-wise fashion*; thus, the approximation might be highly inaccurate for *deep* encoder networks. Instead of the layer-wise approximation, [36] presented Virtual Adversarial Training (VAT) that imposes the local invariance of the neural networks in an *end-to-end fashion*. The end-to-end regularization was empirically shown to achieve excellent performance on supervised and semi-supervised learning [36]. This inspired us to adopt the end-to-end regularization in unsupervised representation learning. Our regularization, SAT, is the direct generalization of VAT to allow users to model other types of invariance: not only the local invariance but also the invariance to other transformations such as affine distortion of images.

6.3   Unsupervised Discrete Representation Learning

Let $\mathcal{X}$ and $\mathcal{Y}$ denote the domains of inputs and discrete representations, respectively. Given training samples, $x_1, x_2, \ldots, x_N \in \mathcal{X}$ drawn i.i.d. from $p(x)$, the task of unsupervised discrete representation learning is to obtain a function,

$f : \mathcal{X} \to \mathcal{Y}$, that maps similar (resp. dissimilar) inputs into similar (resp. dissimilar) discrete representations. The similarity of data is defined according to applications of interest.

Unsupervised discrete representation learning is a general and fundamental machine learning task and includes two important machine learning tasks as special cases. First, it includes the task of clustering when we let $\mathcal{Y}$ be $\{0, \ldots, K-1\}$, where K is the number of clusters. Second, it also includes the task of unsupervised hash learning when we let $\mathcal{Y}$ be $\{0, 1\}^D$, where D is the dimension of binary codes.

In this section, we present an effective and general method for the task of unsupervised discrete representation learning. To this end, we first review the Regularization Information Maximization (RIM) framework [13] for clustering in Sect. 6.3.1. We then build on this framework and explain our proposed method, IMSAT, for unsupervised discrete representation learning in Sect. 6.3.2. We proceed to discuss the use of IMSAT for two important unsupervised learning tasks, namely, clustering and unsupervised hash learning, in Sects. 6.3.3 and 6.3.4, respectively. Finally, in Sect. 6.3.5, we present a simple approximation to the IMSAT objective to scale it to large datasets.

6.3.1   Review of RIM for Clustering

We review RIM [13], a general framework for discriminative clustering, which our proposed method will be built on. At its core, RIM learns a probabilistic classifier $p_\theta(y|x)$ by the following two objectives. First, it maximizes mutual information [8] between inputs and cluster assignments, where θ is a parameter to be learned. Second, RIM regularizes the complexity of the classifier.

More formally, let $X \in \mathcal{X}$ and $Y \in \mathcal{Y} \equiv \{0, \ldots, K-1\}$ denote random variables for data and cluster assignments, respectively, where K is the number of clusters. Then, RIM *minimizes* the objective:

$$\mathcal{R}(\theta) - \lambda \boldsymbol{I}(X;Y), \tag{6.1}$$

where $\mathcal{R}(\theta)$ is the regularization penalty, and $\boldsymbol{I}(X;Y)$ is mutual information between X and Y, which depends on θ through the classifier $p_\theta(y|x)$. Mutual information measures the statistical dependency between X and Y, and is 0 iff they are independent. Hyper-parameter $\lambda \in \mathbb{R}$ trades off the two terms.

6.3.2   Information Maximizing Self-Augmented Training (IMSAT)

Building on RIM, we present our proposed method, which we call Information Maximizing Self-Augmented Training (IMSAT). Following the RIM framework, our IMSAT consists of two objectives: information maximization and regularization. Our key contributions in IMSAT are (1) generalization of the information maximization criterion for clustering [5] to the more general task of *discrete representation learning* and (2) the adoption of *end-to-end regularization* of deep neural networks [36] to the *unsupervised learning scenario*. In the following, we give detailed explanations of our two contributions.

Information Maximization for Discrete Representation Learning. We generalize the information maximization criterion [5] by considering learning M-dimensional discrete representations of data. Let the output domain be $\mathcal{Y} = \mathcal{Y}_1 \times \cdots \times \mathcal{Y}_M$, where $\mathcal{Y}_m \equiv \{0, 1, \ldots, V_m - 1\}$, $1 \leq m \leq M$. Let $Y = (Y_1, \ldots, Y_M) \in \mathcal{Y}$ be a random variable for the discrete representation. Our goal is to learn a *multi-output* probabilistic classifier $p_\theta(y_1, \ldots, y_M | x)$ that maps similar inputs into similar representations. For simplicity, we model the conditional probability $p_\theta(y_1, \ldots, y_M | x)$ by using the deep neural network depicted in Fig. 6.1. Under the model, $\{y_1, \ldots, y_M\}$ are conditionally independent given x:

$$p_\theta(y_1, \ldots, y_M | x) = \prod_{m=1}^{M} p_\theta(y_m | x). \tag{6.2}$$

Following the RIM [13], we maximize the mutual information between inputs and their discrete representations, while regularizing the multi-output probabilistic classifier. The resulting objective to *minimize* looks exactly the same as Eq. (6.1), except that Y is *multi-dimensional* in our setting.

Regularization of Deep Neural Networks via Self-Augmented Training. We present an intuitive and general regularization method, termed *Self-Augmented Training (SAT)*. SAT uses data augmentation to impose the intended invariance on the data representations. Essentially, SAT penalizes representation dissimilarity between the original data points and augmented ones. Let $T : \mathcal{X} \to \mathcal{X}$ denote a pre-defined data augmentation under which the data representations should be invariant. The regularization of SAT made on data point x is

$$\mathcal{R}_{\mathrm{SAT}}(\theta; x, T(x)) = -\sum_{y_1=0}^{V_1-1} \cdots \sum_{y_M=0}^{V_M-1} p_{\widehat{\theta}}(y_1, \ldots, y_M | x) \log p_\theta(y_1, \ldots, y_M | T(x)) \tag{6.3}$$

$$= -\sum_{y_1=0}^{V_1-1} \cdots \sum_{y_M=0}^{V_M-1} p_{\widehat{\theta}}(y_1, \ldots, y_M | x) \sum_{m=1}^{M} \log p_\theta(y_m | T(x)) \tag{6.4}$$

$$= -\sum_{m=1}^{M} \left\{ \sum_{y_1=0}^{V_1-1} \cdots \sum_{y_M=0}^{V_M-1} p_{\widehat{\theta}}(y_1, \ldots, y_M | x) \log p_\theta(y_m | T(x)) \right\} \tag{6.5}$$

$$= -\sum_{m=1}^{M} \left[\sum_{y_m=0}^{V_m-1} \left\{ \sum_{y_i, i \neq m} p_{\widehat{\theta}}(y_1, \ldots, y_M | x) \right\} \log p_\theta(y_m | T(x)) \right] \tag{6.6}$$

$$= -\sum_{m=1}^{M} \sum_{y_m=0}^{V_m-1} p_{\widehat{\theta}}(y_m | x) \log p_\theta(y_m | T(x)), \tag{6.7}$$

where $p_{\widehat{\theta}}(y_m | x)$ is the prediction of original data point x, and $\widehat{\theta}$ is the current parameter of the network. Equation (6.4) follows from the conditional independence assumption in Eq. (6.2). Equation (6.3) is similar to the cross-entropy loss used in ordinary supervised learning except that the target $p_{\widehat{\theta}}(y_1, \ldots, y_M|x)$ is the current prediction of the neural network. Therefore, SAT pushes the predicted representations of the augmented data, i.e., $p_\theta(y_1, \ldots, y_M|T(x))$, to be close to those of the original data, i.e., $p_{\widehat{\theta}}(y_1, \ldots, y_M|x)$. This allows our method to obtain desirable discrete representations that are invariant to the transformation specified by $T(\cdot)$.

The SAT regularization is then the expectation of $\mathcal{R}_{\mathrm{SAT}}(\theta; x, T(x))$ w.r.t. the training density $p(x)$, which can be approximated using unlabeled samples $x_1, x_2, \ldots, x_N$:

$$\mathcal{R}_{\mathrm{SAT}}(\theta; T) \equiv \int \mathcal{R}_{\mathrm{SAT}}(\theta; x_n, T(x))p(x)\mathrm{d}x$$

$$\approx \frac{1}{N} \sum_{n=1}^{N} \mathcal{R}_{\mathrm{SAT}}(\theta; x_n, T(x_n)). \tag{6.8}$$

The augmentation function T can either be stochastic or deterministic. It can be designed specifically for the applications of interest. For example, for image data, affine distortion such as rotation, scaling and parallel movement can be used for the augmentation function.

Alternatively, more general augmentation functions that do not depend on specific applications can be considered. A representative example is local perturbations, in which the augmentation function is

$$T(x) = x + r, \tag{6.9}$$

where r is a small perturbation that does not alter the meaning of the data point. The use of local perturbations in SAT encourages the data representations to be locally invariant. The resulting decision boundaries between different representations tend to lie in low density regions of a data distribution. Such boundaries are generally preferred and follow the low-density separation principle [16].

The two representative regularization methods based on local perturbations are: (1) those based on random perturbations [1, 4, 15, 43], which we call Random Perturbation Training (RPT), and (2) Virtual Adversarial Training (VAT) [36]. In RPT, perturbation r is sampled randomly from hyper-sphere $||r||_2 = \epsilon$, where ϵ is a hyper-parameter that controls the range of the local perturbation. On the other hand, in VAT, perturbation r is chosen to be an *adversarial* direction:

$$r = \arg\max_{r'} \{\mathcal{R}_{\mathrm{SAT}}(\widehat{\theta}; x, x + r'); \; ||r'||_2 \leq \epsilon\}. \tag{6.10}$$

The solution of Eq. (6.10) can be approximated efficiently by a pair of forward and backward passes. For further details, refer to [36].

6.3.3   IMSAT for Clustering

In the case of clustering, we essentially aim to learn one-dimensional discrete representations; hence, $M = 1$. In fact, we can directly apply the RIM [13] reviewed in Sect. 6.3.1. Unlike the original RIM, our method, IMSAT, uses a deep neural network as the classifier and regularizes it via SAT. We can represent the mutual information as the difference between marginal entropy and conditional entropy [8]. Then, we have the objective to minimize:

$$\mathcal{R}_{\mathrm{SAT}}(\theta; T) - \lambda\left[H(Y) - H(Y|X)\right], \tag{6.11}$$

where $H(\cdot)$ and $H(\cdot|\cdot)$ are entropy and conditional entropy, respectively, and the mutual information term in Eq. (6.1) was replaced with the entropy term in Eq. (6.11). The two entropy terms can be empirically approximated as

$$H(Y) \equiv h(p_\theta(y))$$

$$= h\left(\int p_\theta(y|x)p(x)\mathrm{d}x\right) \approx h\left(\frac{1}{N}\sum_{i=1}^{N} p_\theta(y|x_i)\right), \tag{6.12}$$

$$H(Y|X) \equiv \int H(Y|X = x)p(x)\mathrm{d}x \approx \frac{1}{N}\sum_{i=1}^{N} h(p_\theta(y|x_i)), \tag{6.13}$$

where $h(p(y)) \equiv -\sum_{y'} p(y')\log p(y')$ is the entropy function. Increasing the marginal entropy $H(Y)$ encourages the cluster sizes to be uniform, while decreasing the conditional entropy $H(Y|X)$ encourages unambiguous cluster assignments [5].

In practice, we can incorporate our prior knowledge on cluster sizes by modifying $H(Y)$ [13]. Note that $H(Y) = \log K - \mathrm{KL}[p_\theta(y)\|\,\mathcal{U}]$, where K is the number of clusters, $\mathrm{KL}[\cdot\|\cdot]$ is the Kullback-Leibler divergence, and $\mathcal{U}$ is a uniform distribution. Hence, maximization of $H(Y)$ is equivalent to minimization of $\mathrm{KL}[p_\theta(y)\|\,\mathcal{U}]$, which encourages predicted cluster distribution $p_\theta(y)$ to be close to $\mathcal{U}$. [13] replaced $\mathcal{U}$ in $\mathrm{KL}[p_\theta(y)\|\,\mathcal{U}]$ with any specified class prior $q(y)$ so that $p_\theta(y)$ is encouraged to be close to $q(y)$. In our preliminary experiments, we found that the resulting $p_\theta(y)$ could still be far apart from pre-specified $q(y)$. To ensure that $p_\theta(y)$ is actually close to $q(y)$, we consider the following constrained optimization problem:

$$\min_\theta \; \mathcal{R}_{\mathrm{SAT}}(\theta; T) + \lambda H(Y|X),$$
$$\text{subject to} \;\; \mathrm{KL}[p_\theta(y)\|\, q(y)] \le \delta, \tag{6.14}$$

where $\delta > 0$ is a tolerance hyper-parameter that is set sufficiently small so that predicted cluster distribution $p_\theta(y)$ is the same as class prior $q(y)$ up to δ-tolerance. Equation (6.14) can be solved by using the penalty method [3], which turns the original constrained optimization problem into a series of unconstrained optimization problems. More specifically, we introduce a scalar parameter μ and consider minimizing the following unconstrained objective:

$$\mathcal{R}_{\mathrm{SAT}}(\theta; T) + \lambda H(Y|X) + \mu\max\{\mathrm{KL}[p_\theta(y)\|\, q(y)] - \delta, 0\}. \tag{6.15}$$

We gradually increase μ and solve the optimization of Eq. (6.15) for a fixed μ. Let μ^* be the smallest value for which the solution of Eq. (6.15) satisfies the constraint of Eq. (6.14). The penalty method ensures that the solution obtained by solving Eq. (6.15) with $\mu = \mu^*$ is the same as that of the constrained optimization of Eq. (6.14).

In experiments in Sect. 6.4.2, we first set $\mu = \lambda$ and then increased μ in the order of $2\lambda, 4\lambda, 6\lambda, 8\lambda, \ldots$ until the solution of Eq. (6.15) satisfied the constraint of Eq. (6.14).

6.3.4   IMSAT for Hash Learning

In hash learning, each data point is mapped into a D-bit binary code. Hence, the original RIM is not directly applicable. Instead, we apply our method for discrete representation learning presented in Sect. 6.3.2.

The computation of mutual information $\boldsymbol{I}(Y_1, \ldots, Y_D; X)$, however, is intractable for large D because it involves the summation over an exponential number of terms, each of which corresponds to a different configuration of hash bits.

[6] showed that mutual information $\boldsymbol{I}(Y_1, \ldots, Y_D; X)$ can be expanded as the sum of interaction information [35]:

$$\boldsymbol{I}(Y_1, \ldots, Y_D; X) = \sum_{C \subseteq S_Y} \boldsymbol{I}(C \cup \{X\}), \quad |C| \geq 1, \tag{6.16}$$

where $S_Y \equiv \{Y_1, \ldots, Y_D\}$. Note that $\boldsymbol{I}$ denotes interaction information when its argument is a set of random variables. Interaction information is a generalization of mutual information and can take a negative value. When the argument is a set of two random variables, the interaction information reduces to mutual information between the two random variables. Following [6], we only retain terms involving pairs of output dimensions in Eq. (6.16), i.e., all terms where $|C| \leq 2$. This gives us

$$\sum_{d=1}^{D} \boldsymbol{I}(Y_d; X) + \sum_{1 \leq d \neq d' \leq D} \boldsymbol{I}(\{Y_d, Y_{d'}, X\}). \tag{6.17}$$

This approximation ignores the interactions among hash bits beyond the pairwise interactions. It is related to the orthogonality constraint that is widely used in the literature to remove redundancy among hash bits [51]. In fact, the orthogonality constraint encourages the covariance between a pair of hash bits to 0. Thus, it also takes into account the pairwise interactions.

It follows from the definition of interaction information and the conditional independence in Eq. (6.2) that

$$\boldsymbol{I}(\{Y_d, Y_{d'}, X\}) \equiv \boldsymbol{I}(Y_d; Y_{d'} | X) - \boldsymbol{I}(Y_d; Y_{d'})$$
$$= -\boldsymbol{I}(Y_d; Y_{d'}). \tag{6.18}$$

In summary, our approximated objective to minimize is

$$\mathcal{R}_{\text{SAT}}(\theta; T) - \lambda \left(\sum_{d=1}^{D} \boldsymbol{I}(X; Y_d) - \sum_{1 \leq d \neq d' \leq D} \boldsymbol{I}(Y_d; Y_{d'}) \right). \tag{6.19}$$

The first term regularizes the neural network. The second term maximizes the mutual information between data and each hash bit, and the third term removes the redundancy among the hash bits.

6.3.5 Approximation of the Marginal Distribution

To scale up our method to large datasets, we would like our objective to be amenable to optimization based on mini-batch SGD. Recall that the IMSAT objective consists of two parts: SAT regularization and information maximization. The SAT regularization in Eq. (6.8) is the sum of per sample penalties and can be readily adapted to mini-batch computation.

The mutual information in Eq. (6.19) is more complicated. We first decompose it into three parts: (i) conditional entropy $H(Y_d|X)$, (ii) marginal entropy $H(Y_d)$, and (iii) mutual information between a pair of output dimensions $I(Y_d; Y_{d'})$. We see from Eq. (6.13) that (i) the conditional entropy only consists of the sum over per example entropies; thus, can be easily adapted to mini-batch computation. However, (ii) the marginal entropy in Eq. (6.12) and (iii) the mutual information are *non-linear* functions of some marginal distribution $p_\theta(c) \equiv \int p_\theta(c|x)p(x)dx$, where c is some subset of target dimension, i.e., $c \subseteq \{y_1, \ldots, y_M\}$. Therefore, to obtain the accurate approximation of (ii) and (iii), we may need to use the entire training data to approximate the marginal, i.e., $p_\theta(c) \approx \frac{1}{N}\sum_{n=1}^{N} p_\theta(c|x_n)$. Unfortunately, this does not scale well to large datasets, where N is large.

Following [47], we consider approximating the marginal distributions using mini-batch data:

$$p_\theta(c) \approx \frac{1}{|\mathcal{B}|} \sum_{x \in \mathcal{B}} p_\theta(c|x) \equiv \widehat{p_\theta}^{(\mathcal{B})}(c), \tag{6.20}$$

where $\mathcal{B}$ is a set of data in the mini-batch. We empirically confirmed in Sect. 6.4 that this simple approximation yields good performance for a reasonable mini-batch size, i.e., 250. Moreover, in the case of clustering in Eq. (6.15), the approximated objective that we actually minimize, i.e., $\mathbb{E}_\mathcal{B}[\mathrm{KL}[\widehat{p_\theta}^{(\mathcal{B})}(y)||q(y)]]$, turns out to be an upper bound of the exact objective that we try to minimize, i.e., $\mathrm{KL}[p_\theta(y)||q(y)]$. More specifically, by the convexity of the KL divergence [8] and Jensen's inequality, we have

$$\mathbb{E}_\mathcal{B}[\mathrm{KL}[\widehat{p_\theta}^{(\mathcal{B})}(y)||q(y)]] \geq \mathrm{KL}[p_\theta(y)||q(y)] \geq 0, \tag{6.21}$$

where the first expectation is taken with respect to the randomness of the mini-batch selection. Therefore, in the penalty method, the constraint on the exact KL divergence, i.e., $\mathrm{KL}[p_\theta(y)||q(y)] \leq \delta$ can be satisfied by minimizing its upper bound, which is the approximated KL divergence $\mathbb{E}_\mathcal{B}[\mathrm{KL}[\widehat{p_\theta}^{(\mathcal{B})}(y)||q(y)]]$. Obviously, the approximated KL divergence is amenable to the mini-batch setting; thus, can be minimized with SGD.

6.4 Experiments

In this section, we evaluate IMSAT for clustering and hash learning using benchmark datasets.

6.4.1 Implementation

In unsupervised learning, it is not straightforward to determine hyperparameters by cross-validation. Therefore, in all the experiments with benchmark datasets, we used commonly reported parameter values for deep neural networks and avoided dataset-specific tuning as much as possible. Specifically, inspired by [20], we set the network dimensionality to d-1200-1200-M for clustering across all the datasets, where d and M are input and output dimensionality, respectively. For hash learning, we used smaller network sizes to ensure fast computation of mapping data into hash codes. We used rectified linear units [12,22,37] for all the hidden activations and applied batch normalization [21] to each layer to accelerate training. For the output layer, we used the softmax for clustering and the sigmoids for hash learning. Regarding optimization, we used Adam [23] with the step size 0.002. We set the size of mini-batch to 250, and ran 50 epochs for each dataset. We initialized weights following [18]: each element of the weight is initialized by the value drawn independently from Gaussian distribution whose mean is 0, and standard deviation is $scale \times \sqrt{2/fan_{in}}$, where fan_{in} is the number of input units. We set the $scale$ to be 0.1-0.1-0.0001 for weight matrices from the input to the output. The bias terms were all initialized with 0. Our implementation based on Chainer [48] is available at https://github.com/weihua916/imsat.

6.4.2 Clustering

Datasets and Compared Methods. We evaluated our method for clustering presented in Sect. 6.3.3 on eight benchmark datasets. We performed experiments with two variants of the RIM and three variants of IMSAT, each of which uses different classifiers and regularization. Table 6.1 summarizes these variants. We also compared our IMSAT with existing clustering methods including K-means, DEC [54], denoising Auto-Encoder (dAE)+K-means [54].

A brief summary of dataset statistics is given in Table 6.2. In the experiments, our goal was to discover clusters that correspond well with the ground-truth categories. For the STL, CIFAR10 and CIFAR100 datasets, raw pixels are not suited for our goal because color information is dominant. We therefore applied 50-layer pre-trained deep residual networks [19] to extract features and used them for clustering. Note that since the residual network was trained on ImageNet, each class of the STL dataset (which is a subset of ImageNet) was expected to be well-separated in the feature space. For Omniglot, 100 types of characters were sampled, each containing 20 data points. Each data point was augmented 20 times by the stochastic affine distortion described in Appendix 6.C. For SVHN, each image was represented as a 960-dimensional GIST feature [41]. For Reuters

Table 6.1. Summary of the variants.

Method	Used classifier	Regularization
Linear RIM	Linear	Weight-decay
Deep RIM	Deep neural nets	Weight-decay
Linear IMSAT (VAT)	Linear	VAT
IMSAT (RPT)	Deep neural nets	RPT
IMSAT (VAT)	Deep neural nets	VAT

Table 6.2. Summary of dataset statistics.

Dataset	#Points	#Classes	Dimension	%Largest class
MNIST [31]	70000	10	784	11%
Omniglot [29]	40000	100	441	1%
STL [7]	13000	10	2048	10%
CIFAR10 [49]	60000	10	2048	10%
CIFAR100 [49]	60000	100	2048	1%
SVHN [38]	99289	10	960	19%
Reuters [33]	10000	4	2000	43%
20news [30]	18040	20	2000	5%

and 20news, we removed stop words and retained the 2000 most frequent words. We then used *tf-idf* features. Refer to Appendix 6.A for further details.

Evaluation Metric. Following [54], we set the number of clusters to the number of ground-truth categories and evaluated clustering performance with unsupervised clustering accuracy (ACC):

$$\text{ACC} = \max_m \frac{\sum_{n=1}^{N} \mathbf{1}\{l_n = m(c_n)\}}{N}, \tag{6.22}$$

where l_n and c_n are the ground-truth label and cluster assignment produced using the algorithm for x_n, respectively. The m ranges over all possible one-to-one mappings between clusters and labels. The best mapping can be efficiently computed using the Hungarian algorithm [26]. Refer to Appendix 6.B for the details of hyper-parameter selection.

Experimental Results. In Table 6.3, we compare clustering performance across eight benchmark datasets. We see that IMSAT (VAT) performed well across the datasets. The fact that our IMSAT outperformed Linear RIM, Deep RIM and Linear IMSAT (VAT) for most datasets suggests the effectiveness of using deep neural networks with an end-to-end regularization via SAT.

Table 6.3. Comparison of clustering accuracy on eight benchmark datasets (%). Averages and standard deviations over twelve trials were reported. Results marked with † were excerpted from [54].

Method	MNIST	Omniglot	STL	CIFAR10	CIFAR100	SVHN	Reuters	20news
K-means	53.2	12.0	85.6	34.4	21.5	17.9	54.1	15.5
dAE+K-means	79.8 †	14.1	72.2	44.2	20.8	17.4	67.2	22.1
DEC	84.3 †	5.7 (0.3)	78.1 (0.1)	**46.9 (0.9)**	14.3 (0.6)	11.9 (0.4)	67.3 (0.2)	30.8 (1.8)
Linear RIM	59.6 (2.3)	11.1 (0.2)	73.5 (6.5)	40.3 (2.1)	23.7 (0.8)	20.2 (1.4)	62.8 (7.8)	**50.9 (3.1)**
Deep RIM	58.5 (3.5)	5.8 (2.2)	92.5 (2.2)	40.3 (3.5)	13.4 (1.2)	26.8 (3.2)	62.3 (3.9)	25.1 (2.8)
Linear IMSAT (VAT)	61.1 (1.9)	12.3 (0.2)	91.7 (0.5)	40.7 (0.6)	23.9 (0.4)	18.2 (1.9)	42.9 (0.8)	43.9 (3.3)
IMSAT (RPT)	89.6 (5.4)	16.4 (3.1)	92.8 (2.5)	45.5 (2.9)	24.7 (0.5)	35.9 (4.3)	**71.9 (6.5)**	24.4 (4.7)
IMSAT (VAT)	**98.4 (0.4)**	**24.0 (0.9)**	**94.1 (0.4)**	45.6 (0.8)	**27.5 (0.4)**	**57.3 (3.9)**	71.0 (4.9)	31.1 (1.9)

Table 6.4. Comparison of clustering accuracy on the Omniglot dataset using IMSAT with different types of SAT.

Method	Omniglot
IMSAT (VAT)	24.0 (0.9)
IMSAT (affine)	45.1 (2.0)
IMSAT (VAT & affine)	**70.0 (2.0)**

Linear IMSAT (VAT) did not perform well even with the end-to-end regularization probably because the linear classifier was not flexible enough to model the intended invariance of the representations. We also see from Table 6.3 that IMSAT (VAT) consistently outperformed IMSAT (RPT) in our experiments. This suggests that VAT is an effective regularization method in *unsupervised* learning scenarios.

We further conducted experiments on the Omniglot dataset to demonstrate that clustering performance can be improved by incorporating domain-specific knowledge in the augmentation function of SAT. Specifically, we used the affine distortion in addition to VAT for the augmented function of SAT. We compared the clustering accuracy of IMSAT with three different augmentation functions: VAT, affine distortion, and the combination of VAT & affine distortion, in which we simply set the regularization to be

$$\frac{1}{2} \cdot \mathcal{R}_{\mathrm{SAT}}(\theta; T_{\mathrm{VAT}}) + \frac{1}{2} \cdot \mathcal{R}_{\mathrm{SAT}}(\theta; T_{\mathrm{affine}}), \tag{6.23}$$

where T_{VAT} and T_{affine} are augmentation functions of VAT and affine distortion, respectively. For T_{affine}, we used the stochastic affine distortion function defined in Appendix 6.C.

We report the clustering accuracy of Omniglot in Table 6.4. We see that including affine distortion in data augmentation significantly improved clustering accuracy. Figure 6.1 shows ten clusters of the Omniglot dataset that were found using IMSAT (VAT) and IMSAT (VAT & affine distortion). We observe that IMSAT (VAT & affine distortion) was able to discover cluster assignments

Table 6.5. Comparison of hash performance for 16-bit hash codes (%). Averages and standard deviations over ten trials were reported. Experimental results of Deep Hash and the previous methods were excerpted from [11].

Method (Dimensions of hidden layers)	Hamming ranking (mAP)		precision @ sample = 500		precision @ r = 2	
	MNIST	CIFAR10	MNIST	CIFAR10	MNIST	CIFAR10
Spectral hash [52]	26.6	12.6	56.3	18.8	57.5	18.5
PCA-ITQ [14]	41.2	15.7	66.4	22.5	65.7	22.6
Deep Hash (60-30)	43.1	16.2	67.9	23.8	66.1	23.3
Linear RIM	35.9 (0.6)	**24.0 (3.5)**	68.9 (1.1)	15.9 (0.5)	71.3 (0.9)	14.2 (0.3)
Deep RIM (60-30)	42.7 (2.8)	15.2 (0.5)	67.9 (2.7)	21.8 (0.9)	65.9 (2.7)	21.2 (0.9)
Deep RIM (200-200)	43.7 (3.7)	15.6 (0.6)	68.7 (4.9)	21.6 (1.2)	67.0 (4.9)	21.1 (1.1)
Deep RIM (400-400)	43.9 (2.7)	15.4 (0.2)	69.0 (3.2)	21.5 (0.4)	66.7 (3.2)	20.9 (0.3)
IMSAT (VAT) (60-30)	61.2 (2.5)	19.8 (1.2)	78.6 (2.1)	21.0 (1.8)	76.5 (2.3)	19.3 (1.6)
IMSAT (VAT) (200-200)	80.7 (2.2)	21.2 (0.8)	95.8 (1.0)	**27.3 (1.3)**	94.6 (1.4)	26.1 (1.3)
IMSAT (VAT) (400-400)	**83.9 (2.3)**	21.4 (0.5)	**97.0 (0.8)**	**27.3 (1.1)**	**96.2 (1.1)**	**26.4 (1.0)**

that are invariant to affine distortion as we intended. These results suggest that our method successfully captured the invariance in the hand-written character recognition in an unsupervised way.

6.4.3 Hash Learning

Datasets and Compared Methods. We evaluate our method for hash learning presented on two benchmark datasets: MNIST and CIFAR10 datasets. Each data sample of CIFAR10 is represented as a 512-dimensional GIST feature [41]. Our method was compared against several unsupervised hash learning methods: spectral hashing [52], PCA-ITQ [14], and Deep Hash [11]. We also compared our method to the hash versions of Linear RIM and Deep RIM. For our IMSAT, we used VAT for the regularization. We used the same hyper-parameters as our experiments on clustering. See Appendix 6.B for the details.

Evaluation Metric. Following [11], we used three evaluation metrics to measure the performance of the different methods: (1) mean average precision (mAP); (2) precision at $N = 500$ samples; and (3) Hamming look-up result where the hamming radius is set as $r = 2$. We used the class labels to define the neighbors. We repeated the experiments ten times and took the average as the final result.

Experimental Results. The MNIST and CIFAR10 datasets both have 10 classes, and contain 70000 and 60000 data points, respectively. Following [11], we randomly sampled 1000 samples, 100 per class, as the query data and used the remaining data as the gallery set, i.e., a set of data that are compared with query data.

We tested performance for 16 and 32-bit hash codes. In practice, fast computation of hash codes is crucial for fast information retrieval. Hence, small

Table 6.6. Comparison of hash performance for 32-bit hash codes (%). Averages and standard deviations over ten trials were reported. Experimental results of Deep Hash and the previous methods are excerpted from [11].

Method	Hamming ranking (mAP)		precision @ sample = 500		precision @ r = 2	
(Network dimensionality)	MNIST	CIFAR10	MNIST	CIFAR10	MNIST	CIFAR10
Spectral hash [52]	25.7	12.4	61.3	19.7	65.3	20.6
PCA-ITQ [14]	43.8	16.2	74.0	25.3	73.1	15.0
Deep Hash (80-50)	45.0	16.6	74.7	26.0	73.3	15.8
Linear RIM	29.7 (0.4)	**21.2 (3.0)**	68.9 (0.9)	16.7 (0.8)	60.9 (2.2)	15.2 (0.9)
Deep RIM (80-50)	34.8 (0.7)	14.2 (0.3)	72.7 (2.2)	24.0 (0.9)	72.6 (2.1)	23.5 (1.0)
Deep RIM (200-200)	36.5 (0.8	14.1 (0.2)	76.2 (1.7)	23.7 (0.7)	75.9 (1.6)	23.3 (0.7)
Deep RIM (400-400)	37.0 (1.2)	14.2 (0.4)	76.1 (2.2)	23.9 (1.3)	75.7 (2.3)	23.7 (1.2)
IMSAT (VAT) (80-50)	55.4 (1.4)	20.0 (5.5)	87.6 (1.3)	23.5 (3.4)	88.8 (1.3)	22.4 (3.2)
IMSAT (VAT) (200-200)	62.9 (1.1)	18.9 (0.7)	96.1 (0.6)	29.8 (1.6)	95.8 (0.4)	**29.1 (1.4)**
IMSAT (VAT) (400-400)	**64.8 (0.8)**	18.9 (0.5)	**97.3 (0.4)**	30.8 (1.2)	**96.7 (0.6)**	29.2 (1.2)

networks are preferable. We therefore tested our method on three different network sizes: the same ones as Deep Hash [11], d-200-200-M, and d-400-400-M. Note that Deep Hash used d-60-30-M and d-80-50-M for learning 16 and 32-bit hash codes, respectively.

Tables 6.5 and 6.6 list the results for 16- and 32-bit hash codes, respectively. We see that IMSAT with the largest network sizes (400-400) achieved competitive performance in both datasets. The performance of IMSAT improved significantly when slightly bigger networks (200-200) were used, while the performance of Deep RIM did not improve much with the larger networks. We deduce that this is because we can better model the local invariance by using more flexible networks. Deep RIM, on the other hand, did not significantly benefit from the larger networks, because the additional flexibility of the networks was not used by the global function regularization via weight-decay.[1] We empirically analyzed this in Sect. 6.4.4.

6.4.4 Toy Dataset Study of IMSAT with Different Regularizations and Network Sizes

We used a toy dataset to illustrate that IMSAT can benefit from larger networks sizes by better modeling the local invariance. We also illustrate that weight-decay does not benefit much from the increased flexibility of neural networks.

For the experiments, we generated a spiral-shaped dataset, each arc containing 300 data points. For IMSAT, we used VAT regularization and set $\epsilon = 0.3$ for all the data points. We compared IMSAT with Deep RIM, which also uses neural networks but with weight-decay regularization. We set the decay rate to 0.0005. We varied three settings for the network dimensionality of the hidden layers: 5-5, 10-10, and 20-20.

---

[1] Hence, we deduce that Deep Hash, which is only regularized by weight-decay, would not benefit much by using larger networks.

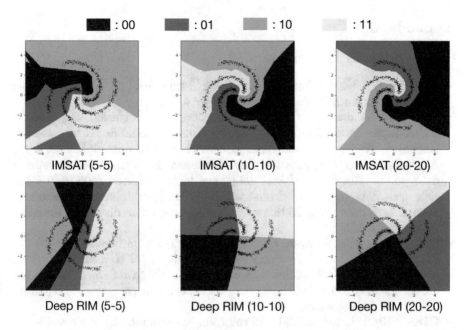

Fig. 6.3. IMSAT with the different regularizations and network sizes using toy datasets.

Figure 6.3 shows the experimental results. We see that IMSAT (VAT) was able to model the complicated decision boundaries by using the increased network dimensionality. On the contrary, the decision boundaries of Deep RIM did not adapt to the non-linearity of data even when the network dimensionality was increased. This observation may suggest why IMSAT (VAT) benefited from the large networks in the benchmark datasets, while Deep RIM did not.

6.5   Conclusion

We presented IMSAT, an information-theoretic method for unsupervised discrete representation learning using deep neural networks. Through extensive experiments, we showed that intended discrete representations can be obtained by directly imposing the invariance to data augmentation on the prediction of neural networks in an end-to-end fashion. This allows us to obtain more interpretable representations and achieve state-of-the-art performance on both clustering and hash learning.

Acknowledgements. MS was supported by KAKENHI 17H01760.

Appendices

6.A   Datasets Description

- **MNIST**: A dataset of hand-written digit classification [31]. The value of each pixel was transformed linearly into an interval [–1, 1].
- **Omniglot**: A dataset of hand-written character recognition [29], containing examples from 50 alphabets ranging from well-established international languages. We sampled 100 types of characters from four alphabets, Magi, Anglo-Saxon Futhorc, Arcadian, and Armenian. Each character contains 20 data points. Since the original data have high resolution (105-by-105 pixels), each data point was down-sampled to 21-by-21 pixels. We also augmented each data point 20 times by thestochastic affine distortion explained in Appendix 6.C.
- **STL**: A dataset of 96-by-96 color images acquired from labeled examples on ImageNet [7]. Features were extracted using 50-layer pre-trained deep residual networks [19] available online as a caffe model. Note that since the residual network is also trained on ImageNet, we expect that each class is separated well in the feature space.
- **CIFAR10**: A dataset of 32-by-32 color images with ten object classes, which are from the Tiny image dataset [49]. Features were extracted using the 50-layer pre-trained deep residual networks [19].
- **CIFAR100**: A dataset 32-by-32 color images with 100 refined object classes, which are from the Tiny image dataset [49]. Features were extracted using the 50-layer pre-trained deep residual networks [19].
- **SVHN**: A dataset with street view house numbers [38]. Training and test images were both used. Each image was represented as a 960-dimensional GIST feature [41].
- **Reuters**: A dataset with English news stories labeled with a category tree [33]. Following DEC [54], we used four categories: corporate/industrial, government/social, markets, and economics as labels. The preprocessing was the same as that used by [54], except that we removed stop words. As [54] did, 10000 documents were randomly sampled, and *tf-idf* features were used.
- **20news**: A dataset of newsgroup documents, partitioned nearly evenly across 20 different newsgroups[2]. As Reuters dataset, stop words were removed, and the 2000 most frequent words were retained. Documents with less than ten words were then removed, and *tf-idf* features were used.

For the STL, CIFAR10 and CIFAR100 datasets, each image was first resized into a 224-by-224 image before its feature was extracted using the deep residual network.

6.B   Hyper-parameter Selection

We fixed hyper-parameters across all the datasets unless there was an objective way to select them. For K-means, we tried 12 different initializations and

---

[2]   http://qwone.com/~jason/20Newsgroups/.

reported the results with the best objectives. For dAE+K-means and DEC [54], we used the recommended hyper-parameters for the network dimensionality and annealing speed.

Inspired by the automatic kernel width selection in spectral clustering [57], we set the perturbation range, ϵ, on data point x in VAT and RPT as

$$\epsilon(x) = \alpha \cdot \sigma_t(x), \tag{6.24}$$

where α is a scalar and $\sigma_t(x)$ is the Euclidian distance to the t-th neighbor of x. In our experiments, we fixed $t = 10$. For Linear IMSAT (VAT), IMSAT (RPT) and IMSAT (VAT), we fixed $\alpha = 0.4, 2.5$ and 0.25, respectively, which performed well across the datasets.

For the methods shown in Table 6.1, we varied one hyper-parameter and chose the best one that performed well across the datasets. More specifically, for Linear RIM and Deep RIM, we varied the decay rate over $0.0025 \cdot 2^i, i = 0, 1, \ldots, 7$. For the three variants of IMSAT, we varied λ in Eq. (6.15) for $0.025 \cdot 2^i, i = 0, 1, \ldots, 7$. We set q to be the uniform distribution and let $\delta = 0.01 \cdot h(q(y))$ in Eq. (6.14) for the all experiments.

Consequently, we chose 0.005 for decay rates in both Linear RIM and Deep RIM. Also, we set $\lambda = 1.6, 0.05$ and 0.1 for Linear IMSAT (VAT), IMSAT (RPT) and IMSAT (VAT), respectively. We henceforth fixed these hyper-parameters throughout the experiments for both clustering and hash learning. In Appendix 6.D, we report all the experimental results and the criteria to choose the parameters.

6.C   Affine Distortion for the Omniglot Dataset

We applied stochastic affine distortion to data points in Omniglot. The affine distortion is similar to the one used by [24], except that we applied the affine distortion on down-sampled images in our experiments. The followings are the stochastic components of the affine distortion used in our experiments. Our implementation of the affine distortion is based on scikit-image[3].

- Random scaling along x and y-axis by a factor of (s_x, s_y), where s_x and s_y are drawn uniformly from interval $[0.8, 1.2]$.
- Random translation along x and y-axis by (t_x, t_y), where t_x and t_y are drawn uniformly from interval $[-0.4, 0.4]$.
- Random rotation by θ, where θ is drawn uniformly from interval $[-10°, 10°]$.
- Random shearing along x and y-axis by (ρ_x, ρ_y), where ρ_x and ρ_y are drawn uniformly from interval $[-0.3, 0.3]$.

Figure 6.4 shows examples of the random affine distortion.

---

[3]   http://scikit-image.org/.

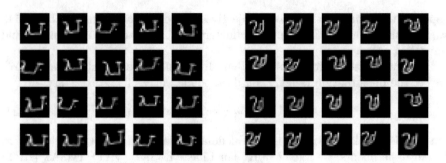

Fig. 6.4. Examples of the random affine distortion used in our experiments. Images in the top left side are stochastically transformed using the affine distortion.

6.D   Hyper-parameter Selection

In Fig. 6.5 we report the experimental results for different hyper-parameter settings. We used Eq. (6.25) as a criterion to select hyper-parameter, β^*, which performed well across the datasets.

$$\beta^* = \text{argmax}_\beta \sum_{\text{dataset}} \frac{\text{ACC}(\beta, \text{dataset})}{\text{ACC}(\beta^*_{\text{dataset}}, \text{dataset})}, \tag{6.25}$$

where β^*_{dataset} is the best hyper-parameter for the dataset, and $\text{ACC}(\beta, \text{dataset})$ is the clustering accuracy when hyper-parameter β is used for the dataset. According to the criterion, we set 0.005 for decay rates in both Linear RIM and Deep RIM. Also, we set $\lambda = 1.6, 0.05$ and 0.1 for Linear IMSAT (VAT), IMSAT (RPT) and IMSAT (VAT), respectively.

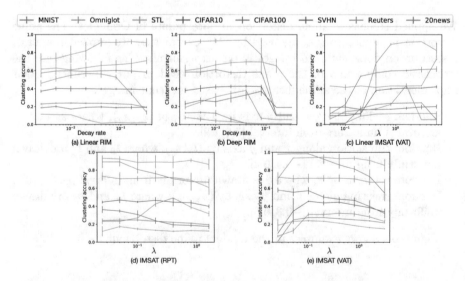

Fig. 6.5. Relationship between hyper-parameters and clustering accuracy for 8 benchmark datasets with different methods: (a) Linear RIM, (b) Deep RIM, (c) Linear IMSAT (VAT), (d) IMSAT (RPT), and (e) IMSAT (VAT).

References

1. Bachman, P., Alsharif, O., Precup, D.: Learning with pseudo-ensembles. In: NIPS (2014)
2. Berkhin, P.: A survey of clustering data mining techniques. In: Kogan, J., Nicholas, C., Teboulle, M. (eds)Grouping Multidimensional Data, pp. 25–71. Springer, Heidelberg (2006). https://doi.org/10.1007/3-540-28349-8_2
3. Bertsekas, D.P.: Nonlinear Programming. Athena Scientific Belmont (1999)
4. Bishop, C.M.: Training with noise is equivalent to tikhonov regularization. Neural Comput. **7**(1), 108–116 (1995)
5. Bridle, J.S., Heading, A.J.R., MacKay, D.J.C.: Unsupervised classifiers, mutual information and 'phantom targets'. In: NIPS, pp. 1096–1101 (1991)
6. Brown, G.: A new perspective for information theoretic feature selection. In: AISTATS (2009)
7. Coates, A., Lee, H., Ng, A.Y.: An analysis of single-layer networks in unsupervised feature learning. Ann Arbor **1001**(48109), 2 (2010)
8. Cover, T.M., Thomas, J.A.: Elements of Information Theory. Wiley, New York (2012)
9. Dilokthanakul, N., et al.: Deep unsupervised clustering with gaussian mixture variational autoencoders. arXiv preprint arXiv:1611.02648 (2016)
10. Dosovitskiy, A., Springenberg, J.T., Riedmiller, M., Brox, T.: Discriminative unsupervised feature learning with convolutional neural networks. In: NIPS, pp. 766–774 (2014)
11. Erin Liong, V., Lu, J., Wang, G., Moulin, P., Zhou, J.: Deep hashing for compact binary codes learning. In: CVPR (2015)
12. Glorot, X., Bordes, A., Bengio, Y.: Deep sparse rectifier neural networks. In: AISTATS (2011)
13. Gomes, R., Krause, A., Perona, P.: Discriminative clustering by regularized information maximization. In: NIPS (2010)
14. Gong, Y., Lazebnik, S., Gordo, A., Perronnin, F.: Iterative quantization: a procrustean approach to learning binary codes for large-scale image retrieval. IEEE Trans. Pattern Anal. Mach. Intell. **35**(12), 2916–2929 (2013)
15. Goodfellow, I., Bengio, Y., Courville, A., Bengio, Y.: Deep Learning, vol. 1. MIT Press, Cambridge (2016)
16. Grandvalet, Y., Bengio, Y., et al.: Semi-supervised learning by entropy minimization. In: NIPS (2004)
17. He, K., Wen, F., Sun, J.: K-means hashing: an affinity-preserving quantization method for learning binary compact codes. In: CVPR (2013)
18. He, K., Zhang, X., Ren, S., Sun, J.: Delving deep into rectifiers: surpassing human-level performance on imagenet classification. In: CVPR (2015)
19. He, K., Zhang, X., Ren, S., Sun, J.: Deep residual learning for image recognition. In: CVPR (2016)
20. Hinton, G.E., Srivastava, N., Krizhevsky, A., Sutskever, I., Salakhutdinov, R.R.: Improving neural networks by preventing co-adaptation of feature detectors. arXiv preprint arXiv:1207.0580 (2012)
21. Ioffe, S., Szegedy, C.: Batch normalization: accelerating deep network training by reducing internal covariate shift. In: ICML (2015)
22. Jarrett, K., Kavukcuoglu, K., Ranzato, M., LeCun, Y.: What is the best multi-stage architecture for object recognition? In: ICCV (2009)
23. Kingma, D., Ba, J.: Adam: a method for stochastic optimization. In: ICLR (2015)

24. Koch, G.: Siamese neural networks for one-shot image recognition. Ph.D. thesis, University of Toronto (2015)
25. Krizhevsky, A., Sutskever, I., Hinton, G.E.: Imagenet classification with deep convolutional neural networks. In: Advances in Neural Information Processing Systems, pp. 1097–1105 (2012)
26. Kuhn, H.W.: The hungarian method for the assignment problem. Naval Res. Logist. Q. **2**(1–2), 83–97 (1955)
27. Kulis, B., Darrell, T.: Learning to hash with binary reconstructive embeddings. In: NIPS (2009)
28. Lai, H., Pan, Y., Liu, Y., Yan, S.: Simultaneous feature learning and hash coding with deep neural networks. In: CVPR (2015)
29. Lake, B.M., Salakhutdinov, R., Gross, J., Tenenbaum, J.B.: One shot learning of simple visual concepts. In: Cognitive Science (2011)
30. Lang, K.: Newsweeder: learning to filter netnews. In: ICML, pp. 331–339 (1995)
31. LeCun, Y., Bottou, L., Bengio, Y., Haffner, P.: Gradient-based learning applied to document recognition. Proc. IEEE **86**(11), 2278–2324 (1998)
32. Leen, T.K.: From data distributions to regularization in invariant learning. Neural Comput. **7**(5), 974–981 (1995)
33. Lewis, D.D., Yang, Y., Rose, T.G., Li, F.: Rcv1: a new benchmark collection for text categorization research. J. Mach. Learn. Res. **5**, 361–397 (2004)
34. Li, W.J., Wang, S., Kang, W.C.: Feature learning based deep supervised hashing with pairwise labels. In: IJCAI (2015)
35. McGill, W.J.: Multivariate information transmission. Psychometrika **19**(2), 97–116 (1954)
36. Miyato, T., Maeda, S.I., Koyama, M., Nakae, K., Ishii, S.: Distributional smoothing with virtual adversarial training. In: ICLR (2016)
37. Nair, V., Hinton, G.E.: Rectified linear units improve restricted Boltzmann machines. In: ICML (2010)
38. Netzer, Y., Wang, T., Coates, A., Bissacco, A., Wu, B., Ng, A.Y.: Reading digits in natural images with unsupervised feature learning. In: NIPS Workshop on Deep Learning and Unsupervised Feature Learning (2011)
39. Ng, A.Y., Jordan, M.I., Weiss, Y., et al.: On spectral clustering: analysis and an algorithm. In: NIPS (2001)
40. Norouzi, M., Blei, D.M.: Minimal loss hashing for compact binary codes. In: ICML (2011)
41. Oliva, A., Torralba, A.: Modeling the shape of the scene: a holistic representation of the spatial envelope. Int. J. Comput. Vis. **42**(3), 145–175 (2001)
42. van den Oord, A., Vinyals, O., et al.: Neural discrete representation learning. In: Advances in Neural Information Processing Systems, pp. 6306–6315 (2017)
43. Reed, R., Oh, S., Marks, R.: Regularization using jittered training data. In: IJCNN, vol. 3, pp. 147–152. IEEE (1992)
44. Rifai, S., Vincent, P., Muller, X., Glorot, X., Bengio, Y.: Contractive auto-encoders: explicit invariance during feature extraction. In: ICML (2011)
45. Sajjadi, M., Javanmardi, M., Tasdizen, T.: Regularization with stochastic transformations and perturbations for deep semi-supervised learning. In: NIPS (2016)
46. Salakhutdinov, R., Hinton, G.: Semantic hashing. Int. J. Approximate Reasoning **50**(7), 969–978 (2009)
47. Springenberg, J.T.: Unsupervised and semi-supervised learning with categorical generative adversarial networks. In: ICLR (2015)

48. Tokui, S., Oono, K., Hido, S., Clayton, J.: Chainer: a next-generation open source framework for deep learning. In: NIPS Workshop on Machine Learning Systems (LearningSys) (2015)
49. Torralba, A., Fergus, R., Freeman, W.T.: 80 million tiny images: a large data set for nonparametric object and scene recognition. IEEE Trans. Pattern Anal. Mach. Intell. **30**(11), 1958–1970 (2008)
50. Vincent, P., Larochelle, H., Bengio, Y., Manzagol, P.A.: Extracting and composing robust features with denoising autoencoders. In: ICML (2008)
51. Wang, J., Liu, W., Kumar, S., Chang, S.F.: Learning to hash for indexing big data–a survey. Proc. IEEE **104**(1), 34–57 (2016)
52. Weiss, Y., Torralba, A., Fergus, R.: Spectral hashing. In: NIPS (2009)
53. Xia, R., Pan, Y., Lai, H., Liu, C., Yan, S.: Supervised hashing for image retrieval via image representation learning. In: AAAI (2014)
54. Xie, J., Girshick, R., Farhadi, A.: Unsupervised deep embedding for clustering analysis. In: ICML (2016)
55. Xu, J., et al.: Convolutional neural networks for text hashing. In: IJCAI (2015)
56. Xu, L., Neufeld, J., Larson, B., Schuurmans, D.: Maximum margin clustering. In: NIPS (2004)
57. Zelnik-Manor, L., Perona, P.: Self-tuning spectral clustering. In: NIPS (2004)
58. Zhang, R., Lin, L., Zhang, R., Zuo, W., Zhang, L.: Bit-scalable deep hashing with regularized similarity learning for image retrieval and person re-identification. IEEE Trans. Image Process. **24**(12), 4766–4779 (2015)
59. Zheng, Y., Tan, H., Tang, B., Zhou, H., et al.: Variational deep embedding: a generative approach to clustering. arXiv preprint arXiv:1611.05148 (2016)
60. Zhou, Z.H.: A brief introduction to weakly supervised learning. Nat. Sci. Rev. **5**(1), 44–53 (2017)

7
Towards Reverse-Engineering Black-Box Neural Networks

Seong Joon Oh$^{(\boxtimes)}$, Bernt Schiele, and Mario Fritz

Max-Planck Institute, Saarbrücken, Germany
{joon,schiele,mfritz}@mpi-inf.mpg.de

Abstract. Much progress in interpretable AI is built around scenarios where the user, one who interprets the model, has a full ownership of the model to be diagnosed. The user either owns the training data and computing resources to train an interpretable model herself or owns a full access to an already trained model to be interpreted post-hoc. In this chapter, we consider a less investigated scenario of diagnosing *black-box neural networks*, where the user can only send queries and read off outputs. Black-box access is a common deployment mode for many public and commercial models, since internal details, such as architecture, optimisation procedure, and training data, can be proprietary and aggravate their vulnerability to attacks like adversarial examples. We propose a method for exposing internals of black-box models and show that the method is surprisingly effective at inferring a diverse set of internal information. We further show how the exposed internals can be exploited to strengthen adversarial examples against the model. Our work starts an important discussion on the security implications of diagnosing deployed models with limited accessibility. The code is available at goo.gl/MbYfsv.

Keywords: Machine Learning · Security · Black box · Explainability

7.1 Introduction

Interpretable artificial intelligence (AI) is becoming more critical. Data-driven learned models have excelled human performance in many domains, but they often lack interpretability: it is difficult to infer the rationale behind their decisions. This limits their applications on safety- and security-critical domains such as self-driving cars, medical analysis, and finance. Increasing amount of work is being devoted to building more interpretable machine learning (ML) systems.

Interpretable AI is studied under different user scenarios with varying degrees of control over the model. We identify three main cases. (1) *Own data.* User owns the training data and computational resources to train a model herself. She may choose model classes that are interpretable by design, such as decision trees or

Supported by German Research Foundation (DFG CRC 1223).

© Springer Nature Switzerland AG 2019
W. Samek et al. (Eds.): Explainable AI, LNAI 11700, pp. 121–144, 2019.
https://doi.org/10.1007/978-3-030-28954-6_7

sparse linear models. (2) *Own model.* User is given a trained model that is not alterable, but she has access to any detail of the model like its function class, optimisation hyperparameters, and trained parameters. The aim of interpretable AI in this case is to turn the complex computational curcuit into a human-friendly explanation (e.g. saliency map for image classifiers). (3) *Black box model.* Again, user is given a fixed trained model, but she can only send query inputs and read off outputs. Note that we use the term "black box" to specifically indicate a system that takes an input and returns the output, as opposed to an incomprehensible system (as commonly used in model interpretability literature). This is a common deployment mode for many public and commercial models. Internal information is often hidden from users because they are proprietary and may increase vulnerability to various attacks.

Progress has been made in all three scenarios, as we will see in Sect. 7.2.1. This chapter focuses on the third scenario, the *black box model* case, with a ML security viewpoint. We show that it is possible to infer neural network hyperparameters (model class, optimisation parameters, and training data) to a surprising level of accuracy even if one can only access the model through queries. Our findings shed light on the security aspect of model interpretability. It has legal implications to intellectual properties (IP) involving neural networks – internal information about the model can be proprietary and a key IP, and the training data may be privacy sensitive. Disclosing hidden details may also render the model more susceptible to attacks from adversaries.

We introduce the term "model attributes" to refer to various types of information about a trained neural network model. We group them into three types: (1) architecture (e.g. type of non-linear activation), (2) optimisation process (e.g. SGD or ADAM?), and (3) training data (e.g. which dataset?). We approach the problem as a standard supervised learning task *applied over models.* First, collect a diverse set of white-box models ("meta-training set") that are expected to be similar to the target black box at least to a certain extent. Then, over the collected meta-training set, train another model ("metamodel") that takes a model as input and returns the corresponding model attributes as output. Importantly, since we want to predict attributes at test time for black-box models, the only information available for attribute prediction is the query input-output pairs. As we will see in the experiments, such input-output pairs allow to predict model attributes surprisingly well.

In summary, we contribute: (1) Investigation of the type and amount of internal information about the black-box model that can be extracted from querying; (2) Novel metamodel methods that not only reason over outputs from static query inputs, but also actively optimise query inputs that can extract more information; (3) Study of factors like size of the meta-training set, quantity and quality of queries, and the dissimilarity between the meta-training models and the test black box (generalisability); (4) Empirical verification that revealed information leads to greater susceptibility of a black-box model to an adversarial example based attack.

The chapter is mostly based on Oh et al. [23] published at the International Conference on Learning Representations, Vancouver 2018. Section 7.7 is based on Oh et al. [24] published at the International Conference on Computer Vision, Venice 2017.

7.2   Related Work

Work in this chapter is closely related to interpretable AI and ML security. We will discuss prior work in both areas.

7.2.1   Interpretable AI

We review prior work in interpretable AI according to different user scenarios where the user's degrees of control over the model differ. We identify three cases in the following as described in the introduction: (1) own data, (2) own model, and (3) black box model.

Own Data. User possesses the training data and can train a model by herself. In particular, user can choose a model that is explainable by design [16]. Often there exists a tradeoff between interpretability and performance. Examples of more interpretable model types include decision trees, sparse linear models, additive models encoding pairwise interactions [2], and certain Bayesian models [15]. Deep neural networks (DNNs), on the other hand, have shown great performance in many domains, but their inner mechanisms are difficult to understand in general. Efforts have been made to make DNNs more interpretable by design. For example, Hendricks et al. [9] have attached a sentence generation module on top of an image classification system to generate captions explaining the positive and negative cues used for the task.

Own Model. Often it is useful to be able to interpret an already trained model post-hoc; user may not have enough computational resources to train models herself, for example. Under this scenario, user *owns* the model and has access to any internal information, such as training data, model type, training hyperparameters, model parameters.

For complex models like deep neural networks, visualisation technique have gained popularity. Salient regions for image classifiers are visualised via image gradient with respect to the prediction [31], and this technique has become an active area of research [4,5]. These techniques typically require full access to the model weights for efficient gradient computation (backpropagation). Other visualisation techniques include network inversion [19], where internal representations are diagnosed by inverting them, and activation visualisation [34], where activation-maximising inputs are visualised. They require access to internal activation values.

Apart from visualisation, decision tree extraction algorithms have been developed to obtain a more interpretable surrogate of complex neural networks [13]. The tree is built using internal node values.

Black Box Model. There are a few interpretation work requiring only black-box access (submit input, observe output). Ribeiro et al. [28] have proposed Local Interpretable Model-agnostic Explanations (LIME) that trains an interpretable-by-design model (e.g. sparse linear model) that maximises the likelihood of input-output pairs from the target network. Importantly, the method does not require access to internal weights, activations, or any other hyperparameters. It can be seen as an instance of model stealing attack to be discussed in Sect. 7.2.2.

While LIME is focused on replicating the target model under an interpretable-by-design constraint, our work is more focused on inferring model hyperparameters, such as the model class and training algorithms. We investigate the security threats that follow from diagnosing models with limited access.

7.2.2   Model Security

Our work is deeply related to the security problems with machine learning. There exists a line of work on extracting and exploiting information from black-box learned models. We first describe papers on extracting information (*model stealing* and *membership inference* attacks), and then discuss ones on attacking the network using the extracted information (*adversarial image perturbations*).

Model Stealing Attacks. Model extraction attacks either reconstruct the exact model parameters or build an *avatar model* that maximises the likelihood of the query input-output pairs from the target model [26,33]. Tramer et al. [33] have shown the efficacy of equation solving attacks and the avatar method in retrieving internal parameters of non-neural network models. Papernot et al. [26] have also used the avatar approach with the end goal of generating adversarial examples. While the avatar approach first assumes model hyperparameters like model family (architecture) and training data, we discriminatively train a meta-model to predict those hyperparameters themselves. As such, our approach is complementary to the avatar approach.

Membership Inference Attacks. Membership inference attacks determine if a given data sample has been included in the training data [1,29]. In particular, Ateniese et al. [1] also trains a decision tree metamodel over a set of classifiers trained on different datasets. This work goes far beyond only inferring the training data by showing that even the model architecture and optimisation process can be inferred.

Adversarial Image Perturbations. Using the obtained cues, one can launch more effective, focused attacks on the black box. We use *adversarial image perturbations* (AIPs) as an example of such attack. AIPs are small perturbations over the input such that the network is mislead. Research on this topic has flourished recently after it was shown that the needed amount of perturbation to completely mislead an image classifier is nearly invisible [6,20,32].

Most effective AIPs require gradients of the target network. Some papers proposed different ways to attack black boxes. They can be grouped into three approaches. (1) Approximate gradients by *numerical gradients* [3, 21]. The caveat is that thousands and millions of queries are needed to compute a single AIP, depending on the image size. (2) Use the *avatar approach* to train a white box network that is supposedly similar to the target [7, 25, 26]. We note again that our metamodel is complementary to the avatar approach – the avatar network hyperparemters can be determined by the metamodel. (3) Exploit *transferability* of adversarial examples; it has been shown that AIPs generated against one network can also fool other networks [17, 20]. [17] in particular have shown that generating AIPs against an ensemble of networks make it more transferable. We show in this work that the AIPs transfer better within an architecture family (e.g. ResNet or DenseNet) than across, and that such a property can be exploited by our metamodel for generating more targetted AIPs.

7.3   Attacker Assumptions

We first set up the attack scenario. We will precisely define the goal as well as the set of possible actions for the attacker. An overview of the attack scenario is given in Fig. 7.1.

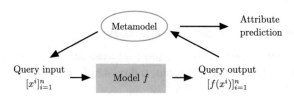

Fig. 7.1. Overview of attack.

Goal. The goal of the attack is to find out the type and amount of internal information about a black-box model. More specifically, the attacker aims to correctly predict model attributes (e.g. which non-linear activation is used?) for a given model in the attribute classification framework. I.e. the attacker is asked to choose one of the attributes in a pre-defined list (e.g. {Tanh, ReLU, PReLU, ELU}).

Knowledge. The attacker can gain knowledge on the target black-box model by sending queries n query inputs $\left[x^i\right]_{i=1}^{n}$ and observing corresponding outputs $\left[f(x^i)\right]_{i=1}^{n}$, which we refer to as **fingerprints** of a model. The degree of knowledge on the model depends on the type of fingerprints. In this work, we consider three types of fingerprints: argmax, top-k, and probability vector. The attacker can send any input as queries to the network as long as pixel values are within the valid range [0, 255]. The attacker does not have access to the actual training data of the model.

7.4   Metamodels

We approach this by first building metamodels for predicting model attributes, and then evaluating their performance on black-box models. In a nutshell, metamodel is a classifier of classifiers. See Fig. 7.1 for an overview. The metamodel submits n query inputs $\left[x^i\right]_{i=1}^n$ to a black box model f; the metamodel takes corresponding model outputs $\left[f(x^i)\right]_{i=1}^n$ as an input, and returns predicted model attributes as output. As we will describe in detail, the metamodel not only learns to infer model attributes from query outputs (model fingerprints) from a static set of inputs, but also searches for query inputs that are designed to extract greater amount of information from the target models.

In this section, our main methods are introduced in the context of MNIST digit classifiers. While MNIST classifiers are not fully representative of *generic* learned models, they have a computational edge: it takes only five minutes to train each of them with reasonable performance. We could thus prepare a diverse set of 11k MNIST classifiers within 40 GPU days for the meta-training and evaluation of our metamodels. We stress, however, that the proposed approach is generic with respect to the task, data, and the type of models. We also focus on 12 model attributes (Table 7.1) that cover hyperparameters for common neural network MNIST classifiers, but again the range of predictable attributes are not confined to this list.

7.4.1   Collecting a Dataset of Classifiers

We need a dataset of classifiers to train and evaluate metamodels. We explain how MNIST-NETS has been constructed, a dataset of 11k MNIST digit classifiers; the procedure is task and data generic.

Base Network Skeleton. Every model in MNIST-NETS shares the same convnet skeleton architecture: "N conv blocks $\rightarrow$ M fc blocks $\rightarrow$ 1 linear classifier". Each conv block has the following structure: "ks $\times$ ks convolution $\rightarrow$ optional 2 $\times$ 2 max-pooling $\rightarrow$ non-linear activation", where ks (kernel size) and the activation type are to be chosen. Each fc block has the structure: "linear mapping $\rightarrow$ non-linear activation $\rightarrow$ optional dropout" This convnet structure already covers many LeNet [14] variants, one of the best performing architectures on MNIST[1].

Increasing Diversity. In order to learn generalisable features, the metamodel needs to be trained over a diverse set of models. The base architecture described above already has several free parameters like the number of layers (N and M), the existence of dropout or max-pooling layers, or the type of non-linear activation.

Apart from the architectural hyperparameters, we increase diversity along two more axes – optimisation process and the training data. Along the optimisation axis, we vary optimisation algorithm (SGD, ADAM, or RMSprop) and the

---

[1] http://yann.lecun.com/exdb/mnist/.

Table 7.1. MNIST classifier attributes. *Italicised* attributes are derived from other attributes.

	Code	Attribute	Values
Architecture	act	Activation	ReLU, PReLU, ELU, Tanh
	drop	Dropout	Yes, No
	pool	Max pooling	Yes, No
	ks	Conv ker. size	3, 5
	#conv	#Conv layers	2, 3, 4
	#fc	#FC layers	2, 3, 4
	#par	*#Parameters*	$2^{14}, \cdots, 2^{21}$
	ens	Ensemble	Yes, No
Opt.	alg	Algorithm	SGD, ADAM, RMSprop
	bs	Batch size	64, 128, 256
Data	split	Data split	All_0, $\text{Half}_{0/1}$, $\text{Quarter}_{0/1/2/3}$
	size	*Data size*	All, Half, Quarter

training batch size (64, 128, 256). We also consider training MNIST classifiers on either on the entire MNIST training set (All_0, 60k), one of the two disjoint halves ($\text{Half}_{0/1}$, 30k), or one of the four disjoint quarters ($\text{Quarter}_{0/1/2/3}$, 15k).

See Table 7.1 for the comprehensive list of 12 model attributes altered in MNIST-NETS. The number of trainable parameters (#par) and the training data size (size) are not directly controlled but derived from the other attributes. We also augment MNIST-NETS with ensembles of classifiers (ens), whose procedure will be described later.

Sampling and Training. The number of all possible combinations of controllable options in Table 7.1 is 18, 144. We also select random seeds that control the initialisation and training data shuffling from $\{0, \cdots, 999\}$, resulting in 18, 144, 000 unique models. Training such a large number of models is intractable; we have sampled (without replacement) and trained 10, 000 of them. All the models have been trained with learning rate 0.1 and momentum 0.5 for 100 epochs. It takes around 5 min to train each model on a GPU machine (GeForce GTX TITAN); training of 10k classifiers has taken 40 GPU days.

Pruning and Augmenting. In order to make sure that MNIST-NETS realistically represents commonly used MNIST classifiers, we have pruned low-performance classifiers (validation accuracy < 98%), resulting in 8, 582 classifiers. Ensembles of trained classifiers have been constructed by grouping the identical classifiers (modulo random seed). Given t identical ones, we have augmented MNIST-NETS with 2, $\cdots$, t combinations. The ensemble augmentation has resulted in 11, 282 final models. Due to large sample size all the attributes are evenly covered.

Train-Eval Splits. Attribute prediction can get arbitrarily easy by including the black-box model (or similar ones) in the meta-training set. We introduce multiple splits of MNIST-NETS with varying requirements on generalization. Unless stated otherwise, every split has $5,000$ training (meta-training), $1,000$ testing (black box), and $5,282$ leftover models.

The Random (R) split randomly (uniform weights) assigns training and test splits, respectively. Under the R split, the training and test models come from the same distribution. We introduce harder Extrapolation (E) splits. We separate a few attributes between the training and test splits. They are designed to simulate more difficult domain gaps when the meta-training models are significantly different from the black box. Specific examples of E splits will be shown in Sect. 7.5.

7.4.2   Metamodel Methods

The metamodel predicts the attribute of a black-box model g in the test split by submitting n query inputs and observing the outputs. It is trained over meta-training models f in the training split ($f \sim \mathcal{F}$). We propose three approaches for the metamodels – we collectively name them kennen[2]. See Fig. 7.2 for an overview.

kennen-o: Reason over Output. kennen-o first selects a fixed set of queries $[x^i]_{i=1\cdots n}$ from a dataset. Both during training and testing, always these queries are submitted. kennen-o learns a classifier m_θ to map from the order-sensitively concatenated n model fingerprints, $[f(x^i)]_{i=1\cdots n}$ ($n \times 10$ dim for MNIST), to the simultaneous prediction of 12 attributes in f. The training objective is:

$$\min_\theta \ \mathbb{E}_{f \sim \mathcal{F}} \left[\sum_{a=1}^{12} \mathcal{L} \left(m_\theta^a \left([f(x^i)]_{i=1}^n \right), y^a \right) \right] \tag{7.1}$$

where $\mathcal{F}$ is the distribution of meta-training models, y^a is the ground truth label of attribute a, and $\mathcal{L}$ is the cross-entropy loss. With the learned parameter $\tilde{\theta}$, $m_{\tilde{\theta}}^a \left([g(x^i)]_{i=1}^n \right)$ gives the prediction of attribute a for the black box g.

In our experiments, we model the classifier m_θ via multilayer perceptron (MLP) with two hidden layers with 1000 hidden units. The last layer consists of 12 parallel linear layers for a simultaneous prediction of the 12 attributes. In our preliminary experiments, MLP has performed better than the linear classifiers. The optimisation problem in Eq. 7.1 is solved via SGD by approximating the expectation over $f \sim \mathbb{F}$ by an empirical sum over the training split classifiers for 200 epochs.

For query inputs, we have used a random subset of n images from the validation set (both for MNIST and ImageNet experiments). The performance is not sensitive to the choice of queries. Next methods (kennen-i/io) describe how to actively craft query inputs, potentially outside the natural image distribution.

---

[2] *kennen* means "to know" in German, and "to dig out" in Korean.

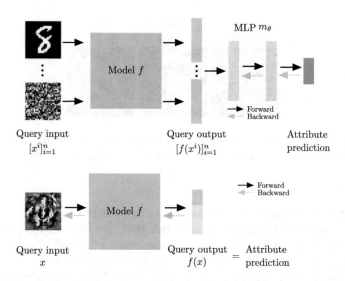

Fig. 7.2. Training procedure for metamodels `kennen-o` (top) and `kennen-i` (bottom).

Note that `kennen-o` can be applied to any type of model (e.g. non-neural networks) with any output structure, as long as the output can be embedded in an Euclidean space. We will show that this method can effectively extract information from f even if the output is a top-k ranking. In this case, top-k ranked labels $(l_1, \cdots, l_k)$ can be represented as a sparse pseudo-output vector $o \in \mathbb{R}^{10}$ where the non-zero values at class $l_{k'}$ is defined by $o_{l_{k'}} := r^{-k'}$ for $k' \in \{1, \cdots, k\}$. $r \in (0, 1)$ is a pre-defined decay factor. For example, if the top-3 ranking is $(3, 4)$ and $r = 0.5$, its pseudo-output is the sparse vector with non-zero entries $(3 : 0.5, 4 : 0.25)$.

`kennen-i`: **Craft Input.** `kennen-i` crafts a *single* query input $\tilde{x}$ over the meta-training models that is trained to repurpose a digit classifier f into a model attribute classifier for a *single* attribute a. The crafted input drives the classifier to leak internal information via digit prediction. The learned input is submitted to the test black-box model g, and the attribute is predicted by reading off its digit prediction $g(\tilde{x})$. For example, `kennen-i` for max-pooling layer prediction crafts an input x that is predicted as "1" for generic MNIST digit classifiers with max-pooling layers and "0" for ones without. See Fig. 7.3 for visual examples.

We describe in detail how `kennen-i` learns this input. The training objective is:

$$\min_{x:\ \text{image}} \mathbb{E}_{f \sim \mathcal{F}} [\mathcal{L}(f(x), y^a)] \tag{7.2}$$

where $f(x)$ is the 10-dimensional output of the digit classifier f. The condition $x :$ image ensures the input stays a valid image $x \in [0, 1]^D$ with image dimension D. The loss $\mathcal{L}$, together with the attribute label y^a of f, guides the digit prediction $f(x)$ to reveal the attribute a instead. Note that the optimisation problem is

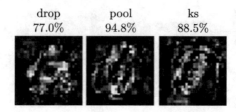

Fig. 7.3. Inputs designed to extract internal details from MNIST digit classifiers. E.g. feeding the middle image reveals the existence of a max-pooling layer with 94.8% chance.

identical to the training of digit classifiers except that the ground truth is the attribute label rather than the digit label, that the loss is averaged over the models instead of the images, and that the input x instead of the model f is optimised. With the learned query input $\tilde{x}$, the attribute for the black box g is predicted by $g(\tilde{x})$. In particular, we do not use gradient information from g.

We initialise x with a random sample from the MNIST validation set (random noise or uniform gray initialisation gives similar performances), and run SGD for 200 epochs. For each iteration x is truncated back to $[0,1]^D$ to enforce the constraint.

While being simple and effective, kennen-i can only predict a single attribute at a time, and cannot predict attributes with more than 10 classes (for digit classifiers). Moreover, training kennen-i can sometimes be difficult, as no interpreting module is trained over the model fingerprints at the same time. kennen-io introduced below overcomes above limitations by simultaneously training the kennen-o module on top. kennen-i may also be unrealistic when the exploration needs to be stealthy: it submits unnatural images to the system. Also unlike kennen-o, kennen-i requires end-to-end differentiability of the training models $f \sim \mathcal{F}$, although it still requires only black-box access to test models g.

kennen-io: **Combined Approach.** We overcome the drawbacks of kennen-i that it can only predict one attribute at a time and that the number of predictable classes by attaching an additional interpretation module on top of the output. Our final method kennen-io combines kennen-i and kennen-o approaches: both input generator and output interpreters are used. Being able to reason over multiple model fingerprints via MLP layers, kennen-io supports the optimisation of multiple query inputs as well.

Specifically, the kennen-io training objective is given by:

$$\min_{[x^i]_{i=1}^n:\,\text{images}}\ \min_{\theta}\ \mathbb{E}_{f\sim\mathcal{F}}\left[\sum_{a=1}^{12}\mathcal{L}\left(m_\theta^a\left([f(x^i)]_{i=1}^n\right),y^a\right)\right]. \tag{7.3}$$

Note that the formulation is identical to that for kennen-o (Eq. 7.1), except that the second minimisation problem regarding the query inputs is added. With learned parameters $\tilde{\theta}$ and $[\tilde{x}^i]_{i=1}^n$, the attribute a for the black box g

is predicted by $m_{\hat{\theta}}^{a}\left([g(\tilde{x}^i)]_{i=1}^{n}\right)$. Again, we require end-to-end differentiability of meta-training models f, but only the black-box access for the test model g.

To improve stability against covariate shift, we initialise m_θ with kennen-o for 200 epochs. Afterwards, gradient updates of $[x^i]_{i=1}^{n}$ and θ alternate every 50 epochs, for 200 additional epochs.

7.5 Reverse-Engineering Black-Box MNIST Digit Classifiers

We have introduced a procedure for constructing a dataset of classifiers (MNIST-NETS) as well as novel metamodels (kennen variants) that learn to extract information from black-box classifiers. In this section, we evaluate the ability of kennen to extract information from black-box MNIST digit classifiers. We measure the *class-balanced* attribute prediction accuracy for each attribute a in the list of 12 attributes in Table 7.1.

Table 7.2. Comparison of metamodel methods. See Table 7.1 for the full names of attributes. 100 queries are used for every method below, except for kennen-i which uses a single query. The "Output" column shows the output representation: "prob" (vector of probabilities for each digit class), "ranking" (a sorted list of digits according to their likelihood), "top-1" (most likely digit), or "bottom-1" (least likely digit).

Method	Output	Architecture								Optim		Data		Avg
		act	drop	pool	ks	#conv	#fc	#par	ens	alg	bs	size	split	
Chance	-	25.0	50.0	50.0	50.0	33.3	33.3	12.5	50.0	33.3	33.3	33.3	14.3	34.9
kennen-o	prob	80.6	94.6	94.9	84.6	67.1	77.3	41.7	54.0	71.8	50.4	73.8	90.0	73.4
kennen-o	ranking	63.7	93.8	90.8	80.0	63.0	73.7	44.1	**62.4**	65.3	47.0	66.2	86.6	69.7
kennen-o	bottom-1	48.6	80.0	73.6	64.0	48.9	63.1	28.7	52.8	53.6	41.9	45.9	51.4	54.4
kennen-o	top-1	31.2	56.9	58.8	49.9	38.9	33.7	19.6	50.0	36.1	35.3	33.3	30.7	39.5
kennen-i	top-1	43.5	77.0	94.8	88.5	54.5	41.0	32.3	46.5	45.7	37.0	42.6	29.3	52.7
kennen-io	prob	**88.4**	**95.8**	**99.5**	**97.7**	**80.3**	**80.2**	**45.2**	60.2	**79.3**	**54.3**	**84.8**	**95.6**	**80.1**

Attribute Prediction. See Table 7.2 for the main results of our metamodels, kennen-o/i/io, on the Random split. Unless stated otherwise, metamodels are trained with 5,000 training split classifiers.

Given $n = 100$ queries with probability output, kennen-o already performs far above the random chance in predicting 12 diverse attributes (73.4% versus 34.9% on average); neural network output indeed contains rich information about the black box. In particular, the presence of dropout (94.6%) or max-pooling (94.9%) has been predicted with high precision. As we will see in Sect. 7.5.3, outputs of networks trained with dropout layers form clusters, explaining the good prediction performance.

It is surprising that optimisation details like algorithm (71.8%) and batch size (50.4%) can also be predicted well above the random chance (33.3% for both). We observe that the training data attributes are also predicted with high accuracy (71.8% and 90.0% for size and split).

Comparing Methods. `kennen-o/i/io`. Table 7.2 shows the comparison of `kennen-o/i/io`. `kennen-i` has a relatively low performance (average 52.7%), but `kennen-i` relies on a cheap resource: 1 query with single-label output. `kennen-i` is also performant at predicting the kernel size (88.5%) and pooling (94.8%), attributes that are closely linked to spatial structure of the input. We conjecture `kennen-i` is relatively effective for such attributes. `kennen-io` is superior to `kennen-o/i` for all the attributes with average accuracy 80.1%.

7.5.1   Factor Analysis

We examine potential factors that contribute to the successful prediction of black box internal attributes. We measure the prediction accuracy of our metamodels as we vary (1) the number of meta-training models, (2) the number of queries, and (3) the quality of query output (fingerprint).

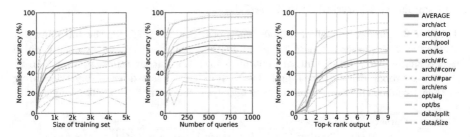

Fig. 7.4. `kennen-o` performance of against the size of meta-training set (left), number of queries (middle), and quality of queries (right). Unless stated otherwise, we use 100 probability outputs and 5k models to train `kennen-o`. Each curve is linearly scaled such that random chance (0 training data, 0 query, or top-0) performs 0%, and the perfect predictor performs 100%.

Number of Training Models. We have trained `kennen-o` with different number of the meta-training classifiers, ranging from 100 to 5,000. See Fig. 7.4 (left) for the trend. We observe a diminishing return, but also that the performance has not saturated – collecting larger meta-training set will improve the performance.

Number of Queries. See Fig. 7.4 (middle) for the `kennen-o` performance against the number of queries with probability output. The average performance saturates after ~500 queries. On the other hand, with only ~100 queries, we already retrieve ample information about the neural network.

Quality of Output. Many black-box models return top-k ranking (e.g. Facebook face recogniser), or single-label output. We represent top-k ranking outputs by assigning exponentially decaying probabilities up to k digits and a small probability ϵ to the remaining.

See Table 7.2 for the `kennen-o` performance comparison among 100 probability, top-10 ranking, bottom-1, and top-1 outputs, with average accuracies 73.4%, 69.7%, 54.4%, and 39.5%, respectively. While performance drops with coarser outputs, when compared to random chance (34.9%), 100 single-label bottom-1 outputs already leak a great amount of information about the black box (54.4%). It is also notable that bottom-1 outputs contain much more information than do the top-1 outputs; note that for high-performance classifiers top-1 predictions are rather uniform across models and thus have much less freedom to leak auxiliary information. Figure 7.4 (right) shows the interpolation from top-1 to top-10 (i.e. top-9) ranking. We observe from the jump at $k = 2$ that the second likely predictions (top-2) contain far more information than the most likely ones (top-1). For $k \geq 3$, each additional output label exhibits a diminishing return.

7.5.2 What if the Black-Box Is Quite Different from Meta-training Models?

So far we have seen results on the Random (R) split. In realistic scenarios, the meta-training model distribution may not be fully covering possible black box models. We show how damaging such a scenario is through Extrapolation (E) split experiments.

Evaluation. E-splits split the training and testing models based on one or more attributes (Sect. 7.4.1). For example, we may assign shallower models (#layers ≤ 10) to the training split and deeper ones (#layers > 10) to the testing split. In this example, we refer to #layers as the *splitting attribute*. Since for an E-split, some classes of the splitting attributes have zero training examples, we only evaluate the prediction accuracies over the non-splitting attributes. When the set of splitting attributes is $\tilde{A}$, a subset of the entire attribute set A, we define *E-split accuracy* or $\text{E.Acc}(\tilde{A})$ to be the mean prediction accuracy over the non-splitting attributes $A \setminus \tilde{A}$. For easier comparison, we report the *normalised accuracy* (N.Acc) that shows the how much percentage of the R-split accuracy is achieved in the E-split setup on the non-splitting attributes $A \setminus \tilde{A}$. Specifically:

$$\text{N.Acc}(\tilde{A}) = \frac{\text{E.Acc}(\tilde{A}) - \text{Chance}(\tilde{A})}{\text{R.Acc}(\tilde{A}) - \text{Chance}(\tilde{A})} \times 100\% \tag{7.4}$$

where $\text{R.Acc}(\tilde{A})$ and $\text{Chance}(\tilde{A})$ are the means of the R-split and Chance-level accuracies over $A \setminus \tilde{A}$. Note that N.Acc is 100% if the E-split performance is at the level of R-split and 0% if it is at chance level.

Results. The normalised accuracies for R-split and multiple E-splits are presented in Table 7.3. We consider three axes of choices of splitting attributes for the E-split: architecture (#conv and #fc), optimisation (alg and bs), and data (size). For example, "E-#conv-#fc" row presents results when metamodel is

Table 7.3. Normalised accuracies (see text) of `kennen-o` and `kennen-io` on R and E splits. We denote E-split with splitting attributes *attr1* and *attr2* as "E-*attr1*-*attr2*". Splitting criteria are also shown. When there are two splitting attributes, the first attribute inherits the previous row criteria.

Split	Train	Test	kennen-	
			o	io
R	-	-	100	100
E-#conv	2, 3	4	87.5	92.0
E-#conv-#fc	2, 3	4	77.1	80.7
E-alg	SGD, ADAM	RMSprop	83.0	88.5
E-alg-bs	64, 128	256	64.2	70.0
E-split	Quarter$_{0/1}$	Quarter$_{2/3}$	83.5	89.3
E-size	Quarter	Half,All	81.7	86.8
Chance	-	-	0.0	0.0

trained on shallower nets (2 or 3 conv/fc layers each) compared to the test black box model (4 conv and fc layers each).

Not surprisingly, E-split performances are lower than R-split ones (N.Acc < 100%); it is advisable to cover all the expected black-box attributes during meta-training. Nonetheless, E-split performances of `kennen-io` are still far above the chance level (N.Acc $\geq$ 70% $\gg$ 0%); failing to cover a few attributes during meta-training is not too damaging.

Comparing `kennen-o` and `kennen-io` for their generalisability, we observe that `kennen-io` consistently outperforms `kennen-o` under severe extrapolation (around 5 pp better N.Acc). It is left as a future work to investigate the intriguing fact that utilising out-of-domain query inputs improves the generalisation of metamodel.

7.5.3   Why and How Does Metamodel Work?

It is surprising that metamodels can extract inner details with great precision and generalisability. This section provides a glimpse of *why* and *how* this is possible via metamodel input and output analyses. Full answers to those questions is beyond the scope of the paper.

Metamodel Input (t-SNE). We analyse the inputs to our metamodels (i.e. fingerprints from black-box models) to convince ourselves that the inputs do contain discriminative features for model attributes. As the input is high dimensional (1000 when the number of queries is $n = 100$), we use the t-SNE [18] visualisation method. Roughly speaking, t-SNE embeds high dimensional data points onto the 2-dimensional plane such that the pairwise distances are best respected. We then colour-code the embedded data points according to the model attributes. Clusters of same-coloured points indicate highly discriminative features.

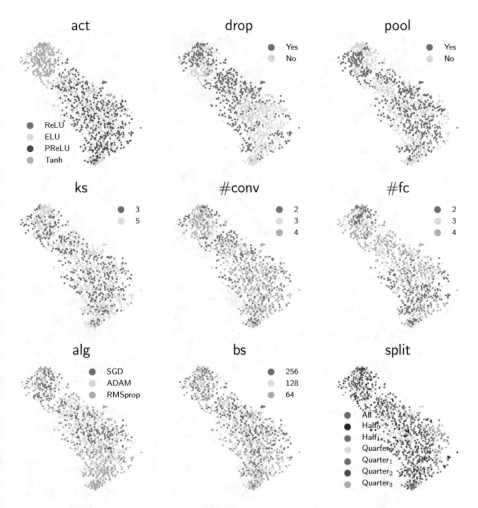

Fig. 7.5. Probability query output (fingerprint) embedded into 2-D plane via t-SNE. The same embedding is shown with different colour-coding for each attribute. These are the inputs to the kennen-io metamodel.

The visualisation of input data points are shown in Fig. 7.5 for kennen-io. For experimental details. We observe that some attributes form clear clusters in the input space – e.g. Tanh in act, binary dropout attribute, RMSprop in alg, max-pooling, and kernel size. For the other attributes, however, it seems that the clusters are too complicated to be represented in a 2-dimensional space.

Metamodel Output (Confusion Matrix). We show confusion matrices of kennen-io to analyse the failure modes. See Fig. 7.6. We observe that the confusion occurs more frequently with similar classes. For attributes #conv and #fc, more confusion occurs between $(2,3)$ or $(3,4)$ than between $(2,4)$. A similar

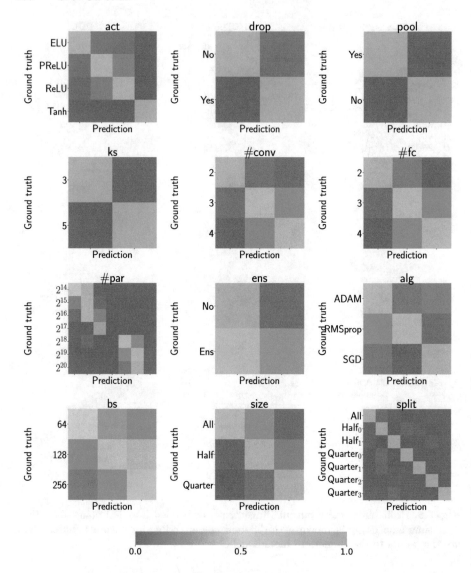

Fig. 7.6. Confusion matrices for `kennen-io`.

trend is observed for #par and bs. This is a strong indication that (1) there exists semantic attribute information in the neural network outputs (e.g. number of layers, parameters, or size of training batch) and (2) the metamodels learn semantic information that can generalise, as opposed to merely relying on artifacts. This observation agrees with a conclusion of the extrapolation experiments in Sect. 7.5.2: the metamodels generalise.

7.5.4   Discussion

We have verified through our novel `kennen` metamodels that black-box access to a neural network exposes much internal information. We have shown that only 100 single-label outputs already reveal a great deal about a black box. When the black-box classifier is quite different from the meta-training classifiers, the performance of our best metamodel – `kennen-io` – decreases; however, the prediction accuracy for black box internal information is still surprisingly high.

While still surprising, a crucial underlying assumption is that the model attributes of the black boxes are taken from a pre-defined list of attributes (closed world assumption). For more practical attacks, future researches shall consider applying open-world recognition methods, such as prediction uncertainties or out-of-distribution detector, to be able to tell whether a black-box model has one of the attributes already known to the attacker or not.

7.6   Reverse-Engineering and Attacking ImageNet Classifiers

While MNIST experiments are computationally cheap and a massive number of controlled experiments is possible, we provide additional ImageNet experiments for practical implications on realistic image classifiers. In this section, we use `kennen-o` introduced in Sect. 7.4 to predict a single attribute of black-box ImageNet classifiers – the architecture family (e.g. ResNet or VGG?). In this section, we go a step further to use the extracted information to attack black boxes with adversarial examples.

7.6.1   Dataset of ImageNet Classifiers

It is computationally prohibitive to train $O(10k)$ ImageNet classifiers from scratch as in the previous section. We have resorted to 19 PyTorch[3] pretrained ImageNet classifiers. The 19 classifiers come from five families: **S**queezenet, **V**GG, **V**GG-**B**atchNorm, **R**esNet, and **D**enseNet, each with 2, 4, 4, 5, and 4 variants, respectively [8,10–12,30]. We observe both large intra-family diversity and small inter-family separability in terms of #layers, #parameters, and performances. The family prediction task is not as trivial as e.g. simply inferring the performance.

7.6.2   Classifier Family Prediction

We predict the classifier family (S, V, B, R, D) from the black-box query output (fingerprint), using the method `kennen-o`, with the same MLP architecture (Sect. 7.4). `kennen-i` and `kennen-io` have not been used for computational reasons, but can also be used in principle. We conduct 10 cross validations (random

---

[3] https://github.com/pytorch.

sampling of single test network from each family) for evaluation. We also perform 10 random sampling of the queries from ImageNet validation set. In total 100 random tries are averaged.

Results: compared to the random chance (20.0%), 100 queries result in high kennen-o performance (90.4%). With 1,000 queries, the prediction performance is even 94.8%.

7.6.3   Attacking ImageNet Classifiers

In this section we attack ImageNet classifiers with adversarial image perturbations (AIPs). We show that the knowledge about the black box architecture family makes the attack more effective.

Adversarial Image Perturbation (AIP). AIPs are carefully crafted additive perturbations on the input image for the purpose of misleading the target model to predict wrong labels [6]. Among variants of AIPs, we use efficient and robust GAMAN [24].

Table 7.4. Transferability of adversarial examples within and across families. We report *misclassification rates*.

AIP generation	Target model family				
	SqueezeNet	VGG	VGG-BN	ResNet	DenseNet
Clean input	38	32	28	30	29
SqueezeNet	64	49	45	39	35
VGG	62	96	96	57	52
VGG-BN	50	85	95	47	44
ResNet	64	72	78	87	77
DenseNet	58	63	70	76	90
Ensenble	70	93	93	75	80

Transferability of AIPs. Typical AIP algorithms require gradients from the target network, which is not available for a black box. Mainly three approaches for generating AIPs against black boxes have been proposed: (1) numerical gradient, (2) avatar network, or (3) transferability. We show that our metamodel strengthens the transferability based attack.

We hypothesize and empirically show that AIPs transfer better within the architecture family than across. Using this property, we will show in later sections that first predicting the family of the black box (e.g. ResNet), and then generate AIPs against a few instances in the family (e.g. ResNet101, ResNet152) improves the attack success rates.

We first verify our hypothesis that AIPs transfer better within a family. Within-family: we do a leave-one-out cross validation – generate AIPs using all but one instances of the family and test on the holdout. Not using the exact test black box, this gives a lower bound on the within-family performance. Across-family: still leave out one random instance from the generating family to match the generating set size with the within-family cases. We also include the use-all case (Ens): generate AIPs with one network from *each* family.

See Table 7.4 for the results. We report the *misclassification rate*, defined as 100−top-1 accuracy, on 100 random ImageNet validation images. We observe that the within-family performances dominate the across-family ones (diagonal entries versus the others in each row); if the target black box family is identified, one can generate more effective AIPs. Finally, trying to target all network ("Ens") is not as effective as focusing resources (diagonal entries).

Metamodel Enables More Effective Attacks. We empirically show that the reverse-engineering enables more effective attacks. We consider multiple scenarios. "White box" means the target model is fully known, and the AIP is generated specifically for this model. "Black box" means the exact target is unknown, but we make a distinction when the family is known ("Family black box").

Table 7.5. Black-box ImageNet classifier misclassification rates (MC) for different approaches.

Scenario	Generating nets	MC (%)
White box	Single white box	100.0
Family black box	GT family	86.2
Black box whitened	**Predicted family**	**85.7**
Black box	Multiple families	82.2

See Table 7.5 for the misclassification rates (MC) in different scenarios. When the target is fully specified (white box), MC is 100%. When neither the exact target nor the family is known, AIPs are generated against multiple families (82.2%). When the reverse-engineering takes place (i.e. the black box model is "whitened" to a certain degree), and AIPs are generated over the predicted family, attacks become more effective (85.7%). We almost reach the family-oracle case (86.2%).

7.6.4 Discussion

Our metamodel can predict architecture families for ImageNet classifiers with high accuracy. We additionally show that this reverse-engineering enables more focused attack on black-boxes.

7.7   Stronger Adversary with Game Theoretic Guarantees

In the previous section we have described how one can narrow down the candidate space for the target black-box neural network by exposing its hyperparameters (e.g. architecture family). This information has been used to improve the adversarial image perturbations (AIP). In practice, however, it may be hard to narrow down the target to the single correct model by sequentially applying kennen without mistake. At certain point, adversary needs to deal with remaining uncertainty.

In the current section, we describe a technique for the adversary that, given a set of candidate target models, provides a particular way to combine attacks against each candidate model. The suggested combination comes with a guarantee on the attack success rate. The technique is based on game theoretic principles that determine the optimal worst-case attack strategy that yields a lower bound on the attack success rate. The two players in this game are (1) the attacker A who wants to find the hyperparameters of the black box and (2) the "attacked" M who can choose the black-box model. This technique, for example, can be used in conjunction with kennen as follows: kennen narrows down the candidate space to the VGG family, {VGG-11,VGG-13,VGG-16,VGG-19}, and our game theoretic tool further determines a strategy to attain the worst-case guarantee for the attacker A against any particular choice of the VGG instance by M.

The technique allows adversary to deal with remaining uncertainty on the target black box after applying kennen. The adversary as a result obtains guarantees on attack success rates without full specification of the target black box. This section further emphasises the security implications of diagnosing access-limited models. This section is based on the conference paper [24].

7.7.1   Game Theory

We provide a background on game theory. It is a tool for obtaining utility guarantee given an opponent whose action is hard to predict with confidence. We are interested in the optimal worst-case strategy against the opponent: the utility one can obtain regardless of the opponent's action. We study a special instance of game theory, namely the **two-player zero-sum game** [22].

We consider a two-player zero-sum game between the adversary A and the model M. We assume a fictitious model chooser M picking a neural network model j from a set of candidate models Θ. Adversary A makes a guess on the target model $i \in \Theta$. Each choice is made without knowledge on the opponent's strategy. As a result of picking strategies, a payoff p_{ij} occurs for A and $-p_{ij}$ for M, satisfying the zero-sum requirement. In our case, p is the chance of fooling the target model.

We allow **mixed (random) strategy** for each player: $\theta^A = (\theta_i^A)_{i \in \Theta}$ and $\theta^M = (\theta_j^M)_{j \in \Theta}$ defined as a distribution over candidate models Θ. With abuse of notation we write $p(\theta^A, \theta^M) := \sum_{i,j} \theta_i^A \theta_j^M p_{ij}$ for the expected payoff for A when the mixed strategies θ^A and θ^M are taken.

Theorem 1 (von Neumann [22], 1928). *For a finite constant-sum game, there exist **optimal** or **minimax** mixed strategies $\theta^{A\star}$ and $\theta^{M\star}$ such that*

$$p(\theta^{A\star}, \theta^M) \le p(\theta^{A\star}, \theta^{M\star}) \le p(\theta^A, \theta^{M\star}) \quad \forall \theta^A, \theta^M \qquad (7.5)$$

*where $v := p(\theta^{A\star}, \theta^{M\star})$ is the **value of the game.***

Equation 7.5 implies that when A plays $\theta^{A\star}$, A is guaranteed to have a payoff of at least v, regardless of M's strategy.

A's optimal strategies can be obtained efficiently via linear programming that solves the following:

$$\arg\max_{\theta^A} \min_{\theta^M} \sum_{i,j} \theta_i^A \theta_j^M p_{ij} \quad \text{s.t.} \quad \theta^A, \theta^M \text{ are distributions.} \qquad (7.6)$$

The resulting optimal AIP combination $\theta^{A\star}$ is the recommended recipe for the adversary to mix different version prepared for each candidate model $j \in \Theta$ that is guaranteed to provide the optimal worst-case utility of $v = p(\theta^{A\star}, \theta^{M\star})$.

7.7.2 Case Study

We have prepared a theoretical background for obtaining adversary's utility (attack success rate) guarantees even when the target model is not fully specified. Here, we provide some case studies to demonstrate the technique in practice. We study a case from prior work on adversarial image perturbations (AIPs), where the candidate set for the target model has been shortlisted to a few models Θ. In each case, we obtain a guarantee on the attack success rate (value of the game) v regardless of the actual model chosen from the candidate set Θ.

Table 7.6. Payoff table for attacker A, using Generative Adversarial Perturbations against each possible model $j \in \Theta$. Shown numbers are fooling rates, or the payoff for A.

Attack $\in \Theta$	Actual target model $\in \Theta$		
	VGG16	VGG19	ResNet152
VGG16	93.9	89.6	52.2
VGG19	88.0	94.9	49.0
ResNet152	31.9	30.6	79.5

We consider the case where the target model is narrowed down to the set $\Theta = \{\text{VGG16, VGG19, ResNet152}\}$. The attacker uses *Generative Adversarial Perturbations* [27] against each possible target model - the resulting attack success rates (payoff p_{ij}) for 3×3 cases are shown in Table 7.6 (taken from Table 7.4 of [27]).

Optimal Deterministic Strategy. We can regard Table 7.6 as the payoff Table p_{ij} for the adversary A with strategies $i, j \in \Theta$. Let's first assume that the players only choose fixed strategies (no stochastic mixture). Then, solving Eq. 7.6 with determinism constraints $\theta_i^A, \theta_j^M \in \{0, 1\}$ yields A's optimal strategy as *AIP against VGG16* with the attack success rate guarantee of at least 52.2%.

Optimal Random Strategy. Game theory suggests that it is sometimes better to randomise strategies. Solving Eq. 7.6 without the integral constraints yield the optimal solutions for A as $\theta^{A\star} = $ (VGG16: 56.7%, ResNet152: 43.3%). Playing $\theta^{A\star}$ guarantees A to allow at least 64.0% attack success rate on average, an improved guarantee than the deterministic case, 52.2%.

Knowledge on M's Strategy. Increasing knowledge on M's strategy, or equivalently narrowing down the candidate target space Θ, can improve the payoff bound for A. Let us consider, for example, that A can safely rule out ResNet152 from the candidate space. Assuming that it is not the actual model, the new optimal solution for A is $\Theta^{A\star} = $ (VGG16: 61.6%, VGG19: 38.4%) with an improved utility lower bound of 91.6%. It benefits to reduce the number of candidates, whenever possible.

7.7.3 Discussion

kennen methods can narrow down the possibilities for target model, only requiring black-box access. After reducing the possibilities to a few models (Θ), game theory can resolve the remaining uncertainty by suggesting the adversary to hedge bets on multiple models to obtain the optimal worst-case strategy. Improved attack rates highlight further dangers of leaking model internals.

7.8 Conclusion

Many deployed ML models only allow for query access (sequence of inputs and corresponding outputs). Our novel metamodel methods, kennen, can successfully predict attributes related not only to the architecture but also to training hyperparameters (optimisation algorithm and dataset) even in difficult scenarios (e.g. single-label output, or a distribution gap between the meta-training models and the target black box). Being able to diagnose such models and expose internal details can lead to security breaches by means of more targetted adversarial attacks. We have shown that the adversary can attack with further utility guarantees by applying game theoretic principles. The work sheds lights on the relationship between diagnosing a model with restricted access and model security.

References

1. Ateniese, G., Mancini, L.V., Spognardi, A., Villani, A., Vitali, D., Felici, G.: Hacking smart machines with smarter ones: how to extract meaningful data from machine learning classifiers. Int. J. Secur. Netw. **10**(3), 137–150 (2015)
2. Caruana, R., Lou, Y., Gehrke, J., Koch, P., Sturm, M., Elhadad, N.: Intelligible models for healthcare: predicting pneumonia risk and hospital 30-day readmission. In: Proceedings of the 21th ACM SIGKDD International Conference on Knowledge Discovery and Data Mining, pp. 1721–1730. ACM (2015)
3. Chen, P.Y., Zhang, H., Sharma, Y., Yi, J., Hsieh, C.J.: Zoo: Zeroth order optimization based black-box attacks to deep neural networks without training substitute models. In: Proceedings of the 10th ACM Workshop on Artificial Intelligence and Security, pp. 15–26. ACM, New York (2017)
4. Dabkowski, P., Gal, Y.: Real time image saliency for black box classifiers. In: Advances in Neural Information Processing Systems, pp. 6967–6976 (2017)
5. Fong, R.C., Vedaldi, A.: Interpretable explanations of black boxes by meaningful perturbation. In: 2017 IEEE International Conference on Computer Vision (ICCV), pp. 3449–3457. IEEE (2017)
6. Goodfellow, I.J., Shlens, J., Szegedy, C.: Explaining and harnessing adversarial examples. In: International Conference on Learning Representations (2015)
7. Hayes, J., Danezis, G.: Machine learning as an adversarial service: learning black-box adversarial examples. CoRR abs/1708.05207 (2017)
8. He, K., Zhang, X., Ren, S., Sun, J.: Deep residual learning for image recognition. In: 2016 IEEE Conference on Computer Vision and Pattern Recognition (CVPR), pp. 770–778 (2016)
9. Hendricks, L.A., Akata, Z., Rohrbach, M., Donahue, J., Schiele, B., Darrell, T.: Generating visual explanations. In: Leibe, B., Matas, J., Sebe, N., Welling, M. (eds.) ECCV 2016. LNCS, vol. 9908, pp. 3–19. Springer, Cham (2016). https://doi.org/10.1007/978-3-319-46493-0_1
10. Huang, G., Liu, Z., Van Der Maaten, L., Weinberger, K.Q.: Densely connected convolutional networks. In: Proceedings of the IEEE Conference on Computer Vision and Pattern Recognition, pp. 4700–4708 (2017)
11. Iandola, F.N., Moskewicz, M.W., Ashraf, K., Han, S., Dally, W.J., Keutzer, K.: SqueezeNet: AlexNet-level accuracy with 50x fewer parameters and <1mb model size. CoRR abs/1602.07360 (2017)
12. Ioffe, S., Szegedy, C.: Batch normalization: accelerating deep network training by reducing internal covariate shift. In: Bach, F., Blei, D. (eds.) Proceedings of the 32nd International Conference on Machine Learning. Proceedings of Machine Learning Research, vol. 37, pp. 448–456. PMLR, Lille (2015). http://proceedings.mlr.press/v37/ioffe15.html
13. Kamruzzaman, S.M., Islam, M.M.: An algorithm to extract rules from artificial neural networks for medical diagnosis problems. CoRR abs/1009.4566 (2010)
14. LeCun, Y., Bottou, L., Bengio, Y., Haffner, P.: Gradient-based learning applied to document recognition. Proc. IEEE **86**, 2278–2324 (1998)
15. Letham, B., Rudin, C., McCormick, T.H., Madigan, D., et al.: Interpretable classifiers using rules and bayesian analysis: building a better stroke prediction model. Ann. Appl. Stat. **9**(3), 1350–1371 (2015)
16. Lipton, Z.C.: The mythos of model interpretability. Queue **16**(3), 30:31–30:57 (2018)

17. Liu, Y., Chen, X., Liu, C., Song, D.: Delving into transferable adversarial examples and black-box attacks. In: International Conference on Learning Representations (2017)
18. van der Maaten, L., Hinton, G.: Visualizing high-dimensional data using t-SNE. J. Mach. Learn. Res. **9**, 2579–2605 (2008)
19. Mahendran, A., Vedaldi, A.: Understanding deep image representations by inverting them. In: Proceedings of the IEEE Conference on Computer Vision and Pattern Recognition, pp. 5188–5196 (2015)
20. Moosavi-Dezfooli, S.M., Fawzi, A., Fawzi, O., Frossard, P.: Universal adversarial perturbations. In: Proceedings of the IEEE Conference on Computer Vision and Pattern Recognition, pp. 1765–1773 (2017)
21. Narodytska, N., Kasiviswanathan, S.P.: Simple black-box adversarial perturbations for deep networks. CoRR abs/1612.06299 (2017)
22. Neumann, J.: Zur Theorie der Gesellschaftsspiele. Math. Ann. **100**, 295–320 (1928). http://eudml.org/doc/159291
23. Oh, S.J., Augustin, M., Schiele, B., Fritz, M.: Towards reverse-engineering black-box neural networks. In: International Conference on Learning Representations (ICLR) (2018)
24. Oh, S.J., Fritz, M., Schiele, B.: Adversarial image perturbation for privacy protection a game theory perspective. In: 2017 IEEE International Conference on Computer Vision (ICCV), pp. 1491–1500. IEEE (2017)
25. Papernot, N., McDaniel, P., Goodfellow, I.: Transferability in machine learning: from phenomena to black-box attacks using adversarial samples. CoRR abs/1605.07277 (2016)
26. Papernot, N., McDaniel, P., Goodfellow, I., Jha, S., Celik, Z.B., Swami, A.: Practical black-box attacks against machine learning. In: Proceedings of the 2017 ACM on Asia Conference on Computer and Communications Security, pp. 506–519. ACM (2017)
27. Poursaeed, O., Katsman, I., Gao, B., Belongie, S.: Generative adversarial perturbations. In: Proceedings of the IEEE Conference on Computer Vision and Pattern Recognition, pp. 4422–4431 (2018)
28. Ribeiro, M.T., Singh, S., Guestrin, C.: Why should I trust you?: Explaining the predictions of any classifier. In: Proceedings of the 22nd ACM SIGKDD International Conference on Knowledge Discovery and Data Mining, pp. 1135–1144. ACM (2016)
29. Shokri, R., Stronati, M., Song, C., Shmatikov, V.: Membership inference attacks against machine learning models. In: 2017 IEEE Symposium on Security and Privacy (SP), pp. 3–18. IEEE (2017)
30. Simonyan, K., Zisserman, A.: Very deep convolutional networks for large-scale image recognition. In: International Conference on Learning Representations (2015)
31. Simonyan, K., Vedaldi, A., Zisserman, A.: Deep inside convolutional networks: visualising image classification models and saliency maps. CoRR abs/1312.6034 (2013)
32. Szegedy, C., et al.: Intriguing properties of neural networks. In: International Conference on Learning Representations (2014)
33. Tramèr, F., Zhang, F., Juels, A., Reiter, M.K., Ristenpart, T.: Stealing machine learning models via prediction APIs. In: 25th {USENIX} Security Symposium ({USENIX} Security 16), pp. 601–618 (2016)
34. Yosinski, J., Clune, J., Nguyen, A.M., Fuchs, T.J., Lipson, H.: Understanding neural networks through deep visualization. CoRR abs/1506.06579 (2015)

Part III
Explaining the Decisions of AI Systems

Explaining the Decisions
of AI Systems – Preface

Among all aspects of XAI that have been studied, a problem that has received particular attention is how to identify input features that have contributed to a given prediction or that are locally relevant for that prediction. Answering this question is important as it allows a human to verify that the decision behavior is based on plausible features rather than spurious correlations or artifacts. Large datasets collected from heterogeneous sources have made machine learning models and other data-driven approaches at high risk of picking the wrong features to support their decisions and effectively becoming "Clever Hans" predictors [5].

A large number of proposals have emerged on how to best explain the decisions of AI models in terms of input features. The following chapters give a sense of the variety of methods that are available, as well as their respective advantages and limitations.

In Chapter 8, Fong and Vedaldi [4] present a technique called "Meaningful Perturbation" which synthesizes a minimal local perturbation of the current data point that maximally affects the ML model decision. Variables that form the perturbation are then deemed relevant for the decision. While synthesis can be computationally expensive, it confers high flexibility in shaping the perturbation, allowing to finely control certain properties of an explanation such as sparsity.

In Chapter 9, Ancona et al. [1] survey a number of Gradient-Based techniques, where the explanation derives from extracting the components of the gradient of the decision function. These techniques can rely on the automatic differentiation mechanism available in most recent neural network libraries. This makes them applicable out-of-the-box to complex and varied architectures. The chapter presents some theoretical justifications for these techniques and draws connections to other classes of explanation techniques such as those based on propagation [3, 8].

In Chapter 10, Montavon et al. [6] present "Layer-Wise Relevance Propagation (LRP)", a technique that explains deep neural networks by propagating the decision backward in the neural network by means of purposely designed propagation rules. The chapter illustrates the dependence of the resulting explanation on the choice of the propagation rule at each layer. It then stresses the need to carefully adapt these rules to the neural network architecture at hand and provides best practices. An appropriate choice of propagation rules yields explanations that have the desired quality and that can be computed quickly.

In Chapter 11, Arras et al. [2] study how the LRP technique presented in Chapter 10 can be extended to another class of machine learning models, LSTMs, a popular deep learning model used for prediction of data that has temporal structure. Following the observation that propagation-based explanation techniques need to be carefully adapted to the given architecture, special propagation rules are consequently designed to handle the special gating and cumulative functions of the LSTM models. Furthermore, this chapter shows how the LSTM model can be simplified to facilitate explanation.

Altogether, these four chapters give an overview of explanation methods with different computational, qualitative, and applicative characteristics. For example, synthesis and gradient-based methods apply effortlessly, but this comes either at the price of a higher computational cost, or explanation stability [7]. Propagation-based methods run cheaply and produce stable explanations, but need to be carefully adapted to the neural network of interest. Furthermore, the obvious differences encountered between explanations produced by various methods will motivate the need for an objective assessment of explanation quality, which we will take on in Part IV of the book.

July 2019

Wojciech Samek
Grégoire Montavon
Andrea Vedaldi
Lars Kai Hansen
Klaus-Robert Müller

References

1. Ancona, M., Ceolini, E., Öztireli, C., Gross, M.: Gradient-based attribution methods. In: Samek, W., Montavon, G., Vedaldi, A., Hansen, L.K., Müller, K.-R. (eds.) Explainable AI: Interpreting, Explaining and Visualizing Deep Learning. LNCS, vol. 11700, pp. 169–191. Springer, Cham (2019)

2. Arras, L., et al.: Explaining and interpreting LSTMs. In: Samek, W., Montavon, G., Vedaldi, A., Hansen, L.K., Müller, K.-R. (eds.) Explainable AI: Interpreting, Explaining and Visualizing Deep Learning. LNCS, vol. 11700, pp. 211–238. Springer, Cham (2019)

3. Bach, S., Binder, A., Montavon, G., Klauschen, F., Müller, K.-R., Samek, W.: On pixel-wise explanations for non-linear classifier decisions by layer-wise relevance propagation. PLoS ONE **10**(7), e0130–140 (2015)

4. Fong, R., Vedaldi, A.: Explanations for attributing deep neural network predictions. In: Samek, W., Montavon, G., Vedaldi, A., Hansen, L.K., Müller, K.-R. (eds.) Explainable AI: Interpreting, Explaining and Visualizing Deep Learning. LNCS, vol. 11700, pp. 149–167. Springer, Cham (2019)

5. Lapuschkin, S., Wäldchen, S., Binder, A., Montavon, G., Samek, W., Müller, K.-R.: Unmasking clever hans predictors and assessing what machines really learn. Nat. Commun. **10**, 1096 (2019)

6. Montavon, G., Binder, A., Lapuschkin, S., Samek, W., Müller, K.-R.: Layer-wise relevance propagation: An overview. In: Samek, W., Montavon, G., Vedaldi, A., Hansen, L.K., Müller, K.-R. (eds.) Explainable AI: Interpreting, Explaining and Visualizing Deep Learning. LNCS, vol. 11700, pp. 193–209. Springer, Cham (2019)

7. Montavon, G., Samek, W., Müller, K.-R.: Methods for interpreting and understanding deep neural networks. Digital Signal Process. **73**, 1–15 (2018)

8. Shrikumar, A., Greenside, P., Kundaje, A.: Learning important features through propagating activation differences. In: Proceedings of the 34th International Conference on Machine Learning. pp. 3145–3153 (2017)

8
Explanations for Attributing Deep Neural Network Predictions

Ruth Fong$^{(\boxtimes)}$ⓘ and Andrea Vedaldiⓘ

University of Oxford, Oxford, UK
{ruthfong,vedaldi}@robots.ox.ac.uk

Abstract. Given the recent success of deep neural networks and their applications to more high impact and high risk applications, like autonomous driving and healthcare decision-making, there is a great need for *faithful* and *interpretable explanations* of "why" an algorithm is making a certain prediction. In this chapter, we introduce 1. Meta-Predictors as Explanations, a principled framework for learning explanations for any black box algorithm, and 2. Meaningful Perturbations, an instantiation of our paradigm applied to the problem of attribution, which is concerned with attributing what features of an input (i.e., regions of an input image) are responsible for a model's output (i.e., a CNN classifier's object class prediction). We first introduced these contributions in [8]. We also briefly survey existing visual attribution methods and highlight how they faith to be both *faithful* and *interpretable*.

Keywords: Explainable artificial intelligence · Computer vision · Machine learning

8.1 Introduction

What is a good explanation? At the minimum, it should be *faithful* and *interpretable*. A faithful explanation is an accurate characterization of a model's behavior, while an interpretable one is easy to understand by a human expert. The weights and architecture of a CNN provide a perfectly accurate explanation of its behavior but is uninterpretable by the human mind. Thus, there has been major research efforts to produce *interpretable* explanations of CNN behavior. However, an interpretable visualization that does not accurately describe CNN behavior is equally problematic, especially when being used to determine whether the model's prediction is trustworthy.

But, what does it mean to *faithfully* explain a model? Consider function f, i.e., a CNN object classifier. Two kinds of explanations answer the questions: 1. *what* has f learned to do, and 2. *how* does it do it? The "what" question is concerned with the *external* properties of the function (i.e., is it invariant to X?) while the "how" question is concerned with the *internal* workings of the function

© Springer Nature Switzerland AG 2019
W. Samek et al. (Eds.): Explainable AI, LNAI 11700, pp. 149–167, 2019.
https://doi.org/10.1007/978-3-030-28954-6_8

(i.e., how do hidden units process information to achieve invariance?) that enable it to possess certain qualities. We focus on answering the "what" question and propose that it can be answered by interpretable *rules* that characterize the input-output relationship of a model. For instance, the rule that "$f(x) = f(x')$ for all images x, x' that are related by a rotation" would characterize whether f is rotationally invariant. Such explanatory rules make *predictions* on the outcome of the black box f. Finding explanations can therefore be formulated as the problem of learning *meta-predictors* that predict the behavior of a model.

In this chapter, we first introduce our framework of using meta-predictors as explanations, building off [29]. We then focus on *local explanations* and reformulate *visual attribution maps* within this framework. A local explanation aims to clarify *why* a black box makes a certain prediction based on local features (i.e., pixels). Since f is a black box, we answer this question by observing its behaviour to *meaningful changes in the input*. For example, we can consider images x obtained from x_0 by *deleting* a subregion R from it. Depending on whether $f(x) = f(x_0)$, we can find out if R contains useful information for f. By finding all such regions, we can plot a visual attribution map of the image that identifies "what" is relevant to the black box f. We identify several issues, such as network vulnerability to adversarial artifacts, that likely constrained previous perturbation-based methods [20, 30] which only work in limited settings and introduce technical solutions to these problems. Finally, we demonstrate that our meaningful perturbations method provide more interpretable and faithful explanations compared to other techniques [22, 24, 26, 30, 31].

8.2   Meta-predictors as Explanations: A Framework

In this section, we develop a formal framework of explanations as *learnable meta-predictors* that predict the input-output behavior of a black box function f in certain conditions.

Preliminaries. Let $f : \mathcal{X} \to \mathcal{Y}$ be the black box function we are interested in explaining. To make our discussion more concrete, we will consider the space of object classifiers that operate on an input space of natural, color images, i.e., $\mathcal{X} \subset \mathcal{I} = \mathbb{R}^{H \times W \times 3}$. The output space could be a boolean, i.e., $y \in \mathcal{Y} = \{-1, +1\}$ in the case of a binary classifier that computes whether an image contains a certain kind of object (i.e., a robin), or a continuous vector, i.e., $y \in \mathcal{Y} \subset [0, 1]^C$ in the case of a multi-class classifier that computes the probability of the C object classes each being present in the image.

8.2.1   Global Explanations

In this sub-section, we consider *global* explanations that explain the global properties of a model such as geometric invariances.

Example 1 (classification). Suppose we have a binary classifier $f : \mathcal{I} \to \{-1, +1\}$ that determines the present of an unknown object class, and we would like to explain what object it detects. After using it a while, we suspect that it is some sort of bird classifier and hypothesize that it's a "robin" classifier.

A rule that describes this explanation of f is as follows:

$$Q_1(x; f) = \{x \in \mathcal{X}_c \Leftrightarrow f(x) = +1\} \tag{8.1}$$

where $\mathcal{X}_c \subset \mathcal{X}$, where $\mathcal{X}_c$ is the subset of all images containing object $c =$ "robin". Q_1 is a boolean-valued predicate function; it evaluates to "true" when specified properties hold and otherwise evaluates to "false". Now, we can quantify the faithfulness of an explanation Q_1 as its expected prediction error, that is, as its performance as a *meta-predictor*:

$$\mathcal{L}_1 = \mathbb{E}_{x \in \mathcal{X}}[1 - \delta_{Q_1(x;f)}] \tag{8.2}$$

where δ_Q is the indicator function of predicate Q_1[1]. In this case, the simple, hand-crafted predicate rule Q_1 is being tested as a meta-predictor directly (i.e., there is no additional meta-predictor being learned).

Learning Explanations. Machine learning algorithms can be used to *discover explanations* automatically, by finding explanatory predicates Q that apply to a certain classifier f out of a large pool of possible rules $\mathcal{Q}$, i.e., Q_1 rules for different bird species in Example 1.

    In particular, finding the *most faithful* explanation Q is similar to a traditional learning problem and can be formulated computationally as a *regularized empirical risk minimization* such as:

$$\min_{Q \in \mathcal{Q}} \lambda \mathcal{R}(Q) + \frac{1}{n} \sum_{i=1}^{n} \mathcal{L}(Q, x_i, f), \; x_i \sim p(x). \tag{8.3}$$

where $\mathcal{L}$ is a generalization of Eq. (8.2) for any predicate Q. Here, the regularizer $\mathcal{R}(Q)$ has two goals: to allow the explanation Q to generalize beyond the n samples $x_1, \ldots, x_n$ considered in the optimization and to pick an explanation Q which is simple and thus, hopefully, more interpretable.

Example 2 (rotational invariance). Now, suppose we wanted to explain to what extent a binary object classifier f was rotationally invariant. Then, we could use a rule of the following form:

$$Q_2(x, x'; f, \theta) = \{x \sim_\theta x' \Rightarrow f(x) = f(x')\} \tag{8.4}$$

where $x \sim_\theta x'$ means that x and x' are related by a rotation of an angle $\leq \theta$. Explanations for larger angles imply the ones for smaller ones, with $\theta = 0$ being trivially satisfied, and this rule is interpretable because the relation $\sim_\theta$ is.

---

[1] Note that Q_1 implicitly requires a distribution $p(x)$ over possible images $\mathcal{X}$.

Like Example 1, we can quantify the faithfulness of this explanation as follows[2]:

$$\mathcal{L}_2 = \mathbb{E}[1 - \delta_{Q_2(x,x';f,\theta)}|x \sim_\theta x'] \tag{8.5}$$

Following Eq. (8.3), we can use the following regularizer to learn the maximal angle for which f is rotationally invariant[3]:

$$\mathcal{R}(Q_2(\cdot;\theta)) = -\theta \tag{8.6}$$

Lastly, previous works [14,30] on quantifying invariances (i.e., scale, translation, rotation) in CNNs fit within our framework. For instance, [30]'s experiment of measuring how object class probabilities change when 5 sample images are rotated $\theta \in [0,360]$ degrees (Figure 5d (col c) in [30]) can be thought of as plotting the continuous form of $\mathcal{L}_2$ for each of those images.

8.2.2   Local Explanations

Explanations can be rather diverse. For example, Q_1 is an absolute statement on the value of f at a point x, whereas Q_2 is a relative statement on the value of f at two different points x and x'. Both are quantified by using a 0–1 loss, but, as exemplified later, rules can make continuous predictions, for which regression losses (e.g., squared error) are appropriate. Both Q_1 and Q_2 are global explanations, as points x are sampled without restriction; in this section, we look at local explanations instead.

A *local explanation* is a rule $Q(x; f, x_0)$ that predicts the response of f in a neighborhood of a certain point x_0. If f is smooth at x_0, it is natural to construct Q by using the first-order Taylor expansion of f:

$$Q(x; f, x_0) = \{f(x) \approx f(x_0) + \langle \nabla f(x_0), x - x_0 \rangle\} \tag{8.7}$$

where x is in a neighborhood of x_0. This formulation provides an interpretation of [24]'s gradient-based attribution map, which visualizes the gradient $M_1(x_0) = \nabla f(x_0)$ as an indication of salient image regions. They argue that large values of the gradient identify pixels that strongly affect the network output. However, an issue is that this interpretation *breaks for a linear classifier*: If $f(x) = \langle w, x \rangle + b$, $S_1(x_0) = \nabla f(x_0) = w$ is independent of the image x_0 and hence cannot be interpreted as proper attribution.

The reason for this failure is that Eq. (8.7) studies the variation of f for arbitrary displacements $\Delta_x = x - x_0$ from x_0 and, for a linear classifier, the

---

[2] For rotation invariance we condition on $x \sim_\theta x'$ because the probability of independently sampling rotated x and x' is zero, so that, without conditioning, Q_2 would be true with probability 1.

[3] Naively, strict invariance for any $\theta > 0$ implies invariance to arbitrary rotations as small rotations compose into larger ones. However, the formulation can still be used to describe rotation insensitivity (when f varies slowly with rotation), or $\sim_\theta$'s meaning can be changed to indicate rotation w.r.t. a canonical "upright" direction for a certain object classes, etc.

| Soup Bowl | Gradient | Stethoscope | Gradient |

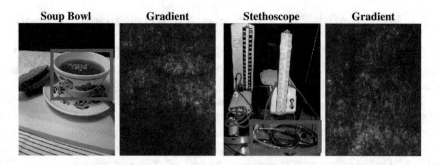

Fig. 8.1. Gradient attribution maps of [24]. A red bounding box highlight the object which is meant to be recognized in the image. Note the strong response in apparently non-relevant image regions.

change is the same regardless of the starting point x_0. For a non-linear black box f such as a neural network, this problem is reduced but not eliminated, and can explain why the attribution map M_1 is rather diffuse, with strong responses even where no obvious information can be found in the image (Fig. 8.1).

We argue that the meaning of explanations depends in large part on the *meaning of varying the input x to the black box*. For example, explanations in Sect. 8.2.1 are based on allowing x vary in image category or in rotation. For attribution, one is interested in finding image regions that impact f's output. Thus, it is natural to consider perturbations x obtained by deleting subregions of x_0. If we model deletion by multiplying x_0 point-wise by a mask m, this amounts to studying the function $f(x_0 \odot m)^4$. The Taylor expansion of f at $m = (1, 1, \ldots, 1)$ is $M_2(x_0) = df(x_0 \odot m)/dm|_{m=(1,\ldots,1)} = \nabla f(x_0) \odot x_0$. For a linear classifier f, this results in the attribution map $M_2(x_0) = w \odot x_0$, which is large for pixels for which x_0 and w are large simultaneously.

Finally, note that both attribution methods M_1 and M_2 can be obtained as the approximate solutions of a learning problem such as Eq. (8.3), both using the loss $\mathcal{L} = (f(x) - Q(x))^2$ where the explanation rule is a linear predictor $Q(x) = \langle v, x - x_0 \rangle + f(x_0)$. The difference is that in M_1 one samples $x \sim \mathcal{N}(x_0, \sigma^2 I)$ as a (small) isotropic Gaussian centered on x_0, whereas in M_2 as $x = x_0 \odot m$ where one samples the mask $m \sim \mathcal{N}((1, \ldots, 1), \sigma^2 I)$ instead.

Other works have also discussed the limitations of using the gradient for attribution [2,17]. [17] provides a similar explanation to the one we present in this section, that is, that the gradient does not provide an explanation of evaluating function f for a specific example x and output class y (i.e., attribution specific to an example and to a target output class) but rather the slope of function f (i.e., weights w in a linear classifier). [2] highlights the limitation of [24]'s gradient visualization in practice, which takes the absolute value of the maximum gradient across input color channels, thereby eliminating knowledge of positive versus negative evidence.

---

[4] $\odot$ is the Hadamard or element-wise product of vectors.

8.3   Meaningful Perturbations: An Attribution Method

In this section, we apply the meta-predictors as explanation framework developed in Sect. 8.2 to the case, briefly considered in Sect. 8.2.2, of learning visual attribution maps for CNNs.

In order to define an explanatory rule for a black box $f(x)$, one must start by specifying which variations of the input x will be used to study f. The aim of attribution is to identify which regions of an image x_0 are used by the black box to produce the output value $f(x_0)$. We can do so by observing how the value of $f(x)$ changes as x is obtained "deleting" different regions R of x_0. For example, if $f(x_0) = +1$ denotes a "robin" image, we expect that $f(x) = +1$ as well unless the choice of R deletes the "robin" from the image. Given that x is a perturbation of x_0, this is a local explanation (Sect. 8.2.2) and we expect the explanation to characterize the relationship between f and x_0.

While conceptually simple, there are several problems with this idea. The first one is to specify what it means to "delete" information. As discussed in detail in Sect. 8.3.3, we are generally interested in simulating naturalistic or plausible imaging effect, leading to more meaningful perturbations and hence explanations.

8.3.1   Perturbation Types

Since we do not have access to the image generation process, we consider three obvious proxies: replacing the region R with a constant value, injecting noise, and blurring the image (Fig. 8.2).

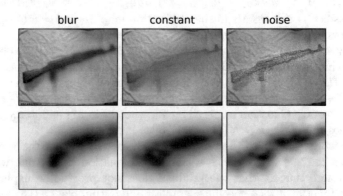

Fig. 8.2. Perturbation types. Bottom: perturbation mask; top: effect of blur, constant, and noise perturbations.

Formally, let $m : \Lambda \to [0,1]$ be a *mask*, associating each pixel $u \in \Lambda$ with a scalar value $m(u)$. Then the perturbation operator is defined as

$$[\Phi(x_0; m)](u) = \begin{cases} m(u)x_0(u) + (1 - m(u))\mu_0, & \text{constant,} \\ m(u)x_0(u) + (1 - m(u))\eta(u), & \text{noise,} \\ \int g_{\sigma_0 m(u)}(v - u)x_0(v)\, dv, & \text{blur,} \end{cases}$$

where μ_0 is an average color, $\eta(u)$ are i.i.d. Gaussian noise samples for each pixel and σ_0 is the maximum isotropic standard deviation of the Gaussian blur kernel g_σ (we use $\sigma_0 = 10$, which yields a significantly blurred image).

8.3.2 Deletion and Preservation

Given an image x_0, our goal is to summarize compactly the effect of deleting image regions in order to explain the behavior of the black box. One approach to this problem is to find deletion regions that are maximally informative.

In order to simplify the discussion, in the rest of the paper we consider black boxes $f(x) \in \mathbb{R}^C$ that generate a vector of scores for different hypotheses about the content of the image (e.g., as a softmax probability layer in a neural network). Then, we consider a "deletion game" where the goal is to find the smallest deletion mask m that causes the score $f_c(\Phi(x_0; m)) \ll f_c(x_0)$ to drop significantly, where c is the target class. Finding m can be formulated as the following learning problem:

$$m^* = \operatorname*{argmin}_{m \in [0,1]^\Lambda} \lambda \|\mathbf{1} - m\|_1 + f_c(\Phi(x_0; m)) \tag{8.8}$$

where λ encourages most of the mask to be turned off (hence deleting a small subset of x_0). In this manner, we can find a highly informative region for the network.

One can also play an symmetric "preservation game", where the goal is to find the smallest subset of the image that must be retained to preserve the score $f_c(\Phi(x_0; m)) \geq f_c(x_0)$: $m^* = \operatorname{argmin}_m \lambda \|m\|_1 - f_c(\Phi(x_0; m))$. The main difference is that the deletion game removes enough evidence to prevent the network from recognizing the object in the image, whereas the preservation game finds a minimal subset of sufficient evidence.

Iterated Gradients. Both optimization problems are solved by using a local search by means of gradient descent methods. In this manner, our method extracts information from the black box f by computing its gradient, similar to the approach of [24]. However, it differs in that it extracts this information progressively, over several gradient evaluations, accumulating increasingly more information over time.

8.3.3 Dealing with Artifacts

When using the simple objective in Eq. (8.8), we notice that the optimization procedure learns subtly structured masks with highly unnatural artifacts. This is not too unexpected, given that neural networks, in particular, are known to be affected by such artifacts. For example, [13] show that a nearly-invisible adversarial perturbation of an image can lead a neural network to classify an object for another; [18] construct abstract synthetic images that are classified arbitrarily; and [15] find deconstructed versions of an image which are indistinguishable from the viewpoint of the neural network from the original image. This is not entirely surprising since neural networks are trained discriminatively on natural image statistics.

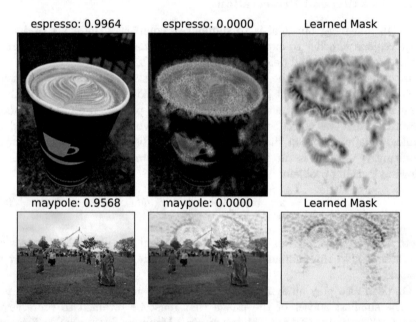

Fig. 8.3. From left to right: an image correctly classified with large confidence by GoogLeNet [28]; a perturbed image that is not recognized correctly anymore; the deletion mask learned with artifacts. Top: A mask learned by minimizing the top five predicted classes by jointly applying the constant, random noise, and blur perturbations. Note that the mask learns to add highly structured swirls along the rim of the cup ($\gamma = 1, \lambda_1 = 10^{-5}, \lambda_2 = 10^{-3}, \beta = 3$). Bottom: A minimizing-top5 mask learned by applying a constant perturbation. Notice that the mask learns to introduce sharp, unnatural artifacts in the sky instead of deleting the pole ($\gamma = 0.1, \lambda_1 = 10^{-4}, \lambda_2 = 10^{-2}, \beta = 3$).

Although the existence and characterization of artifacts is an interesting problem *per se*, we wish to describe the behavior of black boxes under normal operating conditions. Thus, we first identified the sources of artifacts and then propose technical solutions to eliminate them.

Artifacts from the Choice of Perturbation. We noticed that using the blur perturbation was more naturalistic, as perturbing with random noise or an average color allowed the optimization procedure to leverage sharp color-contrasting border artifacts (Fig. 8.3, bottom row).

Artifacts from the Preservation Game. When optimizing for the preservation game, if the network finds little positive evidence for a given class (i.e., a difficult image that yields a low softmax score for its ground truth class), the optimization procedure can yield artifacts that "draw" in parts of an ideal example of target class to maximize its output score. In contrast, the deletion game is more natural: there is usually some positive evidence for the ground truth class that can be "deleted" from an image. If there is no positive evidence for a class (i.e., explaining the network's prediction for a randomly selected class), then the optimization procedure learns that nothing needs to be deleted.

Sharp, Pixel-Level Artifacts. The sharp, pixel-level artifacts learned are highly unnatural, as natural perturbations (i.e., a partially occluded object) are typically smooth (i.e., another object). As noted before, the meaning of an explanation depends on the meaning of the changes applied to the input x; to obtain a mask more representative of natural perturbations we can encourage it to have a simple, regular structure which cannot be co-adapted to such artifacts. We do so by regularizing m with a total-variation (TV) norm to encourage spatial smoothness and upsampling it from a low resolution version to discourage unnatural, pixel-level artifacts. Lastly, a powerful explanation should, just like any predictor, generalize as much as possible. For the deletion game, this means not relying on the details of a singly-learned mask m. Thus, we reformulate the problem to apply the mask m stochastically, up to a small amount of random jitter.

Improved Objective. With these three modifications, Eq. (8.8) becomes:

$$\min_{m \in [0,1]^\Lambda} \lambda_1 \|1 - m\|_1 + \lambda_2 \sum_{u \in \Lambda} \|\nabla m(u)\|_\beta^\beta + \mathbb{E}_\tau[f_c(\Phi(x_0(\cdot - \tau), m))], \quad (8.9)$$

where $M(v) = \sum_u g_{\sigma_m}(v/s - u)m(u)$. is the upsampled mask and g_{σ_m} is a 2D Gaussian kernel. Equation (8.9) can be optimized using stochastic gradient descent.

Implementation Details. Unless otherwise specified, the visualizations shown were generated with Caffe [10] using Adam [11] to minimize (i.e., delete) GoogLeNet's [28] softmax probability of the target class by using the blur perturbation with the following parameters: learning rate $\gamma = 0.1, N = 300$ iterations, $\lambda_1 = 10^{-4}, \lambda_2 = 10^{-2}, \beta = 3$, upsampling a mask ($28 \times 28$ for GoogLeNet) by a factor of $\delta = 8$, blurring the upsampled mask with $g_{\sigma_m=5}$, and jittering the mask by drawing an integer from the discrete uniform distribution on $[0, \tau)$ where $\tau = 4$. Because the optimization is highly non-convex and a few images with large dominant objects had troubling yielding convergent meaningful deletory masks, we initialize the mask as the smallest centered circular mask that suppresses the score of the original image by 99% when compared to that of the fully perturbed image, i.e. a fully blurred image.[5]

8.4   Related Work

8.4.1   Survey of Attribution Methods

Since the renassiance of CNNs [12], numerous attribution methods have been introduced to visualize parts of an input image are responsible for a CNN's prediction, and they fall roughly into four categories based on the information used for visualizations:

1. gradients (Gradient [24], DeConvNet [30], Guided Backprop [16,26], SmoothGrad [25])
2. activations (CAM [33] and DeepLift [23])
3. combination of gradients and activations (LRP [4], Excitation Backprop [31], and Grad-CAM [22])
4. perturbations to inputs and/or activations (Occlusion [30], LIME [20] and Feedback [5])

The first three kinds of techniques are *propagation-based* methods, that is, they only require the propagation of one forward and/or backward pass through the CNN to generate an attribution visualization. In contrast, *perturbation-based* methods are mostly iterative, optimization-based approaches that require multiple passes through a network.

Gradient-Based Methods. Arguably the first attribution method for CNNs, [24] visualized $\frac{dy_k}{dx}$, the gradient of the input image x with respect to a target class y_k (a.k.a., the backpropagated error signal through the CNN), with some post-processing[6]. Because [24]'s gradient method produced noisy visualizations (Fig. 8.1), subsequent methods were developed to produce sharper attribution heatmaps by thresholding the backpropagated signal in different ways(DeConvNet [30] and Guided Backprop [16,26]) or averaging the gradient signal for an input with noise added to it (SmoothGrad [25]).

Activation- and Combination-Based Methods. In contrast to backprogation-based visualizations, Class Activation Mapping (CAM) [33] visualizes a CNN by linearly combining activation maps at the penultimate layer with the last layer's fully-connected weights corresponding to a target class. CAM is limited however by its architectural constraint that the penultimate layer be a global

---

[5] Our source code is available at https://github.com/ruthcfong/perturb_explanations.
[6] [24]'s method visualized the gradient's maximum magnitude across color channels at each pixel location, i.e., $\max_{c \in C} \lVert \frac{dy_k}{dx_{i,j}} \rVert$, where C is the set of color channels.

average pooling (GAP) layer. Grad-CAM [22] relaxes this constraint by weighting the activation maps at given layer by the gradient backpropagated to a that layer. Like DeConvNet [30] and Guided Backprop [26], Layer-Wise Relevance Propagation (LRP) [4] and Excitation Backprop [31] modify backpropagation rules such that a back-propagated signal is weighted by convolution layers' activations and weights. Many propagation-based techniques require architectural or backprop rule modifications [16, 26, 30, 33] and/or access to intermediate layers [4, 22, 31, 33]. The main disadvantage of some of these techniques is their lack of self-interpretability. In contrast to propagation-based methods, perturbation-based approaches are grounded in naturally, self-interpretable edit operations in the input space. Thus, when a image region is highlighted by a perturbation-based methods, it has a easily interpretable meaning, that is, that editing that region in the actual input will have a significant effect on the model's prediction. [1, 16] also demonstrate that several propagation-based attribution methods generate visualizations that are not specific to the target class [16] or even the model weights themselves [1]. They do this by showing that visualizations for randomly selected classes and for models with random weights are very visually similar to those for the top predicted class and for trained models.

Perturbation-Based Methods. A few techniques sought to visualize attribution with perturbations to the input image and/or activations. Occlusion [30] did this by visualizing the change in feature activation magnitude and/or classification score when a fixed-size, gray-color occluding square was slid over an image. RISE [19] extends occlusions by using upsampled, random binary masks to occlude and visualizing the linear combination of their occlusion masks with the target class' classification score. [32] introduced a greedy method of graying out segments of an image until it was misclassified. [5]'s feedback networks relates to our method's preservative version in that they learned to mask all post-ReLU activations to maximize a network's class score. However, our masks are directly interpretable as they are linked to a real edit to an input image, whereas their masks are not. Lastly, [20] is closest to our method, but theirs operates on fixed, super-pixels that are flipped to gray and takes much longer to converge ($N = 5000$ vs. our $N = 300$). Thus, while several perturbation-based methods exist, ours is uniquely unconstrained and allows for the effect of the joint inclusion and exclusion of variable-sized image regions to be considered.

8.4.2   Formalizing and Evaluating Attribution Methods

Other works have formalized axioms for the quality of explanations in other ways. [21] defines the quality of an explanation by its sensitivity to region-specific perturbations and introduce an evaluation metric to capture that quality. Given an attribution heatmap, a list of pixels ordered by importance is retrieved. This ordered list is then used in a greedy, iterative procedure to perturb regions of most to least importance. The effects of these iterative perturbations are plotted against the number of perturbations used. Other works have used similar perturbation-based evaluation metrics [2, 3, 19]. [17] proposes that an explanation should be continuous in nature, that is, if two data points are nearly equivalent, then their explanations should also be nearly equivalent. [27] suggests two principles: The first "sensitivity" axiom they suggest is that every feature for which a difference in input results in a difference in output should have a non-zero attribution. The second "implementation invariance" axiom is that networks that are functionally equivalent (i.e., produce the identical outputs for all inputs, despite implementation differences) should yield identical explanations.

8.5   Faithfulness and Interpretability of Meaningful Perturbations

In this section, we discuss and demonstrate how our attribution technique is both faithful to the model being explained and interpretable to humans in comparison to other attribution methods.

8.5.1   Testability

An advantage of the proposed framework is that the generated visualizations have a clear, interpretable meaning: the deletion game produces a minimal mask that prevents the network from recognizing the object.

When compared to other techniques (Fig. 8.4), this method can pinpoint the reason why a certain object is recognized without highlighting non-essential evidence. This can be noted in Fig. 8.4 for the CD player (row 7) where other visualizations also emphasize the neighboring speakers, and similarly for the cliff (row 3), the street sign (row 4), and the sunglasses (row 8). Sometimes this shows that only a part of an object is essential: the face of the Pekenese dog (row 2), the upper half of the truck (row 6), and the spoon on the chocolate sauce plate (row 1) are all found to be minimally sufficient parts.

While contrastive excitation backprop generated heatmaps were most similar to our masks, our method introduces a quantitative criterion (i.e., maximally suppressing a target class score), and its verifiable nature (i.e., direct edits to an image) allows us to compare differing proposed saliency explanations and demonstrate that our learned masks are better on this metric. In Fig. 8.5, row 2, we show that applying a bounded perturbation informed by our learned mask significantly suppresses the truck softmax score, whereas a boxed perturbation on the truck's back bumper, which is highlighted by contrastive excitation backprop in Fig. 8.4, row 6, actually increases the score from 0.717 to 0.850.

The principled interpretability of our method also allows us to identify instances when an algorithm may have learned the wrong association. In the case of the chocolate sauce in Fig. 8.5, row 1, it is surprising that the spoon is highlighted by our learned mask, as one might expect the sauce-filled jar to be more salient. However, manually perturbing the image reveals that indeed the spoon is more suppressive than the jar. One explanation is that the ImageNet "chocolate sauce" images contain more spoons than jars, which appears to be

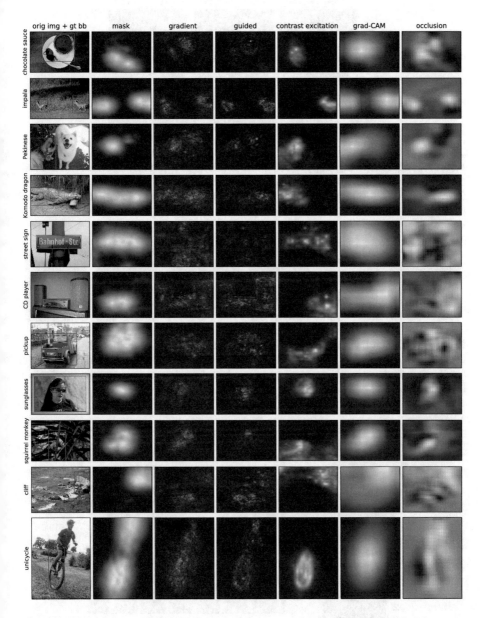

Fig. 8.4. Comparison with other saliency methods. From left to right: original image with ground truth bounding box, learned mask subtracted from 1 (our method), gradient-based saliency [24], guided backprop [16,26], contrastive excitation backprop [31], Grad-CAM [22], and occlusion [30].

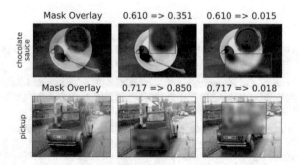

Fig. 8.5. Interrogating suppressive effects. Left to right: original image with mask overlaid; a boxed perturbation of interest (truck's middle box chosen based on [31] from Fig. 8.4); another perturbation based on mask (softmax scores of original and perturbed images listed above).

Fig. 8.6. Selectivity to Output Neuron. In contrast to other methods like Guided Grad-CAM [22] (right), our method (left) is selective to the output neuron, as its attribution maps on random neurons and random directions across neurons are distinct from that on the maximum neuron.

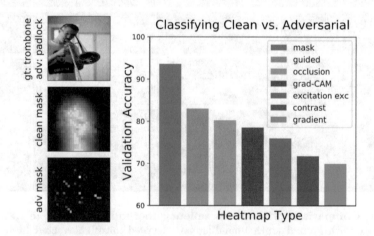

Fig. 8.7. Adversarial defense. (Left) Difference between mask for clean (middle) and adversarial (bottom) images (28×28 masks shown). (Right) Classification accuracy for discriminating between clean vs. adversarial images using heatmap visualizations ($N_{trn} = 4000, N_{val} = 1000$).

true upon examining some images. More generally, our method allows us to diagnose highly-predictive yet non-intuitive and possibly misleading correlations in the data that are identified and exploited by machine learning algorithms.

8.5.2 Selectivity to Output Neuron

The work of [16] shows that the gradient [24], DeConvNet [30], and Guided Backprop [26] methods were not at all selective for the output neuron, that is, they yielded similar visualizations regardless of the output class being explained. For visual attribution, this is quite troubling. In Fig. 8.6, we demonstrate that our method by design does not suffer from this problem[7].

8.5.3 Attribution Map Compactness

In this experiment, we compare our method with other visual attribution methods on the task of correctly identifying a *minimal* region that sufficiently suppresses the target object class score. Given an attribution map, we normalize its intensities to lie in the range $[0, 1]$, threshold it with $h \in [0 : 0.1 : 1]$, and fit the tightest bounding box around the resulting heatmap. We then blur the image in the box and compute the normalized[8] target softmax probability from GoogLeNet [28] of the partially blurred image.

From these bounding boxes and normalized scores, for a given amount of score suppression, we find the smallest bounding box that achieves that amount of suppression. Figure 8.8 shows that, on average, our method yields the smallest minimal bounding boxes when considering suppressive effects of $80\%, 90\%, 95\%$, and 99%. These results show that our method finds a small salient area that strongly impacts the network. While these results are unsurprising, as we regularize for sparsity and smoothness with the L1 and TV norm regularizing terms in Eq. (8.9), it confirms that these regularizing terms properly translate to relatively compact masks.

8.6 Application to Adversarial Defense

In this section, we discuss a novel application of attribution masks for defending against adversarial examples. We show that our method is clearly superior in its ability to defend against certain classes of adversarial attacks. For more applications of our method, like investing hypotheses in data science and weakly supervised localization, please see [8].

Adversarial examples [13] are often generated using a similar, complementary optimization procedure to our method that learns a imperceptible pattern of

---

[7] These experiments were conducted on AlexNet using PyTorch implementations of our method (https://github.com/ruthcfong/pytorch-explain-black-box) and Grad-CAM (https://github.com/ruthcfong/pytorch-grad-cam) respectively.

[8] $p' = \dfrac{p - p_0}{p_0 - p_b}$, where p, p_0, p_b are the masked, original, and fully blurred images' scores.

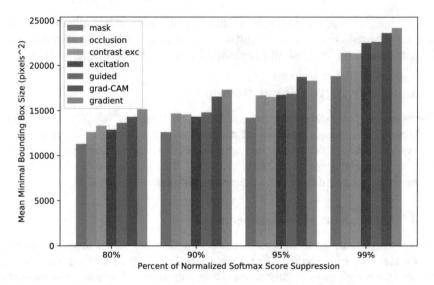

Fig. 8.8. On average, our method generates the smallest bounding boxes that, when used to blur the original images, highly suppress their normalized softmax probabilities (standard error included).

noise which causes an image to be misclassified when added to it. Using our re-implementation of the highly effective one-step iterative method ($\epsilon = 8$) [13] to generate adversarial examples, our method yielded visually distinct, abnormal masks compared to those produced on natural images (Fig. 8.7, left). We train an Alexnet [12] classifier (learning rate $\lambda_{lr} = 10^{-2}$, weight decay $\lambda_{L1} = 10^{-4}$, and momentum $\gamma = 0.9$) to distinguish between clean and adversarial images by using a given heatmap visualization with respect to the top predicted class on the clean and adversarial images (Fig. 8.7, right); our method greatly outperforms the other methods and achieves a discriminating accuracy of 93.6%.

Lastly, when our learned masks are applied back to their corresponding adversarial images, they not only minimize the adversarial label but often allow the original, predicted label from the clean image to rise back as the top predicted class. Our method recovers the original label predicted on the clean image 40.64% of time and the ground truth label 37.32% ($N = 5000$). Moreover, 100% of the time the original, predicted label was recovered as one of top-5 predicted labels in the "mask+adversarial" setting. To our knowledge, this is the first work that is able to recover originally predicted labels without any modification to the training set-up and/or network architecture. These finding paves a new research path of further investigating and re-tooling attribution maps for adversarial defense.

8.7   Discussion and Conclusion

In this chapter, we have proposed a comprehensive, formal framework for learning explanations as meta-predictors. We also present a novel image saliency paradigm that learns *where* an algorithm *looks* by discovering which parts of an image most affect its output score when perturbed. Unlike many previous visual attribution techniques, our method explicitly edits to the image, making it interpretable and testable. We demonstrated numerous applications of our method, such as comparing the suppressive effect of different methods (Figs. 8.5, 8.8) and defending against adversarial examples (Fig. 8.7). Finally, we contributed new insights into the fragility of neural networks and their susceptibility to artifacts, which opens a future research opportunity to adaptively augment networks to make them robust against undesirable artifacts.

Evaluating Attribution Methods. Previous works [19, 31] have evaluated attribution methods via weakly-supervised localization tasks. They do this by extracting bounding boxes and/or maximal points from attribution heatmaps. While these evaluation metrics provide some helpful information, we argue that using these tasks as the sole criterion for evaluating attribution methods is problematic because they do not properly test for attribution (i.e., what does the model 'believe' is responsible for its prediction). If the model has learned an incorrect association (i.e., spoons are responsible for "chocolate sauce" in Fig. 8.5), then we would expect a good attribution method to perform poorly in localization and/or pointing for the affected examples as the model did not learn to properly attribute[9]. Instead, we suggest a few such metrics based on minimal deletion (also known as smallest destroying region [SDR] in [6]) and selectivity to output neuron and network weights (as highlighted as problems in [1, 16]). Additionally, we argue that testability is a valuable property for any attribution method and encourage further research on verifiable attribution techniques like ours.

Future Directions. While we focused our attention on the problem of attribution, our meaningful perturbations method can easily be extended to perturb and explain intermediate activations either along the spatial dimensions or the channel dimensions or both (our subsequent work [7] can be viewed in this light, as we perturb feature channels). Others have also built on our work, demonstrating that our method generalizes to other machine learning domains such as explaining reinforcement learning policies for Atari game play [9] and that it can be sped up by training a mask predictor using learned masks via our method as ground truth [6].

References

1. Adebayo, J., Gilmer, J., Muelly, M., Goodfellow, I., Hardt, M., Kim, B.: Sanity checks for saliency maps. In: NeurIPS, pp. 9525–9536 (2018)
2. Ancona, M., Ceolini, E., Öztireli, C., Gross, M.: Towards better understanding of gradient-based attribution methods for deep neural networks. In: ICLR (2018)

---

[9] For completeness, we tested our method on these metrics; our results can be found in [8].

3. Arras, L., Horn, F., Montavon, G., Müller, K.R., Samek, W.: "What is relevant in a text document?": an interpretable machine learning approach. PLoS ONE **12**(8), e0181142 (2017)
4. Bach, S., Binder, A., Montavon, G., Klauschen, F., Müller, K.R., Samek, W.: On pixel-wise explanations for non-linear classifier decisions by layer-wise relevance propagation. PLoS ONE **10**(7), e0130140 (2015)
5. Cao, C., et al.: Look and think twice: capturing top-down visual attention with feedback convolutional neural networks. In: ICCV, pp. 2956–2964 (2015)
6. Dabkowski, P., Gal, Y.: Real time image saliency for black box classifiers. In: NIPS, pp. 6967–6976 (2017)
7. Fong, R., Vedaldi, A.: Net2vec: quantifying and explaining how concepts are encoded by filters in deep neural networks. In: CVPR, pp. 8730–8738 (2018)
8. Fong, R.C., Vedaldi, A.: Interpretable explanations of black boxes by meaningful perturbation. In: ICCV, pp. 3429–3437 (2017)
9. Greydanus, S., Koul, A., Dodge, J., Fern, A.: Visualizing and understanding atari agents. arXiv preprint arXiv:1711.00138 (2017)
10. Jia, Y., et al.: Caffe: Convolutional architecture for fast feature embedding. arXiv preprint arXiv:1408.5093 (2014)
11. Kingma, D., Ba, J.: Adam: A method for stochastic optimization. arXiv preprint arXiv:1412.6980 (2014)
12. Krizhevsky, A., Sutskever, I., Hinton, G.E.: Imagenet classification with deep convolutional neural networks. In: NIPS, pp. 1097–1105 (2012)
13. Kurakin, A., Goodfellow, I., Bengio, S.: Adversarial examples in the physical world. arXiv preprint arXiv:1607.02533 (2016)
14. Lenc, K., Vedaldi, A.: Understanding image representations by measuring their equivariance and equivalence. In: CVPR, pp. 991–999 (2015)
15. Mahendran, A., Vedaldi, A.: Understanding deep image representations by inverting them. In: CVPR, pp. 5188–5196 (2015)
16. Mahendran, A., Vedaldi, A.: Salient deconvolutional networks. In: Leibe, B., Matas, J., Sebe, N., Welling, M. (eds.) ECCV 2016. LNCS, vol. 9910, pp. 120–135. Springer, Cham (2016). https://doi.org/10.1007/978-3-319-46466-4_8
17. Montavon, G., Samek, W., Müller, K.R.: Methods for interpreting and understanding deep neural networks. Digital Sig. Process. **73**, 1–15 (2018)
18. Nguyen, A., Yosinski, J., Clune, J.: Deep neural networks are easily fooled: high confidence predictions for unrecognizable images. In: CVPR, pp. 427–436 (2015)
19. Petsiuk, V., Das, A., Saenko, K.: Rise: randomized input sampling for explanation of black-box models. In: BMVC (2018)
20. Ribeiro, M.T., Singh, S., Guestrin, C.: Why should I trust you?: explaining the predictions of any classifier. In: Proceedings of the 22nd ACM SIGKDD International Conference on Knowledge Discovery and Data Mining, pp. 1135–1144. ACM (2016)
21. Samek, W., Binder, A., Montavon, G., Lapuschkin, S., Müller, K.R.: Evaluating the visualization of what a deep neural network has learned. IEEE Trans. Neural Netw. Learn. Syst. **28**(11), 2660–2673 (2017)
22. Selvaraju, R.R., Das, A., Vedantam, R., Cogswell, M., Parikh, D., Batra, D.: Gradcam: Why did you say that? visual explanations from deep networks via gradient-based localization. arXiv preprint arXiv:1610.02391 (2016)
23. Shrikumar, A., Greenside, P., Kundaje, A.: Learning important features through propagating activation differences. arXiv preprint arXiv:1704.02685 (2017)
24. Simonyan, K., Vedaldi, A., Zisserman, A.: Deep inside convolutional networks: visualising image classification models and saliency maps. In: ICLR (2014)

25. Smilkov, D., Thorat, N., Kim, B., Viégas, F., Wattenberg, M.: Smoothgrad: removing noise by adding noise. arXiv preprint arxiv:1706.03825 (2017)
26. Springenberg, J.T., Dosovitskiy, A., Brox, T., Riedmiller, M.: Striving for simplicity: the all convolutional net. arXiv preprint arXiv:1412.6806 (2014)
27. Sundararajan, M., Taly, A., Yan, Q.: Axiomatic attribution for deep networks. In: ICML, pp. 3319–3328 (2017)
28. Szegedy, C., et al.: Going deeper with convolutions. In: CVPR, pp. 1–9 (2015)
29. Turner, R.: A model explanation system. In: IEEE MLSP, pp. 1–6 (2016)
30. Zeiler, M.D., Fergus, R.: Visualizing and understanding convolutional networks. In: Fleet, D., Pajdla, T., Schiele, B., Tuytelaars, T. (eds.) ECCV 2014. LNCS, vol. 8689, pp. 818–833. Springer, Cham (2014). https://doi.org/10.1007/978-3-319-10590-1_53
31. Zhang, J., Lin, Z., Brandt, J., Shen, X., Sclaroff, S.: Top-down neural attention by excitation backprop. In: Leibe, B., Matas, J., Sebe, N., Welling, M. (eds.) ECCV 2016. LNCS, vol. 9908, pp. 543–559. Springer, Cham (2016). https://doi.org/10.1007/978-3-319-46493-0_33
32. Zhou, B., Khosla, A., Lapedriza, A., Oliva, A., Torralba, A.: Object detectors emerge in deep scene CNNs. arXiv preprint arXiv:1412.6856 (2014)
33. Zhou, B., Khosla, A., Lapedriza, A., Oliva, A., Torralba, A.: Learning deep features for discriminative localization. In: CVPR, pp. 2921–2929 (2016)

9
Gradient-Based Attribution Methods

Marco Ancona[1(✉)], Enea Ceolini[1,2], Cengiz Öztireli[1], and Markus Gross[1]

[1] ETH Zürich, 8092 Zürich, Switzerland
{anconam,cengizo,grossm}@inf.ethz.ch
[2] University of Zürich, 8006 Zürich, Switzerland
eceoli@ini.uzh.ch

Abstract. The problem of explaining complex machine learning models, including Deep Neural Networks, has gained increasing attention over the last few years. While several methods have been proposed to explain network predictions, the definition itself of explanation is still debated. Moreover, only a few attempts to compare explanation methods from a theoretical perspective has been done. In this chapter, we discuss the theoretical properties of several attribution methods and show how they share the same idea of using the gradient information as a descriptive factor for the functioning of a model. Finally, we discuss the strengths and limitations of these methods and compare them with available alternatives.

Keywords: Attribution methods · Deep Neural Networks · Explainable artificial intelligence

9.1 Introduction

Machine Learning has demonstrated huge potential in solving a variety of problems, mostly thanks to numerous ground-breaking results with Deep Neural Networks (DNNs) [12,14,17,29,36]. As learning-based algorithms are deployed into everyday life products, explaining their predictions becomes of crucial importance, not only to ensure reliability and robustness, but also to make sure the prediction is fair and not discriminating. While machine learning models power an increasing number of applications, the black-box nature of DNNs has become a barrier to the adoption of these systems in those fields where interpretability is crucial. Whether machine learning is employed in medical prognosis, controlling a self-driving car or assessing the risk of committing new crimes, the decisions taken have a deep impact on the life of the people involved and precise guarantees need to be enforced. European regulations are rather strict in this sense, as they introduce the legal notion of a *right to explanation* [10], de facto banning the use of non-explainable machine learning models on some domains.

Interpretability in machine learning can be achieved in different ways. The first approach is to use models that are *inherently interpretable*, like linear models. Although this is the most immediate solution, these models often trade

© Springer Nature Switzerland AG 2019
W. Samek et al. (Eds.): Explainable AI, LNAI 11700, pp. 169–191, 2019.
https://doi.org/10.1007/978-3-030-28954-6_9

interpretability for limited predictive power. A second approach is to design models able to generate predictions and explanations, either in textual or visual form, at the same time. Training this kind of models is very challenging as they require ground-truth explanations to train on. What is more, as the explanation generator is itself a trained model, the problem of evaluating fairness and accuracy is only being transferred from the operational model to the explanation model. Finally, one can build explanation methods on top of existing models. Potentially, this allows generating explanations for any existing black-box model without the need for retraining and without sacrificing the performances of the best models.

Another important dimension to consider is the *scope* of interpretability methods. *Global interpretability* is about understanding how the overall model makes decisions, which input patterns are captured and how these are transformed to produce the output [6]. Global interpretability is very useful to detect biases that might cause unfair or discriminating behavior of the model, but it is arguably very hard to achieve as the number of interacting parameters grows. For this reason, several works on interpretability of DNN models focus on explaining the reasons for a specific decision instead. This is commonly referred to as *local interpretability* [6, 15] as the model behavior is only explained for a single, specific instance. This type of explanation is useful to justify model predictions on a case by case basis, e.g. why a loan application was rejected.

In the remainder of this chapter, we focus on *attribution methods* for DNNs. As they are built on top of existing models, attribution methods belong to the last of the three explainability approaches discussed above. They aim at explaining decisions for existing neural network architectures that would be not explainable otherwise. Moreover, they operate in the scope of *local interpretability*, as they produce explanations specifically for a given model and input instance.

Several attribution methods have been developed specifically for neural networks [4, 18, 25, 27, 30, 32, 33, 37, 38]. However, the lack of a ground-truth explanation makes it very challenging to evaluate these methods quantitatively, while qualitative evaluations have been shown to be insufficient or biased [2, 8, 20]. With the proliferation of attribution methods, we believe a better understanding of their properties, assumptions and limitations becomes necessary.

We analyze some recently proposed attribution methods from a theoretical perspective and discuss connections between them. We show how the gradient with respect to the input features of a neural network is the fundamental piece of information used by several attribution methods to build explanations and we discuss the limitations of this approach.

The content of the chapter is mostly based on the results and considerations of a previous work [3], reorganized to gradually introduce the non-expert reader into the topic of attribution methods for DNNs. In Sect. 9.2, we formally define attribution methods, show how the gradient is used to generate attributions in a simple linear model and discuss some desirable properties of these methods. In Sect. 9.3, we move from linear models to DNNs, showing how the gradient information can be adapted to explain non-linear models. In Sect. 9.4, we discuss strengths, limitations and alternatives to gradient-based methods. Lastly, Sect. 9.5 presents some final considerations.

9.2   Attribution Methods

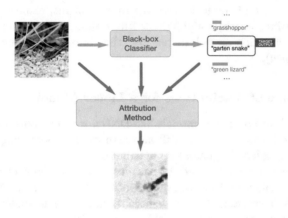

Fig. 9.1. General setting for attribution methods. An attribution map is generated for a specific input, model and target output.

Consider a model that takes an N-dimensional input $x = [x_1, ..., x_N] \in \mathbb{R}^N$ and produces a C-dimensional output $S(x) = [S_1(x), ..., S_C(x)] \in \mathbb{R}^C$. The model could be, for example, a DNN where C is the total number of output neurons. Depending on the application, the input features $x_1, ..., x_N$ can have different nature. For example, in image classification, x is usually a picture and each feature in x is a pixel in the picture. In the case of speech recognition, each feature might be the signal spectral power for a particular time and frequency bin. In the case of natural language processing, each feature is usually a multi-dimensional vector representation of each word in a sentence. Similarly, each output of the network can represent either a numerical predicted quantity (regression task) or the probability of a corresponding class (classification task).

Given their potentially large number, it is desirable to know which of the network input features have a greater impact on the predicted output, as well as the direction of their influence. Even though this is a simplistic notion of explanation, compared to the human notion which usually involves the formulation in textual form, it has been proved nevertheless useful to understand the reasons behind some network (mis)predictions [22].

Formally, attribution methods aim at producing explanations by assigning a scalar *attribution* value, sometimes also called "relevance" or "contribution", to each input feature of a network for a given input sample.

Given a single target output unit c, the goal of an attribution method is to determine the contribution $R^c = [R_1^c, ..., R_N^c] \in \mathbb{R}^N$ of each input feature x_i to the output $S_c(x)$. For a classification task, the target output can be chosen to be the one associated with the label of the correct class (e.g. to verify which input features activated the class) or the one associated with a different class (e.g. to analyze the cause of a wrong classification).

Most often, attributions are visualized as *attribution maps*. These are heatmaps where, for each input feature, a red or blue color indicates the positive or negative influence of the feature to the target output, respectively (Fig. 9.1). Therefore, attribution maps highlight features that are positively contributing to the target activation as well as features that have a suppressing effect on it (counter-evidence).

9.2.1   Example of Attributions for a Linear Model

Before moving into non-linear models like DNNs, we show how attributions can be found in the linear case. This will also give us the opportunity to introduce the role of the gradient in generating attributions.

Linear models have been used for decades by statisticians, economists, computer and data scientists to tackle quantitative problems. Among such models, *Multiple Linear Regression* [13] can be used to model the dependency of a regression target y on a number of input features $x_1, ..., x_N$:

$$y = w_0 + w_1 x_1 + ... + w_N x_N + \epsilon, \qquad (9.1)$$

where the w_i are the learned model weights and ϵ is the residual error. The model weights can be estimated by ordinary least squares (OLS). As the model optimization is not in the scope of this chapter, we refer the reader to [13] for further details. Under the assumptions of independence, linearity, normality and homoscedasticity, the weights of a linear regression model are easy to understand and provide an immediate tool for the model interpretation. Let us consider a minimal example, where a linear regression is used to estimate the future capital asset y_c, based on two investments x_1 and x_2. Let assume the assumptions above are met and the model parameters are estimated as follows:

$$\mathbb{E}[y_c | x_1, x_2] = 1.05 x_1 + 1.50 x_2, \qquad (9.2)$$

We can derive immediately a *global* interpretation of this model. Every dollar invested in fund x_1 will produce a capital of 1.05\$, while every dollar invested in x_2 will produce a capital of 1.50\$, independently of the values x_1 and x_2 might assume in a concrete scenario. Notice that this explanation is purely based on the learned coefficient $w_1 = 1.05$ and $w_2 = 1.50$. These, sometimes called *partial regression coefficients*, are themselves candidate attribution values to explain the influence of the independent variables of the target variable:

$$R_1(x) = 1.05 \quad R_2(x) = 1.50 \qquad (9.3)$$

Notice also that the coefficients are the partial derivatives of the target variable with respect to the independent variable, therefore this attribution reduces to the model gradient:

$$R_i(x) = \frac{\partial y_c}{\partial x_i}(x) \tag{9.4}$$

On the other hand, this is not the only possible attribution scheme for such a model. Let us consider a concrete investment scenario where $100'000\$$ have been invested in x_1 and $10'000\$$ in x_2. The total capital asset, according to our trained model, will be $120'000\$$. One might be interested to know, in the particular case at hand, how x_1 and x_2 influenced the asset, i.e. how the two different investments contributed to the final capital. In this case, we are looking for a *local* explanation, as we are interested in explaining the response for a specific data point.

Again, thanks to the linearity of the model, it is easy to see that the $120'000\$$ can be explained as the sum of two contributions: $105'000\$$ from money invested in the first fund and $15'000\$$ from the money invested in the second one. Reasonable attribution values are, therefore:

$$R_1(x) = 105'000 \quad R_2(x) = 15'000 \tag{9.5}$$

In terms of relation with the gradient, we can formulate attributions as the gradient multiplied element-wise by the input:

$$R_i(x) = x_i \cdot \frac{\partial y_c}{\partial x_i}(x) \tag{9.6}$$

From this toy example, we have found two possible explanations in terms of attribution values. Notice that both are based on the gradient of the model function but significantly different. In the first case, the attribution for variable x_2 is significantly higher than for variable x_1, while in the second case the ranking is inverted. One might ask whether one of these is better than the other in explaining the model. As both attributions were derived with a clear objective, we argue that they are both reasonable explanations of the model. On the other hand, it is clear that they answer different questions: attributions in Eq. 9.3 answer the question *"Where should one invest in order to generate more capital?"*, while attributions in Eq. 9.5 answer the questions *"How the initial investments contributed to the final capital?"*. Depending on the question that needs to be answered, the appropriate attribution methods should be chosen. As they answer different questions, it is also evident how the two attributions cannot be directly compared.

9.2.2 Salience Versus Sensitivity Methods

The two attribution methods described by Eqs. 9.4 and 9.6 differ in that the second one also involves the multiplication by the input itself. In the previous section, we discussed how they explain two very different aspects of the model.

As we will discuss later, several (but not all) attribution methods for DNNs are computed by multiplying point-wise a quantity by the input being explained.

The justification for multiplying by the input has been only partially discussed in previous literature [28,31,33]. It has been noted that, when applied to image classification models, it contributes to making attribution maps sharper [28], although others noticed that it remains unclear how much of this can be attributed to the sharpness of the original image itself [31]. On the other hand, there is a more fundamental justification, which allows distinguishing attribution methods in two broad categories: *salience* and *sensitivity methods* [3].

A *sensitivity method* aims at describing how the output of the network changes when one or more input features are perturbed. In a linear model, this effect is constant for arbitrarily large perturbations. With non-linear models, sensitivity methods still represent the expected effect of a change in the input, but as first-order Taylor expansion of a non-linear function, they are only accurate for infinitesimal perturbations around the original input. While the model sensitivity to a feature perturbation has been regarded as a possible measure for the "importance" of the feature [30], the inherent objective of *sensitivity* methods should always be taken into account.

Conversely, a *salience method* describes the marginal effect of a feature to the output with respect to the same input where such feature has been removed. In other words, the produced values are meant to describe the contributions of the different input variables to the final target output. In this sense, for a *salience* method, it is often considered desirable that all attribution values sum up to the final target score, so that the attributions can be directly related to the output as additive contributions [4,27,33]. In our linear example, the multiplication between the input and the gradient provides a *salience* method that fulfills this property. We will see that the same method does not necessarily satisfy the property when extended to non-linear models. Notice also that *salience* methods must necessarily take the input into account when computing attributions.

9.2.3   Baseline for Salience Methods

Most *salience* methods require to define a baseline value. Since we are interested in the marginal effect of a feature, we are implicitly looking for how the output would change without that feature. As pointed out by others [33], humans also assign blame to a cause by comparing the outcomes of a process including or not such cause. In the particular case of a machine learning model, a feature with a non-zero attribution is expected to play some role in determining the output of the model.

Unfortunately, there is no proper way to *remove* one or more features from the input to a DNN, as most network architectures assume the number of input features is fixed. While we could re-train the network with a reduced set of input features, this would result in a different model whose internal mechanics are not necessarily related to the ones of the original model we want to explain.

In the related literature, this problem is often addressed by *simulating* the absence of a feature, instead of removing it in the strictest sense. First, a baseline input $\bar{x}$ is defined. The baseline should be chosen, depending on the domain, to best represent the absence of information (e.g. the black image). Then, attributions are computed with respect to the baseline, replacing each feature with its corresponding baseline value anytime the absence of the feature needs to be tested.

An important consequence of this setup is that attributions are heavily affected by the choice of the baseline. In particular, explanations are a function of the difference between the input and the baseline, rather than the input alone. Unfortunately, how to choose an appropriate baseline for different domains is still an open research question. Moreover, the baseline must necessarily be chosen in the domain of the input space, which creates an evident ambiguity between a valid input that incidentally assumes the baseline value and the indicator for a missing feature.

For many attribution methods, the zero baseline is the canonical choice [27,33,37]. Sometimes, the zero baseline is also used implicitly by attribution methods that do not let the user define it [4,22]. One possible justification for this particular choice relies on the observation that, for a model that implements a chain of operations of the form $z_j = f(\sum_i (w_{ji} \cdot z_i) + b_j)$, the all-zero input is somehow neutral to the output (i.e. $\forall c \in C : S_c(0) \approx 0$). If the model has no additive bias and all non-linear activations f map zero to zero (e.g. ReLU and Tanh), the output is in fact zero when the network is fed a zero input. Empirically, the output is often near zero even when biases have different values, which makes the choice of zero for the baseline reasonable, although arbitrary.

Other choices are possible. Sometimes, the expected value of each feature over the training set is used as a baseline [16,27]. In the image domain, previous works also suggested to set the baseline to a blurred version of the input images [7]. Finally, it is also possible to marginalize over the features to be removed in order to simulate their absence. For example, it has been shown how local coherence of natural images can be exploited to marginalize over image patches [38]. Unfortunately, this approach is significantly slower. What is more, it can only be applied to images or other domains where a prior about features correlation is known and this can be exploited to make the problem computationally feasible.

9.2.4   Properties and Definitions

We now introduce some definitions and notable properties that will be used in the remainder of this chapter to characterize attribution methods.

Explanation Continuity. We say an attribution method satisfies *explanation continuity* if, given a continuous prediction function to be explained $S_c(x)$, it produces continuous attributions $R^c(x)$. This is a desirable property for any attribution method [19]: if, for two nearly identical data points, the model response is nearly identical, then it is reasonable to expect that the corresponding explanations should also be nearly identical.

Implementation Invariance. We say that two models m_1 and m_2 are *functionally equivalent* if, for any x provided as input to both models, they produce the same output, despite possibly different implementations. More formally, if $\forall x : S_{m_1}(x) = S_{m_2}(x)$.

An attribution method is said to be *implementation invariant* [33] if it always produces identical attributions for functionally equivalent models m_1, m_2 provided with identical input:

$$\forall(m_1, m_2, x, c) : R^{c,m_1}(x) = R^{c,m_2}(x) \tag{9.7}$$

Sensitivity-n. An attribution method satisfies *sensitivity-n* [3] when the sum of the attributions for any subset of features of cardinality n is equal to the variation of the output S_c caused removing the features in the subset. In this context, removing a feature means setting it to a baseline value, often chosen to be zero as discussed in Sect. 9.2.3. Mathematically, a method satisfies *sensitivity-n* when, for all subsets of features $x_S = [x_1, ...x_n] \subseteq x$, it holds:

$$\sum_{i=1}^{n} R_i^c(x) = S_c(x) - S_c(x \setminus x_S), \tag{9.8}$$

where the notation $x \setminus x_S$ indicates a data point x where all features in x_S have been replaced by a baseline value.

When $n = N$, with N being the total number of input features, we have $\sum_{i=0}^{N} R_i^c(x) = S_c(x) - S_c(\bar{x})$, where $\bar{x}$ is an input baseline representing an input from which all features have been removed. This property is known as *efficiency* in the context of cooperative game theory [23] and recognized as desirable for various attribution methods [4, 27, 33]. In related literature, the same property has been variously called *completeness* [33] or *summation to delta* [27].

Most often, the baseline is chosen to be neutral with respect to the model response ($S_c(\bar{x}) \approx 0$), in which case *sensitivity-N*, reduces to

$$\forall x, c : \sum_{i=1}^{N} R_i^c(x) = S_c(x) \tag{9.9}$$

meaning that the output of a model for a specific input x can be decomposed as sum of the individual contributions of the input features.

Clearly, this property only applies to *salience* methods. A notable observation is that no attribution method, as defined in Sect. 9.2, can satisfy *sensitivity-n* for *all* values of n, when applied to a non-linear model. The proof is provided in [3]. Intuitively, this is due to the fact that attribution maps have not enough degrees of freedom to capture non-linear interactions: given a non-linear model, there must exists two features x_i and x_j such that $S(x) - S(x \setminus x_i, x_j) \neq 2 \cdot S(x) - S(x \setminus x_i) - S(x \setminus x_j)$. In this case, either *sensitivity-1* or *sensitivity-2* must be violated since attribution methods assign a single attribution value to both x_i and x_j.

9.3   Gradient-Based Attribution Methods for DNNs

In this section, we discuss how the idea of using the gradient information to generate attributions has been applied in several ways, implicitly or explicitly, to non-linear models, in particular DNNs. In Sect. 9.2.1 we showed how attributions for a linear regression model are generated as a function of the gradient with respect to the input features. Now we show the role of gradient while introducing several popular attribution methods for DNNs. We show how these methods differ in the way the backpropagation rules are modified in order to take into account the non-linearity of the network function. We also discuss how some methods can be revisited as gradient-based methods, despite their different original formulation. This will enable a direct comparison between them as part of a unified gradient-based framework.

9.3.1   From Linear to Non-linear Models

In the case of a linear regression, we found two possible attribution methods:

$$R_i^c(x) = \frac{\partial S_c(x)}{\partial x_i} \qquad R_i^c(x) = x_i \cdot \frac{\partial S_c(x)}{\partial x_i} \tag{9.10}$$

We discussed how these methods can be both considered producing meaningful explanations for a linear model, although answering different questions. As a first attempt to produce explanations for a DNN, one might consider applying the same ideas. Indeed, this is what has been suggested in the related literature over the past decade.

Sensitivity analysis was one of the first methods to be adapted to the deep learning domain [30]. Attributions are constructed by taking the absolute value of the partial derivative of the target output S_c with respect to the inputs x_i:

$$R_i^c(x) = \left| \frac{\partial S_c(x)}{\partial x_i} \right| \tag{9.11}$$

Intuitively, the absolute value of the gradient indicates those input features (e.g. pixels, for image classification) that can be perturbed the least in order for the target output to change the most, discarding any information about the direction of this change. Nevertheless, Sensitivity analysis is usually rather noisy [18, 24, 31] and taking the absolute value prevents the detection of positive and negative evidence that might be present in the input.

Gradient * Input [28] was initially proposed as a technique to improve the sharpness of attribution maps generated by Sensitivity analysis. The attribution is computed by taking the (signed) partial derivatives of the output with respect to the input and multiplying them feature-wise by the input itself.

$$R_i^c(x) = \frac{\partial S_c(x)}{\partial x_i} \cdot x_i \tag{9.12}$$

The reader might recognize in Eq. 9.12 an attribution method that we have previously discussed for linear models. While the multiplication with the input can be theoretically justified if we are interested in *salience* instead of *sensitivity*, as we move from linear to non-linear models, computing *salience* is not as easy. Both Sensitivity analysis and Gradient * Input present clear shortcomings, as the partial derivative $S_c(x)/\partial x_i$ varies not only with x_i but also with the value of other input features.

Sensitivity analysis still provides a valid measure of the variation of the target output for a perturbation of the input variables but, in the case of a non-linear model, this value is only accurate for infinitesimally small perturbations around the original input. In fact, the resulting attributions can be seen as the first-order term of a Taylor decomposition of the function implemented by the network, computed at a point *infinitesimally close* to the actual input [18].

Similarly, as the gradient is not constant, Gradient * Input does not necessarily represent the correct marginal effect of a feature. Let us consider an additive model of the form:

$$y = w_0 + f_1(x_1) + ... + f_N(x_N) \tag{9.13}$$

where f_i are non-linear functions. Since the target y is computed as the sum of contributions of the input variables and there is no cross-interaction between them, we can expect a salience method to detect these contributions exactly and satisfy *sensitivity-N*. Concretely, let us consider the toy example $y = x_1 + \sqrt{x_2}$, evaluated at input $(4, 4)$. In this case, the contributions to the output $(y = 6)$ would be naturally distributed as attributions $R_1 = 4$ and $R_2 = 2$. It is easy to verify that Gradient * Input fails to satisfy *sensitivity-N*, producing attributions $R_1 = 4$ and $R_2 = 1$, which do not sum up to the target value and are hardly justifiable. In order to overcome these limitations, gradient-based methods have been adapted to take into account the non-linear nature of DNNs.

9.3.2   Towards Average Gradients

Notice that in order to produce the expected attributions for the toy example illustrated above, we could simply replace the instant gradient, as in Gradient * Input, with the *average gradient* between the baseline (here $(0, 0)$) and the input value (here $(4, 4)$). This idea, in fact, is at the core of more recent attribution methods: Layer-wise Relevance Propagation (in its variant ϵ-LRP), DeepLIFT Rescale and Integrated Gradients. We now introduce these methods and discuss how they can all be examined under the same gradient-based framework. Notice that the following *post-hoc* considerations might not have been the ones that originally led to the formulation of these methods.

Layer-Wise Relevance Propagation (ϵ-LRP) [4] is computed with a backward pass on the network. Let us consider a quantity $r_i^{(l)}$, called "relevance" of unit i of layer l. The algorithm starts at the output layer L, assigning the relevance of the target neuron c equal to the activation of the neuron itself, and the relevance of all other neurons to zero (Eq. 9.14). Then it proceeds layer by layer, redistributing the prediction score S_i until the input layer is reached. One recursive rule for the redistribution of a layer's relevance to the following layer is the ϵ-rule described in Eq. 9.15, where we defined $z_{ij} = x_i^{(l)} w_{ij}^{(l,l+1)}$ to be the weighted activation of a neuron i onto neuron j in the next layer and b_j the additive bias of unit j. A small quantity ϵ is added to the denominator to avoid numerical instabilities. Once reached the input layer, the final attributions are defined as $R_i^c(x) = r_i^{(1)}$.

$$r_i^{(L)} = \begin{cases} S_i(x) & \text{if unit } i \text{ is the target unit of interest} \\ 0 & \text{otherwise} \end{cases} \tag{9.14}$$

$$r_i^{(l)} = \sum_j \frac{z_{ij}}{\sum_{i'} z_{i'j} + b_j + \epsilon \cdot sign(\sum_{i'} z_{i'j} + b_j)} r_j^{(l+1)} \tag{9.15}$$

LRP, together with the propagation rule described in Eq. 9.15, is called ϵ-LRP, analyzed in the remainder of this chapter. We will briefly discuss a more recent variation of LRP in Sect. 9.4.3. Additionally, we assume a small and fixed ϵ, with the only purpose of avoiding divisions by zero.

We introduced the method according to the original formulation, where the role of the gradient might not appear immediately evident. On the other hand, we can reformulate ϵ-LRP to show how this method actually computes the average gradient in some cases and, based on this, discuss its advantages compared to Gradient * Input, as well as its limitations.

In a DNN where each layer performs a linear transformation $z_j = \sum_i w_{ji} x_i + b_j$ followed by a nonlinear mapping $x_j = f(z_j)$, a path connecting any two units consists of a sequence of such operations. The chain rule along a single path is therefore the product of the partial derivatives of all linear and nonlinear transformations along the path. For two units i and j in *subsequent* layers we have $\partial x_j / \partial x_i = w_{ji} \cdot f'(z_j)$, whereas for any two generic units i and c connected by a set of paths P_{ic} the partial derivative is the sum of the product of all weights w_p and all derivatives of the nonlinearities $f'(z)_p$ along each path $p \in P_{ic}$. We introduce a notation to indicate a modified chain rule, where the derivative of the nonlinearities $f'()$ is replaced by a generic function $g()$:

$$\frac{\partial^g x_c}{\partial x_i} = \sum_{p \in P_{ic}} \left(\prod w_p \prod g(z)_p \right) \tag{9.16}$$

When $g() = f'()$, Eq. 9.16 is the definition of partial derivative of the output of unit c with respect to unit i, computed as the sum of contributions over all paths connecting the two units. Given that a zero weight can be used for non-existing or blocked paths, this is valid for any architecture that involves fully-connected, convolutional or recurrent layers without multiplicative units, as well as for pooling operations.

Notably, given this notation, ϵ-LRP can be reformulated as in the following proposition [3]:

Proposition 1. ϵ-LRP is equivalent to the feature-wise product of the input and the modified partial derivative $\partial^g S_c(x)/\partial x_i$, with $g = g^{LRP} = f_i(z_i)/z_i$, i.e. the ratio between the output and the input at each nonlinearity.

The reader can refer to Table 9.1 for the mathematical formulation, which makes the relation between ϵ-LRP and Gradient * Input more evident. In both cases, the input is multiplied with a quantity that depends on the network and its parameters. In the case of Gradient * Input, this quantity is simply the derivative of the output with respect to the input. In the case of ϵ-LRP, the quantity can be seen as a *modified* gradient, where the instant gradient of each nonlinearity in the chain rule is replaced by the ratio between the output and the input to the nonlinearity.

Furthermore, notice that $g^{LRP}(z) = (f(z) - 0)/(z - 0)$ which, in the case of Rectified Linear Unit (ReLU) or Tanh activations, is the *average gradient* of the nonlinearity in $[0, z]$. It is also easy to see that $\lim_{z \to 0} g^{LRP}(z) = f'(0)$, which explains why g, for these nonlinearities, can not assume arbitrarily large values as $z \to 0$, even without a stabilizer. On the contrary, if the discussed condition on the nonlinearity is not satisfied, for example with Sigmoid or Softplus activations, ϵ-LRP fails to produce meaningful attributions [3]. This is likely due to the fact $g^{LRP}(z)$ can become extremely large for small values of z, being its upper-bound only limited by the stabilizer. As a consequence, attribution values tend to concentrate on a few features. Notice also that the interpretation of g^{LRP} as average gradient of the nonlinearity does not hold in this case.

Table 9.1. Gradient-based formulation of several attribution methods.

Method	Attribution $R_i^c(x)$
Sensitivity analysis	$\left\| \dfrac{\partial S_c(x)}{\partial x_i} \right\|$
Gradient * Input	$x_i \cdot \dfrac{\partial S_c(x)}{\partial x_i}$
ϵ-LRP	$x_i \cdot \dfrac{\partial^g S_c(x)}{\partial x_i}, \quad g = \dfrac{f(z)}{z}$
DeepLIFT (Rescale)	$(x_i - \bar{x}_i) \cdot \dfrac{\partial^g S_c(x)}{\partial x_i}, \quad g = \dfrac{f(z) - f(\bar{z})}{z - \bar{z}}$
Integrated Gradients	$(x_i - \bar{x}_i) \cdot \displaystyle\int_{\alpha=0}^{1} \left. \dfrac{\partial S_c(\tilde{x})}{\partial(\tilde{x}_i)} \right\|_{\tilde{x}=\bar{x}+\alpha(x-\bar{x})} d\alpha$

DeepLIFT Rescale. The use of average gradients to compute attributions has been later generalized by other methods. DeepLIFT [27] proceeds in a backward fashion, similarly to LRP. Each unit i is assigned an attribution that represents the relative effect of the unit activated at the original network input x compared to the activation at some reference input $\bar{x}$ (Eq. 9.17). Reference values $\bar{z}_{ij}$ for all hidden units are determined by running a forward pass through the network, using the baseline $\bar{x}$ as input, and recording the activation of each unit. The baseline is a user-defined parameter often chosen to be zero for the reasons discussed in Sect. 9.2.3. Equation 9.18 describes the relevance propagation rule.

$$r_i^{(L)} = \begin{cases} S_i(x) - S_i(\bar{x}) & \text{if unit } i \text{ is the target unit of interest} \\ 0 & \text{otherwise} \end{cases} \qquad (9.17)$$

$$r_i^{(l)} = \sum_j \frac{z_{ij} - \bar{z}_{ij}}{\sum_{i'} z_{i'j} - \sum_{i'} \bar{z}_{i'j}} r_j^{(l+1)} \qquad (9.18)$$

In Eq. 9.18, $\bar{z}_{ij} = \bar{x}_i^{(l)} w_{ij}^{(l,l+1)}$ is weighted activation of a neuron i onto neuron j when the baseline $\bar{x}$ is fed into the network. The attributions at the input layer are defined as $R_i^c(x) = r_i^{(1)}$. The rule here described ("Rescale rule") is used in the original formulation of the method and it is the one we will analyze in the remainder of the chapter.

Similarly to ϵ-LRP, we can reformulate DeepLIFT (Rescale) to highlight the role of the gradient [3]:

Proposition 2. *DeepLIFT (Rescale) is equivalent to the feature-wise product of the $x - \bar{x}$ and the modified partial derivative $\partial^g S_c(x)/\partial x_i$, with $g = g^{DL} = (f_i(z_i) - f_i(\bar{z}_i))/(z_i - \bar{z}_i)$, i.e. the ratio between the difference in output and the difference in input at each nonlinearity, for a network provided with some input x and some baseline input $\bar{x}$ defined by the user.*

Again, by comparing the formulation of Gradient * Input and DeepLIFT (Table 9.1), it easy to see how the latter replaces the instant gradient of each nonlinearity in the interval that goes from the baseline to the actual input value. In this case, the formulation as average gradient holds also for those nonlinearities that do not cross the origin, such as Sigmoid and Softplus, the reason why DeepLIFT (Rescale) could be considered a generalization of ϵ-LRP that does not assume a zero baseline or a particular shape for the nonlinearity.

The formulation in Table 9.1 also highlights some further connections between Gradient * Input, ϵ-LRP and DeepLIFT. Motivated by the fact that attribution maps for different gradient-based methods look surprisingly similar on several tasks, some conditions of equivalence or approximation have been be derived [3]:

Proposition 3. *ϵ-LRP is equivalent to (i) Gradient * Input if only ReLUs are used as nonlinearities; (ii) DeepLIFT (computed with a zero baseline) if applied to a network with no additive biases and with nonlinearities f such that $f(0) = 0$ (e.g. ReLU or Tanh).*

The first part of Proposition 3 comes directly as a corollary of Proposition 1 by noticing that for ReLUs the gradient at the nonlinearity f' is equal to g^{LRP} for all inputs. This relation has been previously proven in the literature [11, 28]. Similarly, we notice that, in a network with no additive biases and nonlinearities that cross the origin, the propagation of the baseline produces a zero reference value for *all* hidden units (i.e. $\forall i : \bar{z}_i = f(\bar{z}_i) = 0$). Then $g^{LRP} = g^{DL}$, which proves the second part of the proposition.

Integrated Gradients. We have seen how DeepLIFT and, in some cases, ϵ-LRP can be seen as computing a backward pass through the network where the gradient of the nonlinearities is replaced by their average gradient. There is one fundamental problem with this approach though: the chain rule does not hold for discrete gradients in general. As a consequence, the quantity computed by replacing each instant gradient by an average gradient at each nonlinearity does not necessarily result in the average gradient of the function as a whole. Moreover, two different implementations of the same function might lead to different results when the chain rule is applied. In this case, we say that the attribution method fails to satisfy *implementation invariance* [33].

Integrated Gradients [33] can be considered a generalization of DeepLIFT, designed to satisfy *implementation invariance*. It builds on the same idea of previous methods, as it can be interpreted as computing attributions multiplying the input variable element-wise with the average partial derivative, as the input varies from a baseline $\bar{x}$ to its final value x.

However, in this case, the original gradient is used for the nonlinearities, thus preserving the validity of the chain rule. Attributions are defined as follows.

$$R_i^c(x) = x_i \cdot \int_{\alpha=0}^1 \frac{\partial S_c(\tilde{x})}{\partial(\tilde{x}_i)}\Big|_{\tilde{x}=\bar{x}+\alpha(x-\bar{x})} d\alpha \qquad (9.19)$$

Integrated Gradients presents several interesting properties. First, as the gradient of a function only depends on the function itself and not on its implementation, Integrated Gradients has the notable property of being implementation invariant, a property which is not satisfied by ϵ-LRP and DeepLIFT in general. Secondly, it can be immediately applied to any network architecture as it only depends on the function gradient, which is easily obtained thanks to the automatic differentiation of frameworks like Tensorflow [1] or PyTorch [21]. Finally, it always satisfies *sensitivity-N*, meaning that the sum of the produced attributions sum up to the network output minus the output when the network is evaluated at the baseline. Notice that DeepLIFT also satisfies *sensitivity-N* by design, but only if the computational graph does not include multiplicative interactions. This is illustrated in the following counter-example: take two variables x_1 and x_2 and a the function $h(x_1, x_2) = ReLU(x_1 - 1) \cdot ReLU(x_2)$. One can easily show that, by applying the methods as described by Table 9.1, DeepLIFT does not satisfy *sensitivity-N* while Integrated gradients does[1].

One of the limitations of Integrated Gradients is its relatively high computational cost, as evaluating the average gradient requires to numerically evaluate an integral. This means one needs to evaluate the model and its gradient several times, with slightly different inputs, which is computationally expensive for large models. While Integrated Gradients computes the average partial derivative of each feature as the input varies from a baseline to its final value, DeepLIFT

---

[1] DeepLIFT has been designed specifically for feed-forward neural networks and therefore assumes no multiplicative interactions. The gradient-based formulation generalizes the method to other architectures but does not guarantee meaningful results outside the scope DeepLIFT was designed for.

approximates this quantity in a single step by replacing the gradient at each nonlinearity with its average gradient. Although the chain rule does not hold in general for average gradients, it has been shown empirically that DeepLIFT is most often a good approximation of Integrated Gradients in the case of feed-forward architectures [3].

9.4 Discussion

In the previous section, we have introduced five gradient-based methods for DNNs. While Sensitivity analysis, Gradient * Input and Integrated Gradients belong to this category by construction, we have discussed how ϵ-LRP and DeepLIFT (Rescale) can also fit in the definition of gradient-based methods, as they are computed by applying the chain rule for gradients once the instant gradient at each nonlinearity is replaced with a function that depends on the method. We have also suggested a theoretical justification for using the gradient information to produce explanations, starting from linear models and moving to DNNs. In this section, we highlight the advantages and limitations of gradient-based methods and discuss some possible alternatives.

9.4.1 Advantages of Gradient-Based Methods

The strength of gradient-based methods is twofold. First, they are fast. Sensitivity analysis, Gradient * Input and ϵ-LRP only require a single forward and backward pass through the network to produce the attribution map. DeepLIFT requires one more forward pass to set the baselines for all nonlinearities, an operation that is computationally negligible in most of the use-cases. Integrated Gradients is slower than the others as it requires 50–200 backward passes for the numerical evaluation of the integral. Nevertheless, compared to other, not gradient-based methods, it can be still considered very efficient. What is more, the number of network evaluations does not depend on the number of input features to the network, which allows these methods to scale more easily. Notice also that frameworks like Tensorflow and PyTorch provide optimized algorithms to compute the gradients, often evaluated on the GPU to reach the best performance.

The second advantage of gradient-based methods is the ease of implementation. As pointed out by others [33], a desirable property for attribution methods is their immediate applicability to existing models. When the pure gradient is used, like in the case of Gradient * Input or Integrated Gradients, attributions can be computed for any network architecture where a gradient is defined, with very few lines of code. Our gradient-based formulation makes this possible for ϵ-LRP and DeepLIFT (Rescale) as well. Since all modern frameworks for Deep Learning implement backpropagation for efficient computation of the chain rule, it is possible to implement all methods above by overriding the gradient of all nonlinearities in the computational graph, with no need to implement custom layers or operations. Listings 9.1, and 9.2 show an example of how to achieve this on Tensorflow, respectively for ϵ-LRP and DeepLIFT (Rescale).

```
1  @ops.RegisterGradient("GradLRP")
2  def _GradLRP(op, grad):
3      op_out = op.outputs[0]
4      op_in = op.inputs[0]
5      return grad * op_out / (op_in + eps)
```

Listing 9.1. Example of gradient override for a Tensorflow operation. After registering this function as the gradient for nonlinear activation functions, a call to tf.gradients() and the multiplication with the input will produce the ϵ-LRP attributions.

```
1  @ops.RegisterGradient("GradDeepLIFT")
2  def _GradDeepLIFT(op, grad):
3      op_out = op.outputs[0]
4      op_in = op.inputs[0]
5      delta_out = op_out - ref_output
6      delta_in = op_in - ref_input
7      if tf.abs(delta_in) < eps:
8          return grad
9      else:
10         return grad * delta_out / delta_in
```

Listing 9.2. Example of gradient override for a Tensorflow operation (DeepLIFT (Rescale)). Compared to ϵ-LRP, this requires to compute a reference input and output for each hidden unit, with a second forward pass.

9.4.2 Limitations

Unfortunately, gradient-based methods are also strongly affected by noisy gradients, as depicted in Fig. 9.2, which shows the attributions generated for a Convolutional Neural Network (CNN) performing image classification. While most attribution mass is assigned to the area of the picture with the main subject, which seems reasonable, the attribution value assigned to individual pixels is affected by high-frequency variations, with neighboring pixels often being assigned very different attributions, possibly of the opposite sign. This phenomenon is likely to be caused by the violation of *explanation continuity* on gradient-based methods.

To illustrate the problem, let us consider a simple continuous function $y = max(x_1, x_2)$ and compute the attributions for the two input variables (x_1, x_2) as the input varies from $(2, 2 + \epsilon)$ to $(2, 2 - \epsilon)$, assuming the default baseline $(0, 0)$. Notice that this kind of function is very common in CNNs, which often include several *max-pooling* layers. Notice also that the function is continuous as the output varies smoothly from $2 + \epsilon$ to 2. On the other hand, since the gradient for the *max* function acts as a hard switch, all gradient-based methods discussed above[2] present a discontinuity in $(2, 2)$ where the attribution mass suddenly moves from x_2 entirely to x_1, as shown in Table 9.2. Intuitively, assigning all the attribution to the input feature with the highest value ignores the fact that, without that feature, the output would still be significantly high thanks to the influence of the other. While there is no doubt that the two input variables have some interaction to generate the result, generally it is not straight-forward to find a fair mechanism for credit assignment. The problem has been extensively studied in the context of cooperative game theory, where alternative mechanism, often proven to be closer to the human intuition, have been proposed [26]. Unfortunately, these methods are also computationally expensive and only applicable to DNNs with some significant approximations [16], a reason why gradient-based methods are still very popular.

Table 9.2. Example of attributions generated for a continuous function by gradient-based methods (Gradient * Input, Integrated Gradients and most implementations of ϵ-LRP and DeepLIFT (Rescale).

Attributions for $min(x_1, x_2)$		
Input	$(x_1, x_2) = (2, 2 + \epsilon)$	$(x_1, x_2) = (2, 2 - \epsilon)$
Attributions	$(R_1, R_2) = (0, 2 + \epsilon)$	$(R_1, R_2) = (2, 0)$

In general, continuity in the produced explanations is a desirable property for any explanation method [19]. When we move away from a single operation and consider more complex models such as deep CNNs, the violation of *explanation continuity* exacerbates the problem of shattered gradients [5]: a high number of piece-wise linear regions in the learned function causes the gradient to become highly discontinuous and resemble white noise, which turns into high-frequency variations in the attributions produced by gradient-based methods. This makes these explanations particularly sensitive to small variations in the input and not necessarily representative of the overall classification process.

9.4.3 Beyond Gradient-Based Methods

Gradient-based methods are certainly not the only attribution methods proposed in the literature. In particular, the gradient-based methods discussed before can be framed within a broader category of *backpropagation methods*, where the

---

[2] In fact, ϵ-LRP and DeepLIFT (Rescale) are not implementation invariant so the result might change depending on the actual implementation of the *max* function in the network. For example, this can be implemented as a primitive operation (*max-pooling*) or, for positive numbers, it can be implicitly implemented by a two-layer network with three hidden units: $y = 0.5 \cdot (ReLU(x_1 - x_2) + ReLU(x_2 - x_1) + ReLU(x_1 + x_2)$. In both cases, our reference implementation [3] produces the same attributions for all gradient-based methods, including ϵ-LRP and DeepLIFT (Rescale).

influence of the input features on the output is estimated layer by layer, trying to reverse the flow of information of the forward pass.

Instead of considering the model as a black-box that cannot be inspected, backpropagation methods take advantage of lower level access to the model's computational components and of the knowledge of how information flows in a DNN. Most often, backpropagation methods compute attribution maps with a few forward and backward passes through the network (Fig. 9.3a). In the forward pass, normal inference is performed on the input that needs to be explained. Then, a backward pass is performed, starting from a target (output) unit and propagating its activation through the network, layer by layer, until the input layer is reached, where the attribution map is formed.

Backpropagation methods differ in the way information flows in the backward pass. While this might consist in computing the chain rule for gradients (possibly replacing the gradient of the nonlinearities with other quantities), there are also different mechanisms to propagate relevance information from upper layers to the input. Most notably, some recent variants of LRP and DeepLIFT are back-propagation methods that cannot be easily fit in the definition of gradient-based methods. For example, $\alpha\beta$-LRP [4,19] employs a backpropagation rule where the positive and negative information paths are weighted according to two different parameters, chosen by the user. This adaptation enables *explanation continuity* [19] but it also produces attributions that diverge from other gradient-based methods, making it hard to apply the theoretical framework we discussed so far. Similarly, a second variant of DeepLIFT known as "RevealCancel" [27] inherits some considerations from cooperative game theory to fix the problem of *explanation continuity* as discussed in the previous section. Both of these methods produce interesting results but more research will be necessary to derive strong theoretical foundations for these propagation rules, whose heuristics might have limitations not fully understood.

Other notable attribution methods are the so-called *perturbation methods*. In this case, attributions for each input feature (or set of features) are computed by directly removing, masking or altering them, and running a second forward pass on the new input, measuring the effect that this operation has on the output (Fig. 9.3b). Perturbation methods have the advantages of a straightforward interpretation, as they are a direct measure of the marginal effect of some input features to the output. They are also model-agnostic, meaning that they can be applied to any black-box model that provides an evaluation function, without any need to access the internal operations. These methods have been first applied to CNNs in the domain of image classification, visualizing the probability of the correct class as a function of the position of a grey patch occluding part of the image, a method known as Box Occlusion [37]. Other methods are Prediction Difference Analysis [38], Meaningful Perturbation [7] and LIME [22].

A major limitation of perturbation methods is that the number of features that are perturbed altogether at each iteration, as well as the chosen perturbation technique, significantly affect the resulting explanations. Figure 9.4 highlights this problem in the case of Box Occlusion, where different explanations are

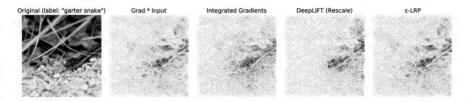

Fig. 9.2. Attribution generated by applying several attribution methods to an Inception V3 network for natural image classification [34]. Notice how all gradient-based methods produce attributions affected by significant local variance.

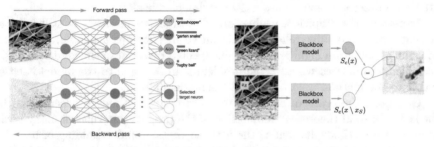

(a) Backpropagation methods   (b) Perturbation methods

Fig. 9.3. Categorization of attribution methods

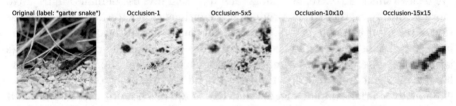

Fig. 9.4. Attributions generated by occluding portions of the input image with squared grey patches of different sizes. Notice how the size of the patches influence the result, with focus on the main subject only when using bigger patches.

generated for different sizes of the occluding box. While an ideal perturbation method would test all possible subsets of input features, this is not computationally feasible with most real-life datasets, as the cardinality of the power-set grows exponentially with the size of the input. In practice, perturbation methods differ by their underlying perturbation technique but the lack of a theoretically-grounded way of choosing it raises questions about the reliability of the resulting explanations. Moreover, notice that perturbation methods tend to be significantly slower than gradient-based methods (up to hours for a single image [38]). As the number of required network evaluations grows with the number of input features, these are often aggregated to obtain attributions within a reasonable time. Which and how features are aggregated is also an hyper-parameter that strongly affects the resulting explanations.

9.5 Conclusions

Understanding and explaining complex machine learning models have become crucially important. While several attribution methods have been proposed in the last decade, we see no silver bullet among them. As discussed in the case of a linear model, the notion itself of "explanation" is not well defined, and therefore attribution methods sometimes answer different questions.

Moreover, the empirical evaluation of attribution methods is still hard to accomplish, as no fully reliable quantitative metrics are available. Therefore, when an explanation highlights some unexpected behavior of the model, it might be difficult to discern whether the problem is in fact due to the model itself or rather to the method used to explain the model [33].

Generally, the problem of validating attribution methods is accentuated by the lack of a solid theoretical foundation of the propagation rules of many back-propagation methods, as well as the little theoretical understanding of how different perturbation techniques affect the result on perturbation methods. Too often, attribution methods are only evaluated qualitatively, for example by comparing the attribution maps generated by different methods for the same model. We believe this is an extremely dangerous approach because humans might judge more favorably methods that produce explanations closer to their own expectations. Take, for example, a DNN trained for image classification: several works have shown that these networks are easily fooled by carefully-crafted adversarial samples, altered images almost indistinguishable from the originals by the human eye, but able to trick the network into a totally wrong classification [9,35]. Adversarial samples suggest that DNNs are much more sensitive to small variations in the intensity of image pixels than the human brain is. So, if the mechanisms underlying the image recognition task in a DNN and in the human brain are different, we would expect the corresponding explanations to reflect this difference. Instead, qualitative evaluations tend to be biased towards what people consider a "good" explanation as humans.

In order to develop better quantitative tools for the evaluation of attribution methods, we first need to define the goal that an ideal attribution method should achieve, as different methods might be suitable for different tasks. Then, as for the properties of *explanation continuity, implementation invariance* and *sensitivity-N*, we can proceed defining those axioms or properties we consider necessary for any good explanation method to fulfill. We believe this is a promising path to follow for future research on this topic.

To conclude, in this chapter we have analyzed five attribution methods and the role of the gradient in defining them. Starting from a linear model, we have shown how the gradient information can be used to generate explanations, explicitly or implicitly. We have also discussed some theoretical properties of these methods and shown that, despite their apparently different formulation, they are strongly related. By reformulating ϵ-LRP and DeepLIFT (Rescale), we have shown how these can be conveniently implemented with modern machine learning frameworks, similarly to other gradient methods. Finally, we have discussed some limitations of gradient-based methods, in the hope of encouraging further exploration of new techniques towards achieving explainable DNN models.

References

1. Abadi, M., et al.: TensorFlow: large-scale machine learning on heterogeneous systems (2015). https://www.tensorflow.org/
2. Adebayo, J., Gilmer, J., Muelly, M., Goodfellow, I., Hardt, M., Kim, B.: Sanity checks for saliency maps. In: Advances in Neural Information Processing Systems, pp. 9524–9535 (2018)
3. Ancona, M., Ceolini, E., Oztireli, C., Gross, M.: Towards better understanding of gradient-based attribution methods for deep neural networks. In: 6th International Conference on Learning Representations (ICLR) (2018)
4. Bach, S., Binder, A., Montavon, G., Klauschen, F., Müller, K.R., Samek, W.: On pixel-wise explanations for non-linear classifier decisions by layer-wise relevance propagation. PLoS ONE **10**(7), e0130140 (2015)
5. Balduzzi, D., Frean, M., Leary, L., Lewis, J.P., Ma, K.W.D., McWilliams, B.: The shattered gradients problem: if resnets are the answer, then what is the question? In: Proceedings of the 34th International Conference on Machine Learning, ICML 2017, vol. 70, pp. 342–350 (2017). JMLR.org
6. Doshi-Velez, F., Kim, B.: Towards a rigorous science of interpretable machine learning. arXiv (2017). https://arxiv.org/abs/1702.08608
7. Fong, R.C., Vedaldi, A.: Interpretable explanations of black boxes by meaningful perturbation. In: Proceedings of the IEEE International Conference on Computer Vision, pp. 3429–3437 (2017)
8. Ghorbani, A., Abid, A., Zou, J.: Interpretation of neural networks is fragile. In: AAAI 2019 (2019)
9. Goodfellow, I.J., Shlens, J., Szegedy, C.: Explaining and harnessing adversarial examples. In: International Conference on Learning Representations (ICLR) (2015)
10. Goodman, B., Flaxman, S.: European union regulations on algorithmic decision-making and a "right to explanation". In: ICML Workshop on Human Interpretability in Machine Learning (WHI) (2016)
11. Kindermans, P., Schütt, K., Müller, K., Dähne, S.: Investigating the influence of noise and distractors on the interpretation of neural networks. In: NIPS Workshop on Interpretable Machine Learning in Complex Systems (2016)
12. Krizhevsky, A., Sutskever, I., Hinton, G.E.: Imagenet classification with deep convolutional neural networks. In: Proceedings of NIPS, pp. 1097–1105 (2012)
13. Kutner, M.H., Nachtsheim, C., Neter, J.: Applied Linear Regression Models. McGraw-Hill/Irwin, New York (2004)
14. LeCun, Y., Bengio, Y., Hinton, G.: Deep learning. Nature **521**(7553), 436–444 (2015)
15. Lipton, Z.C.: The mythos of model interpretability. In: ICML Workshop on Human Interpretability of Machine Learning (2016)
16. Lundberg, S.M., Lee, S.I.: A unified approach to interpreting model predictions. In: Guyon, I., et al. (eds.) Proceedings of Advances in Neural Information Processing Systems (NIPS), pp. 4765–4774 (2017)

17. Mnih, V., et al.: Human-level control through deep reinforcement learning. Nature **518**(7540), 529–533 (2015)
18. Montavon, G., Lapuschkin, S., Binder, A., Samek, W., Müller, K.R.: Explaining nonlinear classification decisions with deep Taylor decomposition. Pattern Recogn. **65**, 211–222 (2017)
19. Montavon, G., Samek, W., Müller, K.R.: Methods for interpreting and understanding deep neural networks. Digital Signal Process. **73**, 1–15 (2018)
20. Nie, W., Zhang, Y., Patel, A.: A theoretical explanation for perplexing behaviors of back propagation-based visualizations. In: ICML 2018 (2018)
21. Paszke, A., et al.: Automatic differentiation in PyTorch. In: NIPS Autodiff Workshop (2017)
22. Ribeiro, M.T., Singh, S., Guestrin, C.: "Why Should I Trust You?": explaining the predictions of any classifier. In: Proceedings of the 22nd ACM SIGKDD International Conference on Knowledge Discovery and Data Mining, KDD 2016, ACM, New York, NY, USA, pp. 1135–1144 (2016)
23. Roth, A.E.: The Shapley Value: Essays in Honor of Lloyd S. Shapley. Cambridge University Press, Cambridge (1988)
24. Samek, W., Binder, A., Montavon, G., Lapuschkin, S., Müller, K.R.: Evaluating the visualization of what a deep neural network has learned. IEEE Trans. Neural Networks Learn. Syst. **28**(11), 2660–2673 (2017)
25. Selvaraju, R.R., Cogswell, M., Das, A., Vedantam, R., Parikh, D., Batra, D.: Grad-CAM: visual explanations from deep networks via gradient-based localization. In: Proceedings of the IEEE International Conference on Computer Vision, pp. 618–626 (2017)
26. Shapley, L.S.: A value for n-person games. Contrib. Theory Games **2**(28), 307–317 (1953)
27. Shrikumar, A., Greenside, P., Kundaje, A.: Learning important features through propagating activation differences. In: Proceedings of the 34th International Conference on Machine Learning, Proceedings of Machine Learning Research, PMLR, International Convention Centre, Sydney, Australia, vol. 70, pp. 3145–3153, 06–11 August 2017
28. Shrikumar, A., Greenside, P., Shcherbina, A., Kundaje, A.: Not just a black box: learning important features through propagating activation differences. arXiv preprint arXiv:1605.01713 (2016)
29. Silver, D., et al.: Mastering the game of go with deep neural networks and tree search. Nature **529**(7587), 484–489 (2016)
30. Simonyan, K., Vedaldi, A., Zisserman, A.: Deep inside convolutional networks: visualising image classification models and saliency maps. In: ICLR Workshop (2014)
31. Smilkov, D., Thorat, N., Kim, B., Viégas, F., Wattenberg, M.: SmoothGrad: removing noise by adding noise. In: ICML Workshop on Visualization for Deep Learning (2017)
32. Springenberg, J.T., Dosovitskiy, A., Brox, T., Riedmiller, M.: Striving for simplicity: the all convolutional net. In: ICLR 2015 Workshop (2015)
33. Sundararajan, M., Taly, A., Yan, Q.: Axiomatic attribution for deep networks. In: Proceedings of the 34th International Conference on Machine Learning, Proceedings of Machine Learning Research, PMLR, International Convention Centre, Sydney, Australia, vol. 70, pp. 3319–3328, 06–11 August 2017
34. Szegedy, C., Vanhoucke, V., Ioffe, S., Shlens, J., Wojna, Z.: Rethinking the inception architecture for computer vision. In: Proceedings of the IEEE Conference on Computer Vision and Pattern Recognition, pp. 2818–2826 (2016)

35. Szegedy, C., et al.: Intriguing properties of neural networks. In: International Conference on Learning Representations (ICLR) (2014)
36. Wu, Y., et al.: Google's neural machine translation system: bridging the gap between human and machine translation. Trans. Assoc. Comput. Linguist. **5**, 339–351 (2017)
37. Zeiler, M.D., Fergus, R.: Visualizing and understanding convolutional networks. In: Fleet, D., Pajdla, T., Schiele, B., Tuytelaars, T. (eds.) ECCV 2014. LNCS, vol. 8689, pp. 818–833. Springer, Cham (2014). https://doi.org/10.1007/978-3-319-10590-1_53
38. Zintgraf, L.M., Cohen, T.S., Adel, T., Welling, M.: Visualizing deep neural network decisions: prediction difference analysis. In: International Conference on Learning Representations (2017)

10
Layer-Wise Relevance Propagation: An Overview

Grégoire Montavon[1](✉), Alexander Binder[2], Sebastian Lapuschkin[3], Wojciech Samek[3], and Klaus-Robert Müller[1,4,5]

[1] Technische Universität Berlin, 10587 Berlin, Germany
{gregoire.montavon,klaus-robert.mueller}@tu-berlin.de
[2] Singapore University of Technology and Design, Singapore 487372, Singapore
alexander_binder@sutd.edu.sg
[3] Fraunhofer Heinrich Hertz Institute, 10587 Berlin, Germany
{sebastian.lapuschkin,wojciech.samek}@hhi.fraunhofer.de
[4] Korea University, Anam-dong, Seongbuk-gu, Seoul 02841, Korea
[5] Max Planck Institute for Informatics, 66123 Saarbrücken, Germany

Abstract. For a machine learning model to generalize well, one needs to ensure that its decisions are supported by meaningful patterns in the input data. A prerequisite is however for the model to be able to explain itself, e.g. by highlighting which input features it uses to support its prediction. Layer-wise Relevance Propagation (LRP) is a technique that brings such explainability and scales to potentially highly complex deep neural networks. It operates by propagating the prediction backward in the neural network, using a set of purposely designed propagation rules. In this chapter, we give a concise introduction to LRP with a discussion of (1) how to implement propagation rules easily and efficiently, (2) how the propagation procedure can be theoretically justified as a 'deep Taylor decomposition', (3) how to choose the propagation rules at each layer to deliver high explanation quality, and (4) how LRP can be extended to handle a variety of machine learning scenarios beyond deep neural networks.

Keywords: Explanations · Deep Neural Networks ·
Layer-wise Relevance Propagation · Deep Taylor Decomposition

10.1 Introduction

Machine learning techniques such as deep neural networks have reached many successes in scientific [9,14,17,33,45] and industrial (e.g. [2,20,32]) applications. A main driver for the adoption of these techniques is the rise of large datasets, enabling the extraction of complex real-world correlations and nonlinearities.

Large datasets, however, are often plagued by the presence of spurious correlations between the different variables [13]. Spurious correlations leave the

© Springer Nature Switzerland AG 2019
W. Samek et al. (Eds.): Explainable AI, LNAI 11700, pp. 193–209, 2019.
https://doi.org/10.1007/978-3-030-28954-6_10

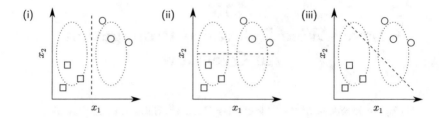

Fig. 10.1. Illustration of the problem of spurious correlations often encountered in high-dimensional data. In this example, both x_1 and x_2 predict the current data, but only x_1 generalizes correctly to the true distribution.

learning machine perplexed when having to decide which of the few correlated input variables should be used to support the prediction. A simple example is given in Fig. 10.1. The model classifies the data perfectly by using either feature x_1, feature x_2, or both of them, yet only the first option will generalize correctly to new data. Failure to learn the correct input features may lead to 'Clever Hans'-type predictors [30].

Feature selection [19] offers a potential solution by presenting to the learning machine only a limited number of 'good' input features. This approach is however difficult to apply e.g. in image recognition, where the role of individual pixels is not fixed.

Explainable machine learning [8,37,52] looks at the problem in the other direction: First, a model is trained without caring too much about feature selection. Only after training we look at which input features the neural network has learned. Based on this explanatory feedback, 'bad' features can be removed and the model can be retrained on the cleaned data [15,57]. A simple method, Taylor Decomposition [7,11], produces explanations by performing a Taylor expansion of the prediction $f(\boldsymbol{x})$ at some nearby reference point $\widetilde{\boldsymbol{x}}$:

$$f(\boldsymbol{x}) = f(\widetilde{\boldsymbol{x}}) + \sum_{i=1}^{d} (x_i - \widetilde{x}_i) \cdot [\nabla f(\widetilde{\boldsymbol{x}})]_i + \dots$$

First-order terms (elements of the sum) quantify the relevance of each input feature to the prediction, and form the explanation. Although simple and straightforward, this method is unstable when applied to deep neural networks. The instability can be traced to various known shortcomings of deep neural network functions:

– *Shattered gradients* [10]: While the function value $f(\boldsymbol{x})$ is generally accurate, the gradient of the function is noisy.
– *Adversarial examples* [53]: Some tiny perturbations of the input $\boldsymbol{x}$ can cause the function value $f(\boldsymbol{x})$ to change drastically.

These shortcomings make it difficult to choose a meaningful reference point $\widetilde{\boldsymbol{x}}$ with a meaningful gradient $\nabla f(\widetilde{\boldsymbol{x}})$. This prevents the construction of a reliable explanation [37].

Numerous explanation techniques have been proposed to better address the complexity of deep neural networks. Some proposals improve the explanation by integrating a large number of local gradient estimates [49,51]. Other techniques replace the gradient by a coarser estimate of effect [60], e.g. the model response to patch-like perturbations [58]. Further techniques involve the optimization of some local surrogate model [41], or of the explanation itself [18]. All these techniques involve multiple neural network evaluations, which can be computationally expensive.

In the following, we place our focus on Layer-wise Relevance Propagation [7], a technique that leverages the graph structure of the deep neural network to quickly and reliably compute explanations.

10.2   Layer-Wise Relevance Propagation

Layer-wise Relevance Propagation (LRP) [7] is an explanation technique applicable to models structured as neural networks, where inputs can be e.g. images, videos, or text [3,5,7]. LRP operates by propagating the prediction $f(\boldsymbol{x})$ backwards in the neural network, by means of purposely designed local propagation rules.

The propagation procedure implemented by LRP is subject to a conservation property, where what has been received by a neuron must be redistributed to the lower layer in equal amount. This behavior is analogous to Kirchoff's conservation laws in electrical circuits, and shared by other works on explanations such as [27,46,59]. Let j and k be neurons at two consecutive layers of the neural network. Propagating relevance scores $(R_k)_k$ at a given layer onto neurons of the lower layer is achieved by applying the rule:

$$R_j = \sum_k \frac{z_{jk}}{\sum_j z_{jk}} R_k.$$

The quantity z_{jk} models the extent to which neuron j has contributed to make neuron k relevant. The denominator serves to enforce the conservation property. The propagation procedure terminates once the input features have been reached. If using the rule above for all neurons in the network, it is easy to verify the layer-wise conservation property $\sum_j R_j = \sum_k R_k$, and by extension the global conservation property $\sum_i R_i = f(\boldsymbol{x})$. The overall LRP procedure is illustrated in Fig. 10.2.

Although LRP clearly differs from the simple Taylor decomposition approach mentioned in the introduction, we will observe in Sect. 10.2.3 that each step of the propagation procedure can be modeled as an own Taylor decomposition performed over local quantities in the graph [36].

LRP was applied to discover biases in commonly used ML models and datasets [28,30]. It was also applied to extract new insights from well-functioning ML models, e.g. in face expression recognition [4,29]. LRP was used to find relevant features for audio source localization [39], to identify points of interest in side channel traces [21], and to identify EEG patterns that explain decisions

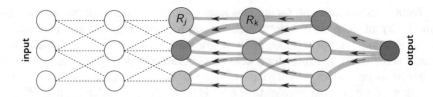

Fig. 10.2. Illustration of the LRP procedure. Each neuron redistributes to the lower layer as much as it has received from the higher layer.

in brain-computer interfaces [50]. In the biomedical domain, LRP was used to identify subject-specific characteristics in gait patterns [24], to highlight relevant cell structure in microscopy [12], as well as to explain therapy predictions [56]. Finally, an extension called CLRP was applied to highlight relevant molecular sections in the context of protein-ligand scoring [23].

10.2.1   LRP Rules for Deep Rectifier Networks

We consider the application of LRP to deep neural networks with rectifier (ReLU) nonlinearities, arguably the most common choice in today's applications. It includes well-known architectures for image recognition such as VGG-16 [48] and Inception v3 [54], or neural networks used in reinforcement learning [35]. Deep rectifier networks are composed of neurons of the type:

$$a_k = \max\left(0, \sum_{0,j} a_j w_{jk}\right). \tag{10.1}$$

The sum $\sum_{0,j}$ runs over all lower-layer activations $(a_j)_j$, plus an extra neuron representing the bias. More precisely, we set $a_0 = 1$ and define w_{0k} to be the neuron bias. We present three propagation rules for these networks and describe their properties.

Basic Rule (LRP-0) [7]. This rule redistributes in proportion to the contributions of each input to the neuron activation as they occur in Eq. (10.1):

$$R_j = \sum_k \frac{a_j w_{jk}}{\sum_{0,j} a_j w_{jk}} R_k$$

This rule satisfies basic properties, such as $(a_j = 0) \vee (w_{j:} = 0) \Rightarrow R_j = 0$, which makes coincide concepts such as zero weight, deactivation, and absence of connection. Although this rule looks intuitive, it can be shown that a uniform application of this rule to the whole neural network produces an explanation that is equivalent to Gradient × Input (cf. [47]). As we have mentioned in the introduction, gradient of a deep neural network is typically noisy, therefore one needs to design more robust propagation rules.

Epsilon Rule (LRP-ϵ) [7]. A first enhancement of the basic LRP-0 rule consists of adding a small positive term ϵ in the denominator:

$$R_j = \sum_k \frac{a_j w_{jk}}{\epsilon + \sum_{0,j} a_j w_{jk}} R_k$$

The role of ϵ is to absorb some relevance when the contributions to the activation of neuron k are weak or contradictory. As ϵ becomes larger, only the most salient explanation factors survive the absorption. This typically leads to explanations that are sparser in terms of input features and less noisy.

Gamma Rule (LRP-γ). Another enhancement which we introduce here is obtained by favoring the effect of positive contributions over negative contributions:

$$R_j = \sum_k \frac{a_j \cdot (w_{jk} + \gamma w_{jk}^+)}{\sum_{0,j} a_j \cdot (w_{jk} + \gamma w_{jk}^+)} R_k$$

The parameter γ controls by how much positive contributions are favored. As γ increases, negative contributions start to disappear. The prevalence of positive contributions has a limiting effect on how large positive and negative relevance can grow in the propagation phase. This helps to deliver more stable explanations. The idea of treating positive and negative contributions in an asymmetric manner was originally proposed in [7] with the LRP-$\alpha\beta$ rule (cf. Appendix 10.A). Also, choosing $\gamma \to \infty$ lets LRP-γ become equivalent to LRP-$\alpha_1\beta_0$ [7], the z^+-rule [36], and 'excitation-backprop' [59].

10.2.2 Implementing LRP Efficiently

The structure of LRP rules presented in Sect. 10.2.1 allows for an easy and efficient implementation. Consider the generic rule

$$R_j = \sum_k \frac{a_j \cdot \rho(w_{jk})}{\epsilon + \sum_{0,j} a_j \cdot \rho(w_{jk})} R_k, \tag{10.2}$$

of which LRP-$0/\epsilon/\gamma$ are special cases. The computation of this propagation rule can be decomposed in four steps:

$\forall_k :\ z_k = \epsilon + \sum_{0,j} a_j \cdot \rho(w_{jk})$	(forward pass)
$\forall_k :\ s_k = R_k/z_k$	(element-wise division)
$\forall_j :\ c_j = \sum_k \rho(w_{jk}) \cdot s_k$	(backward pass)
$\forall_j :\ R_j = a_j c_j$	(element-wise product)

The first step is a forward pass on a copy of the layer where the weights and biases have been applied the map $\theta \mapsto \rho(\theta)$, to which we further add the small increment ϵ. The second and fourth steps are simple element-wise operations. For the third step, one notes that c_j can also be expressed as the gradient computation:

$$c_j = \left[\nabla \left(\sum_k z_k(\boldsymbol{a}) \cdot s_k \right) \right]_j$$

where $\boldsymbol{a} = (a_j)_j$ is the vector of lower-layer activations, where z_k is a function of it, and where s_k is instead treated as constant. This gradient can be computed via automatic differentiation, which is available in most neural networks libraries. In PyTorch[1], this propagation rule can be implemented by the following code:

```
def relprop(a,layer,R):
    z = epsilon + rho(layer).forward(a)
    s = R/(z+1e-9)
    (z*s.data).sum().backward()
    c = a.grad
    R = a*c
    return R
```

The code is applicable to both convolution and dense layers with ReLU activation. The function "rho" returns a copy of the layer, where the weights and biases have been applied the map $\theta \mapsto \rho(\theta)$. The small additive term 1e-9 in the division simply enforces the behavior $0/0 = 0$. The operation ".data" lets the variable "s" become constant so that the gradient is not propagated through it. The function "backward" invokes the automatic differentiation mechanism and stores the resulting gradient in "a". Full code for the VGG-16 network is available at www.heatmapping.org/tutorial. When the structure of the neural network to analyze is more complex, or when we would like to compare and benchmark different explanation techniques, it can be recommended to use instead an existing software implementation such as iNNvestigate [1].

10.2.3   LRP as a Deep Taylor Decomposition

Propagation rules of Sect. 10.2.1 can be interpreted within the Deep Taylor Decomposition (DTD) framework [36]. DTD views LRP as a succession of Taylor expansions performed locally at each neuron. More specifically, the relevance score R_k is expressed as a function of the lower-level activations $(a_j)_j$ denoted by the vector $\boldsymbol{a}$, and we then perform a first-order Taylor expansion of $R_k(\boldsymbol{a})$ at some reference point $\widetilde{\boldsymbol{a}}$ in the space of activations:

$$R_k(\boldsymbol{a}) = R_k(\widetilde{\boldsymbol{a}}) + \sum_{0,j}(a_j - \widetilde{a}_j) \cdot [\nabla R_k(\widetilde{\boldsymbol{a}})]_j + \dots \qquad (10.3)$$

First-order terms (summed elements) identify how much of R_k should be redistributed on neurons of the lower layer. Due to the potentially complex relation between $\boldsymbol{a}$ and R_k, finding an appropriate reference point and computing the gradient locally is difficult.

Relevance Model. In order to obtain a closed-form expression for the terms of Eq. (10.3), one needs to substitute the true relevance function $R_k(\boldsymbol{a})$ by a relevance model $\widehat{R}_k(\boldsymbol{a})$ that is easier to analyze [36]. One such model is the modulated ReLU activation:

$$\widehat{R}_k(\boldsymbol{a}) = \max\left(0, \sum_{0,j} a_j w_{jk}\right) \cdot c_k.$$

---

[1] http://pytorch.org.

The modulation term c_k is set constant and in a way that $\widehat{R}_k(\boldsymbol{a}) = R_k(\boldsymbol{a})$ at the current data point. Treating c_k as constant can be justified when R_k results from application of LRP-0/ϵ/γ in higher layers (cf. Appendix 10.B). A Taylor expansion of the relevance model $\widehat{R}_k(\boldsymbol{a})$ on the activation domain gives:

$$\widehat{R}_k(\boldsymbol{a}) = \widehat{R}_k(\widetilde{\boldsymbol{a}}) + \sum_{0,j}(a_j - \widetilde{a}_j) \cdot w_{jk}\, c_k.$$

Second- and higher-order terms are zero due to the linearity of the ReLU function on its activated domain. The zero-order term can also be made arbitrarily small by choosing the reference point near the ReLU hinge. Once a reference point is chosen, first-order terms can be easily computed, and redistributed to neurons in the lower layer. Figure 10.3(a–c) illustrates how deep Taylor decomposition is applied at a given neuron.

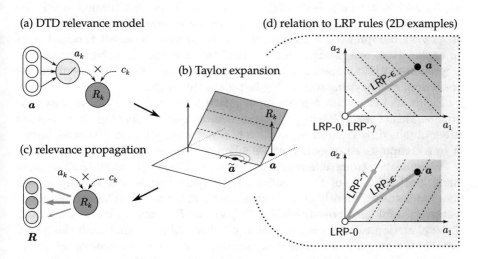

Fig. 10.3. Illustration of DTD: (a) graph view of the relevance model, (b) function view of the relevance model and reference point at which the Taylor expansion is performed, (c) propagation of first-order terms on the lower layer.

Relation to LRP-0/ϵ/γ. Each choice of reference point $\widetilde{\boldsymbol{a}}$ leads to a different way of redistributing relevance. Interestingly, specific choices of reference points reduce to the LRP propagation rules defined in Sect. 10.2.1. LRP-0 is recovered by choosing $\widetilde{\boldsymbol{a}} = \boldsymbol{0}$. LRP-$\epsilon$ is recovered by choosing $\widetilde{\boldsymbol{a}} = \epsilon \cdot (a_k + \epsilon)^{-1}\,\boldsymbol{a}$. LRP-$\gamma$ is recovered by choosing $\widetilde{\boldsymbol{a}}$ at the intersection between the ReLU hinge and the line $\{\boldsymbol{a} - t \cdot \boldsymbol{a} \odot (1 + \gamma \cdot \mathbf{1}_{w_k \succeq 0}) \mid t \in \mathbb{R}\}$, where $\mathbf{1}_{\{\cdot\}}$ is an indicator function applied element-wise. The relation between LRP and DTD root points is further illustrated on simple two-dimensional neurons in Fig. 10.3 (d). For all three LRP propagation rules, one can show that the DTD reference points always satisfy $\widetilde{\boldsymbol{a}} \succeq \boldsymbol{0}$, and therefore match the domain of ReLU activations received as input [36]. A further property of reference points one can look at is the distance

$\|\widetilde{a} - a\|$. The smaller the distance, the more contextualized the explanation will be, and the lower the number of input variables that will appear to be in contradiction. LRP-0 has the highest distance. LRP-ϵ and LRP-γ reduce this distance significantly.

10.3   Which LRP Rule for Which Layer?

As a general framework for propagation, LRP leaves much flexibility on which rule to use at each layer, and how the parameters ϵ and γ should be set. Selecting LRP parameters optimally would require a measure of explanation quality. How to assess explanation quality is still an active research topic [16,38,40,43], and a full discussion is beyond the scope of this chapter. Instead, we discuss LRP in the light of two general and well-agreed desirable properties of an explanation: *fidelity* and *understandability* [52]. In other words, an explanation should be an accurate representation of the output neuron of interest, and it should also be easy to interpret for a human. Note that to visually assess the fidelity of an explanation, one needs to assume that the network has solved the task in a "ground-truth" manner, i.e. using the correct visual features to support its prediction, and ignoring distracting factors in the image.

Figure 10.4 shows for a given input image (of size 224×224), various LRP explanations of the VGG-16 [48] output neuron 'castle'. These explanations are either obtained by uniform application of a single propagation rule at all layers, or by a composite strategy [29] where different rules are used at different layers.

We observe strong differences in the explanations. *Uniform LRP-0* picks many local artifacts of the function. The explanation is overly complex and does not focus sufficiently on the actual castle in the image. The explanation is neither faithful nor understandable. *Uniform LRP-ϵ* removes noise elements in the explanation to keep only a limited number features that match the actual castle in the image. It is a faithful explanation, but too sparse to be easily understandable. *Uniform LRP-γ* is easier for a human to understand because features are more densely highlighted, but it also picks unrelated concepts such as the lamp post, making it unfaithful. *Composite LRP* overcomes the disadvantages of the approaches above. The features of the castle are correctly identified and fully highlighted, thereby making the explanation both faithful and understandable.

The reason why Composite LRP delivers a better explanation can be traced to the qualitative differences between the various layers of the VGG-16 neural network:

Upper layers have only approximately 4 000 neurons (i.e. on average 4 neurons per class), making it likely that the many concepts forming the different classes are entangled. Here, a propagation rule close to the function and its gradient (e.g. LRP-0) will be insensitive to these entanglements.

Middle layers have a more disentangled representation, however, the stacking of many layers and the weight sharing in convolutions introduces spurious variations. LRP-ϵ filters out these spurious variations and retains only the most salient explanation factors.

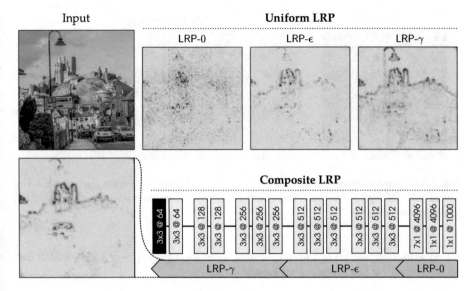

Fig. 10.4. Input image and pixel-wise explanations of the output neuron 'castle' obtained with various LRP procedures. Parameters are $\epsilon = 0.25\,\mathrm{std}$ and $\gamma = 0.25$.

Lower layers are similar to middle layers, however, LRP-γ is more suitable here, as this rule tends to spread relevance uniformly to the whole feature rather than capturing the contribution of every individual pixel. This makes the explanation more understandable for a human.

Overall, in order to apply LRP successfully on a new task, it is important to carefully inspect the properties of the neural network layers, and to ask the human what kind of explanation is most understandable for him.

10.3.1   Handling the Top Layer

The quantity we have explained so far is the score z_c for class c, computed from lower-layer activations $(a_k)_k$ as:

$$z_c = \sum_{0,k} a_k w_{kc}.$$

It is linked to the predicted class probability via the softmax function $\mathrm{P}(\omega_c) = \exp(z_c)/\sum_{c'} \exp(z_{c'})$. Fig. 10.5 (middle) shows an explanation of the score $z_{\mathrm{passenger\_car}}$ for some image containing a locomotive, a passenger car and other elements in the background. The explanation retains the passenger car features, but also features of the locomotive in front of it. This shows that the quantity z_c is not truly selective for the class to explain.

Input   LRP explanations

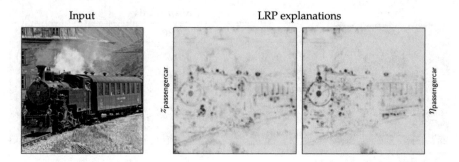

Fig. 10.5. Explanations obtained for the output neuron 'passenger_car' and for the actual probability of the class 'passenger_car'. The locomotive switches from positive to negatively relevant.

Alternately, we can opt for explaining $\eta_c = \log[\mathrm{P}(\omega_c)/(1-\mathrm{P}(\omega_c))]$, which can be expressed by the sequence of layers:

$$z_{c,c'} = \sum_{0,k} a_k(w_{kc} - w_{kc'})$$
$$\eta_c = -\log \sum_{c' \neq c} \exp(-z_{c,c'}).$$

The first layer represents the log-probability ratios $\log[\mathrm{P}(\omega_c)/\mathrm{P}(\omega_{c'})]$, and the second layer performs a reverse log-sum-exp pooling over these ratios. A propagation rule for this type of pooling layer was proposed in [26]: Relevance is redistributed on the pooled neurons following a min-take-most strategy: $R_{c,c'} = z_{c,c'} \cdot \exp(-z_{c,c'})/\sum_{c'' \neq c} \exp(-z_{c,c''})$. These scores can then be further propagated into the neural network with usual LRP rules. Figure 10.5 (right) shows the explanation for $\eta_{\mathrm{passenger\_car}}$. Positive evidence becomes sparser, and the locomotive turns blue (i.e. negatively relevant). This reflects the fact that the presence of the locomotive in the image raises the probability for the class 'locomotive' and thus lowers it for the class 'passenger_car'.

10.3.2   Handling Special Layers

Practical neural networks are often equipped with special layers that facilitate optimization, incorporate some predefined invariance into the model, or handle a particular type of input data. We briefly review how to handle some of these layers within the LRP framework.

Spatial Pooling Layers are often used between convolution layers to promote local translation invariance in the model. A sum-pooling layer applied to positive activations can be easily rewritten as a standard linear-ReLU layer. Thus all LRP rules we have presented here can also be applied to sum-pooling layers. Max-pooling layers, on the other hand, can either be handled by a winner-take-all redistribution scheme [7], or by using the same rules as for the sum-pooling case [36, 37]. In this chapter, we have used the second option.

Batch Normalization Layers are commonly used to facilitate training and improve prediction accuracy. At test time, they simply consist of a centering and rescaling operation. These layers can therefore be absorbed by the adjacent linear layer without changing the function. This allows to recover the canonical neural network structure needed for applying LRP.

Input Layers are different from intermediate layers as they do not receive ReLU activations as input but pixels or real values. Special rules for these layers can also be derived from the DTD framework [36] (cf. Appendix 10.A). In this chapter, we made use of the $z^{\mathcal{B}}$-rule, which is suitable for pixels.

10.4 LRP Beyond Deep Networks

Deep neural networks have been particularly successful on tasks involving classification and regression. Other problems such as unsupervised modeling, time series forecasting, and pairwise matching, have been traditionally handled by other types of models. Here, we discuss various extensions that let LRP be applied to this broader class of models.

Unsupervised Models. Unsupervised learning algorithms extract structures from unlabeled data from which properties such as membership to some cluster or degree of anomaly can be predicted. In order to explain these predictions, a novel methodology called Neuralization-Propagation (NEON) was proposed [25, 26]: The learned unsupervised model is first 'neuralized' (i.e. transformed into a functionally equivalent neural network). Then, an LRP procedure is built in order to propagate the prediction backward in the neural network.

In one-class SVMs [44], predicted anomaly could be rewritten as a min-pooling over support vector distances [25]. Similarly, in k-means, predicted cluster membership could be rewritten as pooling over local linear discriminants between competing clusters [26]. For each extracted neural network, suitable LRP rules could be designed based on the DTD methodology. Overall, the proposed Neuralization-Propagation approach endows these unsupervised models with fast and reliable explanations.

Time Series Prediction. To predict the next steps of a time series, one must ideally be able to identify the underlying dynamical system and simulate it forward. A popular model for this is the LSTM [22]. It uses product interactions of the type

$$h_k = \text{sigm}(\textstyle\sum_j a_j v_{jk} + c_k) \cdot g(\textstyle\sum_j a_j w_{jk} + b_k).$$

The first term is a gate that regulates how the signal is transferred between the internal state and the real-world. The second term is the signal itself. A successful strategy for applying LRP in these models is to let all relevance flow through the second term [6, 40, 42, 56]. Furthermore, when g is chosen to be a ReLU function, and if the gating function is strictly positive or locally constant, this strategy can also be justified within the DTD framework.

Pairwise Matching. A last problem for which one may require explanations is when predicting if two vectors $x \in \mathcal{X}$ and $y \in \mathcal{Y}$ match. This problem arises, for example, when modeling the relation between an image and a transformed version of it [34], or in recommender systems, when modeling the relation between users and products [55]. An approach to pairwise matching is to build product neurons of the type $a_k = \max(0, \sum_i x_i w_{ik}) \cdot \max(0, \sum_j y_j v_{jk})$. A propagation rule for this product of neurons is given by [31]:

$$R_{ij} = \sum_k \frac{x_i y_j w_{ik} v_{jk}}{\sum_{ij} x_i y_j w_{ik} v_{jk}} R_k.$$

This propagation rule can also be derived from DTD when considering second-order Taylor expansions. The resulting explanation is in terms of pairs of input features i and j from each modality.

10.5   Conclusion

We have reviewed Layer-wise Relevance Propagation (LRP), a technique that can explain the predictions of complex state-of-the-art neural networks in terms of input features, by propagating the prediction backward in the network by means of propagation rules. LRP has a number of properties that makes it attractive: Propagation rules can be implemented efficiently and modularly in most modern neural network software and a number of these rules are furthermore embeddable in the Deep Taylor Decomposition framework. Parameters of the LRP rules can be set in a way that high explanation quality is obtained even for complex models. Finally, LRP is extensible beyond deep neural network classifiers to a broader range of machine learning models and tasks. This makes it applicable to a large number of practical scenarios where explanation is needed.

Acknowledgements. This work was supported by the German Ministry for Education and Research as Berlin Big Data Centre (01IS14013A), Berlin Center for Machine Learning (01IS18037I) and TraMeExCo (01IS18056A). Partial funding by DFG is acknowledged (EXC 2046/1, project-ID: 390685689). This work was also supported by the Institute for Information & Communications Technology Planning & Evaluation (IITP) grant funded by the Korea government (No. 2017-0-00451, No. 2017-0-01779).

Appendices

10.A   List of Commonly Used LRP Rules

The table below gives a non-exhaustive list of propagation rules that are commonly used for explaining deep neural networks with ReLU nonlinearities. The last column in the table indicates whether the rules can be derived from the deep Taylor decomposition [36] framework.

Here, we have used the notation $(\cdot)^+ = \max(0, \cdot)$ and $(\cdot)^- = \min(0, \cdot)$. For the LRP-$\alpha\beta$ rule, the parameters α, β are subject to the conservation constraint $\alpha = \beta + 1$. For the $z^{\mathcal{B}}$-rule the parameters l_i, h_i define the box constraints of the input domain ($\forall_i : l_i \leq x_i \leq h_i$).

Name	Formula	Usage	DTD
LRP-0 [7]	$R_j = \sum_k \frac{a_j w_{jk}}{\sum_{0,j} a_j w_{jk}} R_k$	Upper layers	✓
LRP-ϵ [7]	$R_j = \sum_k \frac{a_j w_{jk}}{\epsilon + \sum_{0,j} a_j w_{jk}} R_k$	Middle layers	✓
LRP-γ	$R_j = \sum_k \frac{a_j (w_{jk} + \gamma w_{jk}^+)}{\sum_{0,j} a_j (w_{jk} + \gamma w_{jk}^+)} R_k$	Lower layers	✓
LRP-$\alpha\beta$ [7]	$R_j = \sum_k \left(\alpha \frac{(a_j w_{jk})^+}{\sum_{0,j} (a_j w_{jk})^+} - \beta \frac{(a_j w_{jk})^-}{\sum_{0,j} (a_j w_{jk})^-} \right) R_k$	Lower layers	×[a]
flat [30]	$R_j = \sum_k \frac{1}{\sum_j 1} R_k$	Lower layers	×
w^2-rule [36]	$R_i = \sum_j \frac{w_{ij}^2}{\sum_i w_{ij}^2} R_j$	First layer ($\mathbb{R}^d$)	✓
$z^{\mathcal{B}}$-rule [36]	$R_i = \sum_j \frac{x_i w_{ij} - l_i w_{ij}^+ - h_i w_{ij}^-}{\sum_i x_i w_{ij} - l_i w_{ij}^+ - h_i w_{ij}^-} R_j$	First layer (pixels)	✓

([a]DTD interpretation only for the case $\alpha = 1, \beta = 0$.)

10.B   Justification of the Relevance Model

We give here a justification similar to [36,37] that the relevance model $\widehat{R}_k(\boldsymbol{a})$ of Sect. 10.2.3 is suitable when relevance R_k results from applying LRP-$0/\epsilon/\gamma$ in the higher layers. The generic propagation rule

$$R_k = \sum_l \frac{a_k \cdot \rho(w_{kl})}{\epsilon + \sum_{0,k} a_k \cdot \rho(w_{kl})} R_l,$$

of which LRP-$0/\epsilon/\gamma$ are special cases, can be rewritten as $R_k = a_k c_k$ with

$$c_k(\boldsymbol{a}) = \sum_l \rho(w_{kl}) \frac{\max \left(0, \sum_{0,k} a_k(\boldsymbol{a}) \cdot w_{kl}\right)}{\epsilon + \sum_{0,k} a_k(\boldsymbol{a}) \cdot \rho(w_{kl})} c_l(\boldsymbol{a}),$$

where the dependences on lower activations $\boldsymbol{a}$ have been made explicit. Assume $c_l(\boldsymbol{a})$ to be approximately locally constant w.r.t. $\boldsymbol{a}$. Because other terms that depend on $\boldsymbol{a}$ are diluted by two nested sums, it is plausible that $c_k(\boldsymbol{a})$ is again locally approximately constant, which is the assumption made by the relevance model $\widehat{R}_k(\boldsymbol{a})$.

References

1. Alber, M., et al.: iNNvestigate neural networks!. J. Mach. Learn. Res. **20**(93), 1–8 (2019)
2. Amodei, D., et al.: Deep speech 2 : end-to-end speech recognition in English and Mandarin. In: Proceedings of the 33nd International Conference on Machine Learning, pp. 173–182 (2016)
3. Anders, C., Montavon, G., Samek, W., Müller, K.-R.: Understanding patch-based learning of video data by explaining predictions. In: Samek, W., Montavon, G., Vedaldi, A., Hansen, L.K., Müller, K.R., et al. (eds.) Explainable AI, LNCS, vol. 11700, pp. 297–309. Springer, Cham (2019)

4. Arbabzadah, F., Montavon, G., Müller, K., Samek, W.: Identifying individual facial expressions by deconstructing a neural network. In: 38th German Conference on Pattern Recognition, pp. 344–354 (2016)
5. Arras, L., Horn, F., Montavon, G., Müller, K.R., Samek, W.: "What is relevant in a text document?": an interpretable machine learning approach. PLoS ONE **12**(8), e0181142 (2017)
6. Arras, L., Montavon, G., Müller, K.R., Samek, W.: Explaining recurrent neural network predictions in sentiment analysis. In: Proceedings of the 8th EMNLP Workshop on Computational Approaches to Subjectivity, Sentiment and Social Media Analysis, pp. 159–168 (2017)
7. Bach, S., Binder, A., Montavon, G., Klauschen, F., Müller, K.R., Samek, W.: On pixel-wise explanations for non-linear classifier decisions by layer-wise relevance propagation. PLoS ONE **10**(7), e0130140 (2015)
8. Baehrens, D., Schroeter, T., Harmeling, S., Kawanabe, M., Hansen, K., Müller, K.: How to explain individual classification decisions. J. Mach. Learn. Res. **11**, 1803–1831 (2010)
9. Baldi, P., Sadowski, P., Whiteson, D.: Searching for exotic particles in high-energy physics with deep learning. Nat. Commun. **5**(1) (2014). Article Number 4308
10. Balduzzi, D., Frean, M., Leary, L., Lewis, J.P., Ma, K.W., McWilliams, B.: The shattered gradients problem: if resnets are the answer, then what is the question? In: Proceedings of the 34th International Conference on Machine Learning, pp. 342–350 (2017)
11. Bazen, S., Joutard, X.: The Taylor decomposition: a unified generalization of the Oaxaca method to nonlinear models. Working papers, HAL (2013)
12. Binder, A., et al.: Towards computational fluorescence microscopy: machine learning-based integrated prediction of morphological and molecular tumor profiles. CoRR abs/1805.11178 (2018)
13. Calude, C.S., Longo, G.: The deluge of spurious correlations in big data. Found. Sci. **22**(3), 595–612 (2017)
14. Chmiela, S., Tkatchenko, A., Sauceda, H.E., Poltavsky, I., Schütt, K.T., Müller, K.R.: Machine learning of accurate energy-conserving molecular force fields. Sci. Adv. **3**(5), e1603015 (2017)
15. Clark, P., Matwin, S.: Using qualitative models to guide inductive learning. In: Proceedings of the 10th International Conference on Machine Learning, pp. 49–56 (1993)
16. Doshi-Velez, F., Kim, B.: Considerations for evaluation and generalization in interpretable machine learning. In: Escalante, H.J., et al. (eds.) Explainable and Interpretable Models in Computer Vision and Machine Learning. TSSCML, pp. 3–17. Springer, Cham (2018). https://doi.org/10.1007/978-3-319-98131-4_1
17. Esteva, A., et al.: Dermatologist-level classification of skin cancer with deep neural networks. Nature **542**(7639), 115–118 (2017)
18. Fong, R.C., Vedaldi, A.: Interpretable explanations of black boxes by meaningful perturbation. In: IEEE International Conference on Computer Vision, pp. 3449–3457 (2017)
19. Guyon, I., Elisseeff, A.: An introduction to variable and feature selection. J. Mach. Learn. Res. **3**, 1157–1182 (2003)
20. He, X., Liao, L., Zhang, H., Nie, L., Hu, X., Chua, T.: Neural collaborative filtering. In: Proceedings of the 26th International Conference on World Wide Web, pp. 173–182 (2017)

21. Hettwer, B., Gehrer, S., Güneysu, T.: Deep neural network attribution methods for leakage analysis and symmetric key recovery. IACR Cryptology ePrint Arch. **2019**, 143 (2019)
22. Hochreiter, S., Schmidhuber, J.: Long short-term memory. Neural Comput. **9**(8), 1735–1780 (1997)
23. Hochuli, J., Helbling, A., Skaist, T., Ragoza, M., Koes, D.R.: Visualizing convolutional neural network protein-ligand scoring. J. Mol. Graph. Model. **84**, 96–108 (2018)
24. Horst, F., Lapuschkin, S., Samek, W., Müller, K.R., Schöllhorn, W.I.: Explaining the unique nature of individual gait patterns with deep learning. Sci. Rep. **9**, 2391 (2019)
25. Kauffmann, J., Müller, K.R., Montavon, G.: Towards explaining anomalies: a deep Taylor decomposition of one-class models. CoRR abs/1805.06230 (2018)
26. Kauffmann, J., Esders, M., Montavon, G., Samek, W., Müller, K.R.: From clustering to cluster explanations via neural networks. CoRR abs/1906.07633 (2019)
27. Landecker, W., Thomure, M.D., Bettencourt, L.M.A., Mitchell, M., Kenyon, G.T., Brumby, S.P.: Interpreting individual classifications of hierarchical networks. In: IEEE Symposium on Computational Intelligence and Data Mining, pp. 32–38 (2013)
28. Lapuschkin, S., Binder, A., Montavon, G., Müller, K.R., Samek, W.: Analyzing classifiers: fisher vectors and deep neural networks. In: Proceedings of the IEEE Conference on Computer Vision and Pattern Recognition, pp. 2912–2920 (2016)
29. Lapuschkin, S., Binder, A., Müller, K.R., Samek, W.: Understanding and comparing deep neural networks for age and gender classification. In: IEEE International Conference on Computer Vision Workshops, pp. 1629–1638 (2017)
30. Lapuschkin, S., Wäldchen, S., Binder, A., Montavon, G., Samek, W., Müller, K.R.: Unmasking Clever Hans predictors and assessing what machines really learn. Nat. Commun. **10**, 1096 (2019)
31. Leupold, S.: Second-order Taylor decomposition for Explaining Spatial Transformation of Images. Master's thesis, Technische Universität Berlin (2017)
32. Mao, H., Alizadeh, M., Menache, I., Kandula, S.: Resource management with deep reinforcement learning. In: Proceedings of the 15th ACM Workshop on Hot Topics in Networks, pp. 50–56 (2016)
33. Mayr, A., Klambauer, G., Unterthiner, T., Hochreiter, S.: DeepTox: toxicity prediction using deep learning. Front. Environ. Sci. **3**, 80 (2016)
34. Memisevic, R., Hinton, G.E.: Learning to represent spatial transformations with factored higher-order Boltzmann machines. Neural Comput. **22**(6), 1473–1492 (2010)
35. Mnih, V., et al.: Human-level control through deep reinforcement learning. Nature **518**(7540), 529–533 (2015)
36. Montavon, G., Lapuschkin, S., Binder, A., Samek, W., Müller, K.R.: Explaining nonlinear classification decisions with deep Taylor decomposition. Pattern Recogn. **65**, 211–222 (2017)
37. Montavon, G., Samek, W., Müller, K.R.: Methods for interpreting and understanding deep neural networks. Digital Signal Process. **73**, 1–15 (2018)
38. Narayanan, M., Chen, E., He, J., Kim, B., Gershman, S., Doshi-Velez, F.: How do humans understand explanations from machine learning systems? an evaluation of the human-interpretability of explanation. CoRR abs/1802.00682 (2018)
39. Perotin, L., Serizel, R., Vincent, E., Guérin, A.: CRNN-based multiple DoA estimation using acoustic intensity features for ambisonics recordings. J. Sel. Top. Signal Process. **13**(1), 22–33 (2019)

40. Poerner, N., Schütze, H., Roth, B.: Evaluating neural network explanation methods using hybrid documents and morphosyntactic agreement. In: Proceedings of the 56th Annual Meeting of the Association for Computational Linguistics, pp. 340–350 (2018)

41. Ribeiro, M.T., Singh, S., Guestrin, C.: "Why should I trust you?": explaining the predictions of any classifier. In: Proceedings of the 22nd ACM SIGKDD International Conference on Knowledge Discovery and Data Mining, pp. 1135–1144 (2016)

42. Rieger, L., Chormai, P., Montavon, G., Hansen, L.K., Müller, K.-R.: Structuring neural networks for more explainable predictions. In: Escalante, H.J., et al. (eds.) Explainable and Interpretable Models in Computer Vision and Machine Learning. TSSCML, pp. 115–131. Springer, Cham (2018). https://doi.org/10.1007/978-3-319-98131-4_5

43. Samek, W., Binder, A., Montavon, G., Lapuschkin, S., Müller, K.R.: Evaluating the visualization of what a deep neural network has learned. IEEE Trans. Neural Networks Learn. Syst. **28**(11), 2660–2673 (2017)

44. Schölkopf, B., Williamson, R.C., Smola, A.J., Shawe-Taylor, J., Platt, J.C.: Support vector method for novelty detection. Adv. Neural Inf. Process. Syst. **12**, 582–588 (1999)

45. Schütt, K.T., Arbabzadah, F., Chmiela, S., Müller, K.R., Tkatchenko, A.: Quantum-chemical insights from deep tensor neural networks. Nature Commun. **8**, 13890 (2017)

46. Shrikumar, A., Greenside, P., Kundaje, A.: Learning important features through propagating activation differences. In: Proceedings of the 34th International Conference on Machine Learning, pp. 3145–3153 (2017)

47. Shrikumar, A., Greenside, P., Shcherbina, A., Kundaje, A.: Not just a black box: learning important features through propagating activation differences. CoRR abs/1605.01713 (2016)

48. Simonyan, K., Zisserman, A.: Very deep convolutional networks for large-scale image recognition. In: 3rd International Conference on Learning Representations (2015)

49. Smilkov, D., Thorat, N., Kim, B., Viégas, F.B., Wattenberg, M.: SmoothGrad: removing noise by adding noise. CoRR abs/1706.03825 (2017)

50. Sturm, I., Lapuschkin, S., Samek, W., Müller, K.R.: Interpretable deep neural networks for single-trial EEG classification. J. Neurosci. Methods **274**, 141–145 (2016)

51. Sundararajan, M., Taly, A., Yan, Q.: Axiomatic attribution for deep networks. In: Proceedings of the 34th International Conference on Machine Learning, pp. 3319–3328 (2017)

52. Swartout, W.R., Moore, J.D.: Explanation in second generation expert systems. In: David, J.M., Krivine, J.P., Simmons, R. (eds.) Second Generation Expert Systems, pp. 543–585. Springer, Heidelberg (1993). https://doi.org/10.1007/978-3-642-77927-5_24

53. Szegedy, C., et al.: Intriguing properties of neural networks. In: 2nd International Conference on Learning Representations (2014)

54. Szegedy, C., Vanhoucke, V., Ioffe, S., Shlens, J., Wojna, Z.: Rethinking the inception architecture for computer vision. In: IEEE Conference on Computer Vision and Pattern Recognition, pp. 2818–2826 (2016)

55. Xue, H., Dai, X., Zhang, J., Huang, S., Chen, J.: Deep matrix factorization models for recommender systems. In: Proceedings of the 26th International Joint Conference on Artificial Intelligence, pp. 3203–3209 (2017)

56. Yang, Y., Tresp, V., Wunderle, M., Fasching, P.A.: Explaining therapy predictions with layer-wise relevance propagation in neural networks. In: IEEE International Conference on Healthcare Informatics, pp. 152–162 (2018)
57. Yuan, X., He, P., Zhu, Q., Li, X.: Adversarial examples: attacks and defenses for deep learning. IEEE Trans. Neural Networks Learn. Syst. 1–20 (2019)
58. Zeiler, M.D., Fergus, R.: Visualizing and understanding convolutional networks. In: Fleet, D., Pajdla, T., Schiele, B., Tuytelaars, T. (eds.) ECCV 2014. LNCS, vol. 8689, pp. 818–833. Springer, Cham (2014). https://doi.org/10.1007/978-3-319-10590-1_53
59. Zhang, J., Bargal, S.A., Lin, Z., Brandt, J., Shen, X., Sclaroff, S.: Top-down neural attention by excitation backprop. Int. J. Comput. Vis. **126**(10), 1084–1102 (2018)
60. Zintgraf, L.M., Cohen, T.S., Adel, T., Welling, M.: Visualizing deep neural network decisions: prediction difference analysis. In: International Conference on Learning Representations (2017)

11
Explaining and Interpreting LSTMs

Leila Arras[1], José Arjona-Medina[2], Michael Widrich[2], Grégoire Montavon[3], Michael Gillhofer[2], Klaus-Robert Müller[3,4,5], Sepp Hochreiter[2], and Wojciech Samek[1(✉)]

[1] Fraunhofer Heinrich Hertz Institute, 10587 Berlin, Germany
{leila.arras,wojciech.samek}@hhi.fraunhofer.de
[2] Johannes Kepler University Linz, 4040 Linz, Austria
{arjona,widrich,gillhofer,hochreit}@ml.jku.at
[3] Technische Universität Berlin, 10587 Berlin, Germany
{gregoire.montavon,klaus-robert.mueller}@tu-berlin.de
[4] Korea University, Anam-dong, Seongbuk-gu, Seoul 02841, Korea
[5] Max Planck Institute for Informatics, 66123 Saarbrücken, Germany

Abstract. While neural networks have acted as a strong unifying force in the design of modern AI systems, the neural network architectures themselves remain highly heterogeneous due to the variety of tasks to be solved. In this chapter, we explore how to adapt the Layer-wise Relevance Propagation (LRP) technique used for explaining the predictions of feed-forward networks to the LSTM architecture used for sequential data modeling and forecasting. The special accumulators and gated interactions present in the LSTM require both a new propagation scheme and an extension of the underlying theoretical framework to deliver faithful explanations.

Keywords: Explainable artificial intelligence · Model transparency · Recurrent neural networks · LSTM · Interpretability

11.1 Introduction

In practical applications, building high-performing AI systems is not always the sole objective, and interpretability may also be an important issue [16].

Most of the recent research on interpretable AI has focused on feedforward neural networks, especially the deep rectifier networks and variants used for image recognition [68,79]. Layer-wise relevance propagation (LRP) [6,51] was shown in this setting to provide for state-of-the-art models such as VGG-16, explanations that are both informative and fast to compute, and that could be embedded in the framework of deep Taylor decomposition [52].

L. Arras and J. Arjona-Medina—Contributed equally to this work.

© Springer Nature Switzerland AG 2019
W. Samek et al. (Eds.): Explainable AI, LNAI 11700, pp. 211–238, 2019.
https://doi.org/10.1007/978-3-030-28954-6_11

However, in the presence of sequential data, one may need to incorporate temporal structure in the neural network model, e.g. to make forecasts about future time steps. In this setting it is key to be able to learn the underlying *dynamical system*, e.g. with a recurrent neural network, so that it can then be simulated forward. Learning dynamical systems with long-term dependencies using recurrent neural networks presents a number of challenges. The backpropagation through time learning signal tends to either blow up or vanish [10, 30]. To reduce this difficulty, special neural network architectures have been proposed, in particular, the Long Short-Term Memory (LSTM) [30, 35, 37], which makes use of special accumulators and gating functions.

The multiple architectural changes and the unique nature of the sequential prediction task make a direct application of the LRP-type explanation technique non-straightforward. To be able to deliver accurate explanations, one needs to carefully inspect the structure of the LSTM blocks forming the model and their interaction.

In this chapter, we explore multiple dimensions of the interface between the LRP technique and the LSTM. First, we analyze how the LRP propagation mechanism can be adapted to accumulators and gated interactions in the LSTM. Our new propagation scheme is embedded in the deep Taylor decomposition framework [52], and validated empirically on sentiment analysis and on a toy numeric task. Further, we investigate how modifications of the LSTM architecture, in particular, on the cell input activation, the forget and output gates and on the network connections, make explanations more straightforward, and we apply these changes in a reinforcement learning showcase.

The present chapter elaborates on our previous work [2, 5].

11.2   Background

11.2.1   Long Short-Term Memory (LSTM)

Recently, *Long Short-Term Memory* (LSTM; [30, 35, 37]) networks have emerged as the best-performing technique in speech and language processing. LSTM networks have been overwhelmingly successful in different speech and language applications, including handwriting recognition [24], generation of writings [23], language modeling and identification [22, 78], automatic language translation [73], speech recognition [17, 63], analysis of audio data [49], analysis, annotation, and description of video data [15, 70, 76]. LSTM has facilitated recent benchmark records in TIMIT phoneme recognition, optical character recognition, text-to-speech synthesis, language identification, large vocabulary speech recognition, English-to-French translation, audio onset detection, social signal classification, image caption generation, video-to-text description, end-to-end speech recognition, and semantic representations.

The key idea of LSTM is the use of memory cells that allow for constant error flow during training. Thereby, LSTM avoids the *vanishing gradient problem*, that is, the phenomenon that training errors are decaying when they are back-propagated through time [30, 33]. The vanishing gradient problem severely impedes *credit assignment* in recurrent neural networks, i.e. the correct identification of relevant events whose effects are not immediate, but observed with possibly long delays. LSTM, by its constant error flow, avoids vanishing gradients and, hence, allows for *uniform credit assignment*, i.e. all input signals obtain a similar error signal. Other recurrent neural networks are not able to assign the same credit to all input signals and therefore, are very limited concerning the solutions they will find. Uniform credit assignment enables LSTM networks to excel in speech and language tasks: if a sentence is analyzed, then the first word can be as important as the last word. Via uniform credit assignment, LSTM networks regard all words of a sentence equally. Uniform credit assignment enables to consider all input information at each phase of learning, no matter where it is located in the input sequence. Therefore, uniform credit assignment reveals many more solutions to the learning algorithm, which would otherwise remain hidden.

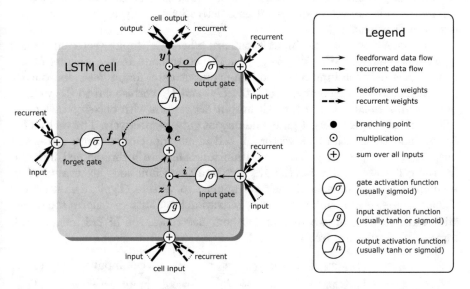

Fig. 11.1. LSTM memory cell without peepholes. z is the vector of cell input activations, i is the vector of input gate activations, f is the vector of forget gate activations, c is the vector of memory cell states, o is the vector of output gate activations, and y is the vector of cell output activations. The activation functions are g for the cell input, h for the cell state, and σ for the gates. Data flow is either "feed-forward" without delay or "recurrent" with a one-step delay. "Input" connections are from the external input to the LSTM network, while "recurrent" connections take inputs from other memory cell outputs y in the LSTM network with a delay of one time step, accordingly to Eqs. 11.1–11.6. The cell state c also has a recurrent connection with one time step delay to himself via a multiplication with the forget gate f, and gets accumulated through a sum with the current input.

LSTM in a Nutshell. The central processing and storage unit for LSTM recurrent networks is the *memory cell*. As already mentioned, it avoids vanishing gradients and allows for uniform credit assignment. The most commonly used LSTM memory cell architecture in the literature [25,66] contains forget gates [19,20] and peephole connections [18]. In our previous work [34,38], we found that peephole connections are only useful for modeling time series, but not for language, meta-learning, or biological sequences. That peephole connections can be removed without performance decrease, was recently confirmed in a large assessment, where different LSTM architectures have been tested [26]. While LSTM networks are highly successful in various applications, the central memory cell architecture was not modified since 2000 [66]. A memory cell architecture without peepholes is depicted in Fig. 11.1.

In our definition of an LSTM network, all units of one kind are pooled to a vector: z is the vector of cell input activations, i is the vector of input gate activations, f is the vector of forget gate activations, c is the vector of memory cell states, o is the vector of output gate activations, and y is the vector of cell output activations.

We assume to have an input sequence, where the input vector at time t is x_t. The matrices W_z, W_i, W_f, and W_o correspond to the weights of the connections between inputs and cell input, input gate, forget gate, and output gate, respectively. The matrices U_z, U_i, U_f, and U_o correspond to the weights of the connections between the cell output activations with one-step delay and cell input, input gate, forget gate, and output gate, respectively. The vectors b_z, b_i, b_f, and b_o are the bias vectors of cell input, input gate, forget gate, and output gate, respectively. The activation functions are g for the cell input, h for the cell state, and σ for the gates, where these functions are evaluated in a component-wise manner if they are applied to vectors. Typically, either the sigmoid $\frac{1}{1+\exp(-x)}$ or tanh are used as activation functions. $\odot$ denotes the pointwise multiplication of two vectors. Without peepholes, the LSTM memory cell forward pass rules are (see Fig. 11.1):

$$z_t = g\left(W_z\, x_t + U_z\, y_{t-1} + b_z\right) \qquad \text{cell input} \qquad (11.1)$$

$$i_t = \sigma\left(W_i\, x_t + U_i\, y_{t-1} + b_i\right) \qquad \text{input gate} \qquad (11.2)$$

$$f_t = \sigma\left(W_f\, x_t + U_f\, y_{t-1} + b_f\right) \qquad \text{forget gate} \qquad (11.3)$$

$$c_t = i_t \odot z_t + f_t \odot c_{t-1} \qquad \text{cell state} \qquad (11.4)$$

$$o_t = \sigma\left(W_o\, x_t + U_o\, y_{t-1} + b_o\right) \qquad \text{output gate} \qquad (11.5)$$

$$y_t = o_t \odot h\left(c_t\right) \qquad \text{cell output} \qquad (11.6)$$

Long-Term Dependencies vs. Uniform Credit Assignment. The LSTM network has been proposed with the aim to learn *long-term dependencies* in sequences which span over long intervals [31,32,36,37]. However, besides extracting long-term dependencies, LSTM memory cells have another, even more important, advantage in sequence learning: as already described in the early 1990s, LSTM memory cells allow for *uniform credit assignment*, that is, the propagation of errors back to inputs without scaling them [30]. For uniform credit assignment of current LSTM architectures, the forget gate f must be one or close to one. A memory cell without an input gate i just sums up all the squashed inputs it receives during scanning the input sequence. Thus, such a memory cell is equivalent to a unit that sees all sequence elements at the same time, as has been shown via the "Ersatzschaltbild" (engl. equivalent circuit diagram) [30]. If an output error occurs only at the end of the sequence, such a memory cell, via backpropagation, supplies the same delta error at the cell input unit z at every time step. Thus, all inputs obtain the same credit for producing the correct output and are treated on an equal level and, consequently, the incoming weights to a memory cell are adjusted by using the same delta error at the input unit z.

In contrast to LSTM memory cells, standard recurrent networks scale the delta error and assign different credit to different inputs. The more recent the input, the more credit it obtains. The first inputs of the sequence are hidden from the final states of the recurrent network. In many learning tasks, however, important information is distributed over the entire length of the sequence and can even occur at the very beginning. For example, in language- and text-related tasks, the first words are often important for the meaning of a sentence. If the credit assignment is not uniform along the input sequence, then learning is very limited. Learning would start by trying to improve the prediction solely by using the most recent inputs. Therefore, the solutions that can be found are restricted to those that can be constructed if the last inputs are considered first. Thus, only those solutions are found that are accessible by gradient descent from regions in the parameter space that only use the most recent input information. In general, these limitations lead to suboptimal solutions, since learning gets trapped in local optima. Typically, these local optima correspond to solutions which efficiently exploit the most recent information in the input sequence, while information way back in the past is neglected.

11.2.2   Layer-Wise Relevance Propagation (LRP)

Layer-wise relevance propagation (LRP) [6] (cf. [51] for an overview) is a technique to explain individual predictions of deep neural networks in terms of input variables. For a given input and the neural network's prediction, it assigns a score to each of the input variables indicating to which extent they contributed to the prediction. LRP works by reverse-propagating the prediction through the network by means of heuristic propagation rules that apply to each layer of a neural network [6]. In terms of computational cost the LRP method is very efficient, as it can be computed in one forward and backward pass through the network. In various applications LRP was shown to produce faithful explanations, even for highly complex and nonlinear networks used in computer vision [6,64]. Besides it was able to detect biases in models and datasets used for training [44], e.g. the presence of a copyright tag that spuriously correlated to the class 'horse' in the Pascal VOC 2012 dataset. Further, it was used to get new insights in scientific and medical applications [39,71,77], to interpret clustering [40], to analyze audio data [9,75], and to compare text classifiers for topic categorization [3].

Conservative Propagation. LRP explains by redistributing the neural network output progressively from layer to layer until the input layer is reached. Similar to other works such as [41,67,80], the propagation procedure implemented by LRP is based on a local conservation principle: the net quantity, or relevance, received by any higher layer neuron is redistributed in the same amount to neurons of the layer below. In this way the relevance's flow is analog to the Kirchhoff's first law for the conservation of electric charge, or to the continuity equation in physics for transportation in general form. Concretely, if j and k are indices for neurons in two consecutive layers, and denoting by $R_{j \leftarrow k}$ the relevance flowing between two neurons, we have the equations:

$$\sum_j R_{j \leftarrow k} = R_k$$
$$R_j = \sum_k R_{j \leftarrow k}.$$

This local enforcement of conservation induces conservation at coarser scales, in particular, conservation between consecutive layers $\sum_j R_j = \sum_j \sum_k R_{j \leftarrow k} = \sum_k \sum_j R_{j \leftarrow k} = \sum_k R_k$, and ultimately, conservation at the level of the whole deep neural network, i.e. given an input $\boldsymbol{x} = (x_i)_i$ and its prediction $f(\boldsymbol{x})$, we have $\sum_i R_i = f(\boldsymbol{x})$[1]. This global conservation property allows to interpret the result as the share by which each input variable has contributed to the prediction.

LRP in Deep Neural Networks. LRP has been most commonly applied to deep rectifier networks. In these networks, the activations at the current layer can be computed from activations in the previous layer as:

$$a_k = \max \left(0, \sum_{0,j} a_j w_{jk}\right)$$

A general family of propagation rules for such types of layer is given by [51]:

$$R_j = \sum_k \frac{a_j \cdot \rho(w_{jk})}{\epsilon + \sum_{0,j} a_j \cdot \rho(w_{jk})} R_k$$

Specific propagation rules such as LRP-ϵ, LRP-$\alpha_1\beta_0$ and LRP-γ fall under this umbrella. They are easy to implement [42,51] and can be interpreted as the result of a deep Taylor decomposition of the neural network function [52].

On convolutional neural networks for computer vision, composite strategies making use of different rules at different layers have shown to work well in practice [43,51]. An alternative default strategy in computer vision is to uniformly employ the LRP-$\alpha_1\beta_0$ in every hidden layer [53], the latter has the advantage of having no free parameter, and delivers positive explanations. On convolutional neural networks for text, LRP-ϵ with a small ϵ value was found to work well [3,57], it provides a signed explanation.

While LRP was described in the context of a layered feed-forward neural network, the principle is general enough to apply to arbitrary directed acyclic graphs, including recurrent neural networks unfolded in time such as LSTMs.

---

[1] The global conservation is exact up to the relevance absorbed by some stabilizing term, and by the biases, see details later in Sect. 11.3.1.

11.3   Extending LRP for LSTMs

We address the question of how to explain the LSTM model's output by expanding the previously described LRP technique to "standard" LSTM architectures, in the form they are most commonly used in the literature [26], i.e. following the recurrence Eqs. 11.1–11.6 and Fig. 11.1 introduced in Sect. 11.2.1, and usually containing the *tanh* nonlinearity as an activation function for the cell input and the cell state.

For this, we first need to identify an appropriate structure of computation in these models, and introduce some notation. Let s, g be the neurons representing the signal and the gate, let p be the neuron representing the product of these two quantities. Let f be the neuron corresponding to the forget gate. Let k be the neuron on which the signal is being accumulated. Let $k - 1, p - 1, \ldots$ be the same neurons at previous time steps. We can recompose the LSTM forward pass in terms of the following three elementary types of computation:

1. linear mappings $\qquad z_s = \sum_{0,j} a_j w_{js}$, $z_g = \sum_{0,j} a_j w_{jg}$

2. gated interactions $\qquad a_p = \tanh\left(z_s\right) \cdot \mathrm{sigm}\left(z_g\right)$

3. accumulation $\qquad a_k = a_f \cdot a_{k-1} + a_p$

These three types of computation and the way they are typically interconnected are shown graphically in Fig. 11.2.

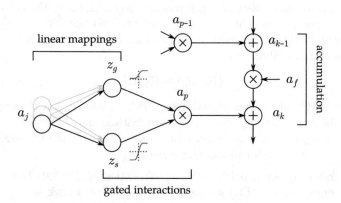

Fig. 11.2. Three elementary computations performed by the LSTM from the perspective of LRP.

Linear mappings form the input of the gated interactions. The output of some of the gated interactions enter into the accumulation function.

11.3.1   Linear Mappings

Each output of this computation is a weighted sum over a large number of input variables. Here, one strategy is to redistribute the relevance in *proportion* to the weighted activations $a_j w_{js}$, as they occur in the linear projection formulas above. One way of implementing this strategy is the epsilon-rule (LRP-ϵ) given by [6]:

$$R_j = \sum_s \frac{a_j w_{js}}{\epsilon_s + \sum_{0,j} a_j w_{js}} R_s$$

where $\epsilon_s = \epsilon \cdot \text{sign}\left(\sum_{0,j} a_j w_{js}\right)$ is a small stabilizer that pushes the denominator away from zero by some constant factor, and has the effect of absorbing some relevance when the weighted activations are weak or contradictory. This type of propagation rule was employed by previous works with recurrent neural networks [2,4,14,57,77]. A large value for ϵ tends to keep only the most salient factors of explanation. Note that, in our notation, neuron biases are taken into account via a constant neuron $a_0 = 1$ whose connection weight is the corresponding bias. This neuron also gets assigned a share of relevance. However its relevance will not be propagated further and will get trapped in that neuron, since the "bias neuron" has no lower-layer connections.

11.3.2   Gated Interactions

These layers do not have a simple summing structure as the linear mappings. Their multiplicative nonlinearity makes them intrinsically more difficult to handle. Recently, three works extended the LRP propagation technique to recurrent neural networks, such as LSTMs [37] and GRUs [12], by proposing a rule to propagate the relevance through such product layers [2,4,14]. These LRP extensions were tested in the context of sentiment analysis, machine translation and reinforcement learning respectively. Arras et al. [4], in particular, proposed the signal-take-all redistribution rule

$$(R_g, R_s) = (0, R_p)$$

referred as "LRP-all" in our experiments. This redistribution strategy can be motivated in a similar way the gates were initially introduced in the LSTM model [37]: the gate units are intended to control the flow of information in the LSTM, but not to be information themselves.

In the following, we provide further justification of this rule based on Deep Taylor Decomposition (DTD) [52], a mathematical framework for analyzing the relevance propagation process in a deep network. DTD expresses the relevance obtained at a given layer as a function of the activations in the lower-layer, and determines how the relevance should be redistributed based on a Taylor expansion of this function. Consider the relevance function $R_p(z_g, z_s)$ mapping the input $z = (z_g, z_s)$ of the gated interaction to the relevance received by the output of that module. We then write its Taylor expansion:

$$R_p(z_g, z_s) = R_p(\tilde{z}_g, \tilde{z}_s) + \left.\frac{\partial R_p}{\partial z_g}\right|_{\tilde{z}} \cdot (z_g - \tilde{z}_g) + \left.\frac{\partial R_p}{\partial z_s}\right|_{\tilde{z}} \cdot (z_s - \tilde{z}_s) + \ldots$$

where $\tilde{z} = (\tilde{z}_g, \tilde{z}_s)$ is a root point of the function, and where the first-order terms can be used to determine on which lower-layer neurons (g or s the relevance should be propagated). In practice, a root point and its gradient are difficult to compute analytically. However, we can consider instead a relevance model [52] which is easier to analyze, in our case, of the form:

$$\widehat{R}_p(z_g, z_s) = \mathrm{sigm}(z_g) \cdot \tanh(z_s) \cdot c_p.$$

The variable c_p is constant and set such that $R_p(z_g, z_s) = \widehat{R}_p(z_g, z_s)$ locally. This model is a reasonable approximation when R_p results from a propagation rule where the activation term naturally factors out (cf. [52]). The relevance model for the gated interaction of the standard LSTM is depicted in Fig. 11.3(left).

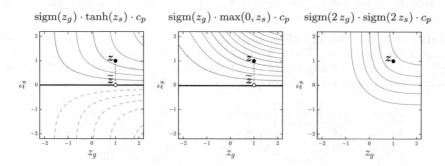

Fig. 11.3. DTD relevance models for different choices of nonlinear functions with nearest root point (white dot). The left model is the standard LSTM. Positive contours are drawn as continuous lines, negative contours as dashed lines, and the dark line represents the zero-valued contour.

Having built the relevance model, we would like to perform a Taylor expansion of it at some root point in the vicinity of the observed point $z = (z_g, z_s)$. The nearest root point of the relevance model is found at $(\widetilde{z}_g, \widetilde{z}_s) = (z_g, 0)$, and more generally any root point satisfies $\widetilde{z}_s = 0$. A Taylor expansion of this simplified relevance model gives:

$$
\begin{aligned}
\widehat{R}_p(z_g, z_s) = \ &\widehat{R}_p(\widetilde{z}_g, \widetilde{z}_s) \\
&+ \mathrm{sigm}'(\widetilde{z}_g) \cdot \tanh(\widetilde{z}_s) \cdot c_p \cdot (z_g - \widetilde{z}_g) && (\, = R_g) \\
&+ \mathrm{sigm}(\widetilde{z}_g) \cdot \tanh'(\widetilde{z}_s) \cdot c_p \cdot (z_s - \widetilde{z}_s) && (\, = R_s) \\
&+ \dots
\end{aligned}
$$

Clearly, the first linear term R_g is zero for the nearest root point, thus, no relevance will be redistributed to the gate, however, the saturation effect of the hyperbolic tangent can create a mismatch between the first-order term, and the function value to redistribute. However, if replacing in the LSTM the hyperbolic tangent by the identity or the ReLU nonlinearity (as this was done, for example, in [59]), then we get an exact decomposition of the relevance model with $(R_g, R_s) = (0, \widehat{R}_p)$, since the Taylor remainder is exactly zero in this case. This corresponds to the LRP-all redistribution rule.

This section has justified the signal-take-all strategy for standard LSTMs. In Sect. 11.4 modified LSTM variants that are tuned for further interpretability will benefit from a different propagation strategy. For example, using sigmoids both for the gate and the signal (cf. Fig. 11.3 right) suggests a different propagation strategy.

A more complete set of propagation rules that have been used in practice [2,4,14,57,59,77], and that we consider in our experiments, is given in Table 11.1. In addition to the definitions provided in Table 11.1, in order to avoid near zero division, one may add a stabilizing term into the denominator of the LRP-prop and LRP-abs variants, similarly to the epsilon-rule stabilization for linear mappings. It has the form $\epsilon \cdot \text{sign}(z_g + z_s)$ in the first case, and simply ϵ in the other case, where ϵ is a small positive number.

Table 11.1. Overview of LRP propagation rules for gated interactions, and whether they derive from a deep Taylor decomposition. LRP-all stands for "signal-take-all", LRP-prop stands for "proportional", LRP-abs is similar to LRP-prop but with absolute values instead, and LRP-half corresponds to equal redistribution.

Name	Proposed in	Received by gate	Received by signal	DTD
LRP-all	[4]	$R_g = 0$	$R_s = R_p$	✓
LRP-prop	[2,14]	$R_g = \frac{z_g}{z_g + z_s} R_p$	$R_s = \frac{z_s}{z_g + z_s} R_p$	✗
LRP-abs		$R_g = \frac{\lvert z_g \rvert}{\lvert z_g \rvert + \lvert z_s \rvert} R_p$	$R_s = \frac{\lvert z_s \rvert}{\lvert z_g \rvert + \lvert z_s \rvert} R_p$	✗
LRP-half	[2]	$R_g = 0.5 \cdot R_p$	$R_s = 0.5 \cdot R_p$	✗

11.3.3 Accumulation

The last type of module one needs to consider is the accumulation module that discounts the LSTM memory state with a "forget" factor, and adds a small additive term based on current observations:

$$a_k = a_f \cdot a_{k-1} + a_p.$$

Consider the relevance R_k of the accumulator neuron a_k for the final time step. Define $R_k = a_k \cdot c_k$. Through the accumulation module, we get the following redistribution:

$$R_p = a_p \cdot c_k$$
$$R_{k-1} = a_f \cdot a_{k-1} \cdot c_k,$$

where we have used the signal-take-all strategy in the product, and the epsilon-rule (with no stabilizer) in the sum. Iterating this redistribution process on previous time steps, we obtain:

$$R_{p-1} = a_f \cdot a_{p-1} \cdot c_k$$
$$R_{p-2} = (a_f \cdot a_{f-1}) \cdot a_{p-2} \cdot c_k$$
$$\vdots$$
$$R_{p-T} = \left(\textstyle\prod_{t=1}^{T} a_{f-t+1} \right) \cdot a_{p-T} \cdot c_k.$$

Note that, here, we assume a simplified recurrence structure over the standard LSTM presented in Fig. 11.1, in particular we assume that neurons a_p do not redistribute relevance to past time steps via z_s (i.e. z_s is connected only to the current input and not to previous recurrent states), to simplify the present analysis.

Now we inspect the structure of the relevance scores $R_p, \ldots, R_{p-T}$ at each time step, as given above. We can see that the relevance terms can be divided into three parts:

1. A product of forget gates: This term tends to decrease exponentially with every further redistribution step, unless the forget gate is equal to one. In other words, only the few most recent time steps will receive relevance.
2. The value of the product neuron a_p at the current time step. In other words, the relevance at a given time step is directly influenced by the activation of its representative neuron, which can be either positive or negative.
3. A term that does not change with the time steps, and relates to the amount of relevance available for redistribution.

These observations on the structure of the relevance over time provide a further justification for the LRP explanation procedure, which we will be validating empirically in Sect. 11.5. They also serve as a starting point to propose new variants of the LSTM for which the relevance redistribution satisfies further constraints, as proposed in the following Sect. 11.4.

11.4   LSTM Architectures Motivated by LRP

A "standard" LSTM network with fully connected LSTM blocks, as presented in Fig. 11.1, is a very powerful network capable of modelling extremely complex sequential tasks. However, in many cases, an LSTM network with a reduced complexity is able to solve the same problems with a similar prediction performance. With the further goal of increasing the model's interpretability, we propose some modifications which simplify the LSTM network and make the resulting model easier to explain with LRP.

11.4.1   LSTM for LRP Backward Analysis: Nondecreasing Memory Cells

The LRP backward propagation procedure is made simpler if memory cell states c_t are nondecreasing, this way the contribution of each input to each memory cell is well-defined, and the problem that a negative and a positive contribution cancel each other is avoided. For nondecreasing memory cells and backward analysis with LRP, we make the following assumptions over the LSTM network from Fig. 11.1 and Eqs. 11.1–11.6:

(**A1**) $f_t = 1$ for all t. That is, the forget gate is always 1 and nothing is forgotten. This ensures uniform credit assignment over time, and alleviates the problem identified earlier in Sect. 11.3.3 that the relevance redistributed via the accumulation module decreases over time.

(A2) $g > 0$, that is, the cell input activation function g is positive. For example we can use a sigmoid $\sigma(x) = \frac{1}{1+\exp(-x)}$: $g(x) = a_g \sigma(x)$, with $a_g \in \{2, 3, 4\}$. Indeed methods like LRP and the epsilon-rule for linear mappings (cf. Sect. 11.3.1) face numerical stability issues when negative contributions cancel with positive contributions [53]. With a positive g all contributions are positive, and the redistribution in the LSTM accumulation module is made more stable. Further, we assume that the cell input z has a negative bias, that is, $b_z < 0$. This is important to avoid the drift effect. The drift effect is that the memory content only gets positive contributions, which leads to an increase of c over time. Typical values are $b_z \in \{-1, -2, -3, -4, -5\}$.

(A3) We want to ensure that for the cell state activation it holds $h(0) = 0$, such that, if the memory content is zero, then nothing is transferred to the next layer. Therefore we set $h = a_h \tanh$, with $a_h \in \{1, 2, 4\}$.

(A4) The cell input z is only connected to the input, and is not connected to other LSTM memory cell outputs. Which means U_z is zero. This ensures that LRP assigns relevance z to the input and z is not disturbed by redistributing relevance to the network.

(A5) The input gate i has only connections to other memory cell outputs, and is not connected to the input. That is, W_i is zero. This ensures that LRP assigns relevance only via z to the input.

(A6) The output gate o has only connections to other memory cell outputs, and is not connected to the input. That is, W_o is zero. This ensures that LRP assigns relevance only via z to the input.

(A7) The input gate i has a negative bias, that is, $b_i < 0$. Like with the cell input the negative bias avoids the drift effect. Typical values are $b_i \in \{-1, -2, -3, -4\}$.

(A8) The output gate o may also have a negative bias, that is, $b_o < 0$. This allows to bring in different memory cells at different time points. It is related to resource allocation.

(A9) The memory cell state content is initialized with zero at time $t = 0$, that is, $c_0 = 0$. Lastly, the memory cell content c_t is non-negative $c_t \geq 0$ for all t, since $z_t \geq 0$ and $i_t \geq 0$.

The resulting LSTM forward pass rules for LRP are:

$$z_t = a_g\, \sigma\left(W_z\, x_t + b_z\right) \qquad \text{cell input} \qquad (11.7)$$

$$i_t = \sigma\left(U_i\, y_{t-1} + b_i\right) \qquad \text{input gate} \qquad (11.8)$$

$$c_t = i_t \odot z_t + c_{t-1} \qquad \text{cell state} \qquad (11.9)$$

$$o_t = \sigma\left(U_o\, y_{t-1} + b_o\right) \qquad \text{output gate} \qquad (11.10)$$

$$y_t = o_t \odot a_h\, \tanh\left(c_t\right) \qquad \text{cell output} \qquad (11.11)$$

See Fig. 11.4a which depicts these forward pass rules for LRP.

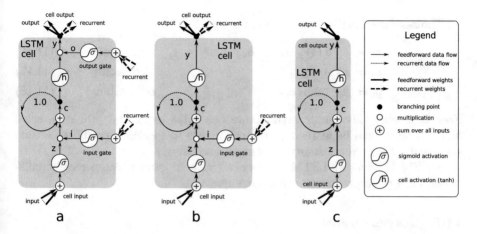

Fig. 11.4. LSTM memory cell used for Layer-Wise Relevance Propagation (LRP). (a) z is the vector of cell input activations, i is the vector of input gate activations, c is the vector of memory cell states, o is the vector of output gate activations, and y is the vector of cell output activations. (b) The memory cell is nondecreasing and guarantees the Markov property. (a and b) Data flow is either "feed-forward" without delay or "recurrent" with a one-step delay. External input reaches the LSTM network only via the cell input z. All gates only receive recurrent input, that is, from other memory cell outputs. (c) LSTM memory cell without gates. External input is stored in the memory cell via the input z.

11.4.2   LSTM for LRP Backward Analysis: Keeping the Markov Property

Forget gates can modify the memory cells' information at some future time step, i.e. they could completely erase the cells' state content. Output gates can hide the cells' information and deliver it in the future, i.e. output gates can be closed and open at some future time, masking all information stored by the cell. Thus, in order to guarantee the Markov property, the forget and output gates must be disconnected.

The resulting LSTM forward pass rules for Markov memory cells are:

$$z_t = a_g\, \sigma\,(W_z\, x_t\, +\, b_z) \qquad\qquad \text{cell input} \qquad (11.12)$$

$$i_t = \sigma\,(U_i\, y_{t-1}\, +\, b_i) \qquad\qquad \text{input gate} \qquad (11.13)$$

$$c_t = i_t\, \odot\, z_t\, +\, c_{t-1} \qquad\qquad \text{cell state} \qquad (11.14)$$

$$y_t = a_h\, \tanh\,(c_t) \qquad\qquad \text{cell output} \qquad (11.15)$$

See Fig. 11.4b for an LSTM memory cell that guarantees the Markov property.

11.4.3   LSTM Without Gates

The most simple LSTM architecture for backward analysis does not use any gates. Therefore complex dynamics that have to be treated in the LRP backward analysis are avoided.

The resulting LSTM forward pass rules are:

$$z_t = a_g\, \sigma\left(\boldsymbol{W}_z\, \boldsymbol{x}_t + \boldsymbol{b}_z\right) \qquad \text{cell input} \qquad (11.16)$$

$$\boldsymbol{c}_t = \boldsymbol{z}_t + \boldsymbol{c}_{t-1} \qquad\qquad\qquad \text{cell state} \qquad (11.17)$$

$$\boldsymbol{y}_t = a_h\, \tanh\left(\boldsymbol{c}_t\right) \qquad\qquad\; \text{cell output} \qquad (11.18)$$

Note that even this simple architecture can solve sequential problems, since different biases can be learned by the cell inputs to specialize on different time steps and activate the memory cell output accordingly.

See Fig. 11.4c for an LSTM memory cell without gates which perfectly redistributes the relevance across the input sequence.

11.5   Experiments

11.5.1   Validating Explanations on Standard LSTMs: Selectivity and Fidelity

First we verify that the LRP explanation is able to select input positions that are the most determinant either in *supporting* or in *contradicting* an LSTM's prediction, using a sentiment prediction task. To that end we perform a perturbation experiment aka "pixel flipping" or "region perturbation" [6,64] commonly used in computer vision to evaluate and generate explanations, e.g. [1,11,47,54]. Here we confirm whether the *sign* and *ordering* of the relevance reflect what the LSTM considers as highly speaking *for* or *against* a particular class.

Another property of the relevance we test is fidelity. To that end we use a synthetic task where the input-output relationship is known and compare the relevances w.r.t some ground truth explanation. By using a synthetic toy task we can avoid problems of disentangling errors made by the model from errors made by the explanation [72]. Here we seek to validate the *magnitude* of the relevance as a continuously distributed quantity. To the best of our knowledge we are the first one to conduct such a continuous analysis of the relevance in recurrent neural networks. Yet another work validated LSTM explanations via a toy classification task [77], however it practically treated the relevance as a binary variable.

Explanation Methods. Now we introduce the various explanation methods we consider in our experiments with standard LSTMs. For the LRP explanation technique we consider all product rule variants specified in Table 11.1 (cf. Sect. 11.3.2), i.e. LRP-all [4], LRP-prop [2,14], LRP-abs and LRP-half [2]. Since the LRP backward pass delivers one relevance value per input dimension, we simply sum up the relevances across the input dimensions to get one relevance value per time step. Besides LRP we also consider gradient-based explanation [13,21,45,68], occlusion-based relevance [46,79], and Contextual Decomposition (CD) [56], as alternative methods.

For the gradient-based explanation we use as the relevance, either the prediction function's partial derivative w.r.t. the input dimension of interest and square this quantity, we denote this variant simply as *Gradient*, or else we multiply this derivative by the input dimension's value, we call it *Gradient × Input* relevance. In both cases, similarly to LRP, the relevance of several input dimensions can be summed up to obtain one relevance value per time step.

For the occlusion-based explanation we take as the relevance, either a difference of prediction function values (i.e. of prediction scores before softmax normalization), we denote this variant as $Occlusion_{f\text{-diff}}$, or else we use a difference of predicted probabilities, we call it $Occlusion_{P\text{-diff}}$, where the difference is calculated over the model's prediction on the original input and a prediction with an altered input where the position of interest (for which the relevance is being computed) is set to zero.

For the CD explanation method [56] we employ the code from the authors[2] to generate one relevance value per time step (this necessitates to run the CD decomposition as many times as there are time steps in the input sequence).

Testing Selectivity. In order to assess the selectivity, we consider a five-class sentiment prediction task of movie reviews. As a dataset we use the Stanford Sentiment Treebank (SST) [69] which contains labels (from very negative, negative, neutral, positive, to very positive sentiment) for resp. 8544/1101/2210 train/val/test sentences and their constituent phrases. As an LSTM model we employ the bidirectional LSTM model from Li et al. [45] already trained on SST[3] and previously employed by the authors to perform a gradient-based analysis on the network decisions. The input consists of a sequence of 60-dimensional word embeddings, the LSTM hidden layer has size 60, and the only text preprocessing is lowercasing. On binary sentiment classification of full sentences (ignoring the neutral class) the model reaches 82.9% test accuracy, and on five-class sentiment prediction of full sentences it achieves 46.3% accuracy.

For the perturbation experiment we consider all test sentences with a length of at least ten words (thus we retain 1849 sentences), and compute word-level relevances (i.e. one relevance value per time step) using as the target output class the *true* sentence class, and considering all five classes of the sentiment prediction task. For the computation of the LRP relevance we use as a stabilizer value, for linear mappings and product layers, $\epsilon = 0.001$[4].

Then, given these word-level relevances, we iteratively remove up to five words from each input sentence, either in *decreasing* or *increasing* order of their relevance, depending on whether the corresponding sentence was initially correctly or falsely classified by the LSTM. We expect this input modification to decrease resp. increase the model's confidence for the true class, which we measure in terms of the model's accuracy. For removing a word we simply discard it from the input sequence and concatenate the remaining parts of the sentence.

---

[2] https://github.com/jamie-murdoch/ContextualDecomposition.

[3] https://github.com/jiweil/Visualizing-and-Understanding-Neural-Models-in-NLP.

[4] Except for the LRP-prop variant, where we take $\epsilon = 0.2$. We tried following values: [0.001, 0.01, 0.1, 0.2, 0.3, 0.4, 1.0], and took the lowest one to achieve numerical stability.

An alternative removal scheme would have been to set the corresponding word embedding to zero in the input (which in practice gave us similar results), however the former enables us to generate more natural texts, although we acknowledge that the resulting sentence might be partly syntactically broken as pointed out by Poerner et al. [57].

Our results of the perturbation experiment are compiled in Fig. 11.5.

When looking at the removal of the most relevant words (Fig. 11.5 left), we observe that the occlusion-based relevance, LRP-all and CD are the most competitive methods, and perform on-par; followed by *Gradient* × *Input*, which performs better than *Gradient*. The remaining methods, which are the other LRP variants LRP-prop, LRP-abs, LRP-half are almost equivalent to random, and thus not adequate to detect words speaking *for* a specific class.

In the removal of the least relevant words (Fig. 11.5 right), $Occlusion_{P\text{-diff}}$ performs best; followed by $Occlusion_{f\text{-diff}}$, LRP-all, CD and *Gradient* × *Input*. Again the remaining LRP variants are almost equivalent to random. However this time *Gradient* performs worse than random, this indicates that low *Gradient* relevance is more likely to identify unimportant words for the classification problem (like stop-words) rather than identifying words speaking *against* a specific class (this was also observed in previous work, see e.g. [4], Table 1).

In summary, our perturbation experiment in sentiment analysis suggests that if one is interested in identifying the most influential positions that strongly *support* or *inhibit* a specific classification decision using a standard LSTM model, then the occlusion-based relevance, the LRP method with the product rule from Arras et al. [4], and the CD method of Murdoch et al. [56] are good candidates to provide this information.

For another evaluation of recurrent neural networks explanations, including a standard LSTM model, we further refer to Poerner et al. [57], in particular to their experiment using a subject-verb agreement task. Here the authors find that LRP and DeepLIFT [67] perform best among the tested explanation methods, both when using the signal-take-all strategy proposed in Arras et al. [4] for product layers[5].

Testing Fidelity. In order to validate the fidelity, we consider a toy task with a linear input-output relationship. In particular we use the addition/subtraction of two numbers. Accordingly we expect the relevances to be linearly related to the actual input values, which we can directly measure in terms of the empirical correlation.

For our purpose we use a variant of the adding problem of Hochreiter et al. [36], where instead of using explicit markers, we use implicit ones; further we remove the sequence start and end positions. This way we enforce the LSTM

---

[5] Ancona et al. [1] also performed a comparative study of explanations on LSTMs, however, in order to redistribute the relevance through product layers, the authors use standard gradient backpropagation. This redistribution scheme violates one of the key underlying property of LRP, which is local relevance conservation, hence their results for LRP are not conclusive.

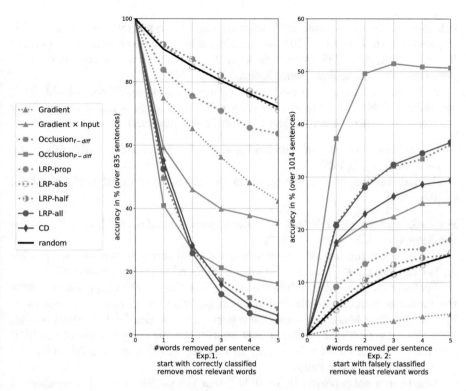

Fig. 11.5. Impact of word removal on initially correctly (left) and initially falsely (right) classified sentences. The relevance target class is the true sentence class, and words are deleted in decreasing (left) and increasing (right) order of their relevance. Random deletion is averaged over 10 runs (std < 0.02). A steep decline (left) and incline (right) indicate selective relevance.

model to attribute non-zero relevance *only* to the relevant numbers in the input and not to markers (since in general it is unclear what "ground truth" relevance should be attributed to a marker, to which we could compare the computed relevance to). Thus our input sequence of length T has the form:

$$\begin{bmatrix} n_1 & 0 \\ \dots & 0 \\ n_{a-1} & 0 \\ 0 & n_a \\ n_{a+1} & 0 \\ \dots & 0 \\ n_{b-1} & 0 \\ 0 & n_b \\ n_{b+1} & 0 \\ \dots & 0 \\ n_T & 0 \end{bmatrix}$$

where the non-zero entries n_t, with $t \in \{1, ..., T\}$, are randomly sampled real numbers, and the two relevant positions a and b are sampled uniformly among $\{1, ..., T\}$ with $a < b$. The target output is $n_a + n_b$ for addition, and $n_a - n_b$ for subtraction. To ensure that the train/val/test sets do not overlap, we use 10000 sequences with $T \in \{4, ..., 10\}$ for training, 2500 sequences with $T \in \{11, 12\}$ for validation, and 2500 sequences with $T \in \{13, 14\}$ as test set. Training is performed by minimizing Mean Squared Error (MSE).

More particularly, we consider two *minimal* tasks, which are solvable by a standard LSTM with only *one* memory cell, followed by a linear output layer with no bias (thus the model has 17 trainable parameters):

- the addition of *signed* numbers (where n_t is sampled uniformly from $[-1, -0.5] \cup [0.5, 1.0]$),
- the subtraction of *positive* numbers (where n_t is sampled uniformly from $[0.5, 1.0]$)[6].

For each task we train 50 LSTM models with a validation MSE $< 10^{-4}$, the resulting test MSE is also $< 10^{-4}$.

Then, using the model's predicted output, we compute one relevance value R_t per time step $t \in \{1, ..., T\}$, for each considered explanation method.

For the occlusion-based relevance we use only the $Occlusion_{f\text{-diff}}$ variant, since the model output is one-dimensional and the considered task is a regression. For the gradient-based relevance we report only the *Gradient × Input* results, since the pure *Gradient* performs very poorly. For the computation of the LRP relevance we didn't find it necessary to add any stabilizing term (therefore we use $\epsilon = 0.0$ for all LRP rules).

Our results are reported in Table 11.2. For the positions a and b, we checked whether there is a correlation between the computed relevance and the input numbers' actual value. Besides, we verified the portion of the relevance (in absolute value) assigned to these positions, compared to the relevance attributed to all time steps in the sequence.

Interestingly several methods pass our sanity check (they are reported in bold in the Table) and attribute as expected a correlation of almost one in the addition task, namely: *Gradient × Input*, *Occlusion*, LRP-all and CD.

However, on subtraction, only *Gradient × Input* and LRP-all assign a correct correlation of near one to the first number, and of near minus one to the second number, while the remaining explanation methods fail completely.

For both addition and subtraction, we observe that methods that fail in the correlation results also erroneously assign a non-negligible portion of the relevance to clearly unimportant time steps.

One key difference between the two arithmetic tasks we considered, is that our addition task is non-sequential and solvable by a Bag-of-Words approach (i.e. by ignoring the ordering of the inputs), while our subtraction task is truly sequential and requires the LSTM model to remember which number arrives in the first position and which number in the second.

From this sanity check, we certainly can not deduce that every method that passes the subtraction test is also appropriate to explain *any* complex nonlinear

---

[6] We use an arbitrary minimum magnitude of 0.5 only to simplify training (since sampling very small numbers would encourage the model weights to grow rapidly).

Table 11.2. Statistics of the relevance w.r.t. the numbers n_a and n_b on toy arithmetic tasks. ρ denotes the correlation and E the mean and for each LSTM model these statistics are computed over 2500 test points. Reported results are the mean (and standard deviation in parenthesis), in %, over 50 trained LSTM models.

	$\rho(n_a, R_a)$	$\rho(n_b, R_b)$	$E[\frac{|R_a|+|R_b|}{\sum_t |R_t|}]$
	Addition $n_a + n_b$		
Gradient × Input	**99.960** (0.017)	**99.954** (0.019)	**99.68** (0.53)
Occlusion	**99.990** (0.004)	**99.990** (0.004)	**99.82** (0.27)
LRP-prop	0.785 (3.619)	10.111 (12.362)	18.14 (4.23)
LRP-abs	7.002 (6.224)	12.410 (17.440)	18.01 (4.48)
LRP-half	29.035 (9.478)	51.460 (19.939)	54.09 (17.53)
LRP-all	**99.995** (0.002)	**99.995** (0.002)	**99.95** (0.05)
CD	**99.997** (0.002)	**99.997** (0.002)	**99.92** (0.06)
	Subtraction $n_a - n_b$		
Gradient × Input	**97.9** (1.6)	$-$**98.8** (0.6)	**98.3** (0.6)
Occlusion	99.0 (2.0)	$-$69.0 (19.1)	25.4 (16.8)
LRP-prop	3.1 (4.8)	$-$8.4 (18.9)	15.0 (2.4)
LRP-abs	1.2 (7.6)	$-$23.0 (11.1)	15.1 (1.6)
LRP-half	7.7 (15.3)	$-$28.9 (6.4)	42.3 (8.3)
LRP-all	**98.5** (3.5)	$-$**99.3** (1.3)	**99.3** (0.6)
CD	$-$25.9 (39.1)	$-$50.0 (29.2)	49.4 (26.1)

prediction task. However, we postulate that an explanation method that fails on such a test with the smallest possible number of free parameters (i.e. an LSTM with one memory cell) is generally a less suited method.

In this vein, our present analysis opens up new avenues for improving and testing LSTM explanation methods in general, including the LRP method and its LRP-all variant, whose results in our arithmetic task degrade when more memory cells are included to the LSTM model, which suggests that gates might also be used by the standard LSTM to store the input numbers' value[7]. The latter phenomenon could be either avoided by adapting the LSTM architecture, or could be taken into account in the relevance propagation procedure by employing alternative propagation rules for products. This leads us to the next subsection, where we use an adapted LSTM model and different product rules, for the task of reward redistribution.

---

[7] The same phenomenon can occur, on the addition problem, when using only positive numbers as input. Whereas in the specific toy tasks we considered, the cell input (z_t) is required to process the numbers to add/subtract, and the cell state (c_t) accumulates the result of the arithmetic operation.

11.5.2   Long Term Credit Assignment in Markov Decision Processes via LRP and LSTMs

Assigning the credit for a received reward to actions that were performed is one of the central tasks in reinforcement learning [74]. Long term credit assignment has been identified as one of the biggest challenges in reinforcement learning [62]. Classical reinforcement learning methods use a forward view approach by estimating the future expected return of a Markov Decision Process (MDP). However, they fail when the reward is delayed since they have to average over a large number of probabilistic future state-action paths that increases exponentially with the delay of the reward [48,58].

In contrast to using a forward view, a backward view approach based on a backward analysis of a forward model avoids problems with unknown future state-action paths, since the sequence is already completed and known. Backward analysis transforms the forward view approach into a regression task, at which deep learning methods excel. As a forward model, an LSTM can be trained to predict the final return, given a sequence of state-actions. LSTM was already used in reinforcement learning [66] for advantage learning [7] and learning policies [27,28,50]. However, backward analysis via sensitivity analysis like "backpropagation through a model" [8,55,60,61] have major drawbacks: local minima, instabilities, exploding or vanishing gradients in the world model, proper exploration, actions being only regarded by sensitivity but not their contribution (relevance) [29,65].

Contribution analysis, however, can be used to decompose the return prediction (the output relevance) into contributions of single state-action pairs along the observed sequence, obtaining a redistributed reward (the relevance redistribution). As a result, a new MDP is created with the same optimal policies and, in the optimal case, with no delayed rewards (expected future rewards equal zero) [2]. Indeed, for MDPs the Q-value is equal to the expected immediate reward plus the expected future rewards. Thus, if the expected future rewards are zero, the Q-value estimation simplifies to computing the mean of the immediate rewards.

In the following experiment we do not evaluate the performance of the agent under this reward redistribution. Instead, the aim of this experiment is to show how different LRP product rules change the explanation of the model and, therefore, the reward redistribution.

LSTM and Markov Properties. For LSTMs with forget gate or output gate [26], as described in Sect. 11.2.1, the cell content does not comply to Markov assumptions. This is because the current contribution of an input to a memory cell can be modified or hidden by later inputs, via the forget gate or output gate. For example, the forget gate can erase or reduce the contribution of the current input in the future due to some later inputs. Likewise, the output gate can hide the contribution of the current input by closing the gate until some future input opens the gate and reveals the already past contribution.

Figure 11.4b shows an LSTM memory cell that complies with the Markov property.

Environment. In our environment, an agent has to collect the *Moneybag* and then collect as many *Coins* as possible in a one dimension grid world. Only *Coins* collected after collecting the *Moneybag* give reward. At each time step, the agent can move to the left or to the right. All rewards are only given at the end of the episode, depending on how many *Coins* the agent collected in the *Moneybag*.

Training the Model. We are given a collection of sequences of state-action pairs. Each sequence represents one episode. Each episode is labeled with a scalar corresponding to the episode return. States and actions in the sequence are encoded as a vector of four binary features representing if the *Moneybag* is collected, if a *Coin* is collected, and the chosen action for the current timestep (one binary feature per action). In this experiment, we use a Long Short-Term Memory (LSTM) [30,37] to predict the return of an episode [2]. Notice that since we are using an LSTM, the input encoding does not have to fulfil the Markov property. Once the LSTM is trained, we use LRP [6] as contribution analysis for backward analysis.

LRP and Different Product Rules. We trained an LSTM network, as depicted in Fig. 11.4b, to predict the return given a sequence of states and actions. Later, we applied different product rules to propagate the relevance through the input gates and the cell inputs (cf. Table 11.1 Sect. 11.3.2). Results are shown in Figs. 11.6 and 11.7. When no relevance is propagated through the input gates (LRP-all),

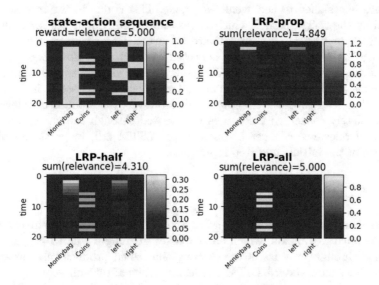

Fig. 11.6. LRP with different product rules as contribution analysis method in backward analysis, for one specific sequence of state-actions. State and action sequence is represented as a vector of four binary features. In this environment, *Coins* only give reward once the *Moneybag* is collected. When relevance is allowed to flow through the gate (LRP-prop and LRP-half rule), the event *Moneybag* is detected. Otherwise, only coin events are detected.

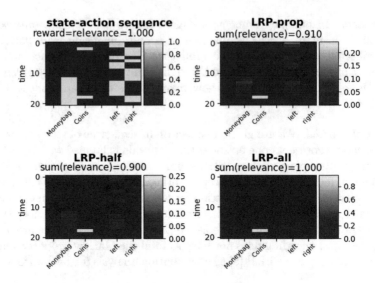

Fig. 11.7. LRP with different product rules as contribution analysis method in backward analysis, for one specific sequence of state-actions. Since *Coins* without *Moneybag* do not count for the reward, no relevance is assigned to these events.

certain important events are not detected by the contribution analysis, i.e. no relevance is assigned to the event *Moneybag*. This is due to the representation learned by the LSTM model, which stores information about the *Moneybag* feature, which in turn is used to activate a learned *Coins* counter via the input gate once the *Moneybag* has been collected. As such, the *Moneybag* event contributes through the input gate. When relevance is allowed to flow through the input gates (LRP-prop and LRP-half), all events can be detected, including the actions that lead to the *Moneybag* event. However, the amount of relevance is not completely conserved when it is propagated through the gates, as a small amount of relevance can get trapped in the LSTM cell, in particular via the relevance of the initial time step input gate.

11.6   Conclusion

We presented several ways of extending the LRP technique to recurrent neural networks such as LSTMs, which encompasses defining a rule to propagate the relevance through product layers. Among the tested product rule variants we showed that, on standard LSTM models, the signal-take-all strategy leads to the most pertinent results, and can be embedded in the deep Taylor framework where it corresponds to choosing the nearest root point in the gated interaction relevance model.

Additionally, we showed that the relevance propagation flow can be made more straightforward and stable by adapting the LSTM model towards the LRP technique and that, in this case, propagating a share of relevance through the gates leads to a detection of relevant events earlier in time. The resulting simplified and less connected LSTM model can potentially solve the same problems as the standard LSTM, although in practice this may necessitate using more memory cells.

More generally, further investigating the representational power of the new proposed LSTM, as well as its interplay with various LRP propagation rules, in particular via controlled experiments, would be a subject for future work.

Acknowledgements. This work was supported by the German Ministry for Education and Research as Berlin Big Data Centre (01IS14013A), Berlin Center for Machine Learning (01IS18037I) and TraMeExCo (01IS18056A). Partial funding by DFG is acknowledged (EXC 2046/1, project-ID: 390685689). This work was also supported by the Institute for Information & Communications Technology Planning & Evaluation (IITP) grant funded by the Korea government (No. 2017-0-00451, No. 2017-0-01779).

References

1. Ancona, M., Ceolini, E., Öztireli, C., Gross, M.: Towards better understanding of gradient-based attribution methods for deep neural networks. In: International Conference on Learning Representations (ICLR) (2018)
2. Arjona-Medina, J.A., Gillhofer, M., Widrich, M., Unterthiner, T., Brandstetter, J., Hochreiter, S.: RUDDER: return decomposition for delayed rewards. arXiv:1806.07857 (2018)
3. Arras, L., Horn, F., Montavon, G., Müller, K.R., Samek, W.: "What is relevant in a text document?": An interpretable machine learning approach. PLoS ONE **12**(8), e0181142 (2017)
4. Arras, L., Montavon, G., Müller, K.R., Samek, W.: Explaining recurrent neural network predictions in sentiment analysis. In: Proceedings of the EMNLP 2017 Workshop on Computational Approaches to Subjectivity, Sentiment and Social Media Analysis (WASSA), pp. 159–168 (2017)
5. Arras, L., Osman, A., Müller, K.R., Samek, W.: Evaluating recurrent neural network explanations. In: Proceedings of the ACL 2019 Workshop on BlackboxNLP: Analyzing and Interpreting Neural Networks for NLP, pp. 113–126. Association for Computational Linguistics (2019)
6. Bach, S., Binder, A., Montavon, G., Klauschen, F., Müller, K.R., Samek, W.: On pixel-wise explanations for non-linear classifier decisions by layer-wise relevance propagation. PLoS ONE **10**(7), e0130140 (2015)
7. Bakker, B.: Reinforcement learning with long short-term memory. In: Advances in Neural Information Processing Systems 14 (NIPS), pp. 1475–1482 (2002)
8. Bakker, B.: Reinforcement learning by backpropagation through an LSTM model/ critic. In: IEEE International Symposium on Approximate Dynamic Programming and Reinforcement Learning, pp. 127–134 (2007)
9. Becker, S., Ackermann, M., Lapuschkin, S., Müller, K.R., Samek, W.: Interpreting and explaining deep neural networks for classification of audio signals. arXiv:1807.03418 (2018)
10. Bengio, Y., Simard, P., Frasconi, P.: Learning long-term dependencies with gradient descent is difficult. IEEE Trans. Neural Networks **5**(2), 157–166 (1994)

11. Chen, J., Song, L., Wainwright, M., Jordan, M.: Learning to explain: an information-theoretic perspective on model interpretation. In: Proceedings of the 35th International Conference on Machine Learning (ICML), vol. 80, pp. 883–892 (2018)

12. Cho, K., et al.: Learning phrase representations using RNN encoder-decoder for statistical machine translation. In: Proceedings of the 2014 Conference on Empirical Methods in Natural Language Processing (EMNLP), pp. 1724–1734. Association for Computational Linguistics (2014)

13. Denil, M., Demiraj, A., de Freitas, N.: Extraction of salient sentences from labelled documents. arXiv:1412.6815 (2015)

14. Ding, Y., Liu, Y., Luan, H., Sun, M.: Visualizing and understanding neural machine translation. In: Proceedings of the 55th Annual Meeting of the Association for Computational Linguistics (ACL), pp. 1150–1159. Association for Computational Linguistics (2017)

15. Donahue, J., et al.: Long-term recurrent convolutional networks for visual recognition and description. IEEE Trans. Pattern Anal. Mach. Intell. **39**(4), 677–691 (2017)

16. EU-GDPR: Regulation (EU) 2016/679 of the European Parliament and of the Council of 27 April 2016 on the protection of natural persons with regard to the processing of personal data and on the free movement of such data, and repealing Directive 95/46/EC (General Data Protection Regulation). Official J. Eur. Union L **119**(59), 1–88 (2016)

17. Geiger, J.T., Zhang, Z., Weninger, F., Schuller, B., Rigoll, G.: Robust speech recognition using long short-term memory recurrent neural networks for hybrid acoustic modelling. In: Proceedings of the 15th Annual Conference of the International Speech Communication Association (INTERSPEECH), pp. 631–635 (2014)

18. Gers, F.A., Schmidhuber, J.: Recurrent nets that time and count. In: Proceedings of the IEEE International Joint Conference on Neural Networks (IJCNN), vol. 3, pp. 189–194 (2000)

19. Gers, F.A., Schmidhuber, J., Cummins, F.: Learning to forget: continual prediction with LSTM. In: Proceedings of the International Conference on Artificial Neural Networks (ICANN), vol. 2, pp. 850–855 (1999)

20. Gers, F.A., Schmidhuber, J., Cummins, F.: Learning to forget: continual prediction with LSTM. Neural Comput. **12**(10), 2451–2471 (2000)

21. Gevrey, M., Dimopoulos, I., Lek, S.: Review and comparison of methods to study the contribution of variables in artificial neural network models. Ecol. Model. **160**(3), 249–264 (2003)

22. Gonzalez-Dominguez, J., Lopez-Moreno, I., Sak, H., Gonzalez-Rodriguez, J., Moreno, P.J.: Automatic language identification using long short-term memory recurrent neural networks. In: Proceedings of the 15th Annual Conference of the International Speech Communication Association (INTERSPEECH), pp. 2155–2159 (2014)

23. Graves, A.: Generating sequences with recurrent neural networks. arXiv:1308.0850 (2014)

24. Graves, A., Liwicki, M., Fernandez, S., Bertolami, R., Bunke, H., Schmidhuber, J.: A novel connectionist system for unconstrained handwriting recognition. IEEE Trans. Pattern Anal. Mach. Intell. **31**(5), 855–868 (2009)

25. Graves, A., Schmidhuber, J.: Framewise phoneme classification with bidirectional LSTM and other neural network architectures. Neural Networks **18**(5–6), 602–610 (2005)

26. Greff, K., Srivastava, R.K., Koutník, J., Steunebrink, B.R., Schmidhuber, J.: LSTM: a search space odyssey. IEEE Trans. Neural Netw. Learn. Syst. **28**(10), 2222–2232 (2017)

27. Hausknecht, M., Stone, P.: Deep recurrent Q-learning for partially observable MDPs. In: AAAI Fall Symposium Series - Sequential Decision Making for Intelligent Agents, pp. 29–37 (2015)

28. Heess, N., Wayne, G., Tassa, Y., Lillicrap, T., Riedmiller, M., Silver, D.: Learning and transfer of modulated locomotor controllers. arXiv:1610.05182 (2016)

29. Hochreiter, S.: Implementierung und Anwendung eines 'neuronalen' Echtzeit-Lernalgorithmus für reaktive Umgebungen. Practical work, Institut für Informatik, Technische Universität München (1990)

30. Hochreiter, S.: Untersuchungen zu dynamischen neuronalen Netzen. Master's thesis. Institut für Informatik, Technische Universität München (1991)

31. Hochreiter, S.: Recurrent neural net learning and vanishing gradient. In: Freksa, C. (ed.) Proceedings in Artificial Intelligence - Fuzzy-Neuro-Systeme 1997 Workshop, pp. 130–137. Infix (1997)

32. Hochreiter, S.: The vanishing gradient problem during learning recurrent neural nets and problem solutions. Int. J. Uncertainty Fuzziness Knowl. Based Syst. **6**(2), 107–116 (1998)

33. Hochreiter, S., Bengio, Y., Frasconi, P., Schmidhuber, J.: Gradient flow in recurrent nets: the difficulty of learning long-term dependencies. In: Kolen, J.F., Kremer, S.C. (eds.) A Field Guide to Dynamical Recurrent Networks, pp. 237–244. IEEE Press, New York (2001)

34. Hochreiter, S., Heusel, M., Obermayer, K.: Fast model-based protein homology detection without alignment. Bioinformatics **23**(14), 1728–1736 (2007)

35. Hochreiter, S., Schmidhuber, J.: Long short-term memory. Technical report, FKI-207-95, Fakultät für Informatik, Technische Universität München (1995)

36. Hochreiter, S., Schmidhuber, J.: LSTM can solve hard long time lag problems. In: Advances in Neural Information Processing Systems 9 (NIPS), pp. 473–479 (1996)

37. Hochreiter, S., Schmidhuber, J.: Long short-term memory. Neural Comput. **9**(8), 1735–1780 (1997)

38. Hochreiter, S., Younger, A.S., Conwell, P.R.: Learning to learn using gradient descent. In: Proceedings of the International Conference on Artificial Neural Networks (ICANN), pp. 87–94 (2001)

39. Horst, F., Lapuschkin, S., Samek, W., Müller, K.R., Schöllhorn, W.I.: Explaining the unique nature of individual gait patterns with deep learning. Sci. Rep. **9**, 2391 (2019)

40. Kauffmann, J., Esders, M., Montavon, G., Samek, W., Müller, K.R.,: From clustering to cluster explanations via neural networks. arXiv:1906.07633 (2019)

41. Landecker, W., Thomure, M.D., Bettencourt, L.M.A., Mitchell, M., Kenyon, G.T., Brumby, S.P.: Interpreting individual classifications of hierarchical networks. In: IEEE Symposium on Computational Intelligence and Data Mining (CIDM), pp. 32–38 (2013)

42. Lapuschkin, S., Binder, A., Montavon, G., Müller, K.R., Samek, W.: The LRP toolbox for artificial neural networks. J. Mach. Learn. Res. **17**(114), 1–5 (2016)

43. Lapuschkin, S., Binder, A., Müller, K.R., Samek, W.: Understanding and comparing deep neural networks for age and gender classification. In: IEEE International Conference on Computer Vision Workshops, pp. 1629–1638 (2017)

44. Lapuschkin, S., Wäldchen, S., Binder, A., Montavon, G., Samek, W., Müller, K.R.: Unmasking clever hans predictors and assessing what machines really learn. Nat. Commun. **10**, 1096 (2019)

45. Li, J., Chen, X., Hovy, E., Jurafsky, D.: Visualizing and understanding neural models in NLP. In: Proceedings of the 2016 Conference of the North American Chapter of the Association for Computational Linguistics: Human Language Technologies (NAACL-HLT), pp. 681–691. Association for Computational Linguistics (2016)
46. Li, J., Monroe, W., Jurafsky, D.: Understanding neural networks through representation erasure. arXiv:1612.08220 (2017)
47. Lundberg, S.M., Lee, S.I.: A unified approach to interpreting model predictions. In: Advances in Neural Information Processing Systems 30 (NIPS), pp. 4765–4774 (2017)
48. Luoma, J., Ruutu, S., King, A.W., Tikkanen, H.: Time delays, competitive interdependence, and firm performance. Strateg. Manag. J. **38**(3), 506–525 (2017)
49. Marchi, E., Ferroni, G., Eyben, F., Gabrielli, L., Squartini, S., Schuller, B.: Multiresolution linear prediction based features for audio onset detection with bidirectional LSTM neural networks. In: IEEE International Conference on Acoustics, Speech and Signal Processing (ICASSP), pp. 2164–2168 (2014)
50. Mnih, V., et al.: Asynchronous methods for deep reinforcement learning. In: Proceedings of the 33rd International Conference on Machine Learning (ICML), vol. 48, pp. 1928–1937 (2016)
51. Montavon, G., Binder, A., Lapuschkin, S., Samek, W., Müller, K.-R.: Layer-wise relevance propagation: an overview. In: Samek, W. et al. (eds.) Explainable AI, LNCS 11700, pp. 193–209. Springer, Heidelberg (2019)
52. Montavon, G., Lapuschkin, S., Binder, A., Samek, W., Müller, K.R.: Explaining nonlinear classification decisions with deep Taylor decomposition. Pattern Recogn. **65**, 211–222 (2017)
53. Montavon, G., Samek, W., Müller, K.R.: Methods for interpreting and understanding deep neural networks. Digit. Signal Proc. **73**, 1–15 (2018)
54. Morcos, A.S., Barrett, D.G., Rabinowitz, N.C., Botvinick, M.: On the importance of single directions for generalization. In: International Conference on Learning Representations (ICLR) (2018)
55. Munro, P.: A dual back-propagation scheme for scalar reward learning. In: Proceedings of the Ninth Annual Conference of the Cognitive Science Society, pp. 165–176 (1987)
56. Murdoch, W.J., Liu, P.J., Yu, B.: Beyond word importance: contextual decomposition to extract interactions from LSTMs. In: International Conference on Learning Representations (ICLR) (2018)
57. Poerner, N., Schütze, H., Roth, B.: Evaluating neural network explanation methods using hybrid documents and morphosyntactic agreement. In: Proceedings of the 56th Annual Meeting of the Association for Computational Linguistics (ACL), pp. 340–350. Association for Computational Linguistics (2018)
58. Rahmandad, H., Repenning, N., Sterman, J.: Effects of feedback delay on learning. Syst. Dyn. Rev. **25**(4), 309–338 (2009)
59. Rieger, L., Chormai, P., Montavon, G., Hansen, L.K., Müller, K.-R.: Structuring neural networks for more explainable predictions. In: Escalante, H.J., et al. (eds.) Explainable and Interpretable Models in Computer Vision and Machine Learning. TSSCML, pp. 115–131. Springer, Cham (2018). https://doi.org/10.1007/978-3-319-98131-4_5
60. Robinson, A.J.: Dynamic error propagation networks. Ph.D. thesis, Trinity Hall and Cambridge University Engineering Department (1989)
61. Robinson, T., Fallside, F.: Dynamic reinforcement driven error propagation networks with application to game playing. In: Proceedings of the 11th Conference of the Cognitive Science Society, Ann Arbor, pp. 836–843 (1989)

62. Sahni, H.: Reinforcement learning never worked, and 'deep' only helped a bit. himanshusahni.github.io/2018/02/23/reinforcement-learning-never-worked.html (2018)
63. Sak, H., Senior, A., Beaufays, F.: Long short-term memory recurrent neural network architectures for large scale acoustic modeling. In: Proceedings of the 15th Annual Conference of the International Speech Communication Association (INTERSPEECH), Singapore, pp. 338–342 (2014)
64. Samek, W., Binder, A., Montavon, G., Lapuschkin, S., Müller, K.R.: Evaluating the visualization of what a deep neural network has learned. IEEE Trans. Neural Netw. Learn. Syst. **28**(11), 2660–2673 (2017)
65. Schmidhuber, J.: Making the world differentiable: on using fully recurrent self-supervised neural networks for dynamic reinforcement learning and planning in non-stationary environments. Technical report, FKI-126-90 (revised), Institut für Informatik, Technische Universität München (1990). Experiments by Sepp Hochreiter
66. Schmidhuber, J.: Deep learning in neural networks: an overview. Neural Netw. **61**, 85–117 (2015)
67. Shrikumar, A., Greenside, P., Kundaje, A.: Learning important features through propagating activation differences. In: Proceedings of the 34th International Conference on Machine Learning (ICML), vol. 70, pp. 3145–3153 (2017)
68. Simonyan, K., Vedaldi, A., Zisserman, A.: Deep inside convolutional networks: visualising image classification models and saliency maps. In: International Conference on Learning Representations (ICLR) (2014)
69. Socher, R., et al.: Recursive deep models for semantic compositionality over a sentiment treebank. In: Proceedings of the 2013 Conference on Empirical Methods in Natural Language Processing (EMNLP), pp. 1631–1642. Association for Computational Linguistics (2013)
70. Srivastava, N., Mansimov, E., Salakhudinov, R.: Unsupervised learning of video representations using LSTMs. In: Proceedings of the 32nd International Conference on Machine Learning (ICML), vol. 37, pp. 843–852 (2015)
71. Sturm, I., Lapuschkin, S., Samek, W., Müller, K.R.: Interpretable deep neural networks for single-trial EEG classification. J. Neurosci. Methods **274**, 141–145 (2016)
72. Sundararajan, M., Taly, A., Yan, Q.: Axiomatic attribution for deep networks. In: Proceedings of the 34th International Conference on Machine Learning (ICML), vol. 70, pp. 3319–3328 (2017)
73. Sutskever, I., Vinyals, O., Le, Q.V.: Sequence to sequence learning with neural networks. In: Advances in Neural Information Processing Systems 27 (NIPS), pp. 3104–3112 (2014)
74. Sutton, R.S., Barto, A.G.: Reinforcement Learning: An Introduction, 2nd edn. MIT Press, Cambridge (2017). Draft from November 2017
75. Thuillier, E., Gamper, H., Tashev, I.J.: Spatial audio feature discovery with convolutional neural networks. In: IEEE International Conference on Acoustics, Speech and Signal Processing (ICASSP), pp. 6797–6801 (2018)
76. Venugopalan, S., Xu, H., Donahue, J., Rohrbach, M., Mooney, R., Saenko, K.: Translating videos to natural language using deep recurrent neural networks. In: Proceedings of the 2015 Conference of the North American Chapter of the Association for Computational Linguistics: Human Language Technologies (NAACL-HLT), pp. 1494–1504. Association for Computational Linguistics (2015)

77. Yang, Y., Tresp, V., Wunderle, M., Fasching, P.A.: Explaining therapy predictions with layer-wise relevance propagation in neural networks. In: IEEE International Conference on Healthcare Informatics (ICHI), pp. 152–162 (2018)
78. Zaremba, W., Sutskever, I., Vinyals, O.: Recurrent neural network regularization. arXiv:1409.2329 (2015)
79. Zeiler, M.D., Fergus, R.: Visualizing and understanding convolutional networks. In: Fleet, D., Pajdla, T., Schiele, B., Tuytelaars, T. (eds.) ECCV 2014. LNCS, vol. 8689, pp. 818–833. Springer, Cham (2014). https://doi.org/10.1007/978-3-319-10590-1_53
80. Zhang, J., Lin, Z., Brandt, J., Shen, X., Sclaroff, S.: Top-down neural attention by excitation backprop. In: Leibe, B., Matas, J., Sebe, N., Welling, M. (eds.) ECCV 2016. LNCS, vol. 9908, pp. 543–559. Springer, Cham (2016). https://doi.org/10.1007/978-3-319-46493-0_33

Part IV
Evaluating Interpretability and Explanations

Evaluating Interpretability
and Explanations – Preface

Explanations provide insights into the functioning of an AI model. They can be used by the human expert to comprehend and verify the predictions and thus have an important trust building role in the use of AI technology. Furthermore, it is very conceivable that explanations will play a pivotal role in the quality assessment (and possibly certification) of future AI systems, e.g., AI-enhanced medical devices. However, this step requires validation that explanations themselves can be trusted unreservedly.

While the plausibility of explanations can be often judged subjectively by a human, a quantitative measure is needed for the objective assessment of explanation quality and for the comparison of different explanation techniques. Due to its practical relevance, the question of how to evaluate interpretability and explanations has recently become an active research topic. The next three chapters discuss different important aspects of this problem.

In Chapter 12, Zhou et al. [8] introduce a technique, called Network Dissection, to quantify the interpretability of neural representations. This method views units of a deep neural network as concept detectors and measures interpretability as the degree of alignment between neuron activations and the real-world concepts. This approach to understanding the internal representations is fully quantitative, thus allowing to compare the semantics of units in various networks and investigate the effect of different training parameters (e.g., pre-training, number of iterations) on the representation.

In Chapter 13, Montavon [5] proposes to assess the correctness of explanation techniques by means of an 'axiomatic approach'. Three axiomatic properties are considered in this chapter and permit to better understand the difference between gradient-based and LRP-type propagation methods, and their respective qualities. By testing for these properties both on the overall explanation and in the intermediate layers, the proposed approach not only allows to objectively assess the properties of the final explanation, but also to understand how the explanation is being formed layer after layer.

In Chapter 14, Kindermans et al. [4] present a study on the quality and reliability of saliency methods. An example is constructed, which shows that input transformations exist which do not change the processing and final decision of the network, but which largely affect the explanation. The authors regard input invariance as a desirable property and show that it is not fulfilled by many explanation methods.

Overall, these three chapters have presented approaches to evaluate interpretability or explanation quality. For explanation quality, further popular methods exist which have not been considered here, e.g., perturbation-based approaches [6], pointing games [7], methods using ground truth information in a toy task [3] and indirect evaluation schemes [1, 2]. Especially, the axiomatic approaches to interpretation are promising, because to some extent they allow to also formalize the explanation problem. However, the discussion on which axioms are desirable is still ongoing and may need future extension depending on the application domain and the recipient's goals. For instance, axioms such as input invariance might not be a generally desirable attribute, e.g., if explanations are supposed to capture the interaction of the model with the input. In linear model, explanations usually display the interaction between the feature dimension and the model's weight, i.e., do not fulfill this axiom. Thus, for deciding which axioms are desirable, the semantic meaning of an explanation needs to be further clarified.

July 2019

Wojciech Samek
Grégoire Montavon
Andrea Vedaldi
Lars Kai Hansen
Klaus-Robert Müller

References

1. Arjona-Medina, J.A., Gillhofer, M., Widrich, M., Unterthiner, T., Hochreiter, S.: RUDDER: return decomposition for delayed rewards. CoRR. (2018) arXiv:1806.07857
2. Arras, L., Horn, F., Montavon, G., Müller, K.-R., Samek, W.: "What is relevant in a text document?": an interpretable machine learning approach. PLoS ONE **12**(8), e0181142 (Aug 2017)
3. Arras, L., Osman, A., Müller, K.-R., Samek, W.: Evaluating recurrent neural network explanations. In: ACL 2019 Workshop on BlackboxNLP: Analyzing and Interpreting Neural Networks for NLP, pp. 113–126. Association for Computational Linguistics (2019)
4. Kindermans, P.-J., et al.: The (Un)reliability of saliency methods. In: Samek, W., Montavon, G., Vedaldi, A., Hansen, L.K., Müller, K.-R. (eds.) Explainable AI: Interpreting, Explaining and Visualizing Deep Learning. LNCS, vol. 11700, pp. 267–280. Springer, Cham (2019)
5. Montavon, G.: Gradient-based vs. propagation-based explanations: An axiomatic comparison. In: Samek, W., Montavon, G., Vedaldi, A., Hansen, L.K., Müller, K.-R. (eds.) Explainable AI: Interpreting, Explaining and Visualizing Deep Learning. LNCS, vol. 11700, pp. 253–265. Springer, Cham (2019)
6. Samek, W., Binder, A., Montavon, G., Lapuschkin, S., Müller, K.-R.: Evaluating the visualization of what a deep neural network has learned. IEEE Trans. Neural Networks Learn. Syst. **28**(11), 2660–2673 (2017)
7. Zhang, J., Bargal, S.A., Lin, Z., Brandt, J., Shen, X., Sclaroff, S.: Top-down neural attention by excitation backprop. Int. J. Comput. Vis. **126**(10), 1084–1102 (2018)
8. Zhou, B., Bau, D., Oliva, A., Torralba, A.: Comparing the interpretability of deep networks via network dissection. In: Samek, W., Montavon, G., Vedaldi, A., Hansen, L.K., Müller, K.-R. (eds.) Explainable AI: Interpreting, Explaining and Visualizing Deep Learning. LNCS, vol. 11700, pp. 243–252. Springer, Cham (2019)

12
Comparing the Interpretability of Deep Networks via Network Dissection

Bolei Zhou[1($\boxtimes$)], David Bau[2], Aude Oliva[2], and Antonio Torralba[2]

[1] The Chinese University of Hong Kong, Sha Tin, Hong Kong, China
bzhou@ie.cuhk.edu.hk
[2] Massachusetts Institute of Technology, Cambridge, MA, USA

Abstract. In this chapter, we introduce Network Dissection (The complete paper and code are available at http://netdissect.csail.mit.edu), a general framework to quantify the interpretability of the units inside a deep convolutional neural networks (CNNs). We compare the different vocabularies of interpretable units as concept detectors emerged from the networks trained to solve different supervised learning tasks such as object recognition on ImageNet and scene classification on Places. The network dissection is further applied to analyze how the units acting as semantic detectors grow and evolve over the training iterations both in the scenario of the train-from-scratch and in the stage of the fine-tuning between data sources. Our results highlight that interpretability is an important property of deep neural networks that provides new insights into their hierarchical structure.

Keywords: Interpretable machine learning · Deep neural networks · Model visualization

12.1 Introduction

Previous effort to interpret the internals of a convolutional neural network has focused on visualizations of the internal units. For example, visualizing image patches that maximize individual unit activations [13,16]; or using optimization to generate patterns and regions salient to a unit [7,9,12,13]; or rendering representation space using dimensionality reduction [5,6]. Though the visualizations give us the intuition about what image patterns the internal units are trying to detect, the results based on visualization are usually qualitative and unable to be interpreted quantitatively, *i.e.* which human interpretable concept some unit detects and how accurate it is. Therefore it is still an open question on how to quantify the interpretability of the deep visual representations and compare them beyond their classification power.

On the other hand, various techniques have been proposed to quantify the visualization for the decision making of deep neural networks. Samek et al. [10]

quantifies the quality of interpretations and correlates network performance over training with the measure using a perturbation based approach. Zhang et al. [14] describes various experiments such as pointing game to quantitatively evaluate and compare explanations. Zhou et al. [17] and Selvaraju et al. [11] uses the weakly-supervised localization for evaluating the generated class-specific maps. These interpretation method for the final prediction could be combined with the work on interpreting the internal units. For example, our recent work [18] uses the semantics of the internal activation to generate the visual explanation for the final prediction.

In this chapter, we focus on how we extract and quantify the semantics of units. A framework called *Network Dissection* has been proposed to quantify the interpretability of any given CNN [1,15]. Network dissection quantifies the interpretability of any given network by measuring the degree of alignment between the unit activation and the ground-truth labels in a pre-defined dictionary of concepts. Based on the quantified interpretability, we compare the semantics of units in various networks, and the effect of training iterations and fine-tuning to the internal representations of the networks. Our results highlight that interpretability is an important property of deep neural networks that provides new insights into their deep hierarchical structure. This chapter is a summary of the results from our work [1,15] on comparing the interpretability of various deep networks.

12.2 Overview of Network Dissection

To measure interpretability, we evaluate the ability of each hidden unit to solve segmentation problems from a dictionary of human-interpretable visual concepts.

12.2.1 Broden: Broadly and Densely Labeled Dataset

As a dictionary of visual concepts, we construct the **Bro**adly and **Den**sely Labeled Dataset (**Broden**), which unifies several densely labeled image data sets: ADE [19], OpenSurfaces [2], Pascal-Context [8], Pascal-Part [3], and the Describable Textures Dataset [4], containing a broad range of labeled classes of objects, scenes, object parts, textures, and materials, with most examples labeled at the pixel level.

12.2.2 Scoring Unit Interpretability

Let c denote any concept within the Broden dataset and let k denote any convolutional unit in a CNN. Network dissection defines the quality of the interpretation c for unit k by quantifying the ability of k to solve the segmentation problem given by c using this IoU score:

$$IoU_{k,c} = \frac{\sum |M_k(\mathbf{x}) \cap L_c(\mathbf{x})|}{\sum |M_k(\mathbf{x}) \cup L_c(\mathbf{x})|}, \qquad (12.1)$$

In the above, $\mathbf{x}$ represents an image in the Broden dataset, $L_c(\mathbf{x})$ is the set of pixels labeled with concept c, and $M_k(\mathbf{x})$ is binary mask selecting those pixels that lie within areas of highest activation of unit k. M_k is computed by (bilinearly) upsampling the activation of k on input $\mathbf{x}$, and applying a threshold T_k that selects a fixed quantile (0.5%) of the pixels over the entire dataset. Because the data set contains some categories of labels (such as textures) which are not present on some subsets of inputs, the sums are computed only on the subset of images that have at least one labeled concept of the same category as c. The summation is over all the images annotated with ground-truth.

The value of $IoU_{k,c}$ is the accuracy of unit k in detecting concept c. In our analysis, we consider a unit k as a detector for concept c if $IoU_{k,c} > 0.04$, and when a unit detects more than one concept, we choose the top scoring label. To quantify the interpretability of a layer, we count the distinct concepts detected, i.e., the number of *unique detectors*. The threshold for IoU is empirically set, fixed as 0.04 for all the networks. In [15], we have a detailed analysis on the effect of different thresholds.

Figure 12.1 summarizes the whole process of scoring unit interpretability: By segmenting the annotation mask using the receptive field of units for the top activated images, we compute the IoU for each concept. Importantly, the IoU which evaluates the quality of the segmentation of a unit is an objective confidence score for interpretability that is *comparable across networks*, enabling us to compare interpretability of different representations and so lays the basis for the experiments below. Note that network dissection results depends on the underlying vocabulary: if a unit matches a human-understandable concept that is absent from Broden, that unit will not score well for interpretability. Future versions of Broden will include a larger vocabulary of visual concepts.

12.3   Experiments

12.3.1   The Emergent Concept Detectors Across Different Networks

Network dissection is applied to the last convolutional layer of different networks (the histograms of concept detectors for each network are available at the project page). Figure 12.2 shows the examples of object detectors grouped by object categories. For the same object category, the visual appearance of the unit as detector varies not only within the same network but also across different networks. DenseNet and ResNet has such good detectors for bus and airplane with IoU more than 0.25.

12.3.2   The Emergence of Concepts over Training Iterations

Figure 12.3 plots the interpretability of snapshots of the baseline model (AlexNet trained on Places205) at different training iterations along with the accuracy on the validation set. We can see that object detectors and part detectors start emerging at about 10,000 iterations (each iteration processes a batch of 256

Top activated images

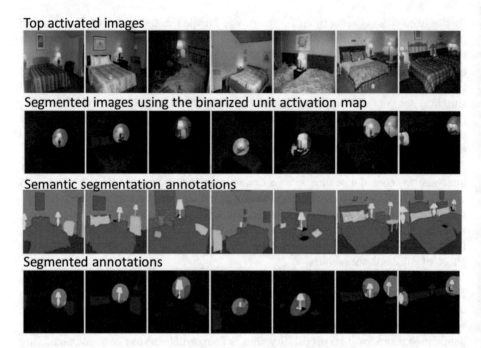

Fig. 12.1. Scoring unit interpretability by evaluating the unit activation for semantic segmentation. Unit activation map is used to segment the top activated images, localizing the favorite image patterns for that unit. The activation map is further used to segment the annotation mask to compute the IoU.

images). We also see there is a strong correlation between the validation accuracy and the emergence of high-level object detectors thus the interpretability might help debug the network during the training.

In Fig. 12.4, we keep track of four units over different training iterations. We observe that the units start converging to the semantic concept at early stage. For example, in the second row the unit starts detecting mountain from iteration 5000. Meanwhile, some units have interesting transition over concepts, for example the unit in the first row detects road first before it detects car.

12.3.3   The Evolution of Units in Transfer Learning

Fine-tuning the pre-trained network such as ImageNet-CNN to another target dataset is a commonly used technique in transfer learning. It makes the training converge faster, while it leads to better accuracy in the case that there is not enough training data at the target dataset. Here we observe that the interpretation of the internal units evolves over different stages of training in the transfer learning.

Given a well trained Places-AlexNet and ImageNet-AlexNet respectively, we fine-tune the Places-AlexNet on ImageNet and fine-tune the ImageNet-AlexNet

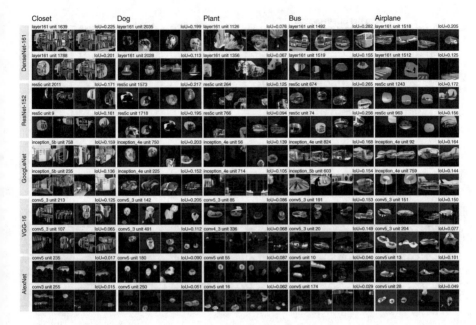

Fig. 12.2. Comparison of several visual concept detectors identified by network dissection in DenseNet, ResNet, GoogLeNet, VGG, and AlexNet. Each network is trained on Places365. The two highest-IoU matches among convolutional units of each network is shown. The four maximally activated Broden images segmented by unit activation map are shown as the visualization of each unit.

on Places respectively. The interpretability results of the snapshots of the networks over the fine-tuning iterations are plotted in Fig. 12.5. We can see that the training indeed converges faster compared to the network trained from scratch on Places in Fig. 12.3. The semantics of units also change over fine-tuning. For example, the number of unique object detectors first drop then keep increasing for the network trained on ImageNet being fine-tuned to Places365, while it is slowly dropping for the network trained on Places being fine-tuned to ImageNet.

Figure 12.6 shows the evolution of the six units in the network fine-tuned from ImageNet to Places365 and reversely. The top associated interpretation for each unit keep evolving during the fine-tuning process. For example, in the network fine-tuned from ImageNet to Places365, the first unit which detects the white dog, evolves to detect the waterfall; the third unit which detects the green concept, evolves to detect the baseball field. On the other hand, in the network fine-tuned from Places365 to ImageNet, units detecting different concepts converge to detect dog-relevant concepts such as ear and dog head. Interestingly though those units evolve to detect different concepts, many of them still remain to have similarity in colors or textures.

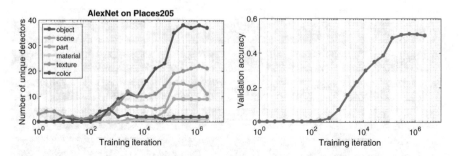

Fig. 12.3. The interpretability of the units at conv5 layer of the baseline model over 300,000 training iterations. The validation accuracy is plotted below.

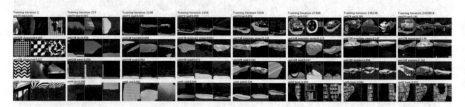

Fig. 12.4. The interpretation of four units evolves at different training iterations.

The fine-tuned model achieves the same classification accuracy than the train-from-scratch model, but the training converges faster due to the feature reuse. For the ImageNet to Places network, 139 out of 256 units (54.4%) at conv5 layer keep the same concepts during the finetuning, while for the network fine-tuned from Places to ImageNet, 135 out of 256 units (52.7%) at conv5 stay have the same concepts. We further categorized the unit evolution into five types based on the similarity between the concepts before and after fine-tuning. Out of the 117 units which evolved in the network fine-tuned from Imagenet to Places, 47 units keep a similar type of shape, 31 units have a similar texture, 18 units have similar colors, 13 units have a similar type of object, and 8 units do not have a clear pattern of similarities (see Fig. 12.7). Figure 12.8 illustrates the evolution history for two units of each model. Units seems to switch their top ranked label times before converging to a concept: unit15 in the fine-tuning of ImageNet to Places365 flipped to white, crystalline, before stabilizing to a waterfall concept. Other units are switching faster: unit132 in the fine-tuning of Places365 to ImageNet goes from hair to dog at an early stage of fine-tuning.

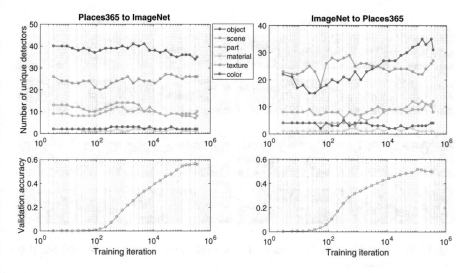

Fig. 12.5. The network interpretability under the fine-tuning between Places and ImageNet. The validation accuracy is plotted below. The network architecture is the same as AlexNet.

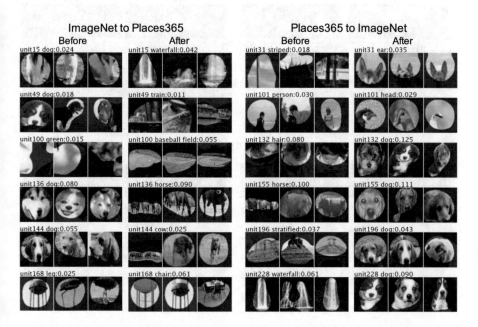

Fig. 12.6. The interpretation of six units before and after fine-tuning between ImageNet and Places.

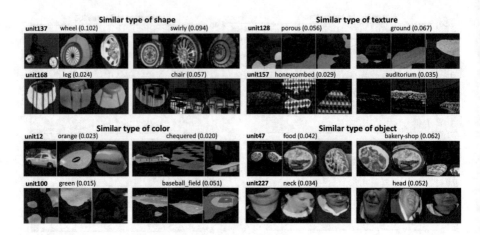

Fig. 12.7. Examples from four types of unit evolutions. Types are defined based on the concept similarity.

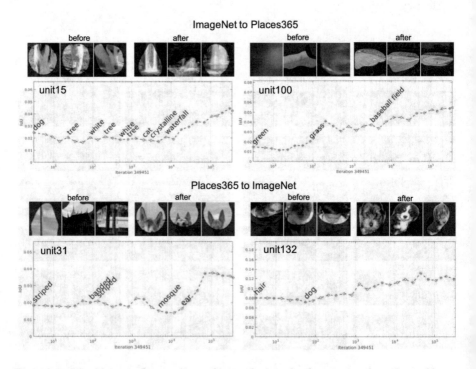

Fig. 12.8. The history of one unit evolution during the fine-tuning from ImageNet to Places365 (top) and Places365 to ImageNet (low).

12.4   Conclusion

Based on the network dissection, we compare the interpretability of deep visual representations for a range of networks trained from different supervisions and training conditions. We show that the interpretability based on unit-concept alignment is an important property of deep neural networks that could be used to compare networks beyond their classification accuracy. Future work will extend the framework of network dissection for interpreting the internals of the generative networks and the networks trained from reinforcement learning.

References

1. Bau, D., Zhou, B., Khosla, A., Oliva, A., Torralba, A.: Network dissection: quantifying interpretability of deep visual representations. In: Computer Vision and Pattern Recognition (2017)
2. Bell, S., Bala, K., Snavely, N.: Intrinsic images in the wild. ACM Trans. Graph. **33**(4), 159 (2014)
3. Chen, X., Mottaghi, R., Liu, X., Fidler, S., Urtasun, R., Yuille, A.: Detect what you can: detecting and representing objects using holistic models and body parts. In: Proceeding CVPR (2014)
4. Cimpoi, M., Maji, S., Kokkinos, I., Mohamed, S., Vedaldi, A.: Describing textures in the wild. In: Proceedings CVPR (2014)
5. Jolliffe, I.: Principal Component Analysis. Wiley Online Library, Hoboken (2002)
6. van der Maaten, L., Hinton, G.: Visualizing data using t-SNE: Visualizing data using t-SNE. J. Mach. Learn. Res. **9**, 2579–2605 (2008)
7. Mahendran, A., Vedaldi, A.: Understanding deep image representations by inverting them. Proceedings CVPR (2015)
8. Mottaghi, R., et al.: The role of context for object detection and semantic segmentation in the wild. In: Proceedings CVPR (2014)
9. Nguyen, A., Dosovitskiy, A., Yosinski, J., Brox, T., Clune, J.: Synthesizing the preferred inputs for neurons in neural networks via deep generator networks. In: Advances in Neural Information Processing Systems (2016)
10. Samek, W., Binder, A., Montavon, G., Lapuschkin, S., Müller, K.R.: Evaluating the visualization of what a deep neural network has learned. IEEE Trans. Neural Netw. Learn. Syst. **28**(11), 2660–2673 (2017)
11. Selvaraju, R.R., Cogswell, M., Das, A., Vedantam, R., Parikh, D., Batra, D.: Grad-CAM: visual explanations from deep networks via gradient-based localization. In: Proceedings ICCV (2017)
12. Simonyan, K., Vedaldi, A., Zisserman, A.: Deep inside convolutional networks: visualising image classification models and saliency maps. In: International Conference on Learning Representations Workshop (2014)
13. Zeiler, M.D., Fergus, R.: Visualizing and understanding convolutional networks. In: Proceedings ECCV (2014)
14. Zhang, J., Bargal, S.A., Lin, Z., Brandt, J., Shen, X., Sclaroff, S.: Top-down neural attention by excitation backprop. Int. J. Comput. Vision **126**(10), 1084–1102 (2018)
15. Zhou, B., Bau, D., Oliva, A., Torralba, A.: Interpreting deep visual representations via network dissection. IEEE Trans. Pattern Anal. Mach. Intell. (2018). https://doi.org/10.1109/TPAMI.2018.2858759

16. Zhou, B., Khosla, A., Lapedriza, A., Oliva, A., Torralba, A.: Object detectors emerge in deep scene CNNs. In: International Conference on Learning Representations (2015)
17. Zhou, B., Khosla, A., Lapedriza, A., Oliva, A., Torralba, A.: Learning deep features for discriminative localization. In: Proceedings CVPR (2016)
18. Zhou, B., Sun, Y., Bau, D., Torralba, A.: Interpretable basis decomposition for visual explanation. In: Proceedings ECCV (2018)
19. Zhou, B., Zhao, H., Puig, X., Fidler, S., Barriuso, A., Torralba, A.: Scene parsing through ADE20K dataset. In: Proceedings CVPR (2017)

13
Gradient-Based Vs. Propagation-Based Explanations: An Axiomatic Comparison

Grégoire Montavon[(✉)]

Technische Universität Berlin, 10587 Berlin, Germany
gregoire.montavon@tu-berlin.de

Abstract. Deep neural networks, once considered to be inscrutable black-boxes, are now supplemented with techniques that can *explain* how these models decide. This raises the question whether the produced explanations are reliable. In this chapter, we consider two popular explanation techniques, one based on gradient computation and one based on a propagation mechanism. We evaluate them using three "axiomatic" properties: *conservation*, *continuity*, and *implementation invariance*. These properties are tested on the overall explanation, but also at intermediate layers, where our analysis brings further insights on how the explanation is being formed.

Keywords: Explanations · Deep neural networks · Axioms

13.1 Introduction

Deep neural networks have been able to predict highly complex datasets and to perform extremely well in competitive benchmarks [7,10,28]. There has been growing interest in understanding how these models come up with their successful decisions. A popular approach is to extract for some examples of interest an *explanation* identifying which input variables (e.g. pixels) the model has used to build its prediction [2,16,19,29].

Two categories of explanation techniques have received considerable attention: The first category views the neural network as a function and relies on the function's *gradient* (readily available from the backpropagation algorithm) to produce explanations; examples include Gradient × Input [1,22], sensitivity analysis [23,32], smoothgrad [25], or integrated gradients [27]. A second category views the prediction as the output of a computational graph (the neural network), and explains by progressively redistributing the output on the lower layers by means of *propagation* rules; examples include layer-wise relevance propagation (LRP) [2], contribution-propagation [8], excitation-backprop [30], and deepLIFT [21].

Although these two categories of explanation techniques differ in their approach, the goal they pursue is the same: scoring input variables according to their

© Springer Nature Switzerland AG 2019
W. Samek et al. (Eds.): Explainable AI, LNAI 11700, pp. 253–265, 2019.
https://doi.org/10.1007/978-3-030-28954-6_13

Input   Gradient × Input   LRP

Fig. 13.1. Example of an image predicted by VGG-16 and explanations for the class ImageNet:Viaduct produced by two explanation techniques. Red color indicates pixels identified as relevant. Gray color indicates irrelevant pixels, blue color indicates negatively relevant (or contradictory) pixels.

importance for the prediction. Figure 13.1 shows the example of an image fed to the trained VGG-16 network [24] and where the evidence found by the network for the class ImageNet:Viaduct is explained by Gradient × Input (gradient-based) and LRP (propagation-based).

We observe that the two explanations diverge substantially, raising the question which one is the most correct. Pixel-flipping [2,18] is a method that evaluates the correctness of an explanation by taking features predicted as relevant and testing if removing these features has a strong effect on the prediction. The method relies on the design of an explicit feature removal scheme which may be specific to the type of data and prediction task.

In this chapter, we adopt instead an "axiomatic approach" [6,9,20,26,27], where an axiom is a self-evident property of an explanation, that we require to hold true for a fairly large class of inputs and models. We consider three axioms: (1) *conservation*, (2) *continuity*, and (3) *implementation invariance*, and scrutinize Gradient × Input and LRP explanations in their light. A peculiarity of our work will be to trace these axioms down to individual neurons of the network, where the explanation is being formed. This will allow us to identify key elements of the explanation techniques, that are responsible for fulfilling or breaking these axioms.

13.2 Explaining Neural Network Predictions

Given a trained neural network $x \mapsto f(x)$, we consider the problem of scoring input variables $x_1, \ldots, x_d$ according to their importance for the prediction $f(x)$. We call the list of produced scores $R_1, \ldots, R_d$ an explanation.

The class of networks we will consider in this chapter are deep rectifier networks. In their basic form, they can be described as a layered composition of ReLU neurons of the type

$$z_k = \sum_j a_j w_{jk} + b_k$$
$$a_k = \max(0, z_k).$$

The neuron parameters w_{jk}, b_k are learned from the data. To simplify the notation we will view the bias as a weight $w_{0k} = b_k$ connected to an input activation $a_0 = 1$, which then gives $a_0 w_{0k} = b_k$. This lets us rewrite the pre-activation as

$$z_k = \sum_{0,j} a_j w_{jk},$$

where the sum is over all input activations including the bias.

13.2.1   Gradient × Input Explanations

Gradient × Input is a gradient-based explanation technique that views the neural network as a function, whose gradient can be evaluated locally. Explanations are obtained by computing the product of the locally evaluated partial derivative and the input activation:

$$R_i = \left.\frac{\partial f}{\partial x_i}\right|_x \cdot x_i$$

In other words, an input variable is relevant if it manifests itself (is non-zero) in the input data *and* if the model positively reacts to it. When applied to a deep rectifier network with zero biases, Gradient × Input can also be seen as extracting the linear terms of a first-order Taylor expansion at root point $\tilde{x} = \lim_{t \to 0} t \cdot x$ (cf. [13]). Another popular gradient-based explanation technique is Integrated Gradient [27]. The latter reduces to Gradient × Input when the function is linear on the integration domain.

13.2.2   LRP Explanations

Layer-wise relevance propagation (LRP) [2] explains a neural network prediction by redistributing the neural network output layer after layer until the input variables have been reached. This is achieved by application of propagation rules at each layer of the network. A general propagation rule is given by:

$$R_j = \sum_k \frac{a_j \cdot (w_{jk} + \gamma w_{jk}^+)}{\epsilon + \sum_{0,j} a_j \cdot (w_{jk} + \gamma w_{jk}^+)} R_k, \tag{13.1}$$

where $(R_k)_k$ are relevance scores associated to neurons at a certain layer, $(R_j)_j$ are relevance scores from neurons in the lower layer, and γ, ϵ are hyperparameters to be set. The rule reduces to LRP-γ [11] when choosing $\gamma > 0$ and $\epsilon = 0$; it reduces to LRP-ϵ [2,11] when choosing $\gamma = 0$ and $\epsilon > 0$, and finally, setting $\gamma, \epsilon = 0$ gives LRP-0 [2,11]. All these rules can be applied to layers receiving ReLU neuron activations as input. For layers that receive pixels as input (e.g. the first layer) special rules such as the z^B-rule are more suitable [12].

For application of LRP to the VGG-16 network, we follow the approach of [11], consisting of applying z^B in the first layer, LRP-γ with $\gamma = 0.25$ in the first three convolutional blocks, LRP-ϵ with $\epsilon = 0.25$ std in the next two convolutional blocks, and LRP-0 for the top-level dense layers.

13.2.3 Propagation View on Gradient × Input

The propagation-based approach to explanation not only allows to engineer specific propagation rules, it can also serve as a framework to express other types of explanation techniques. For example, it is possible to reformulate Gradient × Input as a propagation procedure [22]. For this, let us first write the chain rule for derivatives explicitly:

$$\frac{\partial f}{\partial a_j} = \sum_k w_{jk} \cdot 1_{z_k > 0} \cdot \frac{\partial f}{\partial a_k}.$$

When multiplying both sides of the equation by the activation a_j, and defining $R_j = \partial f / \partial a_j \cdot a_j$ (i.e. gradient × activation), we obtain the propagation rule

$$R_j = \sum_k \frac{a_j w_{jk}}{\sum_{0,j} a_j w_{jk}} R_k. \tag{13.2}$$

which is equivalent to LRP-0 (see also [22]). The purpose of adopting a propagation view on Gradient × Input is to be able to more directly inspect how the latter compares to LRP, for example, in terms of inducing axiomatic properties of Sect. 13.3.

On the VGG-16 network, we will slightly depart from a uniform application of LRP-0 in every layer, and use instead the rule $z^{\mathcal{B}}$ in the first layer. This small modification addresses a technical shortcoming of Gradient × Input of not being able to assign relevance to gray pixels.

13.3 Axioms of an Explanation

Having introduced Gradient × Input and LRP, we now consider the problem of determining which of these two techniques delivers the best explanations. We adopt an approach where explanations are evaluated based on the fulfillment of a certain number of axioms [6,9,20,26,27]. Axioms are self-evident properties of an explanation that should be fulfilled for all possible examples in the input domain and for all possible neural network models in the given model class. In the following, we consider three axioms of an explanation, (1) *conservation*, (2) *continuity* and (3) *implementation invariance*, and study whether Gradient × Input and LRP satisfy or break them. Our analysis will be illustrated on a small two-dimensional example and on the VGG-16 network.

13.3.1 Conservation

A first desirable property of an explanation technique is to produce scores $R_1, \ldots, R_d$ that match in magnitude the evidence $f(\boldsymbol{x})$ found at the output of the network. A possible characterization of conservation is given by

$$\sum_{i=1}^d R_i + \varepsilon = f(\boldsymbol{x}), \tag{13.3}$$

with ε a small positive term containing all unexplained factors. The conservation property is inherent to techniques based on sum-decomposition [15, 31], or Taylor expansions [2, 4]. The conservation property can be further enforced at each layer [2, 8] where the explanation is being built progressively, i.e. $\sum_{i=1}^{d} R_i \approx \cdots \approx \sum_j R_j \approx \sum_k R_k \approx \cdots \approx f(\boldsymbol{x})$. Necessarily, this layer-wise conservation also implies global conservation in the sense of Eq. (13.3). This stronger form of conservation is particularly suited to analyze the construction of explanations by Gradient × Input and LRP. Specifically, we consider the sum of scores obtained at a given layer and observe how it relates to the sum of scores in the next layer. For Gradient × Input, summing scores as defined by Eq. (13.2) gives:

$$\sum_j R_j = \sum_k \frac{\sum_j a_j w_{jk}}{\sum_{0,j} a_j w_{jk}} R_k. \qquad \text{(Gradient × Input)}$$

Here, a sufficient condition for conservation to hold is that the bias w_{0k} is zero. In the case of LRP, summing scores as obtained from Eq. (13.1) gives:

$$\sum_j R_j = \sum_k \frac{\sum_j a_j \cdot (w_{jk} + \gamma w_{jk}^+)}{\epsilon + \sum_{0,j} a_j \cdot (w_{jk} + \gamma w_{jk}^+)} R_k. \qquad \text{(LRP)}$$

A first parameter that affects conservation is the hyperparameter ϵ. The larger ϵ, the more relevance is dissipated when propagating backwards. The parameter γ also influences conservation: When γ is large, the constraint on the bias w_{0k} can be relaxed to being non-positive instead of strictly zero.

Figure 13.2-A tests layer-wise conservation for both methods on the example of Fig. 13.1 where the prediction of the VGG-16 network is being explained. For LRP, we observe that relevance is dissipated in the intermediate layers where the rule LRP-ϵ is being used. Gradient × Input is closer to reaching the conservation property.

In order to avoid a scenario where the explanation would be composed of very positive and negative scores (e.g. $R_1 = 20$, $R_2 = -19$, $f(\boldsymbol{x}) = 1$), one needs to verify that scores of the explanation do not grow unbounded. This can be enforced by requiring the sum of *absolute* scores to not exceed some fixed threshold:

$$\sum_{i=1}^{d} |R_i| \leq A \qquad (13.4)$$

Figure 13.2-B shows the layer-wise evolution of absolute scores, along with a visualization of these scores when summed over feature maps or color channels. While LRP scores decrease on a similar scale as in the previous experiment, Gradient × Input scores exhibit exponential growth. This is also visible from the emergence of massive negative contributions (blue color) in the visualization. The reduction of absolute scores in the last layer is due to the application of the special $z^{\mathcal{B}}$ propagation rule [12] that smooths the explanation, as well as the compression from a large number of feature maps to only three color channels.

Overall, we observe that both methods produce explanations that deviate in some ways from the conservation property. The use of LRP-ϵ has the effect of

A. Layer-wise evolution of *summed* explanation scores

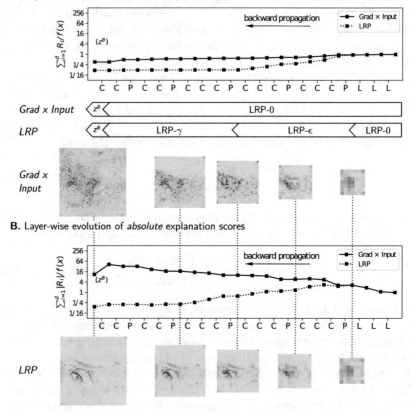

Fig. 13.2. Evolution of explanation scores in the backward propagation pass of Gradient × Input and LRP. In the plot, the redistribution from output to input goes from right to left.

reducing propagated scores layer after layer and the unexplained factors dominate the produced explanation. On the other hand, Gradient × Input scores explode in magnitude, an effect that can also be traced down to the exploding gradient problem [5].

13.3.2 Continuity

A second property we look at is continuity. First, we note that deep rectifier networks produce continuous prediction functions. This is a consequence of them being a composition of ReLU neurons, that are themselves continuous. Consequently, two similar input patterns will lead to similar neural network outputs.

Here, we would like to enforce similar property for the explanations. An explanation function is continuous if for any pair of nearly identical examples and assuming nearly identical predictions, their respective explanations are also nearly identical [13]. This property can be formulated as:

$$\forall_{i=1}^d : R_i(\boldsymbol{x}) \approx R_i(\boldsymbol{x} + \boldsymbol{\varepsilon})$$

for all inputs $\boldsymbol{x} \in \mathbb{R}^d$ and small perturbations $\boldsymbol{\varepsilon} \in \mathbb{R}^d$ of these inputs. Because the gradient of a deep rectifier networks is discontinuous, explanations produced by Gradient × Input are also discontinuous, thus not satisfying the axiom. The discontinuity can be traced down to the rule used to propagate the gradient: $\delta_j = \sum_k w_{jk} \cdot 1_{z_k \geq 0} \cdot \delta_k$, where the middle term is a step function with a discontinuity at $z_k = 0$. In other words, as soon as the neuron k becomes active, the gradient term δ_k, which is potentially large, percolates through that neuron and can significantly alter the gradient in the lower layers. For deep rectified networks the number of discontinuous regions of the gradient may grow exponentially with depth [3,14].

We now ask whether LRP produces continuous explanations. For this, we first express $R_j = a_j \sum_k c_{jk}$ and $R_k = a_k c_k$ so that the propagation rule can be rewritten as:

$$c_{jk} = \begin{cases} (w_{jk} + \gamma w_{jk}^+) \cdot \dfrac{\sum_{0,j} a_j w_{jk}}{\epsilon + \sum_{0,j} a_j \cdot (w_{jk} + \gamma w_{jk})^+} c_k & (a_k > 0) \\ 0 & (a_k = 0) \end{cases}$$

Using composition rules for continuity, we observe that, as long as one of the LRP hyperparameters γ, ϵ is non-zero, the LRP explanation is continuous.

Figure 13.3 illustrates the different behavior of Gradient × Input and LRP with respect to continuity on a simple ReLU neuron model that receives a two-dimensional input $\boldsymbol{a} = (a_1, a_2)$. We observe in this simple example that explanation scores $R_1(\boldsymbol{a})$ and $R_2(\boldsymbol{a})$ produced by LRP are continuous in the space of activations. This is not the case for Gradient × Input where we can observe in the top-right corner of the input domain that explanation scores jump abruptly from zero to large positive or negative values.

Figure 13.4 analyzes the continuity of explanation techniques when applied to the VGG-16 network. We take the image and perform a local occlusion at some relevant location in the image. We then translate this perturbation from left to right. The explanation at each stage of the translation is collected. The sequence explanations are then summarized in PCA plots, where the translation process describes a trajectory. We observe that the explanation produced by Gradient × Input evolves in a discontinuous manner and takes unpredictable steps in the PCA space. Instead, the explanations produced by LRP define a more continuous and predictable path. Thus, LRP is more capable of enforcing the continuity property.

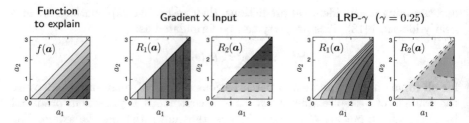

Fig. 13.3. Two-dimensional function $f(a) = \max(0, a_1 - a_2)$ and the explanation produced by Gradient × Input and LRP on the two input variables. White color represents value 0. Red color (solid contour lines) represents positive values and blue color (dashed contour lines) represents negative values.

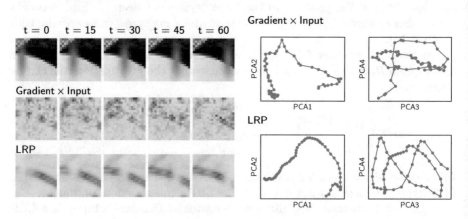

Fig. 13.4. Evolution of the explanation as we translate an occluding pattern from left to right in the image. Plots on the right are PCA embeddings of the sequence of explanations.

13.3.3 Implementation Invariance

A third axiom that has been proposed for explanation is implementation invariance [27]: Consider f_θ and $f_{\theta'}$ two functions with respective implementations θ and θ'. When applying an explanation technique to these two function implementations, the following property should be satisfied:

$$f_\theta = f_{\theta'} \;\;\Rightarrow\;\; \forall_{i=1}^d: \; R_i(x; f_\theta) = R_i(x; f_{\theta'}).$$

In other words, the explanation should be influenced by the function f_θ but not its implementation θ.

Because Gradient × Input relies on the data and the function but never on its implementation, produced explanations are implementation invariant. Instead, one can find examples where LRP is *not* implementation invariant. Figure 13.5 provides one such example, where two distinct neural networks implementing the same function give rise to different explanations.

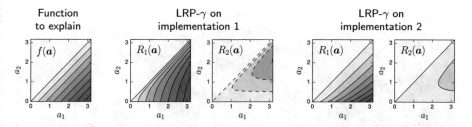

Fig. 13.5. LRP explanations obtained for two different implementations of the same function: The first implementation has a single neuron and computes $f(\boldsymbol{a}) = \max(0, a_1 - a_2)$. The second implementation has three neurons and computes $f(\boldsymbol{a}) = \max(0, \max(0, a_1 + 9a_2) - \max(0, 10a_2))$. In both cases, explanations are produced by applying at each neuron LRP-γ with $\gamma = 0.25$.

We now adopt a more systematic approach to study implementation invariance (or lack of it). A simple process for reimplementing a neural network without changing the actual function is neuron splitting. Consider at a certain layer a neuron a_s in the same layer as the neurons $(a_j)_j$. We split a_s in two neurons $(a_{s'}, a_{s''})$ with $a_s = a_{s'} = a_{s''}$. We choose outgoing weights $w_{s'k} = w_{sk} + \theta$ and $w_{s''k} = -\theta$ with $\theta > 0$. Clearly, the net effect of the splitting operation on a_k is null, thus, maintaining function equivalence.

Relevance scores found by LRP for neuron a_s and its split version $(a_{s'}, a_{s''})$ are given by:

$$R_s = \sum_k \frac{a_s \cdot (w_{sk} + \gamma w_{sk}^+)}{z_k + a_s \cdot (w_{sk} + \gamma w_{sk}^+)} R_k$$

and

$$(R_{s'} + R_{s''}) = \sum_k \frac{a_{s'} \cdot (w_{s'k} + \gamma w_{s'k}^+) + a_{s''} \cdot (w_{s''k} + \gamma w_{s''k}^+)}{z_k + a_{s'} \cdot (w_{s'k} + \gamma w_{s'k}^+) + a_{s''} \cdot (w_{s''k} + \gamma w_{s''k}^+)} R_k$$

$$= \sum_k \frac{a_s \cdot (w_{sk} + \gamma \cdot (w_{sk} + \theta)^+)}{z_k + a_s \cdot (w_{sk} + \gamma \cdot (w_{sk} + \theta)^+)} R_k$$

where $z_k = \epsilon + \sum_{0,j} a_j \cdot (w_{jk} + \gamma w_{jk}^+)$ is the original denominator without the contribution of the neuron s or its split version. We observe that $R_s \neq R_{s'} + R_{s''}$. In particular, when $\gamma > 0$, large values of θ will cause $R_{s'} + R_{s''} \approx \sum_k R_k \gg R_s$. That is, without changing the function, the splitting operation can let the neuron s absorb an arbitrary large fraction of the relevance available from the higher layer. Thus, the result of the LRP procedure will be an explanation of the neuron s rather than of the function f predicted at the output.

Figure 13.6 shows the explanations produced on the original trained image classifier, and an adversarial reimplementation where we have split each feature map at each layer, and set the parameter θ to 10x the standard deviation of weights in the corresponding layer.

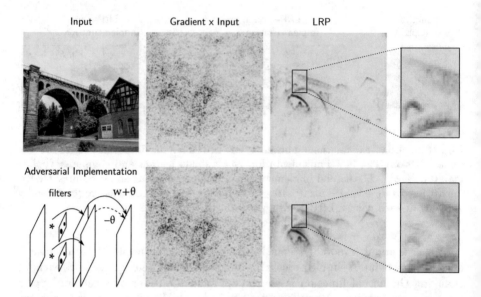

Fig. 13.6. Explanations obtained on the original trained neural network (top), and an adversarial implementation where feature maps at each layer have been split in order to perturb the propagation procedure while keeping the function unchanged (bottom).

As expected, this reimplementation does not affect the Gradient × Input explanation, which is implementation invariant. LRP seems globally implementation invariant, however, a closer inspection of the explanation shows that there are slight pixel-wise differences. LRP is thus influenced by the internal representation. Therefore, to make optimal use of LRP and other propagation techniques, it is not sufficient that the neural network predicts the data well, one also needs to pay particular attention to the structure of the learned model [17].

13.4   Conclusion

In this chapter, we have asked which of Gradient × Input and LRP, two explanation techniques that are prototypical of the gradient-based and propagation-based approaches, delivers the most reasonable explanations. As there are typically no ground-truth explanations to evaluate against, the approach we have pursued here is based on an 'axiomatic' characterization of explanations. More precisely, we have considered three axioms: *conservation, continuity* and *implementation invariance*, that must hold for any input and neural network, and tested Gradient × Input and LRP in their light.

A peculiarity of our analysis has been to view Gradient × Input and LRP in the same propagation-based framework, which allowed us to inspect and relate, at the level of the layer or the neuron, how the explanations are being progressively built, and how the axioms are becoming fulfilled or violated. For example, we could observe that the lack of conservation of Gradient × Input (LRP-0) grows with every layer. We have also shown that specific reimplementations of the neural network function affect the LRP-γ redistribution. Understanding the strengths and limitations of each method or propagation rule allows to use them strategically, e.g. choosing specific rules at specific layers [11], so that the overall explanation process is perturbed minimally.

We can ask the following question: If one would apply the same axioms-based evaluation to a potentially much broader class of explanations and use these axioms as a selection criterion, would we necessarily obtain good explanations? To answer this, consider one such class containing in particular the uniform explanation $\forall_{i=1}^d : R_i = d^{-1} f(\boldsymbol{x})$. It is easy to show that it is optimal with respect to the *conservation, continuity* and *implementation invariance*, but clearly not a reasonable explanation.

Because axioms may not be sufficient to uniquely identify the 'true' explanation and differentiate it from flawed explanations, keeping a restricted class of models, e.g. motivated by an underlying mathematical principle and where the hyperparameters are introduced parsimoniously, remains an important ingredient towards producing good explanations.

Acknowledgements. This work was supported by the German Ministry for Education and Research as Berlin Center for Machine Learning (01IS18037I). Partial funding by DFG is acknowledged (EXC 2046/1, project-ID: 390685689). The author is grateful to Klaus-Robert Müller for the valuable feedback.

References

1. Ancona, M., Ceolini, E., Öztireli, A.C., Gross, M.H.: A unified view of gradient-based attribution methods for deep neural networks. CoRR abs/1711.06104 (2017)
2. Bach, S., Binder, A., Montavon, G., Klauschen, F., Müller, K.R., Samek, W.: On pixel-wise explanations for non-linear classifier decisions by layer-wise relevance propagation. PLoS ONE **10**(7), e0130140 (2015)
3. Balduzzi, D., Frean, M., Leary, L., Lewis, J.P., Ma, K.W., McWilliams, B.: The shattered gradients problem: if resnets are the answer, then what is the question? In: International Conference on Machine Learning, pp. 342–350 (2017)
4. Bazen, S., Joutard, X.: The Taylor decomposition: a unified generalization of the Oaxaca method to nonlinear models. Technical report 2013–32, Aix-Marseille University (2013)
5. Bengio, Y., Simard, P.Y., Frasconi, P.: Learning long-term dependencies with gradient descent is difficult. IEEE Trans. Neural Networks **5**(2), 157–166 (1994)
6. Kindermans, P., et al.: The (un)reliability of saliency methods. CoRR abs/1711.00867 (2017)
7. Krizhevsky, A., Sutskever, I., Hinton, G.E.: Imagenet classification with deep convolutional neural networks. In: Neural Information Processing Systems, pp. 1106–1114 (2012)
8. Landecker, W., Thomure, M.D., Bettencourt, L.M.A., Mitchell, M., Kenyon, G.T., Brumby, S.P.: Interpreting individual classifications of hierarchical networks. In: IEEE Symposium on Computational Intelligence, pp. 32–38 (2013)
9. Lundberg, S.M., Lee, S.: A unified approach to interpreting model predictions. In: Neural Information Processing Systems, pp. 4768–4777 (2017)

10. Mnih, V., et al.: Human-level control through deep reinforcement learning. Nature **518**(7540), 529–533 (2015)
11. Montavon, G., Binder, A., Lapuschkin, S., Samek, W., Müller, K.-R.: Layer-wise relevance propagation: an overview. In: Samek, W., Montavon, G., Vedaldi, A., Hansen, L.K., Müller, K.-R. (eds.) Explainable AI. LNCS, vol. 11700, pp. 193–209. Springer, Cham (2019)
12. Montavon, G., Lapuschkin, S., Binder, A., Samek, W., Müller, K.: Explaining nonlinear classification decisions with deep Taylor decomposition. Pattern Recogn. **65**, 211–222 (2017)
13. Montavon, G., Samek, W., Müller, K.: Methods for interpreting and understanding deep neural networks. Digit. Signal Process. **73**, 1–15 (2018)
14. Montúfar, G.F., Pascanu, R., Cho, K., Bengio, Y.: On the number of linear regions of deep neural networks. In: Neural Information Processing Systems, pp. 2924–2932 (2014)
15. Poulin, B., et al.: Visual explanation of evidence with additive classifiers. In: National Conference on Artificial Intelligence and Innovative Applications of Artificial Intelligence, pp. 1822–1829 (2006)
16. Ribeiro, M.T., Singh, S., Guestrin, C.: Why should I trust you?: Explaining the predictions of any classifier. In: ACM SIGKDD International Conference on Knowledge Discovery and Data Mining, pp. 1135–1144 (2016)
17. Rieger, L., Chormai, P., Montavon, G., Hansen, L.K., Müller, K.-R.: Structuring neural networks for more explainable predictions. In: Escalante, H.J., et al. (eds.) Explainable and Interpretable Models in Computer Vision and Machine Learning. TSSCML, pp. 115–131. Springer, Cham (2018). https://doi.org/10.1007/978-3-319-98131-4_5
18. Samek, W., Binder, A., Montavon, G., Lapuschkin, S., Müller, K.: Evaluating the visualization of what a deep neural network has learned. IEEE Trans. Neural Netw. Learn. Syst. **28**(11), 2660–2673 (2017)
19. Selvaraju, R.R., Cogswell, M., Das, A., Vedantam, R., Parikh, D., Batra, D.: Grad-CAM: visual explanations from deep networks via gradient-based localization. In: IEEE International Conference on Computer Vision, pp. 618–626 (2017)
20. Shapley, L.S.: 17. A value for n-person games. In: Contributions to the Theory of Games (AM-28), Volume II. Princeton University Press (1953)
21. Shrikumar, A., Greenside, P., Kundaje, A.: Learning important features through propagating activation differences. In: International Conference on Machine Learning, pp. 3145–3153 (2017)
22. Shrikumar, A., Greenside, P., Shcherbina, A., Kundaje, A.: Not just a black box: learning important features through propagating activation differences. CoRR abs/1605.01713 (2016)
23. Simonyan, K., Vedaldi, A., Zisserman, A.: Deep inside convolutional networks: visualising image classification models and saliency maps. In: 2nd International Conference on Learning Representations (2014)
24. Simonyan, K., Zisserman, A.: Very deep convolutional networks for large-scale image recognition. In: 3rd International Conference on Learning Representations (2015)
25. Smilkov, D., Thorat, N., Kim, B., Viégas, F.B., Wattenberg, M.: SmoothGrad: removing noise by adding noise. CoRR abs/1706.03825 (2017)
26. Sun, Y., Sundararajan, M.: Axiomatic attribution for multilinear functions. In: ACM Conference on Electronic Commerce, pp. 177–178 (2011)
27. Sundararajan, M., Taly, A., Yan, Q.: Axiomatic attribution for deep networks. In: International Conference on Machine Learning, pp. 3319–3328 (2017)

28. Sutskever, I., Vinyals, O., Le, Q.V.: Sequence to sequence learning with neural networks. In: Neural Information Processing Systems, pp. 3104–3112 (2014)
29. Zeiler, M.D., Fergus, R.: Visualizing and understanding convolutional networks. In: Fleet, D., Pajdla, T., Schiele, B., Tuytelaars, T. (eds.) ECCV 2014. LNCS, vol. 8689, pp. 818–833. Springer, Cham (2014). https://doi.org/10.1007/978-3-319-10590-1_53
30. Zhang, J., Bargal, S.A., Lin, Z., Brandt, J., Shen, X., Sclaroff, S.: Top-down neural attention by excitation backprop. Int. J. Comput. Vision **126**(10), 1084–1102 (2018)
31. Zhou, B., Khosla, A., Lapedriza, À., Oliva, A., Torralba, A.: Learning deep features for discriminative localization. In: IEEE Conference on Computer Vision and Pattern Recognition, pp. 2921–2929 (2016)
32. Zurada, J.M., Malinowski, A., Cloete, I.: Sensitivity analysis for minimization of input data dimension for feedforward neural network. In: IEEE International Symposium on Circuits and Systems, pp. 447–450 (1994)

14

The (Un)reliability of Saliency Methods

Pieter-Jan Kindermans[1(✉)], Sara Hooker[1], Julius Adebayo[1],
Maximilian Alber[2], Kristof T. Schütt[2], Sven Dähne[2], Dumitru Erhan[1],
and Been Kim[1]

[1] Google Brain, Mountain View, CA, USA
{pikinder,shooker}@google.com
[2] Technische Universität Berlin, 10587 Berlin, Germany

Abstract. Saliency methods aim to explain the predictions of deep neural networks. These methods lack reliability when the explanation is sensitive to factors that do not contribute to the model prediction. We use a simple and common pre-processing step which can be compensated for easily—adding a constant shift to the input data—to show that a transformation with no effect on how the model makes the decision can cause numerous methods to attribute incorrectly. In order to guarantee reliability, we believe that the explanation should not change when we can guarantee that two networks process the images in identical manners. We show, through several examples, that saliency methods that do not satisfy this requirement result in misleading attribution. The approach can be seen as a type of unit test; we construct a narrow ground truth to measure one stated desirable property. As such, we hope the community will embrace the development of additional tests.

14.1 Introduction

While considerable research has focused on discerning the decision process of neural networks [2–4, 7–9, 14–20], there remains a trade-off between model complexity and interpretability. In deep neural networks, feature representation is delegated to the model and subsequently we cannot generally say in an informative way what led to a model prediction. Saliency methods aim to infer insights about the function $f(x)$ learnt by the model by ranking the inputs by their explanatory power. While unified in purpose, these methods are surprisingly divergent and non-overlapping in outcome. Evaluating the reliability of these methods is complicated because of the lack of ground truth, as ground truth would depend upon full transparency into how a model arrives at a decision—the very problem we are trying to solve for in the first place [7,17]. This becomes obvious when we consider Fig. 14.1, which shows a typical visualization of attribution methods. In this figure several methods produce very different results, but it is impossible to decide which one can be considered a good explanation.

P.-J. Kindermans and S. Hooker—Contributed equally to this work and Work done as part of the Google AI Residency program.

© Springer Nature Switzerland AG 2019
W. Samek et al. (Eds.): Explainable AI, LNAI 11700, pp. 267–280, 2019.
https://doi.org/10.1007/978-3-030-28954-6_14

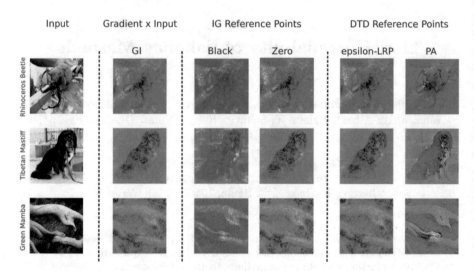

Fig. 14.1. Integrated gradients and Deep Taylor Decomposition determine input attribution relative to a chosen reference point. This choice determines the vantage point for all subsequent attribution. Using two example reference points for each method we demonstrate that changing the reference causes the attribution to diverge. A visualisation as presented here appears to be intuitive, but it is difficult to determine which approach is best. We argue that for this reason effective tests for these methods are needed. The attributions are visualized in a consistent manner with the IG paper [17]. Visualisations were made using ImageNet data. [10] and the VGG16 architecture [14].

A formal methodology to evaluate the relative reliability of different saliency methods is needed. Reliable explanations build trust with users, help identify points of model failure and remove barriers to entry for the deployment of deep neural networks in domains like health care, security and transportation. Several recent works have proposed formal methodologies for comparing the relative merit of saliency methods [1,5,7,11]. In addition, there are multiple works that discuss and formulate desirable properties that saliency methods should fulfill, such as completeness and implementation invariance [2,17].

We propose *input shift invariance* as a property that is necessary to achieve a reliable explanation of the input's contribution to the model prediction. Input shift invariance requires that the saliency method's output remains consistent when the input data is shifted and the model was adjusted to compensate for the shift. In this case, the original image and the modified counter part are processed in exactly the same way. Therefore the saliency method's output should not change either.

We demonstrate that numerous methods do not satisfy input shift invariance. Our results also demonstrate that explanations of a networks predictions can be purposefully manipulated using this surprisingly simple transformation.

14.2   A Unit Test for Saliency Methods

The goal of this work is to develop a setting where we can measure one aspect of reliability. To do so, we construct a unit test where a semantically meaningless transformation of the input (across the entire dataset) does not affect the model function. We then test whether the explanation is sensitive to the transformation despite the model being unchanged. A reliable method should be invariant to any transformation that does not impact the model.

Shifting the entire dataset by a constant vector is such a semantically mean-ingless perturbation. We show that the bias of a neural network can compensate for the constant shift. This results in two networks with identical weights, inter-mediate activations and predictions. Therefore, a reliable saliency method will produce identical explanations for both networks.

To evaluate this unit test we compare the attribution across two networks, $f_1(\boldsymbol{x})$ and $f_2(\boldsymbol{x})$. Here, $f_1(\boldsymbol{x})$ is a network trained on input $\boldsymbol{x}_1^i$ that denotes sample i from training set X_1. The classifier output of network 1 is:

$$f_1(\boldsymbol{x}_1^i) = \boldsymbol{y}^i,$$

Now $f_2(\boldsymbol{x})$ is a network that predicts the classification of a transformed input $\boldsymbol{x}_2^i$. The relationship between $\boldsymbol{x}_1^i$ and $\boldsymbol{x}_2^i$ is the addition of constant vector $\boldsymbol{m}_2$:

$$\forall i, \boldsymbol{x}_2^i = \boldsymbol{x}_1^i + \boldsymbol{m}_2.$$

Given a trained network $f_1(\boldsymbol{x})$ we can construct network $f_2(\boldsymbol{x})$ to make the identical prediction on the modified data. Network $f_2(\boldsymbol{x})$ has the same weights as network $f_1(\boldsymbol{x})$. It only differs in the first layer biases. Consider a first layer neuron before non-linearity in $f_1(\boldsymbol{x})$:

$$z = \boldsymbol{w}^T \boldsymbol{x}_1 + b_1.$$

In network $f_2(\boldsymbol{x})$, we alter the biases in the first layer neuron by compensating for the mean shift: $\boldsymbol{m}_2$. Therefore the bias in the first layer of network $f_2(\boldsymbol{x})$ becomes:

$$b_2 = b_1 - \boldsymbol{w}^T \boldsymbol{m}_2.$$

As a result the first layer activations are the same for $f_1(\boldsymbol{x})$ and $f_2(\boldsymbol{x})$:

$$z = \boldsymbol{w}^T \boldsymbol{x}_2 + b_2 = \boldsymbol{w}^T \boldsymbol{x}_1 + \boldsymbol{w}^T \boldsymbol{m}_2 + b_1 - \boldsymbol{w}^T \boldsymbol{m}_2.$$

Note that the gradient with respect to the input remains unchanged as well:

$$\frac{\partial f_1(\boldsymbol{x}_1^i)}{\partial \boldsymbol{x}_1^i} = \frac{\partial f_2(\boldsymbol{x}_2^i)}{\partial \boldsymbol{x}_2^i}.$$

By construction network $f_2(\boldsymbol{x})$ cancels out the mean shift transformation. This means that $f_1(\boldsymbol{x})$ and $f_2(\boldsymbol{x})$ have identical weights and produce the same output for all corresponding samples, $\boldsymbol{x}_1^i \in X_1, \boldsymbol{x}_2^i \in X_2$:

$$\forall i, f_1(\boldsymbol{x}_1^i) = f_2(\boldsymbol{x}_2^i).$$

In our experiments $f_1(\boldsymbol{x})$ is trained and $f_2(\boldsymbol{x})$ is obtained transforming $f_1(\boldsymbol{x})$ using the bias modification presented above.

14.2.1   Experimental Setup

Now, we describe our experiment setup to evaluate the *input shift invariance* of a set of saliency methods. In the implementation of this experimental framework, network 1 is a 3 layer multi-layer perceptron with 1024 ReLU-activated neurons each. Network 1 classifies MNIST image inputs in a [0, 1] encoding. We consider a negative constant shift of $m_2 = -1$; Network 2 classifies MNIST image inputs in a [−1, 0] MNIST encoding. The first network is trained for 10 epochs using mini-batch stochastic gradient descent (SGD). The final accuracy is 98.3% for both.

14.3   The (In)sensitivity of Saliency Methods to Mean Shifts

In Sect. 14.3.1 we introduce the broad grouping of the saliency methods that we evaluate. In Sect. 14.3.2 we find that gradient and signal methods satisfy input invariance. In Sect. 14.3.3 we find that most attribution methods considered have points of failure.

14.3.1   Saliency Methods Considered

Saliency methods broadly fall into three different categories:

1. **Gradients (Sensitivity)** [3, 13] show how a small change to the input affects the classification score for the output of interest.
2. **Signal methods** such as DeConvNet [19], Guided BackProp (GB) [16] and PatternNet (PN) [7] aim to isolate input patterns that stimulate neuron activation in higher layers.
3. **Attribution methods** such as Gradient times Input (GI), Deep-Taylor Decomposition (DTD) [8], Integrated Gradients (IG) [17] and PatternAttribution (PA) [7] assign importance to input dimensions by decomposing the value y_j at an output neuron j into contributions from the individual input dimensions:

$$s_j = A(\boldsymbol{x})_j.$$

   s_j is the decomposition into input contributions and has the same number of dimensions as $\boldsymbol{x}$, $A(\boldsymbol{x})_j$ signifies the attribution method applied to output j for sample $\boldsymbol{x}$. Attribution methods are distinct from gradients because of the insistence on *completeness*: the sum of all attributions should be approximately equal to the original output y_i.

We consider the input shift invariance of each category separately (by evaluating raw gradients, GB, PN, GI, IG, DTD, PA). We also benchmark the input invariance of SmoothGrad (SG) [15], a method that wraps around an underlying saliency approach and uses the addition of noise to produce an explanation of the saliency heatmap that is often considered visually "sharper".

The experiment setup and methodology is as described in Sect. 14.2. Each method is evaluated by comparing the explanation for the predictions of network 1 and 2, where x_2^i is simply the mean shifted input $(x_1^i + m_2)$. A saliency method that satisfies input shift invariance will produce identical saliency heatmaps for network 1 and 2 despite the constant shift in input.

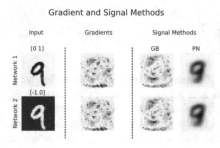

Fig. 14.2. Evaluating the input shift invariance of gradient and signal methods using MNIST with a $[0, 1]$ encoding for network f_1 and a $[-1, 0]$ encoding for network f_2. Both raw gradients and signal methods satisfy input shift invariance by producing identical saliency heatmaps for both networks.

14.3.2 Gradient and Signal Methods

Gradient and signal methods are not sensitive to a constant shift in inputs. In Fig. 14.2 raw gradients, and the signal methods considered (PatternNet [7] and Guided Backprop [16]) produce identical saliency heatmaps for both networks. Intuitively, gradient, PN and GB satisfy input shift invariance given that we are comparing two networks with an identical $f(x)$. Both gradient and signal methods considered determine attribution *entirely* as a function of the network/- pattern weights and thus will be consistent as long as we are comparing networks with identical weights.

In the same manner, we can say that these methods will not be invariant when comparing networks with different weights (even if we consider models with different architectures but identical predictions for every input).

14.3.3 Attribution Methods

We evaluate the following attribution methods: Gradient times Input (GI), Integrated Gradients (IG), Deep-Taylor Decomposition (DTD). Both IG and DTD require that attribution is done in relation to a chosen reference. We find that satisfying input invariance depends upon the choice of reference point and the type of constant shift to the input.

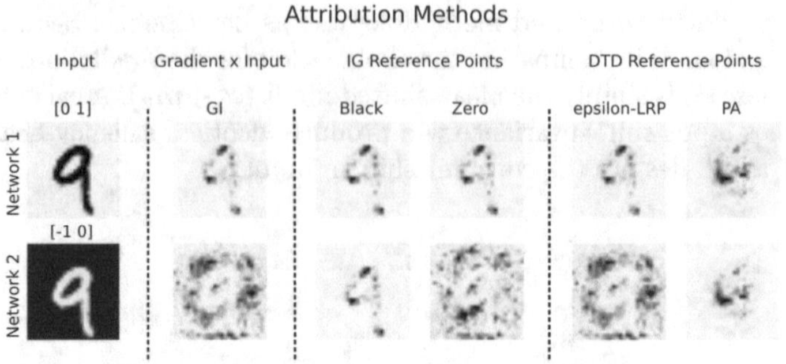

Attribution Methods

Fig. 14.3. Evaluation of attribution method sensitivity using MNIST with a $[0, 1]$ encoding for network f_1 and a $[-1, 0]$ encoding for network f_2. Gradient times input, IG and DTD with a zero reference point, which is equivalent to epsilon-LRP [2,8], are not reliable and produce different attributions for each network. IG with a black image reference point and DTD with a PA reference point are not sensitive to a mean shift in input.

Gradient Times Input (GI). We find that the multiplication of gradients with the image breaks attribution reliability. In Fig. 14.3 GI produces different saliency heatmaps for both networks.

In Sect. 14.3.2 we determined that the gradient does satisfy input shift invariance. This breaks when the gradients are multiplied with the input image.

$$s_j = \frac{\partial f(\boldsymbol{x})_j}{\partial \boldsymbol{x}} \odot \boldsymbol{x}.$$

Multiplying by the input means attribution is no longer reliable because the input shift is carried through to the final attribution. Naive multiplication by the input, as noted by [15], also constrains attribution without justification to inputs that are nonzero.

Integrated Gradients (IG). [17] attribute the predicted score to each input with respect to a baseline $\boldsymbol{x}_0$. This is achieved by constructing a set of inputs interpolating between the baseline and the input.

$$s = (\boldsymbol{x} - \boldsymbol{x}_0) \odot \int_{\alpha=0}^{1} \frac{\partial f(\boldsymbol{x}_0 + \alpha(\boldsymbol{x} - \boldsymbol{x}_0))}{\partial \boldsymbol{x}} d\alpha$$

Since this integral cannot be computed analytically, it is approximated by a finite sum ranging over $\alpha \in [0, 1]$.

$$s = (\boldsymbol{x} - \boldsymbol{x}_0) \odot \sum_{\alpha} \frac{\partial f(\boldsymbol{x}_0 + \alpha(\boldsymbol{x} - \boldsymbol{x}_0))}{\partial \boldsymbol{x}}.$$

We evaluate two possible IG reference points. Firstly, we consider as a reference point a constant vector with the minimum pixel value from the dataset

$(\boldsymbol{x}_0 = min(\boldsymbol{x}))$ (black image). Secondly, we consider as a reference point a zero vector image. In Fig. 14.3, IG with black reference point produces identical attribution heatmaps whereas IG with a zero vector reference point is not input invariant.

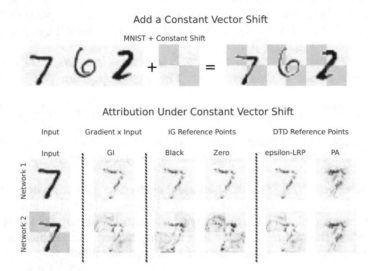

Fig. 14.4. Evaluation of attribution method sensitivity using MNIST. Gradient times input, all IG reference points and DTD with an epsilon-LRP reference point do not satisfy input invariance and produce different attributions for each network. DTD with a PA reference point is not sensitive to the transformation of the input.

It is possible to construct a transformation of the input that will break the reliability of using a black image as a reference point. We consider a transformation $\boldsymbol{x}_2^i$ of the input $\boldsymbol{x}_1^i$ where the constant vector $(\boldsymbol{m}_2)$ added to $\boldsymbol{x}_1^i$ is an image of a checkered box. The difference between $\boldsymbol{x}_1^i$ and the transformed input $\boldsymbol{x}_2^i$ is the addition of the checkered box image vector $\boldsymbol{m}_2$. Network 2 is identical to network 1 by construction.

In Fig. 14.4, we show that we are able to successfully manipulate the attribution map of an MNIST prediction so that the checkered box image appears. Using a black image as a reference point for IG no longer satisfies input invariance.

Deep Taylor Decomposition (DTD). [8] determines attribution relative to a reference point neuron. In the general formulation, the attribution of an input neuron j is initialized to be equal to the output of that neuron. The attribution of other output neurons is set to zero. This attribution is send back to input neurons using the following distribution rule where s_j^l is the attribution assigned to neuron j in layer l:

$$s_j^{output} = y, \qquad s_{k \neq j}^{output} = 0, \qquad s^{l-1,j} = \frac{w \odot (x - x_0)}{w^T x} s_j^l.$$

We evaluate the DTD using a reference point determined by Layer-wise Relevance Propagation (epsilon-LRP) [2] and PatternAttribution (PA) [7]. In Fig. 14.3, DTD satisfies input invariance when using a reference point defined by PA however it is not stable when using a reference point defined by epsilon-LRP.

Epsilon-LRP is sensitive to the input shift because it is a case of DTD where a zero vector is chosen as the root point[1]. The back-propagation rule becomes:

$$s_j^{output} = y, \qquad s_{k \neq j}^{output} = 0, \qquad s^{l-1,j} = \frac{w \odot x}{w^T x} s_j^l.$$

$s^{l-1,j}$ depends only upon the input and so attribution will change between network 1 and 2 because x_1 and x_2 differ by a constant vector.

PatternAttribution (PA) is stable because the reference point x_0 is defined as the natural direction of variation in the data [7]. This natural direction is determined by the covariance of the data and thus compensates explicitly for the constant vector shift of the input. Therefore it is by construction input shift invariant.

To understand this, we start from the PA reference point:

$$x_0 = x - a w^T x \tag{14.1}$$

where $a^T w = 1$.

In a linear model:

$$a = \frac{\text{cov}[x, y]}{w^T \text{cov}[x, y]}. \tag{14.2}$$

For neurons followed by a ReLu non-linearity the vector a accounts for the non-linearity and is computed as:

$$a = \frac{E_+[x, y] - E_+[x]E[y]}{w^T (E_+[x, y] - E_+[x]E[y])}.$$

Here E_+ denotes the expectation taken over values where y is positive.

PA reduces to the following step:

$$s_j^{output} = y, \qquad s_{k \neq i}^{output} = 0, \qquad s^{l-1,j} = w \odot a s_j^l.$$

The vector a depends upon covariance and thus removes the mean shift of the input. Therefore the attribution for both networks is identical.

---

[1] This case of DTD is called the *Z-rule* and can be shown to be equivalent to Layer-wise Relevance Propagation [2,8]. Under specific circumstances, epsilon-LRP is also equivalent to the gradient times input [6,12].

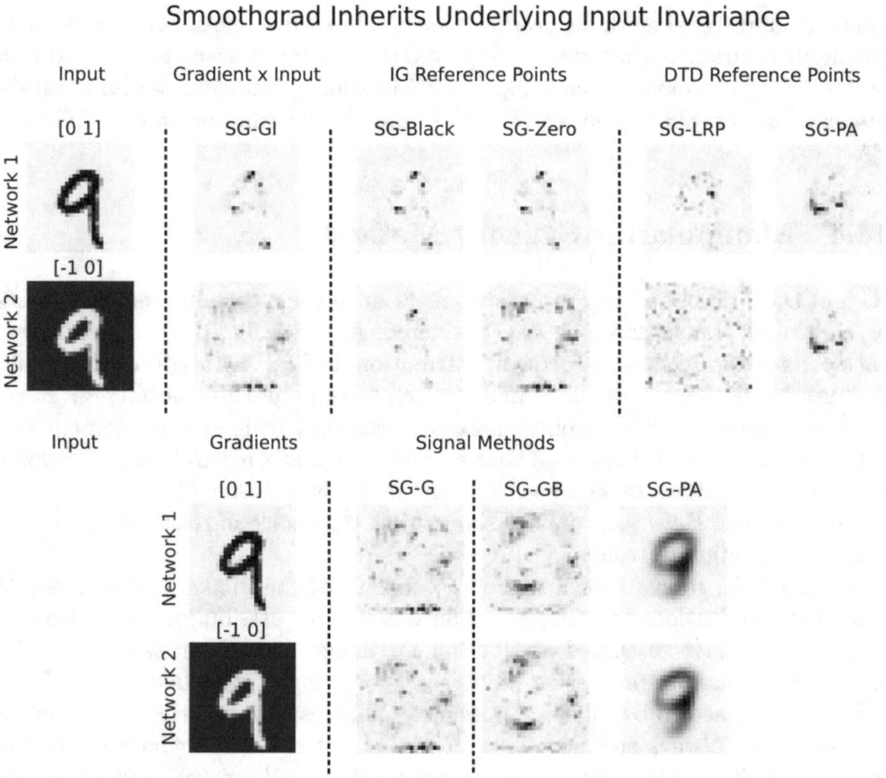

Smoothgrad Inherits Underlying Input Invariance

Fig. 14.5. Smoothgrad (SG) inherits the sensitivity of the underlying attribution method. SG is invariant to the constant input shift when PatternAttribution (SG-PA) or a black image (SG-Black) are used. However, if SG is applied to a method that is not invariant, it will stay as such.

14.3.4   SmoothGrad (SG) [15]

SmoothGrad replaces the input with N identical versions of the input with added random noise. These noisy inputs are injected into the underlying attribution method and final attribution is the average attribution across N. For example, if the underlying methods are gradients w.r.t. the input. $g(\boldsymbol{x})_j = \frac{\partial f(\boldsymbol{x})_j}{\partial \boldsymbol{x}}$ SG becomes:

$$\frac{1}{N}\sum_{i=1}^{N} g(\boldsymbol{x} + \mathcal{N}(0, \sigma^2))_j.$$

SG often results in what is perceived to be aesthetically sharper visualizations when applied to multi-layer neural networks with non-linearities. SG does not alter the attribution method itself so will always inherit the input invariance of the underlying method. Thus, as shown in Fig. 14.5 applying SG on top of gradients and signal methods produces identical saliency maps. SG does not satisfy input invariance when applied to gradient times input, epsilon-LRP and zero vector reference points which compares SG heatmaps generated for all methods discussed so far. SG is insensitive to the input transformation when applied to PA.

14.4   Manipulating Saliency Methods

IG and DTD do not satisfy input shift invariance when certain reference points or/and input transformations are considered. Additionally, the choice of reference point determines all subsequent attribution. In Fig. 14.1 attribution visually diverges for the same method if multiple reference points are considered.

A reasonable reference point choice will naturally depend upon domain and task. For example, [17] suggests that a black image is a natural reference point for image recognition tasks whereas a zero vector is a reasonable choice for text based networks. However, we have shown that the choice of reference point can lead to very different results.

As a result, unintentional misrepresentation of the model is very possible when the implications of using a certain baseline for attribution are unknown. Thus far, we have discussed attribution for image recognition tasks with the assumption that pre-processing steps are known and visual inspection of the points determined to be salient is possible. While visual inspection in the image domain is not always sufficient (e.g. in Fig. 14.1 it is unclear which method is best), for audio and language based models where visual inspection is even more difficult or inappropriate. Therefore identifying failure points or how attribution varies under different baselines poses an additional challenge in other domains.

It is important to realize that if we cannot determine the implications of reference point choice, we are limited in our ability to say anything about the reliability of the method. To demonstrate this point, we construct a constant shift of the input that takes advantage of attribution points of failure discussed thus far. Almost all methods are sensitive to this input shift transformation which results in a misleading explanation of the model prediction. In the following experiment we show using a hand drawn image of cat, how a well chosen vector can be used to purposefully create a misleading explanation of the model prediction.

Network 1 is the same as introduced in Sect. 14.2. We consider a new transformation x_2^i of the input x_1^i where the constant vector m_2 added to x_1^i is a hand drawn image of a cat. The raw image can be seen in Fig. 14.6. Consistent with Sect. 14.2, the relationship between x_1^i and the transformed input x_2^i is the addition of a constant vector m_2.

$$\forall i, x_2^i = x_1^i + m_2.$$

We construct m_2 by choosing a desired attribution $\hat{s}$ that should be assigned to a specific sample $\hat{x}$ when the gradient is multiplied with the input.

By setting m_2 as follows, it will ensure the specific x_2^i receives the desired attribution:

$$m_2 = \frac{\hat{s}}{\frac{\partial f_1(x)}{\partial x}} - x.$$

To make sure that the original image is still recognizable as belonging to its class, we clip the shift to be within $[-.3, .3]$.

In Fig. 14.6 we are able to purposefully misrepresent the explanation of the model prediction for all attribution methods except DTD when using PA as a baseline.

It is important to note that some of these methods would have satisfied *input shift invariance* if the data had normalized prior to attribution. For example, IG with a black baseline will satisfy *input shift invariance* if the data is always normalized to zero mean[2] However, this is far from a systematic treatment of the reference point selection and there are cases outside of our experiment scope where this would not be sufficient.

In many cases, the notion of a black image might not exist (e.g. with audio processing) and the selection of the baseline remains a problem. Since the selection of the baseline for both IG and DTD is crucial, we believe that an open research question is furthering the understanding of reference point choice that guarantee reliability without relying on case-by-case solutions.

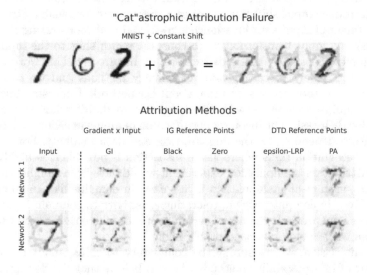

Fig. 14.6. Evaluation of attribution method sensitivity using MNIST. Gradient times input, IG with both a black and zero reference point and DTD with an epsilon-LRP reference point, do not satisfy input invariance and produce different attribution for each network. DTD with a PA reference point are not sensitive to the transformation of the input.

---

[2] A similar reasoning can be applied to the $Z_+ - rule$ for DTD [8].

A first step in this direction is the $Z_{box} - rule$ for DTD [8] and PatternNet/-PatternAttribution [7]. The $Z_{box} - rule$ [8] is designed for analyzing networks where the data is confined to a specific interval. Here, the attribution is done using reference points that are relative to the borders of the interval. Pattern-Net and PatternAttribution explicitly compensate for the mean of the data when learning the reference points.

While existing methods can definitely be applied successfully in specific cases, it is clear from our experiments that they can exhibit undesired behaviour in other settings. Therefore we would encourage the community to adopt the idea of the unit test. By taking part in the iterative process of defining additional tests and developing methods that pass the current set of tests, the community can move towards robust and reliable methods. On top of that, we believe it is crucial to understand the limitations of the current approaches, since this will enable the practitioner to select the best method for this use case.

14.5   Conclusion

Saliency methods are powerful tools to gain intuition about our model. We show that numerous methods fail to attribute correctly when a constant vector shift is applied to the input. More worryingly, we show that we are able to purposefully create a deceptive explanation of the network using a hand drawn cat image.

We introduce input shift invariance as a prerequisite for reliable attribution. Our treatment of input shift invariance is restricted to demonstrating that there is at least one input transformation (a constant vector shift to the input) that causes numerous saliency methods to attribute incorrectly. This work is motivated by the widely perceived value of saliency methods and we belief they remain valuable tools to gain intuition about the network. Understanding where they fail equips researchers with the awareness to decide what is a suitable method for their task. The incorrect classification of inputs as salient will be more of a concern depending on the domain, task and data modality. For example, in image recognition tasks where visual inspection is possible it is highly likely the cat attribution manipulation experiment would have been caught. However, identifying such clear manipulation is less clear in domains like audio or word vectors. Even in computer vision, tolerating sensitivity to common input transformations may preclude the use of certain methods where the cost of a mistake on human welfare may be unacceptably high.

For this reason, we encourage the community to think about the desired behaviour of interpretability methods. We also believe that the development of tests such as the input shift invariance will help the entire community to move towards more robust and reliable methods because we can only build improved methods if we better understand the desired behaviour.

References

1. Adebayo, J., Gilmer, J., Muelly, M., Goodfellow, I.J., Hardt, M., Kim, B.: Sanity checks for saliency maps. In: Neural Information Processing Systems, NeurIPS (2018)
2. Bach, S., Binder, A., Montavon, G., Klauschen, F., Müller, K.R., Samek, W.: On pixel-wise explanations for non-linear classifier decisions by layer-wise relevance propagation. PLoS One **10**(7), e0130140 (2015)
3. Baehrens, D., Schroeter, T., Harmeling, S., Kawanabe, M., Hansen, K., Müller, K.R.: How to explain individual classification decisions. J. Mach. Learn. Res. **11**(Jun), 1803–1831 (2010)
4. Haufe, S., et al.: On the interpretation of weight vectors of linear models in multivariate neuroimaging. Neuroimage **87**, 96–110 (2014)
5. Hooker, S., Erhan, D., Kindermans, P.J., Kim, B.: Evaluating feature importance estimates. arXiv preprint arXiv:1806.10758 (2018)
6. Kindermans, P.J., Schütt, K., Müller, K.R., Dähne, S.: Investigating the influence of noise and distractors on the interpretation of neural networks. arXiv preprint arXiv:1611.07270 (2016)
7. Kindermans, P.J., et al.: Learning how to explain neural networks: PatternNet and PatternAttribution. arXiv preprint arXiv:1705.05598v2 (2017)
8. Montavon, G., Lapuschkin, S., Binder, A., Samek, W., Müller, K.R.: Explaining nonlinear classification decisions with deep Taylor decomposition. Pattern Recogn. **65**, 211–222 (2017)
9. Nguyen, A., Dosovitskiy, A., Yosinski, J., Brox, T., Clune, J.: Synthesizing the preferred inputs for neurons in neural networks via deep generator networks. In: Advances in Neural Information Processing Systems, pp. 3387–3395 (2016)
10. Russakovsky, O., et al.: ImageNet large scale visual recognition challenge. Int. J. Comput. Vis. **115**(3), 211–252 (2015)
11. Samek, W., Binder, A., Montavon, G., Lapuschkin, S., Müller, K.R.: Evaluating the visualization of what a deep neural network has learned. IEEE Trans. Neural Netw. Learn. Syst. **28**(11), 2660–2673 (2017)
12. Shrikumar, A., Greenside, P., Shcherbina, A., Kundaje, A.: Not just a black box: learning important features through propagating activation differences. arXiv preprint arXiv:1605.01713 (2016)
13. Simonyan, K., Vedaldi, A., Zisserman, A.: Deep inside convolutional networks: Visualising image classification models and saliency maps. In: International Conference on Learning Representations, ICLR (2014)
14. Simonyan, K., Zisserman, A.: Very deep convolutional networks for large-scale image recognition. In: International Conference on Learning Representations, ICLR (2015)
15. Smilkov, D., Thorat, N., Kim, B., Viégas, F., Wattenberg, M.: SmoothGrad: removing noise by adding noise. arXiv preprint arXiv:1706.03825 (2017)
16. Springenberg, J.T., Dosovitskiy, A., Brox, T., Riedmiller, M.: Striving for simplicity: the all convolutional net. In: International Conference on Learning Representations, ICLR (2015)
17. Sundararajan, M., Taly, A., Yan, Q.: Axiomatic attribution for deep networks. arXiv preprint arXiv:1703.01365 (2017)
18. Yosinski, J., Clune, J., Fuchs, T., Lipson, H.: Understanding neural networks through deep visualization. In: ICML Workshop on Deep Learning (2015)

19. Zeiler, M.D., Fergus, R.: Visualizing and understanding convolutional networks. In: Fleet, D., Pajdla, T., Schiele, B., Tuytelaars, T. (eds.) ECCV 2014. LNCS, vol. 8689, pp. 818–833. Springer, Cham (2014). https://doi.org/10.1007/978-3-319-10590-1_53

20. Zintgraf, L.M., Cohen, T.S., Adel, T., Welling, M.: Visualizing deep neural network decisions: prediction difference analysis. In: International Conference on Learning Representations, ICLR (2017)

Part V
Applications of Explainable AI

Applications of Explainable AI – Preface

Methods of explainable AI are not only attracting attention in the research community, but are also becoming valuable tools for developers and practitioners. When solving real-world problems, understanding the model and being able to explain its predictions fosters trust in the model and helps to verify its correct functioning (i.e., detect "Clever Hans" predictors [5]). Furthermore, by showing what features the AI system uses for predicting, explanations help to unveil patterns in the data, which may not be obvious to the human expert. This may provide valuable information about the biological, chemical or neural mechanisms involved, and lead to new scientific insights [7, 8, 9].

The following chapters show exemplar applications of explainable AI from three different domains, namely computer vision (Chapters 15 and 16), physical sciences (Chapters 17, 18 and 19), and brain research (Chapters 20 and 21).

In Chapter 15, Hofmacher et al. [4] consider the problem of explainability and inspectability of AI models in autonomous driving. A tiered approach with an inter-mediate, human-interpretable layer is proposed. The main component of the system is a semantic segmentation model, which assigns an object class to every pixel in the input image. These segmentation maps are human-interpretable and can be used as input to the autonomous driving system downstream.

In Chapter 16, Anders et al. [1] take an existing 3D convolutional neural network model that classifies video data, and produce explanations for its predictions. The analysis unveils the model's tendency to focus mainly at the border frames of the video, as if the model wants to look beyond the sequence it receives as input. This insight can be used to adapt the data to the model's needs (e.g., by downsampling) and interest-ingly improve the classification accuracy without retraining the model.

In Chapter 17, Schütt et al. [8] demonstrate the potential of explainable AI when applied to physics. Interpretation techniques are presented for deep neural networks trained to predict chemical properties. By comparing the produced atom-wise or spatial explanations with well-known quantum-chemical models, it becomes possible to assess the level of physical plausibility of the learned model and to produce new insights and hypotheses about the underlying quantum-chemical regularities.

In Chapter 18, Preuer et al. [7] apply methods of explainable AI to the problem of molecular property and bioactivity prediction. The analysis of the learned representa-tion shows that single elements of the neural network model act as detectors for pharmacophore- or toxicophore-like structures in the molecule. It is demonstrated that what the model has learned about the molecules is consistent with the literature.

In Chapter 19, Kratzert et al. [6] look at another application of explainable AI in the physical sciences, here in the field of hydrology. They apply Long Short-Term Memory networks to rainfall-runoff forecasting and show that the learned representations are meaningful, e.g., the LSTM realistically represents short- as well as long-term dynamics in the snow cell storage and their connection to the meteorological inputs. This example shows the power of explainable AI models for understanding complex processes in the field of hydrology.

In Chapter 20, Douglas and Anderson [2] discuss challenges for interpreting AI models in the field of neuroscience. It is shown that even interpreting linear models in functional neuroimaging requires great care, because of the feature redundancy (e.g., hundred thousands of fMRI voxels) and high correlations with noise. The awareness of these potential pitfalls is crucial when applying techniques of explainable AI to brain research.

In Chapter 21, van Gerven et al. [3] investigate the use of interpretable machine learning methods for neural decoding, i.e., the reconstruction of visual experience from neural activity patterns. The results show that deep neural networks trained for this task accurately model hierarchical processing along the visual ventral stream. The improved understanding of how humans process information may help to develop more human-like deep models in the future.

Overall, these seven chapters demonstrate that explanation methods can be applied to very different problems. Understanding the AI model was crucial in all these applications.

July 2019

Wojciech Samek
Grégoire Montavon
Andrea Vedaldi
Lars Kai Hansen
Klaus-Robert Müller

References

1. Anders, C.J., Montavon, G., Samek, W., Müller, K.-R.: Understanding patch-based learning of video data by explaining predictions. In: Samek, W., Montavon, G., Vedaldi, A., Hansen, L.K., Müller, K.-R. (eds.) Explainable AI: Interpreting, Explaining and Visualizing Deep Learning. LNCS, vol. 11700, pp. 297–309. Springer, Cham (2019)
2. Douglas, P.K., Anderson, A.: Feature fallacy: Complications with interpreting linear decoding weights in fMRI. In: Samek, W., Montavon, G., Vedaldi, A., Hansen, L.K., Müller, K.-R. (eds.) Explainable AI: Interpreting, Explaining and Visualizing Deep Learning. LNCS, vol. 11700, pp. 363–378. Springer, Cham (2019)
3. van Gerven, M.A.J., Seeliger, K., Güçlü, U., Güçlütürk, Y.: Current advances in neural decoding. In: Samek, W., Montavon, G., Vedaldi, A., Hansen, L.K., Müller, K.-R. (eds.) Explainable AI: Interpreting, Explaining and Visualizing Deep Learning. LNCS, vol. 11700, pp. 379–394. Springer, Cham (2019)
4. Hofmarcher, M., Unterthiner, T., Arjona-Medina, J., Klambauer, G., Hochreiter, S., Nessler, B.: Visual scene understanding for autonomous driving using semantic segmentation. In: Samek, W., Montavon, G., Vedaldi, A., Hansen, L.K., Müller, K.-R. (eds.) Explainable AI: Interpreting, Explaining and Visualizing Deep Learning. LNCS, vol. 11700, pp. 285–296. Springer, Cham (2019)
5. Lapuschkin, S., Wäldchen, S., Binder, A., Montavon, G., Samek, W., Müller, K.-R.: Unmasking clever hans predictors and assessing what machines really learn. Nat. Commun. **10**, 1096 (2019)

6. Kratzert, F., Herrnegger, M., Klotz, D., Hochreiter, S., Klambauer, G.: NeuralHydrology – Interpreting LSTMs in hydrology. In: Samek, W., Montavon, G., Vedaldi, A., Hansen, L.K., Müller, K.-R. (eds.) Explainable AI: Interpreting, Explaining and Visualizing Deep Learning. LNCS, vol. 11700, pp. 347–362. Springer, Cham (2019)
7. Preuer, K., Klambauer, G., Rippmann, F., Hochreiter, S., Unterthiner, T.: Interpretable deep learning in drug discovery. In: Samek, W., Montavon, G., Vedaldi, A., Hansen, L.K., Müller, K.-R. (eds.) Explainable AI: Interpreting, Explaining and Visualizing Deep Learning. LNCS, vol. 11700, pp. 331–345. Springer, Cham (2019)
8. Schütt, K.T., Gastegger, M., Tkatchenko, A., Müller, K.-R.: Quantum-chemical insights from interpretable atomistic neural networks. In: Samek, W., Montavon, G., Vedaldi, A., Hansen, L.K., Müller, K.-R. (eds.) Explainable AI: Interpreting, Explaining and Visualizing Deep Learning. LNCS, vol. 11700, pp. 311–330. Springer, Cham (2019)
9. Thomas, A.W., Heekeren, H.R., Müller, K.-R., Samek, W.: Analyzing neuroimaging data through recurrent deep learning models (2018). arXiv preprint arXiv:1810.09945

15
Visual Scene Understanding for Autonomous Driving Using Semantic Segmentation

Markus Hofmarcher[✉], Thomas Unterthiner, José Arjona-Medina,
Günter Klambauer, Sepp Hochreiter, and Bernhard Nessler

Johannes Kepler University Linz, 4040 Linz, Austria
{hofmarcher,unterthiner,arjona,klambauer,
hochreit,nessler}@ml.jku.at

Abstract. Deep neural networks are an increasingly important technique for autonomous driving, especially as a visual perception component. Deployment in a real environment necessitates the explainability and inspectability of the algorithms controlling the vehicle. Such insightful explanations are relevant not only for legal issues and insurance matters but also for engineers and developers in order to achieve provable functional quality guarantees. This applies to all scenarios where the results of deep networks control potentially life threatening machines. We suggest the use of a tiered approach, whose main component is a semantic segmentation model, over an end-to-end approach for an autonomous driving system. In order for a system to provide meaningful explanations for its decisions it is necessary to give an explanation about the semantics that it attributes to the complex sensory inputs that it perceives. In the context of high-dimensional visual input this attribution is done as a pixel-wise classification process that assigns an object class to every pixel in the image. This process is called semantic segmentation.

We propose an architecture that delivers real-time viable segmentation performance and which conforms to the limitations in computational power that is available in production vehicles. The output of such a semantic segmentation model can be used as an input for an interpretable autonomous driving system.

Keywords: Deep learning · Convolutional Neural Networks ·
Semantic segmentation · Classification · Visual scene understanding ·
Interpretability

15.1 Introduction

In the context of very complex learning systems there are two main approaches. The traditional approach is based on handcrafted feature functions that pre-

---

M. Hofmarcher, T. Unterthiner and J. Arjona-Medina—Equally contributed to this work.

W. Samek et al. (Eds.): Explainable AI, LNAI 11700, pp. 285–296, 2019.
https://doi.org/10.1007/978-3-030-28954-6_15

process input in a manner deemed useful for humans. A human expert uses his domain knowledge in the design of these features such that the task relevant information is enhanced and irrelevant signals should be suppressed as much as possible. This pre-processing greatly reduced the input dimensionality which was necessary in order to apply traditional machine learning techniques.

The modern principle is the one favored by the nature of deep learning, the so-called end-to-end approach. This approach gives the network the freedom to learn a function that is based on raw inputs and directly produces the final outputs. This end-to-end approach unleashed deep learning to revolutionize AI in the last couple of years [8, 16, 26, 34, 35].

The advantage of the end-to-end principle is clear: the optimization in the learning process has the freedom to access the full input space and build arbitrary functions as needed. However there are a couple of disadvantages. First, a large number of training examples are required to optimize the more complex function. Furthermore, the domain knowledge usually encoded in engineered features is missing. Finally, the resulting function is even more difficult to interpret than in the traditional pipeline.

In the problem setting of autonomous driving the raw inputs are pixel-wise sensor data from RGB cameras, point-wise depth information from LIDAR sensors, proximity measurements from ultrasonic or radar sensors and odometry information from an IMU. The desired output is just the steering angle, torque and brake. In an end-to-end approach the functional model should utilize the input in an optimal fashion to output optimal driving instructions with respect to a given loss function [4, 6, 7].

However, the aforementioned drawbacks of an end-to-end approach quickly turn out to be insurmountable for this application, as the number of training examples required to train such an end-to-end driving model for arbitrary scenarios is huge. Furthermore, it is extremely hard to interpret such a model to answer questions such as why a model decided for a certain action. This is especially problematic in view of legal issues if the decisions of the model lead to erroneous behavior of the vehicle.

Recently, research into the area of attribution methods, in which the goal is to determine, which part of an input was responsible for a model's output, has gained traction [2, 37, 38, 41]. However, in the scenario of autonomous driving with its high-dimensional image inputs such attribution methods would explain to which extent each single pixel has contributed to the driving decision. This will provide some information about the functional correspondence, but this does not suffice to answer the typical human "why"-question, which asks for the inner model of the system and its world understanding.

We propose a tiered approach, whereby the inputs to individual sensory components are directly - without hand-crafted features - fed into a deep neural network whose training target is defined to be a human interpretable abstract representation of the input. In particular, for a video input signal, we want to abstract from the color of the clothing of pedestrians, from the specific texture of a vehicle and from the specific appearances of streets and buildings. We are only interested in their shapes and positions in space. Semantic segmentation achieves this by assigning an object class to every single pixel of the input image. This is similar to interpreting machine learning models by translating from one modality to another [11,32]. Due to the geometry of our real world this leads to smaller or larger continuous patches of single class identities representing the shape of individual objects, like pedestrians, cars, buildings, lanes and pavement (see Fig. 15.1).

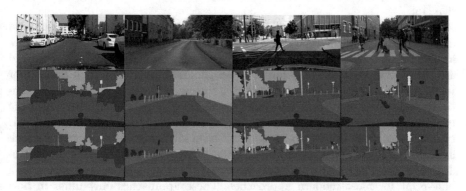

Fig. 15.1. Example output (bottom) of the network with ground truth (center) on images from the Cityscapes validation set.

It is obvious that the output of a semantic segmentation network is of much lower dimensionality when compared to the raw input image. Moreover, it already represents important first decisions of the overall system. Decisions about the presence or absence of humans or vehicles are made at this stage. E.g., whether a human is recognized or not, is fully determined by this intermediate processing of the input, whether other vehicles are recognized as such is decided already at this stage and also the course of the road is already reflected in the output as one of the segments. To a certain extent we are back to a traditional pipeline of engineered features, but this tiered processing is substantially different. We do not hand-craft features, instead we employ human expert knowledge in order to define an internal abstraction layer known that it is suitable for the overall problem. Thus, the raw feature analysis is fully trained and optimized like in end-to-end approaches. The crucial advantage lies in the explanatory power of this layered processing.

In this article, parts of which were published already in [39], we propose novel architectures that are able to infer the semantic segmentation in real-time on embedded hardware, while achieving better accuracy than comparable competitors. In Sect. 15.2 we shortly review the current state-of-the-art and the techniques employed in semantic segmentation with a focus on autonomous driving applications. In Sect. 15.3 we present our proposed architecture for efficient semantic segmentation in autonomous vehicles and show its experimental settings and their evaluation results in Sects. 15.4 and 15.5.

15.2   Semantic Segmentation

Convolutional Neural Networks (CNNs) have emerged as the best performing method for image related tasks [26,35] such as image classification [16,34] or traffic sign recognition [8] and also semantic segmentation [5,28,40,43]. However, performing semantic segmentation might incur a significant computational overhead as compared to end-to-end models. This is especially the case when improved segmentation performance is accomplished by increasing the network size [15].

When employing deep learning for semantic segmentation, the recognition of major objects in the image, such as persons or vehicles is realized at higher levels of a neural network. By design, these layers work on a coarser scale and are translation invariant (e.g. imposed via pooling operations), such that minor variations on a pixel level do not influence the recognition. Furthermore, semantic segmentation requires pixel-exact classification of small features, which are typically only found in lower layers of a network. This trade-off in resolution is typically solved by using skip-connections from lower layers to the output which increase the resolution at layers close to the output. Skip-connections were introduced by the Fully Convolutional Network (FCN) [28], which still serves as a blue-print for most modern approaches. These approaches only differ in how they encode the object level information and how they decode these classifications to pixel-exact labels. The original FCN employed the VGG network [36] that was pre-trained on the LSVRC image classification task. Then FCN added information to higher layers coming from lower layers which is upscaled through a transposed convolution. The FCN architecture was improved by alternative ways to connect to the lower layers, e.g. by accessing the lower-level pooling layers [3], by using enhanced methods to integrate lower level information [31] or forgoing pooling operations for dilated convolutions [27,40]. As a post-processing step, many recent systems apply CRF-based refinement on the output produced by the neural network [27,44]. CRF increases the accuracy of the segmentation at the cost of additional computation.

Reducing the computational burden of semantic segmentation is essential to make it feasible for embedded systems and autonomous driving. Neural networks are trained on servers or workstations with powerful GPUs, and these GPU systems are subsequently used for inference on new data. However, these commodities do not exist in self-driving cars. A self-driving car needs to react to new events instantly to guarantee the safety of passengers and other traffic participants, while it is often acceptable if the borders of objects are not recognized perfectly down to a pixel resolution. To segment an image in real-time is a strong requirement in self-driving applications. Thus, it is critical that any convolutional neural network deployed in these systems fulfills strict requirements in execution speed.

There has been a vast amount of research in reducing the computation required for deep learning. SqueezeNet [21] showed that it was possible to reproduce the image classification accuracy of powerful CNNs, such as AlexNet [24], using 50x less parameters by employing a more efficient architecture. ENet [30] followed the same path and showed that semantic segmentation is feasible on embedded devices in real-time. Another line of research increases the efficiency of existing networks by deriving smaller networks from larger counterparts [1,17], by pruning or quantizing weights [13,14] or tweaking the network for execution on specific hardware designs [12]. These methods can be applied on top of new architectures to speed up execution.

15.3 Methods

15.3.1 Overview

In order to achieve semantic segmentation in real time, we have to trade execution speed against achievable segmentation accuracy. Like most successful segmentation networks, our network is structured as an encoder-decoder pair. An encoder CNN detects higher-level objects such as cars or pedestrians in the input image. A decoder takes this information and enriches it with information from the lower layers of the encoder, supplying a prediction for each pixel in the original input. Figure 15.2 depicts the architecture.

15.3.2 Encoder

The encoder is a modified SqueezeNet 1.1 architecture [21], which was designed as a low-latency network for image recognition while retaining AlexNet [24] like accuracy. The main computational modules of SqueezeNet are the so-called "fire" modules consisting of three convolutional operations, depicted in Fig. 15.3a. The encoder consists of eight "fire" modules, interspersed with a total of three max-pooling layers for downsampling. All rectified linear units (ReLUs) of the original architecture are substituted with exponential linear units (ELUs) [9], which make more efficient use of parameters by also conveying information in the negative part of the activation.

15.3.3 Parallel Dilated Convolutions

The decoder is based on a parallel dilated convolution layer [27] as depicted in Fig. 15.3b. This dilated layer combines the feature maps at the encoder output at different receptive field sizes by using four dilated convolutions of kernel size 3 with different dilation factors. This is equivalent to sampling the layer input with different rates. The contributions from the four dilated convolutions are then fused by an element-wise sum. As a result, the receptive field size is increased and multiscale spatial dependencies are taken into account without having to resort to stacking multiple layers which would be computationally expensive.

15.3.4 Decoder and Bypasses

Pooling layers in the encoder are used to ensure a degree of translational invariance when detecting the parts of an object. However, they in turn reduce the spatial resolution of the output. Transposed convolutions in the decoder are used to upsample the information back to its original size. To improve the upsampling, we do not just use the data that comes directly from the layer immediately before the transposed convolution layer, but combine it with low-level knowledge from lower layers of the encoder. These layers are responsible for detecting finer structures at a higher resolution, which helps with classifying the contours of objects more exactly. Each refinement module combines two streams of information, one coming from the previous upsampling layer, the other one from the encoder. The two convolutional layers in the refinement module learn how to weigh these two streams before passing the information on to the next upsampling layer. We use refinement modules similar to the ones used in the SharpMask approach [31]. We again use ELUs instead of ReLU units (Fig. 15.3c shows the implementation of the module).

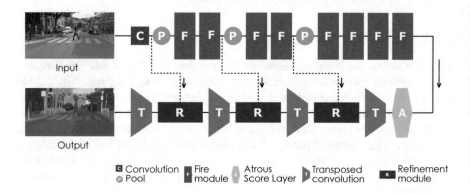

Fig. 15.2. Architecture of the proposed network for semantic segmentation.

Right before every pooling layer in the encoder, a bypass branches off to the refinement module. Once there, a convolution layer weights knowledge from lower layers. Then, it is concatenated with semantic object information from the previous upsampling layer. A second convolutional layer combines the concatenated feature maps from both branches into the class map.

15.3.5 Exponential Linear Units (ELU)

Our network makes extensive use of the exponential linear unit [9] because we empirically found it to work better than ReLU units for our purpose. ELUs were designed to avoid the bias shift in neural network training. The ELU activation function is defined as

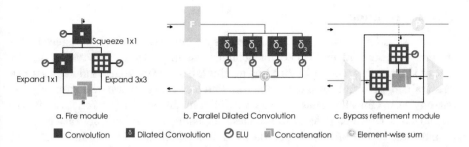

a. Fire module   b. Parallel Dilated Convolution   c. Bypass refinement module

■ Convolution   δ Dilated Convolution   Ⓔ ELU   ▨ Concatenation   ◎ Element-wise sum

Fig. 15.3. (a) SqueezeNet Fire module; (b) Parallel dilated convolution layer; (c) Refinement module

$$f(x) = \begin{cases} x & \text{if } x > 0 \\ \alpha \left(\exp(x) - 1 \right) & \text{if } x \leq 0 \end{cases} , \quad f'(x) = \begin{cases} 1 & \text{if } x > 0 \\ f(x) + \alpha & \text{if } x \leq 0 \end{cases} . \quad (15.1)$$

The parameter α was set to its default value of 1 for all of our experiments. Similar to the often-used ReLU activation, ELUs have a linear positive part which helps to avoid the vanishing gradient [18–20], thus it allows training very deep networks. However, in contrast to the ReLU, the saturating negative part converges to $-\alpha$. This allows the ELU to have a mean activation of 0, thereby avoiding any bias shift effect: In ReLU networks, units will typically have a non-zero mean activation, thus they will act as additional bias unit for units in the next layer. By enabling units to have zero mean, this bias shift effect is reduced, which makes it easier for units to focus solely on actual information processing. This could otherwise only be achieved by using batch normalization [22] or the SELU activation function [23].

15.4 Experiments

15.4.1 Cityscapes Dataset

We trained and evaluated the network on the Cityscapes dataset [10]. Cityscapes is a high quality dataset for semantic street scene understanding. The dataset is split in 2975, 500, and 1525 images of resolution 2048 × 1024 pixels for training, validation, and testing, respectively. It contains 35 annotated classes on pixel-level of which 19 are selected for evaluation in the challenge. Each class belongs to one category: flat, nature, object, sky, construction, human, vehicle. As performance measure the commonly used intersection over union metric is used, which is evaluated for individual classes and categories. Notice that our results were achieved without CRFs as post-processing because that would increase inference time dramatically.

15.4.2 Training

The SqueezeNet encoder was initialized using publicly available ImageNet pre-trained weights and fine-tuned for semantic segmentation on Cityscapes. The rest of the weights were initialized using the MSRA scheme [16] and the network was trained with full resolution images. The loss function was the sum of cross entropy terms for all classes, equally weighted in the overall loss function. It was optimized with Stochastic Gradient Descent, using a fixed learning rate of 10^{-8}, momentum of 0.9 and a weight decay factor of 0.0002. The architecture was implemented using the Caffe framework. Total training time was around 22 h using 2 Titan X Maxwell GPUs with batch size 3 each at full resolution images. In our experiments we trained for the pixel-wise segmentation task using only the fine annotations without any additional training data. Augmentations were not applied in order to establish a baseline for performance.

15.5 Results

Our network compares favourably against the ENet segmentation network [30], a widely-used network architecture for efficient semantic segmentation on embedded devices. Comparable, newer architectures exist [29, 33, 42], but were not compared against.

15.5.1 Segmentation Performance

We evaluated the network on the test set using the official Cityscapes evaluation server. We achieve 59.8 per-class mean IoU and 84.3 per-category mean IoU. Hence the network architecture is able to outperform both ENet as well as SegNet [3] as it can be seen in Table 15.1. We improved on per-class IoU for all but 5 classes (wall, truck, bus, train, motorcycle) compared to ENet. Detailed per-class classification results are presented in Table 15.2. Visual inspection of the predictions of the network show satisfying results on typical urban street scene images (Fig. 15.1). Object contours are segmented very sharply. We believe that this is due to the enhanced ability to integrate pixel-level information from early layers in the encoder into upsampling layers in the decoder by using refinement modules in the bypasses.

Table 15.1. Mean IoU over the 19 individual classes and the 7 categories on the Cityscapes testset. ENet and SegNet results are taken from [30].

	Class IoU	Category IoU
Ours	**59.8**	**84.3**
ENet	58.3	80.4
SegNet	56.1	79.8

15.5.2   Inference Run-Time Performance

Similar to ENet, we are able to surpass the 10 fps design goal on the Nvidia TX1 board on a resolution of 640 × 360, which is a sensible lower limit for enabling self-driving car applications. See Table 15.3 for a comparison of run-times between the different architectures. The run-times were achieved using CUDA 7.5 and cuDNN 4.0, however we expect that timings will improve significantly by switching to newer software versions that support Winograd convolutions [25].

Table 15.2. Per-class IoU on the Cityscapes testset. We improved the ENet results on all but 5 classes (wall, truck, bus, train, motorcycle). ENet results are taken from [30].

	Road	Sidewalk	Building	Wall	Fence	Pole	Trafficlight	Trafficsign	Vegetation	Terrain
Ours	96.9	75.4	87.9	31.6	35.7	50.9	52.0	61.7	90.9	65.8
ENet	96.3	74.2	85.0	32.2	33.2	43.5	34.1	44.0	88.6	61.4

	Sky	Person	Rider	Car	Truck	Bus	Train	Motorcycle	Bicycle	
Ours	93.0	73.8	42.6	91.5	18.8	41.2	33.3	34.0	59.9	
ENet	90.6	65.5	38.4	90.6	36.9	50.5	48.1	38.8	55.4	

Table 15.3. Comparison of inference times on Nvidia Tegra X1. Timings for ENet were taken from the original publication [30].

	480 × 320		640 × 360		1280 × 720	
	ms	fps	ms	fps	ms	fps
Ours	60	16.7	86	11.6	389	2.6
ENet	47	21.1	69	14.6	262	3.8

15.6   Discussion

As a complementary approach to end-to-end deep learning with its lack of explainability we have proposed a tiered approach, whereby only individual components are trained in an end-to-end-like fashion. The intermediate nodes, which are outputs from one tier and inputs to the next, are defined in such a way that their meaning is interpretable by a human expert with knowledge in the domain of the overall system. Semantic segmentation is a powerful instrument that provides a lower-dimensional abstraction of video input signals.

Currently Deep Neural Networks are state-of-the-art systems in semantic image segmentation. However, these deep networks incur high computational cost, which makes them unsuitable for deployment in self-driving cars. In this work we have shown how neural networks can be made small enough to run on embedded devices used in autonomous vehicles while still retaining a level of segmentation performance sufficient for this application. We believe this to be a promising approach towards a modular and interpretable system for autonomous driving.

Subsequent components of the overall system can then take these semantic features as input for their decisions. One such component could be a model for situational awareness, classifying the kind of situation the vehicle is currently in. Another component could be trained to determine an optimal driving path in view of the semantically segmented surroundings and the situation classification. Finally, based on these intermediate human understandable classifications and regressions a controller can be trained on a last tier in order to translate the now interpretable inner model of the system about the real world into specific commands for steering, throttle response or braking. In case of erroneous behavior of the vehicle an expert can investigate such a tiered system by looking at the intermediate nodes of each tier and obtain answers to the "why"-question.

This gain in interpretability comes at a price: a tiered approach allows more fine-grained control and human-interpretable checks of the intermediate steps of driving decisions. However, current research has often showed that end-to-end approaches, while harder to interpret, often allow deep learning systems to achieve higher performance, often even outperforming humans. This is likely because the system is able to process information in a way that is not compatible with typical human perception. For example, while reducing the lower-level camera signals to semantic segmentation maps and discarding more fine-grained information might make sense for humans, it is possible that machine learning approaches can still make use of such information at higher-level decision making processes. Despite these drawbacks, we would argue that, given the accuracy achieved with modern systems, the gain in interpretability is worth the potential loss in overall performance.

Acknowledgements. This work was supported by Audi.JKU Deep Learning Center, Audi Electronics Venture GmbH, Zalando SE with Research Agreement 01/2016, the Austrian Science Fund with Project P28660-N31 and NVIDIA Corporation.

References

1. Ba, J., Caruana, R.: Do deep nets really need to be deep? In: Advances in Neural Information Processing Systems, NIPS (2014)
2. Bach, S., Binder, A., Montavon, G., Klauschen, F., Müller, K.R., Samek, W.: On pixel-wise explanations for non-linear classifier decisions by layer-wise relevance propagation. PLoS ONE **10**(7), 1–46 (2015)
3. Badrinarayanan, V., Kendall, A., Cipolla, R.: Segnet: a deep convolutional encoder-decoder architecture for image segmentation. IEEE Trans. Pattern Anal. Mach. Intell. **39**(12), 2481–2495 (2017)
4. Bojarski, M., et al.: End to end learning for self-driving cars. CoRR abs/1604.07316 (2016)
5. Chen, L., Papandreou, G., Schroff, F., Adam, H.: Rethinking atrous convolution for semantic image segmentation. CoRR abs/1706.05587 (2017)
6. Chen, Z., Huang, X.: End-to-end learning for lane keeping of self-driving cars. In: IEEE Intelligent Vehicles Symposium, pp. 1856–1860. IEEE (2017)
7. Chi, L., Mu, Y.: Deep steering: learning end-to-end driving model from spatial and temporal visual cues. CoRR abs/1708.03798 (2017)

8. Ciresan, D., Meier, U., Masci, J., Schmidhuber, J.: Multi-column deep neural network for traffic sign classification. Neural Netw. **32**, 333–338 (2012)
9. Clevert, D.A., Unterthiner, T., Hochreiter, S.: Fast and accurate deep network learning by exponential linear units (ELUs). In: International Conference on Learning Representations, ICLR (2016)
10. Cordts, M., et al.: The Cityscapes dataset for semantic urban scene understanding. In: IEEE Conference on Computer Vision and Pattern Recognition, CVPR (2016)
11. Donahue, J., et al.: Long-term recurrent convolutional networks for visual recognition and description. IEEE Trans. Pattern Anal. Mach. Intell. **39**(4), 677–691 (2017)
12. Han, S., et al.: Eie: efficient inference engine on compressed deep neural network. In: International Conference on Computer Architecture (2016)
13. Han, S., Mao, H., Dally, W.J.: Deep compression: compressing deep neural networks with pruning, trained quantization and Huffman coding. In: International Conference on Learning Representations, ICLR (2016)
14. Han, S., Pool, J., Tran, J., Dally, W.: Learning both weights and connections for efficient neural network. In: Advances in Neural Information Processing Systems, NIPS (2015)
15. He, K., Zhang, X., Ren, S., Sun, J.: Deep residual learning for image recognition. In: IEEE Conference on Computer Vision and Pattern Recognition, CVPR (2015)
16. He, K., Zhang, X., Ren, S., Sun, J.: Delving deep into rectifiers: surpassing human-level performance on imagenet classification. In: IEEE International Conference on Computer Vision, ICCV (2015)
17. Hinton, G.E., Vinyals, O., Dean, J.: Distilling the knowledge in a neural network. CoRR abs/1503.02531 (2015)
18. Hochreiter, S.: Untersuchungen zu dynamischen neuronalen Netzen. Master's thesis, Technische Universität München, Institut für Informatik (1991)
19. Hochreiter, S.: The vanishing gradient problem during learning recurrent neural nets and problem solutions. Int. J. Uncertain. Fuzziness Knowl. Based Syst. **6**(2), 107–116 (1998)
20. Hochreiter, S., Bengio, Y., Frasconi, P., Schmidhuber, J.: Gradient flow in recurrent nets: the difficulty of learning long-term dependencies. In: Kremer, K. (eds.) A Field Guide to Dynamical Recurrent Neural Networks. IEEE Press (2001)
21. Iandola, F.N., Moskewicz, M.W., Ashraf, K., Han, S., Dally, W.J., Keutzer, K.: Squeezenet: Alexnet-level accuracy with 50x fewer parameters and <1mb model size. CoRR abs/1602.07360 (2016)
22. Ioffe, S., Szegedy, C.: Batch normalization: accelerating deep network training by reducing internal covariate shift. In: Proceedings of the 32nd International Conference on Machine Learning, ICML (2015)
23. Klambauer, G., Unterthiner, T., Mayr, A., Hochreiter, S.: Self-normalizing neural networks. In: Advances in Neural Information Processing Systems, NIPS, Curran Associates, Inc. (2017)
24. Krizhevsky, A., Sutskever, I., Hinton, G.E.: ImageNet classification with deep convolutional neural networks. In: Advances in Neural Information Processing Systems, NIPS (2012)
25. Lavin, A., Gray, S.: Fast algorithms for convolutional neural networks. In: IEEE Conference on Computer Vision and Pattern Recognition, CVPR (2016)
26. LeCun, Y., Bengio, Y., Hinton, G.: Deep learning. Nature **521**(7553), 436–444 (2015)

27. Liang-Chieh, C., Papandreou, G., Kokkinos, I., Murphy, K., Yuille, A.: Semantic image segmentation with deep convolutional nets and fully connected CRFs. In: International Conference on Learning Representations, ICLR (2015)
28. Long, J., Shelhamer, E., Darrell, T.: Fully convolutional networks for semantic segmentation. In: IEEE Conference on Computer Vision and Pattern Recognition, CVPR (2015)
29. Mehta, S., Rastegari, M., Caspi, A., Shapiro, L., Hajishirzi, H.: ESPNet: efficient spatial pyramid of dilated convolutions for semantic segmentation. In: Proceedings of the European Conference on Computer Vision, ECCV (2018)
30. Paszke, A., Chaurasia, A., Kim, S., Culurciello, E.: ENet: a deep neural network architecture for real-time semantic segmentation. CoRR abs/1606.02147 (2016)
31. Pinheiro, P.O., Lin, T.Y., Collobert, R., Dollár, P.: Learning to refine object segments. In: Proceedings of the European Conference on Computer Vision, ECCV (2016)
32. Reed, S., Akata, Z., Yan, X., Logeswaran, L., Schiele, B., Lee, H.: Generative adversarial text-to-image synthesis. In: Proceedings of the 33rd International Conference on Machine Learning, ICML (2016)
33. Romera, E., Álvarez, J.M., Bergasa, L.M., Arroyo, R.: ERFNet: efficient residual factorized convnet for real-time semantic segmentation. IEEE Trans. Intell. Transp. Syst. **19**, 263–272 (2018)
34. Russakovsky, O., et al.: ImageNet large scale visual recognition challenge. Int. J. Comput. Vision (IJCV) **115**(3), 211–252 (2015)
35. Schmidhuber, J.: Deep learning in neural networks: an overview. Neural Networks **61**, 85–117 (2015)
36. Simonyan, K., Zisserman, A.: Very deep convolutional networks for large-scale image recognition. In: International Conference of Learning Representations, ICLR (2015)
37. Simonyan, K., Vedaldi, A., Zisserman, A.: Deep inside convolutional networks: visualising image classification models and saliency maps. CoRR abs/1312.6034 (2013)
38. Sundararajan, M., Taly, A., Yan, Q.: Axiomatic attribution for deep networks. In: Proceedings of the 34th International Conference on Machine Learning, ICML (2017)
39. Treml, M., et al.: Speeding up semantic segmentation for autonomous driving. In: Workshop on Machine Learning for Intelligent Transport Systems, Neural Information Processing Systems (NIPS) (2016)
40. Yu, F., Koltun, V.: Multi-scale context aggregation by dilated convolutions. In: International Conference on Learning Representations, ICLR (2016)
41. Zeiler, M.D., Fergus, R.: Visualizing and understanding convolutional networks. In: Proceedings of the European Conference on Computer Vision, ECCV (2014)
42. Zhao, H., Qi, X., Shen, X., Shi, J., Jia, J.: ICNet for real-time semantic segmentation on high-resolution images. In: Proceedings of the European Conference on Computer Vision, ECCV (2018)
43. Zhao, H., Shi, J., Qi, X., Wang, X., Jia, J.: Pyramid scene parsing network. In: IEEE Conference on Computer Vision and Pattern Recognition, CVPR (2017)
44. Zheng, S., et al.: Conditional random fields as recurrent neural networks. In: IEEE International Conference on Computer Vision, ICCV (2015)

16
Understanding Patch-Based Learning of Video Data by Explaining Predictions

Christopher J. Anders[1], Grégoire Montavon[1(✉)], Wojciech Samek[2], and Klaus-Robert Müller[1,3,4]

[1] Technische Universität Berlin, 10587 Berlin, Germany
{anders,gregoire.montavon,klaus-robert.mueller}@tu-berlin.de
[2] Fraunhofer Heinrich Hertz Institute, 10587 Berlin, Germany
wojciech.samek@hhi.fraunhofer.de
[3] Korea University, Anam-dong, Seongbuk-gu, Seoul 02841, Korea
[4] Max Planck Institute for Informatics, 66123 Saarbrücken, Germany

Abstract. Deep neural networks have shown to learn highly predictive models of video data. Due to the large number of images in individual videos, a common strategy for training is to repeatedly extract short clips with random offsets from the video. We apply the deep Taylor/Layer-wise Relevance Propagation (LRP) technique to understand classification decisions of a deep network trained with this strategy, and identify a tendency of the classifier to look mainly at the frames close to the temporal boundaries of its input clip. This "border effect" reveals the model's relation to the step size used to extract consecutive video frames for its input, which we can then tune in order to improve the classifier's accuracy without retraining the model. To our knowledge, this is the first work to apply the deep Taylor/LRP technique on any neural network operating on video data.

Keywords: Deep neural networks · Video classification · Human action recognition · Explaining predictions

16.1 Introduction

Deep neural networks have set new standards of performance in many machine learning areas such as image classification [12,32], speech recognition [6,19], video analysis [9,10], or in the sciences [2,25,31]. For applications where the input signal is very large in time or space, it has been a common practice to train the model on small patches or clips of that signal [3,7,9]. This strategy reduces the number of input variables to be processed by the network and thus, allows to extract the problem's nonlinearities more quickly by performing more training iterations.

An underlying assumption of patch- or clip-based training is the locality of the label information. This assumption is often violated in practice: For example, discriminative information may only be contained in long-term interactions

© Springer Nature Switzerland AG 2019
W. Samek et al. (Eds.): Explainable AI, LNAI 11700, pp. 297–309, 2019.
https://doi.org/10.1007/978-3-030-28954-6_16

[6, 19, 36] or only reside at specific time steps (e.g. when a particular action occurs). Since such label noise makes the training more difficult [22], recent work investigated ways to cope with this problem, e.g., attention mechanisms [27] or weighted patch aggregation [3].

This paper aims to investigate patch- or clip-based learning from another perspective, namely by analyzing the properties of a model trained with this specific learning procedure. One way to study the properties of a model is to perform introspection into how the model predicts, for example, by explaining its predictions in terms of input variables [21]. Such explanations can now be robustly obtained for a wide range of convolution-type or general deep neural networks [1, 14, 17, 23, 29, 35, 37], and other machine learning models (e.g., [11]).

In this work we analyzed a convolutional neural network [33] trained for human action recognition on the Sports1M dataset [10] using the deep Taylor/Layer-wise Relevance Propagation (LRP) decomposition technique [15, 17]. We first show that this explanation technique reliably captures class-relevant information from videos. We then test how clip-based training affects the prediction strategy of the network and identify two effects induced by this training procedure. The "border effect" describes the observation that the prediction is predominantly focused at the frames close to the temporal boundaries of its given input to compensate for a small amount of frames per input video clip, whereas the "lookahead effect" describes the observation that the model learns to ignore the first few frames of the input video clip and assign more relevance to the later ones. Finally we demonstrate that the insights obtained by explaining predictions can be directly (i.e. without retraining) used to increase the prediction accuracy of the classifier.

While a different approach for human action recognition has been analyzed before [30] using the LRP framework [1], to our knowledge this work is the first to analyze any neural network for video classification using the deep Taylor/LRP decomposition technique [17]. In a recent work, voxel explanations of 3D-CNNs [34] have been produced using different explanation frameworks [26, 39]. Further research has been done on the interpretation [4], description [38] and segmentation of videos [20]. Outside the field of machine learning, some work has been done on saliency detection in videos [8, 16].

16.2   Explaining the Classifier's Predictions

In this paper, we use the deep Taylor/LRP decomposition technique [17] to produce explanations. We give a brief textual description of the method, along with connections to previous work. The method performs a sum-decomposition of the function value $f(x)$ in terms of input variables [21]

$$f(x) = \sum_{p,t} R_{p,t} \tag{16.1}$$

where $R_{p,t}$ is the relevance of pixel p in frame t. These scores are obtained by progressively redistributing the output $f(x)$ backwards in the network, differently

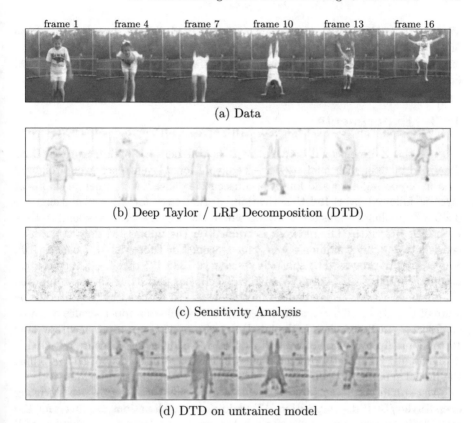

frame 1   frame 4   frame 7   frame 10   frame 13   frame 16

(a) Data

(b) Deep Taylor / LRP Decomposition (DTD)

(c) Sensitivity Analysis

(d) DTD on untrained model

Fig. 16.1. Example of a video along with the DTD explanation of this video belonging to the class 'Tumbling'. High relevance scores are shown in red.

from back-propagation, until the input variables are reached. This redistribution procedure satisfies a conservation principle [1,13], where each neuron passes to the lower-layer as much as it has received from the higher layer. Let i, j be neurons of adjacent layers. Let a_i be the activation of neuron i and w_{ij} be the weight that connects it to neuron j. In linear layers, the redistribution is in proportion to the positive contribution of the input activations $R_{i \leftarrow j} \propto a_i w_{ij}^+$ of each neuron [1,17]. In pooling layers, the redistribution is in proportion to the activations a_i inside the pool [17]. For the first convolutional layer we redistribute in proportion to the signed contributions plus some additive term $R_{i \leftarrow j} \propto a_i w_{ij} - l_i w_{ij}^+ - h_i w_{ij}^-$ where l_i and h_i are the minimal and maximal pixel values respectively [17].

Another popular explanation technique is sensitivity analysis [5,28], which computes importance scores as e.g.

$$S_{p,t} = \left(\frac{df}{dx_{p,t}} \right)^2. \tag{16.2}$$

We note that this analysis can be interpreted as performing a sum-decomposition of the squared gradient norm ($\|\nabla f\|^2 = \sum_{p,t} S_{p,t}$), and is thus closer to an explanation of the function's variation. We refer the reader for a comparison of different explanation methods to [18, 24].

16.3   Experiments

We use the 3-dimensional convolutional neural network architecture C3D as described by [33], with $1+1+2+2+2$ convolutional layers, each group followed by a max-pooling layer and finally 2 consecutive dense layers, where each linear layer is followed by a ReLU activation. Kernel sizes for all convolutions are $3 \times 3 \times 3$, pooling kernels are $1 \times 3 \times 3$ where the dimensions correspond to time by height by width. The network is trained on the Sports-1M data set, which consists of roughly 1 million sports videos from YouTube with 487 classes [10]. Videos are pre-processed by spatially resizing to 128×171 pixels and then center-cropping to 121×121 pixels. We take video clips at particular offsets, composed of 16 frames each. The pre-trained model we use, as supplied by [33], used to be state-of-the-art in human action recognition. It achieves a top-1 accuracy (most confidently predicted class is the label) per clip of 46.1%, a top-1 accuracy over 10 random clips of a single video of 61.1%, as well as a top-5 accuracy (label is in the 5 most confidently predicted classes) for the same setting of 85.2%. Thus, the model successfully performs the classification task and can be analyzed.

We explain predictions for 1000 videos from the test set of Sports-1M using deep Taylor/LRP decomposition [17]. Additional explanations are given for the same 3-dimensional convolutional neural network architecture untrained as well as using gradient-based sensitivity analysis [5, 28] for comparison.

16.3.1   Heatmap Analysis

To get a first impression of the prediction, we take a look at the individual explanation of one specific video clip. In Fig. 16.1, we show an exemplary video and the deep Taylor/LRP decomposition (DTD) for the predicted class label "Tumbling". The hands are identified as relevant, especially when the latter are touching the trampoline, which is characteristic of that class. Other parts of the image such as the trees in the background are not highlighted and therefore found to be non-relevant. The DTD analysis is also less noisy and more focused on the class-relevant features than sensitivity analysis (Fig. 16.1c).

An interesting observation that can be made is that the training procedure tends to make the relevance converge from the center frames of the video clip to its frames closest to the beginning and end respectively as evidenced by the difference between DTD and the same analysis performed on an untrained network (Fig. 16.1d). This so-called border effect will be studied quantitatively in Sect. 16.3.2. The initial focus on the center of the sequence is due to these frames being more densely connected to the output.

Additional examples of different videos are shown in Figs. 16.6 and 16.7. In particular, the aforementioned observation of higher relevance towards the videos' borders is more clearly visible in Figs. 16.6a and b. Furthermore, we can also observe that the final frames receive more relevance than any other ones in Figs. 16.6a, 16.7a and b. This lookahead effect will also be studied quantitatively in Sect. 16.3.2.

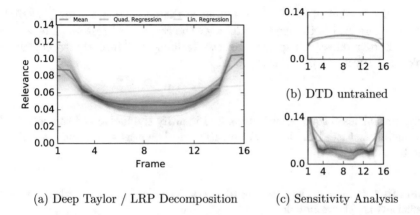

(a) Deep Taylor / LRP Decomposition   (b) DTD untrained

(c) Sensitivity Analysis

Fig. 16.2. Relevance share $(P_t)_t$. Red color shows these vectors for a large number of videos. Lines show the mean relevance share and polynomial fits.

16.3.2   Quantifying Border and Lookahead Effects

To refine the intuition developed in Sect. 16.3.1 about the presence of a border and lookahead effect, we produce DTD explanations for a large number of videos and analyze their average properties. Because the border effect occurs in the temporal domain, we only focus on the temporal axis of explanations $R_{p,t}$ by defining a frame-wise explanation $R_t = \sum_p R_{p,t}$. From these relevance scores, we can define a vector $(P_t)_t$ where $P_t = R_t / \sum_t R_t$ is the share of relevance at time t. Since our input video clips each contain 16 frames, this vector has size 16, which we can visualize in a plot. Results are shown in Fig. 16.2. The red pattern represents the distribution of these 16-dimensional vectors, for which we can compute an average over the dataset (blue line). Results are also compared to sensitivity analysis, as well as DTD on the untrained model.

Results confirm our previous observations of higher relevance in the bordering frames. Note that DTD and sensitivity analysis (Fig. 16.2c) produce consistent results with respect to the border effect. We can further verify that this effect is not due to an architecture-related artifact, by performing the same DTD analysis on the untrained model (Fig. 16.2b): The border effect is present only for the trained model. For the untrained model, relevance at the border is instead lower compared to other frames. The additional lookahead effect can be observed from this analysis where the relevance is slightly higher for the last frame as opposed to the first frame.

In order to determine the strength of the border and lookahead effects, we need a quantitative measure for them. We propose to capture these effects by fitting vectors $(P_t)_t$ using simple quadratic regression. More specifically, we consider the quadratic model

$$q(t) = B \cdot t^2 + C \cdot t + D \tag{16.3}$$

and fit the coefficients B, C, D to minimize the least square error $\sum_t \|E[P_t] - q(t)\|^2$, where $E[\cdot]$ is the expectation over the Sports-1M test set. The strength of the border effect is captured by the variable B. Similarly, to capture the lookahead effect, we fit a linear model

$$l(t) = L \cdot t + A \tag{16.4}$$

using similar least squares objective, and identify the lookahead strength by the parameter L. Fitted models $q(t)$ and $l(t)$ are shown as green and cyan lines in Fig. 16.2.

Table 16.1. Parameters for fitted models $q(t)$ and $l(t)$ as in Eqs. 16.3 and 16.4. Relevant coefficients are shown in bold.

	DTD	SA	DTD-u
B	**0.0010**	**0.0018**	**−0.0005**
C	−0.0168	−0.0322	0.0082
D	0.1085	0.1661	0.0389
L	**0.0007**	**−0.0012**	**−0.0002**
A	0.0558	0.0729	0.0640

These parameters are shown in Table 16.1 for the deep Taylor/LRP decomposition (DTD), sensitivity analysis (SA), and the DTD on the untrained model (DTD-u). Coefficients used for the analysis are shown in bold. We can observe that the border parameter B is positive for both analyses performed on the trained model. The lookahead parameter however has varying signs depending on the choice of analysis. We will see later in Sect. 16.3.4 that this parameter is influenced by the offset of the input sequence.

16.3.3   Border Effect and Step Size

The border effect can be intuitively understood as an attempt by the network to look beyond the sequence received as input. This suggests that upscaling the input sequence may reduce this effect as more context becomes available. For example, Fig. 16.6a is a static scene with barely any motion and shows, compared to other samples, more relevance at the border frames. To test this, we will subsample videos with various step sizes. We start with a step size of $\frac{1}{16}$, which is the same frame repeated 16 times. We then double the step size repeatedly until we reach a value of 32. At each step size, we apply DTD as well as sensitivity analysis. Note that the model is left untouched. The border parameter B for each step size is given in Fig. 16.3. For low step sizes, the border effect is strong. As the step size increases, the border effect is reduced, thus confirming the above intuition.

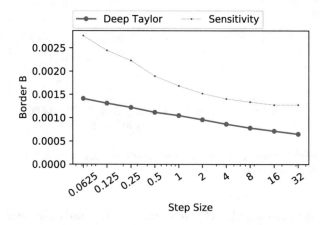

Fig. 16.3. Border parameter B by step size (logarithmic scale)

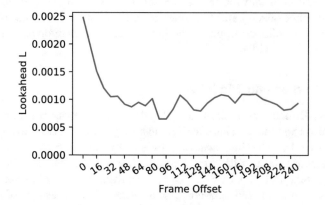

Fig. 16.4. Lookahead parameter L by intra-video frame offset.

16.3.4 Lookahead Effect and Offset

The lookahead effect is the tendency of the network to look predominantly at the end of the sequence. We would like to test whether this effect occurs at every position in the video or mainly at the beginning. One of our suspicions is, that many videos start with some opening screen, where the title of the video, authors etc. are introduced. It would seem natural that the model ignores the first few frames of the video and assigns more relevance to the later frames.

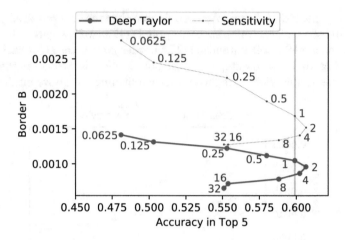

Fig. 16.5. Border parameter B by top-5 accuracy along step size. The grey bar indicates the baseline accuracy.

An example for such a video clip is shown in Fig. 16.7b. We start by taking the input sequence at the beginning of the video, then, we slide the window by 8-framed offsets until we reach an offset of 256. The results are shown in Fig. 16.4. We observe that for offsets 0, 8 and 16, the lookahead parameter is high compared to other offsets, and becomes low and constant for larger offsets. This behavior for small offsets supports the hypothesis of non-informative content at the beginning of the video.

16.3.5   Step Size and Model Accuracy

As a final experiment, we look at how the step size not only controls the border effect, but also the model's classification accuracy. In particular, we test whether we can improve the classifier accuracy by simply choosing a step size different from the training data, without retraining the model. We use the previously defined step sizes and plot in Fig. 16.5 the resulting border parameter in correspondence to the produced classification accuracy. (The measure of accuracy is the membership of the true label to the top five predictions.) A low step size produces few correct predictions. Performance slowly increases until the highest accuracy is reached at a step size of 2, about 1% above the baseline accuracy of 60%. After that, accuracy drops again until a step size of 16. A key observation here is that the optimal step size is different from the step size 1 used for training the model. Thus, the classification accuracy was improved at no cost. Note that we could have made this observation without any model explanation by simple validation over the frame rate. However, the contribution of the explanation module here is the insight of how the model utilizes frames in the input clip, which led to this experiment in the first place.

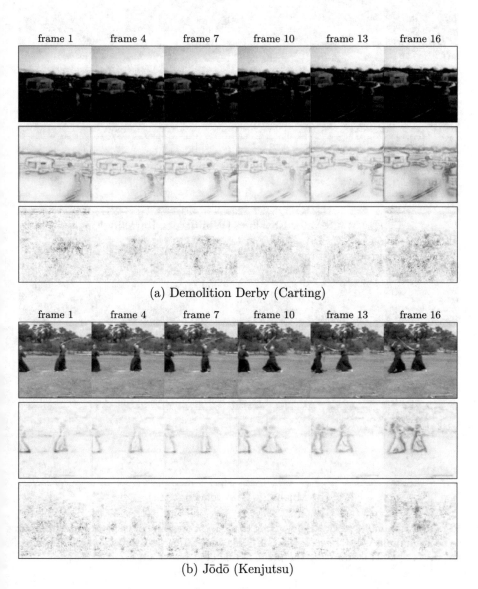

(a) Demolition Derby (Carting)

(b) Jōdō (Kenjutsu)

Fig. 16.6. Examples of videos belonging to different classes. For each example from top to bottom: input video, deep Taylor/LRP decomposition, sensitivity analysis. Captions are the true label followed by the predicted label in parentheses.

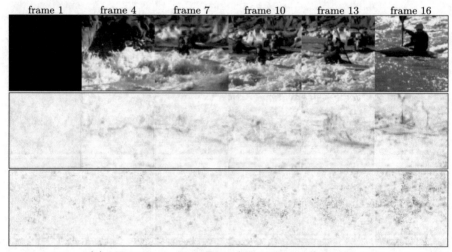

(a) Whitewater Kayaking (Whitewater Kayaking)

(b) Mushing (Gridiron Football)

Fig. 16.7. Examples of videos belonging to different classes. For each example from top to bottom: input video, deep Taylor/LRP decomposition, sensitivity analysis. Captions are the true label followed by the predicted label in parentheses.

16.4   Conclusion

In this work, we have explained the reasoning of a highly predictive video neural network trained on a sports classification task. For this, we have used the recently proposed deep Taylor/LRP framework, which allowed us to robustly identify which frames in the video and which pixels of each frame are relevant for prediction. The method was able to correctly identify video features specific to certain sports. In addition, the analysis has also revealed systematic imbalances in the way relevance is distributed in the temporal domain. These imbalances, that we called "border effect" and "lookahead effect", can be understood as an attempt by the network to look beyond the sequence it receives as input. Based on the result of this analysis, we then explored how transforming the input data reduces/increases these imbalances. In particular, down-sampling the data was shown to reduce the border effect, and also to bring a small increase in classification accuracy (Fig. 16.5), without actually retraining the model. Even though the "lookahead effect" did not immediately lead to a strategy to improve the model, it implied flaws in the preprocessing of the training data. While these specific findings were only shown in this respective context of C3D and Sports1M, we were able to demonstrate to what extent the findings of such an analysis of a video classifier could be used to gain insight of a model's relation to its input data. We speculate that other models might share similar relations.

Acknowledgements. This work was supported by the German Ministry for Education and Research as Berlin Big Data Centre (01IS14013A), Berlin Center for Machine Learning (01IS18037I) and TraMeExCo (01IS18056A). Partial funding by DFG is acknowledged (EXC 2046/1, project-ID: 390685689). This work was also supported by the Institute for Information & Communications Technology Planning & Evaluation (IITP) grant funded by the Korea government (No. 2017-0-00451, No. 2017-0-01779).

References

1. Bach, S., Binder, A., Montavon, G., Klauschen, F., Müller, K.R., Samek, W.: On pixel-wise explanations for non-linear classifier decisions by layer-wise relevance propagation. PLoS ONE **10**(7), e0130140 (2015)
2. Baldi, P., Sadowski, P., Whiteson, D.: Searching for exotic particles in high-energy physics with deep learning. Nat. Commun. **5**, 4308 (2014)
3. Bosse, S., Maniry, D., Müller, K.R., Wiegand, T., Samek, W.: Deep neural networks for no-reference and full-reference image quality assessment. IEEE Trans. Image Process. **27**(1), 206–219 (2018)
4. Donahue, J., et al.: Long-term recurrent convolutional networks for visual recognition and description. In: IEEE CVPR, pp. 2625–2634 (2015)
5. Gevrey, M., Dimopoulos, I., Lek, S.: Review and comparison of methods to study the contribution of variables in artificial neural network models. Ecol. Model. **160**(3), 249–264 (2003)
6. Graves, A., Mohamed, A., Hinton, G.: Speech recognition with deep recurrent neural networks. In: IEEE ICASSP, pp. 6645–6649 (2013)
7. Hou, L., Samaras, D., Kurc, T.M., Gao, Y., Davis, J.E., Saltz, J.H.: Patch-based convolutional neural network for whole slide tissue image classification. In: IEEE CVPR, pp. 2424–2433 (2016)
8. Hu, K.T., Leou, J.J., Hsiao, H.H.: Spatiotemporal saliency detection and salient region determination for H.264 videos. JVCIR **24**(7), 760–772 (2013)
9. Ji, S., Xu, W., Yang, M., Yu, K.: 3D convolutional neural networks for human action recognition. IEEE TPAMI **35**(1), 221–231 (2013)
10. Karpathy, A., Toderici, G., Shetty, S., Leung, T., Sukthankar, R., Fei-Fei, L.: Large-scale video classification with convolutional neural networks. In: IEEE CVPR, pp. 1725–1732 (2014)

11. Kauffmann, J., Esders, M., Montavon, G., Samek, W., Müller, K.R.,: From Clustering to Cluster Explanations via Neural Networks. arXiv preprint arXiv:1906.07633 (2019)
12. Krizhevsky, A., Sutskever, I., Hinton, G.E.: ImageNet classification with deep convolutional neural networks. In: Advances in NIPS, pp. 1097–1105 (2012)
13. Landecker, W., Thomure, M.D., Bettencourt, L.M., Mitchell, M., Kenyon, G.T., Brumby, S.P.: Interpreting individual classifications of hierarchical networks. In: IEEE Symposium CIDM, pp. 32–38 (2013)
14. Lapuschkin, S., Binder, A., Montavon, G., Müller, K.R., Samek, W.: The LRP toolbox for artificial neural networks. J. Mach. Learn. Res. **17**(114), 1–5 (2016)
15. Lapuschkin, S., Wäldchen, S., Binder, A., Montavon, G., Samek, W., Müller, K.R.: Unmasking Clever Hans predictors and assessing what machines really learn. Nat. Commun. **10**, 1096 (2019)
16. Li, J., Liu, Z., Zhang, X., Le Meur, O., Shen, L.: Spatiotemporal saliency detection based on superpixel-level trajectory. Sig. Process. Image Commun. **38**, 100–114 (2015)
17. Montavon, G., Lapuschkin, S., Binder, A., Samek, W., Müller, K.R.: Explaining nonlinear classification decisions with deep Taylor decomposition. Pattern Recogn. **65**, 211–222 (2017)
18. Montavon, G., Samek, W., Müller, K.R.: Methods for interpreting and understanding deep neural networks. Digit. Signal Proc. **73**, 1–15 (2018)
19. van den Oord, A., et al.: WaveNet: a generative model for raw audio. In: The 9th ISCA Speech Synthesis Workshop, Sunnyvale, CA, USA, 13–15 September 2016, p. 125 (2016)
20. Pohlen, T., Hermans, A., Mathias, M., Leibe, B.: Full-resolution residual networks for semantic segmentation in street scenes. In: IEEE CVPR, pp. 4151–4160 (2017)
21. Poulin, B., et al.: Visual explanation of evidence with additive classifiers. In: Proceedings, The Twenty-First National Conference on Artificial Intelligence and the Eighteenth Innovative Applications of Artificial Intelligence Conference, 16–20 July 2006, Boston, Massachusetts, USA, pp. 1822–1829 (2006)
22. Reed, S.E., Lee, H., Anguelov, D., Szegedy, C., Erhan, D., Rabinovich, A.: Training deep neural networks on noisy labels with bootstrapping. In: 3rd International Conference on Learning Representations, ICLR 2015, San Diego, CA, USA, 7–9 May 2015, Workshop Track Proceedings (2015)
23. Ribeiro, M.T., Singh, S., Guestrin, C.: "Why should I trust you?": explaining the predictions of any classifier. In: Proceedings of the 22nd ACM SIGKDD International Conference on Knowledge Discovery and Data Mining, San Francisco, CA, USA, 13–17 August 2016, pp. 1135–1144 (2016)
24. Samek, W., Binder, A., Montavon, G., Lapuschkin, S., Müller, K.: Evaluating the visualization of what a deep neural network has learned. IEEE Trans. Neural Netw. Learn. Syst. **28**(11), 2660–2673 (2017)
25. Schütt, K., Kindermans, P.J., Felix, H.E.S., Chmiela, S., Tkatchenko, A., Müller, K.R.: SchNet: a continuous-filter convolutional neural network for modeling quantum interactions. In: Advances in NIPS, pp. 992–1002 (2017)
26. Selvaraju, R.R., Cogswell, M., Das, A., Vedantam, R., Parikh, D., Batra, D.: Grad-CAM: visual explanations from deep networks via gradient-based localization. In: IEEE CVPR, pp. 618–626 (2017)
27. Sharma, S., Kiros, R., Salakhutdinov, R.: Action recognition using visual attention. CoRR abs/1511.04119 (2015)

28. Simonyan, K., Vedaldi, A., Zisserman, A.: Deep inside convolutional networks: visualising image classification models and saliency maps. In: 2nd International Conference on Learning Representations, ICLR 2014, Banff, AB, Canada, 14–16 April 2014, Workshop Track Proceedings (2014)

29. Springenberg, J.T., Dosovitskiy, A., Brox, T., Riedmiller, M.A.: Striving for simplicity: The all convolutional net. In: 3rd International Conference on Learning Representations, ICLR 2015, San Diego, CA, USA, 7–9 May 2015, Workshop Track Proceedings (2015)

30. Srinivasan, V., Lapuschkin, S., Hellge, C., Müller, K.R., Samek, W.: Interpretable human action recognition in compressed domain. In: IEEE ICASSP, pp. 1692–1696 (2017)

31. Sturm, I., Lapuschkin, S., Samek, W., Müller, K.R.: Interpretable deep neural networks for single-trial EEG classification. J. Neurosci. Methods **274**, 141–145 (2016)

32. Szegedy, C., Liu, W., Jia, Y., Sermanet, P., Reed, S., Anguelov, D., et al.: Going deeper with convolutions. In: IEEE CVPR, pp. 1–9 (2015)

33. Tran, D., Bourdev, L., Fergus, R., Torresani, L., Paluri, M.: Learning spatiotemporal features with 3D convolutional networks. In: IEEE ICCV, pp. 4489–4497 (2015)

34. Yang, C., Rangarajan, A., Ranka, S.: Visual explanations from deep 3D convolutional neural networks for Alzheimer's disease classification. CoRR abs/1803.02544 (2018)

35. Yosinski, J., Clune, J., Nguyen, A.M., Fuchs, T.J., Lipson, H.: Understanding neural networks through deep visualization. CoRR abs/1506.06579 (2015)

36. Yue-Hei Ng, J., Hausknecht, M., Vijayanarasimhan, S., Vinyals, O., Monga, R., Toderici, G.: Beyond short snippets: deep networks for video classification. In: IEEE CVPR, pp. 4694–4702 (2015)

37. Zeiler, M.D., Fergus, R.: Visualizing and understanding convolutional networks. In: Fleet, D., Pajdla, T., Schiele, B., Tuytelaars, T. (eds.) ECCV 2014. LNCS, vol. 8689, pp. 818–833. Springer, Cham (2014). https://doi.org/10.1007/978-3-319-10590-1_53

38. Zhang, C., Tian, Y.: Automatic video description generation via LSTM with joint two-stream encoding. In: ICPR, pp. 2924–2929 (2016)

39. Zhou, B., Khosla, A., Lapedriza, A., Oliva, A., Torralba, A.: Learning deep features for discriminative localization. In: IEEE CVPR, pp. 2921–2929 (2016)

17
Quantum-Chemical Insights from Interpretable Atomistic Neural Networks

Kristof T. Schütt[1], Michael Gastegger[1], Alexandre Tkatchenko[2(✉)], and Klaus-Robert Müller[1,3,4(✉)]

[1] Technische Universität Berlin, 10587 Berlin, Germany
{kristof.schuett,klaus-robert.mueller}@tu-berlin.de
[2] University of Luxembourg, 1511 Luxembourg, Luxembourg
alexandre.tkatchenko@uni.lu
[3] Max-Planck-Institut für Informatik, Saarbrücken, Germany
[4] Korea University, Anam-dong, Seongbuk-gu, Seoul 02841, Korea

Abstract. With the rise of deep neural networks for quantum chemistry applications, there is a pressing need for architectures that, beyond delivering accurate predictions of chemical properties, are readily interpretable by researchers. Here, we describe interpretation techniques for atomistic neural networks on the example of Behler–Parrinello networks as well as the end-to-end model SchNet. Both models obtain predictions of chemical properties by aggregating atom-wise contributions. These latent variables can serve as local explanations of a prediction and are obtained during training without additional cost. Due to their correspondence to well-known chemical concepts such as atomic energies and partial charges, these atom-wise explanations enable insights not only about the model but more importantly about the underlying quantum-chemical regularities. We generalize from atomistic explanations to 3d space, thus obtaining spatially resolved visualizations which further improve interpretability. Finally, we analyze learned embeddings of chemical elements that exhibit a partial ordering that resembles the order of the periodic table. As the examined neural networks show excellent agreement with chemical knowledge, the presented techniques open up new venues for data-driven research in chemistry, physics and materials science.

17.1 Introduction

The discovery of novel molecules and materials is crucial for research in a wide variety of applications ranging from food processing and drug design [3,46] to more efficient batteries [12,23,25] and solar cells [35]. While quantum-chemical calculations [14,28] deliver the means to predict such properties for given atomistic systems, their computational cost as well as the vastness of chemical compound space prevents an exhaustive exploration [30]. In recent years, there

W. Samek et al. (Eds.): Explainable AI, LNAI 11700, pp. 311–330, 2019.
https://doi.org/10.1007/978-3-030-28954-6_17

has been a growing interest in applying machine learning techniques to model quantum-chemical systems [5,9,11,13,16,17,21,22,32,40,43]. While research has focused primarily on predicting chemical properties by applying non-linear regression methods such as Gaussian processes or neural networks to manually crafted features [4,6], there have also been successful approaches to learn molecular representations end-to-end. These include neural circular fingerprints that use chemical graphs as inputs [15,26], mixed approaches that use both graph information as well as atomic positions [20] and architectures that learn purely from first-principles information such as deep tensor neural networks (DTNNs) [42], which represent atomistic systems by modeling subsequent pair-wise interactions of atomic environments with factorized tensor layers. Other architectures fitting into the DTNN framework include SchNet [45], where the interactions are modeled using continuous-filter convolutions [44] as well as more recent variations of this theme such as HIP-NN [31] or crystal graph convolutional networks [50].

As these neural network architectures become increasingly complex, it is crucial that quantum-chemistry researchers are able to acquire an intuition how these models function and how trustworthy predictions are. Beyond a high prediction accuracy, this requires neural networks to demonstrate that they have learned fundamental quantum-chemical principles. Several techniques have been developed that generate explanations for classifier decisions of neural networks [1,2,27,33,48,51,52]. Since quantum-chemical properties are often continuous, such as the prediction of molecular energies with a neural network potential, regression problems are more common in this field than classification. This changes how explanations have to be interpreted. Given a neural network potential, saliency maps based on input gradients [2,48] correspond to the force that acts on atoms. While this might indeed be a reason for high energies, e.g. if two atoms are very close, the gradient is too local to explain the energy level sufficiently. This is especially the case for stable (equilibrium) molecules, which are located in a local energy minimum such that all forces are zero. Therefore, input gradients would indicate that the atom positions are not important, which is clearly wrong. Other explanation methods assign importance or relevance scores to input features through obtaining reverse mappings based on the network parameters [1,33,51], sampling [52] or training for signal reconstruction [23]. Even though some of those alleviate the problem of pure input gradients since their explanations are less local [41], there is another fundamental issue in this application: While pixel-wise relevance scores of images allow for a visual inspection, the influence of the positions and types of individual atoms is not readily interpretable in the quantum chemical picture. Here, we aim for an explanation in the full 3-d space, i.e. beyond positions of nuclear charges.

In the following, we will introduce two neural network potentials, namely (1) Behler-Parrinello networks (BP) [8,9,19] that make use of manually engineered features and (2) SchNet [44,45], which learns atomistic representations directly from atom types and positions. For both architectures, we will demonstrate interpretation strategies that allow for spatially and chemically resolved insights into the inner workings of the neural network as well as the underlying data.

Furthermore, we will show that both kinds of architectures – and deep end-to-end models in particular – not only are highly accurate, but recover fundamental chemical knowledge.

17.2   Atomistic Neural Network Potentials

Due to the spatial structure of atomistic systems and the nature of quantum mechanical laws giving rise to various invariances and scaling behaviors of chemical properties, special adaptations to conventional neural network architectures are necessary in order to model chemical systems efficiently. The first major issue arises from the overall diversity exhibited by molecules. They can vary greatly with respect to the overall number of atoms as well as the combination of chemical elements present, thus rendering purely static architectures ill-suited for obtaining a general description. In addition, molecular properties do not change if atoms of the same element are exchanged and the corresponding invariances with respect to atom types needs to be accounted for by the model.

Second, the properties of molecules originate from interactions between nuclei and electrons. These can be roughly represented by interatomic potentials which are functions in 3d space depending on the types and positions of the atoms. However, atom coordinates – and subsequently all associated molecular properties – can change in a continuous manner. Hence, all grid based methods (e.g. conventional convolutional neural networks) are generally infeasible, as they fail to resolve these incremental changes. Moreover, chemical properties are invariant with respect to translations and rotations in Cartesian space, imposing additional constraints on machine learning models for molecules and materials.

In order to overcome the first of the above issues, so-called atomistic neural network architectures are introduced. Similar to neural networks for graphs, the atomistic system is decomposed into local environments. Specifically, a set of feature vectors is defined for every atom based on which latent atom-wise contributions to a property of interest are predicted. These are used to reconstruct the target property via physically motivated aggregation layers that guarantee permutational invariance of the atoms.

Depending on the strategy used to obtain atom-wise features, two categories of atomistic neural network models can be distinguished (see Fig. 17.1). The first type employs handcrafted features, which are engineered before training. A popular choice in this category are Behler–Parrinello (BP) networks using atom-centered symmetry functions [8,9]. In the second category, all spatial invariances are encoded instead directly into the structure of an atomistic neural network such that atom-wise representations can be obtained during training in an end-to-end fashion. This includes neural networks implementing the DTNN framework, where atomistic representations are constructed through interaction layers such as the continuous-filter convolutional neural network SchNet [44,45].

In the following section, BP and SchNet architectures will be discussed in greater detail. Finally, a short overview will be given on how various chemical properties are obtained in an atomistic machine learning framework.

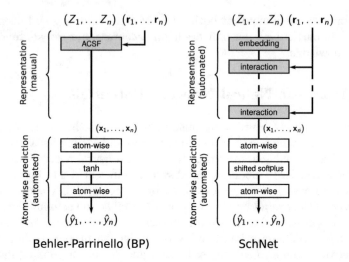

Fig. 17.1. Illustration of the two examined neural network architectures: Behler-Parrinello network with atom-centered symmetry functions (ACSFs, left) and the end-to-end architecture SchNet (right). The softplus activation is shifted by $-\ln(2)$ such that it crosses the origin.

17.2.1 Behler–Parrinello Potentials

BP neural network potentials apply fully-connected neural networks atom-wise to so-called atom-centered symmetry functions (ACSFs) [8]. These ACSFs describe the arrangement and chemical identities of the neighbors surrounding a central atom via sets of specialized distribution functions. Typically, multiple, different types of ACSFs are used to capture radial and angular information.

Radial distribution functions take the form

$$G_i^{\text{rad}} = \sum_{j \neq i}^{N} e^{-\eta(r_{ij}-r_0)^2} f_{\text{cut}}(r_{ij}), \qquad (17.1)$$

where N is the number of atoms in the molecule and r_{ij} the distance between the central atom i and its neighbor j. The parameters η and r_0 control the width and position of the Gaussian. The cutoff function f_{cut} ensures that the contribution of every neighbor to the ACSF becomes exactly zero if it is located too far away from the central atom. As radial functions offer only a limited spatial resolution, they are used in combination with angular ACSFs.

In order to account for different chemical species in an atoms environment, ACSFs are typically defined for pairs (radial) and triples (angles) of chemical elements. In addition, a set of radial and angular ACSFs differing in their respective hyper-parameters is used for every resulting combination in order to provide a sufficiently resolved description of chemical environments. Thus, the number of features and hyper-parameters grows quickly with the number of chemical elements present in the data set. However, strategies have been proposed to overcome some of these problems, such as introducing an element-dependent weighting of ACSFs in order to avoid the combinatorial explosion of features [19].

Due to the above definition, the hyper-parameters of all individual functions need to be determined in a tedious trial and error procedure based on the molecules under investigation. However, ACSFs engineered based on the domain knowledge of a skilled practitioner can be highly efficient in terms of required reference calculations for training [19].

17.2.2   SchNet

In contrast to the previously described architecture, SchNet is able to learn an efficient representation of chemical environments directly from atom types and positions with minimal hyper-parameter tuning. The overall structure of SchNet follows the DTNN framework [42] consisting of three steps:

1. Initialize atom features $\mathbf{x}_i$ with embeddings of chemical element Z_i:

$$\mathbf{x}_i^{(0)} = \mathbf{A}_{Z_i}$$

2. Infuse spatial information of the chemical environment adding pair-wise interaction corrections $\mathbf{v}^{(t)}$ multiple times:

$$\mathbf{x}_i^{(t+1)} = \mathbf{x}_i^{(t)} + \sum_{j \neq i} \mathbf{v}^{(t)}\left(\mathbf{x}_j^{(t)}, r_{ij}\right)$$

3. Obtain property of interest from final atom-wise representations $\mathbf{x}_i^{(T)}$ using physically motivated aggregation (see Sec. 17.2.3).

The crucial difference between various implementations of the DTNN framework is how the interaction corrections $\mathbf{v}^{(t)}$, which present a functional block of SchNet, are modeled. In case of SchNet, we apply a continuous-filter convolution [44] over the atomistic system with a smooth convolution filter generated by a fully-connected neural network depending on the pair-wise distances r_{ij}

$$(\mathbf{x} * W)(\mathbf{r}_i) = \sum_{j=1}^{N} \mathbf{x}_j^{(t)} \circ \underbrace{W^{(t)}(r_{ij})}_{\text{filter-generating network}} \quad ,$$

where "$\circ$" is the Hadamard product. To avoid self-interaction, we mask the filter such that $W^{(t)}(0) = 0$. We obtain the interaction correction $\mathbf{v}^{(t)}$ as a sequence of this convolution and atom-wise layers that facilitate the cross-talk between feature maps. For the detailed architecture, please refer to Ref. [45]. Defining the interaction correction $\mathbf{v}^{(t)}$ using such a convolution on pair-wise distances results in radial filters, i.e. rotational and translational invariances are guaranteed. Due to the repeated interaction corrections, spatial information is propagated across multiple atoms. Thus, many-body interactions can be inferred without having to explicitly include angular or higher-order information [9, 24, 37].

17.2.3 Chemical Properties

In atomistic models, a chemical property is expressed via latent atomistic contributions. Based on these contributions, the original property is then reconstructed via a physically motivated aggregation layer. The exact functional form strongly depends on the property.

A common target of atomistic machine learning approaches is the atomization energy E. It can be seen as a measure of how stable different molecules and their configurations are compared to each other and allows to make predictions about the reactivity of chemical species. In an atomistic framework, the aggregation for the potential energy of a molecule takes the form

$$E = \sum_{i=1}^{N} \hat{E}_i, \tag{17.2}$$

where $\hat{E}_i$ are latent atomic contributions to the energy. In case of BP and SchNet, they are obtained from atom-wise prediction layers that take the respective atom-wise representations as input. Due to the summation in Eq. 17.2, atomistic models implicitly account for permutation invariance and can be applied to molecules of arbitrary size and composition.

Another chemical property of interest is the dipole moment $\boldsymbol{\mu}$ or its magnitude μ [18,47]. Those properties are a measure for the separation of regions of positive and negative charge in a molecule and, for instance, important in infrared spectroscopy. The dipole moment vector $\boldsymbol{\mu}$ can be written as

$$\boldsymbol{\mu} = \sum_{i=1}^{N} \hat{q}_i \mathbf{r}_i. \tag{17.3}$$

where $\hat{q}_i$ are latent partial charges predicted from atom-wise representations. The positions $\mathbf{r}_i$ of atom i are given relative to a reference point, typically the molecules center of mass. Based on expression 17.3, the magnitude of the dipole moment μ simply is

$$\mu = \|\boldsymbol{\mu}\|_2 = \left\| \sum_{i=1}^{N} \hat{q}_i \mathbf{r}_i \right\|_2. \tag{17.4}$$

An important feature of atomistic architectures is that the latent properties are not learned directly, but inferred by the neural network. Only the molecular energies and dipole moments are quantum-mechanical observables and can hence be computed based purely on first principles. Although atomic energies and partial charge distributions can not be derived in a unique manner, they nevertheless constitute important tools to characterize and interpret the properties and behavior of atomistic systems. In this sense, atomistic models represent a new class of purely data driven partitioning schemes for chemical properties.

Table 17.1. Mean absolute errors and root mean squared errors of analyzed models trained on 100k molecules from the QM9 benchmark dataset.

Property	Unit	Behler-Parrinello		SchNet	
		MAE	RMSE	MAE	RMSE
Atomization energy	kcal mol^{-1}	0.77	1.32	0.35	0.94
Dipole moment	Debye	0.073	0.118	0.025	0.050

17.3 Interpretability

As stated in the introduction, conventional interpretation techniques work well for neural networks on images or text, however can not sufficiently explain predictions of continuous chemical properties that depend on interatomic potential spanning the whole 3d space. Instead, we investigate approaches particularly tailored to these kind of problems, exploiting several features of atomistic models in the process. E.g., analyzing latent contributions of chemical environments to a property of interest opens up new venues for interpreting atomistic neural networks from a machine learning perspective [42]. Moreover, many of these explanation schemes are directly related to physical and chemical properties of the molecules under study, allowing to extract chemical insights from the model.

In the following, we will demonstrate three interpretable aspects of atomistic models, namely (1) atom-wise latent contributions, (2) probing representations in 3-d space and (3) embeddings of chemical elements. For all of our analyses, we will employ BP and SchNet models trained on 100k reference calculations at the B3LYP level of theory [7,29] from the popular QM9 molecule benchmark [38]. The dataset consists of all possible molecules with up to nine heavy atoms from the {C, O, N, F} set of chemical elements and are chemically saturated with hydrogen [10,39]. Table 17.1 shows the performance of the trained models. SchNet achieves consistently lower errors since it is able to adapt its representation to the data at hand, while BP employs a fixed feature representation. This is especially advantageous in the chemical compound space setting with a large and diverse set of training molecules. On this ground, we will analyze how both models obtain predictions of chemical properties as well as whether the obtained latent variable agree with chemical intuition and can be employed to extract further insight.

17.3.1 Atom-Wise Partitioning of Chemical Properties

A major feature of atomistic architectures is the access to atom-wise latent variables, providing a framework for atom-wise explanation out-of-the-box. This atom-wise saliency can be seen as the logical extension of the pixel-wise explanations used for images to the domain of molecules. Unlike relevance propagation approaches [1,34], the latent energies $\hat{E}_i$ and charges $\hat{q}_i$ in Eqs. 17.2 and 17.3 are interpretable features that are an implicit part of the model architecture and obtained during training without additional cost, similar to approaches for weakly-supervised object detection [36]. The final prediction is aggregated via physically motivated aggregation layers from the latent variable which thereby get assigned inherent physical interpretations. Since the use of these aggregation layers is not restricted to a particular class of atomistic architectures, valuable information can be gained for any type of model – independent on whether models use hand-crafted features such as BPs or learn representations end-to-end such as SchNet. This makes it possible to compare different models at new levels of abstraction, gaining insights into their inner workings and fundamental differences.

When the property of interest is the atomization energy of an atomistic system, atomic energy contributions are obtained as latent properties. Figure 17.2 depicts the distributions of these energies obtained for the BP and SchNet models and different folds of the QM9 database. While the energy contributions within a model are well conserved in general, we find that this effect is significantly more pronounced for the SchNet architecture. Beyond that, it is possible to discern effects due to the frequency of atom types in the reference data. Less frequent elements such as oxygen show greater variation compared to the abundant hydrogen and carbon atoms.

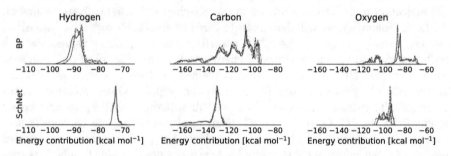

Fig. 17.2. Distribution of energy contributions $\hat{E}_i$ (see Eq. 17.2) for atoms of types H, C, O from QM9 molecules predicted by Behler-Parrinello and SchNet models. The models were trained on 100k examples. Each color corresponds to a model trained on a different subset.

As shown in Fig. 17.2, both atomistic models arrive at qualitatively different partitionings of the atomic energies. The differences observed between the latent variables allow for insight about how energy predictions are obtained. Generally, energy distributions of the BP architecture are wider than their SchNet counterparts and show more distinct features. The main reason for this behavior is the way, how both architectures represent molecular structure. In BP networks, ACSFs are engineered before training to provide a sufficient resolution of different chemical environments. During the learning process, the atomistic energy contributions are adapted based on these predetermined features, which introduce a certain bias. Hence, patterns already present in the descriptors are more or less retained in the latent properties. This is particularly prominent in the case of carbon, where the different peaks of the distribution simply correspond to the various local environments present in QM9. SchNet on the other hand learns appropriate representations in an end-to-end manner exclusively from the reference data. The narrow shape observed for the SchNet energy distributions indicates that this type of model arrives at a simple solution of the learning problem by keeping the deviation of the interaction energies within atom types to a minimum.

These atomic energies can also serve as a basis for constructing novel measures of more abstract chemical concepts. An example for such an application is the use of atomic energies as a stability ranking for aromatic rings with different substitution patterns. We obtain this by summing the contributions of atoms that make up a ring:

$$E_{\text{ring}} = \sum_{i \in \text{ring}} \hat{E}_i$$

The ten most stable rings in the QM9 database determined in this way are shown in Fig. 17.3. The SchNet stability ranking appears to capture central aspects of the chemistry of the investigated systems. For example, the most stable ring is found to be adjacent to a five membered ring involving oxygen. Since the carbon atoms in the smaller ring are connected via a double bond, the π system of the aromatic ring is extended, leading to the high stability. This phenomenon is also referred to as the mesomeric effect in organic chemistry [49]. The same reasoning holds true for alkyne substituents ($-C\equiv CH$, e.g. top right molecule Fig. 17.3), which are found in six out of the ten structures. Another common motif is the presence of a fluorine atom ($-F$, green in Fig. 17.3). Due to its high electronegativity, fluorine forms very strong bonds with carbon, thus contributing greatly to the overall stability of the system. In case of the BP ranking, similar patterns are found for fluorine. Otherwise, the BP model shows preference for groups donating electron density to the central ring, such as hydroxy ($-OH$) and amine ($-NH_2$) groups. This trend is referred to as the inductive effect in organic chemistry and is known to increase ring stability similar to the mesomeric effect observed above [49]. Finally, we find that the BP based model attributes more energy to the ring carbons than SchNet, providing further evidence that SchNet strives to learn a partitioning that minimizes the deviation of the interaction energies within atom types. This interplay between explaining model predictions via chemical reasoning and obtaining new insights into investigated systems themselves constitutes one of the most tantalizing aspects of applying these methods to physically or chemically motivated problems.

Using the molecular dipole moment as the target property, the atomistic networks yield latent atomic partial charges instead of energies (see Eq. 17.4). In direct analogy to the atomic energies, the resulting atom-wise explanations can be used to gain insights not only on a model level, but also on a physical level. Pertaining to model level insights, qualitative differences between the energy and dipole models, as well as between BP and SchNet architectures, can be elucidated based on the distribution of partial charges obtained for all molecules

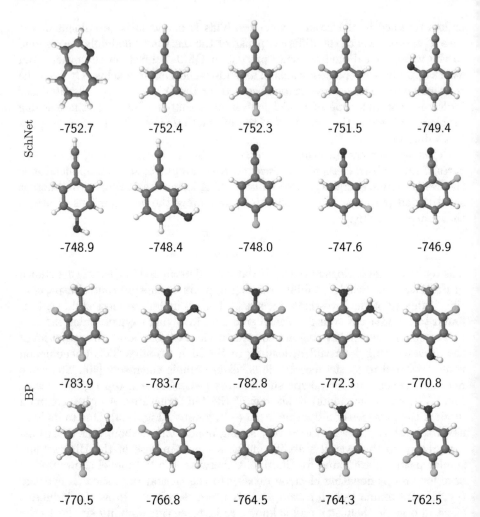

Fig. 17.3. Energy ranking of 6-membered carbon rings in the QM9 dataset obtained from atom-wise energy contributions as predicted by SchNet (top) and a Behler–Parrinello model (bottom). For each architecture, we show the ten most stable 6-membered carbon rings according to this metric. The atom types are colored as follows: hydrogen–white, carbon–gray, nitrogen–blue, fluorine–green.

in QM9 (Fig. 17.4). Comparing the distributions obtained for the same model trained on different subsets of the data, we find that in general the distributions of partial charges are more conserved than those obtained for the atomic energies (Fig. 17.2). The reason for this behavior is the additional structural information present in the dipole aggregation operation (Eq. 17.4). The dependence on the atom positions r_i and hence on the molecular shape introduces additional prior knowledge, thus leading to a more unique partitioning (up to a constant scaling

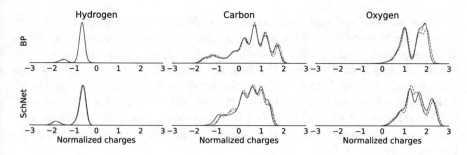

Fig. 17.4. Distributions of latent charges $\hat{q}_i$ (see Eq. 17.4) from Behler-Parrinello and SchNet dipole models.

factor). Further support for this conclusion is offered by the observation that the distribution of charges obtained with BP networks and SchNets shows a much closer agreement than for the atomic energies. This effect is especially pronounced for the hydrogen and carbon partial charge distributions, which exhibit very similar features. Analyzing these features for the carbon atom, one also notices parallels between the energy and charge distribution obtained for the BP type model, whereas the SchNet counterparts show little to no similarity. As stated above, the reason for this phenomenon is the static nature of descriptors employed in BP models, which stay the same irrespective of the target property. SchNet on the other hand is able to infer different, more optimal representations of the molecular structure depending on the modeling task.

In the case of dipole moments and partial charges, interpretation on the physical level takes on particularly interesting characteristics. The ability to obtain partial charges based exclusively on the dipole moment is remarkable, as it offers insights into the internal structure of a molecule – in this case the charge distribution – based on a single global property. These partial charges can in turn be used to rationalize e.g. chemical reaction mechanisms, molecular reactivity or the aggregation behavior of molecules. In the next section, we will explore how to visualize such spatially resolved insights.

17.3.2 Insights from Local Chemical Potentials

Having inspected atom-wise latent contributions, we will now introduce a feature of the DTNN framework that allows us to extend such atom-wise explanations to interpretable visualizations in 3-d space. Since energies are obtained atom-wise through a series of pair-wise interaction corrections, it is possible to obtain an energy contribution for every point in space. To this end, we introduce a test charge p to the atomistic system which we will use to probe the space surrounding the atoms. This enables us to examine the representation regarding spatial changes and interactions. In particular, we obtain a more intuitive visualization of the interactions within the molecule, as they haven been learned by the neural network.

Since we only can represent atoms in SchNet, the test charge is bound to be an atom in our model. This brings the problem that the molecule would be drastically influenced by adding another atom and, moreover, that the resulting molecule is bound to leave the training manifold if we trained the neural network only on equilibrium configuration or single molecular dynamics trajectories with a fixed number of atoms. We solve this by letting the probe atom feel the influence of the molecule, but not vice versa. This allows us to define a local chemical potential $\Omega_{Z_\mathrm{p}}(\mathbf{r})$ as the energy of the test charge of atom type Z_p located at position $\mathbf{r}$:

$$\mathbf{x}_p^{(t+1)} = \mathbf{x}_p^{(t)} + \sum_j \mathbf{v}^{(t)}\left(\mathbf{x}_j^{(t)}, \mathbf{r}_p - \mathbf{r}_j\right) \tag{17.5}$$

$$\Omega_{Z_\mathrm{p}}(\mathbf{r}) = f_\mathrm{out}(\mathbf{x}_\mathrm{p}^{(T)}) \tag{17.6}$$

It is important to note that this potential does not correspond to the actual potential of the molecule, but is a tool for us to visualize the spatial structure of the representation. Since this potential is defined in $\mathbb{R}^3$, we obtain a 3-dimensional continuous explanation. Figure 17.5 visualizes such local chemical potentials using a carbon probe for SchNet trained on QM9 on a smooth iso-surface with constant $\sum_i \|\mathbf{r} - \mathbf{r}_i\|^{-2}$ around a selection of molecules from the dataset. Furthermore, we show cuts through the local chemical potentials of the molecules as contour plots.

The potentials reflect the expected symmetries that stem from the rotational and translational invariance of SchNet. The low- and high-energy regions on the iso-surfaces are clearly separated. In the cuts, we observe a high sensitivity to the probe position (i.e. high density of contour lines) near the atom positions, which is most clearly visible for the molecules with aromatic rings. Both of these findings indicate that the learned representation is localized, which coincides with chemical intuition.

Since our local chemical potentials inherit the locality of atom-wise explanations, they can be similarly used as a visually more intuitive alternative for attributing local relevance. On top of that, the visualizations mirror chemical concepts such as bond saturation as well as different degrees of aromaticity. This makes them a powerful analysis tool for the chemistry researcher.

While the local chemical potentials introduced above deliver valuable and chemically plausible visualizations of the learned representation, they can not correspond to the actual potential generated by the molecule. This is because we are not able to introduce a real point charge for probing into the network, but have to resort to full atoms that would significantly disturb the molecule if we allowed it to influence the other atoms. In contrast, we are able to use the latent partial charges learned during the prediction of dipole moments to obtain an approximation of the electrostatic potential (ESP) of the molecule. The ESP offers insights into the spatial distribution of charges inside a molecule and indicates regions which are attractive or repulsive to the probe atom. This information can in turn be used to interpret e.g. reaction outcomes or coordination to other molecules.

Fig. 17.5. Local chemical potentials obtained with SchNet using a carbon probe for methane, benzene, pyrazine and propane. They are shown on a $\sum_i \|\mathbf{r} - \mathbf{r}_i\|^{-2} = 3.7\text{Å}^{-2}$ isosurface (top) as well as cuts through the center of the molecule (bottom). Dashed lines indicate regions of negative potential.

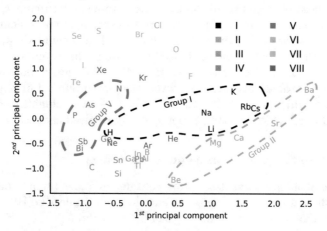

Fig. 17.6. The two leading principal components of the learned embeddings x_0 of sp atoms learned by SchNet from the Materials Project dataset. We recognize a structure in the embedding space according to the groups of the periodic table (shown exemplary for groups I, II and V and color-coded online) as well as an ordering from lighter to heavier elements within the groups, e.g., in groups I and II from light atoms (left) to heavier atoms (right).

The ESP of a molecule is the potential energy experienced by a probe charge q_0 in the electric field of a molecule. Using the latent partial charges $\hat{q}$ obtained above, we can obtain another interpretation in form of a corresponding ESP

$$E(\mathbf{r}_0) = \sum_i^N \frac{\hat{q}_i q_0}{\|\mathbf{r}_i - \mathbf{r}_0\|_2}, \tag{17.7}$$

where $\mathbf{r}_0$ and q_0 are the position and charge of the probe and $\mathbf{r}_i$ and $\hat{q}_i$ are the positions and partial charge of atom i of the molecule. Here, the charge distribution of the molecule is approximated by atom-wise latent partial charges learned in order to predict the dipole moment. Therefore, this approximation only models the part of the ESP that is relevant to describe the dipole of the molecule.

Figure 17.7 gives the ESPs of six molecules from QM9 as computed with latent partial charges from BP and SchNet. Both models give very similar ESPs for the different molecules. This is a consequence of the similarity between the charge distributions produced by the different architectures (see Sect. 17.3.1) and further amplified by the damping introduced via the inverse dependence on the distance between probe and atoms. Looking at the ESPs in general, we find that the obtained maps show excellent agreement with basic chemical reasoning. In the molecules containing only hydrogen and carbon (methane, propane, benzene, toluene), one would expect the hydrogen atoms to carry a slight positive charge and hence lead to unfavorable interactions with the equally positively charged probe. The opposite holds true for the carbon atom. This feature is indeed observed in all the ESP maps. In a similar manner, one would expect the oxygen atoms in phloroglucinol to carry a negative charge, due to their electron-withdrawing properties. Thus, the ESP should show a negative area around these atoms, which is indeed the case in the examined ESPs.

Similar to the local chemical potentials, the ESPs are a valuable tool for analyzing the obtained features. Moreover, they are grounded in physics which makes them readily interpretable. Hence, ESPs present a valuable tool for model validation and allow to directly extract spatially resolved chemical insights.

17.3.3   Insights from Atom Type Embeddings

While a lot of handcrafted descriptors consider different atom types orthogonal [9,21,43] or use nuclear charges to encode atom similarities [19,40], SchNet and DTNN allows for cross-element generalization through the high-dimension embeddings of chemical elements [42,45] If the trained models learn to efficiently make use of this possibility, we should be able to extract element similarities from the embeddings that resemble chemical intuition. Since QM9 only contains five atom types (H, C, N, O, F), we will perform this analysis on the Materials Project dataset of crystal structures as it includes 89 atom types ranging across the periodic table.

Figure 17.6 shows the two leading principal components of the element embeddings of the main group elements of the periodic table. The projection explains only about 20% of the variance, therefore atom types might appear closer than they are in the high-dimensional space. However, we see that atoms belonging to the same group tend to form clusters. This is especially apparent for main groups 1–5, while groups 6–8 appear to be slightly more scattered. In group 1, hydrogen lies further apart from the other members which coincides with its special status, being the element without core electrons. Beyond that,

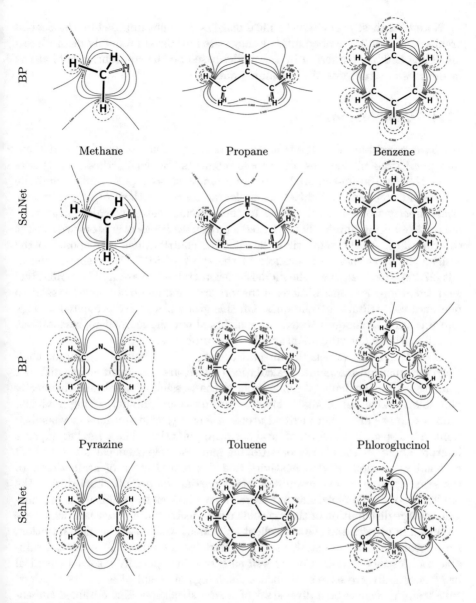

Fig. 17.7. Comparison of electrostatic potentials obtained with the atomic charges yielded by a BP type network and a SchNet and using a probe charge of $q_0 = 1$. Regions of positive potential are indicated with dashed lines. All charges are normalized.

there are partial orderings of elements according to their period within some of the groups. There are orderings from light to heavier elements, e.g. in group 1 (left to right: H - [Na,Li] - [K, Rb, Cs]), group 2 (left to right: Be - Mg - Ca - Sr - Ba) and group 5 (top to bottom: N-[As, P]-[Sb,Bi]).

Note that these extracted chemical insights were not imposed by the SchNet architecture onto the embeddings as they were initialized randomly before training. They had to be inferred by the model based on the co-occurrence of atoms in the crystal structures of the training data.

17.4   Conclusions

We have presented two atomistic neural networks that enable fast and accurate predictions of energies and dipole moments: Behler-Parrinello (BP) networks that use atom-centered symmetry functions as input features and the end-to-end architecture SchNet which learns representations of atomistic systems directly from first-principles. In these architectures, chemical properties are modeled using physically motivated aggregation layers over atom-wise latent contributions. At the same time, latent local contributions correspond to the assignment of atom-wise relevances in the spirit of LRP [1] or similar methods [27,33]. However, since the models are constrained to assemble the final target from atom-wise contributions in the forward pass, we do not have to resort to relevance redistribution techniques. On this ground, we have presented various interpretation techniques to extract insights about the learned representations as well as the underlying quantum-chemical problems.

Both examined models obtain partitionings of the energy – a major challenge for quantum-mechanical calculations – that are consistent across different training splits. Particularly remarkable is the possibility to obtain chemically plausible rankings of aromatic rings regarding their stability. Using a virtual probe atom, we are able to extend atom-wise energy contributions to visualizations in 3-d space in the form of local chemical potentials. These further improve interpretability of the energy partitioning and resemble chemical concepts such as bond saturation, electronegativity and different degrees of aromaticity. In the same spirit, we have examined latent partial charges obtained during the prediction of dipole molecular moments. They allow us to visualize the approximate charge distribution of the molecule using electrostatic potentials, which are grounded in physics and show excellent agreement with basic chemical intuition. Both local chemical potentials as well as electrostatic potentials present a valuable tool for model validation as well as extracting spatially resolved chemical insights. Finally, we have examined embeddings of chemical elements obtained from training SchNet on a diverse set of crystal structures. The obtained embeddings recover knowledge about chemical elements present in the structure of the periodic table. This guides the way to future work, extending the analysis to measure chemical similarity of local structures.

While accurate predictions are a necessary requirement for every machine learning model in quantum chemistry, it is crucial that the model is able to facilitate new research. Here, interpretability constitutes an essential building block for researchers in the respective field to validate, understand and ultimatively trust the machine learning model. Therefore, interpretation techniques should be closely oriented towards analysis methods familiar to the respective field, lowering the initial barrier for researchers unfamiliar with non-linear models of machine learning. For the same reason, it is beneficial if the interpretable properties are directly obtained during the forward pass. This ensures that they are ground truth – i.e. they are the exact decompositon into local contributions that was learned by the model – without having to rely on an approximate redistribution. The excellent agreement of the examined representations with chemical knowledge is a clear demonstration of the ability of atomistic neural networks to open up new venues for data-driven research in the chemistry, physics and materials science.

Acknowledgements. This work was supported by the Federal Ministry of Education and Research (BMBF) for the Berlin Big Data Center BBDC (01IS14013A) and the Berlin Center for Machine Learning (01IS18037A). Additional support was provided by the European Union's Horizon 2020 research and innovation program under the Marie Sklodowska-Curie grant agreement NO 792572. This research was supported by Institute for Information & Communications Technology Promotion and funded by the Korea government (MSIT) (No. 2017-0-00451, No. 2017-0-01779). A.T. acknowledges support from the European Research Council (ERC-CoG grant BeStMo).

References

1. Bach, S., Binder, A., Montavon, G., Klauschen, F., Müller, K.R., Samek, W.: On pixel-wise explanations for non-linear classifier decisions by layer-wise relevance propagation. PLoS One **10**(7), e0130140 (2015)
2. Baehrens, D., Schroeter, T., Harmeling, S., Kawanabe, M., Hansen, K., Müller, K.R.: How to explain individual classification decisions. J. Mach. Learn. Res. **11**, 1803–1831 (2010)
3. Bajorath, J.: Integration of virtual and high-throughput screening. Nat. Rev. Drug Discovery **1**(11), 882 (2002)
4. Bartók, A.P., Kondor, R., Csányi, G.: On representing chemical environments. Phys. Rev. B **87**(18), 184115 (2013)
5. Bartók, A.P., Payne, M.C., Kondor, R., Csányi, G.: Gaussian approximation potentials: the accuracy of quantum mechanics, without the electrons. Phys. Rev. Lett. **104**(13), 136403 (2010)
6. Bartók, A.P., Csányi, G.: Gaussian approximation potentials: a brief tutorial introduction. Int. J. Quantum Chem. **115**(16), 1051–1057 (2015)
7. Becke, A.D.: Density-functional exchange-energy approximation with correct asymptotic behavior. Phys. Rev. A **38**(6), 3098 (1988)
8. Behler, J.: Atom-centered symmetry functions for constructing high-dimensional neural network potentials. J. Chem. Phys. **134**(7), 074106 (2011)
9. Behler, J., Parrinello, M.: Generalized neural-network representation of high-dimensional potential-energy surfaces. Phys. Rev. Lett. **98**(14), 146401 (2007)
10. Blum, L.C., Reymond, J.L.: 970 million druglike small molecules for virtual screening in the chemical universe database GDB-13. J. Am. Chem. Soc. **131**, 8732 (2009)
11. Brockherde, F., Voigt, L., Li, L., Tuckerman, M.E., Burke, K., Müller, K.R.: Bypassing the Kohn-Sham equations with machine learning. Nat. Commun. **8**, 872 (2017)
12. Chen, H., et al.: Carbonophosphates: a new family of cathode materials for Li-Ion batteries identified computationally. Chem. Mater. **24**(11), 2009–2016 (2012)

13. Chmiela, S., Tkatchenko, A., Sauceda, H.E., Poltavsky, I., Schütt, K.T., Müller, K.R.: Machine learning of accurate energy-conserving molecular force fields. Sci. Adv. **3**(5), e1603015 (2017)
14. Hohenberg, P., Kohn, W.: Inhomogeneous electron gas. Phys. Rev. **136**, B864–B871 (1964)
15. Duvenaud, D.K., et al.: Convolutional networks on graphs for learning molecular fingerprints. In: Cortes, C., Lawrence, N.D., Lee, D.D., Sugiyama, M., Garnett, R. (eds.) NIPS, pp. 2224–2232 (2015)
16. Eickenberg, M., Exarchakis, G., Hirn, M., Mallat, S.: Solid harmonic wavelet scattering: predicting quantum molecular energy from invariant descriptors of 3D electronic densities. In: Advances in Neural Information Processing Systems 30, pp. 6543–6552. Curran Associates, Inc., Long Beach (2017)
17. Faber, F.A., et al.: Prediction errors of molecular machine learning models lower than hybrid DFT error. J. Chem. Theory Comput. **13**(11), 5255–5264 (2017)
18. Gastegger, M., Behler, J., Marquetand, P.: Machine learning molecular dynamics for the simulation of infrared spectra. Chem. Sci. **8**(10), 6924–6935 (2017)
19. Gastegger, M., Schwiedrzik, L., Bittermann, M., Berzsenyi, F., Marquetand, P.: wACSF-weighted atom-centered symmetry functions as descriptors in machine learning potentials. J. Chem. Phys. **148**(24), 241709 (2018)
20. Gilmer, J., Schoenholz, S.S., Riley, P.F., Vinyals, O., Dahl, G.E.: Neural message passing for quantum chemistry. In: Proceedings of the 34th International Conference on Machine Learning, pp. 1263–1272 (2017)
21. Hansen, K., et al.: Machine learning predictions of molecular properties: accurate many-body potentials and nonlocality in chemical space. J. Phys. Chem. Lett. **6**, 2326 (2015)
22. Hansen, K., et al.: Assessment and validation of machine learning methods for predicting molecular atomization energies. J. Chem. Theory Comput. **9**(8), 3404–3419 (2013)
23. Hautier, G., Jain, A., Mueller, T., Moore, C., Ong, S.P., Ceder, G.: Designing multielectron lithium-ion phosphate cathodes by mixing transition metals. Chem. Mater. **25**(10), 2064–2074 (2013)
24. Huo, H., Rupp, M.: Unified representation for machine learning of molecules and crystals. arXiv preprint. arXiv:1704.06439 (2017)
25. Kang, K., Meng, Y.S., Bréger, J., Grey, C.P., Ceder, G.: Electrodes with high power and high capacity for rechargeable lithium batteries. Science **311**(5763), 977–980 (2006)
26. Kearnes, S., McCloskey, K., Berndl, M., Pande, V., Riley, P.: Molecular graph convolutions: moving beyond fingerprints. J. Comput. Aided Mol. Des. **30**(8), 595–608 (2016)
27. Kindermans, P.J., et al.: Learning how to explain neural networks: PatternNet and PatternAttribution. In: International Conference on Learning Representations (ICLR) (2018)
28. Kohn, W., Sham, L.J.: Self-consistent equations including exchange and correlation effects. Phys. Rev. **140**, A1133–A1138 (1965). https://doi.org/10.1103/PhysRev.140.A1133
29. Lee, C., Yang, W., Parr, R.G.: Development of the colle-salvetti correlation-energy formula into a functional of the electron density. Phys. Rev. B **37**(2), 785 (1988)
30. von Lilienfeld, O.A.: First principles view on chemical compound space: gaining rigorous atomistic control of molecular properties. Int. J. Quantum Chem. **113**(12), 1676–1689 (2013)

31. Lubbers, N., Smith, J.S., Barros, K.: Hierarchical modeling of molecular energies using a deep neural network. J. Chem. Phys. **148**(24), 241715 (2018)
32. Montavon, G., et al.: Machine learning of molecular electronic properties in chemical compound space. New J. Phys. **15**(9), 095003 (2013)
33. Montavon, G., Lapuschkin, S., Binder, A., Samek, W., Müller, K.R.: Explaining nonlinear classification decisions with deep taylor decomposition. Pattern Recogn. **65**, 211–222 (2017)
34. Montavon, G., Samek, W., Müller, K.R.: Methods for interpreting and understanding deep neural networks. Digit. Signal Process. **73**, 1–15 (2018)
35. Olivares-Amaya, R., et al.: Accelerated computational discovery of high-performance materials for organic photovoltaics by means of cheminformatics. Energy Environ. Sci. **4**, 4849–4861 (2011)
36. Pinheiro, P.O., Collobert, R.: From image-level to pixel-level labeling with convolutional networks. In: Proceedings of the IEEE Conference on Computer Vision and Pattern Recognition, pp. 1713–1721 (2015)
37. Pronobis, W., Tkatchenko, A., Müller, K.R.: Many-body descriptors for predicting molecular properties with machine learning: analysis of pairwise and three-body interactions in molecules. J. Chem. Theory Comput. **14**(6), 2991–3003 (2018). https://doi.org/10.1021/acs.jctc.8b00110
38. Ramakrishnan, R., Dral, P.O., Rupp, M., von Lilienfeld, O.A.: Quantum chemistry structures and properties of 134 kilo molecules. Sci. Data **1**, 140022 (2014)
39. Ruddigkeit, L., Van Deursen, R., Blum, L.C., Reymond, J.L.: Enumeration of 166 billion organic small molecules in the chemical universe database GDB-17. J. Chem. Inf. Model. **52**(11), 2864–2875 (2012)
40. Rupp, M., Tkatchenko, A., Müller, K.R., Von Lilienfeld, O.A.: Fast and accurate modeling of molecular atomization energies with machine learning. Phys. Rev. Lett. **108**(5), 058301 (2012)
41. Samek, W., Binder, A., Montavon, G., Lapuschkin, S., Müller, K.R.: Evaluating the visualization of what a deep neural network has learned. IEEE Trans. Neural Netw. Learn. Syst. **28**(11), 2660–2673 (2017)
42. Schütt, K.T., Arbabzadah, F., Chmiela, S., Müller, K.R., Tkatchenko, A.: Quantum-chemical insights from deep tensor neural networks. Nat. Commun. **8**, 13890 (2017)
43. Schütt, K.T., Glawe, H., Brockherde, F., Sanna, A., Müller, K.R., Gross, E.: How to represent crystal structures for machine learning: towards fast prediction of electronic properties. Phys. Rev. B **89**(20), 205118 (2014)
44. Schütt, K.T., Kindermans, P.J., Sauceda, H.E., Chmiela, S., Tkatchenko, A., Müller, K.R.: SchNet: a continuous-filter convolutional neural network for modeling quantum interactions. In: Advances in Neural Information Processing Systems, vol. 30, pp. 992–1002 (2017)
45. Schütt, K.T., Sauceda, H.E., Kindermans, P.J., Tkatchenko, A., Müller, K.R.: SchNet - a deep learning architecture for molecules and materials. J. Chem. Phys. **148**(24), 241722 (2018)
46. Shoichet, B.K.: Virtual screening of chemical libraries. Nature **432**(7019), 862 (2004)
47. Sifain, A.E., et al.: Discovering a transferable charge assignment model using machine learning. J. Phys. Chem. Lett. **9**, 4495–4501 (2018)
48. Simonyan, K., Vedaldi, A., Zisserman, A.: Deep inside convolutional networks: visualising image classification models and saliency maps. arXiv preprint. arXiv:1312.6034 (2013)

49. Vollhardt, K.P.C., Schore, N.E.: Organic Chemistry; Palgrave Version: Structure and Function. Palgrave Macmillan, Basingstoke (2014)
50. Xie, T., Grossman, J.C.: Crystal graph convolutional neural networks for an accurate and interpretable prediction of material properties. Phys. Rev. Lett. **120**(14), 145301 (2018)
51. Zeiler, M.D., Fergus, R.: Visualizing and understanding convolutional networks. In: Fleet, D., Pajdla, T., Schiele, B., Tuytelaars, T. (eds.) ECCV 2014. LNCS, vol. 8689, pp. 818–833. Springer, Cham (2014). https://doi.org/10.1007/978-3-319-10590-1_53
52. Zintgraf, L.M., Cohen, T.S., Adel, T., Welling, M.: Visualizing deep neural network decisions: prediction difference analysis. arXiv preprint. arXiv:1702.04595 (2017)

18
Interpretable Deep Learning in Drug Discovery

Kristina Preuer[1], Günter Klambauer[1], Friedrich Rippmann[2], Sepp Hochreiter[1], and Thomas Unterthiner[1(✉)]

[1] Johannes Kepler University Linz, 4040 Linz, Austria
{klambauer,hochreit,unterthiner}@ml.jku.at
[2] Computational Chemistry and Biology, Merck KGaA, 64293 Darmstadt, Germany

Abstract. Without any means of interpretation, neural networks that predict molecular properties and bioactivities are merely black boxes. We will unravel these black boxes and will demonstrate approaches to understand the learned representations which are hidden inside these models. We show how single neurons can be interpreted as classifiers which determine the presence or absence of pharmacophore- or toxicophore-like structures, thereby generating new insights and relevant knowledge for chemistry, pharmacology and biochemistry. We further discuss how these novel pharmacophores/toxicophores can be determined from the network by identifying the most relevant components of a compound for the prediction of the network. Additionally, we propose a method which can be used to extract new pharmacophores from a model and will show that these extracted structures are consistent with literature findings. We envision that having access to such interpretable knowledge is a crucial aid in the development and design of new pharmaceutically active molecules, and helps to investigate and understand failures and successes of current methods.

Keywords: Deep learning · Neural networks · Drug development · Target prediction

18.1 Introduction

The central goal of drug discovery research is to identify molecules that act beneficially on the human (or animal) system, e.g., that have a certain therapeutic effect against particular diseases. It is generally unknown how chemical structures have to look like in order to induce the wanted biological effects. Therefore, a large number of molecules have to be investigated to find a potential drug, leading to long drug identification times, and high costs. This is typically done by means of High-Throughput Screening (HTS), where a biological screening experiment is used to identify whether a molecule at a given concentration exhibits a

© Springer Nature Switzerland AG 2019
W. Samek et al. (Eds.): Explainable AI, LNAI 11700, pp. 331–345, 2019.
https://doi.org/10.1007/978-3-030-28954-6_18

certain biological effect or not. However, running a large number of these experiments is expensive and time-intensive. Therefore, using computational models as a means of "Virtual Screening", i.e. to predict these biological effects using computational methods and thereby avoiding physical screening, has a long tradition in drug development [15, 17].

In the past years, the advent of deep learning has allowed neural networks to become the best-performing method for predicting biological activities based on the chemical structure of the molecules [19, 21] mostly because of their ability to exploit the multi-task setting [31]. Recently, deep learning enabled automated molecule generation [22, 28, 35], which has become a new interesting application in the field of drug design. However, some generative models still have problems with mode collapse [33] and are hard to evaluate [25]. Interpretability of neural networks both for predictions and automated drug design could further push their performance, would increase their usability and would especially improve acceptance.

Nowadays, mainly two types of deep neural networks are most frequently used in Virtual Screening: descriptor-based feed-forward neural networks (see Sect. 18.3) and graph convolutional neural networks (see Sect. 18.4). Descriptor-based neural networks rely on predefined features, so-called molecular descriptors, whereas graph convolutional neural networks learn a continuous representation directly from the molecular graph. Neural networks take these discrete or numerical representation of a chemical molecule and calculate their prediction by feeding that representation through several layers of non-linear, differentiable transformations with many, often millions of, adjustable parameters. Unfortunately, the function that is encoded in such a neural network is typically impossible to interpret by humans. In other words: how the neural network reaches a conclusion is usually beyond the understanding of a human user. This work aims at bridging this gap in our understanding of neural network predictions for drug discovery. Although [2, 9, 27] have already focused on the difficult question how machine learning models can be interpreted, none of these works focus on an in depth analysis of both descriptor based and graph based deep learning models for QSAR predictions.

In this work, we first show how a trained neural network can be used to interpret which parts of a molecule are important for its biological properties, and then demonstrate how graph convolutional neural networks can be used to extract annotated chemical substructures, known as pharmacophores or toxicophores. We will empirically show that neural networks rely on pharmacophore-like features to reach their conclusions, similar to how a human pharmacologist would. Concretely, we will show in Sect. 18.3.1 that the units that form the layers of a neural network are pharmacophore detectors. Furthermore, we will demonstrate in Sect. 18.3.2 how indicative substructures can be determined for individual samples. In the second part of our analysis we will focus on graph convolutional neural networks and show that the identified pharmacophores extracted directly from the network match well-known, annotated substructures from the literature.

18.2   Learning from Molecular Structures

There are multiple scales at which molecules such as the example shown in Fig. 18.1 can be represented. Molecules can be represented by their molecular formula (1D), by their structural formula (2D), by their conformation (3D), by their mutual orientation and time-dependent dynamics or combinations of all these [5]. The choice of the right representation is task dependent and crucial for the learning algorithm. Most commonly, molecules are described by so-called Extended Connectivity Fingerprints (ECFPs) [26]. These 2D-descriptors represent the 2-dimensional structure as a bit vector indicating the presence and absence of predefined substructures and showed a high predictive performance in [18, 20, 24, 32]. Therefore, we will use these as descriptors for our first experiments described in Sect. 18.3.

However, newer approaches focus on direct end-to-end methods, where the molecular representation is directly learned from the molecular graph [7, 8, 13]. These graph convolutional methods learn molecular representations during the training process and are therefore able to learn wildcards and flexible substructures. We will analyse the representations learned by a graph convolutional network in Sect. 18.4.

Fig. 18.1. Example of a 2 dimensional structure representation of a molecule.

18.3   Descriptor-Based Feed Forward Neural Networks

A feed forward neural network consists of several layers of computing units. Each layer l takes as its input the vector of outputs $\mathbf{h}^l$ of the layer below it. In the first layer, we use the input data $\mathbf{h}^0 = \mathbf{x}$ instead. The layer l transforms its input according to some parameterized function to produce its own output

$$\mathbf{h}^{l+1} = f(\mathbf{h}^l \mathbf{W}^l)$$

where f is an activation function that is applied to each element, or "hidden unit", h_i^l of the vector individually. Each of these elements can be understood as a feature detector, which detects the presence or absence of some feature in its inputs. The nature of that feature is defined by the learned parameters

$\mathbf{W}^l$, but is usually very difficult to interpret, as the features are typically a highly abstract, non-linear function of the input features. However, we can show that when learned on typical drug development tasks, these hidden units encode features that are very similar to features used by pharmaceutical researchers for decades.

18.3.1   Interpreting Hidden Neurons

A common way to analyze chemical properties of small molecules is by looking at its structures. Atoms that are close together often form functional groups, which may have specific roles for binding to the respective biological targets. These functional groups form larger structures which then are responsible for the biological effect, by modulating a biological target (e.g. a protein or DNA). Work together to build reactive centers that steer chemical reactions. Binding to a specific target can only take place when the necessary active centers are present at exactly the right locations. The exact configuration of active centers is referred to as a pharmacophore [16]. In other words, a pharmacophore is a molecular substructure, or a set of molecular substructures that is responsible for a specific interaction between chemical molecules and biological targets. It is our hypothesis that the hidden units of a neural network learn to detect pharmacophores. To investigate this, we employed a strategy similar to [3], and trained a network that predicts the toxicology of molecules, using the data set from the Tox21 Data Challenge [11]. The data set contains around 12 000 molecules, for each of which twelve biological effects were measured in wet lab experiments with binary outcome ("toxic", "non-toxic"). These twelve biological effects served pose a multi-task classification problem. Deep Learning is the best performing method for this task [14, 20], and we follow the network architecture outlined in [14] for our experiments, using a network with 4 hidden layers of 1024 hidden units with SELU activation function. To represent our molecules, we use ECFPs [26] of radius 1, meaning that the input representation includes presence/absence calls of single atoms and small substructures with at most 5 atoms, but gives no concrete information about larger molecular substructures. The network still performed relatively well, with an average AUC over the 12 targets of 0.77, which would still place it among the top 10 models in the original Tox21 Data Challenge [20].

After training the network, we calculate the activation of the hidden units for all molecules in the training set, and relate them with presence/absence calls of pharmacophores calculated for the same molecules. For this, we used pharmacophores known to be relevant in toxicology [30], the so-called toxicophores. Starting from all the toxicophores in [30], we filter out those that were present in less than 20 of our molecules, leaving us with a total of about 650 toxicophores. For each hidden unit i and each toxicophore j, we then performed a Mann–Whitney U-Test to see if there was a significant difference in the activations between the molecules where a given toxicophore was present and the ones where it was absent. We then looked at correlations that were significant at

$p \leq 0.05$ after adjusting for the multiple testing using a very conservative Bonferoni correction. This leaves us with a total of ≈ 290 toxicophores that were significantly correlated with hidden units of the network.

Next, we investigated whether the hierarchy of the layers is associated with the complexity of the detected toxicophores. If a network learns some biologically meaningful information in one of its layers, it will still need to transport this information through all other layers to use it in its final prediction at the top layer. This means that every important toxicophore which is discovered in a lower layer will usually also reappear in all subsequent layers. Figure 18.2 shows which layers are discovering our known pharmacophores. It appears that the pharmacophores are primarily discovered in the first few layers. The later layers tend to mainly discover pharmacophores that are more complex. Here, we measure the complexity of a pharmacophore by the number of atoms involved in it. The results are well in line with the usual view of deep learning constructing more and more complex features in its higher layers [4].

We have demonstrated that neural networks learn pharmacophore detectors by correlating the hidden units with known toxicophores. However, not all samples contain a known toxicophore. Hence, we will demonstrate in the next section how indicative substructures can be identified for any input molecule.

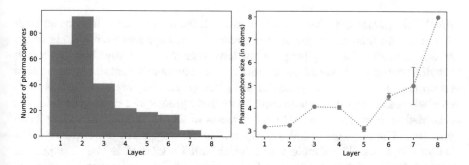

Fig. 18.2. Left: How many pharmacophores were found in each layer of the network. **Right:** Average size of the pharmacophore (in number of involved atoms) that are first discovered in a given layer. Error bars are standard errors. Note that there are no error bars for layer number 8, as only one pharmacophore was first discovered here.

18.3.2 Interpreting the Importance of Input Components

Several ideas have been proposed to explain the predictions from a neural network by attributing its decisions to specific input features. See Ancona et al. [1] for a short overview of gradient-based methods. One of these methods is Integrated Gradients [29], which calculates an attribution value $a_i(\mathbf{x})$ for each input dimension i. The value $a_i(\mathbf{x})$ can be interpreted as the contribution of i to changing the prediction from a baseline input $F(\mathbf{x}')$ to some specific input $F(\mathbf{x})$. It fulfills many useful properties, for example, it is guaranteed that $F(\mathbf{x}) - F(\mathbf{x}') = \sum_i a_i(\mathbf{x})$. Additionally, Integrated Gradients is the only method that works well even when there are multiplicative interactions between features of those considered by [1]. Furthermore, it is independent of the concrete choice of architecture, activation function or other hyperparameters. The method works by aggregating the gradients of the model's output on the straight path between $\mathbf{x}'$ and the target $\mathbf{x}$. When implementing the method, this integral is approximated by a sum:

$$
\begin{aligned}
a_i(\mathbf{x}) &= \int_{\alpha=0}^{1} \frac{\partial F(\gamma(\alpha))}{\partial \gamma_i(\alpha)} \frac{\partial \gamma_i(\alpha)}{\partial \alpha} d\alpha \\
&= (\mathbf{x}_i - \mathbf{x}'_i) \int_{\alpha=0}^{1} \left. \frac{\partial F(\tilde{\mathbf{x}})}{\partial \tilde{\mathbf{x}}_i} \right|_{\tilde{\mathbf{x}}=\mathbf{x}'+\alpha(\mathbf{x}-\mathbf{x}')} d\alpha \qquad (18.1) \\
&\approx (\mathbf{x}_i - \mathbf{x}'_i) \sum_{k=1}^{m} \left. \frac{\partial F(\tilde{\mathbf{x}})}{\partial \tilde{\mathbf{x}}_i} \right|_{\tilde{\mathbf{x}}=\mathbf{x}'+\frac{k}{m}(\mathbf{x}-\mathbf{x}')} \frac{1}{m}
\end{aligned}
$$

where $\gamma(\alpha) = \mathbf{x}' + \alpha(\mathbf{x} - \mathbf{x}')$ describes the interpolation path and m is the number of steps in the approximation that controls how exact the results will be. In our experiments, we obtained good results using an m of 1000. We used a zero vector as baseline for the feed-forward network, which represents a molecule in which all substructures are set to absent.

Alcohol Toy Data Set. As a proof of concept, we investigate if Integrated Gradients can be used to extract interpretable pharmacophores from a feedforward neural network. For this purpose we have constructed a toy data set which classifies compounds based on a simple rule: compounds containing an alcohol group (i.e. a hydroxy group bound to saturated carbon) are classified as positive, whereas compounds containing no hydroxy groups and carboxylic acids are classified as negative. The data set consists of 28 147 samples including 1 236 positives. The negative samples comprise 26 047 oxygen-free molecules and 864 carboxylic acids. The simplest rule which can be learned is that compounds without hydroxyl groups are classified as negative. In a second step a rule has to be found which discriminates between different hydroxyl groups.

In this experiment, we used a fully connected network based on ECFPs of radius 1. Radius 1 is sufficient for this task, because a hydroxyl group bound to a saturated carbon can be distinguished from a carboxylic acid group. In this experiment the model consisted of 4 layers of 1 024 units with SELU activation and achieved a test set AUC of > 0.99. To investigate what was important for the predictions, we used Integrated Gradients. The feed-forward network is based on ECFPs, hence Integrated Gradients provide attributions for each fingerprint. Each fingerprint consists of multiple atoms and one atom is part of multiple fingerprints. Hence, we calculated the atom-wise attribution as the sum of the attributions of all fingerprints in which this atom is part of.

Figure 18.3 shows the attributions for five randomly selected molecules for each of the three different molecule types. In the top, middle and bottom row negative samples without a hydroxyl group, negative samples with a carboxylic acid group and positive samples are displayed, respectively. In the first row, almost all atoms obtain a negative attribution, which is reasonable since non of these atoms are part of a hydroxyl group. Only in a small fraction (1.9%) of the tested atoms small positive attributions were observed. In the second row atoms with carboxylic acids are shown. Atoms not belonging to the acid group are in general classified as negative, whereas the hydroxyl group obtains positive attributions. This means that the network is still able to identify that the hydroxyl group is important for a positive classification. In the third row molecules with hydroxyl groups are displayed. This group was identified as positively contributing to the prediction in 0.83% of the atoms by the network and Integrated Gradients. Due to the overlapping fingerprints, neighboring atoms are also obtaining a slightly positive attribution, whereas atoms further away are still clearly identified as negative contributions. This toy example has shown that the Integrated Gradients can be used to extract the rules underlying the classification.

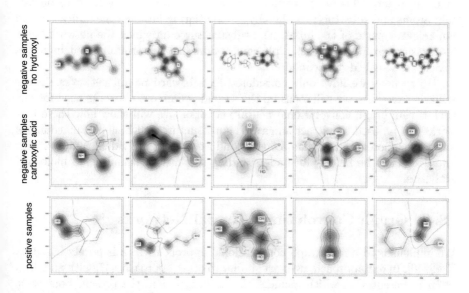

Fig. 18.3. Attributions assigned to the atoms by the model for the three types of compounds. 5 randomly chosen negative samples without hydroxyl groups, negative samples with carboxylic acid groups and positive samples are shown in the top, middle and bottom row, respectively. Dark red indicates that these atoms are responsible for a positive classification, whereas dark blue atoms attribute to a negative classification.

After this toy experiment, in which we knew which rules had to be applied to classify the samples, we will investigate whether the decisions for a more complex task are still interpretable and reasonable. For this purpose, we used the Tox21 data set.

Tox21 Challenge Data Set. In this experiment, we investigated whether Integrated Gradients can be used to extract chemical substructures which are important for classification into toxic and non-toxic chemical compounds on the largest available toxicity data set.

For this purpose, we trained a fully connected neural network consisting of 4 SELU layers with 2048 hidden units each 1024 ECFPs with radius 1 on the Tox21 data set. This network achieved a mean test AUC of 0.78. We followed the same procedure described above which consists of two major steps: applying Integrated Gradients and summarizing feature-wise attributions into atom-wise attributions. Figure 18.4 shows 12 randomly drawn, correctly classified positive test samples. It can be observed that positive attributions cluster together and form substructures. Please note that the model was trained only on small substructures, hence the formation of the larger pharmacophores is a direct result of the learning process. Together with the fact that some attributions are negative or close to zero, this indicates that the neural network is able to focus on certain atoms and substructures thereby differentiating between the indicative and not relevant parts of the input. The substructures on which the network bases its decision can be viewed as a pharmacophore-like substructure that indicates toxicity, a so-called "toxicophore".

Up to now, we have only considered feed-forward neural networks. In the following sections, we will focus on the second prominent networks used for virtual screen: graph convolutional neural networks. We will show how these networks can be used to extract annotated substructures, such as pharmacophores and toxicophores, rather than focusing on interpreting individual samples. This knowledge can be helpful for understanding the basic mechanisms of biological activities.

18.4   Graph Convolutional Neural Networks

We implemented a new graph convolutional approach which is purely based on Keras [6]. In our approach, we start similar to other approaches [7] with an initial atom representation which includes the atom type and the present bond type encoded in a one-hot vector. The network propagates this representation through several graph convolutional layers, whereas each layer performs two steps. In the first step, neighboring atoms are concatenated to form atom pairs. The convolutional filters slide over these atom pairs to obtain a pair representation. The second step is a summarization step, in which a new atom representation is determined. To obtain a new atom representation an order invariant pooling operation is performed over the atom-neighbor pairs. This newly generated representation is then fed into the next convolutional layer. This procedure is illustrated in Fig. 18.5(a). For training and prediction a summarization step which performs a pooling over the atom representations gives a molecular representation. This step is performed to have a molecular representation with a fixed number of dimensions so that the molecule can be processed by fully connected layers. This steps are shown in Fig. 18.5(b).

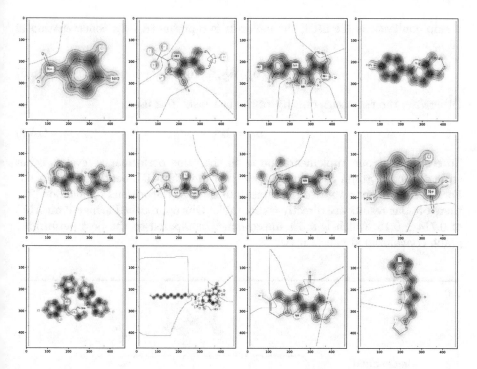

Fig. 18.4. Illustration of atom-wise attribution for 12 randomly drawn positive Tox21 samples. Attributions were extracted from a model trained on ECFP_2 fingerprints. The network clearly bases its decision on larger structures, which were built inside the model out of the small input features.

Formally, this can be described as following. Let G be a molecular graph with a set of atom nodes A. Each atom node v is initially represented by a vector $\mathbf{h}_v^0$ and has a set of neighboring nodes N_v. In every layer l the representations $\mathbf{h}_v^l$ and $\mathbf{h}_w^l$ are concatenated $(.,.)$ if w is a neighboring node of v to form the pair $\mathbf{p}_{vw}^l$. The pair representation $\mathbf{h}_{p_{vw}}$ is the result of the activation function f of the dot product of the trainable matrix $\mathbf{W}^l$ of layer l and the pair p_{vw}^l. The new atom representation $\mathbf{h}_v^{l+1}$ is obtained as a result of any order invariant pooling function g such as max, sum or average pooling.

$$\mathbf{p}_{vw}^l = (\mathbf{h}_v^l, \mathbf{h}_w^l) \quad \forall w \in N_v \tag{18.2}$$

$$\mathbf{h}_{p_{vw}}^l = f(\mathbf{p}_{vw}^l \mathbf{W}^l) \tag{18.3}$$

$$\mathbf{h}_v^{l+1} = g(\{\mathbf{h}_{\mathbf{p}_{vw}}^l | w \in N_v\}) \tag{18.4}$$

A graph representation $\mathbf{h}_G^l$ of layer l is obtained through an atom-wise pooling step.

$$\mathbf{h}_G^l = g(\{\mathbf{h}_v^l | v \in A\}) \tag{18.5}$$

If skip connections are used, the molecule is represented by a concatenation of all h_G^l.

$$\mathbf{h}_G = (\mathbf{h}_G^0, \mathbf{h}_G^1, ..., \mathbf{h}_G^L) \tag{18.6}$$

Otherwise, the representation $\mathbf{h}_G^L$ of the last layer L is used.

$$\mathbf{h}_G = \mathbf{h}_G^L \tag{18.7}$$

To ensure that our implementation is on the same performance level as other state of the art graph convolutions, we used the ChEMBL benchmark data set. For the comparisons we used the same data splits as the original publication [21], therefore our results are directly comparable. Our approached achieved an AUC of 0.714 ± 0.15, which is a 3% improvement compared to the best performing graph convolutional neural network.

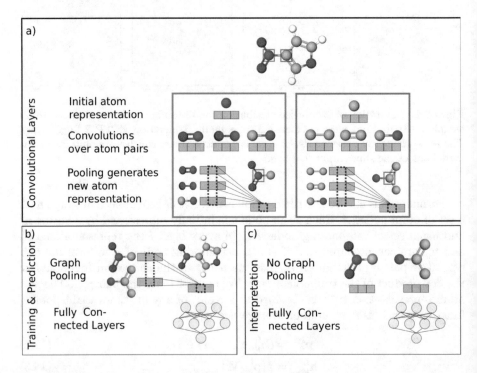

Fig. 18.5. (a) illustrates the convolutional steps for the blue and the grey center atoms. A new atom representation is formed by convolving over the atom pairs and a subsequent pooling operation. (b) shows the graph pooling step which follows the convolutional layers and the fully connected layers at the end of the network. These steps are performed in the training and prediction mode. (c) displays the forward pass which is performed to obtain the most relevant substructures. Here, the graph pooling step is omitted and the substructures are directly fed into the fully connected layers.

18.4.1 Interpreting Convolutional Filters

In this section, we aim at extracting substructures that induce a particular biological effect. This information is useful for designing new drugs and for identifying mechanistic pathways.

In graph convolutional neural networks the convolutional layers learn to detect indicative structures, and later fully connected layers combine these substructures to a meaningful prediction. Our aim is to extract the indicative substructures which are learned within the convolutional layers. This can be achieved by skipping the atom-wise pooling step of Eq. 18.5 and propagating the atom representation h_v^l through the fully connected layers as depicted in Fig. 18.5(c). Please note, that we can skip this step, because pooling over the atoms results again in a graph representation which has the same dimensions as the single atom representations. Therefore, we can use the feature representations of individual atoms in the same way as graph representations. Although the predictions are for single atoms, each atom was influenced by its proximity, therefore the scores can be understood as substructure scores. The receptive field of each atom increases with each convolutional layer by one, therefore h_v^l represents substructures of different sizes, depending on how many layers were employed. The substructures are centered at atom v and have a radius equal to the number of convolutional layers. Scores close to one indicate that the corresponding substructure is indicative for a positive label, whereas substructures with a score close to zero are associated with the negative label.

Ames Mutagenicity Data Set. For this experiment we used a well studied mutagenicity data set. This data set was selected because there exist a number of well-known toxic substructures in the literature which we can leverage to assess our approach. The full data set was published by [10], of which we used the subset originally published by [12] as training set and the remaining data as test set. The training set consisted of 4 337 samples comprising 2 401 mutagenic and 1 936 non mutagenic compounds. The test set consisted in total of 3 315 samples containing 1 690 mutagens and 1 625 non mutagens. We trained a network with 3 convolutional layers with 1 024 filters each followed by a hidden fully connected layer consisting of 512 units. The AUC of the model on the test set was 0.801.

To assess which substructures were most important for the network, we propagated a validation set through the network and calculated the scores for each substructure as described above. The most indicative substructures are shown in Fig. 18.6. Each substructure is displayed together with its SMILES representation and its positive predictive value (PPV) on the test set. These extracted substructures coincide very well with previous findings in the literature [12,23,34]. In Fig. 18.7 some genotoxic structures found in the literature are displayed with a matching substructure identified by our method. The extracted substructures are known to interact with the DNA. Most of the them form covalent bonds with the DNA via uni-molecular and bi-molecular nucleophilic substitutions (SN-1 and SN-2 reactions). Subsequently these modifications can lead severe DNA damage such as base loss, base substitutions, frameshift mutations and insertions [23].

Within this section we have demonstrated that our method for interpreting graph convolutional neural networks yield toxicophores consistent with literature findings and the mechanistic understanding of DNA damage.

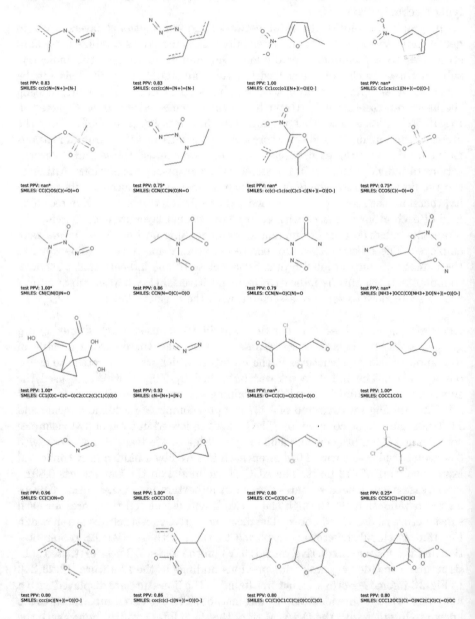

Fig. 18.6. This figure displays the structures extracted with our approach from the graph convolutional neural network. Below the structures the corresponding SMILES representation is shown together with the positive predictive value (PPV) on the test set. PPVs which were calculated on less than 5 samples are marked with an asterisk.

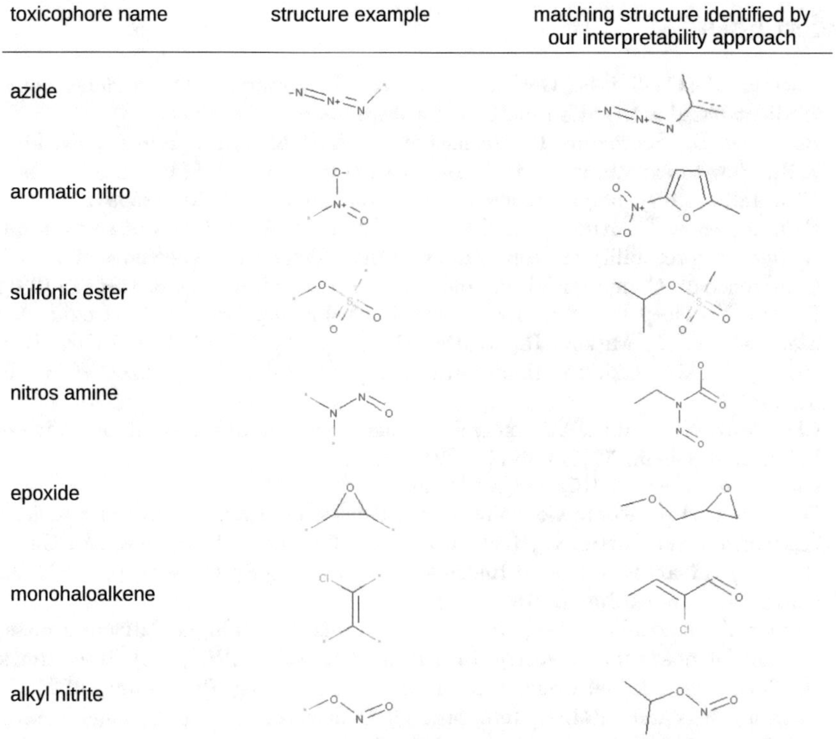

toxicophore name	structure example	matching structure identified by our interpretability approach
azide		
aromatic nitro		
sulfonic ester		
nitros amine		
epoxide		
monohaloalkene		
alkyl nitrite		

Fig. 18.7. This figure shows annotated SMARTS patterns identified in the literature as mutagenic together with matching structures identified by our interpretability approach. The names of the structures are shown in the first column, the SMARTS patterns found in literature are displayed in the second column and the last column shows a matching example of the top scoring substructures identified by our method.

18.5   Discussion

Having a black box model with high predictive performance is often insufficient for drug development: a chemist is not able to derive an actionable hypothesis from just a classification of a molecule into "toxic" or "not toxic". However, once a chemist "sees" the structural elements in a molecule responsible for a toxic effect, he immediately has ideas how to modify a molecule to get rid of these structural elements and thus the toxic effect. Therefore it is an essential goal is to gain additional knowledge and therefore it is necessary to shed light onto the decision process within the neural network and to retrieve the stored information. In this work, we have shown that the layers of a neural network construct toxicophores and that larger substructures are constructed in the higher layers. Furthermore, we have demonstrated that Integrated Gradients is an adequate method to determine the indicative substructures in a given molecule. Additionally, we propose a method to identify the learned toxicophores within a trained network and demonstrated that these extracted substructures are consistent with the literature and chemical mechanisms.

References

1. Ancona, M., Ceolini, E., Öztireli, C., Gross, M.: Towards better understanding of gradient-based attribution methods for deep neural networks (2018)
2. Baehrens, D., Schroeter, T., Harmeling, S., Kawanabe, M., Hansen, K., Müller, K.R.: How to explain individual classification decisions. J. Mach. Learn. Res. **11**, 1803–1831 (2010). http://dl.acm.org/citation.cfm?id=1756006.1859912
3. Bau, D., Zhou, B., Khosla, A., Oliva, A., Torralba, A.: Network dissection: quantifying interpretability of deep visual representations. In: Proceedings of the IEEE Conference on Computer Vision and Pattern Recognition, pp. 6541–6549 (2017)
4. Bengio, Y.: Deep learning of representations: looking forward. In: Dediu, A.-H., Martín-Vide, C., Mitkov, R., Truthe, B. (eds.) SLSP 2013. LNCS (LNAI), vol. 7978, pp. 1–37. Springer, Heidelberg (2013). https://doi.org/10.1007/978-3-642-39593-2_1
5. Cherkasov, A., et al.: QSAR modeling: where have you been? Where are you going to? J. Med. Chem. **57**(12), 4977–5010 (2014)
6. Chollet, F.: Keras (2015). https://keras.io
7. Duvenaud, D.K., et al.: Convolutional networks on graphs for learning molecular fingerprints. In: Cortes, C., Lawrence, N.D., Lee, D.D., Sugiyama, M., Garnett, R. (eds.) Advances in Neural Information Processing Systems 28, pp. 2224–2232. Curran Associates, Inc. (2015)
8. Gilmer, J., Schoenholz, S.S., Riley, P.F., Vinyals, O., Dahl, G.E.: Neural message passing for quantum chemistry. In: Precup, D., Teh, Y.W. (eds.) Proceedings of the 34th International Conference on Machine Learning. Proceedings of Machine Learning Research, PMLR, International Convention Centre, Sydney, Australia, vol. 70, pp. 1263–1272, 06–11 August 2017
9. Hansen, K., Baehrens, D., Schroeter, T., Rupp, M., Müller, K.R.: Visual interpretation of kernel-based prediction models. Mol. Inf. **30**(9), 817–826 (2011)
10. Hansen, K., et al.: Benchmark data set for in silico prediction of ames mutagenicity. J. Chem. Inf. Modeling **49**(9), 2077–2081 (2009)
11. Huang, R., et al.: Profiling of the Tox21 10K compound library for agonists and antagonists of the estrogen receptor alpha signaling pathway. Sci. Rep. **4** (2014)
12. Kazius, J., McGuire, R., Bursi, R.: Derivation and validation of toxicophores for mutagenicity prediction. J. Med. Chem. **48**(1), 312–320 (2005)
13. Kearnes, S., McCloskey, K., Berndl, M., Pande, V., Riley, P.: Molecular graph convolutions: moving beyond fingerprints. J. Comput. Aided Mol. Des. **30**(8), 595–608 (2016)
14. Klambauer, G., Unterthiner, T., Mayr, A., Hochreiter, S.: Self-normalizing neural networks. In: Advances in Neural Information Processing Systems 30 (NIPS) (2017)
15. Lavecchia, A.: Machine-learning approaches in drug discovery: methods and applications. Drug Discovery Today **20**(3), 318–331 (2015)
16. Lin, S.: Pharmacophore perception, development and use in drug design. Edited by Osman F. Güner. Molecules **5**(7), 987–989 (2000)
17. Lionta, E., Spyrou, G., Vassilatis, D.K., Cournia, Z.: Structure-based virtual screening for drug discovery: principles, applications and recent advances. Curr. Top. Med. Chem. **14**(16), 1923–1938 (2014)
18. Lounkine, E., et al.: Large-scale prediction and testing of drug activity on side-effect targets. Nature **486**(7403), 361–367 (2012). https://doi.org/10.1038/nature11159
19. Ma, J., Sheridan, R.P., Liaw, A., Dahl, G.E., Svetnik, V.: Deep neural nets as a method for quantitative structure-activity relationships. J. Chem. Inf. Model. **55**(2), 263–274 (2015)

20. Mayr, A., Klambauer, G., Unterthiner, T., Hochreiter, S.: DeepTox: toxicity prediction using deep learning. Frontiers Environ. Sci. **3**, 80 (2016)
21. Mayr, A., et al.: Large-scale comparison of machine learning methods for drug target prediction on ChEMBL. Chem. Sci. **9**(24), 5441–5451 (2018)
22. Olivecrona, M., Blaschke, T., Engkvist, O., Chen, H.: Molecular de-novo design through deep reinforcement learning. J. Cheminform. **9**(1), 48 (2017)
23. Plošnik, A., Vračko, M., Dolenc, M.S.: Mutagenic and carcinogenic structural alerts and their mechanisms of action. Arch. Ind. Hyg. Toxicol. **67**(3), 169–182 (2016)
24. Preuer, K., Lewis, R.P.I., Hochreiter, S., Bender, A., Bulusu, K.C., Klambauer, G.: DeepSynergy: predicting anti-cancer drug synergy with deep learning. Bioinformatics **34**(9), 1538–1546 (2017)
25. Preuer, K., Renz, P., Unterthiner, T., Hochreiter, S., Klambauer, G.: Fréchet ChemNet distance: a metric for generative models for molecules in drug discovery. J. Chem. Inf. Model. **58**(9), 1736–1741 (2018)
26. Rogers, D., Hahn, M.: Extended-connectivity fingerprints. J. Chem. Inf. Model. **50**(5), 742–754 (2010)
27. Schütt, K.T., Arbabzadah, F., Chmiela, S., Müller, K.R., Tkatchenko, A.: Quantum-chemical insights from deep tensor neural networks. Nat. Commun. **8**, 13890 (2017)
28. Segler, M.H., Kogej, T., Tyrchan, C., Waller, M.P.: Generating focused molecule libraries for drug discovery with recurrent neural networks. ACS Central Sci. (2017)
29. Sundararajan, M., Taly, A., Yan, Q.: Axiomatic attribution for deep networks. In: Proceedings of the 34th International Conference on Machine Learning (ICML) (2017)
30. Sushko, I., Salmina, E., Potemkin, V.A., Poda, G., Tetko, I.V.: ToxAlerts: a web server of structural alerts for toxic chemicals and compounds with potential adverse reactions. J. Chem. Inf. Model. **52**(8), 2310–2316 (2012)
31. Unterthiner, T., et al.: Multi-task deep networks for drug target prediction. In: Workshop on Transfer and Multi-task Learning of NIPS 2014, vol. 2014, pp. 1–4 (2014)
32. Unterthiner, T., et al.: Deep learning as an opportunity in virtual screening. In: Deep Learning and Representation Learning Workshop (NIPS 2014) (2014)
33. Unterthiner, T., Nessler, B., Klambauer, G., Heusel, M., Ramsauer, H., Hochreiter, S.: Coulomb GANs: provably optimal Nash equilibria viapotential fields. In: International Conference of Learning Representations (ICLR) (2018)
34. Yang, H., Li, J., Wu, Z., Li, W., Liu, G., Tang, Y.: Evaluation of different methods for identification of structural alerts using chemical ames mutagenicity data set as a benchmark. Chem. Res. Toxicol. **30**(6), 1355–1364 (2017)
35. Yang, X., Zhang, J., Yoshizoe, K., Terayama, K., Tsuda, K.: ChemTS: an efficient python library for de novo molecular generation. Sci. Technol. Adv. Mater. **18**(1), 972–976 (2017)

19
NeuralHydrology – Interpreting LSTMs in Hydrology

Frederik Kratzert[1]($\boxtimes$), Mathew Herrnegger[2]($\boxtimes$), Daniel Klotz[1],
Sepp Hochreiter[1], and Günter Klambauer[1]

[1] Johannes Kepler University Linz, 4040 Linz, Austria
{kratzert,hochreit,klambauer}@ml.jku.at
[2] University of Natural Resources and Life Sciences, Vienna, 1190 Vienna, Austria
mathew.herrnegger@boku.ac.at

Abstract. Despite the huge success of Long Short-Term Memory networks, their applications in environmental sciences are scarce. We argue that one reason is the difficulty to interpret the internals of trained networks. In this study, we look at the application of LSTMs for rainfall-runoff forecasting, one of the central tasks in the field of hydrology, in which the river discharge has to be predicted from meteorological observations. LSTMs are particularly well-suited for this problem since memory cells can represent dynamic reservoirs and storages, which are essential components in state-space modelling approaches of the hydrological system. On basis of two different catchments, one with snow influence and one without, we demonstrate how the trained model can be analyzed and interpreted. In the process, we show that the network internally learns to represent patterns that are consistent with our qualitative understanding of the hydrological system.

Keywords: Neural networks · LSTM · Interpretability · Hydrology · Rainfall-runoff modelling

19.1 Introduction

Describing the relationship between rainfall and runoff is one of the central tasks in the field of hydrology [21]. This involves the prediction of the river discharge from meteorological observations from a river basin. The basin or catchment of a river is defined by the area of which all (surface) runoff drains to a common outlet [40]. Predicting the discharge of the river is necessary for e.g. flood forecasting, the design of flood protection measures, or the efficient management of hydropower plants.

Within the basin of a river, various hydrological processes take place that influence and lead to the river discharge, including, for example, evapotranspiration, where water is lost to the atmosphere, snow accumulation and snow melt, water movement in the soil or groundwater recharge and discharge (see Fig. 19.1).

© Springer Nature Switzerland AG 2019
W. Samek et al. (Eds.): Explainable AI, LNAI 11700, pp. 347–362, 2019.
https://doi.org/10.1007/978-3-030-28954-6_19

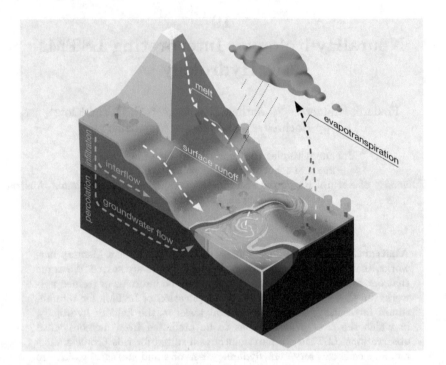

Fig. 19.1. Simplified visualization of processes and fluxes that influence the river discharge, such as precipitation, snow melt, surface runoff or subsurface flows.

The hydrological processes have highly non-linear interactions and depend, to a large degree, on the states of the system, which represent the memory of, e.g. a river basin. Consequently, hydrological models are formulated in a state-space approach where the states at a specific time depend on the input I_t, the system states at the previous time step S_{t-1}, and a set of parameters Θ_i [14]:

$$S_t = f(I_t, S_{t-1}; \Theta_i) \tag{19.1}$$

The discharge at a given time step t is driven by the system states and in consequences by the meteorological events of the preceding time steps. More generally, any output O_t of a hydrological system (e.g. the runoff) can be described as:

$$O_t = g(I_t, S_t; \Theta_j), \tag{19.2}$$

where $g(\cdot)$ is a mapping function that connects the states of the system and the inputs to the system output, and Θ_j is the corresponding subset of model parameters.

For making proficient predictions these non-linearities make it inevitable (at least in classical process-based hydrological models) to explicitly implement the hydrological processes [15,25,32,38]. However, defining the mathematical representations of the processes, including the model structures and determining their effective parameters so that the resulting system exhibits good performance and generalizable properties (e.g. in the form of seamless parameter fields) still remains a challenge in the field of hydrology [11,22,35].

A significant problem and limiting factor in this context is the frequently missing information regarding the physical properties of the system [5,10]. These tend to be highly heterogeneous in space (e.g. soil characteristics) and can additionally change over time, e.g. vegetation cover. Our knowledge of the properties on, or near the surface has increased significantly in the last decades. This is mainly due to advances in high-resolution air- as well as spaceborne remote sensing [7,13,29]. However, hydrology, to a significant part, takes place underground, for which detailed information is rarely available. In essence, the process-based models try to describe a system determined by spatially and temporally distributed system states and physical parameters, which are most of the time unknown.

In contrast, data-driven methods, such as Neural Networks, are solely trained to predict the discharge, given meteorological observations, and do not necessitate an explicit definition of the underlying processes. But these models have not the best reputation among many hydrologists because of the prevailing opinion that models "must work well for the right reasons" [20]. However, due to their predictive power, first studies of using Neural Networks for predicting the river discharge date back to the early 90s [9,12].

Recently, Kratzert et al. [23] used Long Short-Term Memory networks (LSTMs) [17] for daily rainfall-runoff modelling and could show that LSTMs achieve competitive results, compared to the well established Sacramento Soil Moisture Accounting Model [8] coupled with the Snow-17 snow model [2]. LSTM is an especially well-suited network architecture for Hydrological applications, since the evolution of states can be modelled explicitly through time and mapped to a given output. The approach is very similar to rainfall-runoff models defined by Eqs. 19.1–19.2 (in the case of the LSTM the system states are the memory cell states and the parameters are the learnable network weights, [23]).

The aim of this chapter is to show different possibilities that enable the interpretation of the LSTM and its internals in the context of rainfall-runoff simulations. Concretely, we explore and investigate the following questions: How many days of the past influence the output of the network at a given day of the year? Do some of the memory cells correlate with hydrological states? If yes, which input variables influence these cells and how? Answering these questions is important to (a) gain confidence in data-driven models, e.g. in case of the necessity for extrapolation, (b) have tools to understand possible mistakes and difficulties in the learning process and (c) potentially learn from findings for future applications.

19.1.1   Related Work

In the field of water resources and hydrology, a lot of effort has been made on interpreting neural networks and analyzing the importance of input variables (see [6] for an overview). However, so far only feed-forward neural networks have been applied in these studies. Only recently, Kratzert et al. [23] have demonstrated the potential use of LSTMs for the task of rainfall-runoff modelling. In their work they have also shown that memory cells with interpretable functions exist, which were found by visual inspection.

Outside of hydrology, LSTMs found a wide range of applications, which attracted researches to study on analyzing and interpreting the network internals. For example Hochreiter et al. [16] found new protein motifs through analyzing LSTM memory cells. Karpathy et al. [18] inspected memory cells in character level language modelling and identify some interpretable memory cells, e.g. cells that track the line-length or cells that check if the current text is inside brackets of quotation marks. Li et al. [24] inspected trained LSTMs in the application of sentence- and phrase-based sentiment classification and showed through saliency analysis, which parts of the inputs are influencing the network prediction most. Arras et al. [3] used Layer-wise Relevance Propagation to calculate the impact of single words on sentiment analysis from text sequences. Also for sentiment analysis, Murdoch et al. [28] present a decomposition strategy for the hidden and cell state of the LSTM to extract the contributions of single words on the overall prediction. Poerner et al. [33] summarize various interpretability efforts in the natural language processing domain and present an extension of the LIME framework, introduced originally by Reibiero et al. [34]. Strobelt et al. [36] developed LSTMVis, a general purpose visual analysis tool for inspecting hidden state values in recurrent neural networks.

Inspired by these studies, we investigate the internals of LSTMs in the domain of environmental science and compare our findings to hydrological domain knowledge.

19.2   Methods

19.2.1   Model Architecture

In this study, we will use a network consisting of a single LSTM layer with 10 hidden units and a dense layer, that connects the output of the LSTM at the last time step to a single output neuron with linear activation. To predict the discharge of a single time step (day) we provide the last 365 time steps of meteorological observations as inputs. Compared to Eq. 19.1 we can formulate the LSTM as:

$$\{c_t, h_t\} = f_{\mathrm{LSTM}}(i_t, c_{t-1}, h_{t-1}; \Theta_k), \tag{19.3}$$

where $f_{\mathrm{LSTM}}(\cdot)$ symbolizes the LSTM cell that is a function of the meteorological input i_t at time t, and the previous cell state c_{t-1} as well as the previous hidden state h_{t-1}, parametrized by the network weights Θ_k. The output of the system, formally described in Eq. 19.2, would in this specific case be given by:

$$y = f_{\mathrm{Dense}}(h_{365}; \Theta_l), \tag{19.4}$$

where y is the output of a dense layer $f_{\mathrm{Dense}}(\cdot)$ parametrized by the weights Θ_l, which predicts the river discharge from the hidden state at the end of the input sequence h_{365}.

The difference between the LSTM and conventional rainfall-runoff models is that the former has the ability to infer the needed structure/parametrization from data without preconceived assumptions about the nature of the processes. This makes them extremely attractive for hydrological applications.

The network is trained for 50 epochs to minimize the mean squared error using RMSprop [39] with an initial learning rate of 1e−2. The final model is selected based on the score of an independent validation set.

19.2.2   Data

In this work, we concentrate on two different basins from the publicly available CAMELS data set [1,31]. Basin A, which is influenced by snow, and basin B, which is not influenced by snow. Some key attributes of both basins can be found in Table 19.1.

Table 19.1. Basin overview.

Basin	ID[a]	Snow fraction[b]	Area (km^2)	NSE validation	NSE test
A	13340600[c]	56%	3357	0.79	0.76
B	11481200[d]	0%	105	0.72	0.72

[a]USGS stream gauge ID
[b]Fraction of precipitation falling with temperatures below 0 °C
[c]Clearwater river, CA
[d]Little river, CA

For meteorological forcings, the data set contains basin averaged daily records of precipitation (mm/d), solar radiation (W/m^2), minimum and maximum temperature (°C) and vapor pressure (Pa). The streamflow is reported as daily average (m^3/s) and is normalized by the basin area (m^2) to (mm/d). Approximately 33 years of data is available, of which we use the first 15 for training the LSTMs. Of the remaining years the first 25% is used as validation data by which we select the final model. The remaining data points (approx. 13 years) are used for the final evaluation and for all experiments in this study. The meteorological input features, as well as the target variable, the discharge are normalized by the mean and standard deviation of the training period.

One LSTM is trained for each basin separately and the trained model is evaluated using the Nash-Sutcliffe-Efficiency [30], an established measure used to evaluate hydrological time series given by the following equation:

$$\text{NSE} = 1 - \frac{\sum_{t=1}^{T}(Q_m^t - Q_o^t)^2}{\sum_{t=1}^{T}(Q_o^t - \bar{Q}_o)^2}, \tag{19.5}$$

where T is the total number of time steps, Q_m^t is the simulated discharge at time t ($1 \leq t \leq T$), Q_o^t is the observed discharge at time t and $\bar{Q}_o$ is the mean observed discharge. The range of the NSE is (−inf, 1], where a value of 1 means a perfect simulation, a NSE of 0 means the simulation is as good as the mean of the observation and everything below zero means the simulation is worse compared to using the observed mean as a prediction.

In the test period the LSTM achieves a NSE of above 0.7 (see Table 19.1), which can be considered a reasonably good result [27].

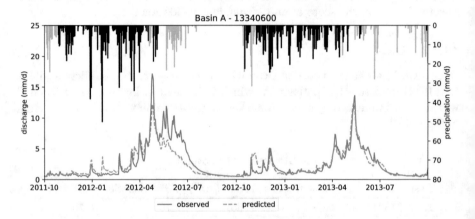

Fig. 19.2. Example of predicted (dashed line) and observed discharge (solid line) of two years of the test period in the snow influenced basin. Corresponding daily precipitation sums are plotted upside down, where snow (temperature below $0\,^{\circ}C$) is plotted darker.

Figure 19.2 shows observed and simulated discharge of two years of the test period in the snow influenced basin A, as well as the input variable precipitation. We can see that the discharge has its peak in the spring/early summer und that the model in the year 2012 underestimates the discharge, while in the second year it fits the observed discharge pretty well. The time lag between precipitation and discharge can be explained by snow accumulation in the winter months and subsequent melt of this snow layer in spring.

19.2.3   Integrated Gradients

Different methods have been presented recently to analyze the attribution of input variables on the network output (or any in-between neuron) (e.g. [3,4,19, 26,37]).

In this study we focus on Integrated gradients by Sundarajan et al. [37]. Here, the attribution of each input to e.g. the output neuron is calculated by looking at the change of this neuron when the input shifts from a baseline input to the target input of interest. Formally, let x be the input of interest, (in our case a sequence of 365 time steps with 5 meteorological observations each), x' the baseline input and $F(\cdot)$ the neuron of interest. Then the integrated gradients, for the i-th input variable x_i, can be approximated by:

$$\text{IntegratedGrads}_i^{\text{approx}}(x) := \frac{x_i - x'_i}{m} \sum_{k=1}^{m} \frac{\partial F(\tilde{x})}{\partial \tilde{x}_i}\bigg|_{\tilde{x}=x'+\frac{k}{m}(x-x')}, \qquad (19.6)$$

where m is the number of steps used to approximate the integral (here $m = 1000$). As baseline x', we used an input sequence of zeros.

19.2.4 Experiments

Question 1: How Many Days of Past Influence the Network Output?
The discharge of a river in a seasonal influenced region varies strongly throughout the year. For e.g. snow influenced basins the discharge usually peaks in the spring or early summer, when not only precipitation and groundwater but also snow melt contributes to the discharge generation. Therefore, at least from a hydrological point of view, the precipitation of the entire winter might be influential for the correct prediction of the discharge. In contrast, in drier periods (e.g. here at the end of summer) the discharge likely depends on far fewer time steps of the meteorological past. Since we provide a constant number of time steps (365 days) of meteorological data as input, it is interesting to see how many of the previous days are really used by the LSTM for the final prediction.

To answer this question, we calculate the integrated gradients for one sample of the test period w.r.t. the input variables and sum the integrated gradients across the features for each time step. We then calculate the difference from time step to time step and determine the first timestep t $(1 \le t \le T)$, at which the difference surpasses a threshold of 2e−3, with T being the total length of the sequence. We have chosen the threshold value empirically so that noise in the integrated gradient signal is ignored. For each sample the number of Time Steps Of Influence (TSOI) on the final prediction can then be calculated by:

$$\text{TSOI} = T - n \tag{19.7}$$

This is repeated for each day of each year in the test period.

Question 2: Do Memory Cells Correlate with Hydrological States?
The discharge of a river basin is frequently approximated by decomposing its (hypothetical) components into a set of interacting reservoirs or storages (see Fig. 19.1). Take snow as an example, which is precipitation that falls if temperatures are below $0\,^\circ\text{C}$. It can be represented in a storage S (see Eq. 19.1), which generally accumulates during the winter period and depletes from spring to summer when the temperatures rise above the melting point. Similarly other components of the system can be modelled as reservoirs of lower or higher complexity. The soil layer, for example, can also be represented by a bucket, which is filled - up to a certain point - by incoming water (e.g. rainfall) and depleted by evapotranspiration, horizontal subsurface flow and water movement into deeper layers, e.g. the groundwater body.

Theoretically, memory cells of LSTMs could learn to mimic these storage processes. This is a crucial property, at least from a hydrological point of view, to be able to correctly predict the river discharge. Therefore the aim of this experiment is to see if certain memory cells c_t (Eq. 19.3) correlate to these hydrological states S_t (Eq. 19.1).

Because the CAMELS data does not include observations for these states, we take the system states of the included SAC-SMA + Snow-17 model as a proxy. This is far from optimal, but since this is a well established and studied hydrological model, we can assume that at least the trend and tendencies of these simulations are correct. Furthermore, we only want to test in this experiment if memory cells correlate with these system states and not if they quantitatively match these states exactly. Of the calibrated SAC-SMA + Snow-17 we use the following states as a reference in this experiment:

- **SWE** (snow water equivalent): This is the amount of water stored in the snow layer. This would be available if the entire snow in the system would melt.
- **UZS** (upper zone storage): This state is calculated as the sum of the UZTWC (upper zone tension water storage content) and the UZFWC (upper zone free water storage) of the SAC-SMA + Snow-17 model. This storage represents upper layer soil moisture and controls the fast response of the soil, e.g. direct surface runoff and interflow.
- **LZS** (lower zone storage): This state is calculated by the sum of LZTWC (lower zone tension water content), LZFSC (lower zone free supplemental water storage content) and LZFPC (lower zone free primary water storage content). This storage represents the groundwater storage and is relevant for the baseflow[1].

For each sample in the test period we calculate the correlation of the cell states with the corresponding time series of these four states.

Question 3: Which Inputs Influence a Specific Memory Cell?
Suppose that we find memory cells that correlate with time series of hydrological system states, then a natural question would be if the inputs influencing these memory cells agree with our understanding of the hydrological system. For example, a storage that represents the snow layer in a catchment, should be influenced by precipitation and solar radiation in a contrarious way. Solid precipitation or snow would increase the amount of snow available in the system during winter. At the same time, solar radiation, providing energy for sublimation, would effectively reduce the amount of snow stored in the snow layer. Therefore, in this experiment we look in more detail at specific cells that emerged from the previous experiment and analyse the influencing variables on this cell. We do this by calculating the integrated gradients from a single memory cell at the last time step of the input sequence w.r.t. the input variables.

---

[1] Following [40] the baseflow is defined as: "Discharge which enters a stream channel mainly from groundwater, but also from lakes and glaciers, during long periods when no precipitation or snowmelt occurs".

19.3   Results and Discussion

19.3.1   Timesteps Influencing the Network Output

Figure 19.3 shows how many time steps with meteorological inputs from the past have an influence on the LSTM output at the time step of prediction (TSOI). The TSOI does thereby not differentiate between single inputs. It is rather the integrated signal of all inputs. Instead of using specific dates, we here show the temporal dimension in the unit day of year (DOY). Because all years of the test period are integrated in the plot, we show the 25%, 50% and 75% quantiles. For the sake of interpretation and the seasonal context, Fig. 19.3 also includes the temporal dynamics of the median precipitation, temperature and discharge.

The left column of Fig. 19.3 shows the results for snow influenced basin A. Here, 3 different periods can be distinguished in the TSOI time series:

(1) Between DOY 200 and 300 the TSOI shows very low values of less than 10–20 days. This period corresponds to the summer season characterised by high temperatures and low flows, with fairly little precipitation. In this period the time span of influence of the inputs on the output is short. From a hydrological perspective this makes sense, since the discharge in this period is driven by short-term rainfall events, which lead to a very limited response in the discharge. The short time span of influence can be explained by higher evapotranspiration rates in this season and lower precipitation amounts. Higher evapotranspiration rates lead to the loss of precipitation to the atmosphere, which is then missing in the discharge. The behaviour of the hydrograph is fairly easy to predict and does not necessitate much information about the past.

(2) In the winter period, starting with DOY 300, the TSOI increases over time reaching a plateau of 140–150 days around DOY 100. In this period the daily minimum temperature is below 0 °C, leading to solid precipitation (snow) and therefore water being stored as snow in the catchment without leading to runoff. This is underlined with the low discharge values, despite high precipitation input. Thus the LSTM has to understand that this input does not lead to an immediate output and therefore the TSOI has to increase. The plateau is reached, as soon as the minimum temperature values are higher than the freezing point. From a hydrological perspective, it is interesting to observe that the TSOI at the end of the winter season has a value which corresponds to the beginning of the winter season (∼DOY 300), when the snow accumulation begins. It should be noted that the transition between the winter period and the following spring season is not sharp, at least when taking the hydrograph as a reference. It is visible that, although the TSOI is still increasing, the discharge is also increasing. From a hydrological point of view this can be explained by a mixed signal in discharge - appart from melting snow (daily maximum temperature is larger than 0 °C), we still have negative minimum temperatures, which would lead to snow fall.

(3) In spring, during the melting season, the TSOI stays constant (DOY 100–160) followed by a sharp decrease until the summer low flows. During the

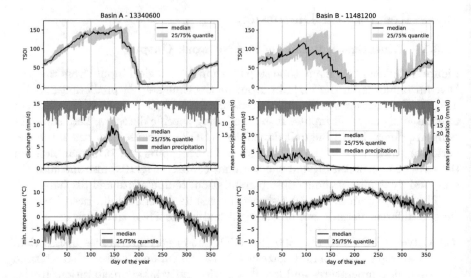

Fig. 19.3. Time steps of influence (TSOI) on the network output over the unit day of year (DOY) for the snow influenced basin A (left column) and the basin B without snow influence (right column). Corresponding median precipitation, discharge and minimum temperature are shown for reference. For the snow-influenced basin A, we can see for example that the TSOI increases during the winter period and is largest during the snow melting period (∼DOY 100–160), which matches our understanding of the hydrological processes.

main melting period, the TSOI of approximately 140–150 days highlights that the LSTM uses the entire information of the winter period to predict the discharge. The precipitation in this period now falls as rain, directly leading to runoff, without increasing the TSOI. At the same time, all the inputs from the winter still influence the river discharge explaining the stable plateau. The sharp decrease of the TSOI around DOY 160 represents a transition period where the snow of the winter continuously loses its influence until all snow has melted.

Although it has the same precipitation seasonality, Basin B (Fig. 19.3, right column) has different characteristics compared to basin A, since it is not influenced by snow. Here, only 2 different periods can be distinguished, where the transitions periods are however more pronounced:

(1) Between DOY 180 and 280, the warm and dry summer season, the catchment is characterised by very low flows. In this period the TSOI is also constantly low, with values of around 10–15 days. The discharge can be predicted with a very short input time series, since rainfall as input is missing and the hydrology does not depend on any inputs.
(2) Following summer, the wet period between DOY 280 and 180 is characterised by a steady increase in the TSOI. The temporal influence of rainfall

on runoff becomes longer, the longer the season lasts. The general level of runoff is now significantly higher compared to the summer. It does not solely depend on single rainfall events, but is driven by the integrated signal of inputs from the past, explaining the increasing TSOI. The TSOI reaches a maximum median value of around 120 days. This peak is followed by a decrease towards the end of the wet period, which is however not as rapid as in basin A. This distinct transition period in TSOI between wet and dry (∼DOY 100–180) season corresponds very well with the observed falling limb in the hydrograph. As the runoff declines, the influence of past meteorological inputs also declines. Compared to basin A, a higher variability in TSOI is evident, which can be explained with a higher variability in precipitation inputs in the single years. In basin A, a high interannual variability in the rainfall is also observable. However, the lower temperatures below freezing level lead to the precipitation falling as snow, and therefore act as a filter. This leads to a lower variability in discharge and in consequence in TSOI.

Overall, the TSOI results of the two contrasting basins match well with our hydrological understanding of the anterior days influencing the runoff signal at a specific day. It is interesting to see that the LSTM shows the capability to learn these differing, basin specific properties of long-term dependencies.

19.3.2   Correlation of Memory Cells with Hydrological States

Figure 19.4 shows the average correlation of every memory cell with the hydrological states considered in this experiment. The correlation is averaged over all samples in the test period and only correlations with $\rho > 0.5$ are shown. We can see, that in both basins some of the memory cells have a particularly high correlation with the provided hydrological states. For both basins several cells exhibit a high correlation with both, the upper (UZS) and lower (LZS), soil states. Although the majority of the cells show a positive correlation, negative correlations are also visible, which are however of a lower absolute magnitude.

The correlation between the LSTM cells and the baseflow influencing state LZS are significantly higher for the drier basin B. However, the baseflow index, a measure to define the importance of the contribution of the baseflow to total runoff, is lower for this basin. In basins A and B the ratios of mean daily baseflow to mean daily discharge are about 66% and 44%, respectively. Currently, we cannot explain this discrepancy. In the snow influenced basin, the trained LSTM also has some cells with high correlation with the snow-water-equivalent (SWE). The occurrence of multiple cells with high correlation to different system states can be seen as an indicator that the LSTM is not yet defined in a parsimonious way. Therefore, hydrologist can use this information to restrict the neural network even further.

In general, the correlation analysis is difficult to interpret in detail. Frequently, high correlations however exist, indicating a strong relationship between LSTM memory cells and system states from a well-established hydrological model.

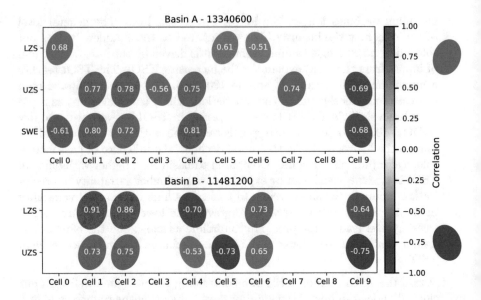

Fig. 19.4. Average correlations between memory cells and hydrological states for basin A (upper plot) and basin B (lower plot). Only correlations with $\rho > 0.5$ are shown. Ellipse are scaled by the absolute correlation and rotated by their sign (left inclined for negative correlation and right inclined for positive correlation)

19.3.3   Inspection of Memory Cells

In the first experiment, we used the integrated gradient method to calculate the attribution of the input variables on the output of the model. In this experiment, we apply it to analyse interactions between arbitrary neurons within the neural network (e.g. here, a memory cell at the last time step). The previous experiment proved that memory cells with a high correlation to some of the hydrological system states exist. The aim of this experiment is therefore to analyse the influences and functionality of a given cell. Here, we can explore (i) which (meteorological) inputs are important and (ii) at what time in the past this influence was high. We chose a *"snow-cell"* from the previous experiment to demonstrate this task, since the accumulation and depletion of snow is a particularly illustrative example. To be more precise, we chose to depict a single sample of the test period from the cell with the highest correlation to the SWE, which is memory cell 4 from basin A (see Fig. 19.4). Figure 19.5 shows the integrated gradients of the meteorological inputs in the top row, the evolution of the memory cell value in the second row and the corresponding change in minimum and maximum temperature in the third row.

One can see that the snow-cell is mainly influenced by the meteorological inputs of precipitation, minimum temperature, maximum temperature and solar radiation. Precipitation shows the largest magnitude of positive influence. Solar radiation in contrast has a negative sign of influence, possibly reproducing the sublimation from the snow layer and leading to a reduction of the snow state.

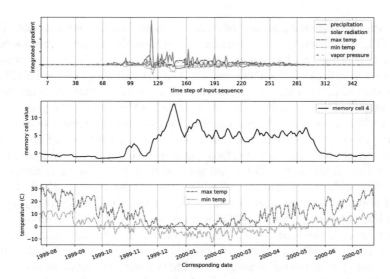

Fig. 19.5. Integrated gradient analysis of the snow-cell (cell 4) of the LSTM trained for basin A. Upper plot shows the integrated gradient signal on each input variable at each time step. The plot in the center shows the memory cell state over time for reference and the bottom plot the minimum and maximum daily temperature.

All influencing factors only play a role at temperatures around or below freezing level. This matches the expected behaviour of a snow storage from a hydrological point of view: Lower temperatures and concurrent precipitation are associated with snow accumulation. Consequently, this leads to an increase in magnitude of the memory cell value (especially for the first temperature below the freezing point). This can be observed e.g. in October 1999, where the temperature values decrease, the influences of the meteorological parameters appear and the snow-cell begins to accumulate. In contrast, as the temperature rises, the value of the cell decreases again, especially when the daily minimum temperature also rises above $0\,^{\circ}C$.

   This suggests that the LSTM realistically represents short- as well as long-term dynamics in the snow cell storage and their connection to the meteorological inputs.

19.4   Conclusion

LSTM networks are a versatile tool for time series predictions, with many potential applications in hydrology and environmental sciences in general. However, currently they do not enjoy a wide-spread application. We argue that one reason is the difficulty to interpret the LSTMs. The methods presented in this book provide solutions regarding interpretability and allow a deeper analysis of these models. In this chapter, we demonstrate this for the task of rainfall-runoff modelling (where the aim is to predict the river discharge from meteorological

observations). In particular, we were able to show that the processes learned by
the LSTM matches our comprehension of a real-world environmental system.

For this study, we focused on a qualitative analysis of the correspondence
between the hydrological system and the learned behaviour of the LSTM. In a
first experiment, we looked at the number of time steps of influence on the network output (TSOI) and how this number varies throughout the year. We saw
that the TSOI pattern matches our hydrological understanding of the yearly
pattern. In the next experiment, we looked at the correlation of the memory
cells of the network with some selected states of the hydrological system (such
as snow or soil moisture). We found some cells that exhibited relatively high
correlation with the chosen states, which strengthens the hypothesis that the
LSTM obtained some general understanding of the runoff-generation processes.
In the last experiment, we inspected a single memory cell that exhibited a high
correlation with the snow state. We analyzed the influencing inputs over time
through the integrated gradient method and could see, that the behavioral patterns manifested in the cell, closely resemble the ones suggested by hydrological
theory. We view this as a further underpinning of the observation that the internally modelled processes of the network follow some sort of physically viable
pattern. We hypothesize that this relation can be seen as a legitimization of
the LSTM usage within environmental sciences applications, and thus believe
that the presented methods will pave the way for its future in environmental-
modelling. The correspondence of the memory cells and the physical states can
be especially useful in novel situations, which often arise in this context. Environmental scientists and practitioners can exploit it (together with the proposed
techniques) to "peek into the LSTM" and argue about potential behaviours.
Our demonstration was certainly not exhaustive and should rather be seen as
indicative application study.

The most important message is that the combination of domain-knowledge
(in this case hydrology) and the insights provided by the proposed interpretation
techniques, provide the fundamentals for designing environmental forecasting
systems with neural networks. Consequently, we expect that the combination of
powerful data driven models (such as LSTMs) with the possibility of interpretation by experts will lead to new insights in the field of application.

References

1. Addor, N., Newman, A.J., Mizukami, N., Clark, M.P.: Catchment Attributes for
   Large-Sample Studies. UCAR/NCAR, Boulder, CO (2017)
2. Anderson, E.A.: National Weather Service River Forecast System - Snow Accumulation and Ablation Model. Technical report, November, US Department of
   Commerce, Silver Spring (1973)
3. Arras, L., Montavon, G., Müller, K.R., Samek, W.: Explaining recurrent neural
   network predictions in sentiment analysis. In: EMNLP 2017 Workshop on Computational Approaches to Subjectivity, Sentiment & Social Media Analysis (WASSA),
   pp. 159–168 (2017)

4. Bach, S., Binder, A., Montavon, G., Klauschen, F., Müller, K.R., Samek, W.: On pixel-wise explanations for non-linear classifier decisions by layer-wise relevance propagation. PLoS ONE **10**(7), e0130140 (2015)
5. Beven, K.: How far can we go in distributed hydrological modelling ? Hydrol. Earth Syst. Sci. **5**(1), 1–12 (2001)
6. Bowden, G.J., Dandy, G.C., Maier, H.R.: Input determination for neural network models in water resources applications. Part 1 - Background and methodology. J. Hydrol. **301**(1–4), 75–92 (2005)
7. Brenner, C., Thiem, C.E., Wizemann, H.D., Bernhardt, M., Schulz, K.: Estimating spatially distributed turbulent heat fluxes from high-resolution thermal imagery acquired with a UAV system. Int. J. Remote Sens. **38**(8–10), 3003–3026 (2017)
8. Burnash, R.J.C., Ferral, R.L., McGuire, R.A.: A generalised streamflow simulation system-conceptual modelling for digital computers. Technical report, US Department of Commerce National Weather Service and State of California Department of Water Resources (1973)
9. Daniell, T.M.: Neural networks-applications in hydrology and water resources engineering. In: Proceedings of the International Hydrology and Water Resources Symposium, vol. 3, pp. 797–802. Institution of Engineers, Perth, Australia (1991)
10. Freeze, R.A., Harlan, R.L.: Blueprint for a physically-based, digitally-simulated hydrologic response model. J. Hydrol. **9**(3), 237–258 (1969)
11. Gupta, H.V., Sorooshian, S., Yapo, P.O.: Status of automatic calibration for hydrologic models: comparison with multilevel expert calibration. J. Hydrol. Eng. **4**(2), 135–143 (1999)
12. Half, A.H., Half, H.M., Azmoodeh, M.: Predicting runoff from rainfall using neural networks. In: ASCE, New York, USA, pp. 760–765 (1993)
13. Hengl, T., et al.: SoilGrids250m: global gridded soil information based on machine learning, vol. 12 (2017)
14. Herrnegger, M., Nachtnebel, H.P., Schulz, K.: From runoff to rainfall: Inverse rainfall-runoff modelling in a high temporal resolution. Hydrol. Earth Syst. Sci. **19**(11), 4619–4639 (2015)
15. Herrnegger, M., Nachtnebel, H.P., Haiden, T.: Evapotranspiration in high alpine catchments - an important part of the water balance!. Hydrol. Res. **43**(4), 460 (2012)
16. Hochreiter, S., Heusel, M., Obermayer, K.: Fast model-based protein homology detection without alignment. Bioinformatics **23**(14), 1728–1736 (2007)
17. Hochreiter, S., Schmidhuber, J.: Long short-term memory. Neural Comput. **9**(8), 1735–1780 (1997)
18. Karpathy, A., Johnson, J., Fei-Fei, L.: Visualizing and understanding recurrent networks. arXiv preprint arXiv:1506.02078 (2015)
19. Kindermans, P.J., et al.: Learning how to explain neural networks: PatternNet and Pattern Attribution, pp. 1–12 (2017)
20. Klemeš, V.: Dilettantism in hydrology: transition or destiny? Water Resour. Res. **22**(9 S), 177S–188S (1986)
21. Klemes, V.: Stochastic models of rainfall-runoff relationship (1982)
22. Klotz, D., Herrnegger, M., Schulz, K.: Symbolic regression for the estimation of transfer functions of hydrological models. Water Resour. Res. **53**(11), 9402–9423 (2017)
23. Kratzert, F., Klotz, D., Brenner, C., Schulz, K., Herrnegger, M.: Rainfall-runoff modelling using Long Short-Term Memory (LSTM) networks. Hydrol. Earth Syst. Sci. **22**(11), 6005–6022 (2018)

24. Li, J., Chen, X., Hovy, E., Jurafsky, D.: Visualizing and Understanding Neural Models in NLP. arXiv preprint arXiv:1506.01066 (2015)
25. Lindström, G., Pers, C., Rosberg, J., Strömqvist, J., Arheimer, B.: Development and testing of the HYPE (Hydrological Predictions for the Environment) water quality model for different spatial scales. Hydrol. Res. **41**(3–4), 295 (2010)
26. Montavon, G., Lapuschkin, S., Binder, A., Samek, W., Müller, K.R.: Explaining nonlinear classification decisions with deep Taylor decomposition. Pattern Recogn. **65**, 211–222 (2017)
27. Moriasi, D.N., Gitau, M.W., Pai, N., Daggupati, P.: Hydrologic and water quality models: performance measures and evaluation criteria. Trans. ASABE **58**(6), 1763–1785 (2015)
28. Murdoch, W.J., Liu, P.J., Yu, B.: Beyond word importance: contextual decomposition to extract interactions from LSTMs. In: International Conference on Learning Representations (2018)
29. Myneni, R.B., et al.: Global products of vegetation leaf area and fraction absorbed PAR from year one of MODIS data. Remote Sens. Environ. **83**(1–2), 214–231 (2002)
30. Nash, J.E., Sutcliffe, J.V.: River flow forecasting through conceptual models part I - a discussion of principles. J. Hydrol. **10**(3), 282–290 (1970)
31. Newman, A., Sampson, K., Clark, M., Bock, A., Viger, R., Blodgett, D.: A large-sample watershed-scale hydrometeorological dataset for the contiguous USA. UCAR/NCAR, Boulder, CO (2014)
32. Perrin, C., Michel, C., Andréassian, V.: Improvement of a parsimonious model for streamflow simulation. J. Hydrol. **279**(1–4), 275–289 (2003)
33. Poerner, N., Schütze, H., Roth, B.: Evaluating neural network explanation methods using hybrid documents and morphosyntactic agreement. In: Proceedings of the 56th Annual Meeting of the Association for Computational Linguistics (Volume 1: Long Papers), vol. 1, pp. 340–350 (2018)
34. Ribeiro, M.T., Singh, S., Guestrin, C.: Why should I trust you? Explaining the predictions of any classifier. In: Proceedings of the 22nd ACM SIGKDD International Conference on Knowledge Discovery and Data Mining, pp. 1135–1144. ACM (2016)
35. Samaniego, L., et al.: Toward seamless hydrologic predictions across spatial scales. Hydrol. Earth Syst. Sci. **21**(9), 4323–4346 (2017)
36. Strobelt, H., Gehrmann, S., Pfister, H., Rush, A.M.: LSTMVis: a tool for visual analysis of hidden state dynamics in recurrent neural networks. IEEE Trans. Visual Comput. Graphics **24**(1), 667–676 (2018)
37. Sundararajan, M., Taly, A., Yan, Q.: Axiomatic attribution for deep networks. In: Proceedings of the 34th International Conference on Machine Learning, vol. 70, pp. 3319–3328. JMLR. org (2017)
38. Thielen, J., Bartholmes, J., Ramos, M.H., de Roo, A.: The European flood alert system – Part 1: concept and development. Hydrol. Earth Syst. Sci. Dis. **5**(1), 257–287 (2008)
39. Tieleman, T., Hinton, G.: Lecture 6.5 - RMSProp, COURSERA: Neural Networks for Machine Learning. Technical report (2012)
40. WMO, UNESCO (United Nations Educational, Scientific and Cultural Organization): International Glossary of Hydrology. No. 12, Geneva, Switzerland (1998)

20
Feature Fallacy: Complications with Interpreting Linear Decoding Weights in fMRI

Pamela K. Douglas[1,2（✉）] and Ariana Anderson[2]

[1] University of Central Florida, Orlando, FL, USA
pkdouglas16@gmail.com
[2] University of California, Los Angeles, CA, USA

Abstract. Decoding and encoding models are popular multivariate approaches used to study representations in functional neuroimaging data. Encoding approaches seek to predict brain activation patterns using aspects of the stimuli as features. Decoding models, in contrast, utilize measured brain responses as features to make predictions about experimental manipulations or behavior. Both approaches have typically included linear classification components. Ideally, decoding and encoding models could be used for the dual purpose of prediction and neuroscientific knowledge gain. However, even within a linear framework, interpretation can be difficult. Encoding models suffer from feature fallacy; multiple combinations of features derived from a stimulus may describe measured brain responses equally well. Interpreting linear decoding models also requires great care, particularly when informative predictor variables (e.g., fMRI voxels) are present in great quantity (redundant) and correlated with noise measurements. In certain cases, noise channels may be assigned a stronger weight than channels that contain relevant information. Although corrections for this problem exist, there are certain noise sources - common to functional neuroimaging recordings - that may complicate corrective approaches, even after regularization is applied. Here, we review potential pitfalls for making inferences based on encoding and decoding hypothesis testing, and suggest a form of feature fallacy also extends to the decoding framework.

Keywords: Encoding · Decoding · fMRI ·
Interpretable artificial intelligence

20.1 Representational Models

Understanding how neural activity gives rise to a range of complex thought and behavior is perhaps the philosopher's stone for modern neuroscience. Early theories suggested that a single neuron may be responsible for representing a

© Springer Nature Switzerland AG 2019
W. Samek et al. (Eds.): Explainable AI, LNAI 11700, pp. 363–378, 2019.
https://doi.org/10.1007/978-3-030-28954-6_20

complex object or concept, often referred to as the grandmother cell hypothesis [20]. This led to a variety of experiments measuring voltage fluctuations in single unit neurons [30], as well as a search for the ever elusive engram [4], a theorized biophysical manifestation of memory in the brain. Although studies using implanted electrodes in humans have demonstrated validity for a sparse representation in the brain [57], a substantial body of work over many decades has provided evidence for a distributed neural code (e.g., [58]). Neurons do not work in isolation; therefore, understanding how neurons interact to represent information may ultimately rest on deciphering the dynamics of complex neural population codes [55].

In humans, functional MRI (fMRI) has been a core tool used to study the functional segregation and specialization in the human brain noninvasively [18]. FMRI measurements do not reflect single neuron activity, but rather local changes in blood oxygen content, thought to indirectly reflect increased firing in neural ensembles [46]. Hemodynamic fMRI signals are temporally smoothed with variable delays and magnitudes across regions of the cortex (e.g., [24,39,44,65]). Nonetheless, these recordings have successfully been used to model representations of basic sensory perception [9,33], categorical object recognition [26,35], semantic content [32], facial recognition [8,34], and belief decisions [15,16].

Early fMRI methods adopted a mass univariate approach for brain mapping purposes (i.e., to determine where activity varied during a task compared to a baseline condition). However, even within this classic general linear model (GLM) framework, incorrect inferences based on the results became an issue of concern. For example, Poldrack [54], pointed out that inferring a cognitive process was engaged based on activation in a particular brain region was not deductively valid, referring to this practice as reverse inference. This conclusion requires that a particular brain region be activated exclusively for a specific cognitive task [54]. Secondly, the extent to which neural code is distributed, the relative modularity, and redundancy in representation has remained unclear. For example, early facial recognition studies in fMRI assumed that the fusiform face area (FFA) was an approximately homogeneous module with similar visual tuning preferences for faces [34]. This assumption was based largely results using classic univariate approaches, where voxels are analyzed independently at the first level of analysis. More recently, patterns of voxel activity in the FFA region were analyzed in combination, revealing multiple specialized subdomains within the FFA, each with specific categorical visual tuning preferences [8]. Therefore analyzing voxel measurements averaged across conditions independently may potentially miss distributed representational patterns related to stimulus categories [49].

One potential reason for this could be that spatial smoothing is typically applied after analyzing voxels independently to improve statistical power and signal-to-noise ratio [64]. Intuitively, the effects of spatial smoothing may potentially diminish or average out unique information in neighboring voxels. However, the hemodynamic fMRI signal is not only temporally delayed, but also spatially extended, particularly in superficial laminar layers of the cortex [39]. Therefore it is unlikely that a voxel is sampling a specific neuronal tuning profile. The effects of spatial smoothing across a variety of kernel widths have been studied extensively for both conventional GLM analysis [48], and for decoding approaches [27]. Interestingly, the effects of spatial smoothing using typical kernel sizes (0–8 mm) appear to have little to no effect on the ability to decode representations [53]. Here, we briefly review encoding and decoding techniques for representational fMRI analysis. We suggest that both of these techniques should be interpreted with care, and the inferences made should reflect the tool used to model the data. Over-interpretation of the tools used to analyze features used for predictive purposes has been referred to as feature fallacy. This issue has been addressed recently with a focus on encoding models [42]. We therefore focus mostly on decoding schemes and the inferences that one can make by applying this framework to fMRI data.

20.1.1   Encoding Models

The goal of representational fMRI analysis is to build models of response patterns, and ideally to additionally test their ability to generalize to new stimuli and conditions [42]. Representational fMRI models have been applied successfully to discriminate between, model, and predict responses across a rich variety of experimental conditions (e.g., [28, 29, 33]). Encoding and decoding are the two most popular multivariate methods used to study representations in fMRI measurements. Both methods have complementary goals, yet anti-correlated analysis pathways. Encoding models are referred to as forward models; these begin with the stimulus and attempt to predict measured responses based on features derived from the stimuli [35, 50, 51]. For example, a set of Gabor functions, derived from natural visual stimuli, were used to describe fMRI responses in early visual processing (V1) areas [35]. Salience and pitch features were used within an encoding framework to predict tonotopically organized cortical processing of naturalistic sounds [9]. The average brain response is typically modeled using a linear combination of these features, and the fit of the models assessed via cross-validation [11].

The ability of these encoding models to predict brain responses is quite impressive. However, as with any modeling approach, the inferences made should reflect the methodology appropriately. For example, in the case of a simple linear encoding model, when the number of features approaches the number of experimental conditions, multiple feature sets may predict activation responses equally well. For example, finger movements, movement synergies, and even random vectors appear to describe representations in sensory motor cortex equally well [12]. Diedrichsen has referred to this issue as feature fallacy, or an over interpretation of the tools used to describe complex activity in a latent space. From a systems identification point of view, this may be analogous to a system that is unidentifiable or quasi-identifiable, where multiple combinations of parameters may describe the data equally well [47]. This aspect of encoding models has motivated the development of other representational techniques including pattern component modeling and representational similarity analysis, for further discussion see [11, 43].

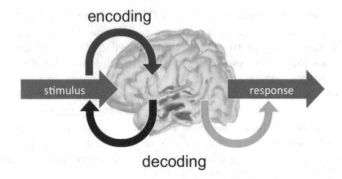

Fig. 20.1. Encoding analyses work in the same direction as information processing in the brain. Features derived from the stimulus (e.g., contours of a visual stimulus) are used as features to predict brain response patterns. Decoding analyses work by utilizing brain response patterns to make predictions (or reconstructions) of the stimulus class or the subjects' response to an experimental paradigm. Less commonly, decoding approaches are used to make predictions about aspects of a behavioral response.

20.1.2   Linear Decoding Models & Explicit Information

Decoding models use machine learning (ML) techniques to find patterns of voxels that collectively discriminate between experimental conditions or predict group membership. Decoding has grown in popularity ever since early applications that demonstrated the ability to discriminate between object categories using fMRI data [26]. Part of the allure of decoding methods is the notion that greater insight into the patchy functional segregation in the brain may be achieved by analyzing voxel measurements in combination as opposed to individually [17]. Decoding, backward models, start with the activity patterns and attempt to see how much can be learned about the stimulus from response patterns [50] (Fig. 20.1). One particularly impressive application of decoding when applied in this fashion is stimulus reconstruction [51]. In certain cases, decoding studies have used fMRI voxel patterns to predict a behavioral response to stimuli (e.g., decision making) [16,23], however this type of application has been less common.

Classification techniques ranging from decision trees to deep neural networks have been applied to neuroimaging data, and non-linear models are now increasingly applied to fMRI data for both decoding [19,21,37,40,60,67] and encoding purposes [62]. However, the most widely adopted practice historically has been to assume that the data from different categories can be shattered linearly with a hyperplane. There are a number of reasons why the linear classification approach has been widely adopted in the fMRI community – beyond computational efficiency. First, linear classifiers (e.g., linear support vector machine) outperformed more complex classifiers in a few of the early applications of ML to fMRI data [7]. Second, linear classifiers were thought to be easier to interpret [33,52]. Lastly, the ability to decode representations linearly is thought to reflect information that is explicit, and closer to the level of read out. For example, visual representations for object category are thought to be hopelessly entangled in early visual areas (V1). However, after many transformations through layers of the visual cortex, the information is thought to be represented more explicitly, and therefore more accessible to linear classification [10]. Consistent with this, the performance of linear classifiers has been shown to increase across levels of visual processing for object category discrimination [31].

20.1.3   Interpretation Pitfalls - Even with Linear Decoders

The process of training and testing a linear classifier furnishes predictive accuracies along with a set of feature weights, typically called the w vector, whose elements collectively influence the classification boundary in feature space. In neuroscience applications, the goal is often not only to classify accurately, but also to interpret the patterns that give rise to a prediction [52]. In numerous studies, feature weights (w) were simply mapped directly back onto their corresponding input voxels, producing weight maps, which resembled brain activation patterns that might result from a conventional GLM analysis. However, there are problems with interpreting weight maps in this manner, even in the simplest case of linear decoders. We will use the simplest case of binary classification from two measurement channels to illustrate this issue.

Suppose we have two time series measurements from two voxels, $v_1(t)$ and $v_2(t)$, sampled at t timepoints and we are trying to discriminate between two tasks or populations. For this particular binary classification task, the first channel, $v_1(t)$ contains class specific information, and is correlated with the task time series $y(t)$. In this $v_1(t)$ channel, the class means differ, and it is therefore informative for this bivariate classification. In the second channel $v_2(t)$, the class means are approximately equal, and this channel may therefore be considered "noise". In Fig. 20.2, case 1, we consider the case when the covariance between the two voxel measurements is approximately zero, and the goal is to predict the class label y, where:
Displayed equations are centered and set on a separate line.

$$y \in \{+1, -1\} \tag{20.1}$$

In the simplest case of a linear discriminant analysis (LDA) binary classification scheme with approximately zero covariance between measurements, the noise voxel would not contribute substantially to either improving sensitivity or to substantially altering the feature weights. Here, the feature weights assigned to each voxel are w_{v_1} and w_{v_2}. Therefore, when the covariance between measurements is approximately zero, the weight map would reflect the contribution of each voxel to the decision label appropriately (Fig. 20.2, case 1). Note that from a geometric perspective, the wLDA weight vector is orthogonal to the decision boundary.

In most cases, some covariance between voxel measurements is expected. This may be due to non-neural latent sources influential across measurements (e.g., motion) or perhaps due to nearby voxels sampling some degree of overlapping fluctuations from the vasculature unrelated to the task. In this case, the covariance between voxels would not be equal, and the covariance between channels would influence the feature weights. In some sense, this aspect of decoding is attractive because it makes it possible to cancel out noise, thereby improving sensitivity and accuracy of a classifier [3,45].

In certain cases, it is possible for the Bayes-optimal classification within an LDA framework to assign a considerably stronger weight to the noise channel than the voxel containing information (see Fig. 20.2, case 2). In this case, strong weights may be observed in spatial locations on weight maps whose measurements are (approximately) statistically independent from the brain process under study. Therefore, it is clear that feature weights should not be interpreted in a direct manner (e.g., [22,25]). In this sense, presenting feature weights as brain maps may lead to an implied interpretation that these images correspond to meaningful representational patterns in the neural code.

20.1.4   Activation Maps Replace Weight Maps

Haufe et al. [25] highlighted this issue of interpreting decoding weights and proposed a solution to this problem. We continue with the same two class problem with two measurement channels. In the linear case, we first express the voxel data as a sum of k latent factors, s, which are weighted by their corresponding activations patterns a plus additive noise. Therefore, the data can be expressed as:

$$v(t) = \Sigma_k a_k s_k(t) + \epsilon(t) \tag{20.2}$$

where $a_k \in R^M$, and $s_k(t) \in \{1, ...K\}$.

This represents the forward model, which is analogous to the encoding case. Decoding models correspond to supervised backward models, where the goal is to extract these latent factors as a function of observations. In the linear case, the mapping from observations to factors can be summarized by an $n \times m$ transformation matrix, W as:

$$W^T v(t) = \hat{s}(t) \tag{20.3}$$

The proposed remedy for the linear square case where $K = M$ is as follows. The extraction filters W form an invertible matrix, and the data can be expressed as a noise free forward model:

$$v(t) = W^{-T} \hat{s}(t) \tag{20.4}$$

where activations patterns in matrix form are:

$$A = W^{-T} \tag{20.5}$$

Although this approach of projecting feature weights or extraction filters onto activation patterns is useful [25], read out from this process remains complex.

20.1.5 Noise May Complicate Activation Corrections

Projecting feature weights onto activation maps may enhance interpretability, redundancy, noise, and regularization can further complicate interpretation – even after projection onto activation maps – depending on the classifier employed. In the presence of non-Gaussian noise seen with artifacts such as scanner drift, motion, and periodic biorhythms, projecting feature weights onto activation maps yields spurious patterns; for example, noise typically associated with scanner drift can cause the activation weights of noise sources to be greater than those of task-associated signals. This suggests that certain decoding or backward models are inherently limited by their approaches to successfully model the structure of incoming noise, and that improper assumptions of this noise structure may yield misleading interpretive maps [13].

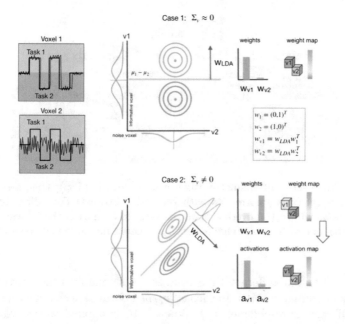

Fig. 20.2. (Top panel) Case 1: two voxel time series with equal variance, but approximately zero covariance (left). Class means differ in voxel 1 $(v_1(t))$, while voxel 2 $(v_2(t))$ does not contain class-specific information, as demonstrated with projections of the data onto each voxel dimension. The w vector, or extraction filter, shown in red, is orthogonal to the decision boundary (grey). In this case, the weights wv1 and wv2 appropriately reflect the information in each channel. (Lower panel) Case 2: Covariance between signal and noise voxels can lead to inappropriate assignment for voxel feature weights and weight maps. However, after projection onto activations (Eq. 20.4), the correct weights are recovered. Figure inspired by Kriegeskorte and Douglas 2019 and Haufe et al. [25].

Different types of noise common in functional MRI recordings, can contaminate the ability to recover information even in the extremely simple case:

a linear discriminant analysis (LDA) classifier with two features. Continuing with the same illustrative example as before, with two voxels measurements v1(t) and v2(t), and and a binary classification task. The first channel is informative, and the second channel contains little class-specific information. Here, we are interested in testing the extent to which back projecting the weights or extraction filters onto activations is effective, when the noise channel varies. In all illustrative cases, the correlation between the output variable and the measurements remained constant with $r = \mathrm{Corr}(y(t), v_1(t)) = 0.75$, and $r = \mathrm{Corr}(y(t), v_2(t)) = 0.09$. For classification, we applied a simple LDA model, assuming Gaussian within-class distributions.

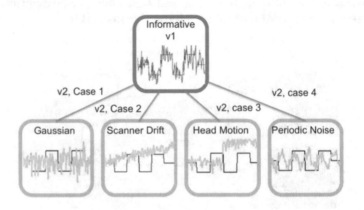

Fig. 20.3. Time series of simulated voxel measurements. (Top) Time series for the informative voxel $(v_1(t))$ correlates with the task. (Bottom) Four different cases of noise measurements $(v_2(t))$ overlaid with the task. In each case, the informative voxel is paired with one of the noise channels. All simulated measurements contained equal variance.

In Fig. 20.3, four different time courses are simulated that represent noise commonly measured in fMRI. In each case, the informative channel (v_1) is paired with a different noise channel (v_2). When LDA is applied to two voxels measurements, one noisy and the other informative, the weight vector assigns a strong weight to the noise channel, and a weak weight to the informative channel (Fig. 20.4). However, when these weights are mapped onto activations using Eq. 20.2, we effectively recover the true information contained, but only for the Gaussian noise case. In cases 2–4, the activation recovery method is ineffective. Scanner drift is very common in the scanning environment, and temporally contiguous portions of drift typically remain in the data, even after high pass filtering. In the case of drift noise, the informative measurement is correctly assigned a higher weight than the noise measurement. However, after projecting onto activations, the reverse happens - the noise measurement is assigned a stronger weight than the channel with class specific information.

Noise due to head motion is also common in the scanning environment. Although motion correction algorithms exist, head motion that remains in the data has continued to cause problems with fMRI analysis [56]. In the case where the motion introduced causes a step change in the noise, the result is similar to that of above in the drift motion case; the activations do not reflect the actual information within the data.

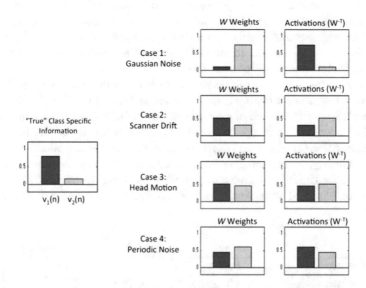

Fig. 20.4. The influence of each of the noise cases (from Fig. 20.3) on fMRI decoding weights and activation recovery. (From left to right, Column 1) The ground truth for information contained in each measurement is the correlation between the voxel time series and the task time series. (Column 2) Weights assigned to the informative channel (blue) and noise channel (gold). (Column 3) Activations recover the "true" weight, but only for the case of Gaussian noise.

20.1.6   Redundancy and Regularization

Redundancy is also thought to be common in fMRI measurements, since spatially contiguous voxels may contain similar information. This observation has has incited debate about the benefit [36] or lack thereof [5] of a separate feature selection step prior to classification. Nonetheless, redundancy also further complicates the issue of interpretation in backward models – even after regularization is applied.

In functional neuroimaging, features can be extracted from a diverse set of variables (e.g., [6]). Interestingly the extent to which features are statistically independent can also influence the ability to interpret decoding output. For example, in the rare circumstance where all features are completely independent and orthogonal, then their inner product is zero, making the weights directly interpretable. In this case, a naive Bayes classifier may be applied since each element is treated as conditionally independent (e.g.,[14]). However, in most cases, the features are not statistically independent (i.e., spatially adjacent neuroimaging voxels) and may contain redundant information.

In early decoding studies, feature selection was applied a separate step for computational and numerical considerations. In the simplest case the data were simply variance thresholded. Since then, t-test filtering, wrapper methods and a priori selection of an ROI have been used to reduce the number of inputs. However, many of these methods favor selection of features that maximize accuracy individually [22]. The searchlight method has also remained popular, whereby spatially contiguous and highly correlated voxels are pooled together. However, this method may still result in spatially distinct searchlight features that have highly correlated temporal information.

Here, we continue with our example with the simple LDA case. However, instead of using a noise channel, we use a redundant channel, $v_j(t)$. Figure 20.5 shows the timecourse of each of example channels, both of which are informative. Figure 20.5 shows what happens to the activation assigned to the initial informative channel $v_1(t)$ when additional redundant features are added to the LDA classifier. Clearly, introducing redundant channels lowers the resulting activation weights for the informative channel. Groups of highly-relevant features may therefore be assigned very small feature weights and activations, despite their relevance.

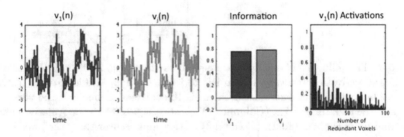

Fig. 20.5. Influence of adding redundant voxels to an LDA classifier. From left to right. Time series of voxel measurements with added Gaussian noise for an informative voxel (blue) and another similar informative voxel (green), each with similar class specific information. (right) As additional approximately redundant voxels are added to the classifier, the activation on v1 diminishes.

20.2   Discussion

Representational models have become core tools for making sense of functional neuroimaging data in the cognitive and computational neurosciences [42,43]. Both encoding and decoding models typically include fitted linear components. Linear models have been widely applied in functional neuroimaging due to their simplicity, speed, and putative ease of interpretation. However, even with linear classifiers, the feature weights or model parameters interact to predict the response pattern label. This multivariate interaction renders the interpretation of feature weights complex, and great care should be taken when making inferences, even within the simple linear case. Both non-Gaussian noise and redundancy may effect the ability to recover information.

In this chapter, we illustrated issues with interpreting decoding weights (and activations) using a very simple LDA decoder on a bivariate task. When classes are Gaussian with shared covariance, the optimal discriminant is linear, and the LDA method rests on the assumptions of multivariate normality and homoscedasticity [1]. Therefore it is unsurprising that noise profiles which deviate from these assumptions would corrupt the reconstructions of weights as shown here. A simple perceptron, which may be considered the building block for feedforward neural networks, can be implemented to perform linear discrimination, and even complex neural networks can be susceptible to adversarial attacks. The most commonly studied adversarial attack is the application of bounded noise to images, which results in perturbations that are imperceivable to the human eye [61]. Understanding the extent to which problems arise due to noise artifacts such as movement, which may produce an intermittent large amount of variance in selected voxels, may be an area of future research.

Within this simple linear framework, redundancy was also problematic. After only a few redundant voxels, activations diminished considerably, and dropped nearly to zero after one hundred. Initially, one hundred redundant features may appear large. However, fMRI data typically contain over 100,000 voxels. If voxels themselves are being used as the features for decoding, it does not seem unreasonable to expect that many would be measuring activations time courses that are similar, and may even be spatially distributed due to the functional connectivity of the human brain. Feature selection methods that reduce redundancy, and or imposing additional sparsity constraints (e.g., L1 norm, elastic method, etc.) may reduce problems with redundancy [66], but may fail to produce the full pattern of activations associated with a representing a stimulus or behavioral phenomenon. This may be dangerous if the goal is to use classification approaches to identify brain tissue (e.g., tumor regions) for resection. Using features that are independent (e.g., independent components) may be a useful avenue for decoding studies moving forward, when the goal is interpretation [2,13,66].

Mapping decoding weights onto activations in combination with sparsity constraints is useful at recovering information when the number of redundant voxels are few [25]. The extent to which this method is effective may depend on the number of (redundant) inputs and the classifier employed. Regularization will assign weights somewhat randomly to voxels that have overlapping yet informative information [43,63]. Therefore, there may be multiple patterns of weights which could yield comparable predictive accuracies. In this sense, the concept of feature fallacy in encoding models also extends to the decoding framework.

Haufe and colleagues suggest that the only inference that can be made from nonzero weights in the two channel scenario is that signal (information) is present in at least one of these channels [25]. Another added complication is that the presence of information does not imply that this information is used by the brain for the particular task under study, or that it serves the function of representing or manipulating a particular stimulus in the context of the brain's overall operation [41]. Therefore, the analogous issue of reverse inference also extends to decoding models (Fig. 20.6).

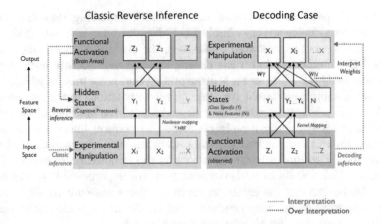

Fig. 20.6. (Left) Classic reverse inference issue in mass univariate fMRI studies. Experimental manipulations (X) putatively engage hidden cognitive processes (Y), leading to functional activations (Z). Reverse inference, or inferring that particular cognitive process is engaged as a result an experimental manipulation, is an over interpretation of the data because it is not clear which (hidden) cognitive processes (Y) or strategies are engaged during a task [54]. Hidden states cannot be inferred on the basis of activation in specific brain regions. (Right) In decoding studies, functional activations (Z) are now the inputs. The presence of information as indicated by weights or activations does not imply that the brain is using that information for a particular task.

Historically, linear models have been the most widely adopted method for classifying 4-dimensional fMRI data (x, y, z, time), perhaps because many computer vision algorithms are designed for inputs with 2 or 3 dimensions. Another factor that has hindered the adoption of more complex non-linear models (e.g., deep neural networks (DNNs)) in the functional neuroimaging community is the idea that these methods were akin to a black box, and couldn't be used for interpretation purposes. However, the application of DNNs to fMRI data is growing in popularity (e.g., [38]), and layer-wise relevance propagation (LRP) has recently provided a principled mechanism for attributing the share that each input variable contributes to the classification decision. LRP has now been applied to both fMRI and EEG data [59,60]. Moving forward DNNs in combination with the LRP method may prove highly useful for both classification and interpretation of neuroimaging data.

References

1. Alpaydin, E.: Introduction to Machine Learning, 3rd edn. MIT Press, Cambridge (2014)
2. Anderson, A., Han, D., Douglas, P.K., Bramen, J., Cohen, M.S.: Real-time functional MRI classification of brain states using Markov-SVM hybrid models: peering inside the rt-fMRI black box. In: Langs, G., Rish, I., Grosse-Wentrup, M., Murphy, B. (eds.) MLINI 2011. LNCS (LNAI), vol. 7263, pp. 242–255. Springer, Heidelberg (2012). https://doi.org/10.1007/978-3-642-34713-9_31

3. Blankertz, B., Lemm, S., Treder, M., Haufe, S., Müller, K.R.: Single-trial analysis and classification of ERP components – a tutorial. NeuroImage **56**, 814–825 (2011)
4. Bruce, D.: Fifty years since lashley's in search of the Engram: refutations and conjectures. J. Hist. Neurosci. **10**, 308–318 (2001)
5. Chu, C., Hsu, A.L., Chou, K.H., Bandettini, P., Lin, C.: Does feature selection improve classification accuracy? Impact of sample size and feature selection on classification using anatomical magnetic resonance images. NeuroImage **60**, 59–70 (2012)
6. Colby, J.B., Rudie, J.D., Brown, J.A., Douglas, P.K., Cohen, M.S., Shehzad, Z.: Insights into multimodal imaging classification of ADHD. Front. Syst. Neurosci. **6**, 59 (2012)
7. Cox, D.D., Savoy, R.L.: Functional magnetic resonance imaging (fMRI) 'brain reading': detecting and a classifying distributed patterns of fMRI activity in human visual cortex. NeuroImage **19**, 261–270 (2003)
8. Cukur, T., Huth, A.G., Nishimoto, S., Gallant, J.L.: Functional subdomains within human FFA. J. Neurosci. **33**, 16748–16766 (2013)
9. De Angelis, V., De Martino, F., Moerel, M., Santoro, R., Hausfeld, L., Formisano, E.: Cortical processing of pitch: model-based encoding and decoding of auditory fMRI responses to real-life sounds. NeuroImage **180**, 291–300 (2018)
10. DiCarlo, J.J., Zoccolan, D., Rust, N.C.: How does the brain solve visual object recognition? Neuron **73**, 415–434 (2012)
11. Diedrichsen, J., Kriegeskorte, N.: Representational models: a common framework for understanding encoding, pattern-component, and representational-similarity analysis. bioRxiv 071472 (2016)
12. Diedrichsen, J., Wiestler, T., Krakauer, J.W.: Two distinct ipsilateral cortical representations for individuated finger movements. Cereb. Cortex **23**, 1362–1377 (2013)
13. Douglas, P.K., Anderson, A.: Interpreting fMRI decoding weights: additional considerations. In: NIPS, Interpretable Machine Learning Workshop (2017)
14. Douglas, P.K., Harris, S., Cohen, M.S.: Naive Bayes classification of belief and disbelief using event related functional neuroimaging data. In: Human Brain Mapping Conference Poster (2009)
15. Douglas, P.K., Harris, S., Yuille, A., Cohen, M.S.: Performance comparison of machine learning algorithms and number of independent components used in fMRI decoding of belief vs. disbelief. NeuroImage **56**, 544–553 (2011)
16. Douglas, P.K., et al.: Single trial decoding of belief decision making from EEG and fMRI data using independent components features. Front. Hum. Neurosci. **7**, 392 (2013)
17. Friston, K.J.: Modalities, modes, and models in functional neuroimaging. Science **326**, 399–403 (2009)
18. Gazzaniga, M.S.: Regional differences in cortical organization. Science **289**, 1887–1888 (2000)
19. Gotsopoulos, A., et al.: Reproducibility of importance extraction methods in neural network based fMRI classification. NeuroImage **181**, 44–54 (2018)
20. Gross, C.G.: Genealogy of the "grandmother cell". Neurosci. **8**, 512–518 (2002)
21. Güçü, U., van Gerven, M.A.J.: Deep neural networks reveal a gradient in the complexity of neural representations across the ventral stream. J. Neurosci. **35**, 10005–10014 (2015)
22. Guyon, I., Elisseeff, A.: An introduction to variable and feature selection. J. Mach. Learn. Res. **3**, 1157–1182 (2003)

23. Hampton, A.N., O'Doherty, J.P.: Decoding the neural substrates of reward-related decision making with functional MRI. Proc. Natl. Acad. Sci. **104**, 1377–1382 (2007)
24. Handwerker, D.A., Ollinger, J.M., D'Esposito, M.: Variation of BOLD hemodynamic responses across subjects and brain regions and their effects on statistical analyses. NeuroImage **21**, 1639–1651 (2004)
25. Haufe, S., et al.: On the interpretation of weight vectors of linear models in multivariate neuroimaging. NeuroImage **87**, 96–110 (2014)
26. Haxby, J.V.: Distributed and overlapping representations of faces and objects in ventral temporal cortex. Science **293**, 2425–2430 (2001)
27. Haynes, J.D.: A primer on pattern-based approaches to fMRI: principles, pitfalls, and perspectives. Neuron **87**, 257–270 (2015)
28. Haynes, J.D., Rees, G.: Predicting the stream of consciousness from activity in human visual cortex. Curr. Biol **15**, 1301–1307 (2005)
29. Haynes, J.D., Rees, G.: Decoding mental states from brain activity in humans. Nat. Rev. Neurosci. **7**, 523–534 (2006)
30. Hodgkin, A.L., Huxley, A.F.: A quantitative description of membrane current and its application to conduction and excitation in nerve. J. Physiol. **117**, 500–544 (1952)
31. Hong, H., Yamins, D.L.K., Majaj, N.J., DiCarlo, J.J.: Explicit information for category-orthogonal object properties increases along the ventral stream. Nat. Neurosci. **19**, 613–622 (2016)
32. Huth, A.G., de Heer, W.A., Griffiths, T.L., Theunissen, F.E., Gallant, J.L.: Natural speech reveals the semantic maps that tile human cerebral cortex. Nature **532**, 453–458 (2016)
33. Kamitani, Y., Tong, F.: Decoding the visual and subjective contents of the human brain. Nat. Neurosci. **8**, 679–685 (2005)
34. Kanwisher, N., Yovel, G.: The fusiform face area: a cortical region specialized for the perception of faces. Philos. Trans. Roy. Soc. B: Biol. Sci. **361**, 2109–2128 (2006)
35. Kay, K.N., Naselaris, T., Prenger, R.J., Gallant, J.L.: Identifying natural images from human brain activity. Nature **452**, 352–355 (2008)
36. Kerr, W.T., Douglas, P.K., Anderson, A., Cohen, M.S.: The utility of data-driven feature selection: Re: Chu et al. 2012. NeuroImage **84**, 1107–1110 (2014)
37. Khaligh-Razavi, S.M., Kriegeskorte, N.: Deep supervised, but not unsupervised, models may explain IT cortical representation. PLOS Comput. Biol. **10**(11), e1003915 (2014)
38. Khaligh-Razavi, S., Kriegeskorte, N.: Object-vision models that better explain IT also categorize better, but all models fail at both. Cosyne Abstracts (2013)
39. Koopmans, P.J., Barth, M., Orzada, S., Norris, D.G.: Multi-echo fMRI of the cortical laminae in humans at 7T. NeuroImage **56**, 1276–1285 (2011)
40. Kriegeskorte, N.: Deep neural networks: a new framework for modeling biological vision and brain information processing. Ann. Rev. Vis. Sci. **1**, 417–446 (2015)
41. Kriegeskorte, N.: Pattern-information analysis: from stimulus decoding to computational-model testing. NeuroImage **56**, 411–421 (2011)
42. Kriegeskorte, N., Douglas, P.K.: Cognitive computational neuroscience. Nat. Neurosci. **21**, 1148–1160 (2018)
43. Kriegeskorte, N., Douglas, P.K.: Interpreting encoding and decoding models. arXiv:1812.00278 (2018)
44. Lee, A.T., Glover, G.H., Meyer, C.H.: Discrimination of large venous vessels in time-course spiral blood-oxygen-level-dependent magnetic-resonance functional neuroimaging. Magn. Reson. Med. **33**, 745–754 (1995)

45. Lemm, S., Blankertz, B., Dickhaus, T., Müller, K.R.: Introduction to machine learning for brain imaging. NeuroImage **56**, 387–399 (2011)
46. Logothetis, N.K., Pauls, J., Augath, M., Trinath, T., Oeltermann, A.: Neurophysiological investigation of the basis of the fMRI signal. Nature **412**, 150–157 (2001)
47. Meshkat, N., Kuo, C.E., DiStefano, J.: On finding and using identifiable parameter combinations in nonlinear dynamic systems biology models and COMBOS: a novel web implementation. PLoS One **9**, e110261 (2014)
48. Mikl, M., et al.: Effects of spatial smoothing on fMRI group inferences. Magn. Reson. Imaging **26**, 490–503 (2008)
49. Naselaris, T., Kay, K.N.: Resolving ambiguities of MVPA using explicit models of representation. Trends Cogn. Sci. **19**, 551–554 (2015)
50. Naselaris, T., Kay, K.N., Nishimoto, S., Gallant, J.L.: Encoding and decoding in fMRI. NeuroImage **56**, 400–410 (2011)
51. Naselaris, T., Prenger, R.J., Kay, K.N., Oliver, M., Gallant, J.L.: Bayesian reconstruction of natural images from human brain activity. Neuron **63**, 902–915 (2009)
52. Norman, K.A., Polyn, S.M., Detre, G.J., Haxby, J.V.: Beyond mind-reading: multivoxel pattern analysis of fMRI data. Trends Cogn. Sci. (Regul. Ed.) **10**, 424–430 (2006)
53. de Beeck, H.P.O.: Against hyperacuity in brain reading: spatial smoothing does not hurt multivariate fMRI analyses? NeuroImage **49**, 1943–1948 (2010)
54. Poldrack, R.A.: Can cognitive processes be inferred from neuroimaging data? Trends Cogn. Sci. (Regul. Ed.) **10**, 59–63 (2006)
55. Pouget, A., Dayan, P., Zemel, R.: Information processing with population codes. Nat. Rev. Neurosci. **1**, 125–132 (2000)
56. Power, J.D., Mitra, A., Laumann, T.O., Snyder, A.Z., Schlaggar, B.L., Petersen, S.E.: Methods to detect, characterize, and remove motion artifact in resting state fMRI. NeuroImage **84**, 320–341 (2014)
57. Quiroga, R.Q., Reddy, L., Kreiman, G., Koch, C., Fried, I.: Invariant visual representation by single neurons in the human brain. Nature **435**, 1102–1107 (2005)
58. Selemon, L., Goldman-Rakic, P.: Common cortical and subcortical targets of the dorsolateral prefrontal and posterior parietal cortices in the rhesus monkey: evidence for a distributed neural network subserving spatially guided behavior. J. Neurosci. **8**, 4049–4068 (1988)
59. Sturm, I., Lapuschkin, S., Samek, W., Müller, K.R.: Interpretable deep neural networks for single-trial EEG classification. J. Neurosci. Methods **274**, 141–145 (2016)
60. Thomas, A.W., Heekeren, H.R., Müller, K.R., Samek, W.: Analyzing neuroimaging data through recurrent deep learning models. arXiv:1810.09945 (2018)
61. Tomsett, R., et al.: Why the failure? How adversarial examples can provide insights for interpretable machine learning. In: 21st International Conference on Information Fusion (2018)
62. VanRullen, R., Reddy, L.: Reconstructing faces from fMRI patterns using deep generative neural networks. arXiv:1810.03856 (2018)
63. Varoquaux, G., Raamana, P.R., Engemann, D.A., Hoyos-Idrobo, A., Schwartz, Y., Thirion, B.: Assessing and tuning brain decoders: cross-validation, caveats, and guidelines. NeuroImage **145**, 166–179 (2017)
64. Worsley, K.J., Marrett, S., Neelin, P., Vandal, A.C., Friston, K.J., Evans, A.C.: A unified statistical approach for determining significant signals in images of cerebral activation. Hum. Brain Mapp. **4**, 58–73 (1996)

65. Wu, G.R., Liao, W., Stramaglia, S., Ding, J.R., Chen, H., Marinazzo, D.: A blind deconvolution approach to recover effective connectivity brain networks from resting state fMRI data. Med. Image Anal. **17**, 365–374 (2013)
66. Xie, J., Douglas, P.K., Wu, Y., Anderson, A.: Decoding the Encoding of functional brain networks: an fMRI classification comparison of non-negative matrix factorization (NMF), independent component analysis (ICA), and sparse coding algorithms. Int. J. Imaging Syst. Technol. **21**, 223–231 (2016)
67. Zhao, S., et al.: Automatic recognition of fMRI-derived functional networks using 3D convolutional neural networks. IEEE Trans. Biomed. Eng. **65**(9), 1975–1984 (2017)

21
Current Advances in Neural Decoding

Marcel A. J. van Gerven$^{(\boxtimes)}$, Katja Seeliger, Umut Güçlü,
and Yağmur Güçlütürk

Donders Institute for Brain, Cognition and Behaviour, Nijmegen, The Netherlands
m.vangerven@donders.ru.nl

Abstract. Neural decoding refers to the extraction of semantically meaningful information from brain activity patterns. We discuss how advances in machine learning drive new advances in neural decoding. While linear methods allow for the reconstruction of basic stimuli from brain activity, more sophisticated nonlinear methods are required when reconstructing complex naturalistic stimuli. We show how deep neural networks and adversarial training yield state-of-the-art results. Ongoing advances in machine learning may one day allow the reconstruction of thoughts from brain activity patterns, providing a unique insight into the contents of the human mind.

Keywords: Neural decoding · Visual Perception ·
Functional Magnetic Resonance Imaging · Deep Neural Networks ·
Adversarial training

21.1 Introduction

A key problem in neuroscience is to understand how our experience is encoded in brain activity patterns. One way to approach this problem is by decoding stimulus properties from measurements of neural activity. Neural decoding has been a core topic in computational neuroscience for many years [10]. It provides us with the means to interpret how representations are encoded in the brain. This is of scientific value since it allows us to understand which properties of the sensory input (or motor output) are encoded in different brain regions. Moreover, it may allow us to reconstruct internal representations that are not otherwise observable in cognitive processes such as imagery, memory maintenance or dreaming. We refer to this use of decoding as *quantitative phenomenology*, since it allows us to uncover phenomenological experience in a quantitative manner, which can normally only be accessed in a qualitative way via introspection. In other words, it allows us to uncover processes related to the mind from neural processed related to the brain, as illustrated in Fig. 21.1.

In practice, neural decoding can be cast as a machine learning problem. Essentially, decoding boils down to a hetero-encoder problem [49], where a high-dimensional input (brain activity) is transformed into a high-dimensional output

© Springer Nature Switzerland AG 2019
W. Samek et al. (Eds.): Explainable AI, LNAI 11700, pp. 379–394, 2019.
https://doi.org/10.1007/978-3-030-28954-6_21

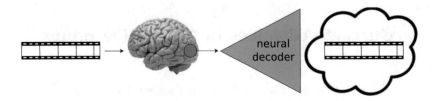

Fig. 21.1. Neural decoding can be used to realize quantitative phenomenology.

(stimulus). Recent advances in machine learning provide new breakthroughs in neural decoding that eventually may allow us to reconstruct arbitrary internal representations from neural activity patterns. This not only provides insights into how representations are organized in the brain but also provides a route towards new neurotechnology that reconstructs phenomenological experience in real time. While there are few labs that are specialized in both machine learning and neuroscience, the availability of preprocessed and directly usable neuroimaging data sets for machine learning on platforms such as `crcns.org`, `studyforrest.org`, `bold5000.github.io` and `data.donders.ru.nl` will enable machine learning groups to contribute to this field. Note, finally, that decoding methods can equally well be applied to artificial neural networks. This allows us to gain insight into the internal representations of artificial systems. In this chapter, we review several decoding methods that have been developed to date and describe how machine learning is driving advances in this field of research.

21.2   Neural Decoding

We start by formulating the problem of interest. We aim to find that stimulus $\mathbf{x} = (x_1, \ldots, x_N)^\top$ which most likely generated observed brain activity $\mathbf{y} = (y_1, \ldots, y_M)^\top$. This stimulus can have an exogenous origin (e.g. a stimulus presented to a subject) or an endogenous origin (e.g. a stimulus retrieved from memory). Decoding refers to predicting $\mathbf{x}$ from $\mathbf{y}$, allowing probing of the representational content of neuronal population recordings [4].

Different variants of neural decoding have been developed, reflecting specific instances of a machine learning problem. For example, if $\mathbf{x}$ can be enumerated using a fixed number of labels then we are dealing with a classification problem. Indeed, standard classification approaches have been heavily used to dissociate different stimulus classes from each other. Classical examples are [27], which showed that different object categories could be decoded from brain activity and [33], which showed that it is possible to decode which of two stimuli a participant is attending to (feature-based attention). Bahramisharif et al. [3] showed that one can also decode the direction to which one is attending without moving one's eyes (covert spatial attention), which boils down to solving a (circular) regression problem. van Gerven et al. [19] showed how the orientation and rotation direction of rotating gratings can be decoded from (slow) functional magnetic resonance imaging (fMRI) responses by employing hidden Markov models and Kalman filters. Note further that decoding does not need to be restricted to the contents of our perceptual system. We can equally well decode processes related to executive function (planning, motor output, navigation) [64].

In this chapter, however, we will focus mostly on what is perceived as a particularly challenging problem in neural decoding, namely *reconstructing* visual experience from neural activity patterns. Early examples of image reconstruction are given by [38,59,60].

21.2.1 MAP Decoding

In this chapter, we formulate decoding as the following maximum a posteriori (MAP) estimation problem:

$$\hat{\mathbf{x}} = \arg\max_{\mathbf{x}} p(\mathbf{x} \mid \mathbf{y}) . \tag{21.1}$$

Here, $\hat{\mathbf{x}}$ is our best guess of $\mathbf{x}$ and $\mathbf{y}$ are brain measurements. For concreteness, we assume that stimuli $\mathbf{x}$ are vectorizations of greyscale images. However, we can easily generalize to other stimuli such as RGB images, video frames or other sensory modalities such as auditory stimuli. The interpretation of the vector of brain measurements $\mathbf{y}$ depends on the neural recording technique used. In case of fMRI, this can be the vectorization of (a number of) brain volumes that reflect blood oxygenation. In case of single-unit recordings, this can be the vectorization of times at which a neuron generates action potentials (spikes). Without loss of generality, both the stimulus and the response are assumed to have zero mean and unit standard deviation.

In practice, the MAP solution also depends on a previously acquired dataset $\mathcal{D} = \{(\mathbf{x}^{(t)}, \mathbf{y}^{(t)})\}_{t=1}^{T}$ consisting of T stimulus-response pairs, left implicit in (21.1). We can compute the MAP solution by plugging in the predictive density

$$p(\mathbf{x} \mid \mathbf{y}, \mathcal{D}) = \int_{\boldsymbol{\theta}} p(\mathbf{x} \mid \mathbf{y}, \boldsymbol{\theta}) p(\boldsymbol{\theta} \mid \mathcal{D}) \tag{21.2}$$

or by further simplifying to $p(\mathbf{x} \mid \mathbf{y}, \mathcal{D}) = p(\mathbf{x} \mid \mathbf{y}, \hat{\boldsymbol{\theta}})$ where $\hat{\boldsymbol{\theta}} = \arg\max_{\boldsymbol{\theta}} p(\boldsymbol{\theta} \mid \mathcal{D})$. In the latter case, we could e.g. use hetero-encoders to directly estimate $\mathbf{x}$ from $\mathbf{y}$; see e.g. [18,63]. Note that, in practice, it is desirable to use many unique stimuli in $\mathcal{D}$ to accurately sample the stimulus space and to use the averaged response $\mathbf{y}$ to the same stimulus when testing decoding model performance, to improve signal-to-noise ratio.

21.2.2 Bayesian Decoding

The approach that is more often followed in literature is to rewrite (21.1) as

$$\mathbf{x}^{*} = \arg\max_{\mathbf{x}} [p(\mathbf{y} \mid \mathbf{x}) p(\mathbf{x})] , \tag{21.3}$$

which immediately follows from Bayes' rule.

From a neuroscientific perspective, this is advantageous because $p(\mathbf{y} \mid \mathbf{x})$ has a direct biophysical interpretation. It basically requires us to specify how a stimulus $\mathbf{x}$ modulates brain activity $\mathbf{z}$ and how brain activity $\mathbf{a}$ causes observed measurements $\mathbf{y}$. Hence, neuroscientific knowledge of human brain function and neurotechnological knowledge of measurement devices can be directly used to construct $p(\mathbf{y} \mid \mathbf{x})$ (in contrast to $p(\mathbf{x} \mid \mathbf{y})$). We also refer to $p(\mathbf{y} \mid \mathbf{x})$ as an *encoding model* [17].

The downside of this approach is that we also need to define a stimulus prior $p(\mathbf{x})$, which is nontrivial for complex (naturalistic) stimulus spaces. Note that this prior implicitly depends on our past experience $\mathcal{X} = \{\mathbf{x}^{(k)}\}_{k=1}^{K}$. We also assume that examples in $\mathcal{X}$ are standardized to have zero mean and unit variance. In explicit form, we write $p(\mathbf{x} \mid \mathcal{X})$. In the following section, we show how (21.3) can be used to *analytically* derive $\hat{\mathbf{x}}$.

21.3   Linear Decoding

Consider again Eq. (21.3), where we write the dependence on $\mathcal{D}$ and $\mathcal{X}$ in explicit form:

$$\mathbf{x}^* = \arg\max_{\mathbf{x}} \left[p(\mathbf{y} \mid \mathbf{x}, \mathcal{D}) p(\mathbf{x} \mid \mathcal{X}) \right] . \tag{21.4}$$

To derive a closed-form expression for $\hat{\mathbf{x}}$ we assume that the likelihood term $p(\mathbf{y} \mid \mathbf{x}, \mathcal{D})$ and prior $p(\mathbf{x} \mid \mathcal{X})$ are given by Gaussians [50].

21.3.1   Gaussian Encoding Model

We assume that the encoding model is given by a multiple-output linear regression model, such that

$$\mathbf{y} = \mathbf{B}^{\top}\mathbf{x} + \boldsymbol{\epsilon} \tag{21.5}$$

with regression coefficients $\mathbf{B} = (\mathbf{b}_1, \ldots, \mathbf{b}_M)$ and where $\boldsymbol{\epsilon} \sim \mathcal{N}(\mathbf{0}; \boldsymbol{\Sigma})$ with $\boldsymbol{\Sigma} = \mathrm{diag}\left(\sigma_1^2, \ldots, \sigma_M^2\right)$. It follows that the encoding model can be written as a multivariate Gaussian

$$p(\mathbf{y} \mid \mathbf{x}, \mathcal{D}) = \mathcal{N}\left(\mathbf{y}; \mathbf{B}^{\top}\mathbf{x}, \boldsymbol{\Sigma}\right)$$

$$\propto \exp\left(-\frac{1}{2}\mathbf{y}^{\top}\boldsymbol{\Sigma}^{-1}\mathbf{y} + (\mathbf{B}\boldsymbol{\Sigma}^{-1}\mathbf{y})^{\top}\mathbf{x} - \frac{1}{2}\mathbf{x}^{\top}\mathbf{B}\boldsymbol{\Sigma}^{-1}\mathbf{B}^{\top}\mathbf{x}\right) \tag{21.6}$$

where (21.6) is its canonical form representation.

We can simultaneously estimate regression coefficients for all responses in closed form, using

$$\hat{\mathbf{B}} = \left(\mathbf{X}^{\top}\mathbf{X} + \lambda\mathbf{I}_N\right)^{-1}\mathbf{X}^{\top}\mathbf{Y}, \tag{21.7}$$

where $\mathbf{X} = \left[\mathbf{x}^{(1)}, \ldots, \mathbf{x}^{(T)}\right]^{\top}$, $\mathbf{Y} = \left[\mathbf{y}^{(1)}, \ldots, \mathbf{y}^{(T)}\right]^{\top}$, $\lambda \geq 0$ is an (optional) regularisation parameter and $\mathbf{I}_N$ an $N \times N$ identity matrix. Alternatively, we can rewrite Eq. (21.7) as

$$\hat{\mathbf{B}} = \mathbf{X}^{\top}(\mathbf{X}\mathbf{X}^{\top} + \lambda\mathbf{I}_T)^{-1}\mathbf{Y}, \tag{21.8}$$

requiring inversion of a $T \times T$ rather than a $N \times N$ matrix [26].

The parameters $\hat{\sigma}_m^2$ are taken to be the residual variance on the responses in $\mathcal{D}$ when using the estimated regression coefficients to predict the responses.

21.3.2   Gaussian Prior

We assume that the image prior is given by a zero-mean multivariate Gaussian of the form:

$$p(\mathbf{x} \mid \mathcal{X}) \propto \exp\left(-\frac{1}{2}\mathbf{x}^{\mathsf{T}}\mathbf{R}^{-1}\mathbf{x}\right) \tag{21.9}$$

with covariance matrix $\mathbf{R}$ given by

$$\mathbf{R} = \frac{1}{K-1}\sum_{\mathbf{x}\in\mathcal{X}}\mathbf{x}\mathbf{x}^{\mathsf{T}}, \tag{21.10}$$

capturing the covariance between image pixels.

21.3.3   Reconstruction

We now combine (21.6) and (21.9) to obtain

$$(\mathbf{x} \mid \mathbf{y}, \mathcal{D}, \mathcal{X}) \propto \exp\left(-\frac{1}{2}\mathbf{y}^{\mathsf{T}}\boldsymbol{\Sigma}^{-1}\mathbf{y} + (\mathbf{B}\boldsymbol{\Sigma}^{-1}\mathbf{y})^{\mathsf{T}}\mathbf{x}\right.$$
$$\left. -\frac{1}{2}\mathbf{x}^{\mathsf{T}}\mathbf{B}\boldsymbol{\Sigma}^{-1}\mathbf{B}^{\mathsf{T}}\mathbf{x}\right) \cdot \exp\left(-\frac{1}{2}\mathbf{x}^{\mathsf{T}}\mathbf{R}^{-1}\mathbf{x}\right). \tag{21.11}$$

Dropping terms not depending on $\mathbf{x}$, this yields

$$p(\mathbf{x} \mid \mathbf{y}, \mathcal{D}, \mathcal{X}) \propto \exp\left((\mathbf{B}\boldsymbol{\Sigma}^{-1}\mathbf{y})^{\mathsf{T}}\mathbf{x} - \frac{1}{2}\mathbf{x}^{\mathsf{T}}\left(\mathbf{R}^{-1} + \mathbf{B}\boldsymbol{\Sigma}^{-1}\mathbf{B}^{\mathsf{T}}\right)\mathbf{x}\right).$$

This is recognized as a multivariate Gaussian in canonical form with mean $\mathbf{m} = \mathbf{Q}\mathbf{B}\boldsymbol{\Sigma}^{-1}\mathbf{y}$ and covariance $\mathbf{Q} = \left(\mathbf{R}^{-1} + \mathbf{B}\boldsymbol{\Sigma}^{-1}\mathbf{B}^{\mathsf{T}}\right)^{-1}$. It immediately follows that

$$\hat{\mathbf{x}} = \mathbf{m} = \left(\mathbf{R}^{-1} + \mathbf{B}\boldsymbol{\Sigma}^{-1}\mathbf{B}^{\mathsf{T}}\right)^{-1}\mathbf{B}\boldsymbol{\Sigma}^{-1}\mathbf{y} \tag{21.12}$$

since the mode of a Gaussian distribution is given by its mean.[1]

For large images, computing (21.12) may be prohibitively expensive since it requires inversion of a $N \times N$ covariance matrix. To resolve this issue, we can make use of the matrix inversion lemma to obtain

$$\hat{\mathbf{x}} = \left(\mathbf{R} - \mathbf{R}\mathbf{B}\left(\boldsymbol{\Sigma} + \mathbf{B}^{\mathsf{T}}\mathbf{R}\mathbf{B}\right)^{-1}\mathbf{B}^{\mathsf{T}}\mathbf{R}\right)\mathbf{B}\boldsymbol{\Sigma}^{-1}\mathbf{y}, \tag{21.13}$$

requiring inversion of an $M \times M$ matrix. Which formulation is most convenient depends on the problem at hand but typically the number of brain responses M is smaller than the number of inputs N, suggesting the latter approach.

---

[1] Eq. (21.12) is also a standard result obtained in Bayesian linear regression when the roles of $\mathbf{B}$ and $\mathbf{x}$ are interchanged [5].

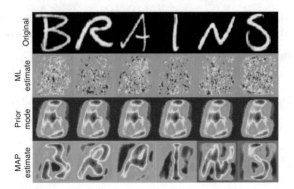

Fig. 21.2. Reconstructing BRAINS from measurements of human brain activity using the linear reconstruction approach. The first row shows the original characters. The second row shows the maximum likelihood estimate that ignores pixel covariances modeled by **R**. The third row shows the mode of the prior. The fourth row shows the reconstructions obtained using (21.13). Adapted from [50].

Using this approach, we have successfully reconstructed handwritten characters from fMRI responses. Figure 21.2 shows the reconstructions that can be obtained.

While these reconstructions looks quite convincing, we remain restricted to the use of Gaussian encoding models and Gaussian priors. While the framework can be extended, e.g. by using a mixture of experts approach [51], this remains a severe restriction. First, the brain is a nonlinear rather than a linear system. Second, natural image statistics are more accurately described by heavy-tailed distributions, thereby violating the Gaussianity assumption. This directly translates into suboptimal performance. This can be critical when moving to more complex settings. For example, when decoding of imagery rather than perception or when decoding naturalistic stimuli rather than handwritten characters. Unfortunately, if we drop the assumptions of linearity and Gaussianity then we cannot resort to the analytical solution anymore.

21.4 Nonlinear Decoding

In this section, we describe a simple approach which allows us to perform reconstruction while being able to exploit nonlinear encoding models. The approach relies on circumventing the need to explicitly solve Eq. (21.3).

21.4.1 Reconstructing with Empirical Priors

In the following, we use a straightforward trick to be able to use nonlinear encoding models during decoding. Using the dataset of stimulus examples $\mathcal{X}$, we can define an empirical prior

$$\hat{p}(\mathbf{x} \mid \mathcal{X}) = \frac{1}{K} \sum_k \delta \left[\mathbf{x} = \mathbf{x}^{(k)} \right], \qquad (21.14)$$

where $\delta[\cdot]$ is the delta function which equals one if its argument evaluates to True and zero if its argument evaluates to False. If we plug this into Eq. (21.4), we obtain

$$\hat{\mathbf{x}} = \arg\max_{\mathbf{x}} \left[p(\mathbf{y} \mid \mathbf{x}, \mathcal{D}) \hat{p}(\mathbf{x} \mid \mathcal{X}) \right]$$
$$= \arg\max_{\mathbf{x} \in \mathcal{X}} p(\mathbf{y} \mid \mathbf{x}, \mathcal{D}). \tag{21.15}$$

Hence, we just pick that stimulus in our empirical prior which maximizes the likelihood. This approach is referred to as *identification* [34]. For large K, we have $\hat{p}(\mathbf{x} \mid \mathcal{X}) \approx p(\mathbf{x})$, motivating the validity of this approach. This approach was used in [41] to obtain reconstructions of natural images using an empirical prior consisting of six million images.

In practice, (21.15) may yield suboptimal reconstructions. This can be caused by a failure to completely cover the stimulus space using $\mathcal{X}$, due to restrictions of the employed encoding model $p(\mathbf{y} \mid \mathbf{x})$ and/or due to noise in the observed responses. These issues can be mitigated by averaging the stimuli with highest posterior probability, referred to as the averaged highest posterior (AHP) reconstruction [41]. Let $\mathcal{L} \subset \mathcal{X}$ be a set of L stimuli such that $p(\mathbf{y} \mid \mathbf{x}, \mathcal{D}) \geq p(\mathbf{y} \mid \mathbf{x}', \mathcal{D})$ for all $\mathbf{x} \in \mathcal{L}$ and $\mathbf{x}' \in \mathcal{X} \setminus \mathcal{L}$. The AHP reconstruction is then given by

$$\hat{\mathbf{x}} = \frac{1}{L} \sum_{\mathbf{x} \in \mathcal{L}} \mathbf{x}, \tag{21.16}$$

which can be interpreted as a Bayesian version of bagging [14].

21.4.2   Nonlinear Encoding Models

The empirical approach allows the use of arbitrary (nonlinear) encoding models since we only need to be able to evaluate $p(\mathbf{y} \mid \mathbf{x}, \mathcal{D})$. In the following, we describe a number of concrete encoding models that make explicit how external stimulation induces observed responses, ranging from basic models that capture responses in early sensory areas to complex models that capture changes in neural dynamics at a whole-brain level. We show some decoding results obtained using these encoding models.

PRF Encoding Models. An elementary encoding model is given by (21.5), which basically implements multiple linear regression. We can however make use of neuroscientific insights to create a more sophisticated encoding model. For a population of neurons, the term *population receptive field* (pRF) is used to refer to those stimulus properties that drive their pooled response [62]. As an example, consider the nonlinear Gabor wavelet pyramid (GWP) model, which uses local contrast energy features computed from 2D Gabor wavelets [34,41]. Gabor wavelets have been used to model the properties of neurons in early visual cortex [9,32,36]. The strength of a response of a Gabor wavelet with unit gain and zero offset at input location (x, y) can be written as

$$w(x,y) = \exp\left(-\frac{\omega^2}{2\sigma^2} - \frac{\rho^2}{2\nu^2}\right)\cos\left(2\pi f\rho + \phi\right) \qquad (21.17)$$

with $\omega = (x - \bar{x})\cos\theta + (y - \bar{y})\sin\theta$ and $\rho = -(x - \bar{x})\sin\theta + (y - \bar{y})\cos\theta$. Here, (f, σ^2, ν^2), ϕ, $(\bar{x}, \bar{y})$ and θ determine the spatial scale, phase, location and orientation of the wavelet, respectively. We can construct a weight vector $\mathbf{w}$ by collecting the response strengths w over all stimulus locations (x, y). By repeating this procedure for multiple Gabor wavelets, we can construct a GWP filter bank $\mathbf{W} = [\mathbf{w}_1, \ldots, \mathbf{w}_K]$. We can use this filter bank to define the following pRF encoding model:

$$\mathbf{y} = \mathbf{B}^\top \phi\left(\mathbf{W}^\top \mathbf{x}\right), \qquad (21.18)$$

where $\phi(\mathbf{x}) = \log(|\mathbf{x}| + 1)$ is a (compressive) nonlinearity which maps Gabor responses to population firing rates. This approach has been used to create reconstructions of natural images [41]. Extensions of the approach, using Gabor wavelets that change over time (motion energy filters), have also been used to reconstruct perceived videos from neural data [43]. See Fig. 21.3.

Fig. 21.3. Reconstruction of video frames based on the motion energy filter model [43]. The shown stimulus frame (left) is an illustration of the original movie shown in fMRI. By courtesy of Shinji Nishimoto.

DNN-Based Encoding Models. Inspecting (21.18), it is evident that the increased sensitivity of pRF encoding models stems from the use of a non-linear transformation of their input before predicting observed measurements. This also suggests that the use of hierarchical models such as deep neural networks (DNNs) [35] may further improve sensitivity. From a neuroscientific point of view, DNNs are of interest since their ability to detect increasingly abstract properties of their environment is reminiscent of the way sensory input is processed across different sensory pathways [8,16,47,56]. DNNs learn a feature space in a supervised manner. Briefly, given a labeled training data set $\mathbf{Z} = \{(\mathbf{x}_1, \mathbf{z}_1), \ldots, (\mathbf{x}_N, \mathbf{z}_N)\}$, consisting, for example, of images $\mathbf{x}_j$ and their categories $\mathbf{z}_j$, a hierarchy of K non-linear transformations ϕ_k is learned using stochastic gradient descent, such that

$$\hat{\mathbf{z}} = (\phi_K \circ \cdots \circ \phi_1)(\mathbf{x}_i) \qquad (21.19)$$

minimizes the distance between $\hat{\mathbf{z}}$ and $\mathbf{z}_i$ is minimized. Any subset of the features embedded in the hierarchical model can be used as an encoding model's feature space, which is then mapped onto the observed responses as in (21.18). The power of using DNNs is illustrated in Fig. 21.4, which shows that the representations learned by DNNs map very closely onto the representations encoded in different areas along the brain's visual ventral stream [22]. Using this approach, the presented stimulus could be identified from a set of 1870 candidate stimuli at up to 96% accuracy.

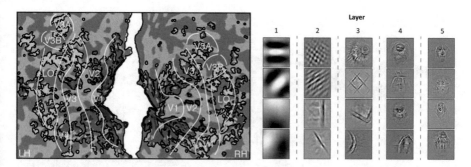

Fig. 21.4. DNNs accurately model hierarchical processing along the visual ventral stream. Left: Representation gradient reveals that different DNN layers map onto different parts of visual cortex. Right: Receptive fields of DNN layers, as visualized by deconvolution [65], increase in complexity, invariance and size. Adapted from [22].

In principle, the more realistic our encoding models become, the better we will be able to decode what information is represented where in the brain. The use of DNNs that are taught to solve tasks such as object recognition [22], music tagging [24] or action recognition [23] to predict brain responses, while effective, hardly constitute accurate models of neural information processing, particularly in downstream areas. We expect further advances using modeling approaches that directly estimate neural computations that take place in individual neuronal populations from brain data [54]. Here, performing gradient descent on the model input can be used to visualize what stimulus properties neuronal populations are maximally sensitive to [15, 39].

21.5 Deep Generative Decoding

So far, we have seen that linear decoding affords an analytical solution to reconstruction, whereas nonlinear decoding increases sensitivity by exploiting more complex encoding models that better capture neural responses to complex stimulus features, though requiring us to resort to the use of empirical priors. In this section we consider a combination of both ideas, which we refer to as deep generative decoding. We first predict a latent representation of the original stimulus from brain activity and then use a generative model to project this prediction into the original stimulus space. Deep generative decoding was pioneered by van Gerven et al. [20], who showed that a deep belief network (DBN) [28] can be conditioned on brain data to obtain stimulus reconstructions. Here, instead, we describe a more recent approach, called deep adversarial neural decoding, which embraces the representational capacity of deep neural networks [35] and the power of adversarial learning [21]. We consider the setting where the aim is to reconstruct perceived faces from fMRI data [25].

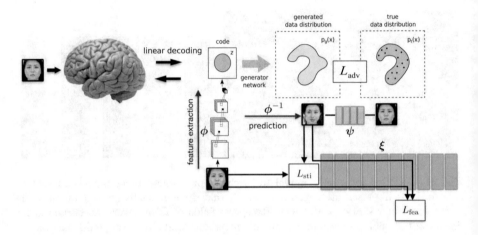

Fig. 21.5. Deep generative decoding through adversarial training. Adapted from [25].

The complete setup is shown in Fig. 21.5. Let $\mathbf{x} \in \mathbb{R}^{h \times w \times c}$ be a stimulus (e.g. a face encoded using RGB channels) and $\phi \colon \mathbb{R}^{h \times w \times c} \to \mathbb{R}^P$ a feature model such that $\mathbf{z} = \phi(\mathbf{x})$. Here, $\mathbf{z}$ represents a meaningful low-dimensional representation of the original input. Specifically, in case of faces we used the VGG-Face network [44] and reduced the output of the 14th layer to a 699-dimensional latent code $\mathbf{z}$ using principal component analysis. To reconstruct faces from this latent code, we define the inverse of the feature model $\phi^{-1}(\mathbf{z})$ (i.e., the image generator) as a convolutional neural network consisting of multiple deconvolution layers.

To train the generator, we make use of two additional neural networks. First, a discriminator network ψ which takes an input and predicts whether the input is real or generated by the generator. Second, a neural network ξ which captures stimulus features, here given by the output of the third layer of the VGG-16 model [58]. The generator is trained by iteratively minimizing a generator loss function, which is a linear combination of an adversarial loss, a feature loss and a stimulus loss:

$$
\begin{aligned}
L_{\text{gen}} = -\lambda_{\text{adv}} L_{\text{adv}} &= \mathbb{E}\left[\log\left(\psi\left(\phi^{-1}(\mathbf{z})\right)\right)\right] \\
&+ \lambda_{\text{fea}}\mathbb{E}\left[||\xi(\mathbf{x}) - \xi(\phi^{-1}(\mathbf{z}))||^2\right] \\
&+ \lambda_{\text{sti}}\mathbb{E}\left[||\mathbf{x} - \phi^{-1}(\mathbf{z})||^2\right].
\end{aligned}
\tag{21.20}
$$

The discriminator is trained by iteratively minimizing a discriminator loss function

$$L_{\mathrm{dis}} = -\mathbb{E}\left[\log \psi(\mathbf{x}) + \log(1 - \psi(\phi^{-1}(\mathbf{z})))\right] . \tag{21.21}$$

We train the generator and the discriminator by pitting them against each other in a two-player zero-sum game, where the goal of the discriminator is to discriminate stimuli from reconstructions and the goal of the generator is to generate reconstructions that are indistinguishable from original stimuli. This adversarial training procedure ensures that reconstructed stimuli are similar to target stimuli on a pixel level and a feature level.

After having trained the generator, we use the linear decoding strategy described in Sect. 21.3 to predict the latent code $\mathbf{z}$ from fMRI data. Figure 21.6 shows the reconstructions that can be obtained when training the model on 700 faces and testing the model on 13 repetitions of 48 faces. Visual inspection of the reconstructions from brain responses reveals that they match the test stimuli in several key aspects, such as gender, skin color and facial features. Identification accuracies within subgroups with the same high-level characteristics (which ranged between 57% and 62%) were significantly above chance-level. This suggests that the low-dimensional code represented by the principal components of a deep neural network provide a biologically meaningful characterization of human faces; see [6] for related work. Results also show that deep adversarial neural decoding massively outperforms alternative approaches such as an eigenface approach [7] or linear decoding at the pixel level. See Güçlütürk et al. [25] for further details about the methods and results.

Deep generative decoding has been employed in a number of other studies [53, 57, 61], confirming the state-of-the-art results that can be achieved using this approach. Shen et al. [57] used a different setup where a decoder is used to predict layer activations of a DNN and pixel values of the input to the DNN are optimized such as to match the predicted layer activations. A deep generator network was used here to further improve decoding results by optimizing the latent code of the generator. Deep generator networks have also been used to evolve artificial stimuli that maximally drive neurons in primate cortex [46].

21.6   Beyond Perceived Image Reconstruction

We now briefly discuss other work which goes beyond the reconstruction of perceived images from fMRI data. We can consider image reconstruction from other modalities. For example, Stanley et al. [59] have reconstructed images from invasive recordings in cat lateral geniculate nucleus. Seeliger et al. [52] have shown that images can be identified from MEG data with reasonable accuracy, also allowing for time-resolved decoding of images. Nishida and Nishimoto [42] extracted verbal descriptions from visual scenes by combining decoding techniques with distributed representations of words (Word2Vec [37]), which have been highly successful in natural language processing. When considering other sensory modalities, Pasley et al. [45] and Akbari et al. [1] have demonstrated speech reconstruction from human auditory cortex based on intracranial EEG.

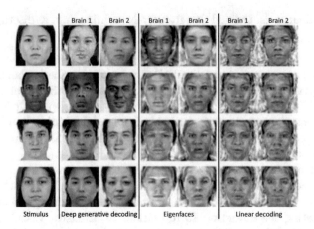

Fig. 21.6. Reconstruction results obtained from two brains using deep generative decoding, an eigenface approach and linear decoding, respectively. In contrast to deep generative decoding, the latter two approaches show little to no correspondence to the original stimuli. Adapted from [25].

The ultimate goal of decoding is to be able to reconstruct the contents of our experience *in the absence of sensory input*. Reconstructions have been obtained in the context of visual imagery [29,40,55,60]. However, so far, reconstruction results for imagery are much less accurate than those obtained for perception. Reasons for this can be that neural processing in perception and imagery only partially overlaps, which makes generalization from perception to imagery hard [12,13] and the fact that subjects can differ widely in their imagery ability [11]. If successful, then imagery decoding may allow us to tap into the contents of our own dreams [30] or reconstruct phenomenological experience in other species. In the auditory domain, it would be a major breakthrough if internal speech could be decoded directly from brain activity patterns since this would allow restoration of communication using an internal speech decoder in people that are unable to communicate otherwise. Evidence that this may one day be feasible is provided in [2], who used recurrent neural networks to synthesize speech from intracranial neural recordings as subjects silently mimed sentences.

21.7 Conclusion

In the past years, neural decoding has witnessed large progress. We expect that this will continue to be the case in the future for two reasons. First, neurotechnology is continuously advancing, allowing us to probe brain activity at ever higher spatial and temporal resolutions [48]. Second, progress in machine learning and biological signal processing will allow us to extract ever more information from the data at hand. Ultimately, these advances allow us to tap into the most private thing we own, that is, our thoughts. While this provides us with new technology to aid people who lost the ability to communicate, it also calls for regulations to use this powerful technology in a responsible manner [31].

References

1. Akbari, H., Khalighinejad, B., Herrero, J.L., Mehta, A.D., Mesgarani, N.: Towards reconstructing intelligible speech from the human auditory cortex. Sci. Rep. **9**(1), 874 (2019)
2. Anumanchipalli, G.K., Chartier, J., Chang, E.F.: Speech synthesis from neural decoding of spoken sentences. Nature **568**, 493–501 (2019)
3. Bahramisharif, A., van Gerven, M.A.J., Heskes, T., Jensen, O.: Covert attention allows for continuous control of brain-computer interfaces. Eur. J. Neurosci. **31**(8), 1501–1508 (2010)
4. Bialek, W., Rieke, F., van Steveninck, R.R.D.R., Warland, D.: Reading a neural code. Science **252**(5014), 1854–1857 (1991)
5. Bishop, C.M.: Pattern Recognition and Machine Learning. Springer, New York (2006)
6. Chang, L., Tsao, D.Y.: The code for facial identity in the primate brain. Cell **169**(6), 1013–1028 (2017)
7. Cowen, A.S., Chun, M.M., Kuhl, B.A.: Neural portraits of perception: reconstructing face images from evoked brain activity. NeuroImage **94**, 12–22 (2014)
8. Cox, D.D., Dean, T.: Neural networks and neuroscience-inspired computer vision. Curr. Biol. **24**(18), PR921–R929 (2014)
9. Daugman, J.G.: Uncertainty relation for resolution in space, spatial frequency, and orientation optimized by two-dimensional visual cortical filters. J. Opt. Soc. Am. A: **2**(7), 1160–1169 (1985)
10. Dayan, P., Abbott, L.F.: Theoretical Neuroscience. MIT Press, Cambridge (2005)
11. Dijkstra, N., Bosch, S.E., van Gerven, M.A.J.: Vividness of visual imagery depends on the neural overlap with perception in visual areas. J. Neurosci. **37**(5), 1367–1373 (2017)
12. Dijkstra, N., Mostert, P., de Lange, F.P., Bosch, S.E., van Gerven, M.A.J.: Differential temporal dynamics during visual imagery and perception. eLIFE, pp. 1–16 (2018)
13. Dijkstra, N., Zeidman, P., Ondobaka, S., van Gerven, M.A.J., Friston, K.: Distinct top-down and bottom-up brain connectivity during visual perception and imagery. Sci. Rep. **7**(5677), 1–9 (2017)
14. Domingos, P.: Why does bagging work? a Bayesian account and its implications. In: Proceedings of the Third International Conference on Knowledge Discovery and Data Mining, pp. 155–158 (1997)
15. Erhan, D., Bengio, Y., Courville, A., Vincent, P.: Visualizing higher-layer features of a deep network. Univ. Montreal **1341**, 1–13 (2009)
16. Fukushima, K.: Neocognitron: a self-organizing neural network model for a mechanism of pattern recognition unaffected by shift in position. Biol. Cybern. **36**(4), 193–202 (1980)
17. van Gerven, M.A.J.: A primer on encoding models in sensory neuroscience. J. Math. Psychol. **76**(B), 172–183 (2017)
18. van Gerven, M.A.J., Chao, Z.C., Heskes, T.: On the decoding of intracranial data using sparse orthonormalized partial least squares. J. Neural Eng. **9**(2), 026017 (2012)
19. van Gerven, M.A.J., Kok, P., de Lange, F.P., Heskes, T.: Dynamic decoding of ongoing perception. NeuroImage **57**, 950–957 (2011)
20. van Gerven, M.A.J., de Lange, F.P., Heskes, T.: Neural decoding with hierarchical generative models. Neural Comput. **22**(12), 3127–3142 (2010)

21. Goodfellow, I., et al.: Generative adversarial nets. In: Advances in Neural Information Processing Systems (NeurIPS) 2014, pp. 2672–2680 (2014)
22. Güçlü, U., van Gerven, M.A.J.: Deep neural networks reveal a gradient in the complexity of neural representations across the ventral stream. J. Neurosci. **35**(27), 10005–10014 (2015)
23. Güçlü, U., van Gerven, M.A.J.: Increasingly complex representations of natural movies across the dorsal stream are shared between subjects. NeuroImage **145**, 329–336 (2017)
24. Güçlü, U., Thielen, J., Hanke, M., van Gerven, M.A.J.: Brains on beats. In: Advances in Neural Information Processing Systems (NeurIPS) 2016, pp. 1–12 (2016)
25. Güçlütürk, Y., Güçlü, U., Seeliger, K., Bosch, S.E., van Lier, R., van Gerven, M.A.J.: Reconstructing perceived faces from brain activations with deep adversarial neural decoding. In: Advances in Neural Information Processing Systems (NeurIPS) 2017 (2017)
26. Hastie, T., Tibshirani, R.J., Friedman, J.H.: The Elements of Statistical Learning: Data Mining, Inference, and Prediction, 2nd edn. Springer, New York (2008). https://doi.org/10.1007/978-0-387-84858-7
27. Haxby, J.V., Gobbini, M.I., Furey, M.L., Ishai, A., Schouten, J.L., Pietrini, P.: Distributed and overlapping representations of faces and objects in ventral temporal cortex. Science **293**, 2425–2430 (2001)
28. Hinton, G.E., Osindero, S., Teh, Y.W.: A fast learning algorithm for deep belief nets. Neural Comput. **18**, 1527–1554 (2006)
29. Horikawa, T., Kamitani, Y.: Hierarchical neural representation of dreamed objects revealed by brain decoding with deep neural network features. Front. Comput. Neurosci. **11**, 1–11 (2017)
30. Horikawa, T., Tamaki, M., Miyawaki, Y., Kamitani, Y.: Neural decoding of visual imagery during sleep. Science **340**(6132), 639–642 (2013)
31. Ienca, M., Haselager, P., Emanuel, E.J.: Brain leaks and consumer neurotechnology. Nat. Biotechnol. **36**(9), 805–810 (2018)
32. Jones, J.P., Palmer, L.A.: An evaluation of the two-dimensional Gabor filter model of simple receptive fields in cat striate cortex. J. Neurophysiol. **58**, 1233–1258 (1987)
33. Kamitani, Y., Tong, F.: Decoding the visual and subjective contents of the human brain. Nat. Neurosci. **8**(5), 679–685 (2005)
34. Kay, K.N., Naselaris, T., Prenger, R.J., Gallant, J.L.: Identifying natural images from human brain activity. Nature **452**, 352–355 (2008)
35. LeCun, Y., Bengio, Y., Hinton, G.E.: Deep learning. Nature **521**(7553), 436 (2015)
36. Marčelja, S.: Mathematical description of the responses of simple cortical cells. J. Opt. Soc. Am. A: **70**(11), 1297–1300 (1980)
37. Mikolov, T., Chen, K., Corrado, G., Dean, J.: Efficient estimation of word representations in vector space. In: International Conference on Learning Representations (ICLR) 2013. Cornell University Library (2013)
38. Miyawaki, Y., et al.: Visual image reconstruction from human brain activity using a combination of multiscale local image decoders. Neuron **60**(5), 915–929 (2008)
39. Mordvintsev, A., Olah, C., Tyka, M.: Inceptionism: going deeper into neural networks (2005). https://research.googleblog.com/2015/06/inceptionism-going-deeper-into-neural.html
40. Naselaris, T., Olman, C.A., Stansbury, D.E., Ugurbil, K., Gallant, J.L.: A voxelwise encoding model for early visual areas decodes mental images of remembered scenes. NeuroImage **105**, 215–228 (2015)

41. Naselaris, T., Prenger, R.J., Kay, K.N., Oliver, M., Gallant, J.L.: Bayesian reconstruction of natural images from human brain activity. Neuron **63**(6), 902–915 (2009)
42. Nishida, S., Nishimoto, S.: Decoding naturalistic experiences from human brain activity via distributed representations of words. NeuroImage **180**, 232–242 (2018)
43. Nishimoto, S., Vu, A.T., Naselaris, T., Benjamini, Y., Yu, B., Gallant, J.L.: Reconstructing visual experiences from brain activity evoked by natural movies. Curr. Biol. **21**, 1–6 (2011)
44. Parkhi, O.M., Vedaldi, A., Zisserman, A.: Deep face recognition. In: British Machine Vision Conference (2015)
45. Pasley, B.N., et al.: Reconstructing speech from human auditory cortex. PLoS Biol. **10**(1), e1001251 (2012)
46. Ponce, C.R., et al.: Evolving images for visual neurons using a deep generative network reveals coding principles and neuronal preferences. Cell **177**, 999–1009 (2019)
47. Riesenhuber, M., Poggio, T.: Hierarchical models of object recognition in cortex. Nat. Neurosci. **2**(11), 1019–1025 (1999)
48. Roelfsema, P.R., Denys, D., Klink, P.C.: Mind reading and writing: the future of neurotechnology. Trends Cogn. Sci. **22**(7), 1–13 (2018)
49. Roweis, S., Brody, C.: Linear heteroencoders. Technical report. GCNU TR 1999-002, Gatsby Computational Neuroscience Unit (1999)
50. Schoenmakers, S., Barth, M., Heskes, T., van Gerven, M.A.J.: Linear reconstruction of perceived images from human brain activity. NeuroImage **83**, 951–961 (2013)
51. Schoenmakers, S., Güçlü, U., van Gerven, M.A.J., Heskes, T.: Gaussian mixture models and semantic gating improve reconstructions from human brain activity. Front. Comput. Neurosci. **8**, 1–10 (2015)
52. Seeliger, K., et al.: Convolutional neural network-based encoding and decoding of visual object recognition in space and time. NeuroImage **180**(A), 253–266 (2017)
53. Seeliger, K., Güçlü, U., Ambrogioni, L., Güçlütürk, Y., van Gerven, M.A.J.: Generative adversarial networks for reconstructing natural images from brain activity. NeuroImage **181**, 775–785 (2018)
54. Seeliger, K., Ambrogioni, L., Güçlütürk, Y., Güçlü, U., Gerven, M.A.J.: Neural system identification with neural information flow. bioRxiv (2019)
55. Senden, M., Emmerling, T.C., van Hoof, R., Frost, M.A., Goebel, R.: Reconstructing imagined letters from early visual cortex reveals tight topographic correspondence between visual mental imagery and perception. Brain Struct. Funct. **224**(3), 1167–1183 (2019)
56. Serre, T., Wolf, L., Bileschi, S., Riesenhuber, M., Poggio, T.: Robust object recognition with cortex-like mechanisms. IEEE Trans. Pattern Anal. Mach. Intell. **29**(3), 411–426 (2007)
57. Shen, G., Horikawa, T., Majima, K., Kamitani, Y.: Deep image reconstruction from human brain activity. PLoS Comput. Biol. **15**(1), 1–23 (2019)
58. Simonyan, K., Zisserman, A.: Very deep convolutional networks for large-scale image recognition. arXiv preprint arXiv:1409.1556 (2014)
59. Stanley, G.B., Li, F.F., Dan, Y.: Reconstruction of natural scenes from ensemble responses in the lateral geniculate nucleus. J. Neurosci. **19**(18), 8036–8042 (1999)
60. Thirion, B., et al.: Inverse retinotopy: inferring the visual content of images from brain activation patterns. NeuroImage **33**(4), 1104–1116 (2006)
61. VanRullen, R., Reddy, L.: Reconstructing Faces from fMRI Patterns using Deep Generative Neural Networks. arXiv preprint arXiv:1810.03856 (2018)

62. Victor, J.D., Purpura, K., Katz, E., Mao, B.: Population encoding of spatial frequency, orientation, and color in macaque V1. J. Neurophysiol. **72**(5), 2151–2166 (1994)
63. Vidaurre, D., van Gerven, M.A.J., Bielza, C., Larrañaga, P., Heskes, T.: Bayesian sparse partial least squares. Neural Comput. **25**(12), 3318–3339 (2013)
64. Wallis, J.D.: Decoding cognitive processes from neural ensembles. Trends Cogn. Sci. **22**(12), 1091–1102 (2018)
65. Zeiler, M.D., Fergus, R.: Visualizing and understanding convolutional networks. In: Fleet, D., Pajdla, T., Schiele, B., Tuytelaars, T. (eds.) ECCV 2014. LNCS, vol. 8689, pp. 818–833. Springer, Cham (2014). https://doi.org/10.1007/978-3-319-10590-1_53

Part VI
Software for Explainable AI

Software for Explainable AI – Preface

AI systems and neural networks have been applied in many disciplines ranging from recommendation systems, modeling of scientific phenomena [7, 8], to extracting content from sound and images [4, 5]. The variety of the tasks, and the need for competitive performance has implied the design of machine learning models that are highly specialized and potentially very large (e.g. GoogleNet, ResNets). The increased network complexity is supported by powerful software libraries such as PyTorch[1] or TensorFlow[2] that bring computational scalability and automatically extract neural network gradients required for learning.

Most of the methods of interpretation that have been presented in this book (e.g., [3, 6]) are relatively simple to implement for standard neural network architectures and can typically be set up with only a few additional lines of code. However, efficiently applying them on the most competitive models preferred in practice can be a much more delicate task. For example, propagation-based explanation methods would need to be extended to handle a wealth of layers types and connectivity structures.—The complexity of implementation increases drastically as a result.—Other explanation methods based on repeated function evaluations may become excessively slow when applied to complex practical neural network models. Applying them thus requires a particularly efficient, e.g. GPU-based implementation, or to tune fine quality-runtime tradeoffs. These practical complications motivate the need for specialized software that makes interpretation techniques accessible to a wider group of users.

In Chapter 22, Alber [1] describes how to implement simple gradient-based technique in the TensorFlow neural network framework, and how to extend this framework to implement propagation-based explanation techniques. The chapter also presents the recent iNNvestigate toolbox [2] which provides a fast implementation for a number of explanation methods and for a range of complex machine learning models. Functionalities offered by iNNvestigate are then tested and benchmarked on state-of-the-art models used in computer vision.

Furthermore, an important challenge for interpretability software and interpretability research in general is to cast the numerous of techniques of explanation that have been proposed into common and modular computational structures. Such a modular approach adopted by iNNvestigate[3] and other frameworks such as deepExplain[4], allows to avoid code redundancy when implementing the multiple explanation techniques and also to facilitate a fair benchmark comparison between them.

As of now, explainability software is an add-on that builds on common machine learning algorithms and machine learning frameworks. As such, it brings useful functionalities for a user who would like to make sense of his trained model. However, for maximum explainability and usefulness, we speculate that once the field of

---

[1] https://pytorch.org/

[2] https://www.tensorflow.org/

[3] https://github.com/albermax/innvestigate

[4] https://github.com/marcoancona/DeepExplain

explainable AI will have further matured, this important functionality will have to be ultimately integrated at the core of machine learning frameworks to serve as a direct validation tool for the learned model and better guide the training process itself.

July 2019

Wojciech Samek
Grégoire Montavon
Andrea Vedaldi
Lars Kai Hansen
Klaus-Robert Müller

References

1. Alber, M.: Software and application patterns for explanation methods. In: Samek, W., Montavon, G., Vedaldi, A., Hansen, L.K., Müller, K.-R. (eds.) Explainable AI: Interpreting, Explaining and Visualizing Deep Learning. LNCS, vol. 11700, pp. 399–433, Springer, Cham (2019)
2. Alber, M., et al.: iNNvestigate neural networks!. J. Mach. Learn. Res. **20**, 1–8 (2019)
3. Ancona, M., Ceolini, E., Öztireli, C., Gross, M.: Gradient-based attribution methods. In: Samek, W., Montavon, G., Vedaldi, A., Hansen, L.K., Müller, K.-R. (eds.) Explainable AI: Interpreting, Explaining and Visualizing Deep Learning. LNCS, vol. 11700, pp. 169–191, Springer, Cham (2019)
4. Graves, A., Mohamed, A., Hinton, G.: Speech recognition with deep recurrent neural networks. In: IEEE ICASSP, pp. 6645–6649 (2013)
5. Krizhevsky, A., Sutskever, I., Hinton, G.E.: Imagenet classification with deep convolutional neural networks. In: Neural Information Processing Systems, pp. 1106–1114 (2012)
6. Montavon, G., Binder, A., Lapuschkin, S., Samek, W., Müller, K.-R.: Layer-wise relevance propagation: An overview. In: Samek, W., Montavon, G., Vedaldi, A., Hansen, L.K., Müller, K.-R. (eds.) Explainable AI: Interpreting, Explaining and Visualizing Deep Learning. LNCS, vol. 11700, pp. 193–209, Springer, Cham (2019)
7. Schütt, K.T., Arbabzadah, F., Chmiela, S., Müller, K.-R., Tkatchenko, A.: Quantum-chemical insights from deep tensor neural networks. Nat. Commun. **8**, 13890 (2017)
8. Thomas, A.W., Heekeren, H.R., Müller, K.-R., Samek, W.: Analyzing neuroimaging data through recurrent deep learning models (2018). arXiv preprint arXiv:1810.09945

22
Software and Application Patterns
for Explanation Methods

Maximilian Alber[✉]

Technische Universität Berlin, 10587 Berlin, Germany
maximilian.alber@tu-berlin.de

Abstract. Deep neural networks successfully pervaded many applications domains and are increasingly used in critical decision processes. Understanding their workings is desirable or even required to further foster their potential as well as to access sensitive domains like medical applications or autonomous driving. One key to this broader usage of explaining frameworks is the accessibility and understanding of respective software. In this work we introduce software and application patterns for explanation techniques that aim to explain individual predictions of neural networks. We discuss how to code well-known algorithms efficiently within deep learning software frameworks and describe how to embed algorithms in downstream implementations. Building on this we show how explanation methods can be used in applications to understand predictions for miss-classified samples, to compare algorithms or networks, and to examine the focus of networks. Furthermore, we review available open-source packages and discuss challenges posed by complex and evolving neural network structures to explanation algorithm development and implementations.

Keywords: Machine learning · Artificial intelligence · Explanation · Interpretability · Software

22.1 Introduction

Recent developments showed that neural networks can be applied successfully in many technical applications like computer vision [18,27,32], speech synthesis [58] and translation [8,56,59]. Inspired by such successes many more domains use machine learning and specifically deep neural networks for, e.g., material science and quantum physics [10,11,39,46,47], cancer research [9,25], strategic games [50,51], knowledge embeddings [3,37,42], and even for automatic machine learning [2,64]. With this broader application focus the requirements beyond predictive power alone rise. One key requirement in this context is the ability to understand and interpret predictions made by a neural network or generally by a learning machine. In at least two areas this ability plays an important role: domains that require an understanding because they are intrinsically critical or

© Springer Nature Switzerland AG 2019
W. Samek et al. (Eds.): Explainable AI, LNAI 11700, pp. 399–433, 2019.
https://doi.org/10.1007/978-3-030-28954-6_22

because it is mandatory by law, and domains that strive to extract knowledge beyond the predictions of learned models. As exemplary domains can be named: health care [9, 16, 25], applications affected by the GDPR [60], and natural sciences [11, 39, 46, 47].

The advancement of deep neural networks is due to their potential to leverage complex and structured data by learning complicated inference processes. This makes a better understanding of such models challenging, yet a rewarding target. Various approaches to tackle this problem have been developed, e.g., [5, 36, 40, 43, 48]. While the nature and objectives of explanation algorithms can be ambiguous [35], in practice gaining specific insights can already enable practitioners and researchers to create knowledge as first promising results show, e.g., [9, 28, 30, 31, 55, 63].

To facilitate the transition of explanation methods from research into widespread application domains the existence and understanding of standard usage patterns and software is of particular importance. This, on one hand, lowers the application barrier and effort for non-experts and, on the other hand, it allows experts to focus on algorithm customization and research. With this in mind, this chapter is dedicated to the software and application patterns for implementing and using explanation methods with deep neural networks. In particular we focus on the explanation techniques that have in common to highlight features in the input space of a targeted neural network [38].

In the next section we address this by a step-by-step showcasing on how explanation methods can be realized efficiently and highlight important design patterns. The final part of the section shows how to tune the algorithms and how to visualize obtained results. In Sect. 22.3 we extend this by integrating explanation methods in several generic application cases with the aim to understand predictions for miss-classified samples, to compare algorithms or networks, and to examine the focus of networks. The remainder, Sects. 22.4, 22.5 and 22.6, addresses available open-source packages, further challenges and gives a conclusion.

22.2   Implementing Explanation Algorithms

Implementing a neural network efficiently can be a complicated and error-prone process and additionally implementing an explanation algorithm makes things even trickier. We will now introduce the key patterns of explanation algorithms that allow for an efficient and structured implementation. Subsequently we complete the section by explaining how to approach interface design, parameter tuning, and visualization of the results.

To make the code examples as useful as possible we will not rely on pseudo-code, but rather use Keras [12], TensorFlow [1] and iNNvestigate [4] to implement our examples for the example network VGG16 [52]. The results are illustrated in Fig. 22.1 and will be created step-by-step. The code listings contain the most important code fragments and we provide corresponding executable code as Jupyter notebook at https://github.com/albermax/interpretable_ai_book_sw_chapter.

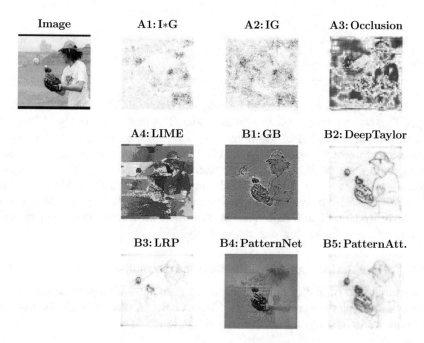

Image	A1: I*G	A2: IG	A3: Occlusion
A4: LIME	B1: GB	B2: DeepTaylor	
B3: LRP	B4: PatternNet	B5: PatternAtt.	

Fig. 22.1. Exemplary application of the implemented algorithms: This figure shows the results of the implemented explanation methods applied on the image in the upper-left corner using a VGG16 network [52]. The prediction- or gradient-based methods (group A) are Input * Gradient [24,49, A1], Integrated Gradients [55, A2], Occlusion [61, A3], and LIME [44, A4]. The propagation-based methods (group B) are Guided Backprop [54, B1], Deep Taylor [38, B2], LRP [30, B3], PatternNet & PatternAttribution [23, B4 and B5]. On how the explanations are visualized we refer to Sect. 22.2.3. Best viewed in digital and color.

Let us recall that the algorithms we explore have a common functional form, namely they map from the input to a equal-dimensional saliency map, e.g., the output saliency map has the same tensor shape as the input tensor. More formal: given a neural network model that maps some input to a single output neuron $f : \mathbb{R}^n \mapsto \mathbb{R}$, the considered algorithms have the following form $e : \mathbb{R}^n \mapsto \mathbb{R}^n$. We will select as output neuron the neuron with the largest activation in the final layer. Any other neuron could also be used. We assume that the target neural network is given as Keras model and the corresponding input and output tensor are given as follows:

```
1  # Create model without trailing softmax
2  model = make_a_keras_model()
3
4  # Get TF tensors
5  input, output = model.inputs[0], model.outputs[0]
6  # Reduce output to response of neuron with largest activation
7  max_output = tf.reduce_max(output, axis=1)
8
```

```
 9  # Select a sample image
10  x_not_pp = select_a_sample_image()
11  # and preprocess it for the network
12  x = preprocess(x_not_pp)
```

The explanation algorithms of interest can be divided into two major groups depending on how they treat the given model. The first group of algorithms uses only the model function or gradient to extract information about the model's prediction process by repetitively calling them with altered inputs. The second group performs a custom backpropagation along the model graph, i.e., requires the ability to introspect the model and adapt to its composition. Methods of the latter are typically more complex to implement, but aim to gain insights more efficiently and/or of different quality. The next two subsections will describe implementations for each group respectively.

22.2.1   Prediction- and Gradient-Based Explanations

Algorithms that only rely on function or on gradient evaluations can be of very simple, yet effective nature [24,44,49,53–55,61,63]. A downside can be the their runtime, which is often a multiple of a single function call.

*Input * gradient.* As a first example we consider input * gradient [24,49]. The name already says it: the algorithm consists of an element-wise multiplication of the input times the gradient. The corresponding formula is:

$$e(x) = x \odot \nabla_x f(x). \tag{22.1}$$

The method can be implemented as follows and the result is marked as A1 in Fig. 22.1:

```
1  # Take gradient of output neuron w.r.t. to the input
2  gradient = tf.gradients(max_output, input)[0]
3  # and multiply it with the input
4  input_t_gradient = input * gradient
5  # Run the code with TF
6  A1 = sess.run(input_t_gradient, {input: x})
```

Integrated Gradients. A more evolved example is the method Integrated Gradients [55] which tries to capture the effect of non-linearities better by computing the gradient along a line between input image and a given reference image x'. The corresponding formula for i-th input dimension is:

$$e(x_i) = (x_i - x_i') \odot \int_{\alpha=0}^{1} \frac{\delta f(x)}{\delta x_i}\bigg|_{x=x'+\alpha(x-x')} d\alpha. \tag{22.2}$$

To implement the method the integral is approximated with a finite sum and, building on the previous code snippet, the code looks as follows (result is tagged with A2 in Fig. 22.1):

```
1  # Nr. of steps along path
2  steps = 32
3  # Take as reference a black image,
4  # i.e., lowest number of the networks input value range.
5  x_ref = np.ones_like(x) * net['input_range'][0]
6  # Take gradient of output neuron w.r.t. to input
7  gradient = tf.gradients(max_output, input)[0]
8
9  # Sum gradients along the path from x to x_ref
10 gradient_sum = np.zeros_like(x)
11 for step in range(steps):
12    # Create intermediate input
13    x_step = x_ref + (x - x_ref) * step / steps
14    # Compute and add the gradient for intermediate input
15    gradient_sum += sess.run(gradient, {input: x_step})
16
17 # Integrated Gradients formula
18 A2 = gradient_sum * (x - x_ref)
```

Occlusion. In contrast to the two presented methods occlusion-based methods rely on the function value instead of its gradient, e.g., [34,61,63]. The basic variant [61] divides the input, typically an image, into a grid of non-overlapping patches. Then each patch gets the function value assigned that is obtained when the patch region in the original image is perturbed or replaced by a reference value. Eventually all values are normalized with the default activation given when no patch is occluded. The algorithm can be implemented as follows and the result is denoted as A3 in Fig. 22.1:

```
1  diff = np.zeros_like(x)
2  # Choose a patch size
3  psize = 8
4
5  # Occlude patch by patch and calculate activation for each patch
6  for i in range(0, net['image_shape'][0], psize):
7    for j in range(0, net['image_shape'][0], psize):
8
9      # Create image with the patch occluded
10     occluded_x = x.copy()
11     occluded_x[:, i:i+psize, j:j+psize, :] = 0
12
13     # Store activation of occluded image
14     diff[:, i:i+psize, j:j+psize, :] = sess.run(
15       max_output, {input: occluded_x})[0]
16
17 # Normalize with initial activation value
18 A3 = sess.run(max_output, {input: x})[0] - diff
```

LIME. The last prediction-based explanation class, e.g., [36,44], decomposes the input sample into features. Subsequently, prediction results for inputs— composed of perturbed features—are collected, yet instead of using the values directly for the explanation, they are used to learn an importance value for the respective features.

One representative algorithm is "Local interpretable model-agnostic explanations" [44, LIME] that learns a local regressor for each explanation. It works as follows for images. First the image is divided into segments, e.g., continuous color regions. Then a dataset is sampled where the features are randomly perturbed, e.g., filled with a gray color. The target of the sample is determined by the prediction value for the accordingly altered input. Using this dataset a weighted, regression model is learned and the resulting weight vector's values indicate the importance of each segment in the neural network's initial prediction. The algorithm can be implemented as follows and the result is denoted as A4 in Fig. 22.1:

```
1   # Segment (not pre-processed) image
2   segments = skimage.segmentation.quickshift(
3     x_not_pp[0], kernel_size=4, max_dist=200, ratio=0.2)
4   nr_segments = np.max(segments)+1
5
6
7   # Create dataset
8   nr_samples = 1000
9   # Randomly switch segments on and off
10  features = np.random.randint(0, 2, size=(nr_samples, nr_segments))
11  features[0, :] = 1
12
13  # Get labels for features
14  labels = []
15  for sample in features:
16    tmp = x.copy()
17    # Switch segments on and off
18    for segment_id, segment_on in enumerate(sample):
19      if segment_on == 0:
20        tmp[0][segments == segment_id] = (0, 0, 0)
21    # Get predicted value for this sample
22    labels.append(sess.run(max_output, {input: tmp})[0])
23
24
25  # Compute sample weights
26  distances = sklearn.metrics.pairwise_distances(
27                 features,
28                 features[0].reshape(1, -1),
29                 metric='cosine',
30  ).ravel()
31  kernel_width = 0.25
32  sample_weights = np.sqrt(np.exp(-(distances ** 2) / kernel_width ** 2))
33
34  # Fit L1-regressor
35  regressor = sklearn.linear_model.Ridge(alpha=1, fit_intercept=True)
36  regressor.fit(features, labels, sample_weight=sample_weights)
37  weights = regressor.coef_
38
39
40  # Map weights onto segments
41  A4 = np.zeros_like(x)
42  for segment_id, w in enumerate(weights):
43    A4[0][segments == segment_id] = (w, w, w)
```

As initially mentioned a drawback of prediction- and gradient-based methods can be slow runtime, which is often a multiple of a single function evaluation—as the loops in the code snippets already suggested. For instance Integrated

Gradients used 32 evaluations, the occlusion algorithm $(224/4)^2 = 56^2 = 3136$ and LIME 1000 (same as in [44]). Especially for complex networks and for applications with time constraints this can be prohibitive. The next subsection is on propagation-based explanation methods, which are more complex to implement, but typically produce explanation results faster.

22.2.2 Propagation-Based Explanations

Algorithms using a custom back-propagation routine to create an explanation are in stark contrast to prediction- or gradient-based explanation algorithms: they rely on knowledge about the model's internal functioning to create more efficient or diverse explanations.

Consider gradient back-propagation that works by first decomposing a function and then performing an iterative backward mapping. For instance, the function $f(x) = u(v(x)) = (u \circ v)(x)$ is first split into the parts u and v—of which it is composed of in the first place—and then the gradient $\frac{\delta f}{\delta x}$ is computed iteratively $\frac{\delta f}{\delta x} = \frac{\delta u \circ v}{\delta v} \frac{\delta v}{\delta x}$ by backward mapping each component using the partial derivatives $\frac{\delta u \circ v}{\delta v}$ and $\frac{\delta v}{\delta x}$. Similar to the computation of the gradient, all propagation-based explanations have this approach in common: (1) each algorithm defines, explicitly or implicitly, how a network should be decomposed into different parts and (2) how for each component the backward mapping should be performed. When implementing an algorithm for an arbitrary network it is important to consider that different methods target different components of a network, that different decompositions for the same method can lead to different results and that certain algorithms cannot be applied to certain network structures.

For instance consider GuidedBackprop [54] and Deep Taylor Decomposition [38, DTD]. The first targets ReLU-activations in a network and describes a backward mapping for such non-linearities, while partial derivatives are used for the remaining parts of the network. On the other hand, DTD and many other algorithms expect the network to be decomposed into linear(izable) parts—which can be done in several ways and may result in different explanations.

When developing such algorithms the emphasis is typically on how a backward mapping can lead to meaningful explanations, because the remaining functionality is very similar and shared across methods. Knowing that, it is useful to split the implementation of propagation-based methods in the following two parts. The first part contains the algorithm details—thus defines how a network should be decomposed and how the respective mappings should be performed. It builds upon the next part which takes care of common functionality, namely decomposing the network as previously specified and iteratively applying the mappings. Both are denoted as "Algorithm" and "Propagation-backend" in an exemplary software stack in Fig. 22.8 in the appendix.

This abstraction has the big advantage that the complex and algorithm independent graph-processing code is shared among explanation routines and allows the developer to focus on the implementation of the explanation algorithm itself.

We will describe in Appendix 22.A.1 how a propagation backend can be implement. Eventually it should allow the developer to realize a method in the following schematic way—using the interface to be presented in Sect. 22.2.3:

```
1  # A backward mapping function, e.g., for convolutional layers
2  def backward_mapping(Xs, Ys, bp_Ys, bp_state):
3    return compute_backward_mapping_magic()
4
5  # A class bundling all algorithm functionality
6  class ExplanationAlgorithm(Analyzer):
7    ...
8    # Defining how to perform the algorithm
9    def _create_analysis(self):
10     # Tell the backend that this mapping
11     # should be applied, e.g., to all convolutional layers.
12     register_backward_mapping(
13       condition=lambda x: is_convolutional_layer(x),
14       backward_mapping)
15     ...
16
17 # Create and build algorithm for a model
18 analyzer = ExplanationAlgorithm(model)
19 # Perform the analysis
20 analyze = analyzer.analyze(x)
```

The idea is that after decomposing the graph into layers (or sub-graphs) each layer gets assigned a mapping, where the mappings' conditions define how they are matched. Then the backend code will take a model and apply the explanation method accordingly to new inputs.

Customizing the Back-Propagation. Based on the established interface we are now able to implement various propagation-based explanation methods in an efficient manner. The algorithms will be implemented using the backend of the iNNvestigate library [4]. Any other solution mentioned in Appendix 22.A.1 could also be used.

Guided Backprop. As a first example we implement the algorithm Guided Backprop [54]. The back-propagation of Guided Backprop is the same as for the gradient computation, except that whenever a ReLU is applied in the forward pass another ReLU is applied in the backward pass. Note that the default back-propagation mapping in iNNvestigate is the partial derivative, thus we only need to change the propagation for layers that contain a ReLU activation and apply an additional ReLU in the backward mapping. The corresponding code looks like follows and can already be applied to arbitrary networks (see B1 in Fig. 22.1):

```
1  # Guidded-Backprop-Mapping
2  # X = input tensor of layer
3  # Y = ouput tensor of layer
4  # bp_Y = backpropagated value for Y
5  # bp_state = additional information on state
6  def guided_backprop_mapping(X, Y, bp_Y, bp_state):
```

```
7    # Apply ReLU to back-propagate values
8    tmp = tf.nn.relu(bp_Y)
9    # Propagate back along the gradient of the forward pass
10   return tf.gradients(Y, X, grad_ys=tmp)
11
12   # Extending iNNvestigate base class with the Guideded Backprop code
13   class GuidedBackprop(ReverseAnalyzerBase):
14
15     # Register the mapping for layers that contain a ReLU
16     def _create_analysis(self, *args, **kwargs):
17
18       self._add_conditional_reverse_mapping(
19         # Apply to all layers that contain a relu activation
20         lambda layer: kchecks.contains_activation(layer, 'relu'),
21         # and use the guided_backprop_mapping to do the backrop step.
22         tf_to_keras_mapping(guided_backprop_mapping),
23         name='guided_backprop',
24       )
25
26       return super(GuidedBackprop, self)._create_analysis(*args, **kwargs)
27
28   # Creating an instance of that analyzer
29   analyzer = GuidedBackprop(model_wo_sm)
30   # and apply it.
31   B1 = analyzer.analyze(x)
```

Deep Taylor. Typically propagation-based methods are more evolved. Propagations are often only described for fully connected layers and one key pattern that arises is extending this description seamlessly to convolutional and other layers. Examples for this case are the "Layerwise relevance propagation" [7], the "Deep Taylor Decomposition" [38] and the "Excitation Backprop" [62] algorithms. Despite different motivation all algorithms yield similar propagation rules for neural networks with ReLU-activations. The first algorithm takes the prediction values at the output neuron and calls it relevance. Then this relevance is re-distributed at each neuron by mapping the back-propagated relevance proportionally to weights onto the inputs. We consider here the so-called Z+ rule. In contrast, Deep Taylor is motivated by a (linear) Taylor decomposition for each neuron and Excitation Backprop by a probabilistic "Winner-Take-All" scheme. Ultimately, for layers with positive input and positive output values—like the inner layers in VGG16—they all have the following propagation formula:

$$
\begin{aligned}
bw\_mapping(x, y, r := bp\_y) &= x \odot (W_+^t z) \\
\text{with } z &= r \oslash (x W_+)
\end{aligned}
\tag{22.3}
$$

given a fully connected layer with W_+ denoting the weight matrix where negative values are set to 0. Using the library iNNvestigate this can be coded in this way:

```
1    # Deep-Taylor/LRP/EB's Z-Rule-Mapping for conv layers
2    # Call R=bp_Y, R for relevance
3    def z_rule_mapping_conv(X, Y, R, bp_state):
4      # Get layer and the parameters
5      layer = bp_state['layer']
6      W = tf.maximum(layer.kernel, 0)
```

```
7
8    Z = tf.keras.backend.conv2d(X, W, layer.strides, layer.padding) + b
9    # normalize incoming relevance
10   tmp = R / Z
11   # map back
12   tmp = tf.keras.backend.conv2d_transpose(
13     tmp, W, (1,)+keras.backend.int_shape(X)[1:],
14     layer.strides, layer.padding)
15   # times input
16   return tmp * X
17
18 # Extending iNNvestigate base class with the Deep Taylor/LRP/EB's Z+-rule
19 class DeepTaylorZ1(ReverseAnalyzerBase):
20   # Register mappings for dense and convolutional layers.
21   # Add Bounded DeepTaylor rule for input layer.
22
23 analyzer = DeepTaylorZ1(model_wo_sm)
24 B2a = analyzer.analyze(x)
```

Unfortunately, this mapping implementation only covers 2D convolutional layers, while other key layers like dense or other convolutional layers are not covered. By creating another mapping for fully-connected layers (Appendix 22.A.2) the code can be applied to VGG16. The result is shown in Fig. 22.1 denoted as B2, where for the constrained input layer we used the bounded rule proposed by [38].

Still, this code does not cover one-dimensional, three-dimensional or any other special type of convolutions. Conveniently unnecessary code-replication can be avoided by using automatic differentiation. The core idea is that many methods can be expressed as pre-/post-processing of the gradient back-propagation. Using automatic differentiation our code example can be expressed as follows and works now with any type of convolutional layer:

```
1  # Deep-Taylor/LRP/EB's Z+-Rule-Mapping for all layers with a kernel
2  # Call R=bp_Y, R for relevance
3  def z_rule_mapping_all(X, Y, R, bp_state):
4    # Get layer
5    layer = bp_state['layer']
6    # and create layer copy without activation part
7    W = tf.maximum(layer.kernel, 0)
8    layer_wo_act = kgraph.copy_layer_wo_activation(
9      layer, weights=[W], keep_bias=False)
10
11   Z = layer_wo_act(X)
12   # normalize incoming relevance
13   tmp = R / Z
14   # map back
15   tmp = tf.gradients(Z, X, grad_ys=tmp)[0]
16   # times input
17   return tmp * X
```

LRP. For some methods it can be necessary to use different propagation rules for different layers. E.g., Deep-Taylor requires different rules depending on the input data range [38] or for LRP it was empirically demonstrated to be useful to apply different rules for different parts of a network. To exemplify this, we show how to use different LRP rules for different layer types as presented in [30]. In more detail, we will apply the epsilon rule for all dense layer and the alpha-beta rule for convolutional layers. This can be implemented in iNNvestigate by changing the matching condition. Using provided LRP-rule mappings this looks as follows:

```
1   class LRPConvNet(ReverseAnalyzerBase):
2
3     # Register the mappings for different layer types
4     def _create_analysis(self, *args, **kwargs):
5
6       # Use Epsilon rule for dense layers
7       self._add_conditional_reverse_mapping(
8         lambda layer: kchecks.is_dense_layer(layer),
9         LRPRules.EpsilonRule,
10        name='dense',
11      )
12      # Use Alpha1Beta0 rule for conv layers
13        self._add_conditional_reverse_mapping(
14        lambda layer: kchecks.is_conv_layer(layer),
15        LRPRules.Alpha1Beta0Rule,
16        name='conv',
17      )
18
19    return super(LRPConvNet, self)._create_analysis(*args, **kwargs)
20
21  analyzer = LRPConvNet(model_wo_sm)
22  B3 = analyzer.analyze(x)
```

The result can be examined in Fig. 22.1 marked with B3.

PatternNet & PatternAttribution. PatternNet & PatternAttribution [23] are two algorithms that are inspired by the pattern-filter theory for linear models [17]. They learn for each neuron in the network a signal direction called pattern. In PatternNet the patterns are used to propagate the signal from the output neuron back to the input by iteratively using the pattern directions of the neurons and the method can be realized with a gradient backward-pass where the filter weights are exchanged with the pattern weights. PatternAttribution is based on the Deep Taylor Decomposition [38]. For each neuron it searches the root point in the direction of its pattern. Given the pattern a the corresponding formula is:

$$bw\_mapping(x, y, r = bp\_y) = (w \odot a)^t r \qquad (22.4)$$

and it can be implemented by doing a gradient backward pass where the filter weights are element-wise multiplied with the patterns.

So far we implemented the backward-mappings as functions and registered them inside an analyzer class for backpropagation. In the next example we will create a single class that takes a parameter, namely the patterns, and the mapping will be a class method that uses a different pattern for each layer mapping (B4 in Fig. 22.1). The following code sketches the implementations which can be found in Appendix 22.A.3:

```
 1  # Extending iNNvestigate base class with the PatternNet algorithm
 2  class PatternNet(ReverseAnalyzerBase):
 3
 4    # Storing the patterns.
 5    def __init__(self, model, patterns, **kwargs):
 6      self._patterns = patterns[:]
 7      super(PatternNet, self).__init__(model, **kwargs)
 8
 9    def _get_pattern_for_layer(self, layer):
10      return self._patterns.pop(-1)
11
12    # Peform the mapping
13    def _patternnet_mapping(self, X, Y, bp_Y, bp_state):
14      ...
15      # Use patterns specific to bp_state['layer']
16      ...
17
18    # Register the mapping
19    def _create_analysis(self, *args, **kwargs):
20      ...
21
22  analyzer = PatternNet(model_wo_sm, net['patterns'])
23  B4 = analyzer.analyze(x)
```

Encapsulating the functionality in a single class allows us now to easily extend PatternNet to PatternAttribution by changing the parameters that are used to perform the backward pass (B5 in Fig. 22.1):

```
 1  # Extending PatternNet to PatternAttribution
 2  class PatternAttribution(PatternNet):
 3
 4    def _get_pattern_for_layer(self, layer):
 5      filters = layer.get_weights()[0]
 6      patterns = self._patterns.pop(-1)
 7      return filters * patterns
 8
 9  analyzer = PatternAttribution(model_wo_sm, net['patterns'])
10  B5 = analyzer.analyze(x)
```

Generalizing to More Complex Networks. For our examples we relied on the VGG16 network [52] which is composed of linear and convolutional layers with ReLU-or Softmax-activations as well as max-pooling layers. Recent networks in computer vision like, e.g., InceptionV3 [57], ResNet50 [18], DenseNet [20], or NASNet [64], are far more complex and contain a variety of new layers like batch normalization layer [21], new types of convolutional layers, e.g., [13], and merge layers that allow for residual connections [18].

The presented code examples either generalize to these new architectures or can be easily adapted to them. Exemplary, Fig. 22.7 in Sect. 22.3 shows a variety of algorithms applied to several state-of-the-art neural networks for computer vision. For each algorithm the *same* explanation code is used to analyze all different networks. The exact way to adapt algorithms to new network families depends on the respective algorithm and is beyond the scope of this chapter. Typically it consists of implementing new mappings for new layers, if required. For more details we refer to the iNNvestigate library [4].

22.2.3   Completing the Implementation

More than the implementation of the methodological core is required to success-fully apply and use explanation software. Depending on the hyper-parameter selection and visualization approaches the explanation result may vary dras-tically. Therefore it is important that software is designed to help the users to easily select the most suitable setting for their task at hand. This can be achieved by exposing the algorithm software via an easy and intuitive interface, allowing the user to focus on the method application itself. Subsequently we will address these topics and as a last contribution in this subsection we will benchmark the implemented code.

Interface. Exposing clear and easy-to-use software interfaces and routines facil-itates that a broad range of practitioners can benefit from a software package. For instance the popular scikit-learn [41] package offers a clear and unified interface for a wide range of machine learning methods, which can be flexibly adjusted to more specific use cases.

In our case one commonality of all explanation algorithms is that they oper-ate on a neural network model and therefore an interface to receive a model description is required. There are two commonly used approaches. The first one is chosen by several software packages, e.g., DeepLIFT [49] and the LRP-toolbox [29], and consists of expecting the model in form of a configuration (file). A drawback of this approach is that the model needs to be serialized before the explanation can be executed.

An alternative way is to take the model represented as a memory object and operate directly with that, e.g., DeepExplain [5] and iNNvestigate [4] work in this way. Typically this memory object was build with a deep learning framework. This approach has the advantage that an explanation can be created without additional overhead and it is easy to use several explanation methods in the same program setup—which is especially useful for comparisons and research purposes. Furthermore, a model, stored in form of a configuration, can still be loaded by using the respective deep learning framework's routines and then being passed to the explanation software.

Exemplary the interface of the iNNvestigate package mimics the one of the popular software package scikit-learn and allows to create an explanation with a few lines of code:

```
1  # Build the explanation algorithm
2  # with the hyper-parameter pattern_type set to 'relu'
3  analyzer = PatternAttribution(model_wo_sm, pattern_type='relu')
4  # fit the analyzer to the training data (if an analyzer requires it)
5  analyzer.fit(X_train)
6  # and apply it to an input
7  e = analyzer.analyze(x)
```

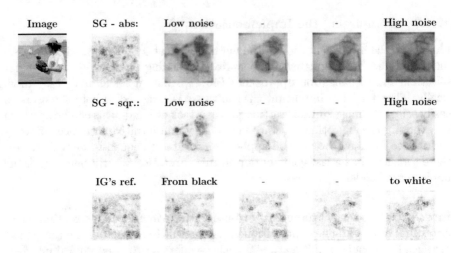

Fig. 22.2. Influence of hyperparamters: Row one to three show how different hyper-parameters change the output of explanation algorithms. Row 1 and 2 depict the Smoothgrad (**SG**) method where the gradient is transformed into a positive value by taking the absolute or the square value respectively. The columns show the influence of the noise scale parameter with low to high noise from left to right. In row 3 we show how the explanation of the Integrated Gradients (**IG**) method varies when selecting as reference an image that is completely black (left side) to completely gray (middle) to completely white (right). Best viewed in digital and color.

Hyper-parameter Selection. Like for many other tasks in machine learning explanation methods can have hyper-parameters, but unlike for other algorithms, for explanation methods no clear selection metric exists. Therefore selecting the right hyperparameter can be a tricky task. One way is a (visual) inspection of the explanation result by domain experts. This approach is suspected to be prone to the human confirmation bias. As an alternative in image classification settings [45] proposed a method called "perturbation analysis". The algorithm divides an image into a set of regions and sorts them in decreasing order of the "importance" each regions gets attributed by an explanation method. Then the algorithm measures the decay of the neural networks prediction value when perturbing the blocks in the given order, i.e., "removing" the information of the most important image parts first. The key ideas is that if an explanation method highlights important regions better the performance will decay faster.

To visualize the sensitivity of explanation methods w.r.t. to their hyper-parameter Fig. 22.2 contains two example settings. The first example application shows the results for Integrated Gradients in row 3 where the image base-line varies from a black to a white image. While the black, nor the white, or the gray image as reference contains any valuable information, the explanation varies significantly—emphasizing the need to pay attention to hyper-parameters of explanation methods. More on the sensitivity of explanation algorithms w.r.t.

Graymap   Heatmap   Scaling   Masking   Blending Back-projection

Fig. 22.3. Different visualizations: Each column depicts a different visualization technique for the explanation of PatternAttribution or PatternNet (last column). The different visualization techniques are described in the text. Best viewed in digital and color.

to this specific parameter can be found in [22]. Using iNNvestigate the corresponding explanation can be generated with the code in Appendix 22.A.4.

Another example is the postprocessing of the saliency output. For instance for SmoothGrad the sign of the output is not considered to be informative and can be transformed to a positive value by using the absolute or the square value. This in turn has a significant impact on the result as depicted in Fig. 22.2 (row 1 vs. row 2). Furthermore, the second parameter of SmoothGrad is the scale of the noise used for smoothing the gradient. This hyper-parameter varies from small on the left hand side to large on the right hand side and, again, has a substantial impact on the result. Which setting to prefer depends on the application. The explanations were created with the code fragment in Appendix 22.A.4.

Visualization. The innate aim of explanation algorithms is to facilitate the understanding for humans. To do so the output of algorithms needs to be transformed into a human understandable format.

For this purpose different visualization techniques were proposed in the domain of computer vision. In Fig. 22.3 we depict different approaches and each one emphasizes or hides different properties of a method. The five approaches are using graymaps [53] or single color maps to show only absolute values (column 1), heatmaps [7] to show positive and negative values (column 2), scaling the input by absolute values [55] (column 3), masking the least important parts of the input [44] (column 4), blending the heatmap and the input [48] (column 5), or projecting the values back into the input value range [23] (column 6). The last technique is used to visualize signal extraction techniques, while the other ones are used for attribution methods [23]. To convert color images to a two-dimensional tensor, the color channels are typically reduced to a single value by the sum or a norm. Then the value gets projected into a suitable range and finally the according mapping is applied. This is done for all except for the last method, which projects each value independently. An implementation of the visualization techniques can be found in Appendix 22.A.5.

For other domains than image classification different visualization schemes are imaginable.

Benchmark. To show the runtime efficiency of the presented code we benchmarked it. We used the iNNvestigate library to implement it and as a reference implementation we use the LRP-Caffe-Toolbox [29] because it was designed to implement algorithms with a similar complexity, namely the LRP-variants which are the most complex algorithms we reviewed.

We test three algorithms and run them with the VGG16 network [52]. Both frameworks need some time to compile the computational graph and to execute it on a batch of images, accordingly we measure both, the setup time and the execution time, for analyzing 512 images.

The LRP-Toolbox has a sequential and a parallel implementations for the CPU. We show the time for the faster parallel implementation. For iNNvestigate we evaluate the runtime on the CPU and on GPU. The workstation for the benchmark is equipped with an Intel Xeon CPU E5-2690-v4 2.60 GHz with 24 physical cores mapped to 56 virtual cores and 256G of memory. Both implementation can use up to 32 cores. The GPU is a Nvidia P100 with 16G of memory. We repeat each test 10 times and report the average duration.

Figure 22.4 shows the measured duration on a logarithmic scale. The presented code implemented with the iNNvestigate library is up to 29 times faster when both implementations run on the CPU. This increases up to 510 times when using iNNvestigate with the GPU compared to the LRP-Toolbox implementation on the CPU. This is achieved while our implementations also considerably reduce the amount and the complexity of code to implement the explanation algorithms compared to the LRP-Toolbox. On the other hand, when using frameworks like iNNvestigate one needs to compile a function graph and accordingly the setup needs up to 3 times as long as for the LRP-Toolbox—yet amortizes already when analyzing a few images.

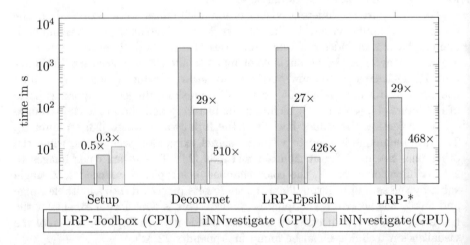

Fig. 22.4. Runtime comparison: The figure shows the setup- and run-times for 512 analyzed images in logarithmic range for the LRP-Toolbox and the code implemented with the iNNvestigate library. Each block contains the numbers for the setup or a different algorithm: Deconvnet [61], LRP-Epsilon [7], and the LRP configuration from [30], denoted as LRP-*. The numbers in black indicate the respective speedup with regard to the LRP-Toolbox.

22.3   Applications

In this section we will use the implemented algorithms and examine common application patterns for explanation methods. For convenience we will rely on the iNNvestigate library [4] to present the following four use cases: (1) Analyzing single (miss-)prediction to gain insights on the model, and subsequently on the data. (2) Comparing algorithms to find a suitable explanation technique for the task at hand. (3) Comparing prediction strategies of different network architectures. (4) Systematically evaluating the predictions of a network.

All except for the last application, which is semi-automatic, typically require a qualitative analysis to gain insights—and we will now see how explanation algorithms support this process. Furthermore, this section will give a limited overview and comparison of explanation techniques. A more detailed analysis is beyond the technical scope of this chapter.

We visualize the methods as presented in Sect. 22.2.3, i.e., use heatmaps for all methods except for PatternNet, which tries to produce a given signal and not an attribution. Accordingly we use a projection into the input space for it. Deconvnet and Guided Backprop are also regarded as signal extraction methods, but fail to reproduce color mappings and therefore we visualize them with heatmaps. This allows to identify the location of signals more easily. For more details we refer to [23].

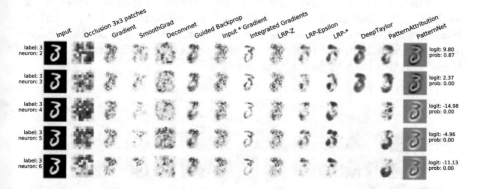

Fig. 22.5.   Analyzing a prediction: The heatmaps show different analysis for a VGG-like network on MNIST. The network predicts the class 2, while the true label is 3. On the left hand side the true label and for each row the respective output neuron is indicated. Probabilities and pre-softmax activation are denoted on the right hand side of the plot. Each columns is dedicated to a different explanation algorithm. LRP-* denotes configuration from [30]. We note that Deep Taylor is not defined when the output neuron is negative.

22.3.1   Analyzing a Prediction

In our first example we focus on the explanation algorithms themselves and the expectations posed by the user. Therefore we chose a dataset without irrelevant features in the input space. In more detail we use a VGG-like network on the MNIST dataset [33] with an accuracy greater than 99% on the test set.

Figure 22.5 shows the result for an input image of the class 3 that is incorrectly classified as 2. The different rows show the explanations for the output neurons for the classes 2, 3, 4, 5, 6 respectively, while each column contains the analyses of the different explanation algorithms.

The true label of the image is 3 and also intuitively it resembles a 3, yet it is classified as 2. Can we retrace why the network decided for a 2? Having a closer look, on the first row—which explains the class 2—the explanation algorithms suggest that the network considers the top and the left stroke as very indicative for a 2, and does not recognize the discontinuity between the center and the right part as contradicting. On the other hand, a look on the second row—which explains a 3—suggests that according to the explanations the left stroke speaks against the digit being a 3. Potential takeaways from this are that the network does not recognize or does not give enough weight on the continuity of lines or that the dataset does not contain enough digit 3 with such a lower left stroke.

Taking this as an example of how such tools can help to understand a neural network, we would like to note that all the stated points are presumptions—based on the assumption that the explanations are meaningful. But given this leap of faith, our argumentation seems plausible and what a user would expect an explanation algorithm to deliver.

We would also like to note that there are common indicators across different methods, e.g., that the topmost stroke is very indicative for a 2 or that the leftmost stroke is not for a 3. This suggest that the methods base their analysis on similar signals in the network. Yet it is not clear which method performs "best" and this leads us to the next example.

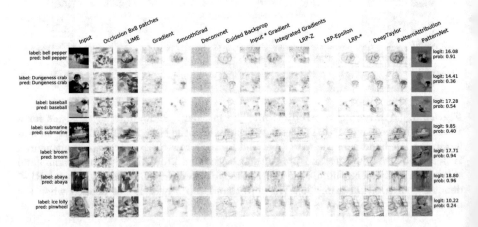

Fig. 22.6. Comparing algorithms: The figure depicts the prediction analysis of a variety of algorithms (columns) for a number of input images (rows) for the VGG16 network [52]. The true and the predicted label are denoted on the left hand side and the softmax and pre-softmax outputs of the network are printed on the right hand side. LRP-* denotes the configuration from [30]. Best viewed in digital and color.

22.3.2   Comparing Explanation Algorithms

For explanation methods there exists no clear evaluation criteria and this makes it inherently hard to find a method that "works" or to choose hyper-parameters (see Sect. 22.2.3). Therefore we argue for the need of extensive comparisons to identify a suitable method for the task at hand.

Figure 22.6 gives an example of such a qualitative comparison and shows the explanation results for a variety of methods (columns) for a set of pictures. We observe that compared to the previous example the analysis results are not as intuitive anymore and we also observe major qualitative differences between the methods. For instance, the algorithms Occlusion and LIME produce distinct heatmaps compared to the other gradient- and propagation-based results. Among this latter group, the results vary in sparseness, but also in which regions the attribution is located. Note despite its results we added the method DeconvNet [61] for completeness.

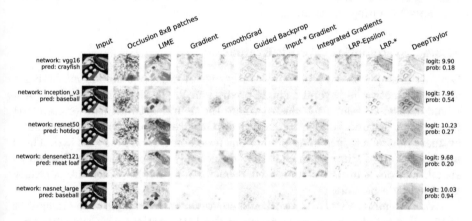

Fig. 22.7. Comparing architectures: The figure depicts the prediction analysis of a variety of algorithms (columns) for a number of neural networks (rows). The true label for this input image is "baseball" and the prediction of the respective network is given on the left hand side. The softmax and pre-softmax outputs of the network are printed on the right hand side. LRP-* denotes the configuration from [30]. Best viewed in digital and color.

Consider the image in the last row, which is miss-classified as pinwheel. While one can interpret that some methods indicate the right part of the hood as significant for this decisions, this is merely a speculation and it is hard to make sense of the analyses—revealing the current dilemma of explanation methods and the need for more research. Nevertheless it is important to be clear about such problems and give the user tools to make up her own opinion.

22.3.3   Comparing Network Architectures

Another possible comparative analysis is to examine the explanations for different architectures. This allows on one hand to assess the transferability of explanation methods and on the other hand to inspect the functioning of different networks.

Figure 22.7 exemplarily depicts such a comparison for an image for the class "baseball". We observe that the quality of the results for the same algorithm can vary significantly between different architectures, e.g., for some algorithms the results are very sparse for deeper architectures. Moreover, the difference between different algorithms applied to the same network seems to increase with the complexity of the architecture (The complexity increases from the first to the last row).

Nevertheless, we note that explanation algorithms give an indication for the different prediction results of the networks and can be a valuable tool for understanding such networks. A similar approach can be used to monitor the learning of a network during the training.

22.3.4   Systematic Network Evaluation

Our last example uses a promising strategy to leverage explanation methods for analysis of networks beyond a single prediction. We evaluate explanations for a whole dataset to search for classes where the neural network uses (correlated) background features to identify an object. Other examples for such systematic evaluations are, e.g., grouping predictions based on their frequencies [31]. These approaches are distinctive in that they do not rely on the miss-classification as signal, i.e., one can detect undesired behavior for samples which are correctly classified by a network.

We use again a VGG16 network and create for each example of the ImageNet 2012 [15] validation set a heatmap using the LRP method with the configuration from [30]. Then we compute the ratio of the attributions absolute values summed inside and outside of the bounding box, and pick the class with the lowest ration, namely "basketball". A selection of images and their heatmaps is given in Table 22.1. The first four images are correctly classified, but one can observe from the heatmaps that the network does not focus on the actual basketball inside the bounding boxes. This suggests the suspicion that the network is not aware of the concept "basketball" as a ball, but rather as a scene. Similarly, in the next three images the basket ball is not identified—leading to wrong predictions. Finally, the last image contains a basketball without any sport scenery and gets miss-classified as ping-pong ball.

One can argue that a sport scene is a strong indicator for the class "basketball", on the other the bounding boxes make clear that the class addresses a ball rather than a scene and the miss-classified images show that taking the scenery rather than a ball as indicator can be miss-leading. The use of explanation methods can support developers to identify such flaws of the learning setup caused by, e.g., biased data or networks that rely on the "wrong" features [31].

Table 22.1. Bounding box analysis: The result of our bounding box analysis suggest that the target network does not use features inside the bounding box to predict the class "basketball". The images have all the true label "basketball" and the label beneath an image indicates the predicted class. We note that for none of the images the network relies on the features of a basketball for the prediction, except for the prediction "ping-pong ball". The result suggest that concept "basketball" is a scenery rather than a ball object for the network. Best viewed in digital and color.

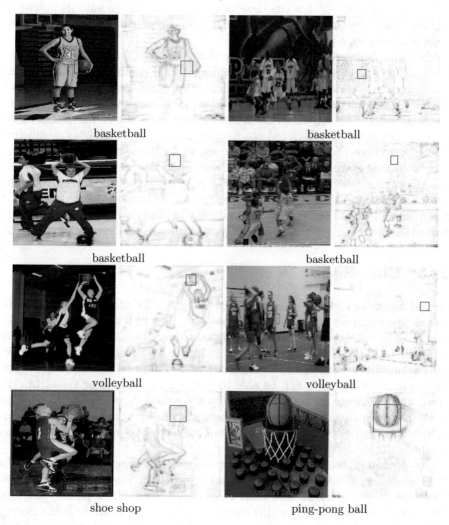

22.4   Software Packages

In this section we would like to give an overview on software packages for explanation techniques.

Accompanying the publication of algorithms many authors released also dedicated software. For the LRP-algorithm a toolbox was published [29] that contains explanatory code in Python and MatLab as well as a faster Caffe-implementation for production purposes. For the algorithms DeepLIFT [49], DeepSHAPE [36], "prediction difference analysis" [63], and LIME [44] the authors also published source code that is based on Keras/Tensorflow, Tensorflow, Tensorflow and scikit-learn respectively. For the algorithm GradCam [48] the authors published a Caffe-based implementation. There exist more GradCam implementations for other frameworks, e.g., [26].

Software packages that contain more than one algorithm family are the following. The software to the paper DeepExplain [5] contains implementations for the gradient-based algorithms saliency map, gradient * input, Integrated Gradients, one variant of DeepLIFT and LRP-Epsilon as well as for the occlusion algorithm. The implementation is based on Tensorflow. The Keras-based software keras-vis [26] offers code to perform activation maximization, saliency algorithms Deconvnet and GuidedBackprop as well as GradCam. Finally, the library iNNvestigate [4] is also Keras-based and contains implementations for the algorithms saliency map, gradient * input, Integrated Gradients, Smoothgrad, DeconvNet, GuidedBackprop, Deep Taylor Decomposition, different LRP algorithms as well as PatternNet and PatternAttribution. It also offers an interface to facilitate the implementation of propagation-based explanation methods.

22.5   Challenges

Neural networks come in a large variety. They can be composed of many different layers and be of complex structure (e.g., Fig. 22.9 shows the sub-blocks of the NASNetA network). Many (propagation-based) explanation methods are designed to handle fully connected layers in the first place, yet to be universally applicable a method and its implementations must be able to scale beyond fully-connected networks and be able to generalize to new layer types. In contrast, the advantage of methods that only use a model's prediction or gradient is their applicability independent of a network's complexity, yet they are typically slower and cannot take advantage of high level features like propagation methods [30,48].

To promote research on propagation methods for complex neural networks it is necessary alleviate researchers from unnecessary implementation efforts. Therefore it is important that tools exist that allow for fast prototyping and let researchers focus on algorithmic developments. One example is the library iNNvestigate, which offers an API that allows to modify the backpropagation easily and implementations of many of state-of-the explanation methods ready for advanced neural networks. We showed in Sect. 22.2.2 how a library like iNNvestigate helps to generalize algorithms to various architectures. Such efforts are promising to facilitate research as they make it easier to compare and develop methods as well as facilitate faster adaption to (recent) developments in deep learning.

For instance, despite first attempts [6,43] LSTMs [19,56] and attention layers [59] are still a challenge for most propagation-based explanation methods. Another challenge are architectures discovered automatically with, e.g., neural architecture search [64]. They often outperform competitors that were created by human intuition, but are very complex. A successful application of and examination with explanation methods can be a promising way to shed led into their workings. The same reasoning applies to networks like SchNet [47], WaveNet [58], and AlphaGo [50]—which led to breakthroughs in their respective domains and a better understanding of their predictions would reveal valuable knowledge.

Another open research question regarding propagation-based methods concerns the decomposition of network into components. Methods like Deep Taylor Decomposition, LRP, DeepLIFT, DeepSHAPE decompose the network and create an explanation based on the linearization of the respective components. Yet networks can be decomposed in different ways: for instance the sequence of a convolutional and a batch normalization layer can be treated as two components or be represented as one layer where both are fused. Another example is the treatment of a single batch normalization layer which can be seen as one or as two linear layers. Further examples can be found and it is not clear how the different approaches to decompose a network influence the result of the explanation algorithms and requires research.

22.6   Conclusion

Explanation methods are a promising approach to leverage hidden knowledge about the workings of neural networks, yet the complexity of many methods can prevent practitioners from implementing and using them for research or application purposes. To alleviate this shortcoming it is important that accessible and efficient software exists. With this in mind we explained how such algorithms can be implemented efficiently by using deep learning frameworks like Tensor-Flow and Keras and showcased important algorithm and application patterns. Moreover, we demonstrated different exemplary use cases of explanation methods such as examining miss-classifications, comparing algorithms, and detecting if a network focuses on the background. By building such software the field will hopefully be more accessible for non-experts and find appeal in the broader sciences. We also hope that it will help researchers to tackle recent developments in deep learning.

Acknowledgements. The authors thank Sebastian Lapuschkin, Grégoire Montavon and Klaus-Robert Müller for their valuable feedback. This work was supported by the Federal Ministry of Education and Research (BMBF) for the Berlin Big Data Center 2 - BBDC 2 (01IS18025A).

Appendices

22.A   Section 2 - Supplementary Content

22.A.1   Propagation Backend

Creating a Propagation Backend. Let us reiterate the aim, which is to create routines that capture common functionality to all propagation-based algorithms and thereby facilitate their efficient implementation. Given the information which graph-parts shall be mapped and how, the backend should decompose the network accordingly and then process the back-propagation as specified. It would be further desirable that the backend is able to identify if a given neural network is not compatible with an algorithm, e.g., because the algorithm does not cover certain network properties.

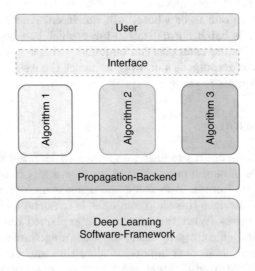

Fig. 22.8. Exemplary software-stack: The diagram depicts exemplary the software stack of iNNvestigate [4]. It shows how different propagation-based methods are build on top of a common graph-backend and expose their functionality through a common interface to the user.

In this regard we see as major challenges for creating an efficient backend the following:

Interface: How shall an algorithm specify the way a network should be decomposed and how should each backward mapping be performed?

Graph matching: Decomposing the neural network according to the algorithm's specifications and, ideally, detecting possible incompatibilities. Note that the specifications can describe the structure of the targeted components as well as their location in the network, e.g., DTD treats layer differently depending where they are located in the network.

Back-propagation: Once determined which backward mapping is used for which part of the network graph, the respective mappings should be applied in the right order until the final explanation is produced.

The first two challenges are solved by choosing appropriate abstractions. The abstractions should be fine-grained enough to enable the implementation of a wide range of algorithms, while being coarse-grained enough to allow for an efficient implementation. The last challenge is in the first place an engineering task.

Interface & Matching. The first step towards a clear interface is to regard a neural network as a directed-acyclic-graph (DAG) of layers—instead of a stack of layers. The notion of a graph of "layers" might not seem intuitive in the first place and comes from the time when neural networks were typically sequential, thus one layer was stacked onto another. Modern networks, e.g., as NASNetA in Fig. 22.9, can be more complex and in such architectures each layer is rather a node in a graph than a layer in a stack. Regardless of that, nodes in such a DAG are still commonly called layers and we will keep this notation.

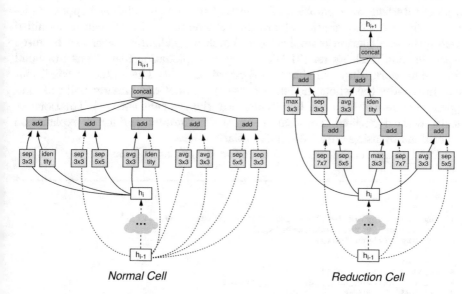

Fig. 22.9. NASNetA cells: The computer vision network NASNetA [64] was created with automatic machine learning, i.e., the architecture of the two depicted building blocks was found with an automated algorithm. The normal cell and the reduction cell have the same purpose as convolutional or max-pooling layers in other networks, but are far more complex. (Figure is from [64].)

A second step is to be aware of DAG's granularity. Different deep learning frameworks represent neural networks in different ways and layers can be composed of more basic operations like additions and dot products, which in turn can be decomposed further. The most intuitive and useful level for implementing explanation methods is to view each layer as node. A more fine-grained view is in many cases not needed and would only complicate the implementation. On the other hand, we note that it might be desired or necessary to fuse layers of networks into one node, e.g., adjacent convolutional and batch normalization layers can be expressed as a single convolutional layer.

Building on this network representation, there are two interfaces to define. One to define where a mapping shall be applied and one how it should be performed.

There are two ways to realize the matching interface and they can be sketched as follows. The first binds a custom backward mapping before or during network building to a method of a layer class—statically by extending a layer class or by overloading its gradient operator. The second receives the already build model and matches the mappings dynamically to the respective layer nodes. This can be done by evaluating a programmable condition for each layer instance or node in order to assign a mapping. Except for the matching conditions, both techniques expose the same interface and in contrast to the first approach the later is more challenging to implement, but has several advantages: (1) It exposes a clear interface by separation of concerns: the model building happens independently of the explanation algorithm. (2) The forward DAG can be modified before the explanation is applied, e.g., batch normalization layer can be fused with convolutional layers. (3) When several explanation algorithms are build for one network, they can share the forward pass. (4) The matching conditions can introspect the whole model, because the model was already build at that point in time. (5) One can build efficiently the gradient w.r.t. explanations by using forward-gradient computation—in the background and for all explanation algorithms by using automatic differentiation.

The two approaches can be sketched in Python as follows:

```
1   # Approach A
2   # Use mapping Y for layer type X
3   register_mapping_for_layer_type(layer_type_X, mapping_Y)
4   build_model_with_custom_mapping()
5   execute_explanation()
6
7   # Approach B
8   model = build_model()
9   graph = extract_and_update_graph(model)
10  for node in graph:
11      # Match node to mapping based on conditions
12      # A node can be a layer or a sub-graph.
13      # Condition can introspect whole model for decision.
14      mapping = match_node_to_mapping(node, model.graph)
15      assign_mapping_to_node(node, mapping)
```

The second interface addresses the backward mapping and is a function that takes as parameters the input and output tensors of the targeted layer, the respective back-propagated values for the output tensors and, optionally, some meta-information on the back-propagation process. The following code segment shows the interface of a backward mapping function in the iNNvestigate library. Due to same purpose other implementations have very similar interfaces.

```
1  # Xs = input tensors of a layer or sub-graph
2  # Ys = output tensors of a layer or sub-graph
3  # bp_Ys = back-propagated values for Ys
4  # bp_state = additional information on state
5  # return back-propagated values for Xs
6  def backward_mapping(Xs, Ys, bp_Ys, bp_state):
7    # the backward mapped tensors correspond in shape
8    # with respective the output tensors of the forward pass
9    assert len(Ys) == len(bp_Ys)
10   assert all(Y.shape == bp_Y.shape for Y, bp_Y in zip(Ys, bp_Ys))
11
12   bp_Xs = compute_backward_mapping_magic()
13
14   # the returned tensors correspond in shape
15   # with the respective input tensors of the forward pass
16   assert len(Ys) == len(bp_Ys)
17   assert all(Y.shape == bp_Y.shape for Y, bp_Y in zip(Ys, bp_Ys))
18   return bp_Xs
```

Note that this signature can not only be used for the backward mapping of layers, but for any connected sub-graph. In the remainder we will use a simplified interface where each layer has only one input and one output tensor.

Back-propagation. Having matched backward mappings with network parts the backend still needs to create the actual backward propagation. Practically this can be done explicitly, as we will show below, or by overloading the gradient operator in the deep learning framework of choice. While the latter is easier to implement it less flexible and has the dis-advantages mentioned above.

The implementations of neural networks is characterized by their layer-oriented structure and the simplest of them are sequential neural networks where each layer is stacked on another layer. To back-propagate through such a network one starts with the model's output value and propagates from top layer to the next lower one and so on. Given mapping functions that take a tensor and back-propagate along a layer, this can be sketched as follows:

```
1  current = output
2  for layer in model.layers[::-1]:
3    current = back_propagate(layer.input, layer.output, current)
4  analysis = current
```

In general neural networks can be much more complex and are represented as directed, acyclic graphs. This allows for multiple input and output tensors for each "layer node". An efficient implementation is for instance the following. First the right propagation order is established using the depth-first search algorithm to create a topological ordering [14]. Then given this ordering, the propagation starts at the output tensors and proceeds in direction of the input tensors. At each step, the implementation collects the required inputs for each node, applies the respective mapping and keeps track of the back-propagated tensors after the mapping. Note, nodes that branch in the forward pass, i.e., have an output tensor that is used several times in the forward pass, receive several tensors as inputs in the backward pass. These need to be reduced to a single tensor before being fed to the backward mapping. This is typically like in the gradient computation, namely by summing the tensors:

```
1   intermediate_tensors = {output: output}
2   execution_order = calculate_execution_order()
3   for layer, inputs, outputs in execution_order[::-1]:
4       # gather corresponding back-propagated tensors for each output tensor
5       back_propagated_values = [
6           # Reduce to single tensor if the forward passed branched!
7           sum(intermediate_tensors[t])
8           for t in outputs
9       ]
10
11      # backprop through layer
12      tmp = back_propagate(inputs, outputs, back_propagated_values)
13
14      # store intermediate tensors
15      for input, intermediate in zip(inputs, tmp):
16          if input in intermediate_tensors:
17              intermediate_tensors[input] = [intermediate]
18          else:
19              # The corresponding forward tensor branched!
20              intermediate_tensors[input].append(intermediate)
21
22  # get the last output
23  analysis = intermediate_tensors[model.input]
```

Despite its relative simplicity, implementing and debugging such an algorithm can be tedious. This among propagation-based methods common operation is part of the iNNvestigate library and as a result one only needs to specify how the back-propagation through specific layers should be performed. Even handier, as default backward mapping the gradient-propagation is used and one only needs to specify whenever the back-propagation should be performed differently.

22.A.2   Deep Taylor

The Deep Taylor mapping for dense layers:

```
1   # Deep-Taylor/LRP/EB's Z+-Rule-Mapping for dense layers
2   # Call R=bp_Y, R for relevance
3   def z_rule_mapping_dense(X, Y, R, bp_state):
4       # Get layer and the parameters
5       layer = bp_state['layer']
6       W = tf.maximum(layer.kernel, 0)
7
8       Z = tf.tensordot(X, W, 1) + b
9       # normalize incoming relevance
10      tmp = R / Z
11      # map back
```

```
12      tmp = tf.tensordot(tmp, tf.transpose(W), 1)
13      # times input
14      return tmp * X
```

22.A.3   PatternNet

The exemplary implementation for PatterNet discussed in Sect. 22.2.2:

```
1   # Extending iNNvestigate base class with the PatternNet algorithm
2   class PatternNet(ReverseAnalyzerBase):
3
4       # Storing the patterns.
5       def __init__(self, model, patterns, **kwargs):
6           self._patterns = patterns[:]
7           super(PatternNet, self).__init__(model, **kwargs)
8
9       def _get_pattern_for_layer(self, layer):
10          return self._patterns.pop(-1)
11
12      def _patternnet_mapping(self, X, Y, bp_Y, bp_state):
13          # Get layer,
14          layer = bp_state['layer']
15          # exchange kernel weights with patterns,
16          weights = layer.get_weights()
17          weights[0] = self._get_pattern_for_layer(layer)
18          # and create layer copy without activation part and patterns as filters
19          layer_wo_act = kgraph.copy_layer_wo_activation(layer, weights=weights)
20
21          if kchecks.contains_activation(layer, 'relu'):
22              # Gradient of activation layer
23              tmp = tf.where(Y > 0, bp_Y, tf.zeros_like(bp_Y))
24          else:
25              # Gradient of linear layer
26              tmp = bp_Y
27
28          # map back along layer with patterns instead of weights
29          pattern_Y = layer_wo_act(X)
30          return tf.gradients(pattern_Y, X, grad_ys=tmp)[0]
31
32      # Register the mappings
33      def _create_analysis(self, *args, **kwargs):
34          self._add_conditional_reverse_mapping(
35              # Apply to all layers that contain a kernel
36              lambda layer: kchecks.contains_kernel(layer),
37              tf_to_keras_mapping(self._patternnet_mapping),
38              name='pattern_mapping',
39          )
40          return super(PatternNet, self)._create_analysis(*args, **kwargs)
41
42  analyzer = PatternNet(model_wo_sm, net['patterns'])
43  B4 = analyzer.analyze(x)
```

22.A.4   Hyper-Parameter Selection

The exemplary hyper-parameter selection for Integrated Gradients:

```
1   IG = []
2   # Take 5 samples from network's input value range
3   for ri in np.linspace(net['input_range'][0], net['input_range'][1], num=5):
4       # and analyze with each.
5       analyzer = innvestigate.create_analyzer(
6           'integrated_gradients',
7           model_wo_sm,
8           reference_inputs=ri,
9           steps=32
10      )
11      IG.append(analyzer.analyze(x))
```

The exemplary hyper-parameter selection for SmoothGrad:

```
1   SG1, SG2 = [], []
2   # Take 5 scale samples for the noise scale of smoothgrad.
3   for scale in range(5):
4       noise_scale = (net['input_range'][1]-net['input_range'][0]) * scale / 5
5       # Smoothgrad with absolute gradients
6       analyzer = innvestigate.create_analyzer(
7           'smoothgrad',
8           model_wo_sm,
9           augment_by_n=32,
10          noise_scale=noise_scale,
11          postprocess='abs'
12      )
13      SG1.append(analyzer.analyze(x))
14
15      # Smoothgrad with with squared gradients
16      analyzer = innvestigate.create_analyzer(
17          'smoothgrad',
18          model_wo_sm,
19          augment_by_n=32,
20          noise_scale=noise_scale,
21          postprocess='square'
22      )
23      SG2.append(analyzer.analyze(x))
```

22.A.5   Visualization

The exemplary implementation of visualization approaches discussed in Sect. 22.2.3:

```
1   def explanation_to_heatmap(e):
2       # Reduce color axis
3       tmp = np.sum(e, axis=color_channel_axis)
4       # To range [0, 255]
5       tmp = (tmp / np.max(np.abs(tmp))) * 127.5 + 127.5
6
7       # Create and apply red-blue heatmap
```

```
 8    colormap = matplotlib.cm.get_cmap("seismic")
 9    tmp = colormap(tmp.flatten().astype(np.int64))[:, :3]
10    tmp = tmp.reshape(e.shape)
11    return tmp
12
13 def explanation_to_graymap(e):
14    # Reduce color axis
15    tmp = np.sum(np.abs(e), axis=color_channel_axis)
16    # To range [0, 255]
17    tmp = (tmp / np.max(np.abs(tmp))) * 255
18
19    # Create and apply red-blue heatmap
20    colormap = matplotlib.cm.get_cmap("gray")
21    tmp = colormap(tmp.flatten().astype(np.int64))[:, :3]
22    tmp = tmp.reshape(e.shape)
23    return tmp
24
25 def explanation_to_scale_input(e):
26    # Create scale
27    e = np.sum(np.abs(e), axis=color_channel_axis, keepdims=True)
28    scale = e / np.max(e)
29
30    # Apply to image
31    return (x_not_preprocessed / 255) * scale
32
33 def explanation_to_mask_input(e):
34    # Get highest scored segments
35    # Segments are reused from the LIME example.
36    segments_scored = [(np.max(e[0][segments == sid]), sid)\
37                        for sid in range(nr_segments)]
38    highest_ones = sorted(segments_scored, reverse=True)[:50]
39
40    # Compute mask
41    mask = np.zeros_like(segments)
42    for _, sid in highest_ones:
43        mask[segments == sid] = 1
44
45    # Apply mask
46    ret = (x_not_pp.copy() / 255)
47    ret[0][mask == 0] = 0
48    return ret
49
50 def explanation_to_blend_w_input(e):
51    e = np.sum(np.abs(e), axis=channel_axis, keepdims=True)
52    # Add blur
53    e = skimage.filters.gaussian(x[e], 3)[None]
54    # Normalize
55    e = (e - e.min())/(e.max()-e.min())
56    # Get and apply colormap
57    heatmap = plot.get_cmap("jet")(e[:, :,:,0])[:,:,:,:3]
58    # Overlap
59    ret = (1.0-e) * (x_not_pp / 255) + e * heatmap
60    return ret
61
62 def explanation_to_projection(e):
63    # To range [0, 1]
64    return (e / np.max(np.abs(e))) + 0.5
```

References

1. Abadi, M., et al.: TensorFlow: a system for large-scale machine learning. In: Proceedings of the 11th USENIX Symposium on Operating Systems Design and Implementation, vol. 16, pp. 265–283 (2016)

2. Alber, M., Bello, I., Zoph, B., Kindermans, P.J., Ramachandran, P., Le, Q.: Back-prop evolution. In: International Conference on Machine Learning 2018 - AutoML Workshop (2018)
3. Alber, M., Kindermans, P.J., Schütt, K.T., Müller, K.R., Sha, F.: An empirical study on the properties of random bases for kernel methods. In: Advances in Neural Information Processing Systems, vol. 30, pp. 2763–2774 (2017)
4. Alber, M., et al.: iNNvestigate neural networks! J. Mach. Learn. Res. **20**(93), 1–8 (2019)
5. Ancona, M., Ceolini, E., Öztireli, C., Gross, M.: Towards better understanding of gradient-based attribution methods for deep neural networks. In: International Conference on Learning Representations (2018)
6. Arras, L., Montavon, G., Müller, K.R., Samek, W.: Explaining recurrent neural network predictions in sentiment analysis. In: Proceedings of the EMNLP 2017 Workshop on Computational Approaches to Subjectivity, Sentiment and Social Media Analysis, pp. 159–168 (2017)
7. Bach, S., Binder, A., Montavon, G., Klauschen, F., Müller, K.R., Samek, W.: On pixel-wise explanations for non-linear classifier decisions by layer-wise relevance propagation. PLoS ONE **10**(7), e0130140 (2015)
8. Bahdanau, D., Cho, K., Bengio, Y.: Neural machine translation by jointly learning to align and translate. In: International Conference on Learning Representations (2015)
9. Binder, A., et al.: Towards computational fluorescence microscopy: machine learning-based integrated prediction of morphological and molecular tumor profiles. arXiv preprint. arXiv:1805.11178 (2018)
10. Chmiela, S., Sauceda, H.E., Müller, K.R., Tkatchenko, A.: Towards exact molecular dynamics simulations with machine-learned force fields. Nat. Commun. **9**(1), 3887 (2018)
11. Chmiela, S., Tkatchenko, A., Sauceda, H.E., Poltavsky, I., Schütt, K.T., Müller, K.R.: Machine learning of accurate energy-conserving molecular force fields. Sci. Adv. **3**(5), e1603015 (2017)
12. Chollet, F., et al.: Keras (2015). https://github.com/fchollet/keras
13. Chollet, F.: Xception: deep learning with depthwise separable convolutions. In: 2017 IEEE Conference on Computer Vision and Pattern Recognition, pp. 1800–1807 (2017)
14. Cormen, T.H., Leiserson, C.E., Rivest, R.L., Stein, C.: Introduction to Algorithms. MIT Press, Cambridge (2009)
15. Deng, J., Dong, W., Socher, R., Li, L.J., Li, K., Fei-Fei, L.: ImageNet: a large-scale hierarchical image database. In: 2009 IEEE Conference on Computer Vision and Pattern Recognition, pp. 248–255 (2009)
16. Gondal, W.M., Köhler, J.M., Grzeszick, R., Fink, G.A., Hirsch, M.: Weakly-supervised localization of diabetic retinopathy lesions in retinal fundus images. In: 2017 IEEE International Conference on Image Processing, pp. 2069–2073 (2017)
17. Haufe, S., et al.: On the interpretation of weight vectors of linear models in multivariate neuroimaging. Neuroimage **87**, 96–110 (2014)
18. He, K., Zhang, X., Ren, S., Sun, J.: Deep residual learning for image recognition. In: 2016 IEEE Conference on Computer Vision and Pattern Recognition, pp. 770–778 (2016)
19. Hochreiter, S., Schmidhuber, J.: Long short-term memory. Neural Comput. **9**(8), 1735–1780 (1997)

20. Huang, G., Liu, Z., van der Maaten, L., Weinberger, K.Q.: Densely connected convolutional networks. In: 2017 IEEE Conference on Computer Vision and Pattern Recognition, pp. 2261–2269 (2017)
21. Ioffe, S., Szegedy, C.: Batch normalization: accelerating deep network training by reducing internal covariate shift. In: Proceedings of the 32nd International Conference on Machine Learning, pp. 448–456 (2015)
22. Kindermans, P.J., et al.: The (Un)reliability of saliency methods. In: Neural Information Processing Systems 2017 - Interpreting, Explaining and Visualizing Deep Learning - Now What? Workshop (2017)
23. Kindermans, P.J., et al.: Learning how to explain neural networks: PatternNet and PatternAttribution. In: International Conference on Learning Representations (2018)
24. Kindermans, P.J., Schütt, K.T., Müller, K.R., Dähne, S.: Investigating the influence of noise and distractors on the interpretation of neural networks. In: Neural Information Processing Systems 2016 - Interpretable Machine Learning for Complex Systems Workshop (2016)
25. Korbar, B., et al.: Looking under the hood: deep neural network visualization to interpret whole-slide image analysis outcomes for colorectal polyps. In: 2017 IEEE Conference on Computer Vision and Pattern Recognition, pp. 821–827 (2017)
26. Kotikalapudi, R., contributors: keras-vis (2017). https://github.com/raghakot/keras-vis
27. Krizhevsky, A., Sutskever, I., Hinton, G.E.: ImageNet classification with deep convolutional neural networks. In: Advances in Neural Information Processing Systems, vol. 25, pp. 1097–1105 (2012)
28. Lapuschkin, S., Binder, A., Montavon, G., Müller, K.R., Samek, W.: Analyzing classifiers: Fisher vectors and deep neural networks. In: 2016 IEEE Conference on Computer Vision and Pattern Recognition, pp. 2912–2920 (2016)
29. Lapuschkin, S., Binder, A., Montavon, G., Müller, K.R., Samek, W.: The layerwise relevance propagation toolbox for artificial neural networks. J. Mach. Learn. Res. 17(114), 1–5 (2016)
30. Lapuschkin, S., Binder, A., Müller, K.R., Samek, W.: Understanding and comparing deep neural networks for age and gender classification. In: IEEE International Conference on Computer Vision Workshops, pp. 1629–1638 (2017)
31. Lapuschkin, S., Wäldchen, S., Binder, A., Montavon, G., Samek, W., Müller, K.R.: Unmasking clever hans predictors and assessing what machines really learn. Nat. Commun. 10, 1096 (2019)
32. LeCun, Y.A., Bengio, Y., Hinton, G.E.: Deep learning. Nature 521(7553), 436–444 (2015)
33. LeCun, Y.A., Cortes, C., Burges, C.J.: The MNIST database of handwritten digits (1998). http://yann.lecun.com/exdb/mnist/
34. Li, J., Monroe, W., Jurafsky, D.: Understanding neural networks through representation erasure. arXiv preprint. arXiv:1612.08220 (2016)
35. Lipton, Z.C.: The mythos of model interpretability. In: International Conference on Machine Learning 2016 - Human Interpretability in Machine Learning Workshop (2016)
36. Lundberg, S.M., Lee, S.I.: A unified approach to interpreting model predictions. In: Advances in Neural Information Processing Systems, vol. 30, pp. 4765–4774 (2017)
37. Mikolov, T., Sutskever, I., Chen, K., Corrado, G.S., Dean, J.: Distributed representations of words and phrases and their compositionality. In: Advances in Neural Information Processing Systems, vol. 26, pp. 3111–3119 (2013)

38. Montavon, G., Bach, S., Binder, A., Samek, W., Müller, K.R.: Explaining nonlinear classification decisions with deep Taylor decomposition. Pattern Recogn. **65**, 211–222 (2017)

39. Montavon, G., et al.: Machine learning of molecular electronic properties in chemical compound space. New J. Phys. **15**(9), 095003 (2013)

40. Montavon, G., Samek, W., Müller, K.R.: Methods for interpreting and understanding deep neural networks. Digital Signal Process. **73**, 1–15 (2018)

41. Pedregosa, F., et al.: Scikit-learn: machine learning in Python. J. Mach. Learn. Res. **12**, 2825–2830 (2011)

42. Pennington, J., Socher, R., Manning, C.: GloVe: global vectors for word representation. In: Proceedings of the 2014 Conference on Empirical Methods in Natural Language Processing, pp. 1532–1543 (2014)

43. Poerner, N., Schütze, H., Roth, B.: Evaluating neural network explanation methods using hybrid documents and morphosyntactic agreement. In: Proceedings of the 56th Annual Meeting of the Association for Computational Linguistics (Volume 1: Long Papers), pp. 340–350 (2018)

44. Ribeiro, M.T., Singh, S., Guestrin, C.: "Why should I trust you?": explaining the predictions of any classifier. In: Proceedings of the 22nd ACM SIGKDD International Conference on Knowledge Discovery and Data Mining, pp. 1135–1144 (2016)

45. Samek, W., Binder, A., Montavon, G., Lapuschkin, S., Müller, K.R.: Evaluating the visualization of what a deep neural network has learned. IEEE Trans. Neural Netw. Learn. Syst. **28**(11), 2660–2673 (2017)

46. Schütt, K.T., Arbabzadah, F., Chmiela, S., Müller, K.R., Tkatchenko, A.: Quantum-chemical insights from deep tensor neural networks. Nat. Commun. **8**, 13890 (2017)

47. Schütt, K.T., Kindermans, P.J., Felix, H.E.S., Chmiela, S., Tkatchenko, A., Müller, K.R.: SchNet: a continuous-filter convolutional neural network for modeling quantum interactions. In: Advances in Neural Information Processing Systems, vol. 30, pp. 991–1001 (2017)

48. Selvaraju, R.R., Cogswell, M., Das, A., Vedantam, R., Parikh, D., Batra, D.: Gradcam: visual explanations from deep networks via gradient-based localization. In: Proceedings of the 2017 International Conference on Computer Vision, pp. 618–626 (2017)

49. Shrikumar, A., Greenside, P., Kundaje, A.: Learning important features through propagating activation differences. In: Proceedings of the 34th International Conference on Machine Learning, pp. 3145–3153 (2017)

50. Silver, D., et al.: Mastering the game of go with deep neural networks and tree search. Nature **529**(7587), 484–489 (2016)

51. Silver, D., et al.: Mastering the game of go without human knowledge. Nature **550**(7676), 354–359 (2017)

52. Simonyan, K., Zisserman, A.: Very deep convolutional networks for large-scale image recognition. arXiv preprint. arXiv:1409.1556 (2014)

53. Smilkov, D., Thorat, N., Kim, B., Viégas, F., Wattenberg, M.: SmoothGrad: removing noise by adding noise. In: International Conference on Machine Learning 2017 - Workshop on Visualization for Deep Learning (2017)

54. Springenberg, J.T., Dosovitskiy, A., Brox, T., Riedmiller, M.: Striving for simplicity: the all convolutional net. In: International Conference on Learning Representations - Workshop Track (2015)

55. Sundararajan, M., Taly, A., Yan, Q.: Axiomatic attribution for deep networks. In: Proceedings of the 34th International Conference on Machine Learning, pp. 3319–3328 (2017)

56. Sutskever, I., Vinyals, O., Le, Q.V.: Sequence to sequence learning with neural networks. In: Advances in Neural Information Processing Systems, vol. 27, pp. 3104–3112 (2014)
57. Szegedy, C., Vanhoucke, V., Ioffe, S., Shlens, J., Wojna, Z.: Rethinking the inception architecture for computer vision. In: 2016 IEEE Conference on Computer Vision and Pattern Recognition, pp. 2818–2826 (2016)
58. Van Den Oord, A., et al.: WaveNet: a generative model for raw audio. arXiv preprint. arXiv:1609.03499 (2016)
59. Vaswani, A., et al.: Attention is all you need. In: Advances in Neural Information Processing Systems, vol. 30, pp. 5998–6008 (2017)
60. Voigt, P., von dem Bussche, A.: The EU General Data Protection Regulation (GDPR): A Practical Guide. Springer, Cham (2017). https://doi.org/10.1007/978-3-319-57959-7
61. Zeiler, M.D., Fergus, R.: Visualizing and understanding convolutional networks. In: Fleet, D., Pajdla, T., Schiele, B., Tuytelaars, T. (eds.) ECCV 2014. LNCS, vol. 8689, pp. 818–833. Springer, Cham (2014). https://doi.org/10.1007/978-3-319-10590-1_53
62. Zhang, J., Bargal, S.A., Lin, Z., Brandt, J., Shen, X., Sclaroff, S.: Top-down neural attention by excitation backprop. Int. J. Comput. Vision **126**(10), 1084–1102 (2018)
63. Zintgraf, L.M., Cohen, T.S., Adel, T., Welling, M.: Visualizing deep neural network decisions: prediction difference analysis. In: International Conference on Learning Representations (2017)
64. Zoph, B., Vasudevan, V., Shlens, J., Le, Q.V.: Learning transferable architectures for scalable image recognition. In: 2018 IEEE Conference on Computer Vision and Pattern Recognition, pp. 8697–8710 (2018)

Subject Index

Author Index

Printed in the United States
By Bookmasters